FIFTH EDITION

THE WHOLE CHILD

Developmental Education for the Early Years

JOANNE HENDRICK
University of Oklahoma

Merrill, an imprint of
Macmillan Publishing Company
New York

Maxwell Macmillan Canada
Toronto

Maxwell Macmillan International
New York   Oxford   Singapore   Sydney

Cover art/photo: Richard Hutchings/InfoEdit
Editor: Linda A. Sullivan
Developmental Editor: Kevin M. Davis
Production Editor: Sheryl Glicker Langner
Art Coordinator: Peter A. Robison
Text Designer: Debra A. Fargo
Production Buyer: Patricia A. Tonneman

This book was set in Palatino by The Clarinda Company and was printed and bound by Arcada Graphics/Halliday. The cover was printed by Lehigh Press, Inc.

Macmillan Publishing Company
866 Third Avenue
New York, NY 10022

Macmillan Publishing Company is part of the Maxwell Communication Group of Companies.

Maxwell Macmillan Canada, Inc.
1200 Eglinton Avenue East, Suite 200
Don Mills, Ontario M3C 3N1

Library of Congress Cataloging-in-Publication Data
Hendrick, Joanne, (date)
    The whole child : developmental education for the early years /
    Joanne Hendrick. — 5th ed.
        p. cm.
    Includes bibliographical references and index.
    ISBN 0-02-353150-9
    1. Education, Preschool—United States.   2. Early childhood education—United States.   3. Preschool teachers—Training of—United States.   I. Title.
    LB1140.23.H46   1992
    372.21—dc20   91-20939
                                                                        CIP

Printing: 3   4   5   6   7   8   9   Year: 3   4   5

PREFACE

OVERVIEW

The Whole Child is a practical methods book that explains how to go about teaching young children in ways that foster healthy development. It shifts the attention of the teacher away from "art" or "science" to what the child *is* and what he needs from the learning environment in order to thrive. For that reason it focuses on the child and pictures him as composed of a number of selves: the physical self, the emotional self, the social self, the creative self, and the cognitive self.

The physical self includes not only large and fine muscle development but also handling routines, since such things as eating, resting, and toileting contribute much to physical comfort and well-being. For the emotional self the book considers ways to increase and sustain mental health, to cope with crises, to use discipline to foster self-control, to cope with aggression, and to foster self-esteem. Under the heading of the social self are ways to build social concern and kindliness, learning to enjoy work, and learning to value the cultures of other people. The creative self covers the areas of self-expression through the use of art materials and creativity as expressed in play and applied in thought. Finally, the cognitive, or intellectual, self is considered in terms of language development and the development of specific reasoning abilities.

The Whole Child is based on the premises that physical and emotional health are fundamental to the well-being of children, that education must be developmentally appropriate if that well-being is to prosper, and that children need time to be children—time to be themselves—to do nothing, to stand and watch, to repeat again what they did before—in short, they need time to live *in* their childhood rather than *through* it. If we offer the young children we teach rich and appropriate learning opportunities combined with enough time for them to enjoy and experience those opportunities to the full, we will enhance childhood, not violate it.

MAJOR CHANGES AND ADDITIONS

The most significant change in this revision is the addition of a new chapter entitled "Fostering the Emergence of Literacy". Other major modifications include splitting the chapter on developing thinking and reasoning skills in half to make mastery of that material easier. The chapter on trends has also been completely rewritten.

As always, considerable new material has been added to assure currency of information. This includes material on protecting teachers from accusations of abuse, a review of working with children who may have AIDS, and, on a happier note, new information on the effects of bilingualism, more extended discussions of the Piagetian Constructivist approach to early education, and a review of the history of early childhood education during the past century.

The 4th edition saw the addition of Self-Check Questions for Review. This section has now been expanded to include higher order thought processes under the heading of "Integrative Questions". These require readers to apply what they have learned by synthesizing, predicting, comparing, and evaluating.

As always, the research and information base of the text has been heavily updated. This edition includes more than 450 new citations as well as an extensively updated annotated bibliography for every chapter. Classic references have, of course, been retained.

Once again, the majority of the photographs are new. I thank the children and staff of the Institute of Child Development, University of Oklahoma, the Oaks Parent Child Workshop, Santa Barbara, California, and Oscar Rose State College, Oklahoma City for their gracious cooperation. If some of the reader's favorites are no longer included, I can only say, "I miss them, too!" But I also enjoyed taking the new ones and hope they will find a place in the reader's affections as they have in mine.

ACKNOWLEDGMENTS

I owe so much to so many people that it is a well-nigh impossible task to mention them all. The contributions of students and parents to my knowledge and point of view have been considerable, as have the contributions of the members of my staff. In addition, I am forever in the debt of my mother, Alma Berg Green, who not only began some of the first parent education classes in Los Angeles, but also taught me a great deal about young children and their families.

I am also indebted to Sarah Foot and her wonderful Starr King Parent/Child Workshop, which convinced me that my future lay in early childhood education, and to my own children who bore with me with such goodwill while I was learning the real truth about bringing up young people.

The fifth edition has moved with the times and includes much new material. For their many suggestions in this regard I wish to thank my reviewers: Eleanor Cook, Central Connecticut State University; Ione Garcia, Illinois State University; Karen Peterson, Washington State University; Phyllis Povell, Long Island University—C. W. Post Campus; and John Worobey, Rutgers University. Their help has been invaluable.

As far as the book itself is concerned, I would like to thank Murray Thomas for teaching me, among other things, how to write and John Wilson for convincing me that some things remained to be said and changed in early education. To Chester and Peggy Harris I am forever indebted for a certain realistic attitude toward research, particularly in the area of cognitive development.

The people at Merrill/Macmillan have been of great assistance. In particular I want to thank Linda Sullivan and Kevin Davis for their encouragement. The contributions of Laura Larson, free-lance copyeditor, and Sheryl Langner, production editor, also deserve notice. Without their careful help, the book would not exist.

Revising this book about early childhood education is always stimulating—it has been an interesting task for me to set down what I know about this area and then to witness the changing needs that the past few years have brought to the fore. If it is also helpful to beginning teachers and to the children they serve, I will be pleased indeed.

Joanne Hendrick

BRIEF CONTENTS

CONTENTS

PART FOUR
Fostering Social Development

PART FIVE
Enhancing Creativity

PART SIX
Developing Language Skills and Mental Ability

PART SEVEN
Working With Special Situations

PART EIGHT
What Lies Ahead?

Appendices

There was a child went forth every day,
And the first object he look'd upon, that object
  he became,
And that object became part of him for the day
  or a certain part of the day,
Or for many years or stretching cycles of years.

The early lilacs became part of this child,
And grass and white and red morning-glories,
  and white and red clover, and the song of
  the phoebe-bird,
And the Third-month lambs and the sow's
  pink-faint litter, and the mare's foal and the
  cow's calf,
And the noisy brood of the barnyard or by the
  mire of the pond-side,
And the fish suspending themselves so
  curiously below there, and the beautiful
  curious liquid,
And the water-plants with their graceful flat
  heads, all became part of him.

The field-sprouts of Fourth-month and Fifth-
  month became part of him,
Water-grain sprouts and those of the light-
  yellow corn, and the esculent roots of the
  garden,
And the apple-trees cover'd with blossoms and
  the fruit afterward, and wood-berries, and
  the commonest weeds by the road,
And the old drunkard staggering home from
  the outhouse of the tavern whence he had
  lately risen,
And the schoolmistress that pass'd on her way
  to the school,
And the friendly boys that pass'd, and the
  quarrelsome boys,
And the tidy and fresh-cheek'd girls, and the
  barefoot negro boy and girl,
And all the changes of city and country
  wherever he went.

His own parents, he that had father'd him and
  she that had conceiv'd him in her womb and
  birth'd him,
They gave this child more of themselves than
  that,
They gave him afterward every day, they
  became part of him.

The mother at home quietly placing the dishes
  on the supper-table,
The mother with mild words, clean her cap
  and gown, a wholesome odor falling off her
  person and clothes as she walks by,
The father, strong, self-sufficient, manly, mean,
  anger'd, unjust,
The blow, the quick loud word, the tight
  bargain, the crafty lure,
The family usages, the language, the company,
  the furniture, the yearning and swelling
  heart,
Affection that will not be gainsay'd, the sense
  of what is real, the thought if after all it
  should prove unreal,
The doubts of day-time and the doubts of
  night-time, the curious whether and how,
Whether that which appears so is so, or is it all
  flashes and specks?
Men and women crowding fast in the streets, if
  they are not flashes and specks what are
  they?
The streets themselves and the facades of
  houses, and goods in the windows,
Vehicles, teams, the heavy-plank'd wharves,
  the huge crossing at the ferries,
The village on the highland seen from afar at
  sunset, the river between,
Shadows, aureola and mist, the light falling on
  roofs and gables of white or brown two miles
  off,
The schooner near by sleepily dropping down
  the tide, the little boat slack-tow'd astern,
The hurrying tumbling waves, quick-broken
  crests, slapping,
The strata of color'd clouds, the long bar of
  maroon-tint away solitary by itself, the
  spread of purity it lies motionless in,
The horizon's edge, the flying sea-crow, the
  fragrance of salt marsh and shore mud,
These became part of that child who went forth
  every day, and who now goes, and will
  always go forth every day.

—Walt Whitman
There Was a Child Went Forth (1871)

PART ONE
Beginning to Teach

CHAPTER 1

How to Survive While Teaching
Suggestions and guidelines for the first few weeks

Wanting to teach is like wanting to have children or to write or paint or dance or invent or think through a mathematical problem that only a few have been able to solve. It has an element of mystery, involving as it does the yearly encounter with new people, the fear that you will be inadequate to meet their needs, as well as the rewards of seeing them become stronger because of your work. And as is true of the other creative challenges, the desire to teach and the ability to teach well are not the same thing. With the rarest of exceptions, one has to learn how to become a good teacher just as one has to learn how to become a scientist or an artist.

— Herbert Kohl (1984)

Childhood is a unique and valuable stage in the life cycle. Our paramount responsibility is to provide safe, healthy, nurturing, and responsive settings for children. We are committed to supporting children's development by cherishing individual differences, by helping them learn to live and work cooperatively, and by promoting their self-esteem.
— National Association for the Education of
Young Children (1989)

Have you ever wondered . . .

Whether you'll ever get used to teaching?

What to do about feeling helpless and incompetent?

Whether anyone else ever hated a child in his class?

Why you felt terribly tired?

If you have, the material in the following pages will help you.

Teaching preschool children can be one of the best, most deeply satisfying experiences in the world. Children ages 2 to 5 go through fascinating, swiftly accomplished stages of development. They are possessed of vigorous personalities, rich enthusiasms, an astonishing amount of physical energy, and strong wills. With the exception of infancy there is no other time in human life when so much is learned in so brief a period (Bloom, 1964).

This phenomenal vigor and burgeoning growth present a challenge to the beginning teacher that is at once exhilarating and frightening. The task is a large one: the teacher must attempt to build an educational climate that enhances the children's development and whets their appetites for further learning. The milieu must also nourish and sustain emotional health, encourage physical growth and muscular prowess, foster satisfying social interactions, enhance creativity, develop language skills, and promote the development of mental ability. Moreover, this must all be garbed in an aura of happiness and affection in order to establish that basic feeling of well-being that is essential to successful learning.

With such a large task at hand, it is not surprising that the beginning teacher may wonder somewhat desperately where to begin and what to do—and that is what this chapter is all about. It is intended to start you on the right track and help you survive those first perilous but exciting days of student teaching.

Granted, the first weeks of teaching are not easy, but they need not be impossible either. However, it is wise for you to make allowances for possible stress and not to be disappointed if you feel more tired than usual, or occasionally disheartened, or bewildered. These feelings will become less frequent as time passes and the children, staff, and routine become more familiar. They will also diminish as you gain more skill and confidence.

SOME THOUGHTS ABOUT GETTING STARTED

Think of Yourself As Providing a Life-Affirming Environment and Use That As a Yardstick When Working with Children

Life-affirming teachers see children and themselves as being involved in a positive series of encounters, intended to facilitate growth and happiness. They have faith that children want to do the right thing—that they can grow and change for the better—and they have confidence that teachers and parents can assist them in that task.

Such teachers accept their own humanness and that of other people, and they know it takes strength, determination, and knowledge to sustain these life-affirming policies in situations where children are just learning the rudiments of socially acceptable behavior, in a time when many families are disorganized and unhappy.

They realize that sometimes a child can seem lost in a morass of angry feelings and strike out at others, but they also have confidence she knows deep

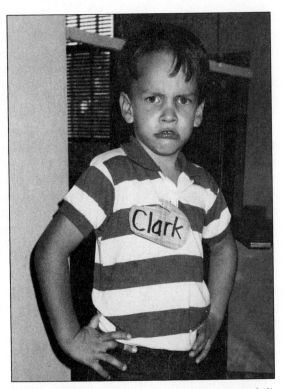

Sometimes children can be lost in a morass of angry feelings.

inside that this behavior is not working well. They know it is possible for a life-affirming teacher to lead that child onto the firmer ground of being socially acceptable if he is patient, positive, and consistent.

Increase Your Self-Esteem by Realizing You Are Part of a Noble, Though Young, Tradition

Interest in the study of children and awareness of the value of educating their parents in wholesome child-rearing practices began to grow around the turn of the century. My own mother was one of the first parent education leaders in Los Angeles, and I well remember her going off to speak to other earnest mothers at various school-sponsored gatherings more than 50 years ago. That this interest continues today is shown by the continued popularity of child-rearing books and the growing awareness that what parents and teachers do during the early years of childhood can make a significant contribution to the future well-being of the child. The newest indication of such concern is the addition of parenting classes by many high schools throughout the United States.

Along with the burgeoning interest in child development came a companion interest in nursery-level education and child care. This began abroad where such leaders as Maria Montessori and the McMillan sisters pioneered child care as a means of improving the well-being of children of the poor.

In 1907 Maria Montessori, an ardent young reformer-physician, began her *Casa dei Bambini* (Children's House). That child care center was originally founded as part of an experiment in refurbishing slum housing in an economically distressed quarter of Rome. Supporters of that cooperative housing venture found that young children left unattended during the day while their parents were away at work were getting into trouble and destroying the property that people had worked so hard to restore. Therefore, they wanted to work out some way for the children to be cared for. Under Montessori's guidance, Children's House emphasized health, cleanliness, sensory training, individual learning, and the actual manipulation of materials (Montessori, 1912). Since Montessori felt that individual experience with self-correcting materials must come before other learning could take place, language experience, the use of imagination, and dramatic play were not recognized as being of much importance (Braun & Edwards, 1972). Montessori stressed that the teacher should be a cultivated woman and that she should live in the community wherein she taught.

In England, too, the pathetic condition of young slum children was being recognized. In 1911 two English sisters, Margaret and Rachel McMillan, founded their open-air nursery school. The McMillans had been interested in socialism and the women's movement and through these concerns came to know the condition of the London poor. They were horrified to discover there were many children running loose in the London slums suffering from lice, malnutrition, and scabies. Like Children's House, their school stressed good health, nourishing food, and adequate medical care. Unlike Children's House, it emphasized the value of outdoor play, sandboxes, and regular baths. (The school featured deep tubs wherein the children were regularly bathed.) The McMillans advocated teaching children together in small groups. They also believed that young girls had natural gifts working with children, so they gave them paid, on-the-job training as they worked with the children (McMillan, 1929).

Nursery education in the United States witnessed a flowering of interest in the early 1920s. In 1915 a short-lived Montessori school was founded in New York by Eva McLin. However, the Montessori philosophy was severely criticized on a variety of grounds, including that there was no opportunity for self-expression, children were not encouraged to play together, and the conception of freedom was inadequate (White & Buka, 1987). Therefore, that school of thought failed to take strong root in the United States until the 1950s, when increasing concern about cognitive learning sparked by *Sputnik* combined with the war on poverty produced renewed interest in the Montessori program.

At about the same time the McLin school was established, a group of women at the University of Chicago began the first parent cooperative nursery school in 1916 (Osborn, 1980). In 1919 Harriet Johnson opened the City and County School that later metamorphosized into Bank Street. Abigail Eliot began the Ruggles Street Nursery School in Boston in 1921—the same year that Patty Smith Hill founded a laboratory nursery school at Columbia Teachers College.

As interest in nursery-level education grew, the academic community began to offer training in the field and professional associations were formed. For example, at the Merrill Palmer School of Motherhood and Home Training (which later became the prestigious Merrill Palmer Institute), a nursery school was provided where students participated in an 8-hour laboratory experience each week. They studied child care management, health, nutrition, and social problems—not very different from what students do, at least in part, today! Other academically based centers included ones at Iowa State, Ohio State, Cornell, Georgia, Purdue, Kansas, Nebraska, Oklahoma A&M, Cincinnati, and Oregon State (Osborn, 1980).

Shortly after that, in 1925, Patty Smith Hill called a meeting of early leaders in the field to discuss issues of concern in the care of young children. In 1929 the National Association of Nursery Education was founded. That association has continued to the present day and is now known as the National Association for the Education of Young Children.

Various government agencies in the United States have participated in the field of child care and education from time to time, but they have never been a consistent, encompassing source of support. During the Great Depression of the 1930s the government added impetus to the growth of child care by sponsoring nearly 3,000 such programs in 31 states. These were intended to provide work for unemployed women as well as care for children for the poor. This federal support continued during World War II so that women could have their children cared for as they worked in war-related industries. (I recall Edith Dowley, a longtime professor of early childhood education, telling me what it had been like to work in one of those 24-hour-a-day centers during the war. At one point she suddenly realized she was tripping over her feet because her shoes were so loose. When she weighed herself, she found she had lost 40 pounds in 3 months while struggling to get one of the wartime centers started.)

Although these federally supported programs are now largely defunct (one one or two states, such as California, have continued to operate them), they may have helped pave the way for the most widely known government-supported program currently in place: Head Start. Head Start provides education and services to young children and their families who are poor. Title XX also makes money available for child care for some families on welfare, and the federal government offers some support to middle-class families by providing them with the Dependent Care Tax Credit deduction—a benefit that only indirectly supports child care programs. The majority of half- and full-day early education programs, however, have never received major government support. Their growth has been gradual and marked by inspired teachers, hard work, and somewhat precarious financing.

Today the demand for child care continues to rise as more and more women join the work force, yet government support remains meager. In 1990 more than 58% of preschool-aged children in the United States had mothers working outside the home, and that number is expected to rise to 65% by 1995 (Children's Defense Fund, 1989). This phenomenal increase in employment creates a continuing need for children's centers as the demand for quality, licensed care continues to outstrip the supply (Hofferth, 1989). The field is likely to continue to expand astronomically in the near future.

Choosing a Place to Teach

The manner by which students are assigned to their practice-teaching schools varies considerably among colleges. Sometimes students are allowed to select their placement from a list of satisfactory schools; sometimes the practice-teaching experience takes place in a demonstration school; and sometimes the student is assigned at the discretion of the supervising teacher.

Regardless of the method of assignment, you should know there are many kinds of situations in which to receive training in the field of early childhood education. These can be divided into seven main types: private schools, cooperatives, "compensatory" programs, full-day centers, kindergartens, Montessori schools, and demonstration or laboratory schools.

Private Schools

Private schools are so named because they do not depend on public funding for support. They are often half-day programs that tend to offer traditional nursery school curriculum based on the individual needs of the children. The program is likely to stress creativity and social and emotional adjustment. Such schools usually serve middle-class families, and they meet a real need for early childhood education in this portion of the community. They are often located in church buildings since many churches offer these facilities at nominal cost. The Ecumenical Child Care Network (1989) reports that in 1988 churches furnished either direct or indirect support for more than 18,000 day care programs serving more than 1,700,700 children. Although some of these are church related, many others are not, and the building is provided during the week as a community service.

Cooperatives

Cooperatives usually have fewer professional teachers and more mothers and fathers participating than private schools do, although they are private in the sense that they too do not usually have public funds for support. They offer the special enrichment provided by a high adult-child ratio, and the children who attend them also profit from the abundance of ideas furnished by so many different adults. As previously noted, the cooperative nursery school has been a tradition in this country since 1916 (Lesser & Gold, 1988; Stevenson, 1990). The movement is flourishing anew on many college campuses where young families are banding together to provide care for their children by this relatively inexpensive method (Sussman, 1984). It is still the case that many teachers enter the profession by participating in a well-run co-op when their children are young, finding that they love to teach and going on to further training in early childhood education.

Compensatory Programs

Head Start, a federally funded program, is the best known of the compensatory programs, since it exists on a nationwide basis. Some states also fund additional preschool programs designed to educate children from low-income families. Although termed *compensatory* because they were originally intended to compensate for lacks in the child's home environment, current investigations have found greater strengths in the homes than had previously been noted. Now the programs seek to honor these strengths as well as to compensate for lags in verbal and mental development.

Day Care Centers

Day care centers offer full-day child care. They usually serve the children of working parents, some of whom are fairly well-to-do and some of whom are not. Funds for such care are provided both by parents and by state or public agencies. Good day care programs are delightful and valuable because of the leisurely pace and the extended learning experiences that they provide. Mediocre, custodial day care services are still a stain on the conscience of some communities and need to be remedied and modified for the welfare of the children.

The 1980s witnessed a phenomenal growth of chains of for-profit centers, ranging from an annual rate of 8 to 10%. However, that trend may be changing since growth slowed to less than 2% in 1989 and 1990 (Neugebauer, 1991). Despite this slowdown, these enterprises continue to offer teachers such possibilities as packaged curricula written by professionals, centralized methods of accounting, and clearly prescribed policies that keep cost down while, in many cases, maintaining a reasonable level of care for children.

Kindergarten Programs and Public School Programs for 4-Year-Olds

During training, some students have the opportunity to split their teaching experience between the kindergarten, first, or second grade, and the preprimary level in a public school setting. Such assignments, which are more typically the case for university rather than community college students, are almost always arranged between colleges of education and the public school in question. Even in that circumstance it may be possible for students to express interest in working with a particular teacher if they are willing to be a little assertive. A good way to identify a teacher who would be congenial is to keep your eyes open during visitations or during early aiding experiences and to ask other students for their opinions, too. Just bear in mind that different students can have radically different feelings about the same teacher, so reserve the right to make the final decision for yourself.

Montessori Schools

Placement in schools that base their curriculum on the teachings of Maria Montessori is usually quite difficult to arrange unless the student is participating in an academic program philosophically based in the same tradition. This is because Montessori schools require their teachers to undergo training specifically related to Montessori's precepts. Occasionally students who do not meet this criterion can find employment as an aide or during the summer in such schools, thereby gaining at least some exposure to the methods and philosophy of that distinguished educator.

Demonstration or Laboratory Schools

Demonstration or laboratory schools are typically connected with teacher-training institutions or with research programs. They can be wonderful places for young students to begin their teaching, since they are the most likely of all the kinds of schools to be child and *student* centered. Ideally students should have teaching opportunities in both laboratory and real-life schools so that they receive a balance of ideal and realistic teaching experiences.

SOME COMFORTING THOUGHTS

Do Teachers Matter?

Two of the outstanding characteristics of beginning teachers are the caring and involvement that they bring with them to their work, and it is heartening to remember that these characteristics are important factors in achieving success. Weikart and Lambie (1970), for example, found that no matter what kind of curricular model was followed (that of Piaget or Bereiter, or a more traditional model), the involvement of the teacher and his or her implementation of the curriculum were fundamental to the success of the outcome. Another researcher (Katz, 1969) attributed the failure of a program she studied to the fact that the teachers gave lip service to the curriculum and failed to carry it through in practice.

In summing up a number of studies of the impact of teachers' behavior on children, Phyfe-Perkins (1981) reports that successful teachers encouraged independent activity, planned a variety of activities, and used criticism and negative commands "sparingly." Such teachers were aware of several activities at the same time and could do more than one thing at a time. Their transitions between activities were smooth, and they were *involved with the children* but did not constantly try to direct their behavior.

So on days when things may not have gone just right, it may be a comfort to remember that involvement and caring are valuable qualities already possessed by the student. It is, of course, an ancient truth that the more one puts into any experience, the more one gets out of it—and teaching is no exception.

The Master Teacher Is Probably Ill at Ease, Too

Sometimes students are so wrapped up in their own shyness that they fail to realize that the teachers they are working with are shy of them as well. They attribute all the awkwardness of the first days on the job to their own insecurities and inexperience. Actually the master teacher is willing to help but may also be a little uncomfortable, particularly if he has not had many students before. It will help him help the student if he knows that the student likes him.

One Poor Experience with a Student Will Not Ruin a Child's Life

Some conscientious new teachers are almost too sensitive to the effect their actions will have on the children. It is true that young children are more vulnerable to influences than older children are, and for this reason everyone attempts to do his or her very best. But the significance of the single traumatic experience has been overrated. It is usually the continuing approach or climate that molds the child (Dugan & Coles, 1989; Werner & Smith, 1982). Therefore,

The ability to enjoy children is one of the basic elements of good teaching.

A LET'S-FIND-OUT PROJECT: WHAT MIXES WITH WHAT!*

I set up my Let's-Find-Out project at the science table. I had three large plastic containers with water in them mixed with salt, sand, and dirt so the children could shake them and see what happened. Plastic tubs of soap powder, sand, salt, flour, sugar, oil, baking soda, cornstarch, and dirt were placed out on a food tray with spoons. I had 10 small plastic jars with water in them for mixing these things with. I placed out towels, paper towels, and a large metal bowl of water for cleanup. The questions and information sheets were taped onto the board in that area with a blue background of construction paper to make it look more attractive.

How I Changed It During the Week

Because this was such a messy project and because it required constant replenishing for every group, I found myself having to be at the Institute before every class. My schedule did not allow me to reset the project up on Tuesday afternoon or on Thursday morning. Some of the other teachers did that for me on Tuesday afternoon, but from what I understand the activity was not there for the 3-year-olds on Thursday morning.

I had some ideas of how to change the activity during the week by providing new things to mix, such as paint or food coloring, but after seeing and hearing how the children reacted to the project, I dumped my own ideas. The children were really using the activity as a trial-and-error cooking project so I went with their ideas. I deleted the sand and dirt from the plastic containers on Thursday afternoon and carried the stove over to the area to promote cooking experiments. Friday, I noticed that the class of 4-year-olds had decided to have the teacher write down what they were making or make their own recipes. It would have been a good idea for me to include a pencil and pad of paper to encourage this.

Evaluation of Activity

The most noticeable aspect of this project was how messy it was. It really made me uncomfortable that I had planned an activity that made such a mess and required a teacher's assistance at all times when I wasn't present. But in the same light I took

---

*Courtesy Melissa Kyle, Fundamentals of Instruction I student paper. Institute of Child Development, University of Oklahoma, Norman.

the student need not agonize over one mishandled situation on the grounds that it may have scarred the child for life; this is a most unlikely result.

Evaluating Activities Can Turn a Student into a Better Teacher

Analyzing an activity after presenting it by noting its strengths as well as its weaknesses is one of the quickest ways to improve one's teaching. When things

this positively because this meant that the activity was really being used. For any activity to be as meaningful as possible, it does require the teacher's presence to expand and explain. I think, and other teachers told me, that the children really enjoyed the activity. No matter how messy and inconvenient it was for the teachers, it was beneficial for the children and that's what counts! The children got a good idea of how different things mix or don't mix with water. They also got to see what happened when you mix things with water simultaneously.

Since I have been at the Institute, I have never seen a Let's-Find-Out activity be used and enjoyed as much as this one. I think this is because the children could actually do so much instead of watching or looking. I also think it went over well because there were so many different possible combinations to test.

Suggestions for Improvement

This activity brought to my attention how important it is to have a teacher involved in Let's-Find-Out projects. There's no telling how many wonderful learning opportunities have been passed by because there was no teacher on the spot in this area to draw out ideas and extend the learning. It would be very beneficial to assign one teacher each week for each age group to get the full benefit.

At first I thought that this would have been better as a 1-day activity; but as I saw it being used by the same children day after day, I decided that I was wrong. The children that were using it were the same ones that had used it the day before. This discovery brought to my attention how important it is to repeat activities so that children are able to enjoy and learn as much as they wish to.

Another suggestion is to remind the teachers to use the information and questions posted to help extend the learning experience. Many more avenues could have been explored by using that information.

I toyed with the idea of using an evaporation project with this, and I'm glad I didn't. I think that would have been too overwhelming, and the educational value of it would have been lost. What was provided was enough to keep their minds full, especially when the teachers used their imagination and the children's, too.

Next time it would be nice to have some things to mix that have some color; but then again, I think the all white and cream colors are what promoted the cooking play. I think if I could have been around more, I would have switched off to food coloring and paint towards the end of the week to extend the children's learning in another direction.

may not have gone exactly right, it's easy to dwell on the negative aspects and forget the positive ones. Even when things could have gone better, rather than investing a lot of energy in regretting the errors, it is more healthy and productive to figure out what went wrong and decide how to be more effective next time. It is also helpful to repeat the experience as soon as possible (rather like getting back on a horse and riding again right after you've fallen off) so that bad memories are supplanted by better ones.

The excerpts on pages 12 to 13 illustrate how one student analyzed an activity and improved the situation as the week progressed. Note, in particular, how sensitive she was to building on the interests of the children.

Remember There Is a Wide Variety of Places to Use Your Training in Addition to Conventional School Situations

Sometimes students become baffled and discouraged when after giving it a fair chance they just do not like teaching a group of children in a half- or full-day setting of any kind, yet they know in their hearts they wish to continue working with young children. For people in that quandary, it can be helpful to turn to the reference published by the National Association for the Education of Young Children (Seaver, Cartwright, Ward, & Heasley, 1983) to review the array of careers for which training in working effectively with the young can form a base. These possibilities range from becoming a childlife specialist in a children's hospital, to going into business for oneself and operating a family day care home, to working in child care licensing.

Remember That Age Need Not Be a Negative Factor When Learning to Teach Young Children

One of the most interesting trends in recent years has been the return to school by women who, for one reason or another, have decided to reenter the working world outside the home. Sometimes it can be a bit daunting to women in their middle years to take classes surrounded by people newly graduated from high school. A number of such women have confided to me that it is frightening to return and have to compete with those they perceive as brighter or at least younger than they.

The truth is that every age brings with it some special assets. It may well be the case that younger students are more accustomed to managing the routines of studying and campus life. However, it can be a comforting thought to more mature learners to remember they, in turn, bring special skills and benefits to the college experience. These usually include more experience with children (there's nothing like having a couple of children of your own to breed humility and compassion for other parents) and also a wider perspective on life that can serve reentry students well as they work to increase their teaching skills.

BASIC PROFESSIONAL ETHICS

Now that the student is becoming a member of a profession, it will be helpful to know from the beginning some ethical guidelines that are observed by most teachers. The National Association for the Education of Young Children has recently released a complete summary of those guidelines, included in Appendix A (National Association for the Education of Young Children, 1989).

Some of the most fundamental ethical principles teachers should observe include the following items.

When in Doubt About the Value of a Decision, Put the Child's Welfare First

Granted, what is "best" may not always be easy to determine. There will always remain special circumstances where we cannot be certain what is best for the child's welfare. For example, is it better for a 3-year-old to stay with a loving but emotionally disturbed and disoriented single parent, or to place her with a less disturbed but apparently cold and emotionally remote grandmother? But it is also true that much of the time, if the teachers honestly try to do what is best for the child rather than what is merely convenient or "the rule," they will be on the right ethical track.

Strive to Be Fair to All Children

Another important guideline to observe is that all children deserve a fair chance and a reasonable amount of concern from each teacher. Perhaps the student will recall situations in his or her own school life where a teacher made a scapegoat of some child and picked on her continually, or where another teacher never seemed to notice some of the youngsters. Although nobody intends to have this kind of thing happen, sometimes it does, and teachers should be warned against behaving this way. Every child is important and is entitled to be valued by the teacher.

Keep Personal Problems Private During the Day

Teachers should not discuss their personal problems or emotional difficulties with the parents, nor should they discuss them with other teachers while school is in session. Teachers need to leave personal problems at the door as they begin the day, since the time at school rightfully belongs to the children. The discussion of personal matters should take place after the children have gone home. Many a teacher has discovered that shutting such troubles out during the teaching day can provide interludes of relief and happiness that can make otherwise intolerable situations bearable.

Show Respect for the Child

One important way teachers of young children demonstrate basic respect for others is by refraining from discussing a child in her presence unless she is included directly in the conversation. Sometimes teachers thoughtlessly talk over the children's heads, assuming that the youngsters are unaware of what is being said. But students who have had the experience of eavesdropping while people were discussing them will no doubt remember the special potency of that overhead comment. Anything said about a child in her presence needs to be said with her included. Thus it is more desirable to say, "Peg, I can see you're feeling pretty tired and hungry" than to cock an eyebrow in her direction and remark to another teacher, "Oh, brother! We are in a nasty temper today!"

An even more fundamental aspect of respect between teacher and child can best be described as a valuing of the person: the teacher who truly respects and values the child pauses to listen to her with full attention whenever this is possible, remembering that each child is a unique person, relishing her for her differences from her companions, and allowing her to generate ideas of her own rather than subtly teaching her it is better to accept unquestioningly the teacher's ideas as being best.

This kind of respect is, of course, a two-way street. Teachers who hold the child in such respectful regard set a model for the youngster, who will in time reflect this same fundamental consideration back to them. This process can be accelerated and strengthened if the teacher quietly makes a point of protecting his own rights, as well as the children's. He may say something as simple as, "Now, Margaret, I've listened to you; take just a minute and hear what I want to say," or he may make this same point with another child by saying, "You know, my desk is just like your cubby. I don't take your things out of that, and you must never take anything from my desk, either."

Observe Professional Discretion

Still another aspect of respect for people is respect for the family's privacy. Family affairs and children's behavior should not be discussed with people outside the school who have no need to know about them. Even amusing events should never be told unless the names of the children either are not mentioned or are changed. Most communities are smaller worlds than a beginning teacher may realize, and news can travel with astonishing rapidity.

In general, student teachers should be wary of being drawn into discussions with parents about their own or other families' children. This kind of discussion is the teacher's prerogative, and it is a wise student who passes off questions about youngsters by making some pleasant remark and referring the parent to the teacher. Nobody is ever antagonized by a student who does this in a tactful way, but disasters can result from well-meant comments by ill-informed or tactless beginners.

In addition, students should not discuss situations they disapprove of at the school where they work or say anything critical about another teacher to outsiders. These remarks have an unpleasant way of returning to the source, and the results can be awkward, to say the least. The principle "If you don't say it, they can't repeat it" is a sound one here. It is better, instead, to talk the problem over in confidence with the college supervisor.

Observe the Chain of Command

In just about every organization there is a chain of command. It is always wise to avoid going over anyone's head when making a comment or request. Understandably, teachers hate being put in a bad light by a student's talking a problem over with the school director or principal before talking it over with the teacher first.

A related aspect of this authority structure is being sure to get permission before planning a special event such as a field trip or getting out the hoses after a videotape on water play. Answers to such requests are generally yes, but it is always best to check before embarking on a major venture.

SOME RECOMMENDATIONS FOR STARTING OUT

Although not always possible, it helps to find some things out before beginning the first student-teaching day. For example, it is helpful to talk with the teacher and determine the expected arrival time and the recommended style of clothing. Most schools are reasonable and will recommend sensible but professional-looking clothes. Many teachers, both men and women, wear some sort of apron since the pockets and protection it provides are real assets. When clothing is protected, it is much more likely teachers will gather a painty or messy child onto their laps and give them a hug than when they are dressed for classes later that day.

Some schools have written guidelines they can give the student to read. Time schedules and lists of rules are also very helpful to review. (For a typical schedule, see chapter 3.) If the school does not have these items written down, ask the teacher how basic routines such as eating and taking children to the toilet are handled, and ask about crucial safety rules and for a brief review of the schedule. If the student can come for a visit when the children are not there, the teacher will have a better opportunity to chat. During this visit make a special point of finding out where the children's cubbies are, where sponges and cleanup materials are kept, and where various supplies are stored. Don't hesitate to ask questions; just do your best to remember the answers!

PRACTICAL THINGS TO DO
TO INCREASE COMPETENCE

Gain Confidence in Your Ability to Control the Group

Almost invariably the first thing students want to discuss is discipline. Since this is the point everyone seems most concerned about, it is recommended that the reader begin preparation for work by reading the chapters on discipline and aggression in order to build skills in this area. Those reviews will help, but observation, practice, and seeing situations all the way through are the best ways to gain competence in controlling children.

Get to Know the Children As Soon As Possible

One way to become familiar with each child is to make a list of their names from the sign-in sheet and then jot down a few adjectives or facts to remember about each one. Calling the children by name at every opportunity will help, too. It will not take more than a day or two to become well acquainted, and it will help you belong to the group more quickly.

Develop the Proverbial "Eyes in the Back of the Head"

One of the most common failings of inexperienced teachers is their tendency to focus on only one child at a time. It is pleasant and much "safer" to sit down and read a favorite book with one or two lovable children and ignore the chaos going on in the block corner, but good teachers form the habit of total awareness. They develop a sense of what is happening in the entire area. This is true outdoors as well as inside. But to say that the teacher should never plan to settle down with any group would be an exaggeration. Of course, teachers have to center their attention on specific children from time to time or there is little satisfaction to the experience for teacher or child, but teachers must keep tuned to the whole room as well. Sometimes such a simple technique as learning to look up frequently will help build skills in this area. Another technique is sitting so that the whole room or whole playground can be seen. Many beginning students sit with their backs to half the room—this is simply courting trouble.

Take Action in Unsafe Situations Immediately

Since students are sometimes afraid of appearing too restrictive in a liberal atmosphere, they allow dangerous things to happen because they do not know the rule or school policy about it. The general rule of thumb is that when one is unsure whether the activity is dangerous, it is better to stop it and then check to see what the teacher thinks. Stopping a few activities that are safe is better than letting two children wrestle each off the top of the slide while the student debates indecisively below. Things generally look less dangerous to students as they gain experience and feel less anxious, *but it is always better to be safe than sorry.*

Encourage the Growth of Independence and Competence; Avoid Overteaching, Overhelping, and Overtalking

As a general principle, we encourage children at the preprimary level to do everything they can for themselves. This is different from the behavior of the teacher who sees the role as doing *to* and doing *for* children. It takes self-control to wait while Katy fumbles for the zipper, insight to see how to assist her without taking over, and self-discipline not to talk too much while she is learning. But building competencies in the children by letting them do things for themselves increases their self-esteem so much that practicing restraint is worth the effort.

Encourage Originality of Self-Expression

One of the most frowned-on things students can do is to make models of something for the children to copy when they are working with creative materials. It is easy to be trapped into making someone a snake or drawing a man for another youngster, but early childhood teachers dislike providing such models because they limit children's expression of their own feelings and ideas. It is better to relish the materials with the children and help them use them for their own purposes.

Keep Contacts with the Children As Quiet and Meaningful As Possible

Except in a real emergency, walk over to the child to talk with her rather than calling across the room. Use a low voice, and bend down so she can see your face and be less overwhelmed by your size. (An excellent way to find out how big an adult is from a child's point of view is to ask a friend to stand up and teach you something while you remain sitting on the floor. It's enlightening.)

Expect to Do Menial Tasks

No other profession requires the full range of abilities and effort that preschool teaching does. These extend from inspiring children and counseling parents to doing the most menial types of cleanup. Sometimes students do not realize this, so they feel imposed upon when they are asked to change a pair of pants or mop the floor or clean the guinea pig. This kind of work is expected of almost all early childhood teachers as just part of school life. Not only is cleaning up to be expected, but also continual straightening up is necessary as the day progresses. Blocks should be arranged on shelves and dress-up clothes rehung several times to keep the room looking attractive. (Unfortunately there is no good fairy who will come along and do this.)

Learn from the Start to Be Ingenious About Creating Equipment and Scrounging Materials

Early childhood programs almost always operate on lean budgets, and every school develops a number of ingenious ways to stretch money and invent equipment. Students can learn from each place they work by picking up these economical ideas from the staff, and they can contribute much by sharing their

Allowing children to do things "on their own" helps them build sound feelings of self-esteem.

own ideas about the creative use of materials and new sources of free supplies. Be on the lookout for so-called waste materials that other businesses throw away. The carpet company's colorful scraps can make handsome additions to the collage box, for example, and rubber tires can be used in fascinating ways to make sturdy play equipment.

Organize Yourself Before Beginning to Teach

It is very helpful to arrive early on each teaching day so there is time to get everything together in advance for the morning or afternoon. Nothing beats the feeling of security this preparation breeds. Life is also easier if before going home the student asks what will be happening during the next teaching session. It is important to check in advance and make certain needed supplies are on hand. Asking in advance also makes reading up on activities ahead of time possible—a real security enhancer!

It increases confidence if you know the schedule well enough to tell what is going to happen next, as well as what time it is likely to happen. This allows time for cleanup and also helps avoid the disappointment of moving into a new activity just as the group is expected to wash up for lunch. For these reasons, it is advisable to always wear a watch.

When You Need Help, Ask for It

People usually are not critical if beginners admit they do not know something and have the courage to ask, but they are inclined to resent students who protect themselves by appearing to know everything already or who defend themselves by making constant excuses. When one is unsure of a policy at the school, it never does any harm to say to the child, "I don't know if it's all right to climb on the fence. Let's ask Mrs. Green and then we'll both know."

The chance to chat with the master teacher while cleaning up at the end of the morning, or at some other convenient time of day, is an invaluable time to raise problems and ask questions. During the day itself, students often have to "muddle through"—learning by observation and using their own common sense. Nothing disastrous is likely to take place, and teachers are usually too busy to be corralled for more than a sentence or two of explanation while school is in progress.

RECOGNIZE STRESS AND DEAL WITH IT AS EFFECTIVELY AS POSSIBLE

It is inevitable to feel stress when dealing with a new situation such as beginning teaching, and it is valuable to recognize this fact so that you can deal with it effectively rather than just feeling anxious, overwhelmed, or disappointed because sometimes you are exhausted at the end of the day. So much about the experience is new. There are so many personalities to deal with and so much to learn, so much uncertainty and excitement, and such a great desire to please without knowing exactly what is expected. This situation is clearly a lot to handle. These stresses do not mean that teaching is bad or unpleasant. Many novel situations such as getting married or receiving a promotion are delightful; but they are stressful nonetheless because they represent change, and change requires learning and adaptation.

Symptoms of stress vary with the individual. Some people lose their appetites, while others try to comfort themselves by eating too much. Still others suffer from loss of sleep or find they get angry at the slightest provocation.

Wise teachers acknowledge the possibility of stress and make practical plans for coping so they can avoid coming down with various ailments or experiencing the excessive fatigue that prevents them from functioning effectively. Unfortunately such plans require a certain amount of self-discipline. Deciding to get plenty of rest, for example, is rarely a favorite prescription for the young, and yet it really does reduce stress, as does adequate nutrition and provision for having fun off the job (Shafer, 1982).

Truthful analysis of what is causing the most intense stress also helps. It might be apprehension about a child's threat to bite you, or it might be worry over how to keep the group attentive during story time, or it might be concern about whether other teachers or parents like you. Whatever it is, identifying the source is the first step toward reducing worry and strain. Solutions beyond that point vary according to case, but after identification, successful reduction of stress depends on making some kind of plan for coping with it and then having the fortitude to carry the plan through. Selye (1981) was certainly correct when he commented that "action absorbs anxiety." For example, rather than just worrying over the coming group time, it is better to take action by acquainting yourself with the materials in advance, planning for variety, choosing activities the children are interested in, and having them actively participate.

Making realistic estimates about how long it will take you to accomplish something takes the strain and worry out of trying to get it done at the last minute. It is better to allow yourself too much time for planning than to come up short. Prioritizing helps, too. Choosing things that must be done and doing those first is a great stress-reducer. Concentrating on just one thing at a time also blocks out worry and helps you appreciate the present experience to its fullest. After all, all anyone really has is the present moment of existence. Why not seek to be aware of it fully while it is here?

Deliberately creating opportunities for relaxation is still another effective way of handling stress. Finding a quiet place and letting go from the toes all the way to the forehead and ears can be quieting and refreshing. Such strategies need not take long, but it is necessary to make a point of remembering to use them from time to time.

The final thing that can help reduce stress is having a safety valve available. Everyone should be aware of things they can do for themselves that take the pressure off for a while when life is too demanding. These solutions vary a lot. I have had people tell me they do everything from going shopping, taking a swim, or reading a detective story, to telling another person how they feel. The important thing about such strategies is that they should not be used as ways of permanently avoiding the stressful situation because ultimately they can increase anxiety. At best they are stopgap measures that provide temporary relief and refreshment so that the person can pick up and go on in a reasonable period of time. When they are resorted to, I believe they should be used deliberately, purposefully, and without guilt. When used in that manner, such indulgence provides maximum refreshment and benefit.

SOME SPECIAL PROBLEMS

The following problems have come up often enough with students that they deserve discussion. Of course, because each situation is different, recommendations are risky. Nevertheless the following suggestions may provide solutions that may not have occurred to the student.

What to Do If You Hate the School to Which You Are Assigned

We have already mentioned that there are several different types of nursery school, child care, and kindergarten situations and that even the same type varies a good deal from school to school. Some schools seem to suit some students, and others fit other students better. Therefore do not conclude that teaching is not for you just because one placement is less than satisfactory. Maybe a change to another school is the answer to the problem; maybe it is not. At any rate, the place to begin solving the difficulty is by talking over the reason for the unhappiness with the supervising teacher from the college. This is a more productive, as well as a more ethical, solution than complaining to a friend.

It is also wise to refrain from making snap judgments about a teacher or placement. The first 2 or 3 weeks in any school will be some of the most stressful weeks of the student's career, and it is essential to realize that some people react to stress by attacking what is frightening them and by criticizing it; others shrink up and feel paralyzed or disillusioned. As time passes, the strain will probably lessen, and the school may seem more attractive, a little the way hospital food mysteriously improves as the patient recovers.

What to Do If You Don't Like a Child

It's no sin to dislike a child, but it *is* a sin not to admit your dislike, come to terms with it, and try to do something about it. Sometimes what will help most is getting to know him or her better, since insight often breeds compassion. Sometimes making progress of some sort with the child helps. Sometimes figuring out why you dislike the youngster will ease the feeling. With beginning students this often be traced to the fact that some children challenge adults or put them on the spot. Students who already feel insecure find this behavior particularly trying. Whatever the reason, it is more healthy to risk admitting your dislike to yourself and perhaps to your master teacher, if you feel safe with that person, and then to work toward resolving the problem. Although the suggested remedies may not overcome the dislike completely, they should help. At the very least, it is always possible to be fair and decent to all the children. Probably the liking will come in time.

THE WAY TO YOUR MASTER TEACHER'S HEART

We have already talked about the fact that it takes time to feel at home and to build a friendship with the master teacher. There are five more specific practices the student can follow that will help generate friendliness. The first is to be prepared to make the small, extra contribution of time and energy *beyond* what is expected. The student who stays the extra 10 minutes on potluck night to dry the coffee pot is well on the way to becoming a popular member of the staff.

The second thing sounds simple but is often overlooked because new teachers tend to be nervous. It is to *listen* to what the teacher tells you, and do your best to remember it!

The third thing is to offer help *before* being asked to lend a hand. Some students are so afraid of being pushy or of making mistakes that they never volunteer. But always having to request help gets tiresome for the master teacher, even if the student is willing when asked. It is better to develop an eye for all the little things that must be done and then to do them quietly. Such students are treasured by their master teachers.

Besides volunteering help, teachers also appreciate the student who contributes ideas for projects and activities. After all, it is not the master teacher's responsibility to provide all the ideas for your teaching days. Come prepared with a variety of suggestions so that, if one or two turn out to be impractical, you can be flexible and propose alternative possibilities.

Finally, the student should let enthusiasm show through. The vast majority of teachers follow their profession because they love it; the rigors of the job and the relatively low pay weed the others out very quickly. The teachers are, therefore, enthusiastic themselves. They are often "born" teachers, and they love teaching students as well as young children. Expressing thanks by being enthusiastic yourself will encourage them to keep on making the extra effort entailed in guiding student teachers.

SUMMARY

The student should grasp three basic principles before beginning to teach: master teachers are human, too; one poor experience won't ruin a child's life; and mistakes can be turned into valuable learning opportunities.

Even beginning students need to observe professional ethics when they are teaching. It is particularly important to respect each child and to preserve the privacy of the families whose children attend the school.

Gaining knowledge of the school's basic routines, schedules, and policies will make the early days of teaching a more comfortable experience for the young teacher. Some practical things to do that will increase the student's competence include gaining confidence in handling discipline situations, getting to know the children, being alert to the whole environment, taking swift action in situations that are dangerous, encouraging the growth of independence and originality of self-expression, making contact with the children as quietly and meaningfully as possible, being organized, realizing that age need not be a negative factor when learning to teach, and asking for help when it is needed.

Probably no other time in the life of the teacher is so exciting, unsettling, and challenging as the first days of student teaching. Teachers are fortunate who manage to retain at least some of this flutter of anticipation throughout their teaching lives.

QUESTIONS AND ACTIVITIES

1. Getting started in the first days of student teaching can be a special challenge, and it is helpful to know yourself and your own reactions well enough to be able to control them. How do you anticipate you will cope with the strangeness and unfamiliarity of

the student-teaching experience when you are just beginning? Close your eyes and think back to the last two or three occasions when you entered a new group and got acquainted. What was your personal mode of adapting? Did you talk a lot? Clam up? Act extremely helpful?

2. If you were guiding a young, new teacher, what advice would you give him or her that might help that person through the first days of teaching?

3. Do you believe that master teachers and professors are ever nervous or frightened when dealing with students, or do they seem invulnerable to such difficulties?

4. If you have ever had the good fortune to exist in a "life-affirming environment," identify the qualities you feel helped create that kind of emotional climate.

5. List some effective *do's* and *don'ts* for getting acquainted with young children. What are some effective ways of establishing friendly yet respectful relationships with them?

6. Do you know of some remedies that seem to help other people deal effectively with stress but do not seem to help you? What might these be, and why do you think they work for some people and not for others?

SELF-CHECK QUESTIONS FOR REVIEW

Content-Related Questions

1. Briefly outline the general history of the child care movement in the United States.

2. The text discusses the educational philosophies of two women who lived in England and Italy and helped begin the child care movement there. What are their names and what are some facts about the schools they founded?

3. Name several different kinds of child care situations and describe each of them in a general way.

4. What are some of the teacher behaviors identified by Phyfe-Perkins that have an important influence on young children?

5. Give some examples of ethical principles that teachers of young children should follow.

6. Name some practical things beginning teachers can do that will help them become competent as quickly as possible.

Integrative Questions

1. The book begins with a poem by Walt Whitman. What does the poem really mean, and how is it related to teaching young children?

2. The book lists some basic tenets of the Montessori and McMillan nursery schools. Compare the two schools. What do they have in common and how do they differ?

3. At this point in your experience, which kind of school (private, Head Start, cooperative, etc.) do you feel would best meet your needs as a student teacher? Discuss what might be the strong points and drawbacks of making that particular choice.

4. This chapter offers a number of suggestions for coping successfully with stress. Which of these suggestions do you personally feel would be the most helpful ones to use?

REFERENCES FOR FURTHER READING

Overviews

Morrison, G. (1988). *Early childhood education today* (4th ed.). Columbus, OH: Merrill. This helpful book offers a current overview of the kinds of early childhood settings that exist in the United States.

Maintaining Good Relationships with Children

Ashton-Warner, S. (1965). *Teacher*. New York: Bantam. In this classic, the author provides a fascinating description of how she, a beginning teacher, came to know the Maori children and how she developed a system of teaching reading based on what was significant in the children's lives. A not-to-be-missed book.

Ayers, W. (1989). *The good preschool teacher: Six teachers reflect on their lives*. New York: Teachers College Press. This book is a collection of interviews given by six very different teachers of preschool children combined with descriptions of events in their child care situations. It provides insights into a variety of viewpoints about what good teachers of young children think about and how they put their philosophies into action.

Read, K., Gardner, P., & Mahler, B. C. (1987). *Early childhood programs: Human relationships and learning* (8th ed.). New York: Holt, Rinehart & Winston. This is the all-time classic of nursery school education. As the title implies, it concentrates on the value of human relationships in the nursery school. A must for beginning teachers.

Maintaining Good Relationships with Other Adults

Blanchard, K., & Johnson, S. (1982). *The one minute manager*. New York: Berkeley. What this book has to say about communicating with people is valuable for all of us, not only managers!

Information About Approaches to Teaching Young Children

Bijou, S. W. (1981). Behavior analysis applied to early childhood education. In M. Kaplan-Sanoff & R. Yablans-Magid (Eds.), *Exploring early childhood: Readings in theory and practice*. New York: Macmillan. Bijou conducts a spirited attack on other philosophies of early education and then presents his case for using behavior modification techniques as a philosophical base.

Greenberg, P. (1970). *The devil has slippery shoes: A biased biography of the Child Development Group of Mississippi*. New York: Macmillan. The trials and tribulations of the Child Development Group of Mississippi in the early days of Head Start are described; still the best book for a sense of what Head Start was really like.

Montessori, M. (1967). *The discovery of the child*. (M. J. Costelloe, Trans.) Notre Dame, IN: Fides. There are many books about and by Dr. Montessori that expound her theories. This one gives an overview and so is probably most useful for the beginning teacher.

Neill, A. D. (1960). *Summerhill*. New York: Hart. Although this book describes a progressive English school for older children, it has delighted teachers who teach all ages by its emphasis on trusting the young to act on their own best behalf.

Pratt, C. (1948). *I learn from children*. New York: Harper & Row. (Reprinted 1990) It is wonderful having this classic of early childhood literature available once again. *Highly recommended.*

Regan, I. M., Mayfield, M. I., & Stange, B. L. (1988). Canadian alternatives in early childhood programs. *International Journal of Early Childhood Education, 20*(1), 3–11. This article reviews the alternatives of ethnically oriented, employer-supported, and parent-child centers.

Stevenson, J. H. (1990). The cooperative preschool model in Canada. In I. M. Doxey (Ed.), *Child care and education: Canadian dimensions*. Scarborough, Ontario: Nelson. Stevenson reviews the history and philosophy of the cooperative movement in Canada and also provides practical suggestions for operating that kind of school.

Taylor, K. W. (1981). *Parents and children learn together* (3rd ed.). New York: Teachers College Press. In Part One Taylor discusses general problems of parents and children. In Part Two she goes on to describe how parent-child cooperatives can function effectively.

Washington, V., & Oyemade, U. J. (1987). *Project Head Start: Past, present, and future trends in the context of family needs*. New York: Garland. This wide-ranging book presents a comprehensive survey of information about Head Start coupled with recommendations for potential changes in the system.

Histories of Early Childhood Education

Cunningham, C. E., & Osborn, D. K. (1979). A historical examination of Blacks in early childhood education. *Young Children, 34*(3), 20–29. This article traces the beginning of Black education in the United States back to 1620 when the Virginia Colony established a public school "for Negroes and Indians" all the way through to the present day. Makes interesting reading.

Greenberg, P. (1990). Before the beginning: A participant's view. *Young Children, 45*(6), 41–52. Greenberg reminisces about and summarizes the beginning of the Head Start program—and reminds us all of its basic, valuable intentions.

Hymes, J. L., Jr. (1991). *Early childhood education: Twenty years in review. A look at 1971–1990.* Washington, DC: National Association for the Education of Young Children. This one-of-a-kind reference is a readable and invaluable historical resource.

Osborn, D. K. (1980). *Early childhood education in historical perspective.* Athens, GA: Education Associates. This is a chronology of significant events in early childhood education with brief synopses of their significance. Dull unless you are interested in the subject, and then fascinating! A one-of-a-kind book.

White, S., & Buka, S. L. (1987). Early education: Programs, traditions, and policies. In E. Z. Rothkopt (Ed.), *Reviews of research in education* (Vol. 14). Washington, DC: American Educational Research Association. In this chapter, White and Buka provide a concise review of early childhood encompassing both the kindergarten and preschool level.

Dealing Effectively with Stress

Early Childhood Director's Association. (1983). *Survival kit for directors.* St. Paul, MN: Toys 'n Things Press (distributor). The Survival Kit singles out specific problems, and then explains step by step how the difficulty was solved. Highly recommended for its positive approach to problem solving and stress reduction.

Jorde, P. (1982). *Avoiding burnout: Strategies for managing time, space, and people in early childhood education.* Washington, DC: Acropolis Books. This is a wonderful, relevant book stuffed with ideas for managing one's life as a teacher and as a human being. *Highly recommended.*

Shafer, M. (1982). *Life after stress.* New York: Plenum Press. This sensible, very good book provides matter-of-fact advice about how to deal with stress—identifying it, resisting it, and coping with it when it happens. *Highly recommended.*

For the Advanced Student

deMause, L. (Ed.). (1974). *The history of childhood.* New York: The Psychohistory Press. This history covers such subjects as the middle-class child in urban Italy in the 14th century and childhood in Imperial Russia. It is a scholarly work that draws heavily on original sources, interesting to browse through.

Feeney, S., & Chun, R. (1985). Effective teachers of young children: Research in review. *Young Children, 41*(1), 47–52. The authors analyze teacher effectiveness from the perspective of personal characteristics, values, apparent behavior, sex, education, experience, and situational factors.

Roopnarine, J. L., & Johnson, J. E. (Eds.). (1987). *Approaches to early childhood education.* Columbus, OH: Merrill. This survey of programs stresses the research procedures and findings associated with their implementation in the preschool classroom.

Selye, H. (1981). The stress concept today. In I. L. Kutash, L. B. Schlesinger, & Associates (Eds.), *Handbook on stress and anxiety.* San Francisco: Jossey-Bass. After a review of the physiological reactions to stress, this "father of stress theory" concludes with some general recommendations for handling this condition successfully.

Relevant Journals

Child Care Information Exchange. P.O. Box 2890, Redmond, WA 98073. Stuffed with timely, practical articles, *CCIE* has filled a gap in the literature on how to work in and operate child care centers successfully.

CHAPTER 2

What Makes a Good Day for Children?

In the evaluation of the dominant moods of any historical period it is important to hold fast to the fact that there are always islands of self-sufficient order—on farms and in castles, in homes, studies, and cloisters—where sensible people manage to live relatively lusty and decent lives: as moral as they must be, as free as they may be, and as masterful as they can be. If we but knew it, this elusive arrangement is happiness.

—Erik Erikson (1958)

Have you ever wondered . . .

What to reply when a friend says your job is really just baby-sitting?

Whether early education makes any difference?

What a good program should include?

If you have, the material in the following pages will help you.

No doubt the reader is anxious to press on to discussions of discipline or eating problems or teaching children to share—these are valid concerns of all teachers of young children. However, it seems wise to take time first for an overview of whether early education is effective and what should go into a good day for young children. What elements should be included when planning the overall curriculum? Once these elements are clearly in mind, we can turn to a consideration of more specific problems and recommendations.

CAN EARLY EDUCATION MAKE A DIFFERENCE?

For more than a decade, research on approaches to early childhood education has sought to investigate the effectiveness of various kinds of programs in changing the behavior and enhancing the development of young children. The results of these investigations have been at times discouraging and at times heartening. On one hand the Westinghouse Report (Cicerelli, Evans, & Schiller, 1969), the Hawkridge study (Hawkridge, Chalupsky, & Roberts, 1968), and a report by Abt Associates (Stebbins et al., 1977) have found little evidence of persistent, across-program change on measures of intellectual ability.

If IQ tests are to be accepted as the one indicator of valuable changes that can result from early education, then these investigators are quite correct. Preschool programs have not been shown to produce measurable, very long-term (continuing beyond the fourth grade) changes in the intelligence quotient of children attending such programs.

However, if some additional measures of school success are taken into account, research now indicates that early education intervention can and *does* make a significant difference. For example, it has turned out that the young adults who participated in some experimental programs carried out in the 1960s repeated fewer grades while in school, and fewer of them spent time in classes for the educationally mentally retarded.

It is important to know about the results of such studies because most members of the general public, including parents and legislators, are still uninformed about the potential value of early education and persist in seeing it as "just baby-sitting." If we are tired of this misguided point of view, we need to have the results of these studies on the tips of our tongues so that we can explain the value of our work with young children to those who need to be better informed about it.

The first of these retrospective studies was published by Irving Lazar (Lazar & Darlington, 1978; Lazar, Hubbell, Murray, Rosch, & Royce, 1982). Additional studies of the Perry Preschool Project detailed in *Changed Lives* (Berrueta-Clement, Schweinhart, Barnett, Epstein, & Weikart, 1984); by Gray, Ramsey, and Klaus, in *From 3 to 20* (1982); and by McKey and colleagues (1985) who reviewed 210 Head Start studies, have supported and enriched these findings. More recently the work of Burchinal, Lee, and Ramey (1989) has emphasized the positive contribution quality group day care can make to the intellectual development of low-income children. Moreover, in a study of high-risk premature babies, the benefits of intensive early education have been confirmed once again (Infant Health and Development Program, 1990).

Lazar's Consortium Study (Lazar et al., 1982) followed up a number of infant and preschool programs (including work by Gray and Weikart) that took place in the 1960s. These programs were special, high-quality ones that used both experimental and control groups and drew their subjects from families of the poor. Members of each experimental group participated in a preschool program while their similar control companions did not have that advantage.

At the time of the follow-up, the questions Lazar and coworkers (1977, 1978, 1982) wanted to answer about both groups were "Now that these children are either in their teens or early twenties, what has become of them?" "How have they turned out?" "Did early intervention make a difference in their lives?" To answer these questions, each project traced as many of the experimental and control children as possible, retested them on the Wechsler Intelligence Test, and, among many questions, asked whether they had ever repeated a grade in school or had been placed in a class for educable mentally retarded children (an EMR classroom).*

An analysis of the intelligence test material (both current and prior tests) led the investigators to conclude that "although evidence showed that early education can produce significant increases in IQ (over a control group) which lasts for up to three years after the child leaves the program . . . it appears that the effect . . . is probably not permanent" (1977, pp. 19, 20).

However, the information related to grade retention and placement in EMR classrooms was much more encouraging, in part because of its implications for saving public monies (Barnett & Escobar, 1987; Weikart, 1989) but also because of what the findings mean in terms of human happiness.

Even though these data (shown in Figures 2.1 and 2.2) vary considerably between programs (probably because different school districts have different policies on having children repeat grades), they clearly indicate that early education can reduce the rate of repeating grades for low-income children, thereby preventing much humiliation and loss of self-esteem. And if repetition of a grade is humiliating to a youngster, one can only surmise how bad it feels to be placed in a classroom for retarded children. Here, once again, the Lazar data provide convincing evidence that early education is worthwhile, since substantially fewer project children were found to have been placed in such classes.

The research on children in the Perry Preschool Project carried these studies even further. Begun in 1962, that research is still continuing, and the data have been consistent over more than three decades of investigation. Table 2.1 illustrates the substantial differences between the experimental group who had experienced the benefits of a good preschool program combined with home visiting and a similar group of children who had not had those experiences (Weikart, 1990). Note that fewer of the Perry Preschool children had been in

---

*For a more complete interpretation and explanation of this study, the reader should refer to the original reports, which are well worth reading.

FIGURE 2.1 Percent of program and control children held back a grade

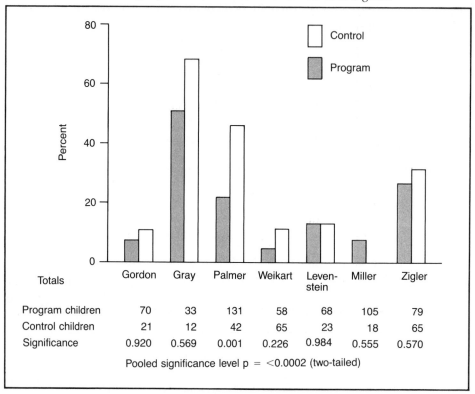

Totals	Gordon	Gray	Palmer	Weikart	Leven- stein	Miller	Zigler
Program children	70	33	131	58	68	105	79
Control children	21	12	42	65	23	18	65
Significance	0.920	0.569	0.001	0.226	0.984	0.555	0.570

Pooled significance level p = <0.0002 (two-tailed)

From I. Lazar, V. R. Hubbell, H. Murray, M. Rosche, and J. Royce, *Summary Report: The Persistence of Preschool Effects* (Washington, DC: U.S. Department of Health, Education, and Welfare, 1977), OHDS 78-30129.

trouble with the law, more of them had graduated from high school, and more of them had jobs after graduation.

The two studies discussed were selected because they are the most widely publicized pieces of research on this subject, but the reader should realize that they are but two of many studies that now support the value of well-planned early education for children who come from families of low income.*

UNDERLYING PHILOSOPHY OF THIS BOOK

Despite these encouraging results, there remains a tantalizing question the research did not answer. It has not told us just exactly which ingredients in these programs have what effect on children, since examination reveals that equally successful programs differ in many respects in their philosophy, teaching techniques, and program content (Berrueta-Clement et al., 1984; Chattin-

*For additional information, the reader should refer to Howes (1986) or Cotton and Conklin (1989).

FIGURE 2.2   Percent of program and control children in special education

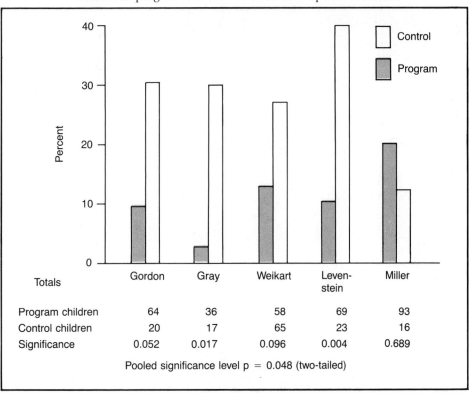

Totals	Gordon	Gray	Weikart	Leven-stein	Miller
Program children	64	36	58	69	93
Control children	20	17	65	23	16
Significance	0.052	0.017	0.096	0.004	0.689

Pooled significance level p = 0.048 (two-tailed)

From I. Lazar, V. R. Hubbell, H. Murray, M. Rosche, and J. Royce, *Summary Report: The Persistence of Preschool Effects* (Washington, DC: U.S. Department of Health, Education, and Welfare, 1977), OHDS 78-30129.

McNichols, 1981; Schweinhart, Weikart, & Larner, 1986). Apparently, as long as the teachers have made a commitment to the program (Weikart, 1971) and the educational intention of the program is clearly defined, a variety of instructional approaches can be successful in producing a good day for children.

The Whole Child uses an eclectic approach that makes use of three theoretical bases: the application of behavior modification strategies where appropriate, application of Piagetian principles where these clarify understanding, and an overall approach best described by the term *developmental interactionist*, which goes beyond those narrower points of view to stress the value of educating the whole child in an open educational setting.

Uses and Values of Behavior Modification

The term *behavior modification* tends to bring scowls to the faces of many teachers who object to the potential for manipulation inherent in that approach. However, it is important to understand its positive value as well. Learning theorists

TABLE 2.1   Summary of the results of the Perry Preschool Project[a]

	Experimental Group (%)	Control Group (%)
IN EDUCATION		
Classified as mentally retarded	15	35
Completed high school	67	49
Attended college or job-training programs	38	21
IN EMPLOYMENT		
Hold jobs	50	32
Support themselves or are supported by spouse	45	25
Satisfied with work	42	26
IN THE COMMUNITY		
Arrested for criminal acts	31	51
Birth rate[b]	64[a]	117[a]
Public assistance	18	32

[a]Age of subjects was 19 years.

[b]Birth rates are per 100 women.

From Weikart, D. (1990). *Quality preschool programs: A long-term social investment*. New York: Ford Foundation (p. 7). Used by permission.

who practice behavior modification have accumulated a great deal of carefully documented research that substantiates their claims that this approach, which rewards desirable behavior and discourages undesirable actions, can be a powerful avenue for teaching (Thomas, 1985; Witt, Elliott, & Gresham, 1988).

Behavior modification theorists stress the importance of the influence of environment on behavior. They maintain that children learn various behaviors as a result of experiencing pleasant or unpleasant outcomes or reinforcements. Pleasant outcomes or rewards such as teacher attention, praise, or candy tend to cause the behavior to persist, while unpleasant negative consequences such as scolding or writing the child's name on the blackboard discourage it. If the child receives neither positive nor negative reinforcement, then he will gradually abandon the behavior. Critics complain that this approach to human develop-ment emphasizes the role of external rewards and sees the child as a passive recipient of stimuli that regulate behavior rather than as a human being capable of initiating novel ideas and behavior.

It is true that the cut-and-dried, deliberately orchestrated manipulation of behavior that might be possible if such a program were carried out in its purest form is repugnant, but it is also true that all teachers use this technique constantly and extensively whether they realize it or not. Every smile, every frown, every positive or negative bit of attention the child receives either encourages or discourages future behavior. Therefore, rather than blindly condemning such theory, why not become aware of how often we employ such strategies on an informal basis and acknowledge their power? To use behavior modification effectively it is not necessary to agree with Skinner (1974) that

No matter what philosophy is involved, warm, caring relationships are the cornerstones of all good early childhood programs.

positive or negative reinforcement is the only activator of behavior. Indeed, it seems impossible to use learning theory satisfactorily to explain how people generate original ideas or how they formulate language patterns they have not heard before. In the author's opinion, learning theory is simply a useful tool that explains a great deal, but not all, of why human beings behave as they do. As such, it cannot be ignored.

Uses and Values of Piagetian Theory

The reader will find that the work of the great theorist and investigator Jean Piaget is referred to again and again throughout this volume. His more than half century of reseach into the developmental stages and characteristics of children's cognitive processes is invaluable, as is his emphasis on the impor-tance of dynamic interaction between the child and the environment, and the significance of play as a medium for learning.

The constructivist approach to early education favored by DeVries and Kohlberg (1990) provides a current example of how some theorists are basing their early childhood curriculum entirely on Piagetian theory. However, many scholars and teachers, including the author, are not satisfied with restricting themselves to only Piagetian theory because they feel Piaget did not say enough about social relationships, creativity, or emotional health to warrant doing that. Piaget's primary interest was the investigation of children's thought processes. In a text of this scope, although we must incorporate his work, we cannot limit ourselves to just his theory.

The Developmental-Interactionist Approach: Philosophy of This Book

To do a comprehensive job of teaching and provide a good day for the children in our care, we must move beyond seeing children as pawns to be moved about at the whim of externally applied reinforcements or as swiftly developing intellects perceiving the world in changing ways as they attain maturity, although behavior modification and Piagetian theory possess undeniable merit and make valuable contributions to our understanding of children.

The development-interactionist approach as exemplified in the Bank Street program described by Biber (1981, 1984) sees children as developing human beings who pass through a variety of stages or steps as they mature—human beings in whom knowing about things (the intellectual self) combines with feeling about them (the emotional self). In this point of view, the impetus for growth lies in part within the maturing individual but also occurs in part as a result of the interaction between the child and the environment.

This interaction is important because the child is regarded as being an active participant in his own growth. He learns by constructing and reconstructing what he knows as he encounters a variety of experiences that widen and enrich his knowledge. The teacher's role is one of guiding, questioning, and enabling—not stuffing the child with an assortment of facts and rewards for good behavior.

Because the child is a complex being composed of many attributes and aspects, we must see teaching as stimulating and enhancing the development of all these aspects. That is why this book concentrates on the five selves of the child rather than on specific topics such as art or science. It is an attempt to shift the attention of the teacher to what the child *is* and what he needs from the learning environment in order to thrive. Only when this is done can it be truly said that we are educating the whole child.

Besides advocating that curriculum be provided for every self, there are a number of additional basic premises on which this book is based. The first is that children pass through various stages as they develop. Piaget has, of course, demonstrated this par excellence in regard to intellectual development, but it has been heavily documented for the other selves as well (Allen & Marotz, 1990; Brittain, 1979; Gesell, Halverson, Thompson, & Ilgn, 1940; Shotwell, Wolf, & Gardner, 1979; Wickstrom, 1983). Once we have identified the stage, then we must provide education which fits that level for each self.

The second premise is that the purpose of education is to increase competence in all aspects of the developing self. It is much more important to teach children to cope by equipping them with skills than to stuff them full of facts. This is because it is confidence in their coping ability that underlies children's sense of self-worth.

The third premise is that physical and emotional health is absolutely fundamental to the well-being of children. Any program that ignores that fact is building its curriculum on a foundation of sand. The fourth is that children learn most easily by means of actual, involving experience with people and activities. This is best accomplished in an open, carefully planned environment where children must take responsibility and make decisions for themselves and where they have ample opportunity to learn through play.

The final premise is that children need time to be children. The purpose of preprimary education and child care should not be to pressure and urge youngsters on to the next step in a hurried way. The current term, *hothousing*, well describes the effect of such forced learning on the unfortunate children who experience it. Recent research now provides evidence that placing academic pressure on preschool children was a precursor to negative attitudes toward school and decreased creativity in kindergarten (Hyson & Hirsh-Pasek, 1990).

Children need time and personal space in which to grow. They need time to be themselves—to do nothing, to stand and watch, to repeat again what they did before; in short, they need time to live *in* their childhood rather than *through* it. If we offer the young children we teach rich and appropriate learning opportunities combined with enough time for them to enjoy and experience those opportunities to the full, we will be enhancing that era of childhood, not violating it.

PUTTING PREMISES INTO PRACTICE: PLANNING A GOOD DAY FOR CHILDREN

Good Human Relationships Are a Fundamental Ingredient of a Good Day

All good programs are built on the foundation of sound human relationships. Warmth and empathic understanding have been shown to be effective means of influencing young children's positive adjustment to school (Truax & Tatum, 1966). It is apparent that genuine caring about the children and about other adults in the program is fundamental to success.

For warmth and personal contact to flourish, the day must be planned and paced so there are numerous opportunities for person-to-person, one-to-one encounters. In practical terms this means that groups must be kept small and that the ratio of adults to children must be as high as possible. Many occasions must also be provided where the children move freely about, making personal choices and generating individual contacts. Such arrangements permit numerous interludes where informal learning experiences can be enjoyed and where human caring can be expressed. The moments may be as fleeting as a quick hug when the teacher ties a pair of trailing shoelaces or as extended as a serious discussion of where babies come from. It is the *quality* of individualized, personal caring and the chance to talk together that are significant.

Parents Should Be Included As Part of the Life of the School

The day is past when parents were expected to pay their bill but leave their children at the center's door. Of course, cooperative schools have long demonstrated the feasibility of including the family in the school experience, but today we can also point to mounting research that confirms that inclusion of the parent in the educational process, whether in home tutoring programs or the school itself, results in longer lasting educational gains for the child (Anthony & Pollock, 1985; Garber & Heber, 1981; Gray et al., 1982; Levenstein, 1988; Swick, 1989).

Nowadays, parent involvement goes far beyond attending parent education meetings and open houses. Parents serve as indispensable volunteers in the classroom where they do everything from tutoring to sharing their cultural backgrounds with the youngsters. They serve on powerful advisory boards, raise money, and provide ideas and criticism about the curriculum.

Rather than feeling threatened by this vigorous interest, wise teachers do all they can to get to know the children's parents well in order to use their talents most effectively. There is no more valuable way to widen everyone's horizons than by strengthening the link between home and school. Chapters 12 and 18 provide more detailed suggestions of practical ways of welcoming parents into the life of the school.

A Good Program Must Be Developmentally Appropriate

Developmentally appropriate means that the learning activities planned for the children are placed at the correct level for their age and are suited to individual children's tastes and abilities as well. This fact is important because if the material is at the right developmental level, the children will be drawn to it and want to learn about it (Bredekamp, 1987).

On the other hand, when children are pushed too far ahead of their levels and the curriculum is unsuited to their abilities, it's like pushing them into deep water before they can swim—they're likely to dread the water and avoid it when they can.

At this early stage of schooling it is crucial for children to decide that learning is something to be pursued with verve, not that it is difficult and anxiety-provoking. For this reason it is vital that teachers have a good grasp of what children are like at various ages, understand they move from stage to stage as they develop, and plan the curriculum accordingly (Miller, 1985).

There Should Be a Balance Between Self-Selection and Teacher Direction—Both Approaches Are Valuable

Value of Self-Selection

The idea that young children can be trusted to choose educational experiences for themselves that will benefit them goes all the way back in educational theory to Jean Jacques Rousseau and John Dewey. At present this concept is being used in the British Infant School, as well as continuing its tenure in the majority of American child care centers.

Philosophical support for the value of self-selection of activities comes from such disparate sources as the self-selection feeding experiments of Clara Davis (1939) and the psychoanalytic theory of Erikson, who speaks of the preschool child's "sudden, violent wish to have a choice" (1950, p. 252). The virtue of self-selection is that it fosters independence and builds within the child responsibility for making his own decisions. It also provides an excellent way to individualize the curriculum because each child is free to pursue his own interests and to suit himself when he is free to choose.

But self-selection needs to be balanced with opportunities for group experiences, too. Some of those experiences are small, casual, and informal, as when a group of interested children gather around the teacher to talk about where the snow went. Some, such as large-group times (chapter 16) and meal times (chapter 4), require more management by the teacher. These more formal situations are essential ingredients in the early childhood program because they provide opportunities to make certain all the children are included in thinking and reasoning activities every day. Without these planned participation times, occasional children might graduate from preschool with a degree in trike riding coupled with a deadly inability to put five words together into a coherent sentence.

The self-selection parts of the program also require careful planning. This point is sometimes overlooked by visitors and beginning student teachers who are most aware of the children circulating freely from one activity to another as their interests dictate. But this appearance of openness and freedom can be deceptive. In actuality, the available choices have been carefully thought through in advance by the teacher, and every activity in the room is there because it provides educational experiences for one or another of the child's selves.

Of course, one would not want the use of a plan to be interpreted so rigorously that there was no room for spontaneity. There are times when the marvelous welling up of an idea or activity occurs, and these teachable moments are to be sought after and treasured—but this does not happen all the time. Nor does reliance on such events assure that every important area will be covered, that necessary goals will be achieved, or that the needs of individual children will be considered. *Only planning coupled with consistent evaluation can accomplish these objectives.*

A Good Program Should Be Comprehensive

An aspect of planning that deserves special consideration is that curriculum should be comprehensive in coverage. As mentioned earlier, a valuable way to think about this is to picture the child as being composed of a number of selves: the physical self, the emotional self, the social self, the creative self, and the cognitive self. This book is based on this division of the child into selves, because experience has shown that various aspects of curriculum fall rather neatly under these headings and that the five selves succeed in covering the personality of the child.

The physical self includes not only large and fine muscle development but also handling routines, since such things as eating, resting, and toileting contribute much to physical comfort and well-being. For the emotional self we consider ways to increase and sustain mental health, to use discipline to foster self-control, to cope with aggression, and to foster self-esteem. Under the heading of the social self are placed ways to build social concern and kindliness, learning to enjoy work, and learning to value the cultures of other people. The creative self covers the areas of self-expression through the use of art materials and creativity as expressed in play and applied in thought. Finally, the cognitive, or intellectual, self is considered in terms of language development and the development of specific reasoning abilities. This last self is the newest one to receive intensive consideration and analysis in early childhood education, and much remains to be learned in this area.

Formulating an Effective Plan

One way of assuring that the curriculum is both comprehensive and purposeful is to discipline oneself by filling out the Curriculum Analysis and Planning Chart each week (shown in Figure 2.3) to make certain there is something deliberately planned for each self of the child every day to purposely enhance his growth.

In the space where Activity is specified, the name of the activity, for example, clay, should be written in. The specific purpose that day for offering clay might be "to relieve aggressive feelings." If so, clay would best fit the Emotional category. Or, if the primary purpose was to provide the material as an opportunity for creative self-expression, then the clay activity would be listed in the Creative space.

Another more in-depth way of planning curriculum involves the use of a daily plan wherein the provision of more detail is possible. An example of part of such a plan recently done by a student is included in Figure 2.4. The theme was selected to combine learning about the spring season with the needs of a hospitalized classmate.

While I would not advocate such detailed planning as a usual thing, the Institute staff has found it helpful for beginning teachers to use because it requires them to think the purposes of their curriculum through carefully. The bonus is that once teachers learn to think this clearly, they not only stop offering educational trash to children but also have no difficulty justifying the educational purposes of the activities to inquiring parents.

Value of Suiting Curriculum to Each Individual Child

We have already reviewed research which indicates that teachers will experience greater success if they identify their educational goals clearly and carry out activities designed to reach these goals. The real art of teaching lies in the ability to clothe these bare-boned goals in the raiment of individual children's interests and pleasures. Fortunately the small size and intimacy of preschool groups make it possible for teachers to know each youngster well and to plan with particular individuals in mind.

Not only should broad goals be personalized to fit the children's interests, but specific goals should be formulated to suit individual children, since every child is different and learns at his own rate. Prompt assessment of the children's skills is invaluable because it can help the teacher identify specific needs of individual children and plan in accordance with these revealed needs.

A Simple Test to Determine
Whether Curriculum Is Individualized

There are three questions the teacher can use to determine whether the curriculum is individualized:

1. Are there some recent instances where curriculum was based on a child's specific interests?
2. Can examples be identified where a child was deliberately provided with opportunities to learn what evaluations had indicated that he especially needed to know?
3. Can examples be cited where curriculum plans were changed because a child revealed an unanticipated interest or enthusiasm during the day?

A Good Program Has Stability and
Regularity Combined with Flexibility

Young children need to know what is likely to happen next during the day. This means that the order of events should be generally predictable. Predictability enables the child to prepare mentally for the next event; it makes compliance with routines more likely and helps children feel secure.

At the same time, time schedules and routines should not be allowed to dominate the school. Sometimes this happens because of a strong-minded custodian or cook. I once knew a school where it was necessary for the children to use only half the space from 10:30 until nap time because of the custodian's routine. Sometimes overconformance to time schedules happens because teachers are creatures of habit and simply do not realize that juice and raisins do not have to be served at exactly 9:15. Rather than sticking right to the clock, it is better to maintain an orderly but elastic schedule, where play periods can be extended when those moments occur when the majority of the children are involved in activities that interest them intensely.

FIGURE 2.3 Curriculum analysis and planning chart

Plans for week of:

Focus or theme:

Part of self being developed	Physical: Gross motor	Physical: Fine motor	Emotional under-standing, feelings	Social	Multi-cultural	Nonsexist	Creative	Cognitive: Mental ability	Cognitive: Language
MONDAY Activity									
Purpose									
TUESDAY Activity									
Purpose									

42

W E D N E S D A Y	Activity							
	Purpose							
T H U R S D A Y	Activity							
	Purpose							
F R I D A Y	Activity							
	Purpose							

43

FIGURE 2.4 Example of a curriculum analysis and planning chart

Plans for week of: 5/1/89

Focus or theme: Spring Flowers

	Physical: Gross motor	Physical: Fine motor	Emotional under-standing, feelings	Social	Multi-cultural	Nonsexist	Creative	Cognitive: Mental ability	Cognitive: Language
Activity	Trike ride to pick flowers	Collage	Hospital play	Send picked flowers to hospital	Lunch	Discuss gardeners	Collage	Let's-find-out table	Dictate let-ter to in-jured child
Purpose	Extended physical ex-ercise; con-trol of trikes so they do not run into each other on narrow sidewalk	Eye-hand control (use of scissors, glue, ar-range small pieces of things)	Clarify ideas about what is happening to injured friend; work through fears.	Express care and concern for injured playmate by sending flowers and note; work together to plan how to do that.	Food from another culture tastes good (tacos, fruit salad, milk).	Both mother and father care for garden they vis-ited.	Foster de-sign, plea-sure in dif-ferent colors; use own inspi-rations and ideas.	*Cause/effect* (flower wilting) *Temporal ordering* (arrange pictures of growing flowers in order) *Common re-lations* (pair pictures with picked flowers)	Writing is useful; it goes from left to right.

W
E
D
N
E
S
D
A
Y

Note: On this particular day the teacher had several purposes in mind. She wanted to help the children clarify some of their worries about a member of their group who had been in an accident and was hospitalized; she wanted them to express their concern about him in some way; she wanted to continue to provide practice on some thinking and reasoning skills; and she wanted to tie these purposes together by using the theme of spring flowers where it was possible to do that. Using the Curriculum Analysis and Planning Chart enabled her to jot down the highlights she planned for the day so that she could be sure she had planned something to benefit all five selves.

Having animals visit is a delightful way to add variety to the program.

A Good Program Has Variety

Children Need Many Different Kinds of Experiences As Well As Changes in Basic Experiences

Research on the effects of stimulus deprivation (Dennis, 1960; Walk, 1981) on early stimulation (White, 1979) has highlighted the value of supplying a variety of experiences even for babies, and variety should certainly be incorporated into a program for preschool children.

Many teachers think of variety of experience in terms of field trips or covering different topics, such as families or baby animals. But another kind of variety that should also be considered is variety in everyday basic learning experiences. What a difference there is between the school that has the same pet rat and bowl of goldfish all year and the school that first raises a rabbit, then borrows a brood hen, and next has two snakes as visitors. Lack of variety is also apparent in schools that offer the omnipresent easel as their major "art" experience or others that set out all the blocks at the beginning of the year and leave it at that.

Children Should Be Offered Various Levels of Difficulty in Activity Materials

If the children's center combines age levels during the day so that 3-, 4-, and 5-year-olds play together, it is important to provide materials that are challenging for all the ages within the group. Teachers need to be especially careful to offer materials that are genuinely interesting to the older 4-year-olds and young 5-year-olds. A dearth of stimulating, fresh curricula is the most common cause of a posse of children galloping through block areas and housekeeping corners, spreading destruction as they go.

Even when the group is composed of predominantly one-age children, the teacher will still need to provide a variety of activities for different developmental levels because there is so much difference, for example, between what younger and older 4-year-olds can achieve.

The curriculum not only should offer a variety of levels of difficulty every day but also *should become more challenging and move from simple to more complex activities as the year progresses* and as the children mature and gain competence. The curriculum should not look the same in May as it did in September.

Children Need Changes of Pace During the Day to Avoid Monotony and Fatigue and to Maintain a Balance of Kinds of Experiences for Them

The most obvious way to incorporate variation of pace is to plan for it in the overall schedule. For example, a quiet snack can be followed by a dance period.

Additional opportunities to meet individual temperamental requirements of children must be allowed for. The quieter, less gregarious child needs to have places available where he can retreat from the herd, and the more active youngster needs the escape hatch of moving about when the group has sat beyond his limit of endurance.

Some kinds of programs appear to have special problems associated with pacing. For example, some compensatory programs attempt to cram so much into such a short time (playtime, story time, snack, lunch, special activity time, not to mention visits from the psychologist, field trips, and special visitors) that the day goes by in a headlong rush of children being hurried from one thing to the next without the opportunity to savor any experience richly and fully. At the other extreme, some day care programs offer a variety of activities and changes of pace during the morning but turn the children loose in the play yard for 3 interminable hours in the afternoon. Such consistent conditions of hurried stress or unalleviated boredom, unless analyzed thoughtfully and modified, can ultimately have only a deleterious effect on children.

Learning Must Be Based on Actual Experience and Participation

Anyone who has ever taken a young child to the market knows how strong his impulse is to touch and smell and taste everything he encounters. Although occasionally inconvenient, the child's behavior illustrates a fundamental fact of early childhood learning: children learn best if allowed to use all their senses as avenues of learning. Participatory experience is an essential ingredient in preschool education. This means that the curriculum of the preschool must be based on real experiences with real things rather than limited to the verbal discussions and pictures commonly (though not necessarily ideally) used when teaching older children.

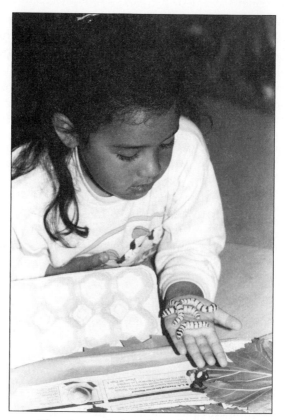

There is no substitute for real experience.

Because educators of young children have emphasized the value of real experience as being fundamental to successful education since the turn of the century and because Piaget has also stressed the importance of participatory experience in the development of intelligence (Hunt, 1961), one might think that this principle need not be reiterated. However, the current influx of word-oriented rather than action-oriented teaching materials on display in the commercial exhibits of most conferences on early childhood and the fact that these materials continue to sell make it evident that this point must be stated very clearly: young children learn best when they can manipulate material, experiment, try things out, and talk about what is happening as it takes place. Talking without doing is largely meaningless for a child of tender years.

Play Is an Indispensable Avenue for Learning

Another long-held value in early childhood education is an appreciation of play as a facilitator of learning. Although research is still lacking in this area, evidence is beginning to accumulate (Bergen, 1988; Fein & Rivkin, 1986) that lends support to something generations of teachers of young children have learned through experience. Teachers who have watched young children at play know the intent, purposeful seriousness they bring to this activity. Play is the medium used by children to translate experience into something internally meaningful to them. Piaget (1962) agrees with teachers and maintains that children use it as an important symbolic activity, but it serves many purposes beyond this function. Play clarifies concepts, provides emotional relief, facilitates social development, and creates periods of clearly satisfying delight. Sometimes teachers see its value only as a teacher-controlled, structured experience used to achieve a specific educational end (role playing after visiting the fire station, for example), but it is crucial that there be ample time in the curriculum for self-initiated play.

The Program Should Be Evaluated Daily

Once planned and put into action, it is also necessary to evaluate the results, and these evaluations need to go beyond such statements as "My gosh! What a terrible day!" or "Things went well!"

Instead, teachers should ask themselves:

How did the day go? Were there any "hitches and glitches"?

If so, how can I rearrange things so they move more smoothly for the children next time?

What did the children learn today?

How are the children with special problems getting along?

What special interests came up that I can build on in curriculum?

And finally, the most valuable question of all:

How can I help each child experience success tomorrow?

Thoughtful answers to questions like these will go a long way in helping build a more effective curriculum for the children as the year moves on.

The Day Should Be Pleasurable

Probably the most significant value a teacher can convey to children is the conviction that school is satisfying fun and that they want to return the next day. This point has been deliberately left until last in order to give it special emphasis, in case the reader, having waded through the other elements of a good program, has begun to feel bogged down with the sober-sided responsibilities of running a good program for young children.

The experience not only should be pleasurable for the children, but it also should be a joy for the adults. Young children have their trying moments, but they are also delightful. They see the world in a clear-sighted way that can lend fresh perspective to the eyes of their teacher, and their tendency to live for the present moment is a lesson to us all. Pleasure, enjoyment, humor, and laughter should be very much a part of each preschool day.

PUTTING THE ELEMENTS TOGETHER

What Does a Day Look Like That Combines These Basic Elements into a Coherent Whole?

The setting is established with children in mind: furniture is scaled to the right size; the building has easy access to the yard; and there is a general air of orderly, yet easygoing comfort and beauty that does not put people off because of its newness or perfection. This kind of atmosphere goes a long way toward making parents feel at home and part of the school family.

When it is necessary to form groups, the children are broken into small gatherings. Story hours and snack tables of four or five children and a grown-up, for example, should be the rule in order to facilitate conversation and participation. (My staff refers to this as Hendrick's law: "The larger the group, the smaller the learning.") The daily pace is easy enough and the staff unharrassed enough that there are many intimate little opportunities for teachers to talk with the children individually.

There is a reasonably repetitious scheduling of basic experiences planned to provide alternate periods of quiet and active experience. These periods include a morning welcome for each child as he arrives, a snack in the morning and afternoon, and lunch and rest in the middle of the day.

In between these landmark times many interesting events take place. These are developed with individual and group goals in mind, and they should include, every day, some activity that is creative, another that is messy, something that is new, something that requires the children to think, some carefully varied activities that foster motor development, some opportunity for the children to engage in meaningful work, and many chances to use books, pictures, poetry, and to listen and be listened to. Intertwined among these activities lie all the situations that the teacher must seize and use as they arise to develop social learning and emotional strength in the children.

For at least one generous block of time during the morning and afternoon, materials and possibilities are set out, and the child is expected to take the responsibility of selecting for himself what he wants to pursue. During this time the teacher moves from one place to another as the occasion demands, talking first with one child, helping another group settle a fight, and getting out a piece of equipment for a third. Another part of the day involves more focused participation but should not be cast in the mold of 15 children doing the identical thing in one large group at the same time.

If staffing and weather permit, children have access to inside and outdoors as they prefer. Failing this, large muscle activities are available indoors, and small muscle and more cognitive and creative materials are available outdoors to avoid the "recess" concept so common in elementary school.

This, then, is the overall framework of a sound preschool day. It provides opportunities for children to learn all kinds of things and to enjoy both the process and the satisfaction of the results. It includes many diverse things and many diverse people. The miracle of a good school is that, somehow, these all go together to produce a good day for both children and staff.

SUMMARY

After more than a decade of research, evidence has accumulated that early intervention in the form of education for young children and their families can make a difference. Moreover, certain elements are emerging that appear to be common to the majority of effective early childhood programs. These include concern for the quality of human relationships, inclusion of the parent as part of the life of the school, a balance of self-selected and teacher-directed activities, the formulation of a well-thought-out plan for the curriculum, and a curriculum that is comprehensive and individualized.

A good program for young children is basically orderly but also flexible; it provides for variety in experience, levels of difficulty, and pacing; it is based on the principles that learning should be the result of actual experience, that play is a significant mode of learning, and, above all, that the center should be a place of joy for both children and staff.

QUESTIONS AND ACTIVITIES

1. *Problem:* Suppose a parent said to you after touring the school, "My heavens, your fees are high. Why, my baby-sitter charges less than you do, and she comes to the house and does the ironing while she takes care of little Carolyn. I don't see what costs so much about just taking care of little children!" What should you reply?

2. What are some situations in your own educational background where the learning was primarily by means of language and others where there was an emphasis on experience and participation? Which method did you prefer? What were the advantages and disadvantages of each of these approaches?

3. What guidelines would you suggest to help a teacher determine whether there are enough free choices or if there is too much structure in the children's day?

4. As a beginning teacher, how do you feel about the prospect of having parents at school? If a mother is helping at school on the day her youngster has a temper tantrum and refuses to come in to lunch, would it be easier to handle this situation if the mother were not there? Do you agree completely that parents should be welcomed at school? Why or why not?

5. Select a basic activity, such as using tricycles or easel painting, that tends to stay the same throughout the year in many schools, and suggest some variations that would add interest and learning to the activity.

SELF-CHECK QUESTIONS FOR REVIEW

Content-Related Questions

1. What are the names of two important research studies having to do with the effectiveness of preschool education? List three or four important findings from these studies.

2. *The Whole Child* uses both behavior modification and Piagetian theory as a partial theoretical base. According to the author, what are the strengths and weaknesses of these two theories?

3. Name the five selves discussed in the chapter and tell what aspects of the child each self includes.

4. List and discuss the ingredients that should go into a good day for young children.

Integrative Questions

1. Suppose a friend says to you, "What I don't understand is why you have to go to school so long to learn to take care of little kids—

after all, it's just glorified baby-sitting." Explain what you might produce in the way of evidence to educate that person.

2. Compare the findings for the experimental and control groups from the Perry Preschool Project (Table 2.1). In which categories did the greatest differences between the groups show up? Imagine you are explaining these differences to a state legislator. What basic points would you stress from the results as being most likely to influence her or him to vote for more money to finance preschool programs?

3. Give an example of a situation with a 3-year-old where it would be appropriate to use a behavior modification technique.

4. Compare the developmental-interactionist philosophy of teaching to a behavior modification approach. What do they have in common and where do they differ?

5. Describe some of the benefits children receive from the self-select parts of an early childhood program, and contrast these to the benefits they gain from activities they participate in together as a group. Be sure to include consideration of social and emotional benefits as well as cognitive ones.

6. During the past year the following topics were proposed as possible educational themes to be used with 3-year-old children: kittens, shapes, space travel, Hawaii, air, and snow. Which of these would you select as being more appropriate and which least appropriate? Explain the reasoning behind your answer.

REFERENCES FOR FURTHER READING

Overviews

Beardsley, L. (1990). *Good day, bad day: The child's experience of child care.* New York: Teachers College Press. This book contrasts fictitious good and mediocre schools by describing imaginary situations and how the schools handle them. These are followed by knowledgeable comments. *Highly recommended.*

Kantrowitz, R., & Wingert, P. (1989). How kids learn. *Young Children, 44*(6), 4–10. For a quick overview of early childhood education, this article, reprinted from *Newsweek,* presents a readable summary of good current practice.

Weikart, D. P. (1989). *Quality preschool programs: A long-term social investment* (Occasional Paper 5). New York: Ford Foundation. Weikart summarizes the positive effects of quality preschool education with an emphasis on the Perry Preschool Project.

Developmentally Appropriate Curriculum

Bredekamp, S. (Ed.). (1987). *Developmentally appropriate practice in early childhood programs serving children from birth through age 8: Ex-* *panded edition.* Washington, DC: National Association for the Education of Young Children. This indispensable resource spells out both good and undesirable teaching practices. It is the most influential publication on this subject in the field.

Cassidy, D. J., Myers, B. K., & Benion, P. E. (1987). Early childhood planning: A developmental perspective. *Childhood Education, 64*(1), 2–8. The authors pose useful questions to ask when developing curriculum and demonstrate how to suit curriculum to children with varying developmental needs in the same group.

Elkind, D. (1987). *Miseducation: Preschoolers at risk.* New York: Knopf. This champion of the right of children to be children argues against building "superkids" and overaccelerating the development of intellectual and physical skills.

Miller, K. (1985). *Ages and stages: Developmental descriptions & activities birth through eight years.* Marshfield, MA: Telshare. This concise book does a good job of linking developmental characteristics to recommendations for curriculum. Quick, easy reading.

Developing Good Human Relationships

Griffin, E. F. (1982). *Island of childhood: Education in the special world of the nursery school.* New York: Teachers College Press. Griffin conveys a sense of the atmosphere that should surround children and teachers during these early years. *Highly recommended.*

Importance of Play

Bergen, D. (Ed.). (1988). *Play as a medium for learning and development: A handbook of theory and practice.* Portsmouth, NH: Heinemann. This is a good overview of the values of play written in readable form by well-known specialists in the field.

For the Advanced Student

Berrueta-Clement, J. T., Schweinhart, L. J., Barnett, W. S., Epstein, A. S., & Weikart, D. P. (1984). *Changed lives: The effect of the Perry Preschool Program on youths through age 19.* Ypsilanti, MI: High/Scope Educational Research Foundation. *Changed Lives* summarizes not only the Perry Preschool research, but also various other longitudinal studies that report the effects of early childhood programs on later development. The High/Scope work is also distinguished by an analysis contained in C. U. Weber, P. W. Foster, and D. P. Weikart (1978), an economic analysis of the Ypsilanti Perry Preschool Project, *Monograph of the High/Scope Educational Research Foundation (5).* This discussion details the significant amount of money saved by the school system and society because the children did not need to be placed in classes for the educationally mentally retarded.

DeVries, R., & Kohlberg, L. (1990). *Constructivist early education: Overview and comparison with other programs.* Washington, DC: National Association for the Education of Young Children. DeVries and Kohlberg contrast the Piagetian constructivist point of view with the Montessori and Bank Street approaches. They make a good case for fostering autonomy in children through independent inquiry.

Early Childhood Research Quarterly. (1987). Entire issue deals with hothousing children. 2(3), 201–304.

International Development Research Centre. (1983). *Preventing school failure: The relationship between preschool and primary education.* Ottawa: The Centre. The articles included here provide a fascinating insight into what is happening in early childhood education in countries as diverse as India, Colombia, Canada, and Thailand.

Lazar, I., Darlington, R., Murray, H., Royce, J., & Snipper, A. (1982). Lasting effects of early education: A report from the Consortium for Longitudinal Studies. *Monographs of the Society for Research in Child Development,* 47(2–3, No. 195). The discussion presents the results and in-depth descriptions of that carefully constructed research investigation.

Meisels, S. J., & Shonkoff, J. P. (1990). *Handbook of early childhood intervention.* New York: Cambridge University Press. This intensive, thorough review of difficulties and results of strategies of early intervention is an outstanding reference.

National Association for the Education of Young Children. (1984). *Accreditation criteria & procedures of the National Academy of Early Childhood Programs.* Washington, DC: The Association. The accreditation guide provides a list of students that explicitly spell out the ingredients of a sound child care program—an indispensable resource.

PART TWO

Fostering Physical Well-Being

CHAPTER 3
Handling Daily Routines

The lunch period should be an occasion for the enjoyment of good food in a social situation. I can remember my first experience as an assistant teacher in an all-day program. Lunch was rolled into the classroom on a wagon. Children (already bibbed) were lying on cots for a pre-lunch rest. Teachers served the plates and summoned the children to the tables. Everything on the plate had to be eaten before melba toast chunks were distributed (these were great favorites!) and finally dessert and milk. There was one particularly dismal meal which appeared weekly: a barely poached egg (the white still transparent) sitting on top of some dreary spinach. No one liked it, and one little girl finally refused to eat it. She sat stolidly before the offensive plate, quietly but firmly asserting, "I won't eat it. I hate it. It's not even cooked." The teacher finally removed the plate to the kitchen with the comment that it would be waiting for her after her nap.

After nap, Jill was escorted to the kitchen to be confronted with the cool mess of uncooked egg and spinach. She was told that she could return to the playroom after she had eaten it.

When she returned to the playroom, the teacher asked her if she had eaten her lunch, Jill answered, "Yes, and then I throwed it up." And she had!

—Evelyn Beyer (1968)

Have you ever wondered . . .

> How to stop nagging the children through transition times?
>
> What children from differing cultures like to eat?
>
> How to get that youngster off the climbing gym when it's time for lunch?

If you have, the material in the following pages will help you.

R outines, those omnipresent recurring sequences of behavior, constitute the backbone of full- and half-day programs and serve as landmarks that divide the day into different sections. They typically include the activities of arriving, departing, eating, toileting, and resting and the transitions between them and the other daily activities of preschool life.

Adequate handling of routines can foster both emotional and physical health, but in recent years teachers have tended to be more aware of the significance of routines in relation to emotional health than of the physical significance of good nutrition and adequate rest. However, the pasty faces, vulnerability to illness, and low energy levels of many children in compensatory programs now serve to remind us that physical health is vital to well-being and that our young children need these routines to help them build strong bodies as well as stable personalities.

It was surprising to discover that although routines involve a good portion of the day and although strong feelings and convictions of what is "right" abound, little research has been carried out in these areas. What research there is deals with nutrition and the emotional process of attachment and separation rather than with the investigation of alternative ways to handle routines in school. Therefore, readers should understand that the following discussion is based on a consensus of generally followed practice and that the recommendations rest on experience and opinion and are not validated by research.

One other note of caution about routines: if the teacher is unwise enough to go to war with a child on the subject of routines, the child, if she is so inclined, can always win. Thus a child who absolutely will not eat, will not use the toilet, or refuses to go to sleep can win any time she wants to; there is little the teacher can do about it. Fortunately teachers and children rarely reach this kind of impasse, but it is important to understand that such power struggles *can* happen and *have* happened and that the most common way to bring about such a disaster is to reduce oneself to attempting to force a child to comply with any routine absolutely against her will. It just does not work.

The best way to prevent conflicts from developing is to realize that children usually find comfort in reasonable routines that contribute to their physical well-being. It also helps if the teacher determines what the most important learnings are to be derived from each routine and then works toward achieving those goals rather than becoming caught up in "winning" for its own sake. For example, it is more important that a child learn to enjoy food and take pleasure in mealtimes than it is that she clear her plate, wait until everyone is served, or not rap her glass on the table. Bearing this primary goal in mind will reduce the amount of criticism and control that may otherwise mar snack and lunch times.

SCHEDULES AND TRANSITIONS INTO ROUTINES

Schedules

Routines and transitions are best understood when seen in the perspective of the overall schedule, so a sample full-day schedule is provided (Figure 3.1).

FIGURE 3.1 Daily schedule for a full-day center: 3- and 4-year-olds

7:00–7:30	Some teachers arrive—set out materials—ready the environment for children.
7:30	Children begin to arrive. One teacher or the director is specially assigned to greet children and parents, chat, and carry out the health check. If possible, another staff member provides a cozy time reading books with those who desire it. Self-select materials are also available.
8:30–9:15	Breakfast available for children who want it. Breakfast area set up near schoolroom sink to facilitate hand washing before and after eating. Self-selected activity continues until 9:15 for those who are not hungry.
9:15–9:45	Small- or large-group time: this often continues quite a while for 4-year-olds, less time for younger children. Its length should vary each day in order to adapt to the changing needs of the group.
9:45–10:00	Transition to activities.
10:00–11:40/11:45	Mingled indoor-outdoor experience or outdoor followed by indoor activity, depending on staffing and weather. Small-group experiences and field trips occur during this time. Self-selected activities, changed from the ones available in the early arrival period, are also provided.
11:40–11:45/12:00	Children help put things away, prepare gradually for lunch. Children go to toilet; children *and teachers* wash hands.
12:00–12:35/12:45	Family style lunchtime; children are seated with adults in groups as small as possible.
12:35–12:45/1:00	Children prepare for nap—toilet, wash hands, brush teeth, disrobe, snuggle down.
1:00–2:30/3:00	Nap time; children get up as they wake up, toilet, dress, and move out of nap area. Snack ready as they arrive and desire it.
By 3:30	All snacks completed. Indoor/outdoor self-select continues, again with special activities planned and provided for.
4:40	Children begin to put things away, freshen up (wash hands and faces, etc.), and have quiet opportunities to use manipulatives or sit with teacher for songs, stories, and general quiet, relaxing time as parents call for them.
5:30	Children picked up (except for the inevitable emergencies of course!)

Note: For a sample plan, see chapter 18, Developing Thinking and Reasoning Skills.

Remember that a schedule should be regarded as a guide not as dogma. Allowance should always be made for deviations when these are desirable. Perhaps it took longer for the bread to rise than anticipated, or perhaps dramatic play is involving most of the group in an intensely satisfying way. There needs to be give and stretch in schedules to accommodate these kinds of possibilities. This is why lap-over ties and approximate times are listed in the sample. Even a modest amount of latitude allows children to proceed gradually from one activity to the next without being hassled by the teachers.

Note, also, that this schedule allows for breakfast to be served only to those children who desire it. For years our center was plagued with the problem of having some children arrive at 8:30 or 9:00 stuffed to the gills while others were clearly famished. If we waited until 10:00 for snack when everyone had at least a little appetite, then they were not hungry for lunch! We finally decided to solve this problem by offering breakfast on a self-select basis with food kept appetizing on warming trays, and with a friendly member of the staff sitting in the breakfast corner at all times to assist the children and welcome them for a quiet personal chat as they ate. This solution, though unconventional, has done a much better job of meeting all the children's needs by freeing more of the staff to work with the youngsters who are not hungry and providing a homey, comfortable, slow-paced beginning of the day for children who are just waking up and who do want breakfast. It also helps settle down children who may have been rushed off to school in too much of a hurry to have had more than a bite before departure.

The same policy of eating-by-choice is followed after nap since children drift out of the nap area a few at at time. Almost all of them at that point, of course, are ready for something good to eat, but it is still made a matter of self-decision for them. This not only prevents wasted food but also is part of our effort to encourage children to be aware of what their bodies are saying to them. Are they eating just because it is the thing to do, or is their body telling them they are really hungry?

The primary rule that applies to both breakfast and snack time is that, once seated, the child stays until finished eating. No one walks around with food in her hands, and a staff member is always seated at the table to keep the children company.

Transition Times

A study of several different kinds of nursery schools (Berk, 1976) makes the point that transitions (the time spent in moving from one activity to the next) occupy from 20 to 35% of activity time in nursery school depending on the school, the particular day, and the skill and planning contributed by the teacher. This surprising statistic certainly emphasizes that transitions are worth thinking about and managing well so that children can move as smoothly as possible from one activity to the next. It also reminds us how necessary it is to plan for enough time when shifting, for instance, from music to lunch, or from lunch to nap, so that children are not unnecessarily harried in the process.

If you find yourself continually nagging and urging the children to hurry through their paces, here are some suggestions you may want to try in order to make transitions easier for you and them. In addition to allowing a realistic amount of time for transitions to take place, it always helps to warn *once* in advance when a change is in the offing, saying, "It's almost story time" or "You can have a little more time with the beads, but then we'll have to put them away." This gives the children a chance to finish what they are doing and makes their compliance more likely. It also helps to remember that transitions do not usually present an opportunity for a real choice (the child is supposed to come, not linger in the yard), so it is best not to ask, "Would you like to come?" or "It's time to come in, OK?" but to say more definitely, "In just a minute it's going to be time for lunch, and we will go indoors. What do you suppose we're having to eat today?" Occasionally singing a simple song such as "Here We Go A' Marching" will also help get children moving in the desired direction. Avoiding situations where all the children have to do something at once is the best help of all because this avoids the noisy, crowded situations that seem to happen with particular frequency in the toilet room.

ROUTINES OF ARRIVAL AND DEPARTURE

It is natural for young children to feel anxious when their mothers or fathers leave them at school. This feeling, called *separation anxiety,* appears to be strongest in American children between the ages of 10 and 24 months (Skolnick, 1986). Even beyond this age, however, separation requires time and tactful handling by the staff in order that the child and the parent come to feel comfortable about parting.

Although some research (Schwartz & Wynn, 1971) indicates that by the time children are 4 years old many can adjust rapidly to a school situation without their parents having to linger, it is not safe to make a blanket rule about this, since there are always individual cases where a child becomes panicky

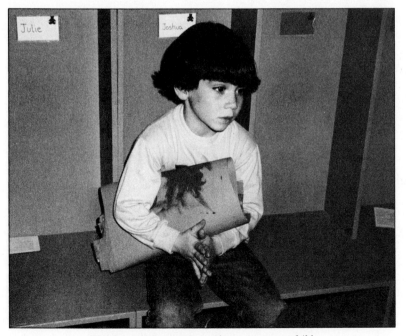

Waiting can seem an eternity to a young child.

when left at school. This seems to be particularly true for 3-year-olds (Cox & Campbell, 1968), 2-year-olds (Provence, Naylor, & Patterson, 1977), and for retarded children (Kessler, Gridth, & Smith, 1968).

Introduce the Child to School Gradually

It is common practice and good sense to recommend a visit by parent and child for the first day, then another short stay while the parent leaves briefly, followed by a gradual extension of time as the child's ability to endure separation increases.

Another way of helping children become comfortable is by having an open house where families can come and go at their convenience. Still other schools begin the term with half the children coming on one day, and the other half, the next. At our center we send each child a personal letter with a name tag, an invitation to the open house, and a short description of what we will be doing

Parting isn't always easy.

at school. The children love these letters, and this preliminary contact does seem to overcome some of their initial apprehension.

These suggestions about gradual adaptation to the new environment are fine for many families where schedules can be somewhat flexible, but they do not work for parents whose jobs demand they appear promptly at 8:00 no matter what the teacher recommends or how hard the child is crying. If at all possible, special arrangements should be made for such families when their children begin attending. A grandfather or aunt might be pressed into service and stay while the child makes friends. Sometimes the parent can bring the child by for a visit around lunchtime, the teacher can make a Saturday visit to the home, or the child can come to school with a friend. Any of these arrangements, while not ideal, is preferable to allowing the child to walk in and simply be left in a strange place with strange people for 9 hours on her first day.

Handling Outbursts of Emotion

It helps to recognize that a child must often deal with three feelings when her mother leaves her: grief (the emotion that seems most obvious and logical), fear (also not very surprising), and anger (the emotion that the teacher is least likely to recognize in these circumstances) (Bowlby, 1973). It is often necessary not only to comfort and reassure the child but also to recognize with her that she feels angry with her mother because she left her at school. I recall one forthright 3-year-old who took real pleasure in biting the mama doll with our toothy rubber hippopotamus as soon as her mother departed. The teacher may also see this angry reaction at being left behind come out at the end of the day when the child insists (with just a touch of malice) that she wants to stay at school "for ever and ever" and does not want to go home. If the teacher interprets this reaction to her mother as being a way of relieving angry feelings, it will help maintain friendly relations all around.

Actually it is the children who make a forthright fuss as their mothers leave who seem to work through their feelings of loss with the greatest expedition, whereas the child who apparently makes an easy adjustment by becoming instantly involved in activities often becomes downcast a few weeks later as she lowers her defenses. If this happens 3 to 4 weeks after entry to school, the parent is likely to assume something has happened there that makes her want to stay home. The best protection against this conclusion is to explain casually to her parent *before her facade crumbles* that the child may show her grief at a later time and that most children feel some sadness and loneliness when left at school.

It is also wise to prepare parents for the fact that children may go through a milder attack of separation anxiety again when they return from vacation. Otherwise this repeated behavior can discourage parents who underwent a difficult separation experience at the beginning of school.

Other unexpected circumstances can also trigger anxiety. One spring the children in our center walked to the college cafeteria and met their parents there for lunch. All went well until it came time to part, and suddenly we had several very unhappy children on our hands. The unusual circumstances had made parting difficult once again for our small charges.

But learning to let go is part of becoming mature. A nice balance of comfort combined with a matter-of-fact expectation that she will feel better soon usually gets the child started on the day. Having something at hand that she especially enjoys will help, too. The teacher must take care to permit the child to form a relationship with him as a bridge to the other children yet at the same times does not encourage this so much that the youngster droops around longer than necessary or becomes a careerist handholder.

ROUTINES THAT CENTER AROUND EATING

Importance of Adequate Nutrition

In these days of imitation foods and casual eating habits it is important to emphasize the value of good food for young children. Too many schools depend on artificial juices and a cracker for snack, supposedly on the grounds that the children are well fed at home, but the underlying reasons for serving this kind of food are that it is convenient and cheap. Yet studies continue to accumulate that indicate that good nutrition is closely linked to the ability to pay attention and learn (Dobbing, 1987).

Although nutritional problems are most severe among the poor, it is not only the children in compensatory programs who are "orphans of wealth." We must also include our more well-to-do youngsters, some of whom subsist on sugared cereals, candy bars, and soft drinks.

So, no matter what the income level of the children served by the center, careful planning of nutritious meals is so important that considerable attention will be paid to it in the following pages.

Planning Appealing and Nutritious Meals

One of the fortunate things about teaching at the preprimary level is that teachers and directors usually have opportunities to participate in planning what the children will eat. Therefore, it is helpful to have some basic principles of menu planning clearly in mind.

A useful place to begin such planning is to become acquainted with the preschool lunch pattern required by the Department of Agriculture (Table 3.1), since so many children's centers use funding from that agency to support their food services.* These standards can serve as the basic guidelines, but there are some additional points to consider as well.

Variety, particularly as the year progresses and the children feel at ease, should be a keynote of the food program. Snacks should be different every day

---

*For further information on obtaining funding, contact the U.S. Department of Agriculture office in your state capital.

TABLE 3.1   School lunch pattern requirements for preschool children†*

Food Components	Preschool Children	
	Group 1 (1 and 2 years)	Group 2 (3 to 4 years)
Meat and meat alternatives		
Meat	1 oz. equivalent	1½ oz. equivalent
A serving (edible portion as served) of cooked lean meat, poultry, or fish, or meat alternatives		
Cheese	1 oz. equivalent	1½ oz. equivalent
Meat alternatives		
Eggs, large	½ egg	¾ egg
Cooked dry beans or peas (½ c may replace 2 oz. cooked lean meat)	¼ c	⅜ c
Peanut butter (2 T may replace 1 oz. cooked lean meat)	2 tbsp	3 tbsp
Vegetables and fruits	½ c	½ c
Two or more servings consisting of vegetables or fruits or both; a serving of full-strength vegetable or fruit juice can be counted to meet not more than half the total requirement		
Bread and bread alternates	5 slices or alternates/week	8 slices or alternates/week
A serving (1 slice) of enriched or whole-grain bread; or a serving of biscuits, rolls, muffins, etc., made with whole-grain or enriched meal or flour; or a serving (½ c) of cooked enriched or whole-grain rice, macaroni, or noodle products		
Milk, fluid	½ c	¾ c
At least one of the following forms of unflavored milk must be offered: • Low-fat milk • Skim milk • Buttermilk This requirement does not prohibit offering other milks along with one or more of the above.		

†Based on school lunch requirements, *Federal Register* (1982), *47*, 162.

*Source: From *Food, Nutrition, and the Young Child* (2nd ed., p. 193) by J. B. Endres and R. E. Rockwell, 1985, Columbus, OH: Merrill. © 1985 by Merrill. Reprinted by permission.

TABLE 3.2   Sample lunch menus*

Monday	Tuesday	Wednesday	Thursday	Friday
Week I				
Oven-baked fish	Beef balls	Stewed chicken	Simmered steak	Ground chicken &
Green beans	Lima beans	Buttered noodles	Scalloped potatoes	egg sandwiches
Carrot sticks	Tomato wedges	Grated carrot-	English peas	Buttered beets
Cheese biscuits	Whole wheat toast	raisin salad	Whole wheat	Lettuce pieces &
Milk	strips	Whole wheat	muffins	tomato wedges
Fresh pear halves	Milk	bread w/apricot	Milk	Milk
	Stewed prunes	spread	Fresh fruit cup	Bananas in gelatin
		Milk		made w/orange
		Orange slices		juice
Week II				
Meat loaf	Creamed chicken	Oven-baked fish	Toasted cheese	Ham
Buttered carrots	Buttered rice	Buttered mixed	sandwich	Bkd potato w/
and peas	French green	vegetables	Tomato soup	cheese
Whole wheat	beans	Whole wheat toast	Chopped broccoli	Celery & carrot
bread and butter	Cornbread sticks	strips	Milk	sticks
Milk	Milk	Milk	Cantaloupe slices	Whole wheat
Oatmeal muffins	Seedless grapes	Apple wedges		strips
				Milk
				Plain cake with
				orange sauce
Week III				
Baked salmon	Meat balls with	Cheese cubes	Beef stew w/peas,	Chicken casserole
croquettes	tomato sauce	Twice-baked	carrots &	Buttered broccoli
Scalloped potatoes	Green beans	potatoes	potatoes	Bran muffins
Okra with	Enriched bread	Buttered beets	French bread	Milk
tomatoes	and butter	Cooked spinach	pieces	Fresh pineapple &
Whole wheat	Milk	w/egg slices	Milk	banana slices
bread	Banana bread	Milk	Cottage cheese &	
Milk		Vanilla ice cream	peach slices	
Apple slices				
Week IV				
Hard-boiled eggs	Braised calves	Tuna fish	Creamed chicken	Beef patty & gravy
Green beans with	liver	sandwiches	Buttered spinach	Peas & potatoes
bacon	English peas	Lettuce pieces	Grated carrot-	Tomato wedges
Drop biscuits	Perfection salad	Buttered summer	raisin salad	Milk
Milk	Whole wheat toast	squash	Whole wheat	Sliced bananas in
Orange slices in	strips	Milk	bread	orange juice
gelatin	Milk	Fresh fruit cup	Milk	
	Baked apple		Applesauce	

*Source: Reprinted, by permission, from ''Ideas for Administrators,'' *The Idea Box*, by the Austin Association for the Education of Young Children, © 1973, National Association for the Education of Young Children, 1834 Connecticut Ave., NW, Washington, DC 20009.

and can be based on seasonal fruits and vegetables to help keep budgets within reason.

Dessert should be unsugared fruit and should be regarded as a nutritional component of the meal, not a reward to be bargained for (Rogers & Morris, 1986).

If the food is plain and familiar and a lot of it can be eaten with the fingers, the children will eat more. As a general rule, young children are deeply suspicious of casseroles and food soaked in sauces and gravies. They prefer things they can recognize, such as carrot sticks, hamburger, and plain fruit.

Table 3.2 provides some sample lunch menus showing how appealing plain, relatively inexpensive food can be. Even if all the children are from one particular ethnic group, it is desirable to vary the suggestions in Table 3.2 by incorporating food from many cultures, bit by bit. For example, menus might include black-eyed peas with ham or pinto beans with melted cheese. Introduction of such foods at this time of the child's life is particularly desirable for two reasons. Good-tasting food that is identified as coming from a particular culture helps children feel friendly toward that culture. Secondly, research indicates that learning plays a big part in developing food preferences and that the preschool years may be a particularly sensitive period in the formation of such preferences (Birch, 1980b). If we wish to extend the range of children's food preferences, this is a good time to begin.

Of course, if there are children at the center of various ethnic and cultural backgrounds, it is even more crucial to include foods they like and that are familiar to them. White, middle-class teachers need to remember that some foods they have eaten all their lives can be dishearteningly unfamiliar to the Navajo youngster who is accustomed to mutton and sheepherder's bread, or the Mexican-American child whose diet staple is the tortilla. Since many of us are unfamiliar with food preferences of various groups, it may be convenient to refer to Tables 3.3 and 3.4 for suggestions about the kinds of food to include. Ethnic

TABLE 3.3   Foods common to most ethnic food patterns*

Meat and Alternates	Milk and Milk Products	Grain Product	Vegetables	Fruits	Others
Pork† Beef Chicken Eggs	Milk, fluid Ice cream	Rice White bread Noodles, macaroni, spaghetti Dry cereal	Carrots Cabbage Green beans Greens (especially spinach) Sweet potatoes or yams Tomatoes	Apples Bananas Oranges Peaches Pears Tangerines	Fruit juices

†May be restricted due to religious customs.

*Source: From *Food, Nutrition, and the Young Child* (3rd ed., p. 227) by J. B. Endres and R. E. Rockwell, 1990, Columbus, OH: Merrill. © 1990 by Merrill Publishing Co. Reprinted by permission.

TABLE 3.4 Characteristic food choices for seven groups*

	Vegetables	° Fruits	Meats and Alternatives	Grain Products	° Others
Black	Broccoli, corn, greens (mustard, collard, kale, turnips, beet, etc.), lima beans, okra, peas, pumpkin	Grapefruit, grapes, nectarine, plums, watermelon	Sausage, pig's feet, ears, etc., bacon, luncheon meat, organ meats, turkey, catfish, perch, red snapper, tuna, salmon, sardines, shrimp, kidney beans, red beans, black-eyed peas, peanuts, and peanut butter	Corn bread, hominy grits, biscuits, muffins, cooked cereal, crackers	Chitterlings, salt pork, gravies, buttermilk
Hispanic-American	Avocado, chilies, corn, lettuce, onion, peas, potato, prickly pear (cactus leaf called *nopales*), zucchini	Guava, lemon, mango, melons, prickly pear (cactus fruit called *tuna*), zapote (or sapote)	Lamb, tripe, sausage (*chorizo*), bologna, bacon, pinto beans, pink beans, garbanzo beans, lentils, peanuts, and peanut butter	Tortillas, corn flour, oatmeal, sweet bread (*pan dulce*)	Salsa (tomato, pepper, onion relish), chili sauce, guacamole, lard (*manteca*) pork cracklings
Japanese	Bamboo shoots, broccoli, burdock root, cauliflower, celery, cucumbers, eggplant, gourd (*kampyo*), mushrooms, napa cabbage, peas, peppers, radishes (daikon or pickles called *takuwan*), snow peas, squash, sweet potato, turnips, water chestnuts, yamaimo	Apricot, cherries, grapefruit, grapes, lemon, lime, melons, persimmon, pineapple, pomegranate, plums (dried pickled *umeboshi*), strawberries	Turkey, raw tuna or sea bass (*sashimi*), mackerel, sardines (*mezashi*), shrimp, abalone, squid, octopus, soybean curd (*tofu*), soybean paste (*miso*), soybeans, red beans (*azuki*), lima beans, peanuts, almonds, cashews	Rice crackers, noodles (whole-wheat noodle called *soba* or *udon*), oatmeal, rice	Soy sauce, Nori paste (used to season rice), bean thread (*komyaku*), ginger (*shoga*; dried form called *denishoga*)
Chinese	Bamboo shoots, bean sprouts, bok choy, broccoli, celery, Chinese cabbage, corn, cucumbers, eggplant, greens (collard, Chinese, broccoli, mustard, kale), leeks, lettuce, mushrooms, peppers, scallions, snow peas, taro, water chestnuts, white turnips, white radishes, winter melon	Figs, grapes, kumquats, loquats, mango, melons, persimmon, pineapple, plums, pomegranate	Organ meats, duck, white fish, shrimp, lobster, oyster, sardines, soybeans, soybean curd (*tofu*), black beans, chestnuts (*kuri*)	Barley, millet, rice, wheat	Soy sauce, sweet and sour sauce, mustard sauce, ginger root, plum sauce, red bean paste

Ethnic group	Vegetables	Fruits	Meat/Protein	Bread/Cereal	Seasonings/Other
Vietnamese†	Bamboo shoots, bean sprouts, cabbage, carrot, cucumber, greens, lettuce, mushroom, onion, pea, spinach, yams	Apples, bananas, eggfruit (o-ma) grapefruit, jackfruit, lychee, mandarin, mango, oranges, papaya, pineapple, tangerines, watermelon	Beef, blood, brain, chicken, duck, eggs, fish, goat, kidney, lamb, liver, pork, shellfish, soybeans	French bread, rice, rice noodles, wheat noodles	Fish sauce, fresh herbs, garlic, ginger, lard, MSG, peanut oil, sesame seeds, sesame seed oil, vegetable oil
Indian‡	Cauliflower, carrots, cucumbers, corn-gourds, leeks, eggplant, beets, radishes, hot pepper, bell pepper, peas, French beans, okra, pumpkin, red and white cabbage, mung sprouts, bean sprouts, potatoes, tapioca root, sweet potatoes	Oranges, limes, grapes, watermelon, mango, guava, honeydew, chiku, cantaloupe, pineapple, green, yellow, and red bananas, berries, custard apples	Lamb, beef, duck, chicken, shrimp, catfish, buffalo, sunfish, sardines, fresh crab, lobster, peanuts, cashews, almonds-chickpeas, split peas, black-eyed peas, dry mung beans	Rice pancakes, wheat chapati, puri, mixed grain flour bread	Fresh coconut juice, curries, tomato sauce, tamarind sauce, dried grain curries (pulses), yogurt-curry garnished with coriander (fresh leaves)
Navajo§‖	Home-grown corn, squash, melons, pumpkins, and some beans; some fresh vegetables available from trading posts; carrots, cabbage, lettuce, potatoes, and onions; also canned vegetables (these items take second priority to staples)	Canned or a little fresh fruit; fruit regarded as luxury	Mutton (name applies to both sheep and goat meat), horse, and beef; when meat is home slaughtered, almost all of animal is consumed; very little poultry	White flour has supplanted corn meal as most basic flour; blue corn flour regarded as specially nutritious	Canned, evaporated milk used almost exclusively; soft drinks in summer very popular

†Information supplied by Hanh-Trang Tran-Viet, Carbondale, IL.

‡Refers to East Indian.

§From "A Study of the Dietary Background and Nutriture of the Navajo Indian" by W. J. Darby, C. M. Adams, M. Pollard, E. Dalton, and P. McKinley, 1956, *Journal of Nutrition, 60* (Supplement), pp. 3–83.

‖There is little variation to daily food patterns. Bread and meat are the most crucial items. The chapter from which this material was taken also includes an interesting list of 20 native plants used as food by some Navajo families. Directions for preparing these plants are also included. Information on the Navajo Tribe was selected as an example of American Indians and is not intended to be used as guidelines for menus for other American Indian groups.

*Source: From *Food, Nutrition, and the Young Child* (2nd ed., pp. 182–183) by J. B. Endres and R. E. Rockwell, 1985, Columbus, OH: Merrill. © 1985 by Merrill. Reprinted by permission. Please note that foods common to most ethnic groups have been omitted and are presented in Table 3.3.

cookbooks and family recipes will help, too, as will a cook who comes from a background similar to that of the children if such a person can be found.

The following checklist, adapted from Endres and Rockwell (1990), provides some additional points to consider when planning menus. If the following questions can be answered with "yes!" the food should be both nutritious and appealing for the children.

Menu Checklist

1. Do the lunches meet the minimum requirements for the group served?
2. Are raw vegetables or fruits included daily for preschoolers and finger foods for toddlers?
3. Is a carotene-rich fruit or vegetable included at least twice a week? Is a dark green vegetable included almost every day?
4. Is a vitamin-C-rich fruit or vegetable included each day?
5. Are foods that are good sources of iron (5 mg) included daily?
6. Are sugar and salt used in limited quantities (e.g., potato chips not served with ham or lunch meats, no sweet desserts)?
7. Do the lunches include a good balance of color, texture, shape, flavor, and temperature?
8. Are the foods varied from day to day and week to week?
9. Is at least one new food or preparation method introduced each week?
10. Are new foods introduced in combination with popular foods?
11. Can the lunches be prepared successfully within the time available?
12. Can the lunches be prepared with the staff, facilities, and equipment available?
13. Can food be purchased with money budgeted?
14. Do the menus reflect both the children's own culture and that of unfamiliar cultures?
15. Do the menus give the child an opportunity to develop motor skills (e.g., preschooler—foods for spoon, knife, and fork; toddler—finger foods and foods for spoon)?

Some Basic Principles Having to Do with Eating

There is perhaps no area in our social life (except sex) that has as many restrictions and regulations attached to it as eating. A class of mine once counted up the rules enforced by their families about mealtimes. We thought of 43 rules within 10 minutes. They ranged from "no dessert until you clear your plate" to "wait until the men are fed before you sit down." We will content ourselves here with enumerating only the principles that the majority of preprimary teachers have come to feel are important as they work with young children.

Some Children Eat More Than Others Do

The quantity a child consumes is related to her physiological makeup as well as to her growth rate. Also, emotional states and needs can affect her appetite. All these factors must be considered when deciding whether a child's nutrition patterns are adequate. As long as the youngster remains healthy and her color is good, there is little need to worry about whether she is eating a lot or a little.

Eating Should Be a Pleasure but Food Should NOT Be Used as a Reward

Most of us are shocked when we hear of parents punishing their children by sending them to bed with no dinner, but how many of us would feel equally concerned about the adult who habitually rewards a child with a cookie or other desired food for being good? And yet this tying food together with behavior is one of the links in developing eating disorders in later years. Certainly eating should be (and is!) a satisfying pleasure, but that pleasure needs to be kept

Lunch provides a fine opportunity for children to do things for themselves.

within bounds—it should not become the primary source of gratification in life. Food should not be used to punish or to bribe or to reward.

Eating Together Should Convey a Sense of Happy Family Life to the Children

There should be time both to eat and to chat. Discipline situations should be avoided whenever possible. It can also be a time to enjoy each other and to help the group by going for seconds, passing food to each other, and group cleanup.

Eating Should Help a Child Be Independent

When I think of the reason we encourage children to serve themselves, I remember the little girl who commented that when teachers are cold they make children put their sweaters on. The same thing is true of eating. When teachers are hungry, they serve the children too much; but if food is passed around the table, each child can take what she desires. It is up to her to choose. She knows how hungry she is, and she knows her preferences far better than her teacher does. Then, too, by serving herself she has the opportunity to learn to observe the social rule "Take some and leave some."

Having sponges close at hand also helps children become independent because they can mop up their own spills. Advertisements that stress the joys of carpeting to the contrary, it is much easier to clean up food from uncarpeted floors, so it is best to eat over a linoleum floor or even outdoors when possible.

Another way to help children retain independence is to make sure the children do not have to wait to be fed. When children are hungry and their blood glucose level is low, they are in poor control of themselves; so food should be ready to be served as the children sit down. If it is placed on a low table or nearby shelf, the teacher can start passing it out as soon as everyone has arrived.

Eating Should Be a Positive Experience

Although the quickest way to teach a child to hate a new food is to make her eat it all, it is desirable to encourage (but not force) everyone to take a taste of everything served. Generally the teacher can count on the combination of good appetites and enthusiasm to foster venturesomeness, but sometimes a child will refuse to try something new. One teacher of my acquaintance handles these outright refusals by simply remarking, "Well, when you're older, I expect you'll want to try it," and then he changes the subject.

Some interesting and carefully controlled research by Birch (1980a) indicates that children can also be influenced toward food in a positive way by the reactions of their peers. After determining who liked which vegetable, Birch studied a number of groups of children where she seated a child who preferred one kind of vegetable with a group who most preferred a second kind. After several days during which the first child witnessed the others choosing his unpreferred vegetable as their first choice, Birch found the child changed to selecting the second vegetable first, also. This change in preference remained constant over a number of weeks.

Unfortunately, negative comments can be just as influential as positive examples. Remarks such as, "It looks like dog pooh pooh!" should be discouraged. A wave of this kind of talk can sweep through a group of 4-year-olds and actually spoil a meal if not controlled. The policy of "You don't have to eat it, but I won't let you spoil it for other people" is a sound one to enforce.

Perhaps one of the best ways to encourage children to try a new food is to allow them to prepare it. Cooking is a fine learning experience as well as a pleasure for preschoolers. Making vegetable soup, deviling eggs, or baking whole-wheat muffins can introduce them to a whole range of taste experiences that they might otherwise shun.

Eating Can Be a Learning Experience

Although the most important goal of the eating situation is to furnish nourishment and pleasure, this experience can provide many opportunities for intellectual learning, too (Goodwin & Pollen, 1980; Whitener & Keeling, 1984). The lunch table is a fine place for conversation and the development of verbal fluency. Children can be encouraged to talk about their pets, what they did on the weekend, what they like best to eat, and what was fun at school during the morning. The opportunity can also be taken to talk about food, textures, colors, and more factual kinds of information, but some teachers seem to do this to excess and forget to emphasize the more valuable goal of fluency. No matter what kinds of learning experiences go along with the meal, the teacher should

Learning social skills is an important part of the lunch experience.

always remember that eating should, first and foremost, be pleasurable and satisfying.

Children with Special Eating Problems

Allergies and Other Food Restrictions

Children who have allergies can have a difficult time at the lunch table and so deserve special mention. The allergy that comes up most frequently is the restriction on milk and milk products. When this is the case, the mother should be asked to supply whatever the child requires instead. A simple explanation to the other children that the child's doctor has said she should not drink milk has always been sufficient at our center. It is wise to be as matter-of-fact as possible in order to avoid making the child feel regretful or persecuted about the restriction.

Sometimes there are other reasons for dietary restrictions. For example, we have had several Black Muslim children and children from vegetarian families in our school, and we always do our best to honor their prohibitions. However, it can be very hard to see a little vegetarian hungrily eyeing the hamburger her neighbor is consuming with gusto. If the problem becomes too difficult, perhaps the teacher will want to invite the parent to a lunch and ask what to do about it.

The Child Who Won't Eat

Not eating and obesity are luxuries that very few countries in the world can afford, so I suppose we should count our blessings. For most children, taking the pressure off eating at mealtimes and allowing a child to skip a meal if she so chooses will gradually solve the problem of not eating. Although it may seem hardhearted, I feel it is a mistake to allow a recalcitrant child to suddenly repent when she realizes that the food is going back to the kitchen. Good food should be set forth; a pleasant opportunity to eat should transpire; and when that time is past, it is past for everyone until it is time for snack. This policy should be carried out without vacillation or guilt on the teacher's part. It is up to the child to choose to eat or not eat; it is not the teacher's role to coax, bargain, or wheedle. No one ever starved to death because she missed her lunch.

There are rare occasions when the teacher will come across a youngster who either compulsively insists on eating only a narrowly circumscribed number of foods or who refuses to eat altogether. This behavior is almost always duplicated at home as well. Taking the pressure off and handling mealtimes in a casual manner may not be enough in these special cases, and the condition can be difficult to ameliorate. Under these circumstances *it is important to suggest counseling promptly* for the family in order to relieve the situation.

The Child Who Grabs Everything

Whereas the noneater is likely to make teachers anxious, the grabber is likely to make them angry. Some grabbing is due to lack of social experience and consideration of others, some is due to enthusiasm or hunger, but some is due to feelings of emotional deprivation.

The teacher may need to remind the child many times to take some and leave some, as well as recognize her feelings by commenting, "It looks so good to you that you just feel like taking it all, don't you?" It is also sound strategy to make sure the hungry one gets a second helping and that she is delegated to go to the kitchen for refills. When she remembers to leave enough for the other children, her thoughtfulness should be commended.

When the grabbiness seems to be a symptom of emotional deprivation, particularly when children cram their mouths so full they cannot swallow, a more indirect approach is required that emphasizes meeting the youngster's emotional needs rather than stressing consideration of others. Here, again, extreme cases may require psychological counseling.

PROCESS OF TOILETING

Taking Children to the Toilet

In general, preschools use the same toilet rooms for boys and girls. However, there are always exceptions to this rule, such as some schools who serve mostly Mexican-American youngsters, where families may feel strongly that open toileting violates the modesty of the little girls.

The benefits of toileting together are that the children learn to treat sexual differences quite casually. They will ask or comment about differences from time to time, and this provides golden opportunities to give straightforward, simple explanations. (Please refer to chapter 12 for a more detailed discussion about sex education.) Open toileting has the advantage of reducing the peeking and furtive inspections that may go on otherwise. It promotes a healthier attitude toward sexual differences and therefore should be encouraged.

The majority of children of preschool age can be expected to go to the toilet when they feel the need, but an occasional child will have to be reminded. Rather than lining everyone up at once and insisting that they use the toilet, it is better to remind children while washing up for lunch or before nap that they will be more comfortable if they use the toilet first.

It will encourage children to take this responsibility for themselves if their parents dress them in pants with elastic tops or other easily managed clothing. It is also sound to remark to children that it certainly feels good to go to the toilet, a point of view with which most of them will concur.

Handwashing should be a consistent part of the toilet routine. Children generally enjoy doing that and will gladly slick their hands with soap if reminded. *Teachers should always take time to wash their hands, too, and use soap as well.* Although this takes a little extra time, the reduction in colds and diarrhea that results for everyone is well worth the effort (Kendrick, Kaufmann, & Messenger, 1988).

Thoughts About Flushing

Some children, most commonly between the ages of 2 and 3, are really afraid of sitting on a toilet while it is being flushed (perhaps they fear vanishing down the hole with their product). Therefore, as a general practice it is wise to wait until the child gets off before asking her to flush the toilet. We have achieved good cooperation by suggesting to the children that it is thoughtful to flush the toilet so that it is fresh for the next person, rather than constantly reminding, "Don't forget to flush it; go back and flush it."

Handling Mishaps

When children wet themselves or have a bowel movement in their pants, they should be changed without shaming or disgust but without an air of cozy approval, either. Such loss of control often happens when children are new to the school, are overly fatigued, or are coming down with something, as well as when children have not yet acquired the rudiments of control. Many children are humiliated by wet or soiled underwear, and the teacher should be sensitive to this and help them change in a quiet place. The inexperienced student may find it helpful to know that it is easier to clean a child who has had a bowel movement if the child helps by bending over during the process.

Theoretically, the children should always have a dry pair of pants stowed in their cubby, but actually these are often not there when needed; so it is necessary to have some extras on hand, with the name of the school written prominently across the seat. It is helpful to have these changes of clothing available in a bureau in the toilet room itself.

Children with Special Problems

Once in a while a mother will worry aloud to the teacher that her child "never" has a bowel movement. By this she usually means the child does not have a bowel movement every day. This may be her natural pattern of defecation, or it may be true constipation. If the child is constipated, it is best to refer the mother to her pediatrician for help.

The same thing goes for a 3- or 4-year-old who leaks a little bowel movement in her pants from time to time and refuses to use the toilet. The child is often "clean" at school but messes her pants frequently at home. The name of this condition is *encopresis*, and it often becomes such a touchy issue between parent and child and can be so hard to treat that it requires help from a pediatrician or, more likely, from a competent psychologist (Schaefer, 1979).

HANDLING NAP TIMES

If eating in a strange place with unknown people is disturbing to young children, going to sleep under such circumstances can be even more so. Releasing oneself into sleep is, among other things, an act of trust, and it is not surprising that this can be difficult for a young child to allow during her first days at school. Fortunately there are some things that the teacher can do to make this task easier for her.

Regularize the Routine

Keep daily expectations and the order of events the same when approaching the nap period. That is, try to do things the same quiet, steady way every day. One pattern that works well is to send the children one by one as they finish lunch to use the toilet, wash their hands, and brush their teeth. Then they are expected to settle down on their cots or mats with a book to look at quietly until all the children are ready to begin resting. Next the room is darkened, and the teacher moves quietly about, helping children take their shoes off; find their blankets, stuffed rabbits, and so forth; and set their books aside. This process should be accomplished with quiet affection combined with the clearly projected expectation that the youngster is going to settle down.

When the children are all snuggled in their blankets, some teachers prefer to read a story, while others sing softly or play a quiet record. It helps to have the children spread out as far from each other as possible and to have them lie head to toe; this reduces stimulation and also keeps them from breathing in each other's faces. Restless children should be placed in out-of-the-way corners. Teachers need to be quiet and not talk among themselves, and other people must not be allowed to tiptoe in and out.

It takes at least two teachers to settle a roomful of children, and it may take as long as half an hour or 45 minutes before the whole school goes to sleep. Some children will need their backs rubbed in a monotonous way to soothe them into slumber.

Allow Children to Get Up As They Wake Up

Usually after about an hour some of the children will wake up by themselves and begin to stir about. This gradual awakening is convenient because it means that each child can be greeted and helped to dress one by one, and it presents a nice opportunity for friendly, quiet chats with the teacher. Children are more likely to wake up in a good mood if they are wakened gradually by the activity around them rather than by having the teacher wake them up. They need time to collect themselves and to regain awareness before they begin their afternoon activities. It often works well to have a few staff members getting children up; the rest of the adults are in the play area, with snack being available as the children desire it and some quiet, attractive activity also available that the children may select when they feel ready for it.

How Long Should Children Sleep?

It is unfair to the parent to allow a child to sleep all afternoon, unless, of course, she does not feel well. A sleep of an hour or so is about right for most youngsters, but this does not include the time it takes for them to settle down.

Should All Children Nap?

All children of preschool age should be expected to lie down and relax for a while in the middle of the day. The need for sleep itself varies considerably with different children, and this difference needs to be taken into consideration. There will be some youngsters, particularly older children who are approaching kindergarten age, who never go to sleep. They should not be expected to lie stiffly on their mats for 2 hours. Instead, following a reasonable rest period, they should be permitted to go outside or to another room and play under the supervision of a staff member. These more mature children often vastly enjoy helping prepare the afternoon snack. It makes them feel important and pays tribute to their own grown-up status.

Occasionally there will be a child who needs to rest but who is so high strung and active that she disturbs everyone at nap time. Our staff has concluded that it is more satisfactory to take these youngsters out of the nap room and give them something quiet to do in the director's office than to become involved in angry, usually noisy confrontations, which upset all the children as well as frighten the restless one.

A Practical Note About Cots

Storage of cots can be a real problem in some schools. In some states licensing laws permit the use of folding mats instead of cots if the floor is not too drafty. These work well except for children who wet their beds at nap time. Saran-covered cots are better to use with these youngsters so that the urine drips through and does not collect in a puddle on the mat. Tiled floors are, of course, indispensable to use in areas where children wet their beds.

SUMMARY

Routines, which consist of arriving and departing, eating, toileting, and resting, are an important part of the child's day. If they are handled well, they can contribute to both the physical health and emotional well-being of young children.

Teachers will experience greatest success in handling routines if they avoid trying to win for the sake of winning, but work instead toward the more worthwhile goals of helping the children become competent, independent people who have healthy attitudes toward their bodily needs and who look forward to eating, toileting, and resting because of the comfort and pleasure associated with these activities.

QUESTIONS AND ACTIVITIES

1. What foods do you particularly dislike? Can you remember the reason for your original dislike? Do you feel you learned anything from that situation that could be transferred to the way you handle eating situations with young children?

2. List all the rules you can think of that applied to eating, sleeping, or toileting in your own family as you grew up. After recalling the stated rules, think of some of the deeper, unspoken ones that were also observed.

3. *Problem:* You are the staff teacher who is delegated to greet children at the door every morning, and there is one little boy who always begins to whimper as he arrives. At that point the father jollies him along and finally gives him a smack on the bottom, telling him firmly, "Little boys don't cry!" You have learned in your student teaching days that it is important for children to express their feelings. How would you handle this situation?

4. Try an experiment wherein you just tell the children for 3 or 4 days that it is time to come in for snack, and then for the next few days try warning them ahead of time that it will soon be time to come in. Is there any difference in the way they respond?

5. *Problem:* Although you never meant to have things arrive at such an impasse, you have inadvertently made such an issue of a child's going to the toilet that he has become so balky about it he will not use the toilet anymore but wets his pants instead. At this point, what approach would you try next to solve this difficulty?

SELF-CHECK QUESTIONS FOR REVIEW

Content-Related Questions

1. Why is it wise to avoid "going to war" with a child about conforming to a particular routine?

2. Name two things teachers can do to help children move easily through transitions.

3. Describe some sound procedures for helping children adjust to the new situation during their first days at the children's center.

4. What basic principles can you think of regarding the management of routines such as eating, naps, and toileting?

Integrative Questions

1. Identify two different transition times that take place at the school where you teach. Which one of the two goes most smoothly? Analyze why that is the case. Can procedures that are effective in managing that transition be applied to the less effective one?

2. Using Table 3.4, "Characteristic Food Choices for Seven Groups," select one particular cultural group and plan a week's lunch menus using its preferred foods that also meet the requirements of the Department of Agriculture guidelines in Table 3.1.

REFERENCES FOR FURTHER READING

Handling Routines

Cherry, C. (1981). *Think of something quiet: A guide for achieving serenity in early childhood classrooms.* Belmont, CA: Pitman Learning. Chapter 5, "Getting the Most from Rest Times," is filled with practical suggestions about nap and alternative approaches to rest times that are helpful for "difficult" nappers.

Read, K., Gardner, P., & Mahler, B. C. (1987). *Early childhood programs: Human relationships and learning* (8th ed.). New York: Holt, Rinehart & Winston. The chapter entitled "Helping Children in Routine Situations" has a detailed discussion of toileting that will be of particular interest to students devoted to the psychoanalytic point of view.

Schedules

Maxim, G. (1989). *The very young* (3rd ed.). Columbus, OH: Merrill. Maxim provides interesting examples showing how schedules can reflect the educational values of the school.

Seefeldt, C., & Barbour, N. (1986). *Early childhood education: An introduction.* Columbus, OH: Merrill. In chapter 5, the authors offer a variety of schedules as well as a clear discussion of how to go about planning curriculum to meet the needs of children.

Separation

Balaban, N. (1985). *Starting school: From separation to independence.* New York: Teachers College Press. Every teacher of young children should read this practical, insightful book.

Gottschall, S. (1989). Understanding and accepting separation feelings. *Young Children, 44*(6), 11–16. Sensitive, practical strategies for helping young children bridge the gulf between home and school are included here.

Kleckner, K. A., & Engel, R. E. (1988). A child begins school: Relieving anxiety with books. *Young Children, 43*(5), 8–14. This annotated bibliography will help children deal with their separation feelings.

Nutrition

Brody, J. (1981). *Jane Brody's nutrition book.* New York: W. W. Norton. This book has been reviewed by the Center for Science in the Public Interest as "the best all-around nutrition text currently available." Well-written "popular" reading.

Endres, J. B., & Rockwell, R. E. (1990). *Food, nutrition and the young child* (3rd ed.). Columbus, OH: Merrill. This is the best book on feeding young children I have ever seen. Full of practical information, it covers everything from extensive information on menu planning to nutrition education and preparing baby formula.

Rothlein, L. (1989). Nutrition tips revisited: On a daily basis, do we implement what we know? *Young Children, 44*(6), 30–36. This article is packed with information about adding new foods, successful cooking with children,

and general nutrition information. *Highly recommended.*

Teaching About Good Nutrition and Cooking with Young Children

Baxter, K. M. (1978). *Come and get it: A natural foods cookbook for children.* Ann Arbor, MI: Children First Press. This cheerful book offers a wide array of simple, wholesome recipes that children can make. *Highly recommended.*

Ferreira, N. (1986). *Learning through cooking: A cooking program for children two to ten.* Palo Alto, CA: R & E Associates. This is a revised edition of an old friend, *The Mother Child Cookbook.* If you could afford just one such book for your school, I believe this would be the one to choose. All the recipes pay careful attention to nutrition and have been used with children of prekindergarten age. There are lists of no-heat recipes and ones that can be cooked outdoors as well as inside.

Goodwin, M. T., & Pollen, G. (1980). *Creative food experiences for children* (rev. ed.). Washington, DC: Center for Science in the Public Interest. This is partly a cookbook (the only one I have seen for children that has completely healthy recipes) and partly a book about things to do with children to help them learn about food and sound nutrition. First-rate and inexpensive.

Whitener, C. B., & Keeling, M. H. (1984). *Nutrition education for young children: Strategies and activities.* Englewood Cliffs, NJ: Prentice-Hall. This book offers rich resources on nutrition, feeding procedures, recipes (including ethnic ones), and carry-over nutrition activities. *Highly recommended.*

Wishik, C. S. (1982). *Kids dish it up . . . Sugar-free.* Port Angeles, WA: Peninsula. The recipes in this book are free of sugar, molasses, honey, and artificial sweeteners. They are accompanied by clear illustrations of recipes that older 4-year-olds could learn to interpret.

Advice on Menu Planning

Aronowitz, V., & Turner, S. (1989). *Health wise quantity cookbook.* Washington, DC: Center for Science in the Public Interest. Contained here are 200 particularly healthy recipes that feed 50 people.

United States Department of Agriculture. (1985). *Your money's worth in foods. Home and garden bulletin #183.* Washington, DC: Superintendent of Documents. *Highly recommended.*

Taking Cultural Food Preferences into Account

Goodwin and Pollen offer many recipes from various countries. I also suggest the Sunset series on foreign foods published by the Land Publishing Company. Their books are relatively low in cost, reasonably authentic, and sensible.

Knight, F. D. (1962). *The Ebony cookbook: A date with a dish.* Chicago, IL: Johnson. Because the Sunset line does not include a book of recipes from the Black culture, I include this one from *Ebony Magazine.*

Smith, J. (1990). *The frugal gourmet on our immigrant ancestors: Recipes you should have gotten from your grandmother.* New York: William Morrow. Smith provides recipes from 35 countries accompanied by vignettes about the countries themselves. Fun and useful.

Tharlet, E. (1987). *The little cooks: Recipes from around the world for boys and girls.* New York: UNICEF. Colorful step-by-step illustrations plus the one-world flavor and costumes of the children make this a recipe book to be used and treasured.

Special Problems Related to Eating

Kessler, J. W. (1966). *Psychopathology of childhood.* Englewood Cliffs, NJ: Prentice-Hall. This book is written for the serious student who wants to know more about handling special behavior problems. It devotes an entire chapter to eating and toileting problems. A helpful, classic reference.

Wishon, P. M., Bower, R., & Eller, B. (1983). Childhood obesity: Prevention and treatment. *Young Children, 39*(1), 21–27. Practical advice about a problem that children in very few countries have to face.

Special Problems Related to Toileting

Schaefer, C. E. (1979). *Childhood encopresis and enuresis: Causes and therapy.* New York: Van Nostrand Reinhold. Schaefer reviews prominent theories about bowel movement retention and wetting and concludes with lists of practical recommendations.

Special Problems Related to Sleeping

Ferber, R. (1985). *Solve your child's sleep problems.* New York: Simon & Schuster. Ferber, who is director of the Center for Pediatric Sleep Disorders at Boston Children's Hospital, offers practical advice about this sometimes difficult problem.

For the Advanced Student

Blatchford, P., Battle, S., & Mays, J. (1982). *The first transition: Home to pre-school. A report on the "Transition from Home to Pre-school" project.* Windsor, Berkshire, England: NFER-Nelson. This research study recounts what did happen during separation at nursery school rather than suggesting what should happen. The case studies are particularly interesting.

Dobbing, J. (Ed.). (1987). *Early nutrition and later achievement.* London: Academic Press. Dobbing repeatedly documents the significant effect malnutrition has on pre- and postnatal development.

Bowlby, J. (1982). Attachment and loss: Retrospect and prospect. *American Journal of Orthopsychiatry, 52*(4), 664–678. This article summarizes how Bowlby, who has done important work on the effect of long-term separation of child from parent, developed his theory and supported it with research.

Powell, G. J. (1983). *The psychosocial development of minority group children.* New York: Brunner Mazel. Powell offers information on specific nutrition problems of Black, Hispanic, and Indian children.

Journals and Organizations of Particular Interest

Center for Science in the Public Interest, 1875 Connecticut Avenue, NW, Washington DC 20009-5728. CSPI publishes a first-rate bulletin entitled *Nutrition Action* plus various attractive charts and books about nutrition. The Goodwin and Pollen book, previously listed, is one of their efforts.

CHAPTER 4

Development of the Physical Self

For children are made so that if they are well, and well cared for, they are very fair to look upon, beautiful, arresting to the eye and heart.
— Margaret McMillan (1929)

So many yards and play spaces remind us more of sensory-deprivation chambers or post-holocaust deserts than anything else. There is no magic in them because very little can be created in a vacuum. We prefer an environment rich in possibilities, abounding with stuff, *with no sense of scarcity.*
— James Talbot and Joe L. Frost (1989)

The habit of exercise is one of the important gifts adults can give to their children. Exercise can not only be beneficial, but also fun, when it becomes part of a child's playtime, building strength, coordination, balance and confidence. In a loving and secure atmosphere, a child can play and prepare to master each physical development stage successfully. . . . A deliberate effort to develop a child's physical and mental capabilities should be made before s/he enters the school system. This responsibility lies with the parent and/or caregiver.
— Canadian Child Day Care Federation
(No date)

Have you ever wondered . . .

How to send a sick child home without hurting his feelings?

Whether it's really all right to admit a child to school whose parents are "going to get his booster shots just as soon as they can"?

What in the world you can do to provide some variety and range to large muscle play?

If you have, the material in the following pages will help you.

Good food, reasonable toilet procedures, and adequate rest are important factors in maintaining the physical and emotional well-being of young children. Additional factors that affect the physical development of children include health and safety and the provision of maximum opportunities for their bodies to grow and develop in the healthiest way.

PROMOTION OF HEALTH AND SAFETY IN THE CHILDREN'S CENTER

Providing Safe Transportation to School Is a Must!

As information accumulates that safety seats and seat belts help save lives, it becomes clear that teachers must help encourage their consistent use (Kendrick et al., 1988). Preprimary teachers have a unique opportunity to foster automobile safety because they meet parents as they deliver their youngsters to school.

Many schools now insist that any child delivered to their premises be transported there "buckled up," and it is a policy that *every* school should institute. Since some children don't like these restraints, teachers should also support the parents' efforts by discussing the value of safety restraints during large group, explaining in a matter-of-fact, nonalarmist way how lucky we are that we have this practical way to keep us safe. Scott (1985) lists numerous

Sometimes the only toothbrushing children do is at school.

low-cost or free educational materials that can be used to add interest to such group times.

Basic Ways to Protect and Foster the Physical Health of Children

Beginning teachers who come from middle-class homes sometimes do not realize how necessary it is for early childhood centers to take the lead in making sure young children have adequate health care. Many families served by preschool centers have very low incomes but do not understand how to make use of free services available to them through Medicare or other health facilities. Families from the lower middle-income bracket are often even more hard-pressed to find the money that medical care requires. Both these groups may need advice from the teacher about how to make use of free or inexpensive community health resources. Even more well-to-do families need to be encouraged to make sure their children have health checkups and immunizations.

Since the first edition of this book was published in 1975, some encouraging progress has taken place in the area of immunization. For example, polio (infantile paralysis) has been virtually eliminated in the United States. We still have much more to do, however, because data gathered in 1988 reveal that more than 40% of children under age 4 have not received the complete basic series of immunizations (National Association of Children's Hospitals and Related Institutions, 1989).

We must be aware that outbreaks of such diseases as measles* are on the rise. For example, the Centers for Disease Control reported a total of 16,236 cases of measles in 1989, compared with 4,866 during the previous year (*Education Week*, 1991).

The problem with rubella (often called 3-day measles) is particularly serious because children who become infected with it may expose their unvaccinated pregnant mothers to this disease—a circumstance that often has deadly implications for the fetus, particularly in the first trimester of pregnancy. Teachers of young children need to take special care that they, themselves, are also vaccinated against it.

Such flare-ups as the measles epidemics have caused many states to pass stricter immunization laws and enforce those already in existence more firmly. However, a recent survey indicates that specific immunization requirements are included in the licensing regulations by only half the states for child care centers and less than one-third for family day care homes (American Public Health Association/American Academy of Pediatrics, 1988).

To make matters worse, even when these regulations exist they are often only laxly enforced or are applied only as the child enters kindergarten or first grade—far too late to protect the vulnerable youngster of preschool age. For this

---

*The seriousness of measles should never be underestimated. It is reported that measles and its aftereffects kill 1.5 million children each year throughout the world (*Children Today*, 1982).

reason, *half- and full-day child care programs serving young children should be particularly adamant about requiring up-to-date immunization records from parents.* Such certification not only protects the child in question but all the other children and adults in the school as well.

Physical Examinations Should Be Required Before the Child Enrolls

Because the preschool is often the first institution that comes into contact with families of young children in a formal way, it is particularly valuable for each school to require preentry physical examinations as well as inoculations. Careful evaluation of potential vision and hearing problems should be a part of this process. Some states already make this part of their licensing regulations for day care centers and nursery schools; those that do not should be encouraged to add this requirement to their regulations promptly.

The Teacher Should Be Prepared to Help Parents Find Health Care During the Year Whenever Possible

There are a variety of free health services and examinations available in many communities, and teachers need to make it their business to become acquainted with each one so that they can refer families who need their help. These services range from university-sponsored speech and hearing clinics to eye examinations paid for by service organizations and the special services offered by the Crippled Children's Society. Sometimes arrangements can be made with training schools

Equipment need not be expensive to be attractive.

to supply health services in return for the opportunity to work with young children. Dental hygienists, for example, may be willing to clean children's teeth in order to obtain experience with preschoolers.

A good way to locate information about such services is to contact the public health nurses in the community. These people are usually gold mines of practical information about sources of assistance.

The Teacher Should Act as a Health Screener

An alert teacher can often spot problems that have been overlooked by families and even by pediatricians, who, though expert, lack the teacher's opportunity to see the child over an extended period of time. The teacher should particularly watch for children who do not seem to see or hear well, who are very awkward, who seldom talk, or who are unusually apathetic or excessively active. The behavior may be only an idiosyncrasy, or it may require professional help, and the sooner help is sought the better. (See chapter 19 for further details on identification of special problems.)

The teacher should make a health check of every child as he arrives at school each day. This serves the purpose of assuring a personal greeting and provides a quick once-over so that a child who is not feeling up to par may be sent home before his parent departs. Although there are some standard things to check for, such as faces that are flushed or too pale, rashes, and marked lethargy, the most important symptom to be aware of is any significant change in the child's appearance. Teachers who see the same children every day get to know how they usually look and behave and can often spot such variations promptly, and thus avoid exposing other children in school to the condition. (See Appendix B for a list of common diseases, their symptoms, and incubation periods.)

Providing care for sick children is a particularly difficult problem for families in which both parents work outside the home. It is encouraging to find that some hospitals are now offering day care for such youngsters. The cost is generally reasonable, and the strategy has helped alleviate the empty-bed syndrome for the hospitals.

Since this service is still rare, parents should also be encouraged to develop a safety net of alternative care arrangements to use when their youngster is too sick to go to school and they must go to work anyway.

The Teacher Must Know What to Do
When a Child Becomes Ill at School

No matter how careful the teacher and conscientious the parent, an occasional child is going to come down with something during the day. Ideally the child should be sent home immediately, but in practice this can be very difficult to do (Aronson, 1986). Even when parents have been asked to make alternative arrangements for emergency care, these arrangements sometimes fall through, and the school and youngster have to make the best of it. Reputable schools try to keep children who are ill apart from the rest; usually the office serves this purpose fairly well. The child should have a place to lie down located as close to a bathroom as possible, and he will need to be comforted and reassured so that he does not feel bereft and lonely.

Because sending a child home from school often embarrasses and angers the parent and hurts the child's feelings as well, it is desirable to be firm but gentle when doing this. Sending something home along with the youngster, such as a book, will help him feel less rejected and make his return to school easier when he is feeling better.

General Health Precautions Should Be Observed Consistently by Children and Staff

Blowing noses on disposable tissue, washing hands before handling food and after toileting, and not allowing children to share food, cups, or utensils they have had in their mouths are basic precautions that must always be observed. If teachers form the habit of washing their hands whenever they have children

"But I don't want to put on my jacket!"

participate in that routine, it not only sets a good example but helps maintain the teachers' good health as well (Moukaddem, 1990). Most schools make it a practice never to administer medication (including aspirin) without the express request of the physician and parent in writing.

It is also important to be aware of the temperature of the day and to take jackets off indoors and dress the children warmly enough outdoors, but not too warmly. Particularly in the fall, mothers tend to weigh their children down with too much clothing, and the children may be so absorbed in their play that they can be dripping with sweat and not realize it. The teacher needs to remind them about staying comfortable and help them adjust their clothing to suit the temperature when necessary.

Maintaining the Physical Safety of Children

Teachers must never forget that the children in their care are not their own and that supervising them carries with it a special responsibility.

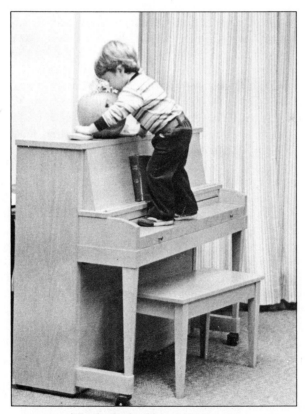

All schools should carry insurance.

Even though insurance costs are high, it is very important for all schools to carry it both to protect them against being sued and also to provide accident coverage for the children. One solution for financing such protection is to include a one-time insurance fee when the child is first enrolled.*

In addition, the entire school needs to be checked continually to make sure it is maintained in safe condition (Frost & Wortham, 1988). Broken equipment such as tricycles without pedals and wobbly jungle gyms *must be removed or repaired promptly.* Sticks, particularly those with nails in them, should be discarded. Safety precautions such as using swings with canvas seats should be observed. The danger area around swings must be clearly marked, and children should be taught to wait on the bottom step of the slide (which can be painted red to make it easier to identify.)

Disinfectants, ant poisons, scouring powders, bleaches, and antiseptics, which are all commonly found in centers and schools, should be kept on high shelves in the kitchen where children are not permitted or, better yet, in locked cabinets.

In chapter 1 it was suggested that inexperienced teachers stop an activity if it looks dangerous to them rather than permit an accident to happen. One other safety rule has proved to be generally helpful: the teacher should never lift a child onto a piece of play equipment if he cannot manage to get on it by himself (swings are an exception to this rule). Of course, youngsters sometimes climb up on something, feel marooned, and must be helped down; but that is different from lifting them onto the top of the jungle gym or boosting them onto a tippy gangplank before they are really able to cope with these situations.

A study of Atlanta child care centers found that accidents occurred most frequently at 11 A.M. and 4 P.M., that the accident rate was highest for 2-year-olds, and that the peak days for accidents were Mondays and Fridays (Sacks et al., 1989). It appears that these are times when teachers should be particularly careful while supervising the children.

It is particularly important to remember that high places such as slides and monkey bars are dangerous for young children because accident records reveal 7 out of 10 playground injuries are the result of falls either from climbing apparatus, jumping or falling from swings, or fooling around on the top of slides (U.S. Consumer Product Safety Commission, 1981).

The concern for safety has to be moderated by the teacher's good sense and self-control. Children must be protected, but they also need the chance to venture and try things out. This venturesomeness is a hallmark of 4-year-olds in particular. Occasional small catastrophes are to be expected, and teachers should not become so overly protective that they hover over the children and remonstrate with them constantly to be careful. Instead they should try to maintain a generally high level of safety combined with the opportunity for the

---

*The reader may wish to check with the National Association for the Education of Young Children as well as with other sources for information on potential insurance policies.

children to experiment with the mild risks that build feelings of competence as they are met and mastered.

BASIC PRINCIPLES OF PHYSICAL DEVELOPMENT

Before reading about specific ways to foster psychomotor development, the student needs to understand some developmental principles that have important implications for education.

Development Occurs in Predictable Patterns and Sequences

Although some investigators have questioned the concept that chronological age should determine when children are taught various skills (Bruner, 1964; Gagné, 1968), it is still generally agreed that children progress through a predictable sequence of developmental stages (Schickedanz, Hansen, & Forsyth, 1990). The examples provided in Table 4.1 illustrate this clearly. (Appendix C provides a chart of normal development from infancy to 6 years of age, organized according to the various selves.) This is as true of physical development as it is true of intellectual development (Piaget & Inhelder, 1967). Children usually sit before they stand, stand before they walk, and walk before they run (Curtis, 1982). In addition, specific skills such as running, jumping, and throwing progress through a number of substages of competency before they emerge as mature physical abilities (Wickstrom, 1983).

Teachers need to be able to recognize these stages of development so they can adjust their curriculum offerings to provide a good balance between opportunities for practice in order to consolidate the skill and opportunities for accepting the challenge of a slightly more difficult activity to go on to.

TABLE 4.1   Age at which a given percentage of children perform locomotor skills*

	25%	50%	75%	90%
Rolls over	2.3 mo	2.8 mo	3.8 mo	4.7 mo
Sits without support	4.8 mo	5.5 mo	6.5 mo	7.8 mo
Walks well	11.3 mo	12.1 mo	13.5 mo	14.3 mo
Kicks ball forward	15 mo	20 mo	22.3 mo	2 yr
Pedals trike	21 mo	23 mo	2.8 yr	3 yr
Balances on one foot 10 seconds	3 yr	4.5 yr	5 yr	5.9 yr
Hops on one foot	3 yr	3.4 yr	4 yr	4.9 yr
Catches bounced ball	3.5 yr	3.9 yr	4.9 yr	5.5 yr
Heel-to-toe walk	3.3 yr	3.6 yr	4.2 yr	5 yr

*Source: From *Developing Motor Behavior in Children: A Balanced Approach to Elementary Physical Education* by D. D. Arnheim and R. A. Pestolesi, 1973, St. Louis: C. V. Mosby. Selected items from the Denver Developmental Screening Test by permission of William K. Frankenburg, MD, and Josiah B. Dodds, PhD, University of Colorado Medical Center.

The Course of Development Moves from Head to Tail

This *cephalocaudal* principle means that children are able to control the region around their head and shoulders before they can control their hands and feet. This is an easy principle to remember if one recalls that babies can sit up and manipulate playthings long before they are able to stand on their feet and walk. Quite simply, children are able to reach, grasp, and use their hands with considerable skill before they are able to master the art of skipping or kicking accurately. The curriculum of the preschool should be planned accordingly.

The Course of Development Moves from Large to Fine Muscle Control

Large muscle activities have been identified by Guilford (1958), who factor-analyzed activities from motor proficiency tests, as including activities involving static balance, dynamic precision, gross body coordination, and flexibility. *Fine muscle* activities include such things as finger speed, arm steadiness, arm and hand precision, and finger and hand dexterity. Development from large to fine muscle control means that children gain control over their larger muscles first and then gradually attain control over the finer muscle groups. Thus a child is able to walk long before he is able to construct a table-top house of tiny plastic bricks.

The educational implications of this developmental principle for early childhood teachers are that preschool children need ample opportunities to use their large muscles in vigorous, energetic, physical play. It can be torment for young children to remain confined too long at chairs and tables. However, since the finer muscle, eye-hand skills are also beginning to develop during this period, activities that stimulate the children to practice these skills should also be offered—but not overdone so that excessive demands are made on the children's self-control.

FOSTERING LARGE MUSCLE DEVELOPMENT IN YOUNG CHILDREN

Use of Apparatus to Promote Large Muscle Skill

In general the school should furnish a large assortment of big, sturdy, durable equipment that provides many opportunities for all kinds of physical activity, and it should also provide a teacher who values vigorous large muscle play and who encourages the children to participate freely in this pleasure.

Equipment good for crawling through, climbing up, balancing on, and hanging from should be included. The children will need things they can lift, haul, and shove around to test their strength and use to make discoveries about physical properties the equipment possesses. They need things they can use for construction, and they need equipment that provides opportunities for rhythmic activities, such as bouncing and jumping and swinging. In addition, there must be places of generous size for them to carry out the wonderful sensory experiences that involve mud, sand, and water. Finally, they need plenty of space in which to simply move about.

I have been deliberately nonspecific about suggesting particular pieces of large muscle equipment in the hope that talking about the children's activity requirements will encourage the teacher to consider afresh what might be used to meet these needs. However, for those who wish to pursue this question in detail, an excellent publication provides detailed lists of indoor and outdoor equipment and firms that manufacture it: *Selecting Educational Equipment and Materials for School and Home* (Moyer, 1986).

There is a continuing and heartening trend toward designing play equipment that is novel, often beautiful, and occasionally cheaper than our more mundane playground furnishings (Eriksen, 1985; Greenman, 1988; Talbot & Frost, 1989).

Equipment need not be expensive to provide sound play value, and several references that give suggestions about how to combine economy with beauty and ingenuity are included at the end of this chapter (Werner & Simmons, 1990). It is wise to remember, though, that poorly constructed, cheap equipment can be the poorest kind of economy in the long run. Children are hard on things, and it does not pay to buy or make playthings that are flimsy—better to have a bake sale and raise money for better quality equipment than be stuck with buying two cheap swing sets 2 years in a row.

In general the more movable and versatile the equipment is, the more stimulating and interesting it will remain for the children. Observation of many schools has convinced me that movable outdoor equipment is one of the things in shortest supply in the play yard; yet it is vital to have plenty of boards, sawhorses, large hollow blocks, ropes, rubber tires, and barrels lest the children feel starved when they cannot complete their more ambitious projects. Schools should budget for more of this kind of equipment every year; there is no such thing as owning too much of it.

Before buying outdoor equipment, however, every teacher should read the discussion by Kritchevsky and Prescott (1977) about how to plan and develop play centers that will have maximum attractiveness and play value for young children. Material explaining the English concept of adventure playgrounds should also be investigated (Allen, 1968; Eriksen, 1985). These wonderfully messy, casual-looking playgrounds place great emphasis on freedom to try out and explore.

Once the equipment has been acquired, it is important to maintain it carefully. Hollow blocks, which are very costly, should be used on grass or outdoor, grass-type carpeting, not on cement or asphalt, where they will splinter badly when knocked down. Most wood equipment has to be sanded and varnished every year to keep it smooth, and over a period of time this treatment can make it beautiful as well. Wooden items must be stored under cover at night. Metal items should be stored under cover when possible to avoid rust.

Of course, children's vigorous activities do not need to be restricted to the school yard. Children will be delighted with the chance to visit parks with large open spaces where they can run freely and roll down hills. Many communities have wading pools for preschoolers or special play areas set aside for younger children. Even a trike expedition around the block with a pause at an interesting long set of steps can offer challenges that should not be overlooked, particularly in a full-day program.

Role of the Teacher in Fostering Large Muscle Play

In addition to providing equipment to enhance large muscle play, teachers can do much to encourage this kind of activity. Probably the most important thing they can do is provide enough uninterrupted time for satisfying play to transpire. Children need time to develop their ideas and carry them through, and if they build something, they need time to use it after they build it.

Outdoor playtime at the preprimary level is not treated as teachers often handle recess in the elementary school. Playtime at this level requires active involvement of the teacher with the children. She does not do this by participating as a companion in their play, but by observing and being alert to ways to make the play richer by offering additional equipment or tactfully teaching an intrusive child how to make himself more welcome to the group. Because her function is encouraging play to continue, she tries to be as facilitative yet unobtrusive as possible.

The teacher needs to keep the environment safe, but at the same time she should keep an open mind about the uses to which equipment can be put. If encouraged, children often come up with original or unconventional uses of materials that are not dangerous and that should be welcomed by the teacher because they are so creative and satisfying to the child. For example, one of our center children recently got together all the beanbags to use as a pillow in the playhouse, and another youngster used the hose to make a worm tunnel in the sandbox. These harmless, innovative activities are all too easily squelched if the teacher is insensitive to their value or too conventional in her thinking.

Finally, the teacher should keep on the lookout for children who are at loose ends and involve them in activities before they begin to run wildly and aimlessly about. Teachers need to be comfortable with a good deal of noise and to welcome the vigorous activity so characteristic of 4-year-olds because they need this opportunity for vigorous assertion and movement in order to develop fully.

USE OF PERCEPTUAL-MOTOR ACTIVITIES TO ENHANCE PHYSICAL DEVELOPMENT

Reports concerning the general level of physical fitness in young children are not encouraging. A recent study that assessed activity patterns and fitness levels of

children aged 6 to 9 years reported that schools do not offer enough scheduled physical education time and that recess times provide inadequate physical education experience also (Ross & Pate, 1987).

Preschool teachers, too, are inclined to turn the children loose during outdoor play and just supply an assortment of equipment such as swings and slides, hoping that the children will seek out the experiences they need by using this apparatus in a variety of ways (Poest, Williams, Witt, & Atwood, 1989). But we now know that perceptual-motor activities can go beyond this sort of thing without requiring children to be regimented and drilled. We really should offer them a broader selection of physically developmental activities than we formerly did if we wish to enhance the full range of their skills. Moreover, children should be encouraged to play vigorously and to sustain their efforts while avoiding overfatigue so that they increase the level of their physical fitness while playing. Just as wholesome eating habits contribute to better lifelong health, so, too, does the establishment of healthy habits of exercise in early childhood (Aronson, 1988).

There are two ways to approach the area of planned perceptual-motor activities: the first provides opportunities for practice in specific skills, and the second uses physical activity to promote creative thought and self-expression. Both approaches have merit.

Planning for Specific Perceptual-Motor Activities

After considerable review of the literature I have concluded that a moderate program offering the clearest language combined with a structure easily understood by teachers and applicable to preschool children is the one utilized by Arnheim and Sinclair in their book *The Clumsy Child* (1979). They divide motor tasks into the following categories: locomotion, balance, body and space perception, rhythm and temporal awareness, rebound and airborne activities, projectile management, management of daily motor activities (including many "fine muscle" tasks), and tension releasers.

It is relatively simple to think of motor activities in relation to these headings once they have been identified and to make certain that opportunities for repeated practice in each of the categories are included in curriculum plans. The trick lies in concocting ways of presenting them that appeal to children. Obstacle courses, simple want-to-try-this kind of noncompetitive games (Orlick, 1982), or movement activities can all be used effectively if only the teacher will keep in mind the diversity of action that should be incorporated. Fortunately the mere challenge of having such possibilities available often provides attraction enough since youngsters are almost irresistibly drawn to physical activities that are just challenging enough without being too difficult. As a matter of fact, if encouraged to experiment, they will often develop the next hardest task for themselves following mastery of its simpler elements.

Fostering Fine Muscle Development (Daily Motor Activities)

Table 4.2 primarily stresses large muscle involvement; but the reader should remember that fine muscle (eye-hand) skills are just as important. These skills include sewing, pegboards, puzzles, beads, and put-together materials (often termed *manipulatives*). Block building, which taps stacking and balancing skills, pouring and spooning in their many forms, and manipulating art materials, most particularly pencils, brushes, scissors, and crayons, also require careful coordination of eye and hand, as does woodworking—it takes a good deal of skill to hit a nail with something as small as a hammerhead.

Things to Remember When Presenting Fine Muscle Activities

Offering a range of challenge in levels of difficulty is particularly important in a group of mixed ages, but even in a relatively homogeneous group of 3-year-olds provision must be made for the fact that the level of fine muscle skill, not to mention the amount of emotional control and ability to concentrate, will vary considerably from child to child. Rather than setting out three or four puzzles of 16 pieces each, the children's range of abilities will be better met if one or two inset puzzles, and perhaps 7-, 15-, and 22-piece puzzles, are set out and changed as they become boring.

Sometimes it adds interest to offer two levels of otherwise identical material. Large and small wood beads make an interesting contrast, or occasionally puzzles that have the same picture but vary in the number of cut pieces can be purchased and made available for use. Children enjoy having access to both levels and like to put into words what it is that makes the materials similar and what it is that makes them different.

Fine muscle activities should be of reasonably short duration. It is difficult for young children to hold still very long, much less sit and concentrate on a fine muscle task that requires considerable self-control. For this reason, several activities should be available at the same time, and children should always be free to get up, move around, and shift to more or less taxing experiences as they feel the need. Quiet periods such as story hours or snack times should not be followed by additional quiet, fine muscle play but by more vigorous large muscle activity.

When children are using fine muscle materials, the teacher should watch out for signs of unusual frustration. I once had a little boy in my nursery school who participated with enthusiasm and happiness in almost everything we did, with one notable exception. Whenever he played with floor blocks, he would work a while and then in a rage send them flying. Yet he was drawn to them as a moth to a flame. His mother and I were baffled; he seemed well adjusted and easygoing, with only this exception. The staff tried building his skills, investigated whether he was happy at home, and watched to see whether other children interfered with his work and made him angry, but we could find no satisfactory answer. Finally one day his mother arrived beaming at school with the following tale. Alan and his father had been looking out the window the

TABLE 4.2 Categories of physical activities and some suggestions for providing practice of these skills at the preschool level*

Category	Illustrative Activities	Comments
Locomotion		
Rolling	Roll over and over, sideways, both directions. Forward roll (somersault).	Nice to have tumbling mats but not essential—rug, grass, or clean floor also works.
Crawling, creeping	Move by placing weight on elbows only, dragging feet. Crawl using arm and leg in unison, on same side of body, or use alternating arm/leg crawl.	Works well to give these movements animal names such as "bear walk," "duck waddle."
Climbing	Apparatus valuable here—good to incorporate stretching, hanging, and reaching in this activity.	Necessary to be careful of safety.
Walking	Can vary with big, little steps, fast or slow. Encourage movement in different directions.	Good to do walking activities barefoot on contrasting surfaces for sensory input.
Stair climbing	Nice to use this during an excursion unless the school has a five- to six-step stairway.	This is an interesting indicator of developmental level: younger children take steps one at a time, drawing second foot up to meet leading foot. Older children alternate feet in this task.
Jumping, hopping, and skipping	Children can jump over lines or very low obstacles, as well as jump down from blocks of various heights. Hopping is difficult for young children; it is a prelude to skipping. Encourage learning to hop on either foot and alternating feet. Skipping often too difficult for nursery school youngsters. Valuable skill to ultimately acquire, since it involves crossing midline in a rhythmical alternating pattern.	Can use animal names here, also. Don't encourage running backward—young children often catch feet and trip themselves.
Running and leaping	Nice to find large, grassy area for these kinds of activities; makes a nice field trip.	Often provides emotional relief, too. Gives marvelous feeling of freedom, power, and satisfaction.

TABLE 4.2 *continued*

Category	Illustrative Activities	Comments
Balance Static (balance while still)	Balance lying on side. Balance standing on tiptoes. Balance on one foot, then the other, for short periods of time.	
Dynamic (balance while moving)	Use balance beam many ways, or use large hollow blocks as stepping stones, or walk on lines. Build a beam that tapers from wide to narrow for the children to use.	A swinging clatter bridge of loosely joined boards to step on, if available, is a particularly challenging task; may overwhelm some children.
Balance using an object	Balance beanbags on hands, or back, or head. Work with unbalanced objects—pole with weight on one end, for example.	
Body and space perception	Movement education techniques apply to this category particularly well. How big can you be? How little? Can you make a "sad" face? Can you fit inside this circle? Can you fill up this circle (a very big one)? How much of you can you get in the air at once? Use shadow dancing for effective awareness building.	Helps to refer to other people's bodies, too, for example, "Where is Henry's elbow?" Listening, imitative actions such as "Simon says" are fun if not carried on too long. Can stress position in space—"over," "under," and so on; tedious if overdone.
Rhythm and temporal awareness	Any moving in time to music or to a rhythmic beat. Can be varied in many ways—fast, slow, or with different rhythmic patterns. Important to keep patterns simple and clear with preschoolers. Remember that many nursery school activities, such as swinging and using rocking horses, also fit this category; fun to add music to these for a change.	Creative dance is the usual medium—"rhythm band" is typical kindergarten-level activity, which is essentially conforming rather than creative. (See also material on dancing in chapter 13.)

Rebound and airborne activities	At preschool age these are generally thought of as "bouncing" activities; mattresses, bouncing boards, and large inner tubes offer various levels of difficulty.	Do not use a trampoline; it requires extraordinarily careful supervision. Many insurance companies absolutely refuse to provide insurance for this piece of equipment.
Projectile management	Swings and hand-over-hand bars are also, in a sense, airborne.	
Throwing and catching	Throwing and catching usually require teacher participation. Children throw best using relatively small objects but catch best using large ones! Can throw objects at target such as wall, or into large box. For catching, older children can use a pitchback net; useful for understanding effect of force in relation to throwing.	Problem is to use objects that move slowly enough and are harmless; Nerf balls, beanbags, large rubber balls, whiffle balls, and fleece balls meet this requirement. Children whose families are interested in soccer are particularly fond of this activity. Need lots of beanbags; not much fun to have to run and pick them up every two or three throws.
Kicking	Begin with kicking a "still" ball, then go to a gently rolling one.	
Striking	Hit balloons with hands and then with paddle. Can hit ball balanced on traffic cone with light plastic bat (whiffle ball good for this).	Many teachers are nervous about striking activities, but these activities are challenging to children and worth the careful supervision and rule setting they require.
Bouncing	Best with large rubber ball; use two hands and then go to one hand; bounce to other children.	
Daily motor activities (fine muscle activities)	Includes many self-help skills such as buttoning and even toothbrushing! Also includes use of almost all self-expressive materials and use of tools in carpentry and cooking. See discussion on fine muscle activities in text.	Be careful of overfatigue.
Tension releasers and relaxation techniques	Refer to material in text.	

*Source: Based on *The Clumsy Child* (2nd ed.) by D. D. Arnheim and W. A. Sinclair, 1979, St. Louis: C. V. Mosby. These activities are only a handful of a great many possibilities. For more extensive material see Arnheim and Sinclair (1979) or Hendrick (1990).

week before, and he had said, "Oh, look Papa, see those two kitties!" But his father had looked and asked, "What two kitties?" since he could see only one. "Why, those two little black kitties right over there," said Al. Shortly thereafter, when his eyes were examined, the answer to his block problem became clear—he was slightly cross-eyed, just enough so that stacking small blocks was a particularly irritating problem for him to solve, and it was this condition that caused him to send them tumbling down when his self-control was exceeded by the difficulty of the task.

This story may help other teachers remember to be alert to activities that seem to provoke consistent frustrations in some children. Such a reaction can often be a symptom of a physical problem that warrants further investigation, since early remediation makes correction more likely.

Relaxation and Tension-Relieving Activities

Sometimes we do not think of relaxation as being a motor skill but rather the absence of one, since "all the child has to do is hold still!" However, the ability to relax and let go can be learned (Jacobson, 1976), and the ever-increasing stress of life as people mature in our culture (Selye, 1981) makes acquiring these techniques invaluable. Moreover, since day care centers invariably include naps as part of their routine, knowledge of relaxation techniques is doubly valuable there. Tension, of course, is intimately tied to emotional states as well as to activity level. We all know that children who are emotionally overwrought find it more difficult to relax. It is worth taking extra time and pains with such youngsters to teach them relaxation skills because of the relief they experience when they can let down even a little.

When one is encouraging children to relax, reducing stimulation from the outside is a good principle to bear in mind. This is often done by darkening the room, playing quiet music, and providing regular, monotonous sensory experience such as rocking or gently rubbing backs.

Yawning, breathing slowly, shutting eyes, and lying somewhat apart from other children will make relaxation easier. The attitude of the teacher moving slowly about and talking quietly is a significant influence as well. Sometimes young children are able to use imagery, also, and picture a quiet place they would like to be. For very young children it is usually necessary to suggest such places—perhaps rocking in their mothers' laps, or lying on a water bed, or resting on the grass on a warm, sleepy day.

During movement and dance activities, children should alternate quiet and active activities. They can be encouraged to sense their own bodies and purposefully relax themselves by being floppy dolls or boiled noodles or melting ice cream. Relaxation should be contrasted with its opposite state of intense contraction. Even young children can learn to make their bodies stiff and hard and then become limp and soft, thereby applying Jacobson's techniques of progressive relaxation (1976). Stretching, holding the stretch, and then relaxing are also easily understood by children of preschool age, and it does feel

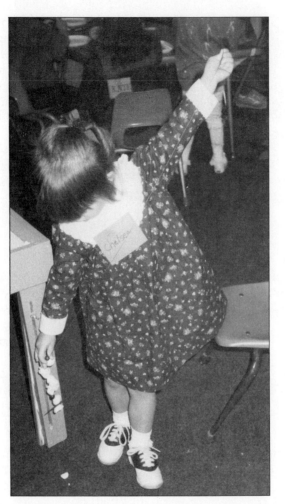

Christmas activities furnish a nice opportunity for fine muscle practice.

wonderful. As we come to understand more about meditation, it is evident that some of these techniques can be used with children, also. An interesting example of such an application is *The Centering Book*, which lists many kinds of awareness and relaxation activities, some of which can be adapted for preschool children (Hendricks & Wills, 1975). Cherry's book *Think of Something Quiet* (1981) also provides many practical ideas of ways to help even very young children learn to attain at least a modicum of inner peace by using various relaxation and meditative techniques.

Even more fundamental than relaxation techniques, however, should be the goal of alleviating whatever is generating tension in the first place. There are numberless reasons why children or adults feel tense, ranging from suppressed anger to shyness or that general feeling of apprehension commonly termed anxiety. Since methods of fostering emotional health and reducing anger are

Stretching is a wonderful way to relieve tension.

discussed in considerable detail later on, suffice it to say here that perhaps the most basic way to help people become less tense is to enable them to become more competent in as many areas of their lives as possible. This feeling of competency—being in command of oneself and one's life—is a highly effective, long-term antidote for tension.

Using Physical Activity to Promote Creative Thought and Self-Expression

Using Movement Exploration

One of the newer aspects of creative physical education is termed *movement education* (Benzwie, 1987; Bresson, 1990). It is a nice blend of physical activity and problem solving that can be considerable fun for children. The teacher may ask a youngster, "Is there some way you could get across the rug without using your feet?" and then, "Is there another way you could do that?" Or she might question, "What could you do with a ball with different parts of your feet?" or "Can you hold a ball without using your hands?"

It is obvious how this kind of teaching fosters the development of fluency in ideas, and some research by Torrance (1970) indicates that when this approach was used with first and second graders in a dance class, they placed significantly higher on tests of creativity than did untrained third graders.

Movement education also contributes to knowing more about the body—being aware of various parts such as elbows or toes and all the things they can do, not only independently, but when used together. According to Tillotson, when thinking about movement education, it is helpful to understand that each action "demands the use of three elements (1) space—straight-line action and indirect biplane action; (2) time—fast or slow speed; and (3) force—strong or light effort. Emphasis is also placed on smooth, controlled performance regardless of the movement pattern" (1970, p. 34). I have found that using these kinds of movement education experiences to begin a dance session leads quite naturally into dance. If the problems presented are simple and fun, children soon begin laughing and trying out possibilities with enthusiasm. This has a very desirable, freeing effect.

Using Creative Dance as a Means of Self-Expression

Dancing can be the freest and most joyful of all large motor activities. For young children, dancing usually means moving rhythmically to music in a variety of relatively unstructured ways. The quandary beginning teachers often feel is just how unstructured this should be. It is rarely effective to just put on a record, no matter how appealing, and expect the children to "dance." On the other hand, the teacher who sets out to teach specific patterns, often in the guise of folk dances, surely limits the creative aspects of this experience. Besides that limitation, patterned dances are usually too complicated for young children to learn unless these are stripped to very simple levels.

What works best is to have an array of records or tapes on hand with which the teacher is very familiar and that provide a selection of moods and tempi. It is important also to have several activities thought out in advance to fall back on if something does not "go over" and to plan on participating with the children. Finally, as the session moves along, more and more ideas and movements can be drawn from the children themselves—an approach that makes the activity truly creative and satisfying for them.*

FOSTERING SENSORY EXPERIENCE

It has been maintained that 80% of everything we learn comes to us through our eyes, but it seems to me that our society encourages use of this one sense far more than is necessary. One has only to watch the deodorant and disinfectant advertisements on television to become aware of the tremendous emphasis on the desirability of smelling only a few choice fragrances. Children are con-

---

*Please refer to chapter 13 for more detailed suggestions.

Remember how your stomach used to feel?

tinually admonished not to touch things, and as they mature, they are also taught not to touch other people except under carefully restricted circumstances. As for tasting, how many times have you heard a mother warn, "Don't put that in your mouth; it's dirty." The latest victim of the war against the senses appears to be hearing. In self-defense, people seem to be learning to tune out the continual piped-in music of the supermarket and the constant noise of the television set.

Teachers need to contend with this narrowing and restricting of the use of the senses by deliberately continuing to use *all* of them as avenues of learning. Children should be encouraged to make comparisons of substances by feeling them and smelling them, as well as by looking at them. Science displays should be explored by handling and manipulation rather than by looking at bulletin board pictures or observing demonstrations carried out by the teacher. Stress should be placed on developing auditory discrimination skills (telling sounds apart) as well as on paying attention to what is said by the teacher. Learning through physical, sensory participation should be an important part of every preschool day.

The Sensory Experience of Close Physical Contact Is Important to Children

The recent handful of sensational court cases concerning sexual abuse in children's centers has made some teachers of young children uneasy about

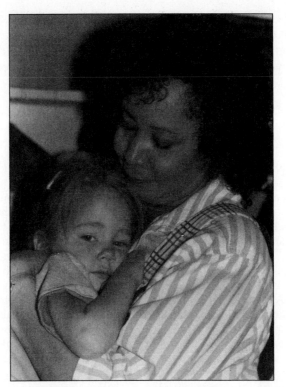

There's just no substitute for cuddling.

touching or cuddling youngsters lest they, too, be accused (Mazur & Pekor, 1985). They feel torn between the desire to protect themselves and the knowledge, well substantiated by practical experience, that young children require the reassurance and comfort of being patted, rocked, held, and hugged from time to time.

Research as well as experience supports the value of close physical contact. Montagu (1986) has reviewed numerous studies illustrating the beneficial effect of being touched and the relationship of tactile experience to healthy physical and emotional development. Investigations documenting the link between touching and the development of attachment confirm those findings (Brown, 1984).

Yet staff must realize that parents are understandably concerned about the possibility of sexual abuse. Centers need to do everything in their power to reassure them. No one, teachers included, wants children to be molested, and parents worry particularly about this when children are away from home. To allay these fears, centers should have clearly stated policies encouraging parents to drop in for unannounced visits, and they should create opportunities for families and teachers to become well acquainted so a climate of trust develops between them. If the center is staffed so that more than one person is with the children at all times, so much the better.

When such openness is the case, parents are reassured, and children and staff are more comfortable, too. In these circumstances the children will grow and thrive, and Cornelia Goldsmith's statement will prove as true today as when she said it 40 years ago—"The teacher's most important piece of equipment is her lap!"

SUMMARY

The promotion of health and safety is vital to the physical well-being of young children. During the hours children are at school, it is the teacher's responsibility to see they follow good health practices and to keep the children as safe as possible without nagging them or being overprotective.

In addition, it is desirable to offer equipment and activities that foster large and fine muscle development. Attaining competence in these physical areas enhances the children's self-esteem and provides opportunities for them to gain social expertise as they develop wholesome feelings of vigor and good health.

Equipment for large muscle activities should be versatile, sturdy, safe, and well maintained. The teacher can encourage active play by tuning in on what is happening and being alert to ways to add to its richness rather than by regarding large muscle playtime as a recess period when she can sit down and relax.

Fine muscle activity is also valuable to offer, but it is important to provide an assortment of levels of difficulty and to be sure that such activities do not continue for too long a time without relief.

Increasing knowledge of perceptual-motor development has made it necessary for preprimary teachers to broaden the range of activities offered to young children in order to provide opportunities for practice in specific motor skills: locomotion, balance, body and space perception, rhythm and temporal awareness, rebound and airborne activities, projectile management, fine muscle activities, and relaxation techniques. Movement activities that encourage creative thinking and self-expression should also be included.

Use of all the senses is important in education. Encourage children to touch, taste, and listen as well as look in order to make the fullest use of these potential pathways for learning.

By using this comprehensive approach involving large and fine muscle skills and various sensory abilities, teachers can assure themselves that the physical development of the child is brought to its fullest potential.

QUESTIONS AND ACTIVITIES

1. *Problem:* A little girl has just fallen out of the swing and is brought into the office bleeding heavily from the mouth. Examination reveals that her front tooth is still whole but has cut entirely through her lower lip. As the teacher in charge, how would you handle this emergency? Remember to think about both short- and long-term aspects of the situation.

2. Are there any conditions in the school where you are teaching that are particularly well handled in terms of safety precautions?

Are there some possible hazards that warrant attention?

3. Suppose you were beginning a new school and had a budget of $3,000 for large muscle equipment. In your opinion, what would be the most satisfactory way to invest this money? What would you buy and why?

4. Could there be advantages to putting children through a planned series of physical exercises on a regular basis? This might not be calisthenics as such; it might be tumbling or learning ball skills. What might be the

disadvantages of this approach to physical education?

5. Some preprimary teachers, particularly male ones, appear to avoid physical contact with the children. What do you think might be the reasons for this restraint? Is it always fear of being accused of sexual abuse, or could there be other reasons for this behavior?

6. What are some examples from your own experience where you are aware that the use of every sense except vision is restricted or curtailed?

SELF-CHECK QUESTIONS FOR REVIEW

Content-Related Questions

1. Explain why it is so important for children's centers to insist that children be immunized and that they have a physical examination before attending school.

2. List some general health precautions teachers should follow when caring for children.

3. List three principles of physical development.

4. Name the categories of large muscle behaviors discussed in the text and give an example of an activity that would fit each category.

5. What are some typical fine muscle activities offered to young children in preprimary schools? Why is it important not to keep children doing these for too long periods of time?

6. Discuss some effective ways to help children learn to relax.

7. What are some effective policies schools might follow that would reassure parents their children are safe from sexual abuse?

Integrative Questions

1. You are now the director of a child care center, and the annual visit by the licensing agency is due very soon. When you check the immunization records of the children in preparation for that visit, to your surprise you find that about a third of the children's immunizations are not up-to-date. You send out a notice requesting parents to take the children to the doctor to have the necessary shots. Three weeks later, only two parents have turned in updated reports. What steps would you take next to ensure compliance with the regulations?

2. The teacher in the room next door is very interested in promoting physical fitness, so she usually organizes her 4-year-olds into teams and has them compete to see which team can get through the obstacle course fastest. Explain whether you would include that kind of activity in your plans for the children in your room. Be sure to include reasons why you would or would not do this.

3. An obstacle course that includes crawling through a cement pipe, swinging across the grass holding onto a rope with both hands, and walking along a narrow line drawn on the sidewalk has been planned for outdoor play. Which of the eight categories described in this chapter are included in this activity? What categories are *not* included? Suggest activities to add to the obstacle course that would provide practice for two more categories.

REFERENCES FOR FURTHER READING

Overviews

Gearheart, B. R., & Gearheart, C. J. (1989). *Learning disabilities: Educational strategies* (5th ed.). Columbus, OH: Merrill. This book has several good chapters that describe the most important schools of thought on perceptual-motor development.

Payne, V. G., & Isaacs, L. D. (1987). *Human motor development: A lifespan approach.* Mountain View, CA: Mayfield. This comprehensive text treats the subject of motor development in depth. Useful for the serious student of this subject.

Poest, C. A., Williams, J. R., Witt, D. D., & Atwood, M. E. (1990). Challenge me to move: Large muscle development in young children. *Young Children, 45*(5), 4–10. The authors present a well-reasoned case for improving the quality of large muscle experiences for young children.

Health and Safety

Kendrick, A. S., Kaufmann, R., & Messenger, K. P. (Eds.). (1988). *Healthy young children: A manual for programs.* Washington, DC: National Association for the Education of Young Children. This practical book covers everything from descriptions of common diseases to ideas for nutritious snacks. *Highly recommended.*

Moukaddem, V. (1990). Preventing infectious diseases in your child care setting. *Young Children, 45*(2), 28–29. Lists of practical do's and don'ts are included in this succinct summary of important precautions for disease control in day care settings. The value of consistent handwashing is particularly stressed.

Sensory Awareness

Brown, C. C. (Ed.). (1984). *The many facets of touch. The foundation of experience: Its importance through life, with initial emphasis for infants and young children.* Skillman, NJ: Johnson & Johnson Baby Products. An interesting and unusual book, this volume documents current research on the relation of touch to healthy human development.

Activities That Foster Balanced Physical Development*

Benzwie, T. (1987). *A moving experience: Dance for lovers of children and the child within.* Tuc-

son, AZ: Zephyr. The subtitle is somewhat misleading because this book deals more with what is often termed "movement education" than with creative dance. It offers many good ideas, including useful ones about how to move children gradually into the experience. It also includes a good list of appropriate records for various activities.

Kelly, N. T., & Kelly, B. J. (1985). *Physical education for pre-school and primary grades.* Springfield, IL: Charles C Thomas. The Kellys offer many stimulating suggestions for physical activities to do with young children. There is a nice emphasis on inexpensive equipment that preschool teachers will appreciate.

Kruger, H., & Kruger, J. (1989). *The preschool teacher's guide to movement education.* Baltimore, MD: Gerstung. Carefully divided according to developmental stages, this book is rich with ideas and practical suggestions for fostering movement exploration.

Miller, K. (1989). *The outside play and learning book: Activities for young children.* Mount Rainier, MD: Gryphon House. Many age-appropriate, attractive, fresh suggestions for outdoor activities are included here. Topics range from ideas for riding-toy play to snow and woodworking activities.

Sullivan, M. (1982). *Feeling strong, feeling free: Movement exploration for young children.* Washington, DC: National Association for the Education of Young Children. *Movement Exploration* provides suggestions for children from ages 3 to 5 and 5 to 8. Sullivan does not hesitate to discuss how to obtain and retain control of the group. She also provides many suggestions for activities. *Highly recommended.*

Teaching Children to Relax

Humphrey, J. H. (1988). *Teaching children to relax.* Springfield, IL: Charles C Thomas. After discussing the causes of tension, Humphrey provides instructions for progressive relaxation, meditation, and other techniques. Many of the suggestions could be used successfully with preschool children.

---

*References on creative dance are included in chapter 13.

Playground Design and Equipment

Frost, J. L., & Klein, B. L. (1979). *Children's play and playgrounds.* Boston: Allyn & Bacon. This is a well-illustrated book rich with ideas for contemporary playgrounds and how to facilitate play within them. It contains a good chapter on playgrounds for children with handicaps.

Frost, J. L., & Wortham, S. (1988). The evolution of American playgrounds. *Young Children, 43*(5), 19–28. After providing a historical review of playground development, the authors suggest a series of guidelines for planning a developmentally appropriate playground for young children.

Greenman, J. (1988). *Caring spaces, learning places: Children's environments that work.* Redmond, WA: Exchange Press. Greenman provides wonderful ideas for anyone redesigning or designing space for children. The book is delightful to read—written with humor and experienced insight.

Werner, R. H., & Simmons, R. Q. (1990). *Homemade play equipment.* Reston, VA: American Alliance for Health, Physical Education, Recreation, and Dance. Although some of the equipment described is intended for older children, many useful, inexpensive ideas appropriate for young children are included, too.

Protecting Schools from Accusations of Child Abuse

Stephens, K. (1988). The First National Study of Sexual Abuse in Child Care: Findings and recommendations. *Child Care Information Exchange, 60,* 9–12. The findings in this valuable research study have important implications for schools that wish to avoid any possibility that sexual abuse might take place on their premises.

For the Advanced Student

Allen, Lady of Hurtwood. (1968). *Planning for play.* Cambridge, MA: The MIT Press. Lady Allen, a progressive thinker, was among the first to advocate the development of adventure playgrounds. She describes the purpose of this book as being "to explore some of the ways of keeping alive and sustaining the innate curiosity and natural gaiety of children." It does that. A classic.

Finkelhor, D., Williams, L. M., & Burns, N. (1988). *Nursery crimes: Sexual abuse in day care.* Newbury Park, CA: Sage. The authors of this disturbing study reviewed a significant number of sexual abuse cases occurring in centers and family day care situations. They conclude the rate is low but not nonexistent. Study includes recommendations for teacher protection.

Fraiberg, S. (1977). *Insights from the blind.* New York: Basic Books. For an absolutely fascinating account of the effect of the deprivation of one sense (vision) on the development of the infant, the reader should not miss this book. The interplay between stimulation by the environment and developmental readiness is nowhere better documented than in this well-written research report.

Gärling, T., & Valsiner, J. (1985). *Children within environments: Toward a psychology of accident prevention.* New York: Plenum. An international publication, this book presents interesting new perspectives on the psychology of safety as it relates to young children.

Kane, D. N. (1985). *Environmental hazards to young children.* Phoenix: Oryx. Kane includes grim evidence documenting the importance of safety. The author explains the necessity of protecting children from hazards such as traffic, fire, and poisonous substances.

McLeod, B. (1990). The status of early childhood (physical) education in Canada. In W. J. Stinson, (Ed.), *Moving and learning for the young child.* Reston, VA: American Alliance for Health, Physical Education, Recreation, and Dance. The author presents a brief overview of Canadian early education and closes with a discussion of movement education in that country.

Stinson, W. J. (Ed.). (1990). *Moving and learning for the young child.* Reston, VA: American Alliance for Health, Physical Education, Recreation, and Dance. This book has a touch of everything in it because it is a collection of papers from a conference about preschool children and physical education.

Publications and Associations Having Related Interests

American Alliance for Health, Physical Education, Recreation, and Dance. 1900 Association Dr., Reston, VA 22091. The Alliance offers many publications and media materials related to an astonishing range of physical activities.

Child Health Alert, PO Box 338, Newton Highlands, MA 02161. This monthly publication covers subjects ranging from head lice to sports injuries.

Child Health Talk. National Black Child Development Institute, 1463 Rhode Island Ave., NW, Washington, DC 20005. *Child Health Talk* presents brief, basic information on various aspects of health care; a special emphasis on nutrition seems always to be included.

PART THREE

Nourishing and Maintaining Emotional Health

CHAPTER 5
Fostering Mental Health in Young Children

Children of all ages need an atmosphere of warmth in which to thrive, the warmth of close, honest human contacts. They need the feeling that adults, teachers, and parents like them, are interested in them, enjoy them, and feel ready to be responsible for them, to protect them even from themselves when occasion demands.

—Barbara Biber (1984)

Have you ever wondered . . .

How to get a child to say what she's feeling instead of hitting somebody?

What to do for a child who just won't stop crying?

How to tell whether a child is mentally healthy?

If you have, the material in the following pages will help you.

The valuable contribution early childhood programs can make to fostering mental health was emphasized as long ago as 1970 when the Joint Commission on the Mental Health of Children repeatedly pointed out that day care centers, nursery schools, and compensatory programs present outstanding opportunities for carrying out preventive and remedial work in this area.

In an era when it is estimated that 12% of the children in the United States under age 18 suffer from mental disorders requiring special treatment, the importance of such work is clear (Institute of Medicine, 1989). We *must* give careful consideration to practical things teachers can do that are likely to foster mental health in children. For this reason, several chapters of this book are devoted to establishing general therapeutic policies, dealing with crisis situations, handling discipline and aggression, and building self-esteem, because these are all important aspects of developing emotional health. Additional aspects of mental health, covered under the development of the social self, include learning to care for other people, valuing cross-cultural education, and taking pleasure in meaningful work.

IMPORTANCE OF DEVELOPING BASIC ATTITUDES OF TRUST, AUTONOMY, AND INITIATIVE IN YOUNG CHILDREN

The most fundamental thing the teacher can do to foster mental health in young children is to provide many opportunities for basic, healthy emotional attitudes to develop. Erikson (1959, 1963, 1982) has made a significant contribution to our understanding of what these basic attitudes are. He hypothesizes that during their life span, individuals pass through a series of stages of emotional development wherein basic attitudes are formed. Early childhood encompasses three of these: the stages of trust versus mistrust, autonomy versus shame and doubt, and initiative versus guilt. Although children at the preprimary level are likely to be working on the second and third sets of attitudes, it is important to understand the implications of the first set, also, since Erikson theorizes that the resolution of each stage depends in part on the successful accomplishment of the previous one.

In the stage of *trust versus mistrust* the baby learns (or fails to learn) that other people can be depended on and also that she can depend on herself to elicit needed responses from them. This development of trust is deeply related to the quality of care that the mother provides and is often reflected in feeding practices, which if handled in a manner that meets her needs, help assure the infant that she is valued and important. Although by the time she enters child care the balance between trust and mistrust will have been tipped in favor of one attitude or the other, the need to experience trust and to have it reaffirmed remains with people throughout their lives. This is also true for the other attitudes as they develop.

Therefore, it is vital that the basic climate of the center encourage the establishment of trust between everyone who is part of that community. If the

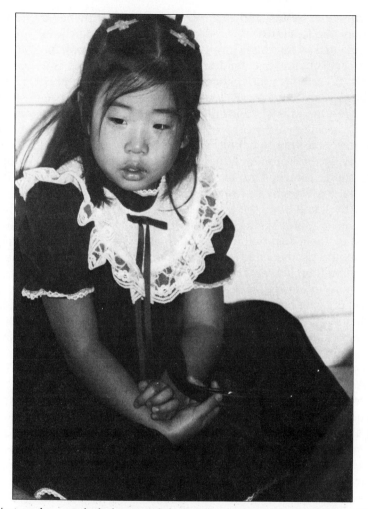

Debbie is in tears because she had to attend the morning party with her little sister. Of course, when she returned to the 4-year-old afternoon gala, the tears were gone.

teacher thinks of establishing trust in terms of letting the children know they can depend on him, it will be fairly easy for him to implement this goal. For example, consistent policies and regularity of events in the program obviously contribute to establishing a trustful climate. Being reasonable also makes it clear to the children that they can depend on the teacher. In addition, if he is sensitive to the individual needs of the children and meets these as they arise, the teacher can once again confirm the message that they are worthy of love and thus further strengthen trust and self-esteem.

In our society the attitudes of *autonomy versus shame and doubt* are formed during the same period in which toilet training takes place. During this time the child is acquiring the skills of holding on and letting go. This fundamental exercise in self-assertion and control is associated with her drive to become independent and to express this independence by making choices and decisions so often couched in the classic imperatives of the 2-year-old: No! Mine! and Me do it! Erikson maintains that children who are overregulated and deprived of the opportunity to establish independence and autonomy may become oppressed with feelings of shame and self-doubt, which result in losing self-esteem, being defiant, trying to get away with things, and in later life in developing various forms of compulsive behavior.

The desirable way to handle this strong need for choice and self-assertion is to provide an environment at home and school that makes many opportunities available for the child to do for herself and to make decisions. This is the fundamental reason why self-selection is an important principle in curriculum design. At the same time, the teacher must be able to establish decisive control when necessary, since young children often show poor judgment and can be tyrannized by their own willfulness unless the teacher is willing to intervene.

Gradually, as the child develops the ability to act independently, she embarks on building the next set of basic attitudes. Around the age of 4 or 5 she becomes more interested in reaching out to the world around her, in doing things, and in being part of the group. At this stage she wants to think things up and try them out; she is interested in the effect her actions have on other people (witness her experimentation with profanity and "bad" language); she formulates concepts of appropriate sex roles; she enjoys imaginative play; and she becomes an avid seeker of information about the world around her. This is the stage Erikson has so aptly named *initiative versus guilt*.

To feel emotionally satisfied, a child of this age must be allowed to explore, to act, and to do. Preprimary schools are generally strong about meeting the children's need to explore and create, but they often underestimate the ability of older 4- and 5-year-olds to participate in making plans and decisions for their group or to attempt challenging projects. Of course, the teacher must make allowance for the fact that 4- and 5-year-olds are better planners and starters than they are finishers. Satisfaction in completing projects is more likely to be part of the developmental stage that follows this one: the stage of *industry versus inferiority*, which is characteristic of the child during early years in primary school. But encouraging the ability to initiate plans and take action will enhance the child's feeling of self-worth and creativity as well as her ability to be a self-starter—all highly desirable outcomes necessary for future development and happiness.

HALLMARKS OF AN EMOTIONALLY HEALTHY YOUNG CHILD

To determine whether the child is in good emotional health, the teacher should ask the following questions about her. If the majority of them can be answered affirmatively, chances are good that she is emotionally healthy.

Is the Child Working on Emotional Tasks That Are Appropriate for Her Age?

We have already talked about the fundamental need for planning a curriculum that provides many opportunities for children to exercise their autonomy and initiative. When looking at individual children, the teacher should consider whether they are taking advantage of these opportunities. He will find that the majority of them are achieving independence, choosing what they want to do, and generating their own ideas with zest and enthusiasm; but there will be a handful of youngsters who need sensitive help to venture forth. This usually involves taking time to build a strong foundation of trust between the child and teacher and then helping her advance to increased independence as her confidence grows (Balaban, 1989).

Is the Child Learning to Separate from Her Family Without Undue Stress and to Form an Attachment with at Least One Other Adult at School?

In chapter 3 considerable space was devoted to handling separation anxiety in a constructive way because the ability to separate from significant others and form additional relationships is an important skill. The teacher should realize that most children, particularly shy ones and those who are younger, make friends with a teacher at school before they branch out to make friends with other children. This link between teacher and child is, of course, not so strong as the bond between parent and child (Balaban, 1985). However, it seems reasonable to propose that in a milder way a wholesome attachment between teacher and child encourages the youngster to explore and venture out in the center setting, just as has been demonstrated by Ainsworth and her colleagues (1978) that toddlers who are well attached to their mothers are more likely to venture and explore new experiences when that parent is present. The teacher who is aware that this is a typical and valuable pattern can relax and enjoy this process without fretting about the child's dependency because he has confidence that in time most children will leave his side in favor of being with other youngsters. This bond between teacher and child may not be so evident in socially able 4-year-olds as it is with younger children, but it should exist all the same. If the child has not formed a relationship with some adult after she has been at school for a while, she should be encouraged to do so. Being attached to the teacher makes it more probable that she will use the teacher as a model or come to him for help when it is needed. Affection between teacher and child is also important because it is a fundamental ingredient of good discipline—but more about that later.

At the same time, the teacher has to be sensitive to the quality of the attachment. Oversolicitude for the child's feelings of loneliness or the teacher's own unmet needs for affection can occasionally create a form of dependency that is undesirable because it restricts the child's venturing out and making friends with her peers. This situation should, of course, be avoided. The teacher must learn to tell the difference between a youngster who genuinely needs the emotional support of a close relationship to begin with and the one who is using him as an emotional crutch.

Is the Child Learning to Conform to Routines at School Without Undue Fuss?

Of course, conforming to routines varies with the age of the child and her temperament, and teachers anticipate some balkiness and noncompliance as being not only inevitable but healthy. Two-year-olds are particularly likely to be balky and at the same time insist that things should be done the same way every time. Self-assertiveness appears again rather prominently between the ages of 4 and 5. The quality of the behavior seems different though: the assertiveness of age 2 comes across as being more dogmatic and less logical, whereas the assertiveness of age 4 seems to be more of a deliberate challenge and trying out of the other person. However, consistent refusal to conform differs from these healthy behaviors because it goes beyond these norms. When this is the case, it should be regarded as a warning sign that the child needs help working through the behavior.

Is the Child Able to Involve Herself Deeply in Play?

A characteristic of severely disturbed children in mental institutions is that they cannot give themselves up to the experience of satisfying play. Indeed, when they become able to do so, it is encouraging evidence that they are getting ready to be released from the hospital. Being able to play is also important for more typical children. The child's ability to enjoy participating in play by herself or with other children as she grows older is not only a hallmark of emotional health but contributes to maintaining mental health as well.

Is the Child Developing the Ability to Settle Down and Concentrate?

Children may be distractible or restless for a variety of reasons, and no child is able to pay attention under all circumstances. Excitement, boredom, the need to go to the toilet, fatigue, interesting distractions, or not feeling well can all interfere from time to time with any child's ability to concentrate. But occasionally the teacher will come across a child who never seems to settle down: she flits continually from place to place and seems to give only surface attention to what she is doing. There are a multitude of reasons for this behavior, ranging from poor habits to birth injuries, but a common cause of distractibility is tension or anxiety.

The ability to lose oneself in play is a fine indicator of emotional health.

One study that followed children who were particularly restless at age 3 to age 8 found that restlessness predicted an antisocial outcome at age 8 (Richman, Stevenson, & Graham, 1982), so teachers need to be aware of this behavior and make efforts to encourage such youngsters to settle down to an activity as often as possible. Since maternal depression appears to be linked to the child's restlessness, a possible referral for counseling for the mother and child may be desirable.

Is the Child Unusually Withdrawn or Aggressive for Her Age?

One of the great advantages teachers have is that by becoming acquainted with hundreds of children over a period of time, they are able to develop some norms for behavior that make it relatively easy to identify youngsters who behave in extreme ways. Very withdrawn behavior is more likely to be overlooked than aggressive behavior because it is much less troublesome to the teacher. He should be aware, however, that either response is a signal from the child that she is emotionally out of balance and needs some extra thought and plans devoted to helping her resolve whatever is causing her to cope in that manner.

Does the Child Have Access to the Full Range of Her Feelings, and Is She Learning to Deal with Them in an Age-Appropriate Way?

Some children have already learned by the age of 3 or 4 years to conceal or deny the existence of their feelings rather than to accept and express them in a tolerable way. Early childhood teachers can help children stay in touch with the full repertoire of their emotions by showing them that they, too, have all sorts of feelings and that they understand that children have feelings as well, whether these be anger, sadness, or affection (Locke & Ciechalski, 1985). Healthy children should also begin to learn during their early years to express their feelings to the people who have actually caused them and to do this in a way that does not harm themselves or others. Learning to do this successfully takes a long time but has its roots in early childhood.

PERSONAL QUALITIES THAT WILL HELP THE TEACHER ESTABLISH A THERAPEUTIC CLIMATE IN THE NURSERY CENTER[*]

Early childhood teachers should use their personal qualities as well as what is commonly referred to as "teaching techniques" to foster a therapeutic, growth-enhancing climate for young children. Such a climate consistently favors the active development and maintenance of an atmosphere conducive to mental health. It frees people to develop to their fullest potential as balanced, happy individuals, and the personal qualities of a "therapeutic" teacher have a lot to do with establishing this desirable climate. For this reason they are discussed next.

Consistency

One way to build a sense of trust between teachers and children is to behave in ways children can predict and to be consistent about maintaining guidelines and schedules—a very basic form of being "trustworthy" and dependable. Thus, the children know what to expect and do not live in fear of erratic or temperamental responses to what they do. For this reason, emotional stability is a highly desirable trait for teachers of young children to possess. Of course, consistency does not mean that rules must be inflexible, but their enforcement should not depend on the whim of the teacher or the manipulative power of various children.

Reasonableness

Coupled with the steadiness of consistency should go the trait of reasonableness, which I define as "expecting neither too much nor too little from children." One practical way to increase reasonableness is to learn the characteristics of the developmental stages when these are discussed in child development courses. The brief developmental summaries presented in this book are intended to remind the student of general developmental characteristics. Knowledge of these characteristics prevents inexperienced teachers from setting their stan-

---

[*]The work in this section owes much to the humanistic philosophy of Carl Rogers and his client-centered approach to psychotherapy.

dards too high or too low. They do not expect a 2-year-old to have the self-control of a 4-year-old. On the other hand, when a 4-year-old starts making demands more typical of a 2-year-old, they know that she is regressing and that they must search for and alleviate the stresses causing her retreat.

Another excellent way to help children (and other adults also) see that the teacher is reasonable is to really listen when people try to tell you something. Walter Hodges (1987) describes this kind of active listening to perfection:

> Active listening requires giving undivided attention to children and accepting what they say without blame, shock, or solving their problems for them. Giving undivided attention is signaled by positioning squarely in front of a child, getting close to the child's eye level, and leaning forward without crowding. Active listening enables us to reflect the feelings of the child, respond appropriately, and to check to see if we understand. Active listening communicates respect, warmth, and empathy. Children know that they are important and that they belong when they are heard (p. 13).

I am indebted to one of my students for the following example of what can happen when one "shuts out" such information.

> We were in the playhouse corner and Heidi was wearing a coat while doing all her kitchen duties. Jennifer came in and stood beside me and said, "I want that coat!" I was about to see if maybe Heidi was wearing Jennifer's coat when a nearby student teacher said it was Heidi's and that Jennifer had a sweater in her cubby.
> "Jennifer, why don't you get your sweater from your cubby?" I suggested.
> "But I want that coat!" she said, on the verge of tears.
> "I can see you want that coat very much, but I can't take it away from Heidi," I said.
> "But it's mine; I don't want a sweater."
> "Do you have a coat at home that looks like that? Is that why you think it's yours?" I asked.
> "Uh-huh. Give it to me!" she demanded (tears still there in the eyes).
> "I'm sorry, Jenny, I can see that you're very unhappy not to have your coat, but I can't take Heidi's," I said.
> "My mommy said I could have it!"
> By now I was finally suspicious, so I checked the coat Heidi was wearing. There, written across the collar, was the name, Jennifer!
> Heidi gave up the coat without a fuss, Jenny put it on, I apologized to her, and she went out to play!

The student concludes by commenting, "All I can say is that I would make sure next time of what I was talking about. It taught me, 'Look before you leap!' to which I would add the advice, 'Take time to listen—you may learn something important.'"

Courage and Strength of Character

Particularly when dealing with outbursts of anger, the student will find that courage and the strength of character commonly called fortitude are required to see such outbursts through. Understandably the embarrassment and insecurity of fearing that the scene may not turn out all right may make it easy to placate an angry child or, more usually, to allow her to run off or have her way. But the trouble with allowing this to happen is that the child will repeat the behavior and feel contemptuous of the adult who permits it. Therefore, being courageous and seeing a problem through are worth the struggle when coping with the strong emotional reactions so common at this age. (Please refer to chapters 9 and 10 for more detailed discussions of how to do this.)

Trustful Confidence

Trustful confidence is the teacher's faith that the child wants to grow and develop in a healthy way. Interestingly enough, psychoanalysts maintain that this ability to have trust or confidence in the good intentions of other people goes back to the individual's own experiences as an infant when she found she could or could not generally depend on her environment to be a nurturing one. Be that as it may, research bears out what many teachers and parents have determined empirically: children respond to what is genuinely expected of them by the people who matter to them (Rosenthal & Jacobson, 1968). The teacher who optimistically trusts children to act in their own best behalf is likely to obtain this response from most of the children most of the time.

Congruence

The teacher also promotes trustful confidence between himself and the child by being honest with himself and with the youngster about his own feelings. This is what Rogers and Dymond (1954) call congruence and Patterson (1977) terms genuineness. A congruent person attempts to recognize and accept his own feelings and be truthful about them to other people. Thus, a teacher might "level" with one child by saying, "I don't want you to kick me again; I feel really angry with you when you do that to me" or with another by saying, "I'm glad to see you today. I've been looking forward to hearing about your new kittens."

However, a note of caution is in order. Rogers advocates revealing such feelings *when it is appropriate to do so*. Children should not be subjected to outbursts of temper or angry attacks by adults in the name of congruence. Uncontrolled outbursts are too disturbing to children, since they know they are relatively helpless and at the mercy of the teacher.

Empathy

Empathy is the ability to feel as other people feel, to feel *with* them rather than *for* them. Empathy is valuable not only because it allows teachers to put themselves in the child's place, but also because it helps them identify and clarify for the child how she is feeling. Research supports the value of this quality. A study by Truax and Tatum (1966) has shown that the teacher's empathic ability combined with the ability to express warmth are effective in fostering positive adjustments to the preschool setting and to peers.

Warmth

Warmth is so important and deserves special emphasis because its presence has been linked to the development of positive self-concepts in children (Rohner, 1986). The warm teacher lets the children and staff know that he likes them and thinks well of them. Both children and adults flourish in this climate of sincere approval and acceptance. But being warm and accepting does not mean that the teacher just sits around and smiles at the children no matter what they do. There is a difference between expressing warmth and being indulgently permissive, and there are times when the teacher must exert control because a child is unable to. But when a teacher does this for a child, he must make it plain that he is taking control because he truly cares for her and not because he wants to obtain power for its own sake or have the satisfaction of winning.

Appreciation

Teaching must be unbearable, or at least much less satisfying, for those who fail to take time to relish and enjoy the children in their care. What a shame it would

Being warm and close with children is an important part of teaching.

be to overlook the comment, "Oh see! That little cat is licking her sweater!" or not sense the impact for a 2-year-old who bids her mother adieu and then says stoutly, "I'm my own Mommy, now!" Such precious moments can be a major reward of teaching if only teachers take the time to savor and appreciate the children and their reactions.

I hope "appreciation" is not interpreted by the reader to mean "be amused by the children." Appreciation is not the same thing as amusement. Appreciation is composed of perceptive understanding and empathy—with a dash of delight thrown in! When children sense this attitude, they blossom because they feel the approval it also implies. I suspect it feels to them as if a generous sun were shining in the room.

Good Health

The longer I teach and observe students teaching, the more firmly I become convinced it is necessary to emphasize the significance of valuing and taking care of oneself if one wishes to facilitate health in others.

We all have times when there seems to be no other choice than to operate on the ragged edge of energy. Some teachers, however, appear to accept this as being a continuing, necessary style of life. Teachers who wish to do their best with children, as well as with their other personal relationships, need to recognize what their bodies and spirits need and honor these needs to remain physically and emotionally healthy. The prescription includes adequate rest, exercise, wholesome food, and someone to care about who cares in return. Providing oneself with these requisites should be viewed as being part of one's own basic *self*-respect as well as being plain good sense.

Attaining These Qualities

Some of the aforementioned qualities, such as consistency, fortitude, and reasonableness, can be acquired through practice and experience. The others— empathy, trustful confidence, congruence, warmth, and the ability to appreciate others—can often be enhanced by participation in well-run encounter groups or through psychological counseling if they do not seem to "come naturally." Many teachers have found that such experiences have improved both their teaching abilities and their personal relationships.

PRACTICAL THINGS THE TEACHER CAN DO TO HELP YOUNG CHILDREN ACHIEVE HEALTHY EMOTIONAL DEVELOPMENT

Before turning to a discussion of more concrete things the teacher can do to contribute to a therapeutic milieu, the students should remember two principles. The first principle is that young children respond with encouraging quickness to a change in atmosphere or approach. It is possible to quickly bring about positive changes in their feelings and behavior by using appropriate methods.

The other principle has been mentioned before: children are resilient (Anthony & Cohler, 1987; Werner, 1984). They bounce back from their own and others' mistakes, and it is unlikely that one imperfect handling of a situation will inflict permanent damage on a child (Yarrow, 1980). This is not said to sanction irresponsible actions by teachers but to reassure beginners that when dealing with difficult situations they should not be unduly hesitant on the grounds they may injure the child. It is the repetition of procedures and the overall quality of the milieu, rather than the single episode, that are likely to enhance or damage.

Develop Friendly, Close Relationships with Each Family

Entrance to the children's center usually marks the occasion in the child's and parents' lives when she leaves their protection for the first time on a regular basis. If the school and family establish a feeling of closeness and a shared interest in the child's welfare, it is easier for her to make this transition, since her world is thereby widened rather than split into two pieces.

Teachers are quick to see the advantage that a friendly, comfortable atmosphere means the family is more likely to seek advice from the school. But another advantage should not be overlooked: the teacher is also in a better position to accept advice and suggestions from the parents when a "caring-sharing" atmosphere is established. This two-way respect fosters genuine mutuality and lays the basic foundation for emotional health at school.

Reduce Frustration for the Child When Possible

Children should not have to spend time waiting for things to happen when this can be prevented. Children's needs are *immediate, intense,* and *personal,* and the longer they are kept waiting the more irritable they become. Snack should be available as the children sit down, and someone should be outside for supervision as the children are dressed and ready to go out and play. Duplicates of equipment mean that there is generally enough to go around; two or three toy trucks are much more satisfactory than just one. A good assortment of developmentally appropriate activities must be available so that 3-year-olds are not expected to stack tiny plastic blocks and 5-year-olds do not have to make do with eight-piece puzzles. The day should be planned so that few and moderate demands are made on children at points where they are likely to be tired and hungry.

Of course, the teacher cannot and should not seek to eliminate all frustrating circumstances. Comparative animal studies indicate that a moderate amount of adversity may foster socialization (Elliot & King, 1960; Hess, 1960). But so many interruptions and frustrations happen in even well-run nursery schools (Jackson & Wolfson, 1968) that the elimination of unnecessary sources of frustration makes sense.

Learn to Identify and Describe the Children's Feelings to Them and Help Them Express These Feelings to the Relevant People

In our society we seem to have reached the conclusion that it is dangerous to allow some emotions to be expressed, the assumption being that if they are expressed they will become stronger or the person will act the feeling out, but if we ignore them or deny their presence they will vanish. Actually the opposite of this premise is psychologically true. The following stanza from William Blake's "A Poison Tree" puts this neatly:

> I was angry with my friend,
> I told my wrath, my wrath did end.
> I was angry with my foe,
> I told it not, my wrath did grow.

Negative emotions that are recognized, accepted, and expressed usually fade but if not expressed they seem to generate pressure that causes the person to relieve them ultimately in a more explosive or veiled, yet hostile way. Also, if children are *not* provided with ways of telling others how they feel, they are almost inevitably driven to show them how they feel by acting the feelings out.

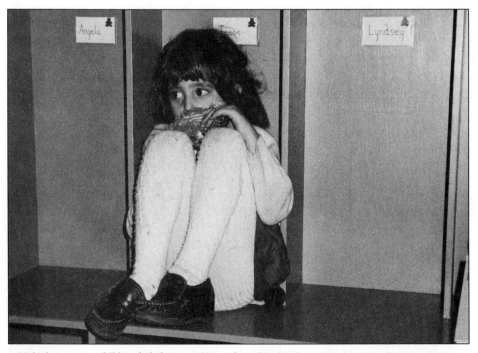

Nobody wants a child to feel the way Aimee does, but it's better to share the feeling with her than just to try cheering her up.

The advantage of helping the child know how she feels is not only that she avoids these overwhelming explosions or complicated emotional displacements but also that she learns that all emotions are acceptable and that, therefore, an important part of herself is acceptable. As she matures, this self-knowledge forms a foundation for learning to express feelings in a way that harms neither herself nor other people.

It takes practice and sensitivity to acquire the skills of describing the child's feelings to her and helping her express them, but research shows that teachers can learn these skills (Kane, Wiszinckas, & Fourquer, 1981). There is more to it than just saying to an angry child, "You're feeling really mad at him, aren't you?" Some examples will help illustrate the technique.

> Evelyn says goodbye to her mother and then hangs by the gate, looking after her sadly as she drives away. Her teacher bends down, picks her up, and says, "You look like you wish she'd stay this morning, Evelyn." "I do, I do, I want her to stay—[emphatically] I hate her, that mean old mommy of mine, I hate her, and I wish she'd stay!" "Yeah, I know how it is—you feel sad she's left you, and it makes you mad because you wanted her to stay." "Yes! And I'm never, never going to speak to her again." (They move toward the nursery school room and go inside.) "And I'm just going to feed her turnips and beans for dinner—turnips and beans, turnips and beans, turnip and beans!" But this is said with decreasing venom and increasing humor as she trails off toward the housekeeping corner to embark on her busy day.

Sometimes it helps to look at the other side of the coin. A student submitted the following example and analysis when asked to submit an insensitive response that did *not* take the child's feelings into account.*

> One evening I was staying with Vickie, age 3, while her father visited her mother in the hospital. Grandmother had dropped by with a covered dish for supper and some sweetrolls for breakfast. Vickie hadn't eaten a very big dinner. She went over to the counter and tried to reach the rolls.
>   "Can I have a roll?"
>   "No Vickie, those are for breakfast."
>   "But I need just one."
>   "You can have one for breakfast."
>   A few minutes later she said, "How about a roll?"
>   "No, Vickie." Later as I was cleaning the kitchen, Vickie was coloring at the table while Stephen, age 1½ watched. He snatched a crayon.
>   "No, Stevie, no!"
>   "Vickie, maybe we could let Stevie use a crayon."
>   "Well, I think maybe a roll would help."
>   "How about some cheese? Are you hungry? Would you like some cheese and bread?"
>   "Yes!"

---

*Courtesy Paige Gregory, University of Oklahoma, Norman.

Rather than giving Vickie reasons, next time I would try to look at the real problem first. I would have liked the scene to have gone more like this:

"Can I have a roll?"

"Those rolls look awfully good to you, don't they?"

"Yes! I want one—my tummy says so!"

"You really want one because you feel kind of empty inside! But there are just enough for breakfast. I can't give you a roll now."

"Oh!" (Vickie looks pensive.)

"How about some cheese?—you like that?"

"OK!"

(Then I'd pick her up and rock her while she ate it and talk about feeling empty because she was missing her mommy—and that her mother would be coming home on Sunday—I also realize, now, I should have put those rolls out of sight!)

In the following example the teacher, working with an older child, encourages him not only to express his feelings but to deal with the person who is causing the unhappiness.

Jonathan arrives at the wookworking bench very excited by the box of new wood he has spied from across the play yard. He reaches for Henry's hammer as it is laid down and is really surprised when Henry snatches it back. The teacher tells Jonathan that all the hammers are in use and he will have to wait. Jonathan stands on one foot and then the other—his hand obviously itching to snatch Henry's hammer. At this point, rather than trying to redirect him to the swings, the teacher says to him, "It's hard to wait, isn't it? I can see how much you want that hammer." "Yes, it is. I wish old Henry'd hurry." "Well, tell him so. Tell him what you want." "Henry, you son of a bitch, I want that hammer when you're done." (The boys grin at each other.) The teacher suggests, "Why don't you saw some wood while you're waiting?" "Don't mind if I do," says Jonathan.

In these examples the teacher did not content herself with the simple statement "You feel angry" or "You're hungry" or "You feel impatient." Instead she tried to describe to the child what he felt like doing and to name the feeling for him since she was fairly sure she could identify it. Describing feelings or intended actions is particularly helpful when working with young children because they understand the statement "You want her to stay" or "It's hard to wait," better than they grasp the label "angry" or "impatient." In addition, description has the advantage that it stands a better chance of being correct and that it is always better to talk about what a person does rather than what he is.

With a younger child or a less controlled one the teacher may need to go further and reassure him by saying, "It's OK to want to grab it as long as you don't really do it." Sometimes she will need to go even further than that and actually restrain him, saying, "I can see you want to hit Henry, but I won't let you hurt him. Tell him you feel like taking his hammer." It takes many experiences for a young child to reach the level of the children in our examples, but it can be done.

Teach Children the Difference
Between Verbal Attack and Self-Report

Also, in the examples presented the teacher neither moralized, "Of course you really love your mother" or said, "If you'd eaten your dinner you wouldn't be hungry now!" nor offered an involved interpretation to the children of the reasons behind their behavior. Instead she concentrated on letting the children know that she understood what they felt, that it was all right to talk about it, and that she would help them draw the line between feeling and acting if they needed that help.

When teaching children to express their feelings, we must teach them gradually to understand the difference between saying how one feels about something (self-report) and telling another person what they are (verbal attack). There's a big difference between allowing a child to attack by shouting, "You selfish pooh pooh pants! You nerd! If you don't give me that shovel right now, I'm never going to play with you again!" and teaching him to tell the same child, "I need that shovel—I'm dying for it! I can't wait another minute!"

Admittedly this is a sophisticated concept for little children to grasp. Sad to say, even some adults seem unable to make this distinction. Nevertheless it is such an extraordinarily valuable emotional and social skill to acquire that teachers should begin to model and teach the rudiments of self-report very early to children. Acquisition of this skill will benefit them all their lives.

There are many additional ways to express feelings through play and through the use of sublimative and expressive materials, which are discussed later on, but the ability to acknowledge feelings openly is the soundest and most fundamental therapeutic skill to use to foster mental health.

Learn to Recognize Signs of Stress
and Emotional Upset in Children

Children give many signals besides crying or fussing that indicate emotional stress. Reverting (regressing) to less mature behavior is a common signal. We are all familiar with the independent 4-year-old who suddenly wants to be babied while recovering from the flu or the child who wets his bed after the baby arrives.

Various nervous habits, such as hair twisting, sighing deeply, nail biting, or thumb sucking, also reveal that the child is under stress. Increased irritability, sometimes to the point of tantrums, is another indicator, as is lethargy or withdrawing from activities. Sometimes children suddenly begin to challenge rules and routines; sometimes they cry a lot; sometimes expressions of tension or stress are more subtle and are conveyed only by a strained look about the eyes or a tightened mouth; sometimes stress is expressed in the more obvious form of excessive activity and running about (Honig, 1986a).

In addition to this knowledge of common symptoms, as the year progresses and the teacher gets to know the children well, he will have the additional advantage of knowing how each child usually behaves. This makes it easier for him to spot changes and identify children who are signaling for special help.

Know What to Do for Children Who Are Emotionally Upset

Emotional upsets have to be handled on a short-term basis and sometimes on a long-term basis as well. (See also chapter 7.)

Short-Term, Emergency Treatment

The first thing to do for a child who is upset to the point of tears is to comfort her. But the manner of comfort will vary from child to child: some youngsters need to be held and rocked, whereas others do best if allowed to reduce themselves to hiccupping silence while the teacher putters about nearby. Children who are using emotional outbursts as a means of controlling

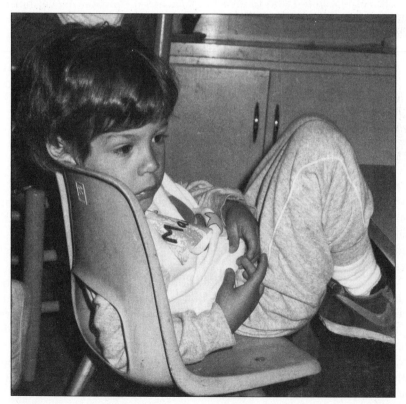

Teachers need to be aware of the more subtle signs of tension in children as well as some of the more obvious ones.

the adult's behavior require still a third response—mildly ignoring them until they subside.

No matter why a child is crying hard, it is a waste of energy to try to reason with her until she has calmed down. However, it can help soothe her to repeat something in a quieter and quieter tone of voice so that she gradually quiets herself to hear what is being said. This may be as simple a sentence as, "When you've stopped crying, we'll talk things over" or "I'm waiting to help you when you've stopped crying." Occasionally it can also be helpful to remark matter-of-factly if the occasion warrants, "You know, I will keep on holding you, even when you've stopped crying."

As the child calms down, getting a drink of water or wiping her eyes may also soothe her. It is often effective at this point to talk over the difficulty, but sometimes it is better to wait and discuss it in a casual way later in the day to clarify how she felt or why she broke down. Each situation has to be judged in its own context.

Finally the teacher should either help the child return and resolve the problem in the group, or, if he deems it wiser, he should help her get started on another satisfying activity. Activities that are particularly helpful at such times include swinging, water play, or messy activities such as finger painting or clay. Water play generally seems to be the best choice.

Long-Term Treatment

It is always wise before deciding that an emotional upset represents a serious long-term difficulty to wait and see if the child is coming down with something; incipient illness is a frequent source of loss of emotional control. It is also wise to consider whether an approaching holiday could be causing the disturbance. Christmas and Halloween are notorious tension increasers, and we have found in our campus children's center that the weeks before and during college examinations are likely to be edgy ones also. Many episodes of fighting, crying, and other exaggerated responses to minor crises will disappear after such times have passed.

If the symptoms of stress do not subside, it is necessary to find out more about what is causing tension in the child. The behavior may be due to something going on at home or to something going on at school, or to a combination of these things.

One helpful way to locate the cause is to think back to the point when the signs of stress appeared and then to confer with the parent about what else changed in the child's life at about the same time. Perhaps the youngster was moved to another room at school, or her close friend was absent because of chicken pox; perhaps her grandfather died, or her father was away, or houseguests were visiting. Once the cause has been discovered, steps can be taken to help the youngster feel more at ease. Sometimes just recognizing the source helps a lot, without doing anything more.

Other signals of disturbance can be traced to continuing environmental situations. Perhaps discipline policies are erratic at home, or affection is lacking, or the child is excessively fatigued because she watches the late show on television. These are more difficult situations to deal with, but even they can often be successfully resolved by working together with the family.

If the situation is too complicated or difficult to be quickly eased by the teacher's intervention, he must encourage the family to seek counseling from a psychologist or a psychiatrist. The area of guidance and referral is such an extensive one that it cannot be treated in detail here. The reader is invited to pursue the subject further in chapters 7, 18, and 19.

SUMMARY

Growth-enhancing child care seeks to create as many opportunities as possible for young children to develop their sense of autonomy and initiative in a setting that is reasonable, consistent, trustful, empathic, warm, and appreciative. Children who are mentally healthy are working on emotional tasks appropriate for their age. They are learning to separate from their families and to conform to school routines without undue stress. They can involve themselves deeply in play, and they are developing the ability to settle down and concentrate. Emotionally healthy children are not excessively withdrawn or aggressive; they have access to the full range of their feelings and are beginning to learn to deal with these feelings in appropriate ways.

Teachers can help the children in their care develop in emotionally healthy ways by forming good relationships with their families, reducing frustration for them where possible, identifying and describing the children's feelings for them and helping them express these to the relevant people, recognizing the signs of stress that signal that help is needed, and handling emotional problems on a short-term and long-term basis when necessary.

QUESTIONS AND ACTIVITIES

1. What are some matter-of-fact ways to express warmth and liking to young children?

2. Looking back on your own education, give an example of a teacher who had unreasonably high expectations of you as a pupil. What was the effect on your learning?

3. With other members of the class set up some role-playing situations that provide opportunities for "children" to express their feelings and "teachers" to practice phrasing responses that would help the child identify how she feels and show that the teacher understands her. Practice this a lot!

4. Do you believe it is always wise to be forthright about your own feelings? What limitations might be helpful to remember? On the other hand, can you think of times when it would have been better to take the risk and be more open and frank in your response? What did you do instead of being direct? Do you think that it was a satisfactory solution?

5. What are some examples where you have seen adults ignore, suppress, or mislabel a child's feelings? Could you see how the child was immediately affected by this kind of response? What would you predict might be the long-term effects of a child's experiencing many such responses to his feelings?

SELF-CHECK QUESTIONS FOR REVIEW

Content-Related Questions

1. What percentage of children in the United States are estimated to suffer from mental disorders severe enough to require special treatment?

2. Name the first three stages of emotional development identified by Erikson, and list some things early childhood teachers can do to foster the successful mastering of each stage.

3. Identify the hallmarks of an emotionally healthy child.

4. Select four personal qualities of teachers that would help foster emotional health in the children, and explain why each is important.

5. What are some common behaviors of children that might alert you to the fact they are experiencing stress?

Integrative Questions

1. What is the difference between feeling sympathy for someone and feeling empathy for him? Provide an example of some emotional situation with a child and explain what you would say if you were expressing sympathy and what you would say to show you were experiencing empathy.

2. Analyze the following gem contributed by a student and suggest what the adult might have said, instead, that would have described the children's feelings to them.*

I was baby-sitting two children in their backyard late in the afternoon. Robby is about 5 years old and Joel is about 3.

Robby: "Hey, look at this rock I found!"
Me: "Make sure you don't throw it at somebody."
Joel: "I'm gunna throw that rock at Jimmy's mean cat!"
Me: "You'd better not, young man."
Robby: "I wanna throw rocks!"
Me: "Not now Robby, it's time to go in and eat dinner, OK?"
Both boys: "No!"
Me: "Why don't you want to eat dinner?"
Robby: "I'm not hungry. I wanna stay out here and play."
Me: "You've played long enough; now you need to get your vitamins."
Robby: "Mom said I already have enough vitamins."
Me: "You'll really like what we're having; meat loaf and baked potatoes, and spinach."
Joel: "I hate spinach!"
Me: "You should eat it, it's good for you!"

3. Analyze the following statements and categorize them according to whether they are examples of "self-report" or "verbal attack."

"I feel pretty worried when you climb that high."

"Let Suzanne have some crackers too. Don't be so selfish!"

"You're always so quick to criticize others!"

Then change each statement into the opposite form. For example, if the original statement was "You're always making me do things I don't want to do," you might change it into "I just feel too shy to do that—please don't press me to try it."

REFERENCES FOR FURTHER READING

Overviews

Curry, N. (Ed.). (1986). *The feeling child: Affective development reconsidered.* New York: Haworth Press. These articles will help the reader understand the significance and role that emotions play in the lives of developing children.

Developmental Stages and Emotional Needs of Children

Curry, N., & Bergen, D. (1987). The relationship of play to emotional, social, and gender/sex role development. In D. Bergen (Ed.), *Play as a medium for learning and development:*

*Courtesy Sarah Strain, University of Oklahoma, Norman.

A handbook of theory and practice. Portsmouth, NH: Heinemann. This chapter provides a comprehensive review of how the emotional self develops.

Erikson, E. H. (1963). *Childhood and society* (2nd ed.). New York: W. W. Norton.

Erikson, E. H. (1971). A healthy personality for every child. In R. H. Anderson & H. G. Shane (Eds.), *As the twig is bent: Readings in early childhood education.* New York: Houghton Mifflin.

Erikson, E. H. (1982). *The life cycle completed: A review.* New York: W. W. Norton. These publications contain original source material that explains in detail Erikson's concepts of the eight stages of man and the emotional attitudes of paramount importance at various stages of development.

Greenspan, S. I., & Greenspan, N. T. (1985). *First feelings: Milestones in the emotional development of your baby and child.* New York: Viking Press. Greenspan proposes six steps in emotional development occurring in the very early years. Interesting reading that also provides practical recommendations.

Building Sound Emotional Relationships with Children

Balaban, N. (1989). Trust: Just a matter of time. In J. S. McKee & K. M. Paciorek (Eds.), *Early childhood: 89/90.* Guilford, CT: Dushkin. The author presents a number of practical examples of ways teachers can build trust with children.

Brazelton, T. B. (1984). *To listen to a child: Understanding the normal problems of growing up.* Reading, MA: Addison-Wesley. Although this book deals mainly with toddlers and babies, it is so full of good sense it should be read by everyone who cares for young children.

Faber, A., & Mazlish, E. (1980). *How to talk so kids will listen, & listen so kids will talk.* New York: Avon Books. Numerous examples of describing and sharing feelings make this book a treasure trove of helpfulness.

Rogers, C. R. (1961). *On becoming a person.* Boston: Houghton Mifflin. Rogers sets forth his philosophy that desirable emotional relationships between people are facilitated by the presence of warmth, congruence, and empathy.

Roemer, J. (1989). *Two to four from 9 to 5: The adventures of a daycare provider.* New York: Harper & Row. Insightful, sensitive encounters with children are a hallmark of this delightful reading. *Highly recommended.*

Samalin, N., & Jablow, M. M. (1987). *Loving your child is not enough.* New York: Viking Press. The chapter on acknowledging feelings provides many examples of how to reflect and describe feelings to children. Helpful reading.

For the Advanced Student

Cicchetti, D., & White, J. (1989). Emotional development and the affective disorders. In W. Damon (Ed.), *Child development today and tomorrow.* San Francisco: Jossey-Bass. The relative lack of research on emotions and their development is cited here, and many promising areas for future research are identified.

Dougherty, D. M., Saxe, L. M., Cross, T., & Silverman, N. (1987). *Children's mental health: Problems and services: A report by the Office of Technology Assessment.* Durham, NC: Duke University Press. The authors present basic information on what constitutes emotional health and the current status of delivery services for children in the United States.

Institute of Medicine. (1989). *Research on children and adolescents with mental, behavioral, and developmental disorders: Mobilizing a national initiative.* Washington, DC: National Academy Press. This book surveys the current status of children with emotional problems and presents recommendations for further progress. *Highly recommended* for its up-to-date, comprehensive, concise presentation of a serious problem.

Powell, G. J. (1983). *The psychosocial development of minority group children.* New York: Brunner/Mazel. Powell's excellent book devotes over 200 pages to the emotional development and mental health of children from a wide variety of ethnic groups.

Strayhorn, J. M. (1988). *The competent child: An approach to psychotherapy and preventive mental health*. New York: Guilford Press. Strayhorn includes a valuable list of psychological skills children need in order to function successfully in the social world and then proposes practical ways of increasing these.

Journals of Continuing Interest

American Journal of Orthopsychiatry. American Orthopsychiatric Association, 49 Sheridan Ave., Albany, NY 12210. The journal describes itself as being dedicated to providing information "relating to mental health and human development from a multidisciplinary and interprofessional perspective."

Pediatric Mental Health. PO Box 1880, Santa Monica, CA 90406-1880. A bimonthly newsletter, this publication covers research and practice on such topics as supporting parenting, play, and preparation for hospitalization.

CHAPTER 6

Developing Self-Esteem
in Young Children

The deepest urge in human nature is the desire to be important.
—John Dewey as quoted in J. M. Harris (1989)

Have you ever wondered what to do about . . .

> The child who habitually protests, "I can't—I know I can't—don't make me!"

> Or the one who always wants to know, "Did I do it right?"

> Or the youngster who says sadly, "Nobody likes me—nobody!"

If you have, the material in the following pages will help you.

Perceiving oneself as a person who has something worthwhile to contribute to the life around one is such an important aspect of being mentally healthy that it is necessary to devote an entire chapter to this concept. It is this feeling of internal worth I have in mind when describing individuals who possess self-esteem. People who feel like this are able to venture out into the world, work toward attaining what they hope for, and welcome life with pleasurable anticipation.

On the other hand, individuals who suffer from low self-esteem fit, to varying degrees, the following description.

> The child with low self-worth focuses on failure instead of success, problems instead of challenges, difficulties instead of possibilities. A child with low self-esteem experiences the world as a dark and gloomy place, filled with danger and threat (Smith, 1988, p. 5).

Moreover an English study of young adolescents found that "individuals who were anxious, depressed, neurotic or *have poor self-esteem* [italics mine] do tend to be more prejudiced than others. They have to a greater extent chosen the cultural symbols of racism as a means of protecting their identity, or enhancing their view of themselves" (Bagley, Verma, Mallick, & Young, 1979, p. 194).

More recently Mecca, Smelser, and Vasconcellos (1989) have published an extensive analysis of the interrelationships between low self-esteem and child abuse, poor school achievement, teenage pregnancy, crime, and drug and alcohol overuse.

It is clear from a perusal of these findings and others like them that a good self-concept and adequate self-esteem are highly desirable qualities to foster in young children, since no one wants children to suffer from the feelings and experiences just described. What teachers and parents need to understand more clearly is how to help children generate good feelings about themselves that are based on reality. It is these good feelings that form the basis for healthy self-esteem.

RELATIONSHIP OF SELF-ESTEEM TO SELF-CONCEPT

Self-esteem and self-concept are closely related to each other. Self-concept refers to an individual's idea of who he is, and self-esteem is a part of this because his feelings of self-esteem result from his reaction to what he judges himself to be and to his anticipation of being accepted or rejected (Marshall, 1989). Thus a youngster who is well coordinated, who is sought after by his playmates, and who gets along well with his teacher will probably see himself as adequate and will possess good feelings of self-esteem, whereas an overweight high school girl suffering from a poor complexion and few friends may come to think of herself as being unattractive and unlovable and as a result will hold herself in low esteem.

SOURCES OF SELF-ESTEEM

Although individuals should ultimately develop internal resources for generating self-esteem, in the early stages of growth the child's feelings of self-esteem come from the people around him. Parents are very significant influences (Coopersmith, 1967; Cotton, 1983). As children move out into the larger world, the opinions of other adults, such as teachers, become important, too, as do the opinions of their peers. That society also has an impact is evident from studies indicating that a higher percentage of people of minority groups possess low self-esteem than people of nonminorities do (Mejia, 1983; Powell, 1983a). Because the unhappy effects of persistent prejudice on the self-image and self-esteem of minority children cannot be overestimated, an entire chapter is devoted to a discussion of ways to sustain or improve the self-image of such youngsters (chapter 12).

Since there are so many powerful factors that influence the development of self-esteem, teachers should not believe they can completely alter the way a child sees himself. However, the numerous research studies cited by Curry and Johnson (1990), Geraty (1983), and Yawkey (1980) support the idea that teachers can establish policies in their classrooms that will help build a child's self-esteem, and they can meticulously avoid employing practices that are likely to have destructive side effects.

COMMON SCHOOL PRACTICES
LIKELY TO REDUCE SELF-ESTEEM

One way to think of self-esteem is to picture it as a balloon—a balloon that just a little prick of criticism will puncture and wither. Unfortunately, there are many ways teachers prick these balloons every day, often when they do not intend to.

Using Comparison and Competition to Motivate Good Behavior

Competitiveness reaches a peak in children around the age of 4 to 5 years (Stott & Ball, 1957). It is all too easy for the teacher to use this fact to obtain quick results by asking, "I wonder who can get his coat on quickest today?" or by commenting, "See how carefully Shirley is putting her blocks away? Why can't you do it like that?" The trouble with motivating behavior by drawing such comparisons and setting up competitive situations is that only a few children "win" under this system. Even the child who turns out to be "best" and whose self-esteem has presumably been enhanced pays an unfortunate price, since he has obtained his self-esteem at the expense of the other children's well-being and may have earned their dislike in the process.

A more desirable way to use comparison is by invoking it in relation to the child's own past performance. This can be a true source of satisfaction for him when the teacher says, "My goodness, John, you're learning to pump better and better every time you try!" or "Remember the way you used to bite people? You haven't done that in a long time now. I'm proud of you!"

Overhelping and Overprotecting Children

Teachers may unintentionally lower a child's self-esteem by doing too much for him. Thus they rush in to carry the bucket of water so that it will not slop or without thinking put all the shoes and socks on the children following nap. Helping in these ways has the virtue of saving time and assuring that the job will be done properly, as well as keeping the teacher busy. But it is much more desirable to wait and let children do things for themselves, since this allows them to experience the triumph of independence that such achievement brings.

Judging Children Within Their Hearing

Children often develop ideas of who they are from hearing what other people say about them. Sometimes this happens in direct form, as when the teacher says impatiently, "Come along now; you're always so slow," or asks, "How can you be so selfish?" Other children are also prone to deliver pronouncements such as "You pig! You never share anything" or "Hazel is a pooh-pooh pants, Hazel is a pooh-pooh pants!" Labels such as these tend to stick; enough of them plastered on a child can convince him that he is neither liked nor worth much, so he might as well not try. This is one of the reasons why teaching children to use self-report rather than verbal attack is so important. Verbal attacks are destructive to other people's self-esteem.

Consider the difference in effect between the child who shouts, "I'm so mad I'm gonna stamp my feet through the floor! You just gotta let me play!" and the one who sneers, "Aw, I don't like you anyway—you stink!"

Sometimes negative evaluations are not delivered directly to the child, but are said over his head to someone else instead: "My, aren't we in a terrible temper today!" "I see he's having a hard day again!" "There's no point in asking *him*—he always holds on like grim death" (Kostelnik, Stein, & Whirin, 1988). Somehow, overheard comments have a special, painful power to compel belief. Teachers should avoid making them not only for this reason, but also because they may hurt a child's feelings and can strengthen a negative self-image. On a more subtle level, talking over children's heads implies that they are not important enough to be included directly in the conversation.

POSITIVE METHODS OF ENHANCING SELF-ESTEEM

Unconditional Positive Regard

The most effective way to help a child build a basic feeling of self-esteem is, unfortunately, also the most elusive for some teachers to achieve: it is the ability

Sharing a child's satisfaction is a fine way to increase her self-esteem.

to feel and project what Rogers terms *unconditional positive regard.* This kind of fundamental acceptance and approval of each child is not contingent on his meeting the teacher's expectations of what he should be; it simply depends on his being alive, being a child, and being in the group. A good test of being accepting or not is to become aware of what one is usually thinking about when looking at the children. Ask yourself, "Am I taking time to enjoy the children, or am I looking at each one with a critical eye—noting mainly what behavior should be improved?" If you catch yourself habitually noting only what should be changed, this is a sign you are losing sight of half the pleasure of teaching, which is to appreciate the children and enjoy who they are right now, at this particular moment in time—no strings attached.

This ability to be uncritical implies a kind of faith in the way the child will turn out, an attitude that subtly makes him aware that the teacher has confidence he will grow in sound directions. There is no substitute for these underlying feelings of trust and confidence in the child. Some teachers are fortunate enough to have developed optimism about people as a result of their own trust-building childhood experiences, some gain it from long experience with children themselves, and some acquire it by means of psychotherapeutic treatment, which helps restore their own confidence as well as their faith in others.

Acceptance of the child as he is also includes accepting his right to be different from the teacher and from other children. Here again, ethnic and cultural differences come particularly to mind. Teachers can make a significant contribution to increasing the self-esteem of the minority child by unconditionally valuing him and by using themselves as models to influence the attitude of the other children and their families.

Honest Recognition and Praise

Rewarding a child with praise is usually the first way teachers think of to build self-esteem. Unfortunately, sometimes praise is the *only* method they think of. Actually it is only one of several and perhaps not one of the better ways to enhance a child's feelings of self-worth.

In recent years, more than 80 research projects have been carried out on the effects such external rewards as praise or prizes have on motivating repeated behavior (Morgan, 1984). These studies have asked the question "Do children work harder when they receive a reward?" (praise is one kind of reward) and the answer, generally, has been "No!" Children tend to exhibit reduced interest in trying harder or working longer at tasks when receiving tangible rewards.

Even the effects of praise vary a lot (Cannella, 1986). To be an effective esteem raiser and motivator, praise should include information about something specific a child has achieved; that is, praise should be based on performance. Used in that context it can heighten the inner *intrinsic* satisfaction of the child. For example, it is better to say to a 4-year-old, "Thanks for letting Mary Lou play—it cheered her up" than to say, "You sure are a nice little girl!" Erikson is right when he says, "Children cannot be fooled by empty praise and condescending encouragement" (1963).

We must be wary of teachers who use praise continually as a means of reinforcing behavior and who often dole it out in such a mechanical way that it comes to have almost no meaning at all. On the other hand, some teachers hardly ever take time to comment favorably on what a child has done. They seem to feel that praise weakens character and that individuals should do things simply because it is right to do them. But praise that is merited should surely be given; everyone who has experienced it knows that honest recognition is sweet indeed.

Using encouragement rather than praise is another effective way of building self-esteem while recognizing what a child is accomplishing (Hitz & Driscoll, 1988). Such comments as "I bet you can do it if you try," or "Look how much work you've done," or "Atta girl!" encourage children without passing judgment on what they've done.

Children need to learn that failing at something is not the end of the world. For this reason it is also important to appreciate the effort of children when they have not been successful. They particularly need encouragement at this point, since the reward inherent in successful accomplishment has not be realized. The teacher can say "I see how hard you've worked on that," or "I'm proud of you; you really tried," or "It takes a while to learn to do that. You've really stuck with it; it's *hard* to learn things sometimes, isn't it?"

Respect

Respecting the child is such a high-minded phrase that examples of behavior must be provided in order to see how respect can be implemented when working with young children. One basic way to show respect is to abide by the child's decision when he has been given a valid choice (also see chapter 9). When a teacher does this, she is really saying, "What you want is important. I have confidence that you know yourself better than I do, and I count on you to choose what will enhance your existence most." Children also feel respect when the teacher asks their opinion and listens carefully to their replies. Even young children can answer "Do you think we should . . ." kinds of questions.

Another way to show respect, and thus sustain the child's self-esteem, is to avoid humiliating a child in front of other people. It is best to carry out discipline measures as unobtrusively as possible. Belittling a child's behavior at any time is, of course, fundamentally disrespectful as well as destructive of self-esteem.

A third valuable way to show respect is to pay the child the compliment of explaining the reason behind the rule. Coopersmith (1967), who carried out an extensive study of children possessing high self-esteem, found that parents of such youngsters were firm in their control of them but also took time to explain the reason for their actions. Such reasoning confers respect because it assumes that the child is important enough to be entitled to an explanation and intelligent enough to comprehend it.

Finally, we must never lose sight of the fact that children are intensely aware of how teachers feel about their families. Teachers who truly respect and value the child's family show this each day in the way they welcome them to the classroom, by the way they avoid making derogatory remarks about them, and by the way they really listen to a family member who has something to say.

HELPING THE CHILD ACHIEVE COMPETENCE

Positive regard, respect, and merited praise are sound in that they help build positive self-pictures for children, but they have one weakness in common; *they all depend on the good will of another person for implementation.* Yet the ultimate goal should be the internalization of esteem so that the individual will not remain permanently dependent on others to supply her feelings of self-worth.

But how can children be helped to shift from relying on external praise or other supports to experiencing *intrinsic* satisfaction from within themselves? The most effective answer is that helping children achieve competence is the surest

Here Karla is applying just the touch of support Miles needs to experience success.

way to instill internal feelings of self-worth. Every time a youngster does something that works out well, whether it be standing up for his rights in the trike area or pumping himself on the swing, the reward of success is inherent in the act, and the child feels competent because of what he *did*, not because of what someone said (Strayhorn, 1988). This knowledge of capability makes children (and adults, too, for that matter) feel good about themselves, feel they are worth something—*and in that knowledge lies the foundation of inner self-esteem.*

White (1968, 1976) summed this up when he pointed out that people have a continuing drive toward competence, which is a powerful motivating agent in their lives. He defined competence as "effectiveness in dealing with the environment." It is this sense of being effective that builds the child's self-esteem internally. No one can take it away from him, and no one, as White comments, "can confer this experience. No one can give another person a sense of competence" (1976, p. 9). What teachers *can* do is provide many opportunities for children to *become* competent. A good place to begin is by asking oneself, at the start of every morning, "How can I help each child experience success today?" Once a child is able to do something well, whether it is practicing diplomacy in the housekeeping corner or using the brace and bit, he has gained a small portion of confidence in himself that does not require the plaudits of others to sustain it.

Allow Children to Experience Mastery by Making Their Own Choices and by Being as Independent as Possible

These are two ways to encourage competence that have already been discussed. Maccoby (1980) speaks of this as keeping the *locus of control* as much within the hands of the child as possible. She cites a number of studies that support the value of encouraging children to feel they are in control of their environment at least part of the time. Of course, this should not be interpreted as meaning that the teacher or parent should submit unquestioningly to every passing whim. Rather, it does mean that encouraging children to make choices and decisions and to do things for themselves is worth encouraging whenever reasonable and possible, because granting them such "power" reduces their feelings of helplessness and increases their feelings of mastery by placing the locus of control within rather than outside themselves (Honig, 1986c).

Coupled with allowing children to do things for themselves goes the establishment of reasonable standards of achievement. For instance, a teacher who wishes to build self-esteem in a newly generous little girl appreciates her helpfulness when she volunteers to pass the snack and overlooks the fact that she has served herself first, just as she thanks the child who has stuffed his boots away in his cubby and refrains from telling him to fix them so the toes point out.

Provide Many Different Ways for Children to Experience Success

Sheer variety of activities is important here, since one child may excel at assembling puzzles, whereas another's forte may be hanging by her heels on the jungle gym. It is important, also, not to be too hidebound when selecting curriculum activities, since a youngster may possess a special skill not usually thought of as being age appropriate but one that, when well used, can confer distinction on her and enrich the lives of the other children. Our center, for example, had a child attending who loved to embroider. She knew several stitches, and two or three of the older children relished learning them from her, although "everyone knows" that embroidery is too difficult for preschool children to carry out successfully.

Emphasize the Value of Building Cross-Sex Competencies of Various Kinds

It is still the case that girls often grow up unable to use power saws or drills or lacking even rudimentary understanding of the combustion engine, and boys are sometimes described as limited in their ability to express emotion. Most women (and many men) have only to recall the last time they dealt with a garage mechanic to realize the sense of inferiority such incompetence produces. Methods of remedying these deficiencies are discussed at greater length in the chapter on achieving equity, so it will only be noted here that broader and more various educational experiences for both sexes should be encouraged.

Offer Creative Activities, Since They Provide Excellent Opportunities for Experiencing Competence

There is so much latitude for individual abilities and differences in creative areas. It feels good to make something that is attractive. If the materials and colors provided by the teacher are harmonious, most things made by the children will have a satisfying outcome and thus enhance the children's feelings of self-esteem.

Provide Opportunities That Are Challenging But Not Excessively Difficult to Give the Children the Chance to Test Themselves Against Difficulties

The derring-do of 4-year-olds is a prime example of this desire to make things a little bit harder every time they attempt them. (The reader may recall learning the game of jacks and its steady progression from *Rolling-Down-Broadway* to the more difficult game *Around the World,* and finally on to *Eggs-in-a-Basket* and *Shooting Star.*) In general, children should always be allowed to attempt more difficult feats as they think of them unless it is evident that they have not anticipated any serious dangers that may be involved.

Something else students sometimes forget is that it takes practice to acquire a new skill. I have seen students offer an activity once and assume that would be sufficient opportunity for the children to learn how to do it. Whether it be using the scooter or cutting around a circle or playing lotto, other things being equal, repeated practice increases competence, so it is important to provide chances for children to do something more than once if you want them to become skillful.

In Addition to Competence in Activities and Motor Skills, Interpersonal Competence Is of Great Importance

The child who feels that he can get along with others, that he is liked by them, and that he generally manages to have his needs met is likely to feel pretty adequate. Chapters 8, 9, and 10 present more detailed discussions of how to help children gain skill and competence in interpersonal relationships.

SUMMARY

Early childhood teachers who wish to increase feelings of self-esteem in the children in their care have at their disposal many ways of accomplishing this. However, practices such as using comparison and competition, being over-protective, and judging children within their hearing should be avoided since they tend to lower self-esteem.

Esteem-building practices that should be part of the child's life include the expression of unconditional positive regard, the provision of recognition and praise when warranted, and the expression of genuine respect for every child.

Finally, the attainment of competence should be valued highly. The more opportunities children have to acquire instrumental and interpersonal skills, the more likely they are to acquire an inner conviction of their own ability to cope. This inner conviction of basic competence is, in the long run, the most satisfactory builder of self-esteem.

QUESTIONS AND ACTIVITIES

1. Pick a school or family life situation (perhaps a trip to the grocery) for role playing and include in it as many possible ways you can think of to deflate and lower the self-esteem of the "children" who are involved.

2. Select a youngster in your school who seems to suffer from low self-esteem. As far as you can tell, what are some principal reasons for this self-image? What could you do to modify it in a more positive direction?

3. Many activities, even for college students, center on externalized sources of self-esteem. Grades are a prime example of external input. What college-related policies appear likely to produce internalized sources of positive self-esteem?

4. This chapter questions the value of competition to motivate behavior, since competition often reduces feelings of self-esteem. Is this necessarily true in all cases? Are there times when competition is both satisfying and desirable?

5. Listen to yourself for several days while you are working with the children. Every day put 10 pennies in your pocket, and whenever you hear yourself talking about a child in front of him, transfer a penny to your other pocket. Can you go an entire day without shifting any pennies?

6. Go down your roster and try to identify opportunities during the past week where each child had the chance to gain competence in some activity. Did each youngster have a chance to accomplish this in some manner?

SELF-CHECK QUESTIONS FOR REVIEW

Content-Related Questions

1. Explain how low self-esteem and being prejudiced against other people are related.

2. What are three common things teachers might do that tend to lower the self-esteem of the children in their care?

3. Is praise the most effective way of increasing the self-esteem of a young child? Explain the reasoning behind your answer.

4. Why is competence such an effective builder of self-esteem?

5. What is the difference between extrinsic and intrinsic methods of increasing self-esteem? Which does the author feel is more desirable?

Integrative Questions

1. Imagine that a new rule has been passed at your school: you may not praise a child for anything during the day, and yet you must increase his self-esteem substantially. How would you go about doing this?

2. Give an example other than praise of something that could be an extrinsic source of self-esteem for an adult, and then give a second example of something that could be an intrinsic source of self-esteem for an adult.

3. Briefly describe three children whom you know well and propose something you could do that would help them gain a new skill.

4. How does nonsexist education contribute to girls' sense of self-esteem? How does it contribute to boys' sense of self-esteem? Might it detract from boys' self-esteem? Explain your conclusions about that answer.

REFERENCES FOR FURTHER READING

Briggs, D. C. (1970). *Your child's self-esteem: The key to his life*. Garden City, NY: Doubleday. Brigg's book deals with building self-esteem in children and its influence on the entire life of the child.

Curry, N. E., & Johnson, C. N. (1990). *Beyond self-esteem: Developing a genuine sense of human value*. Washington, DC: National Association for the Education of Young Children. Curry and Johnson provide a good balance of reviews of research coupled with much practical information about how to foster the growth of self-esteem.

Harter, S. (1985). Competence as a dimension of self-evaluation: Toward a comprehensive model of self-worth. In R. L. Leahy (Ed.), *The development of the self*. New York: Academic Press. This chapter explores the relationship between competence and feelings of self-esteem.

Honig, A. S. (1986). Stress and coping in children. Part 2: Interpersonal family relationships. *Young Children, 41*(5), 47–60. In this article, Honig explains the link between self-esteem, mastery, and adequate coping skills.

Maccoby, E. E. (1980). *Social development: Psychological growth and the parent-child relationship*. New York: Harcourt Brace Jovanovich. This excellent book has an entire chapter, "The Sense of Self," that reviews Coopersmith's work and also discusses locus of control in clear detail.

Practical Ways to Increase Self-Esteem

Harris, J. M. (1989). *You and your child's self-esteem: Building for the future*. New York: Carroll & Graf. This book is filled with practical recommendations that are useful for parents and teachers, too.

Kostelnik, M. J., Stein, L. C., & Whiren, A. P. (1988). Children's self-esteem: The verbal environment. *Childhood Education, 65*(1), 28–32. The authors provide many examples of positive and negative ways teachers use the verbal environment to construct self-concepts in children. *Highly recommended.*

Marshall, H. H. (1989). The development of self-concept. *Young Children, 44*(5), 44–51. Marshall traces developmental stages and includes practical suggestions for positively influencing self-concept.

Factors That Contribute to Poor Self-Esteem

Peplau, L. A., Miceli, M., & Morasch, B. (1982). Loneliness and self-evaluation. In L. A. Peplau & D. Perlman (Eds.), *Loneliness: A sourcebook of current theory, research and therapy*. New York: John Wiley & Sons. There is good material here on loneliness as a cause of low self-esteem. Readers should realize that loneliness may occur even in the lives of very young children as the result of loss of parental attachment through death, divorce, or extended separation.

Zimbardo, P. G. (1977). *Shyness*. Menlo Park, CA: Addison-Wesley. Many children and adults react to stress with undue shyness. This readable book provides insight and practical advice on how to deal with this agonizing emotion so closely related to poor self-esteem.

For the Advanced Student

Cannella, G. S. (1986). Praise and concrete rewards: Concerns for childhood education. *Childhood Education, 62*(4), 297–301. This is a first-rate summary of recent research on the effect of extrinsic (external) rewards.

Coopersmith, S. (1967). *The antecedents of self-esteem*. San Francisco: W. H. Freeman. Coopersmith recounts a classic study that sought to identify the factors within the family that influence self-esteem either positively or negatively.

Mack, J. E., & Ablon, S. L. (Eds.). (1983). *The development and sustaining of self-esteem in childhood*. New York: International Universities Press. The well-written chapters in this book cover most of the aspects of self-esteem that are of interest to teachers.

Mecca, A. M., Smelser, N. J., & Vasconcellos, J. (1989). *The social importance of self-esteem*. Berkeley: University of California Press. This book provides extensive documentation about the value of promoting good self-esteem as a preventive against a wide variety of social ills. *Highly recommended.*

Thomas, A. (1989). Ability and achievement expectations: Implications of research for classroom practice. *Childhood Education, 65*(4), 235–238. The chilling effects of "learned helplessness" are detailed by Thomas together with an analysis of how children come to see themselves as unworthy and incapable.

White, R. W. (1976). *The enterprise of living: A view of personal growth* (2nd ed.). New York: Holt, Rinehart & Winston. The chapter on competence, which discusses its importance in relation to development, traces its growth through various stages, and talks about why the concept is significant, is excellent. The entire book is superlative reading.

Publications of Continuing Interest

Cornerstones: Nurturing self-esteem in young children. Extension Human Development, Department of Human Development and Family Studies, Room 343 Justin Hall, Kansas State University, Manhattan, KS 66506. Six issues a year touch on various aspects of children's lives related to self-esteem. A useful resource for the teacher of young children.

CHAPTER 7

Tender Topics
Helping children master emotional crises*

I, a stranger and afraid
In a world I never made.
— A. E. Houseman (1922)

Have you ever wondered . . .

What to advise a parent who asks if he should tell his son his grandfather is dying?

How to help a 3-year-old get ready to have a hernia repaired?

What you should do when you are helping a child undress for nap and find something that looks like a cigarette burn under her arm?

If you have, the material in the following pages will help you.

---

*I am indebted to Donna Dempster (McClain) of Cornell University for suggesting that a chapter on "tender topics" be included in the revised edition of *The Whole Child*.

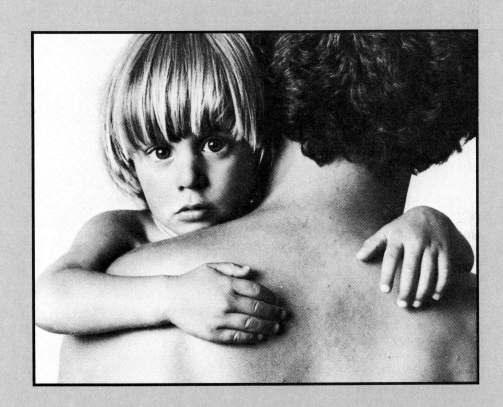

Young children are as subject to stress and strain when a crisis strikes their families as the adults are, but this may be difficult for the family to recognize. They often hope that if nothing is said, the child will be unaware of the problem, or they may be so overwhelmed by the crisis that they have little emotional reserve available to help their children through their troubles at the same time. But children are keen sensors of emotional climates, and they are aware of telephone conversations, comments by neighbors, and so forth. As Furman says,

> Children are so observant of and sensitive to their parents moods and nuances of behavior that, in our experience, it is impossible to spare them from knowing or to deceive them about the true nature of events. (1974, p. 18)

Indeed the secrecy and avoidance often practiced by families when crises occur may serve only to deepen the child's anxiety (Schaefer, 1984). It is far better, then, to reduce this misery where we can by facing facts squarely and providing as much stability as possible than to worsen the problem by failing to deal with it.

Moreover, the experience of crisis is not always undesirable in itself. If well handled, a crisis may actually strengthen character. It is important to realize that experiencing a crisis does not always weaken children. In their book *Vulnerable but Invincible* (1982), Werner and Smith trace the development of children living under the stressful conditions of chronic poverty on Kauai. They found that many children succeeded despite such adversity. In comparing these "resilient" children with their less successful peers, they found that the children were generally active, good-natured, affectionate, and socially adept. Familial factors that contributed to their success included positive attention from caregivers during their first 5 years and a home that had some structure to its life patterns, rules, and values that were shared in common.

Dugan and Coles (1989) also present evidence that some children can find purpose and hope in some of the most hopeless-appearing situations. So, as we approach this discussion of the perils and problems that will confront many of the children we teach, we should remember what Werner and Smith (1982) say so well:

> The terrors of our nature and the world remind us forever how vulnerable we are. Hence biological and behavioral scientists have spent a great deal of time, energy, and resources exploring the roots of our aggression, alienation, disease, and unease. What is often overlooked, but seems more awesome and miraculous, is our resilience as a species. (p. 152)

Crisis *can* constitute "a dangerous opportunity" for growth if it is handled well. Needless to say, this is not always the case. Young children seem particularly vulnerable to potential disaster, in part because they lack experience and in part because they are relatively powerless and helpless (Maccoby, 1983). If they are lucky, they *do* have adults who can help them through these difficult times. Because preprimary teachers occasionally have such opportunities, the following material is included.

WHAT CONSTITUTES A CRISIS?

We usually think of a crisis as being something sudden, and surely death or illness or a trip to the emergency room falls in this category. Other crises are of longer duration—the mental illness of a parent, a divorce, a new baby, physical abuse, moving to a new neighborhood, or even adjusting to child care outside the home.

Some crises are unhappy events—loss of a job, for example—and some are happier occasions—a marriage, perhaps, or the adoption of a child. The one thing all crises have in common whether sudden or chronic, unhappy or joyful, is that they all involve change. These changes occur far more commonly than one would wish. For example, one study estimates that 1 child in 20 experiences the death of a loved one by age 5 (Kliman, 1968). And even though the divorce rate is declining slightly, between 40 and 50% of children born in the late 1970s and early 1980s will experience the divorce of their parents (Glick & Lin, 1986).

Fortunately some of the effects of these events can be mitigated if families and teachers know where to turn and what to do. It is my hope that the following material will be useful in this regard. *However, because of the nature and gravity of the crises presented, the reader should understand that this chapter represents only the barest minimum of information and that it is intended only as a starting point, not as a comprehensive guide.*

For an inexperienced 2-year-old, Halloween masks can constitute a crisis unless the child is prepared for the experience.

SOME GENERAL PRINCIPLES

There is no other time in life when the parent is more important to the child than during a time of crisis (Wallerstein & Blakeslee, 1989). Teachers, psychologists, social workers, and sometimes police officers may also offer meaningful aid, but the family is the most significant influence; for this reason the fundamental goal of the teacher should be to support the family as well as possible. There are a number of ways to accomplish this.

Things to Do for the Family

Make Certain the Parents Understand That It Is Better to Include the Child in the Situation Than to Exclude Her

Particularly in matters of death, serious parental illness, or job loss, adults may attempt to shield children from what is happening, but as mentioned before, children always know when something is wrong. Parents may not realize how frightened this can make youngsters if they are left to fantasize about the nature of the trouble or the reason for it. It is the primeval "fear of the unknown." To remedy this, the teacher should encourage the family to explain in simple terms *but not gory detail* the nature of the emergency.

The same recommendation applies to expressing feelings—children should be allowed to participate in feelings of concern or grief rather than be excluded. Again, I would caution that this principle should be followed within reason. The point to get across to the family is that it is all right for children to understand that grown-ups sometimes feel sad or frightened or upset—as long as this is mingled with steady assurances from family members that life will continue and that the child will be taken care of.

Try Not to Overreact, No Matter What the Parent Tells You

Teachers can be of little help if they allow themselves to become as upset as the parents are over a crisis, though I cannot deny that crises such as suicide or the rape of a 4-year-old are deeply shocking to everyone. However, if teachers can present a model of relative calmness as well as concern, they can influence the parent to behave in the same manner. By providing information on what will help the child, they can encourage the institution of rational steps in dealing with the situation.

Teachers should also guard themselves against being overcome with pity for a youngster or the parents, because pity is not beneficial for the family, either. I recall one situation where a little boy, returning to school after his mother died, was greeted by a teacher who threw her arms around him and burst into tears, saying, "Oh, you poor child! Whatever will you and your poor papa do now?'' This unfortunate response overwhelmed the boy and froze him into an inexpressive state from which it was very difficult to retrieve him. One would think an adult would have more sense, but crises do strange things to people.

Of course, pity is not always so obvious. It may manifest itself in the more subtle forms of overindulgence or spoiling, and this is equally undesirable. Pity is a weakening experience for the person who is its object. It encourages feelings of despair, self-pity, and helplessness (Garber & Seligmann, 1980)—the exact opposites of competence. It is far better to substitute compassionate understanding and to express quiet confidence that, although the family and child feel bad right now, you are certain they are ultimately going to come through the experience all right and that you are there to do whatever you can to help them.

Do Not Violate the Privacy of the Family

Particularly when something sensational has happened, whether it be a car accident or a home burning to the ground, it can be tempting to participate in the tragedy by gossiping about it with other parents. It is impossible to avoid discussion of such events entirely when they are common knowledge in the community, but care should be taken to keep private details private. For one thing, any parents who hear the teacher repeat such personal details are bound to conclude that the teacher will gossip about their personal affairs also. For another, behaving this way is a breach of professional ethics.

Offer Yourself as a Resource

Being a good listener is one way to do this (see chapter 20, ''What Parents Need''), as long as parents do not come to feel that you are mostly interested in the sensational aspects of the crisis or that you cannot wait for them to stop talking so you can offer advice. Remember, also, that sometimes families do not want any help, and this desire must be respected, too.

Sometimes, after the emergency aspect has subsided, parents find it helpful if the teacher has a good reference to lend them, such as Furman's article (1982) or Atkins and Rubin's *Part-Time Father* (1976). If the center has a reserve of at least a few such basic books on hand, they can be instantly available when needed. (A few books of this kind are suggested at the end of this chapter.)

Finally, the teacher can also be a resource for referral to other supporting agencies. This ticklish matter is discussed in greater detail in chapter 21, ''Working with Exceptional Children,'' so I will only comment here that it is necessary to be careful of offering referral resources too hastily lest the family interpret this as wanting to get rid of them and their uncomfortable problem. On the other hand, crises that result from a sudden deep shock or trauma, such as being in a severe automobile accident, experiencing rape, or witnessing a murder or suicide, require immediate psychiatric attention.

Things to Do for the Child

Don't Ignore the Situation by Pretending It Hasn't Happened*

It takes a sensitive teacher to achieve a matter-of-fact facing of a crisis with a child without overdoing it or rubbing it in. Nor should the teacher imply that everything is fine and dandy and that getting over the disaster will be easy or that everything will be just like it was before. It is better to admit that it is not a happy time, while making the point that it is not the end of the world, either.

It helps to be alert to clues that the child wants to talk about her feelings or that she has the problem on her mind. Sometimes this occurs long after the event in question. For example, one of the children in our center suffered a serious burn on her arm that caused her a good deal of misery. Although she seemed fully recovered, later events proved she had not come to terms with it completely at that time. Several months afterward, she happened to be part of a group of youngsters who went on a field trip to inspect the skeleton in the biology department. She was very quiet while she surveyed the bones, and slipping her hand into the teacher's on the way home, she whispered to her, "But what happened to the skin?" To which the teacher responded, "Are you wondering if it got burned off?"—and all of Amy's concerns about skin and injuries came tumbling forth.

But it is best if the situation can be dealt with while it is happening. If the child is unable to bring the problem up, the teacher can provide play experiences for working the event through, or include a book on the subject at story time, or mention the problem casually himself when the opportunity for a quiet private interlude presents itself. Sometimes this can be done tactfully by saying, "I remember when I was little and had my tonsils out—I didn't know what was going to happen in the hospital. I wondered if my mother would stay. And if . . . [include a shrewd guess about what is troubling the particular child]. I wonder if you are wondering about that, too."

The focus of such discussions should be on what the child thinks and what she is worried about. Reassurance and explanation have their place in talking problems over with young children, but they are not nearly so helpful as listening and encouraging youngsters to express their worries through talk and, most valuably, through play (McFadden, 1990).

Remember, It Is All Right for Children
(and Adults) to Cry and to Feel Bad

We early childhood teachers do better than most people at accepting children's right to cry about everyday matters, but sometimes we find ourselves feeling very uncomfortable when children sob over more serious situations, such as the

---

*For further discussion of coping with emotional disturbance in children refer to chapter 21, "Working with Exceptional Children." Indications of disturbance are discussed in chapter 5, "Fostering Mental Health in Young Children."

death of someone they love or a parent's going to jail. Perhaps this is because we know these griefs represent more serious situations, and so we feel more concerned and sorry that the child must go though those experiences. It is natural, when you care about someone, not to want them to feel bad.

But it is important to remember that crying brings relief in serious situations just as it does in more mundane ones, and this relief is valuable and helpful to the child. Therefore it is important for us not to cut off such a response because of our own discomfort and consequent need to comfort the child. Unfortunately, feeling bad is a part of life, just as feeling joyful is. Teachers who realize this learn to endure and accept children's expressions of grief rather than blocking them by providing too swift reassurance, hastily distracting them, or telling them, "Don't feel bad . . . it's all right!"

This does not mean, of course, that one stands coldly by while a youngster sobs forlornly in a corner; supportive warmth and cuddling are appropriate comforts to provide for grieving children. It *does* mean that children should be encouraged to cry as well as talk about their feelings if they feel the need to do so.

Provide Play Opportunities to Express and Clarify Feelings About the Crisis, and Try to Be on Hand to Help the Child Interpret Them

Imaginative play is a very satisfactory way for children to resolve their feelings about crises. Some kinds of play, such as hospital play, benefit children most if special equipment is provided. This might include a set of crutches, something that can stand in for shot needles (we use turkey basters for this purpose), aprons, surgical gowns, and masks.

Hand puppets, little rubber dolls, dollhouse furniture, and a housekeeping corner well equipped with dolls and other paraphernalia of family life are props that can be used to express concerns related to the family situation.

An alert teacher can be aware of the turn the play is taking and help a troubled child ease her feelings. She might, for example, remain close enough to a housekeeping group to comment quietly to a 3-year-old pounding on a baby doll. "Gosh! You really want to show that baby she makes you mad! You want her to stop bothering you and crying so much. That's OK—it's OK to feel that way. You can pretend anything you want. Of course we can't do that to the real baby even when we feel that way, but we can *pretend* anything we want. We can *feel* what we wish, but we must control what we do."

Play opportunities that permit the sublimated expression of feelings are also valuable (see chapter 10, "Aggression: What to Do About It"). Some materials are especially good as aggression relievers—dough and finger paint that can be pounded and squished, and simple hammering come to mind—and some are more relaxing and tension relieving—water play and swinging, for example. In general, unstructured materials that make few demands for performance are the most effective ones to use for such purposes.

Absolve the Child from Guilt

Young children are not good reasoners about cause and effect. Piaget has provided us with many examples where they have reasoned that effect was the cause. (For instance, a child may see trees bending in the wind and conclude that trees bending make the wind blow!) Piaget also teaches us that young children are self-centered and see things mainly in relation to themselves. And, finally, we know that children are prone to magical thinking, tending to believe that the wish has the same power as the act.

If we think about the implications of these developmental facts, it becomes easier to understand why children often conclude that they are the cause of the family's disaster—something usually so far from the actual truth it may not even occur to adults that the child is blaming herself for the trouble and feeling guilty and unhappy as a result. Warren (1977) in her excellent pamphlet *Caring* suggests that the teacher can offer comfort in this kind of situation by helping the child separate adult from child business. For example, she suggests that the teacher might say:

> When your parents fight, that is very hard for you and sometimes makes you cry. But grown-ups' fighting is really grown-up business. Even if they are fighting about you, it is because they are mad at each other and not because of you or anything you did. (p. 22)

Another Way to Help the Child Is to Maintain as Stable and Dependable an Atmosphere as Possible for Her While She Is in Your Care

This means that the child is expected to adhere to regular routines and that, in general, the same rules are applied to her conduct as are usually applied. It does not mean that allowances are not made—they must be. The teacher needs to be extra understanding and tolerant if the youngster cannot eat or is particularly irritable or has trouble falling asleep or cries a lot. However, keeping the routines and rules as steady as possible means that at least part of the child's world has not changed, and this offers substantial comfort to a child whose home world is in turmoil (Skeen & McKenry, 1982).

Help the Child Know What to Expect

Sometimes families know in advance that a crisis is approaching, since they can generally anticipate such events as having a new baby, routine surgery, or moving to a new city. Here it is important not to build up unrealistic ideas of what such a change entails. The new baby will *not* be a wonderful little playmate for the preschooler as soon as she arrives, and ice cream is *not* going to taste wonderful after a tonsillectomy.

It is not necessary to be negative about changes and build undue apprehension. It just helps to talk over what will happen in advance to reduce the element of the unexpected (Wiszinckas, 1981–82). This is particularly true if the teacher and family talk to the youngster in terms of the plans being made for

Advance preparation helps reduce anxiety.

her—how her pet dog will get to the new house and where the family will have dinner on the day of the move. It is this kind of simple detail that children find reassuring and that adults sometimes forget to tell them, since they already know the answers or consider them unimportant.

Help the Child Retain a Sense of Being in Control

During stormy times of crisis when children are upset, they often revert to less mature, more uncontrolled behavior; it may seem paradoxical to recommend they be given as many opportunities to control their lives as possible during such difficult periods. But there is a sound reason for urging this strategy. It is because feeling "in charge" combats the sense of helplessness and panic the youngster must also contend with.

Fortunately, there are some age-appropriate, commonsense ways of helping even young children retain at least some confidence that they can control what is happening to them.

For example, I have already alluded to the value of providing, when possible, appropriate information about what is going to happen. This frankness not only relieves the child of the burden of free-floating anxiety but also provides opportunities for her to make simple plans about how to cope with the change.

"I hear you're going to your grandma's while Mommy's in the hospital. What will you do when you get there?"

Opportunities to make simple choices and decisions also contribute to the child's sense of being in command. "Would you like to paint a picture to take to her, or is there something else you'd rather make?"

Knowing what to do beforehand helps, too. For that reason earthquake, fire, and tornado drills have value the goes beyond the commonsense one of improving safety. By helping children know how to protect themselves, such drills also increase their confidence and sense of control. This is an important alleviator of panic.

Finally, it can restore a child's feelings of being in control if she is encouraged to do something for someone else—even such simple things as helping the teacher set out the cups or hammering in a nail can help a youngster retain her sense of being an able, effective person.

HELPING CHILDREN COPE WITH SPECIFIC CRISES

Adjusting to School and Dealing with the Parent Who Picks the Child Up Late

In chapter 3, "Handling Daily Routines," I have already discussed ways of helping the child adjust to the center, but it should at least be pointed out here also that coming to school can represent such a change in the child's life that it may be a real crisis from her point of view. Particularly if the adjustment is a difficult one, we should not underestimate the anguish she is experiencing when separated from her mother, and we should do all we can to alleviate it.

Another part of attending school that can be a crisis to a child is a late pickup by her parent. I have known children to fly into a panic over this if it is not handled well by the teacher, so a few suggestions are in order. First of all, be careful to reassure the child that her parent *will* come and that you will stay with her until he does. It also is reassuring to say that you know there are some good reasons why he is delayed (and avoid speculating within the child's hearing over what various disasters may have befallen the parent along the way). Second, locate an alternative person to come as soon as possible. Part of the entry record for each child should be a list of the telephone numbers of at least three people to be contacted in case the child becomes ill during the day or when the parent is late. However, do not let the child stand beside you as you dial number after number, getting no response! Remember, *no child should ever be released to any adult who is not on the parent's list.*

Third, hold your temper and do not make the child pay for the parent's sins. It is really hard at the end of a long day to wait and maybe miss the bus, but it is not the child's fault her parent is tardy. In some schools where parents are consistently inconsiderate, policies are established of charging extra for overtime care or not allowing the child to attend the next day, or asking the parent to drive the teacher home if he missed the bus, but these penalties should

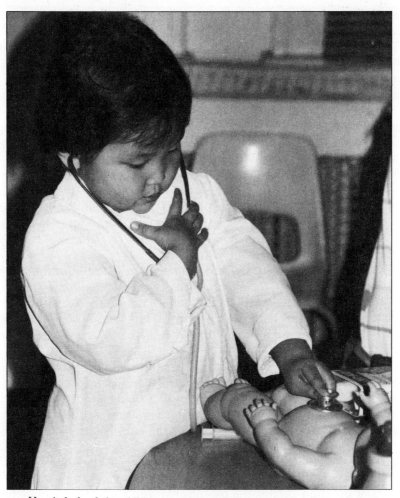

Hospital play helps children work through fears and misunderstandings.

be avoided if possible because they breed ill will. It is usually sufficient to explain, when tempers have cooled, why the teacher prefers to leave on time and to ask the parent to be more considerate in the future.

Arrival of a New Baby

Parents are often quite skillful about preparing a youngster for a new baby during the 9-month wait, yet once the infant has arrived they somehow assume the preschooler will be delighted and certainly not jealous! But the reality of the mother's going to the hospital, possibly having someone unfamiliar take over meanwhile, and then seeing her world changed by the homecoming of the baby with all the demands on the parents' time and energy can turn out to be an unpleasant surprise to a preschooler.

These demands on parents' time that common sense and experience tell us are likely to take place have also been measured in a study of firstborn children (Dunn & Kendrick, 1981). They found that the arrival of the second child really *did* change the mother-firstborn relationship since the mother no longer spent as much time playing with the child or beginning conversations with her. This was coupled (not surprisingly) with a significant rise in the number of negative confrontations that took place between them. No wonder the arrival of a baby constitutes a crisis in the lives of some youngsters!

Some simple remedies that the teacher can apply to help alleviate these feelings of intrusion and jealousy are not to dwell on how wonderful it is to have a new baby in the family and to provide plenty of opportunities for the preschooler to act like a baby if she wants to. I recall one youngster who derived deep satisfaction from sitting in my office being rocked and fed a bottle occasionally—she especially liked being burped!

It also helps to be realistic about the situation—point out the things the baby *can't* do, as well as all the obvious privileges and attention accruing to the preschooler. Help the older child find satisfaction in her own abilities and competencies that are related to being more mature, and make it clear that she will retain this advantage for a long time to come. After all, she will always be the older child.

Finally, if jealousy is interpreted to the parents as *the fear of being left out*, it may enable them to stop deploring or denying it and make plans that show the child she is definitely included. These can be as simple as reading to her by herself for a little while before bedtime, or making a special time of going to the store while the baby remains at home. When the baby begins to crawl, it is only fair to provide a safe place for the older child's belongings. Sometimes older children appreciate having a barrier across their doors so that they can hook it to keep the baby out. (It is an interesting fact of human nature that the more protection of the child's rights the parent provides, the less protective the child will feel driven to be.)

Hospitalization

Preparation in Advance

When surgery or other treatment can be anticipated in advance, there is time for home and school to help the child grasp what will happen, and she is entitled to this information (Trawick-Smith & Thompson, 1986). After all, it is her body that will, in a sense, be violated. There are several good books for children about doctors and hospitals, and a bibliography of such books is included in the References for Further Reading. Hospital play and discussion of the forthcoming hospitalization will also help—not only to reassure the child herself but also to comfort her playmates. In these discussions I have found that using the word "fix" is helpful. Saying the doctor is going to fix a bad leg or the infected tonsils seems to be a concept that children can grasp and that they find comforting. Haller (1967) comments that using hospital masks in dramatic play is of special value, since such masks are often one of the more frightening aspects of hospitalization (remember how upsetting masks are to some children at Halloween?).

Some hospitals permit children to visit first. This possibility should be suggested to the parents, even if it means they must ask the doctor to make special arrangements. (I will never forget the relief of one of my own children, aged 6, when she went for such a visit and discovered there would be a television set in her room, something it had not occurred to me to mention. Since she was not allowed to watch TV during the day at home, this was indeed a selling point for the hospital!)

Another encouraging trend is the policy of admitting children for minor surgery on a day basis only. Under these circumstances the youngster is admitted early in the morning before surgery and released to go home as soon as the effects of the anesthesia have worn off. This sensible procedure not only cuts hospital costs but reduces the potential for misery and fright caused by parental separation as well.

While the child is recovering and out of school, it is important to consider the feelings of her playmates as well as the youngster herself and to provide something they can do for their friend. Children often have very good ideas about this, such as baking something special or making a card with all their handprints on it.

Once again, upon the child's return, more hospital play is definitely of value. This enables the child to work out her feelings and clarify them and helps inform the other children of what went on as well. Incidentally, the mastery role of being doctor or nurse as well as that of victim is particularly satisfying to children who are struggling to overcome their feelings of angry helplessness often generated while under treatment. Many children find that giving shots to someone else feels best of all.

Information for Parents

Parents should be encouraged to stay with their children as much of the time as possible while their youngsters are hospitalized (Pediatric Mental Health, 1986). Many hospitals today maintain open visiting privileges with no time limits for parents, but a few still do not. It is worthwhile becoming acquainted with the policies of various hospitals in your area so you can inform parents about these in advance. Older 4- and 5-year-olds can also maintain contact with their families, particularly siblings, by talking with them on the phone, and this should be encouraged.

Parents are usually cowed by hospitals and apprehensive of antagonizing staff. They do not know their rights, and they are also likely to be upset and worried. A chat beforehand can alleviate some of their concerns and enable them to insist on what is best for their particular child. Moreover, they should be reassured that it is desirable for children to express their feelings. Indeed it is the quiet, passive child conforming unquestioningly to hospital routine who arouses the greatest concern among psychological consultants (Bowlby, 1973; Robertson & Robertson, 1989). Children should not be admonished ("Don't cry") or lied to ("This will just sting a little") or threatened ("You do it, or I'm going to go home!"). It is truly surprising that parents sometimes expect more of their children in these difficult and especially trying situations than they normally would dream of expecting at home.

They may also need to be prepared for the fact that children sometimes reject their mothers when they finally return home. This can come as a painful shock to families unless they have been prepared with an explanation of the reasons for the hostility. This reaction is thought to really be an expression of the child's anger at being separated from her parents, particularly the mother, so in a way the hostility expressed by the child is a kind of compliment to the family for the strength of their emotional bonds. But it can be a confusing compliment if misunderstood (Robertson & Robertson 1989).

The Emergency Room

One of the most trying crises for young children to experience is a visit to the emergency room. This is because no advance preparation is possible, the parents are maximally upset, time is short, and the reason for being there is generally serious and painful. It will come as no news to experienced parent-readers of these pages to learn that accidents are most likely to occur between 3 and 11 P.M. and that twice as many boys as girls require emergency care (Resnick & Hergenroeder, 1975).

One can make a very good parents' night out of offering a discussion of what to do in the emergency room to buffer the child from the worst shocks. Recommendations for parents include (a) staying with the child as much as possible, (b) staying as calm as possible, (c) explaining very simply to the child what is going to happen next so she is not taken completely by surprise when a doctor suddenly materializes with a shot needle, and (d) modeling fortitude by explaining, with assurance, that it may not feel good, but the doctor has to do whatever he is doing because it will help the child get well.

Hospitalization of Parents

A rare series of three studies reported by Rice, Ekdahl, and Miller (1971) reveals that emotional problems are likely to result for children whenever a parent is hospitalized for any length of time, whether it be for physical or mental illness. The impact of mental illness, particularly illness of the mother, causes the most marked difficulties. At least half the children studied gave evidence of such disturbance. This is due to several factors. There is the unhappiness and disorganization that typically precede confinement in a mental institution as well as the fact that families usually have no time to prepare children for the hospitalization. Child abuse or neglect may have taken place before hospitalization, and incarceration of the mother makes it more probable that the child will have to be cared for outside her home—often thereby losing the security of her familiar surroundings and friends as well.

Of course, the center plays only one part in solving the overall problems of families involved in such difficulties, but it can be a significant one if the provision of child care means the child can stay within the home and that she is provided with a stable, understanding environment while at school. The general recommendations given at the beginning of this chapter capsulize what will help these children; here are three additional suggestions:

1. In such circumstances the children's center should make a special effort to coordinate its services with those of other agencies and be prepared to report undue distress to the social worker or psychologist along with a request for help.

2. Young children are often particularly distressed over the unpredictability of the disturbed parent's behavior (Sameroff & Seifer, 1983). Because of the possibility that angry encounters took place between parent and child or that a depressed parent may have been unreachable by the child, it is of great importance to explain in simple terms to the youngster that she was not the reason her mommy went to the hospital.

3. Despite the prehospitalization difficulties that may have troubled the child, remember she is also feeling pain over separation from her parent. This produces deep feelings of loneliness, confusion, and anger.

4. Finally, it is still true that many, perhaps the majority, of people regard mental illness as a shameful stigma, and being near former mental patients fills them with unease. The preschool teacher who can master this apprehension by behaving naturally with recovered patients offers a gift of acceptance much appreciated by the family.

Helping Children Through Divorce

Some useful facts to have in mind about divorce are that children's reactions to divorce vary widely in relation to their age, gender, emotional resources, subsequent life experience, and interpersonal relationships. In general, boys have more difficulty adjusting than girls do; younger children seem to cope more easily with the situation than older ones do; and children from divorced families are allowed more responsibility, independence, and decision-making opportunities than children of nondivorced families are. Eighty percent of men and 75% of women remarry following a divorce, so it is probable that children will need to make a further adjustment by joining a mingled family as part of that long-term divorce experience (Hetherington, 1989).

Occasionally teachers are aware in advance that families are having marital difficulties, but the announcement of an impending divorce often takes them as much by surprise as it does the child. Here are a few points to remember when this happens.

For one thing, try not to take sides. This is difficult to avoid, in part because blame assigning by friends and acquaintances seems to be part of the cultural pattern of divorce, and in part because the parent who confides in the teacher tends, understandably, to present the other parent in a bad light. Something else the teacher should remember is to invite each parent to make appointments with him when it is time for parent-child conferences. All too often, the father is ignored by the school following a divorce, and yet the majority of men remain deeply concerned for their children and greatly appreciate being included. Third, be prepared for the fact that the child herself is likely to exhibit irritability, regression, confusion, and anxiety during and after the divorce.

Still another difficulty that may be encountered by the center is related to custody. Occasionally members of the school staff are subpoenaed to testify in custody altercations. This is usually the case when one parent wishes to prove neglect by the other one. Here, written records of attendance, written reports of parent conferences, and observational records of the child are valuable to have available for citation.

Potential custody problems constitute an additional reason for requiring written, signed lists of individuals to whom a child may be released when the parent is not picking the youngster up from school. Refusing release can create temporary inconvenience and bad feeling, but the school is legally responsible for the child while not in her parent's care. This explanation will usually appease irritated would-be helpers, and enforcement of the rule may protect the child from "parentnapping."

All parents, should, of course, be welcome visitors at school—although once or twice I have found it necessary to make it clear they are welcome just as long as the occasion remains a happy one for the youngster and is not used by parents to generate an upsetting scene.

When a parent remarries, it is equally important for the school to welcome the stepparent and additional siblings into the life of the school. Children in newly blended families often experience bewildering mixtures of feelings ranging from delight and relief to jealousy and insecurity about who is in charge. The teacher who is able to accept the child's positive and negative comments about the remarriage in a matter-of-fact, nonjudgmental way can hasten the child's adjustment to the changed situation.

Explaining the Divorce to the Child

The effects of divorce on children have been found to be long lasting and painful (Hetherington, 1989). Wallerstein and Blakeslee (1989) maintain that it is one of the most severe stressors children can experience—even more severe than the death of a well-loved person—since divorce carries with it an additional burden of uncertainty because it may not seem as final to the child as death does. The possibility of continuing and repeated tension between parents also complicates the situation.

Children are also confused because many parents give their children no explanation at all about the divorce, leaving them to sad fantasies concerning reasons and their own possible role in the breakup (Mitchell, 1985). For these reasons, then, it is of *great* importance that parents be encouraged to provide children with truthful, clear information so that various misapprehensions and possible guilt may be allayed.

Pitcher (1969) recommends that the child be provided with simple explanations of what has happened, and she suggests that parents should explain, "Your father and I don't want to be married anymore. We aren't going to live together anymore," which is preferable to saying "Your father and I don't love each other anymore." This is because loving is not necessarily related to marriage in the child's mind. She is loved also, and yet she is not married. If loving can stop, perhaps she too is in jeopardy.

Commonly seen behavior changes include fear of separation in routine situations such as coming to the center or going to bed at night, sleep disturbances, and being more tearful, irritable, more aggressive, and more likely inhibited in play (Wallerstein, 1983).

But parents should also know that divorce is not always perceived as being unfortunate, even by young children. Youngsters are often well aware that their parents are unhappy and may experience real relief when the final separation takes place. Indeed, a few studies indicate that children from frankly split homes

Using a blanket is a common way children comfort themselves when feeling upset.

generally do better than those from intact but unhappy households (Hethering-ton, Stanley-Hagen, & Anderson, 1989).

If parents are advised to avoid degrading the other parent within the child's hearing, the youngster will be less distressed. Children are usually feeling pain enough over divided loyalties anyway, and being party to the denigration of the other parent only complicates their emotional problems further. It is also of great value to explain to the child which parent she will be living with and reassure her that she will (ideally) have many regular opportunities to be with the other parent as well.

Divorce frequently means a move, often from a house to an apartment. In the child's eyes this may mean the loss of a beloved pet, a change of friends, and sometimes even a change of schools. It almost always includes financial hardship as well. Her mother may be leaving her for a fulltime job for the first time, too. No wonder Mitchell (1985) likens the experience of divorce to death for young children, since so many often painful adjustments must transpire.

Building Sensitivity to Single-Parent Families Within the School

The teacher needs to be especially sensitive to single-parent children at school, not only because they may be unhappy or exhibit various kinds of emotional distress, but also because so many activities in a children's center typically revolve around family life. Contemporary teachers need to broaden their cultural awareness to include the many patterns of single parenting that now exist and must divest themselves of the tacit assumption that most of the children in the school undoubtedly come from two-parent families. At least in day care this is not likely to be true.

Teachers may also need to divest themselves of ingrained prejudices against divorce and divorced people. There is not necessarily anything "wrong" with people who are no longer married or perhaps never have been (Ball, Newman, & Scheuren, 1984). Indeed many single parents, men and women, should be admired for the extraordinary manner in which they have held their families together and continued to care for them. As Herzog and Sudia (1975) put it in their review of research on fatherless homes, "To focus only on problems and weaknesses [of fatherless homes] is to distort the picture and obscure some clues to ways of building on strengths" (p. 202). It is kinder also if the teacher learns to speak of "single-parent families" rather than speaking of children from "broken homes."

In terms of curriculum, Mother's Day and Father's Day can take on a peculiar significance for single-parent children, as can vacations. Unless the teacher is careful, some children will be routinely expected to make gifts for parents they rarely or never see. Rather than have this happen it is better to be well acquainted with the youngster's living arrangements. It may be that she would prefer to make something for a grandparent or her baby-sitter or her mother's boyfriend.

The teacher also should take care in selecting books, so that all kinds of family structures are represented. It is as unfortunate for some children to be continually confronted with the stories of the happy, two-parent family going on a picnic as it was for Black children of the last generation to be exposed only to "Dick and Jane." A list of such books is included in the bibliography at the end of this chapter and in Skeen and McKenry (1982).

Research on the relation of father absence to the establishment of adequate male and female role concepts remains inconclusive, but it is probably an especially good idea to employ male teachers in centers that serve single parents because divorce makes it more likely that children will be deprived of male companionship outside the school. Surely it is more desirable for children of both sexes to have some regular opportunities to relate to men rather than to be raised during their preschool years entirely by women.

Helping Children Understand Death

Although death remains a taboo subject for many people, the increasing frequency of publications and discussion about it (there is even a *Journal of Thanatology* devoted solely to this topic) provides evidence that at least a few people are no longer pretending that death does not exist. And, even though we might prefer to deny it, we must face the fact that death is a part of life for young children as well as for their elders. Five percent of American children will lose a parent through death before they reach age 18 (Wessel, 1983). Children are also exposed to the deaths of grandparents, other family members, friends, and beloved animals, not to mention the continual accounts of death and murder reported endlessly on television. For these reasons it is necessary to learn how to help children cope with this subject, even though we may be barely learning to talk about it ourselves.

What Can the Teacher Do?

It is heartening to learn that in the area of death education there *is* something the early childhood teacher can do that can be of real assistance to young children. Kliman (1968) terms this *psychological immunization* and describes it as helping children acquire at least a modicum of "mastery in advance." By this he means that it is helpful if the subject of death is included matter-of-factly as part of the curriculum of the center in order to desensitize children by providing both information and mild experiences with it before a more emotionally laden death occurs. This can be accomplished in many ways.* Perhaps the most effective of them is based on the death of animals at school. This should include talking about how the animals have changed and what will become of them, as well as helping children carry out the simple burials that are of such intense interest to them at that age. Books and discussions are also helpful, and some schools even advocate visiting cemeteries, which are, after all, quite beautiful places (Riley, 1989).

---

*For a more complete discussion of teaching about death in the curriculum, please refer to Hendrick, 1990, *Total Learning: Curriculum for the Young Child* (3rd ed.), Columbus, OH: Merrill, chapter 9, "Teaching Children to Understand and Value Life."

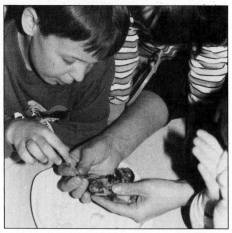

Although adults are often squeamish about dead animals, children can find them deeply interesting. Here Deb Parkinson helps our 4-year-olds grasp what being dead means, while also helping them appreciate the delicacy and wonder of the little chicken's feet.

Helping the Child and the Family When Death Occurs

Kliman also points out that teachers and other nonmedical personnel, such as clergy, are more likely to be asked for help when a death occurs than doctors are, probably because the families feel less hostile toward such people than they do toward the medical profession following bereavement. For this reason the teacher should be well prepared with some down-to-earth suggestions for helping the children by supplying resources for further information and providing knowledge of possible referral sources should these be requested.

Once again I must repeat that the fact of a death should not be avoided by telling a child that her father has gone away on a long trip or that Grandma will come back in the spring or that Snowball is just asleep. This principle must be reiterated because studies reveal such statements are *particularly prevalent* when families deal with death and preschool children (Johnson, 1987). Children need to be allowed to participate in the family's grief because it strengthens their feelings of belonging instead of feeling isolated, and it helps them express their own sadness, too.

As time passes, a child should be encouraged to reminisce about the absent parent. All too often once the initial crisis has passed, families and teachers hesitate to reawaken memories, but recall actually helps ventilate feelings so that the emotional wound can heal cleanly. It also helps the child retain her identification with and feelings of affection for her parent. Family stories about "Do you remember when . . .," photographs, and even movies and tapes have been found to be helpful.

Reliving old memories is also the second of three stages of mourning. The first one is the acceptance of loss, the second is remembering the past, and the third is substitution of a new relationship.

Parents can do a better job if they also understand that the emotion of grief for children (and for adults as well) is not composed only of sadness. There is also a component of anger (Bowlby, 1980; Robertson & Robertson, 1989). Just as children feel a mixture of grief and anger when left at the center, so too do they experience, to a much stronger degree, these same feelings when a parent abandons them in death. It is doubly important to understand this, because young children often connect this anger back to some angry interlude before death and conclude they have caused the parent to die (just as they may believe this about divorce). They then may reason that the death is a punishment for their misbehavior—truly a terrible burden of guilt for a child to bear.

To counteract this, simple reasons for the death must be given ("Your father didn't want to leave us, but he was so sick the medicine couldn't help any more"), combined with reassurances that the surviving parent and child are not likely to die for a long time yet (Furman, 1984). A child should also be told that the surviving parent is going to go right on taking care of her and be reminded that there is also Grandma, Grandpa, and Aunty Margaret, all of whom love her and care for her. The presence of siblings can provide an additional source of strength and family feeling, particularly among children who are older. The anger should be acknowledged by mentioning its presence and its naturalness. Statements such as "I guess you feel mad your dad died and left us. . . . I see you feel like socking things a lot. . . . We know he couldn't help dying, but it's hard to take sometimes, isn't it?'' usually relieve some of the hostile impulses.

Adults must also be cautioned against likening death to sleep. We surely do not want anxious children to guard themselves against sleep because they fear death may come while they are sleeping. A second, less obvious reason for this recommendation has to do with the way some researchers believe that preschool children perceive death. They maintain that inexperienced young children view it as being a temporary condition, one from which the person can be revived (Kastenbaum, 1986; Kübler-Ross, 1969). However, with experience comes understanding. Even though young children may experience initial difficulties grasping the finality of death, experts also agree they can learn to accept its permanency if the event is handled truthfully (Bowlby, 1980; Johnson, 1987). On the other hand, when adults speak of death as "being asleep" it perpetuates serious misunderstandings and promotes false hopes. Even more fundamentally, equating it with sleep is untruthful. Why speak euphemistically of "sleep" and "slumber rooms" when what we mean is "death" and "a visiting room where people can view the body"? Why not face facts?

Finally, student teachers often ask me what to do about religious beliefs and children in relation to death. In general, writers on this subject maintain that talking about religion tends to be confusing to young children and should not be stressed when death occurs (Furman, 1982). Surely it is not the teacher's place to do this, anyway, although he may find it helpful to be conversant with the points of view of the major religions.

The question really raised by students, however, is what to do about statements by children with which they cannot agree. For example, a child may say, "My mommy says my puppy went to heaven, and now the angels are singing over him. Someday I'll see him up there" or, "You know what? My grandmother has it all fixed so she'll be froze solid when she dies—then she can come alive again when she wants to."

Actually it is not necessary to agree or disagree with such statements. All one has to do is show that you respect the family's teaching by listening, and then either ask the child what she thinks or say something that responds to the feelings, such as "I can see you really miss him" and "You'd like to see your puppy again," or at least say something noncommittal, such as, "So that's what your grandma is planning."

AIDS (HIV Infection)—A Serious New Crisis in the Lives of Children

The question of AIDS (acquired immunodeficiency syndrome) and young children is a terribly troublesome one. For one thing, there is the question of what if anything to tell children of preschool age about the condition and, for another, what to do about admitting children with AIDS (also known as HIV—human immunodeficiency virus) to the preschool.

What Is Appropriate AIDS Education for Preschoolers?

Very little has been written on this subject to date, and yet, with the media constantly bombarding us with the word and precautionary recommendations, it seems impossible that it has entirely escaped young children's awareness.

Once again, matter-of-fact explanation is the best approach to take. When a youngster appears concerned, these explanations could include the information that AIDS can make people very sick, so sick they often die; that it is very hard "to get"; that it is a grown-up sickness that hardly ever afflicts children; and that people can take care of themselves and protect themselves from becoming infected. Because of the emphasis on needles that is so prevalent in some commercials, one or two mothers have reported their 5-year-olds objected more strenuously than usual when they had injections. For this reason, it may also be helpful to realize that occasionally children may require additional reassurance that the needles the doctors are using are brand-new ones so nobody has to worry about getting sick from them.

For the more anxious child it may also be necessary to add, just as one does when discussing death, that there will always be particular people who will take care of her—even if something did happen to Mother or Daddy—and reiterate, if she is worried, that there is almost no chance the child could become infected.

Of course, it is true that these statements are all only "mostly true," and tragic exceptions to them do occur. However, for most young children they are still adequate.

Admitting HIV-Infected Children to the Preschool

The incidence of pediatric AIDS cases in the United States is still very low, but it is growing swiftly so that, sooner or later, it is likely that teachers of the coming generation of children will be confronted with the problem of admitting or not admitting infected children to the early childhood center. As of November 1988, the Centers for Disease Control reported a total of 1,230 cases (Task Force on Pediatric AIDS, 1989). However, the National Academy of Sciences estimates cases will grow to 3,000 by the end of 1991, with an additional 10,000 children also infected but not diagnosed. Four-fifths of these cases are due to maternally transmitted infections either before birth or during delivery. The remainder are due to transfusions from contaminated blood. The current guidelines issued by the American Public Health Association/American Academy of Pediatrics (1988) include the following points. Admission to a group program must take into consideration the well-being of the infected child and that of the group. Children too young to walk pose no threat, but infected children who bite others or have open, oozing sores might theoretically transmit the disease, though this has not been proven yet.

Two additional points discussed in the guidelines have to do with requiring testing and maintaining confidentiality of information. The report definitely recommends *against* a policy of screening all children for the HIV antibody. It also states that parents of the other children in the program do *not* have the right to know if a child is infected. Caregivers *do* need to know the child has an immunodeficiency but not that it is the result of HIV infection. (However, it seems highly probable to this author that any caregiver so informed would very likely reach a diagnosis of the problem on his own.)

Separate schools for children with HIV infection are *not* recommended because they are thought to be unnecessary if reasonably sound hygienic practices are followed. These practices include careful, consistent handwashing by children and staff; disinfecting soiled surfaces with one tablespoon bleach to 1 quart water, prepared daily; using paper towels and tissues; and avoiding exposure of mucous membranes or open skin lesions to blood or blood-contaminated body fluids by using disposable gloves for protection (*Young Children*, 1989).

Child Abuse, Neglect, and Sexual Molestation

Child abuse constitutes one of the most terrible crises of childhood. The occurrence of such attacks is fundamentally repugnant to most people, and for a long time the subject went virtually ignored and uninvestigated. Statistics only began to accumulate as late as 1962, when Kempe (1962) initiated the first survey on the subject. In 1989 more than 2,400,000 incidents of child abuse or neglect were reported to child protective agencies. Included in that figure are 1,200 children who died from those abusive situations (Jennings, 1990).

Neglect is also a serious problem (Tzeng & Hanner, 1988), and studies of severe neglect are coming into the literature under such headings as *failure-to-thrive* (Helfer & Kempe, 1987). But these discussions center on extreme cases of neglect, and data remain thin on the results of less flagrant cases of neglect and on the results of psychological abuse, although the effects of such adverse experiences are undoubtedly serious for children.

Much activity continues to center on problems resulting from physical attack, and there is growing awareness and concern about sexual abuse as well. Perhaps this is because physical and sexual abuse are particularly horrifying, since they may result in the death of the child; and perhaps it is also because, though still difficult to prove in court, such abuse is easier to substantiate than is psychological abuse or neglect.

Whereas the average age of children involved in abuse/neglect cases is 7 years, the average age of children experiencing major physical abuse is age 5 and the average age of children who are fatally injured is about 2½ (Tzeng & Hanner, 1988). This may be because very young children are unable to retaliate or tell others of their peril, or it may be due in part to other reasons discussed later in this chapter. Although many of these cases occur in infancy and toddlerhood, children of preschool and early elementary school age are not immune. Teachers of young children must learn to identify possible cases of abuse and understand what to do and *what not to do* when our suspicions are aroused, not only for moral reasons but also because we must report abuse (Broadhurst, 1986). In fact, in recent times a number of lawsuits have been brought against educators who did not do this (Rothman, 1990). Children's center teachers need special advice about how to handle such problems, not only because they are more likely than most teachers to note evidence, since they undress children for naps or toileting, but also because most centers operate autonomously without benefit of advice from school nurses, principals, social workers, and so on.

What to Do When Abuse Is Suspected

Teachers who discover evidence of abuse are very upset about it. They may find it hard to believe that such a "nice" family could do a thing like that and thus deny it, or they may be so frightened for the child's safety that they do not think clearly and therefore act impulsively. For this reason, before going any further with this discussion, *I want to emphasize that handling such cases requires skill and delicacy.* The first approach made to the parents is thought to be crucial in successful management of the case (Helfer & Kempe, 1987). The consequences of unsuccessful management may be so serious that we cannot risk jeopardizing such chances by acting in an ill-considered way. *Therefore, teachers must not suddenly plunge into the problem by accusing the parents or even reveal suspicions by questioning them or the child too closely.* Instead, if they suspect a case of abuse, they should contact whatever agency or individual in their community has the responsibility for handling such cases and report it. *They should ask these people for advice and do what they tell them to, to the best of their ability.*

How to Find Help

The agency the teacher should seek out is whatever agency in the community is responsible for children's protective services. These agencies go by different names in different parts of the country: Department of Social Services, Social Rehabilitation Service, Bureau of Children and Family Services, and so forth. Still another way to locate protective services is to ask the public health nurse whom to call. If no such agency exists, as is sometimes the case in small or rural communities, a mental health clinic, a child psychologist or psychiatrist, or a knowledgeable pediatrician should be asked for help.

Action Should Be Prompt

Because abusers often repeat their behavior, prompt action is advisable; yet teachers sometimes hesitate to get involved. The teacher should realize that all states now have mandatory reporting laws and that many of these specifically identify teachers as being among those people *required* to report cases where abuse is suspected (National Center on Child Abuse, 1975). Even where teachers are not specifically mentioned, the law is generally on the side of anyone reporting such a case "in good faith" (National Committee for Prevention of Child Abuse, 1985). Besides the necessity of conforming to the law, *reporting such cases is an ethical and moral responsibility that the teacher must not overlook.*

A publication by the National Center on Child Abuse (1975) suggests the following guidelines concerning referrals:

> You should be aware of the official policy and specific reporting procedures of your school system, and should know your legal obligations and the protections

from civil and criminal liability in your state's reporting law. (All states provide immunity for mandated, good-faith reports.).

Although you should be familiar with your state's legal definition of abuse and neglect, you are not required to make legal distinctions in order to report. Definitions should serve as guides. If you suspect that a child is abused or neglected, you should report. The teacher's value lies in noticing conditions that indicate a child's welfare may be in jeopardy.

Be concerned about the rights of the child—the rights to life, food, shelter, clothing, and security. But also be aware of the parents' rights—particularly their rights to be treated with respect and to be given needed help and support.

Bear in mind that reporting does not stigmatize a parent as "evil." The report is the start of a rehabilitative process that seeks to protect the child and help the family as a whole.

A report signifies only the suspicion of abuse or neglect. Teachers' reports are seldom unfounded. At the very least, they tend to indicate a need for help and support to the family.

If you report a borderline case in good faith, do not feel guilty or upset if it is dismissed as unfounded upon investigation. Some marginal cases are found to be valid.

Don't put off making a report until the end of the school year. Teachers sometimes live with their suspicions until they suddenly fear for the child's safety during the summer months. A delayed report may mean a delay in needed help for the child and the family. Moreover, by reporting late in the school year, you remove yourself as a continued support to both the child protective agency and the reported family.

If you remove yourself from a case of suspected abuse or neglect by passing it on to superiors, you deprive child protective services of one of their most competent sources of information. For example, a teacher who tells a CPS worker that the child is especially upset on Mondays directs the worker to investigate conditions in the home on weekends. Few persons other than teachers are able to provide this kind of information. Your guideline should be to resolve any question in favor of the child. When in doubt, report. Even if you, as a teacher, have no immunity from liability and prosecution under state law, the fact that your report is made in good faith will free you from liability and prosecution. (pp. 70–71)

What to Look For

Many of us are so inexperienced in identifying the results of abuse that it is necessary to include the following information, which has been extrapolated primarily from the work of Helfer & Kempe (1987), as well as from my own experience.

The teacher should be alert for evidence of bruises, particularly a combination of old and fresh ones, or ones on soft parts of the body, or of burns such as cigarette burns. These are likely to occur in relatively concealed places, often on the small of the back or the buttocks. Red wheals or strap marks should also arouse suspicion, as most certainly should a black eye (although children also suffer black eyes for a multitude of other reasons) or swollen ears. Bite marks are another fairly frequent sign of abuse. One author cautions that the soles of the feet should be checked also since this is a "popular location" (Weston, 1980). If a child arrives at school smelling of alcohol or under the influence of drugs, this is also evidence of abuse—and this *does* happen.

A more general reason for concern exists when the parent's voluntary account of the accident does not match the kind or extent of the injury. The usual excuse for bruises is falling down stairs or out of a crib or bed (Weston, 1980), but common sense often tells the teacher that such an event could not possibly have caused the series of diagonal welts across the child's bottom. Still another cause for suspicion of abuse, or at least neglect, occurs when the child is subject to repeated injuries. The laughing comment by a mother that she "guesses her child is just accident-prone" should not be repeatedly accepted by the teacher, particularly when the level of the child's physical coordination at school does not support this parental conclusion.

Literature on the emotional symptomatology of these children describes their behavior as generally either very passive or very aggressive (Martin, 1976; Mirandy, 1976). Mirandy, reporting on the first 19 preschoolers admitted to Circle House Playschool (a center for abused young children), comments that most of them were very passive and inhibited, and she describes their behavior during their first months in school as

> overly compliant, anxious to please, seeking out permission before initiating any new action. They were quite hypervigilant to the total environment of the pre-school. None of the children demonstrated any separation anxiety in leaving mother, and they were indiscriminately and often physically affectionate with adult strangers. They were oblivious to peer interaction. There was often a hollow smile on a child's face and a complete void of emotions. . . . All lacked true joy. The children rarely expressed anger or pain, they had a poor sense of safety, frequently injuring themselves. Crying was either *highly* infrequent or continual. . . . Most abused children appeared compulsively neat. . . . Play was often noncreative and use of materials highly repetitive, the majority of such children appear to be lacking basic play skills. . . . Most have poor expressive language skills.
>
> It is crucial to stress that most of these traits, such as neatness, perseverance, quietness, compliance and politeness, are valued in the "normal" child and that if the teacher is not aware of the abused child's special needs, these traits may be further reinforced. An abused child has the ability to initially blend in too well and slip by unnoticed.* (pp. 217–218)

Finally, there are some commonsense indications of possible abuse to which the teacher should be sensitive. Children who startle easily and cringe or duck if the teacher moves suddenly may be revealing the fact they are often struck at home. Then, too, it is sometimes evident in conversations with parents that they expect too much or are too dependent on their children, or that they

---

*From "Preschool for Abused Children" by J. Mirandy, in *The Abused Child: A Multidisciplinary Approach to Developmental Issues and Treatment* (pp. 217–218) by H. P. Martin (Ed.), 1976, Cambridge, MA: Ballinger. Copyright 1976 by Ballinger. Reprinted by permission.

know, themselves, they get too angry and "do things they shouldn't" or "wish they hadn't." Such statements are really cries for help and should not be brushed aside on the grounds that everyone feels like that sometimes. These people often benefit from referrals to Parents Anonymous or to local child abuse hot lines.

Evidence of Sexual Molestation

Based on recent findings, it appears that sexual abuse typically begins when the child is between 4 and 12 years old. At the younger ages this is attributed to children's naiveté and sexual curiosity and at the older age to their loyalty, desire to please, and trust of the adult (Wolfe, Wolfe, & Best, 1988). This finding reminds us that we must be alert to the possibility of such abuse when young children complain they "hurt down there" or when genitals are inflamed or when underclothes or odors reveal the presence of pus or infection. Although venereal disease may seem an unthinkable condition in children so young, we cannot afford to blot this possibility from our minds entirely because instances of this have also been reported. When venereal disease is present, it is almost always an indication of sexual abuse (Hibbard, 1988).

Some sexual attacks are perpetrated by strangers, and these are deeply upsetting to families who, nevertheless, often prefer not to report them rather than risk notoriety for the child and endless rehashing of the event with authorities. Of course, if such attacks go unreported, the attacker is immune from arrest, but this can be a difficult and touchy situation to deal with. Actually such an attack is likely to be more extraordinarily upsetting to the parent than to the child until the child picks up his parent's anxiety about it (Layman, 1985). *Referral for psychological help for both parent and child is strongly recommended.*

However, the majority of sexual molestations are *not* perpetrated by strangers. Eighty-nine percent of them are carried out by people the child knows, and almost half of that total are family members (Conte & Berlinger, 1981).

Children need to be empowered to protect themselves, too. They should be taught never to take anything (typically candy) from any stranger and never to get in a car with strangers (even if a stranger knows the child's name). They need to understand the difference between "good touching," such as snuggling and hugging, and "bad touching" that doesn't feel right (i.e., behavior that is inappropriate). They should be assured that their bodies belong to themselves, that it's OK to say "No!" and that, no matter what the threat, they should tell their parents right away if anyone makes that kind of advance to them. In recent years a number of educational programs have become available that offer guidelines in such preventive kinds of instruction. In general they stress, "If an older, more powerful person touches you on any part of the body covered by a bathing suit, except for health reasons, say NO and tell someone" (Kraizer, Witte, & Fryer, 1989).

It can certainly be difficult to teach all this without frightening children too much, so it is important to be definite but matter of fact in order to avoid arousing too much anxiety during such discussions.

Helping the Child's Family After the Referral Has Been Made

Even when teachers have taken the expert's advice, have handled the referral successfully, and the family is receiving help, they must still deal with their feelings about the child and the parent or parents if they believe it is important to retain the child in the center. The relief to parents that such respite provides, as well as the protection and education of the child it affords, means that continuing at school is usually *very* important. Here we are confronted with a paradox. Teachers are more than likely experiencing feelings of revulsion and outrage over what the parents have done, and their impulse may be to judge and punish them. Yet experts tell us that what the parents need, among many other things, is understanding and acceptance—something they may have been woefully short on in their own childhoods. This is because a characteristic of abusers is that many of them are social isolates. The question is, how can teachers possibly behave in a nurturing fashion toward people they regard with aversion?

One thing that may help teachers master their feelings, or at least control them, is to understand the dynamics of child abuse as far as they are understood at the present time. It has become commonplace to assert that abusing adults were abused as children, and it is true that there may be generational links in some instances. However, research now documents the fact that the great majority of abused children do *not* grow up to physically abuse their own youngsters (Starr, Jr., 1982).

Steele (1987) points out that, in many such situations, adequate attachment bonds never formed between the child and the parents and that the parents (or parent) appear to lack a sense of empathy for the child (an inability to put themselves in the child's place). He states also that almost all the parents he has had in treatment felt they had been victims of high parental expectations combined with a true disregard of their own needs as children—a real absence of caring. In essence then, the parent transmits the same unreasonable expectations and severe responses they learned from their first family to their own children. These high expectations combined with a belief in the efficacy of violent punishment, poor impulse control, and a terrible insensitivity to the child's needs and feelings may be reflected in such obvious ways as beating a child or burning her with a cigarette when she cannot stop crying or wetting herself. Or it may be evident in more subtle ways when the parent, seeking the affection he has never had, demands "love" and "caring" from his child by being dependent on her to an unreasonable, unrealistic extent. A mother of my acquaintance, for example, thought it wonderful that her 4-year-old son would get up, feed himself, and then bring her breakfast in bed.

This same dependent behavior is also characteristic of these adults when dealing with other grown-ups. Steele (1987) points out that dependency demands are a noteworthy part of the particularly difficult relationship between social workers and such clients and that these demands must be accepted by the worker to an unusual degree if successful treatment is to occur. It is important for teachers to be cognizant of this trait, too, in order that they may be more tolerant of this emotionally needy behavior than they might otherwise be.

The reader should understand that there is more involved in generating an abusive situation than the basic structure outlined above. For example, Steele (1987) points out that there has to be a precipitating circumstance that tips the scale into violence. It may be alcohol, or a mother's being at home all day with a colicky baby, or the loss of a job, or anything else that arouses feelings of helpless frustration.

Surely anyone who has ever cared for a baby agrees that there are times when young children can be persistently and tenaciously irritating; but several researchers have pointed out that some children appear to especially elicit abuse, whereas others in the same family do not (Freidrich & Einbender, 1983; Kadushin & Martin, 1981). But this fact can in no way be permitted to justify the behavior of an abusing parent.

Then, too, there is a whole additional point of view about abuse that emphasizes sociological causes related to environmental stress, such as unemployment, poverty, and between-parents violence.

The basic generalization that can be safely drawn at this point is that the causes of child abuse are rooted in a complex mixture of personality traits of parents and children combined with various malign environmental influences.

It may also help teachers moderate their reactions to the parents if they realize that only a few of these people are estimated to suffer from serious psychotic disorders (Emery, 1989). It is more realistic to think of the majority of child abusers not as "crazy people" but as people who are often deeply ashamed of their behavior, who have been unable to control it, and who are the products of their own childhoods and environments as perhaps their parents were before them. Many of them lack even rudimentary knowledge of practical, wholesome, child-rearing techniques. The statement that "abusive parents care much for their children but do not care well" about sums it up.

Finally, teachers will benefit by doing some thinking about the reasons why they themselves are so angry over what these parents have done. Certainly part of the reaction stems from the ugly painfulness of seeing a child suffer and from the teacher's commitment to helping children, but it seems to me that there is more to the anger than that. Perhaps some of the reaction comes also because, more than most people, teachers have had to learn to control their own angry impulses toward children. Teachers who are honest with themselves must admit there have been times when they too have felt rage toward a child surge within them. Their anger toward the abusive parent may turn to compassion if they realize that the difference between themselves and those parents at that instant was that they were able to stop in time!

Helping the Child While Her Family Is in Treatment

As Starr (1988) correctly points out, most of the material having to do with the treatment of child abuse deals with the treatment of the adults or amelioration of the family's environment, but the child needs help, too—help that must go beyond the simple level of physical rescue. In addition to whatever may be prescribed in the way of special therapies, nursery school and children's centers are frequently recommended, and Starr places considerable faith in what can be accomplished in that environment to help the child. The points he makes as being desirable ones in caring for abused children are those generally stressed throughout *The Whole Child* as being important in the care of all children.

In particular it is important with such youngsters to emphasize the building of trust and warmth between them and their teachers; steadiness and consistency are invaluable elements of such trust building. The enhancement of self-esteem is also important to stress. Since developmental delays of various kinds appear to be characteristic of these children, a careful analysis of these deficits should be made and attention paid to remediating them when this can be done without undue pressure. (Both Martin [1976] and Mirandy [1976] comment particularly on apparent deficits in perceptual-motor development skills and expressive language ability.)

Above all, every effort should be made to retain the child in school; to maintain consistent, regular contact with the other people who are working with the family; and to be as patient and caring with both the child and her family as possible.

Protecting the Center from False Accusations of Abuse

As the Mcmartin case demonstrated, child care centers need to protect themselves as well as the children against abuse (Wakefield & Underwager, 1988). Some of the recommendations offered by Strickland and Reynolds (1989) that will reduce the possibility of false accusations include

1. Having two adults present with the children whenever possible.
2. Never allowing new or volunteer people to be alone with the children.
3. Establishing a well-publicized open-door visiting policy for parents.
4. Welcoming each child as she arrives, taking a careful look for obvious signs of injury before admitting her, and mentioning these to the parent.
5. Encouraging the director to tour center rooms on a consistent but irregular basis.
6. Making certain the center's insurance policies cover court cases related to abuse.

SUMMARY

Practically all young children experience some form of crisis during their preschool years, and there are many things parents and teachers can do to help them come through these experiences in good condition and perhaps with added strengths. Teachers should encourage parents to *include* rather than exclude the child at such times. They should try not to overreact

to the problem or violate the family's privacy and should offer themselves as a resource of information when the family needs such assistance.

The teacher can help the child and her family by facing the reality of the crisis with her, making certain she does not blame herself for situations she has not caused, keeping her life at school steady and calm, providing play opportunities for her that help her work through and understand her feelings, and helping her anticipate what will happen next.

A discussion of various specific crises of particular concern to children concludes the chapter. Problems related to sending the child to the children's center, the arrival of a new

baby, and hospitalization of either the child or one of her parents are some of these important crises. Additional ones discussed specifically include problems related to divorce, death, AIDS, and child abuse and molestation. Information and recommendations are provided to help teachers and families cope with each of these situations.

QUESTIONS AND ANSWERS

1. One of the youngsters at your school has been scratching her head a lot, and upon inspection, you discover that she has lice. How would you handle this minor but important crisis with the child and her family?

2. The rat at your preschool has been getting fatter and fatter, and it is obvious he has a tumor. The veterinarian pronounces it inoperable—what to do? How would you approach this matter with the children?

3. Keep a list for a month noting all the crises that happen to children and staff during this time. How many were there? How were they handled?

4. Are there some crises children should *not* know about? What might these be, and how would you protect the children from them?

5. Can you recall being jealous of a brother or sister? What did it feel like? Would you han-

dle it as your parents did if you had a child in a similar situation?

6. *Problem:* A child comes to school acting listless and looking pale and washed out. At nap time, when she undresses, you find she has several bruises on her chest and around her arms, and she complains that her neck hurts. There has been a previous occasion where she arrived with a bump on her head and a black eye, which her mother said were due to her falling down a flight of steps. Under these circumstances do you think it wisest to approach the parent with your concern, or are there alternative solutions that should be explored? If the parent, in your judgment, should not be approached, what agencies in your own community would be the most appropriate and effective ones to contact?

SELF-CHECK QUESTIONS FOR REVIEW

Content-Related Questions

1. Are crises always events that happen very suddenly?

2. Name four ways the teacher might help a family that was experiencing a crisis.

3. Explain why it's important to tell children the truth when a crisis occurs.

4. What are the basic principles teachers should remember when helping children work through a crisis?

5. Review the specific crises discussed in the chapter and explain, for each, what a teacher could do to help.

6. Does the author recommend that the teacher confront the parents immediately if he suspects the child has been abused in some manner?

Integrative Questions

1. I've stated that crises *can* strengthen people. Select from your personal experience or from history an individual who experienced a crisis and explain how it strengthened that person.

2. Granted that marrying and starting on a first job both represent a change in life, analyze

other aspects of the two experiences that are similar.

3. A child arrives at school and tells you that his father was in a car accident the night before. Give two examples of what you might say that would tend to deny his concerns about his father. What might you say that would reflect his concern?

4. The talk about the accident continues. The child tells you that his brother socked him and he yelled, and that's what made his father run into the bridge. Predict how you think the child is feeling about his behavior, and then give an example of what you would reply and explain why you chose that particular reply.

5. One of the 4-year-olds caught her foot in a railroad tie, and it was crushed by a switching engine and later amputated. She is due back at school in a week. Basing your plans on recommendations from this chapter, explain how you would handle this situation with the other children in the group.

6. What are some ways the crises of death and divorce are similar, and how might the experiences differ?

7. Do you think that preschool-aged children with HIV infections should be admitted to child care? Why or why not? In your opinion should other parents be informed of that child's condition?

REFERENCES FOR FURTHER READING

Overviews

Brenner, A. (1984). *Helping children cope with stress.* Lexington, MA: D. C. Heath. This very good book unites research with practical recommendations. It includes a chapter on alcoholism and one on ways nontherapists can help.

Garbarino, J., & Stott, F. M. (1989). *What children can tell us: Eliciting, interpreting, and evaluating information from children.* San Francisco: Jossey-Bass. This book reviews many ways adults can be sensitive and perceptive about what children have to tell about themselves and their lives. *Highly recommended.*

Kersey, K. (1986). *Helping your child handle stress: The parent's guide to recognizing and solving childhood problems.* Washington, DC: Acropolis Books. Kersey offers helpful advice on problems and crises ranging from jealousy to alcoholism.

Stress and Resiliency in Childhood

Anthony, E. J., & Cohler, B. J. (Eds.). (1987). *The invulnerable child.* New York: Guilford Press. A refreshing change in emphasis is provided by these authors because they recount several studies where the wholesome emotional process of coping and adapting successfully have been studied.

Honig, A. (1986b). Stress and coping in children: Part 1. *Young Children, 41*(4), 50–63.

Honig, A. (1986c). Stress and coping in children: Part 2. *Young Children, 41*(5), 47–60. Honig identifies many stresses, reviews research, and includes recommendations for coping.

Sheehy, G. (1987). *Spirit of survival.* New York: Bantam Books. I know of no other book that presents the contrasting views of an American adult with a child from another culture so clearly. The book also provides warm testimony of how a Khmer child survived deeply traumatic experiences of war and escape and was still able to make the transition to a new country. Good reading.

Moving to a New Community

Jalongo, M. R. (1985). When young children move. *Young Children, 40*(60), 51–57. A first-rate article on a rarely discussed subject. *Highly recommended.*

Hospitalization

Robertson, J., & Robertson, J. (1989) *Separation and the very young.* London: Free Association Books. *Separation* recounts the long battle the Robertsons fought to improve the care of children enduring separation from their families. It also reviews past and current conditions related to hospitalization and foster care. A very special book.

Trawick-Smith, J., & Thompson, R. H. (1986). Preparing young children for hospitalization. In J. B. McCracken (Ed.), *Reducing stress in young children's lives*. Washington, DC: National Association for the Education of Young Children. Helpful advice is provided for helping children adjust to this crisis.

Divorce

Hetherington, E. M., Stanley-Hagen, M., & Anderson, E. R. (1989). Marital transitions: A child's perspective. *American Psychologist, 44*(2), 303–312. This article provides an excellent review of current literature and findings concerning divorce.

Wallerstein, J. S., & Blakeslee, S. (1989). *Second chances: Men, women, and children a decade after divorce*. New York: Ticknor & Fields. As the title implies, this is, in part, a follow-up of case studies. Teachers will find it particularly interesting because of the down-to-earth analysis of the psychological tasks resulting from a divorce that must be mastered by adults and children.

Death and Dying

Furman, E. (1984). Children's patterns in mourning the death of a loved one. In H. Wass & C. A. Corr (Eds.), *Childhood and death*. Washington, DC: Hemisphere. This is an extraordinarily helpful reference—not to be missed.

Johnson, S. E. (1987). *After a child dies: Counseling bereaved families*. New York: Springer. This book has a wider scope than the title implies. It includes much helpful information on helping children cope with death. *Highly recommended.*

Knowles, D., & Reeves, N. (1983). *But won't Granny need her socks? Dealing effectively with children's concerns about death and dying*. Dubuque, IA: Kendall/Hunt. This is a first-rate primer on how the subject of death can be approached with children of various ages, as well as on helping adults come to terms with their feelings about it. *Highly recommended.*

Oakley, M. (1984). The year we had Aaron. In J. L. Thomas (Ed.), *Death and dying in the classroom: Readings for reference*. Phoenix: Oryx Press. A touching but unsentimental account of how a teacher worked with her second graders to welcome a child with a fatal illness and helped them face the fact of his approaching death. Incidentally, the entire book by Thomas is particularly helpful for the early childhood teacher because it includes several articles focusing on children of preschool age.

Schaefer, D. J. (1987). The status of parent-child communication on death and early-stage grief and loss. In J. E. Schowalter, P. Buschman, P. R. Patterson, A. H. Kutscher, M. Tallmer, & R. G. Stevenson (Eds.), *Children and death: Perspectives from birth through adolescence*. New York: Praeger. This chapter provides excellent advice for parents from an experienced funeral director.

AIDS/HIV Infections

Anderson, G. R. (Ed.). (1990). *Courage to care: Responding to the crisis of children with AIDS*. Washington, DC: Child Welfare League of America. This is really a good, *rare* book. The chapter by Lelyveld on caring for children with AIDS in a day care setting describes the operation of an early childhood setting that serves only youngsters with this condition. It also offers a discussion valuable for teachers in more typical settings who may have to cope with children with these difficulties. *Highly recommended.*

Children Today. (1988). Special report: Pediatric HIV infection. *Children Today, 17*(3), 1–19. This issue of the magazine provides an overview of AIDS and its effects on young children.

Quackenbush, M., & Villarreal, S. (1988). *"Does AIDS hurt?" Educating young children about AIDS*. Santa Cruz, CA: Network Publications. The authors provide guidelines for age-appropriate education on this subject.

Child Abuse

Emery, R. E. (1989). Family violence. *American Psychologist, 44*(2), 321–328. Emery provides an excellent, brief overview of research about violence toward children and women.

Helfer, R. E., & Kempe, R. S. (Eds.). (1987). *The battered child* (5th ed.). Chicago: University of Chicago Press. This is *the* classic handbook for individuals interested in reading more about child abuse.

MacFarlane, K., Waterman, J., Conerly, S., Damon, L., Durfee, M., & Long, S. (1986). *Sexual abuse of young children: Evaluation & treatment*. New York: Guilford Press. This is a comprehensive reference that deals with molestation of preschool children.

Recommended Bibliographies

Bernstein, J. E., & Rudman, R. R. (1989). *Books to help children cope with separation and loss* (Vol. 3). New York: R. R. Bowker. This useful reference includes annotated bibliographies of books for children aged 3 to 16 years covering every kind of separation—the first days at school, divorce, death, AIDS, suicide, homelessness, etc.

For the Advanced Student

Bowlby, J. (1980). *Attachment and loss: Vol. III. Loss: Sadness and depression*. New York: Basic Books. Bowlby discusses the effects of loss for adults and children, paying particular attention to its effects on 2- to 4-year-olds.

Hetherington, E. M. (1989). Coping with family transitions: Winners, losers, and survivors. *Child Development, 60*(1), 1–14. The author describes findings from a landmark longitudinal study of the effects of divorce and remarriage on children. It is of particular interest to preschool teachers because the children in the study were 4 years old at the beginning of the research.

Kübler-Ross, E. (1969). *On death and dying*. New York: Macmillan. This classic work is significant today because it opened the way for study and discussion of a previously taboo subject.

Schlesinger, B. (1985). *The one-parent family in the 1980's. Perspectives and annotated bibliography 1978–84*. Toronto: University of Toronto Press. The title is self-explanatory.

Tzeng, O. C. S., & Jacobsen, J. J. (Eds.). (1988). *Sourcebook for child abuse and neglect: Intervention, treatment, and prevention through crisis programs*. Springfield, IL: Charles C Thomas. A readable overview that includes discussions ranging from trends in legislation to treatment of sexual abuse offenders.

Van Hesselt, V. B., Morrison, R. L., Bellack, A. S., & Hersen, M. (Eds.). (1988). *Handbook of family violence*. New York: Plenum Press. This extensive overview of violence covers all kinds of family-related abuse.

Wass, H., & Corr, C. A. (Eds.). (1984). *Childhood and death*. Washington, DC: Hemisphere. This book covers just about every aspect of death and young children—valuable for the serious reader.

Yawkey, T. D., & Cornelius, G. M. (1990). *The single parent family: For helping professionals and parents*. Lancaster, PA: Techtonic. The authors provide useful reviews of research concerning both male and female single parents, stress, and the learning needs of children. Good research source.

Resources of Special Interest

The Compassionate Friends. P.O. Box 1347, Oak Brook, IL 60521. An organization for parents whose child has died.

The Foundation for Children with AIDS. 77B Warren St., Brighton, MA 02135. (617) 783-7300. The Foundation publishes a bimonthly newsletter, *Children with AIDS Newsletter*, that provides many current resources on this subject.

National Center for the Prevention and Treatment of Child Abuse and Neglect, 1205 Oneida St., Denver, CO 80220.

National Committee for Prevention of Child Abuse, 332 S. Michigan Ave., Suite 1250, Chicago, IL 60604-4357.

Parents Anonymous. Toll-free number outside California is 800-421-0353. An organization for parents who wish to stop abusing their children.

PART FOUR

Fostering Social Development

CHAPTER 8

Developing Social Competence in Young Children

This point was brought home to me by the comments of a distinguished Soviet psychologist, an expert on development during the preschool years. He had been observing in an American day-care center for children of working mothers. The center was conducted under university auspices and reflected modern outlooks and methods in early childhood education. It was therefore with some concern that I noted how upset my colleague was on his return.

"I wouldn't have believed it," he said, "if I hadn't seen it with my own eyes. There were four children sitting at a table, just as in our nurseries. But each was doing something different. What's more, I watched them for a whole ten minutes, and not once did any child help another one. They didn't even talk to each other. Each was busy in his own activity. You really are a nation of individualists."

—Urie Bronfenbrenner (1969)

The social life of a classroom is a slowly evolving, ever-changing phenomenon. Today's enemies are tomorrow's friends. "You can't come to my birthday" frequently turns into "Do you want to play good guys and bad guys?" Teachers play an important role in helping young children learn what it means to be a friend when they demonstrate friendliness, compassion, and respect for children. This model of an adult who is an enabler provides the most meaningful lesson to the young. In an atmosphere of acceptance, children learn to be accepting; in an atmosphere of empathy, children learn to be empathic; in an atmosphere that encourages autonomy, children learn to be autonomous.

—Nancy Balaban (1985)

Have you ever . . .

Thought that young children were just naturally selfish and that nothing could be done about this?

Wondered whether children felt generous *inside* when *you* made them share and take turns?

Wanted to know how to get children to help each other and work together?

If you have, the material in the following pages will help you.

E arly childhood is a time that can be rich in social learnings; it is a dynamic period characterized by many beginnings but few completely attained learnings in the development of social skills and interactions. Although the home is profoundly influential in this area, early childhood teachers can also make a valuable contribution to social development. Before pursuing important social goals for the young children in their care, however, teachers should review the developmental theories of social growth discussed here in order for them to know what social behavior to expect from the children.

DEVELOPMENTAL TRENDS IN SOCIAL GROWTH

In the past many people tended to view young children as generally self-centered human beings who were insensitive and uncaring about others. However, recent research now supports a more encouraging view of young children's nature. Prosocial behavior—behavior intended to help or benefit someone else—begins at an early age. For example, one study by Rheingold (1982) found that all the 2-year-olds included in the research spontaneously helped their mothers complete at least one household chore within a 25-minute period. Another study found that, although most helping behavior in the nursery school happened because the teacher asked for it, during the observations two-thirds of the children also volunteered help of one sort or another (Eisenberg et al., 1987). Moreover, several longitudinal studies reveal that children who are prosocially inclined during the early years continue that behavior as they become older and that children who are helpful in one situation are often (though not always) likely to be helpful in other situations (Eisenberg & Mussen, 1989).

Tables 8.1 and 8.2 summarize some of the many additional social behaviors characteristic of children at various ages.

How Do Children Become Socialized?

Although opinion remains divided about how children become socialized (Eisenberg & Mussen, 1989), social learning theory provides some matter-of-fact explanations of the way it comes about that are helpful for teachers to understand. That theory emphasizes that children learn to become like other people and to get along with them as a result of identifying with and imitating them and also by being reinforced for desirable social behaviors.

Considerable evidence indicates that children learn by observing grown-ups and other children and that, particularly if the person is nurturing and powerful, they will seek to be like the model and imitate his behavior (Bandura, 1986). There is also some evidence that indicates that children are more likely to be influenced by behavioral models than by moral preachments (Bryan, 1975; Rosenhan, 1972), so it behooves teachers to model the behavior they wish to encourage rather than just talk about it or, worse yet, to preach something they do not practice.

TABLE 8.1   Progress indicators of social development, first 3 years*

Behavior Item	Age Expected†
	(Weeks)
Responds to smiling and talking	6
Knows mother	12
Shows marked interest in father	14
Is sober with strangers	16
Withdraws from strangers	32
Responds to "bye-bye"	40
Responds to inhibitory words	52
Plays pat-a-cake	52
Waves "bye-bye"	52
	(Years, months)
Is no longer shy toward strangers	1, 3
Enjoys imitation of adult activities (smoking, etc.)	1, 3
Is interested in and treats another child like an object rather than a person	1, 6
Plays alone	1, 6
Brings things (slippers, etc.) to adult (father)	1, 6
Shows beginning of concept of private ownership	1, 9
Wishes to participate in household activities	1, 9
Has much interest in and watches other children	2
Begins parallel play	2
Is dependent and passive in relation to adults	2
Is shy toward strangers	2
Is not sociable; lacks social interest	2, 3
Is ritualistic in behavior	2, 6
Is imperious, domineering	2, 6
Begins to resist adult influence; wants to be independent	2, 6
Is self-assertive; difficult to handle	2, 6
Is in conflict with children of own age	2, 6
Refuses to share toys; ignores requests	2, 6
Begins to accept suggestions	3
Has "we" feeling with mother	3
Likes to relive babyhood	3
Is independent of mother at nursery school	3
Tends to establish social contacts with adults	3
Shows imitative, "me, too" tendency	3
Begins strong friendships with peer associates, with discrimination against others in group	3, 6

*Abridged from *The Longitudinal Study of Individual Development*, by L. H. Stott, 1955, Detroit: Merrill-Palmer Institute. © 1955 by the Merrill-Palmer Institute. Reprinted by permission.

†As is true in all developmental charts, these ages should be regarded as approximate.

Research indicates that children also learn socially acceptable responses as a result of reinforcement either by adults (Grusec & Redler, 1980) or by peers (Furman & Masters, 1980). This can be negative reinforcement in the form of punishment that may suppress behavior (Parke, 1972), or positive reinforcement in the form of recognition, praise, approval and admission to the group, or other

TABLE 8.2   Progress indicators of social development, ages 4 through 10*

Behavior Item	Age Expected (Years)
Is assertive, boastful	4
Has definite preference for peer mates	4
Tries to gain attention; shows off	4
Tends to be obedient, cooperative; desires to please	5
Seeks approval; avoids disapproval of adults	5
Shows preference for children of his own age	5
Shows protective mothering attitude toward younger sibling	5
Is sensitive to parents' and others' moods, facial expressions	6
Has strong desire to be with father and do things together (especially true of boys)	6
Insists on being "first" in everything with peers	6
Bosses, teases younger siblings	6
Has rich capacity to "pretend" in social play	6
Shows compliance in family relations	7
Desires to be "good"	7
Begins to discriminate between sexes	7
Forms close friendships with one of the same sex; the age of "bosom pals"	8
Sex cleavage is definite; girls giggle, whisper; boys wrestle, "roughhouse"	9
The age of "clubs"	9
Sex differences are pronounced: girls show more poise, more folk wisdom, more interest in family, marriage, etc., and in their own personal appearance	10

*Abridged from *The Longitudinal Study of Individual Development,* by L. H. Stott, 1955, Detroit: Merrill-Palmer Institute. © 1955 by the Merrill-Palmer Institute. Reprinted by permission.

positively reinforcing responses and satisfactions that come from without or within themselves. In addition, a study by Thompson (1944) shows that teachers can facilitate the development of some specific social behaviors by assuming an active, guiding role.

A differing point of view about how children become socialized has been contributed by the developmental interactionists typified by Piaget (1948), Kohlberg (1985), and Damon (1983). Supporters of this theory contend that the intricacies of learning to exist successfully in the social world require explanations that go far beyond the simplicities of reinforcement and modeling theory. They maintain that social development occurs as a result of interaction between people. The cognitive, intellectual learnings that result from the experience of that interaction coupled with maturation produce the widening range of social knowledge and skills necessary for social survival (Edwards & Ramsey, 1986).

It is not only interaction between adults and children, of course, that enhances such learning. Child-child interaction becomes of ever-increasing importance during the early years as groups of children make it clear to their members that they favor positive, friendly behavior and dislike aggression and selfishness (Hartup, Glazer, & Charlesworth, 1967). Such groups rate socially competent children highly (Vaughn & Waters, 1980), and these attitudes, which

It's a good idea to choose equipment that requires more than one child for satisfactory play.

are often frankly expressed, help shape the behavior of the children in the group. Then, too, as children become 4 or 5 years old, they turn to their peers more frequently for help than they turn to adults for it (Stith & Connor, 1962). This aid seeking promotes additional opportunities for positive social interactions and learning to take place.

The quality of emotional attachment between mother and child is an additional important influence on socialization. Children who are closely attached to their mothers tend to be more compliant, that is, conform more readily to the wishes and instructions of their families (Honig 1985c) and are better liked and accepted by their peers (Sroufe, 1983). Securely attached children also tend to be more sensitive to other people's feelings (Ianotti, Zahn-Waxler, Cummings, & Milano, 1987).

Implications for Teaching

As far as teachers of young children are concerned, both of these explanations of socialization have merit since both make it plain that teachers need to do more than sit idly by while the children grow and develop: teachers should assume a role based on active teaching. Since one way children acquire social behaviors is by identifying with models and imitating their behavior, obviously teachers should provide good examples (Moore, 1982). In addition, the relationship between themselves and the child should be based on mutual liking (Bandura & Huston, 1961; Damon, 1977) and warmth (Yarrow, Scott, & Waxler, 1973). Because young boys may tend to imitate male models more readily than they do female ones, it is also desirable to include male teachers and volunteers in the center whenever possible.

Because children learn as a result of positive reinforcement, teachers need to be sure that children receive satisfaction from acting in socially desirable ways. Sometimes this reinforcement will be in the form of a pleasant comment or expression of affection, but a more desirable approach is for the teacher to point out to the child that it feels good to help other people so that the pleasure stems from this inherent reward rather than from a calculated external one.

In addition to these teacher-child interactions, plentiful opportunities for the children to interact together must also be included during the day because so much social learning takes place during play (Asher, Renshaw, & Hymel, 1982; Rubin, 1980). As Hartup (1977) put it, "Children learn many things through rough-and-tumble activity that would not be possible in adult-child relations" (p. 5). This, then, furnishes us with yet another reason for including ample opportunities in the center day for social learning to occur between children.

SUGGESTIONS FOR TEACHING APPROPRIATE SOCIAL SKILLS

When young children want something, be it attention, assistance, or possession of an article, their need is *immediate, intense, and personal*. Their reactions, therefore, to having to wait or to consider the rights of others can be very strong, and it takes patient teaching backed by fortitude to help them develop the ability to wait a little, to control their feelings to a degree, and to consider the rights and desires of others when necessary. All these skills are central to the process of getting along in a social world. If teachers remember to take into account the strength of these immediate, intense, and personal needs as they read about more specific social learnings, they will gain an added appreciation for the magnitude of the child's task in learning to become a socialized human being.

There are, of course, many more social goals than the seven listed here, but these goals have been selected because they are frequently listed by teachers of young children in the United States as being important and as having real social value.

Goal I: Help Children Develop Empathy

Being able to feel what another person is feeling is a valuable social skill for many reasons. As Flavell, Botkin, Fry, Wright, and Jarvis (1968) have said:

Making good inferences about what is going on inside these objects (i.e., other people) permits us some measure of understanding, prediction, and control in our daily interactions with them. (p. v)

Piaget (1926, 1959) long maintained that young children are egocentric and are unable to put themselves in the place of another. But recent reviews of research, as well as the experience of many early childhood teachers, indicate that this egocentrism is not an all-or-nothing condition. As children grow from 2 to 5, they become increasingly able to assume roles and to perceive complex feelings (Grusec & Arnason, 1982; Rubin & Pepler, 1980). With training they can also become more sensitive to other people's feelings and to the effect their actions have on these feelings.

As they become more sensitive to those feelings, they can begin to feel concern for the person who expresses them. In one study (Zahn-Waxler, Radke-Yarrow, & King, 1979) a 17-month-old was reported comforting her mother when she began to cry. I recall my own 21-month-old daughter hugging me and patting my back after I shut the door on my finger, consoling me with tears in her eyes as she murmured, "Tired and hungry! Tired and hungry! We fix! We fix."

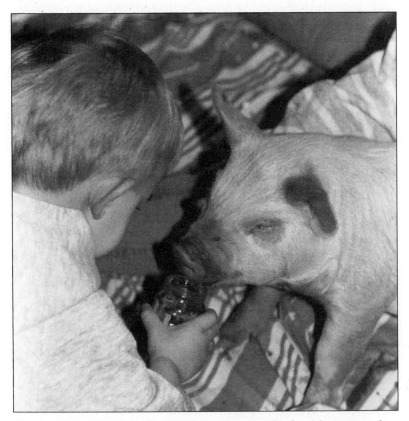

"I just bet that little pig's thirsty," said Bill—a nice example of social concern and empathy.

The interesting thing about Zahn-Waxler and colleagues' study was the consistency of the style of empathic response displayed by youngsters as they developed. For example, a little boy who pushed a child aside to protect another child at age 2, protected his grandmother when someone pushed ahead of her in line when he was 7 years old.

Encourage Role Playing

There are several things the teacher can do to increase the awareness of how it feels to be someone else. One of the most obvious of these is to provide many opportunities for dramatic and imaginative play involving taking roles about what people do. Most nursery centers maintain housekeeping corners, which facilitate the role playing of family life so dear to 3- and 4-year-olds. We have seen that as children reach 4 and 5 years of age, their interest in the world around them increases and extends beyond the family and the school. For these youngsters, enriched role opportunities can be offered with accessories for doctors and nurses, bus drivers, preschool teachers, or anyone else who is familiar to the children. The costumes need not be complete. Indeed it seems wise to leave something to exercise the children's imaginations; but hats are particularly fun, and it is good to have a variety of them representing different characters. For example, our Oklahoma children relish wearing the farm caps given away by seed and feed companies.

Help the Child Understand How the Other Person Feels

Teaching children how other people *feel* in addition to what they *do* is more difficult but not impossible. One virtue of encouraging children to tell each other what they want or how they feel is that in addition to relieving the speaker's feelings, it informs the other child about someone else's emotions and desires. The other important reason for doing this, according to Piaget, is that children are freed of egocentrism by experiencing interactions with other people. He maintained that social conflict and discussion facilitate cognitive growth and the accompanying ability to put the self in another's place (Piaget, 1926; Smedslund, 1966).

Teachers can increase empathy for another's feelings by explaining how a child is feeling in terms that are personal to the observing child, relating the feeling to one they have also experienced. For example:

> Henry, who has just caught his finger in the door, is crying bitterly as the teacher holds him and comforts him. Frankie comes in and stands watching silently, his thumb in his mouth. He looks interested and worried, and as the teacher pats Henry on his back, she explains to Frankie, "Henry hurt his finger in the door. Remember when I rocked on your toe with the rocking chair?" Frankie nods. "Well, his finger feels like that." "It hurt," says Frankie. "It hurt a lot. But we put cold water on it and that made it stop. Let's put his finger in cold water." The teacher says, "That's a great idea! Henry, Frankie is telling you something." Frankie says, "Come on, Hennie, we'll put your finger in water—that will help." And off they go.

Here, the teacher related Henry's feelings directly to what Frankie already knew from his own experience. This helped make the feeling real to him and also encouraged him to use this insight to provide practical comfort for his friend.

During group time, showing pictures of people expressing strong emotions is still another way to build awareness and sensitivity. Children can often identify the feeling (remember, it can be a positive as well as a negative one) and talk over what might have made that person happy or sad and how they might offer help or comfort if that is deemed necessary.

Goal II: Help Children Learn to Be Generous, Altruistic, and Able to Share Equipment, Experiences, and People with Other Children

It is worthwhile to do what we can to develop the ability in children to feel empathy because it appears that this ability to sense someone else's feelings is related at least in younger children to a second prosocial skill as well (Eisenberg, McCreath, & Ahn, 1988): the development of altruistic behavior—behavior performed by a child with the unselfish intention of making another person feel good or happy.

Although much of the research on social development dates back to the 1930s, renewed interest has blossomed in the development of such altruistic behavior (Damon, 1988; Eisenberg & Mussen, 1989). This research has indicated that when affection from the teacher is combined with verbal comments about what is happening, the greatest number of charitable responses is produced in children (Midlarsky & Bryan, 1967). Modeling generosity also increases this behavior (Grusec & Arnason, 1982; Rosenhan, 1972), and paternal nurturing facilitates generosity in boys of nursery school age (Rutherford & Mussen, 1968). Thus we again find support for the recommendation that *teaching a prosocial behavior is accomplished most effectively by a teacher who sets a good example and expresses affection while at the same time clarifying what is happening by discussing it with the children.*

Help Children Learn to Share Equipment

Teaching a specific aspect of generosity such as sharing (a social skill of real concern in the center) requires something more than nurturing and setting a good example. It requires carrying through clear-cut policies directed toward building the generous impulse within the child rather than relying on externally enforced generosity supervised by the teacher. As one of my students put it, "I want him to share from his heart, not because I make him do it."

Many teachers try to teach sharing by regulating turn taking ("You can have it for 2 minutes, then he can have it for 2 minutes"). They seem to interpret sharing as meaning that the child has to hand over anything he is using almost as soon as another child says he wants it. Teachers who enforce taking turns on this basis find they are constantly required to monitor and referee the turn taking themselves. This is not only tiresome *but puts the locus of control and decision making outside the child rather than within him.* It also means that a child may not be permitted to have enough of an experience to be filled up and truly satisfied by it. Such deprivation builds a kind of watchful hunger and avarice that should be avoided. It is still true that one doesn't cure hunger by snatching the bread away.

Rather than struggling to institute the policelike control of the previous procedure, the teacher can establish a climate of generosity by making sure the child has enough of most experiences. Therefore, she does not limit him to two paintings or allow him to ride the trike around the course only three times because another child is waiting. Instead she follows the rule that the child may keep what he has or do what he is doing until he has had enough of it. This means that children do not have to be calculating and defensive about hanging on to things. It also makes settling arguments easier, because it is relatively simple to base decisions on who was using it first and then to state the rule, "Whoever had it first may keep it until he's done with it."

Once assured his own rights and desires will be protected, it becomes much easier for a child to share. When another child is waiting, the teacher can point this out, perhaps saying, "John, when you're done with the swing would you remember to tell Helen? She'd like a turn when you're through." The final step in this process is recognizing when he *does* remember to tell Helen that he is through by commending him and pointing out, "Look how pleased Helen is that you remembered. She's really smiling at you. I guess you're her friend."

It helps in such situations to have enough equipment available that children do not have to wait and wait. Several easels are better than one, and feeling free to improvise in order to meet peak demands will help, too. For example, if painting is suddenly very popular, setting out paint tables might help, or giving children cans of water and old brushes to paint the fence could satisfy their need and reduce waiting.

Help Children Learn to Share the Teacher

Children not only have to learn to share equipment, they also have to learn to share their teacher and her attention with other children. Again, the best model is the generous one, where each gets what he needs rather than each getting an identical, metered amount. This may mean that only one child is rocked while several others play nearby in the block corner rather than every child's being rocked a little. As long as each child receives comfort when he needs it, teachers do not have to worry about whether they are being "fair." They can explain to the children that different people get different special things according to what they need, and then, to remind them that this policy applies to everyone, they can cite examples of times when those children received special attention.

Sometimes individual satisfactions have to be put off, since it is not possible for one child to monopolize the teacher's attention throughout lunch or story time. To handle such demands the teacher might say, "You know, lunch is for everyone to talk together, but I can see you really want to talk just to me. I promise we'll have time for that while I'm getting you ready for nap."

Goal III: Help Children Learn That It Feels Good to Help Others

I agree with the Soviet psychologist's implication at the beginning of this chapter that American children are not encouraged to help their friends as much as they might be. Providing opportunities for children to experience the satisfaction and pleasure that come from helping someone else appears to be a sound way to generate willingness to take prosocial action because the resulting good feeling reinforces the behavior (Bar-Tal & Raviv, 1982). Sometimes helping others takes the form of comforting another child; sometimes it is as simple as passing the cups at snack; sometimes it is as sophisticated as thinking of an excursion everyone will enjoy.

Children should be *encouraged and expected* to help each other. The teacher should emphasize that helping other people is a worthwhile, important thing to do. Here are some simple examples furnished by student teachers* of how this can be clearly and consistently taught at the preschool level when teachers are sensitive to incorporating these values.

Sometimes opportunities to help someone else come up unexpectedly.

---

*My thanks to Mary Kashmar, Lauren Davis, Sandi Coe, and the children for the following episodes.

This episode took place in the hollow block area with some cardboard blocks that have foam packing glued to their insides. Janelle, Timothy, and Jenny were all climbing around on them.

Timothy: "Watch, I can climb out of here by myself." He proceeds to do so.

Me: "Boy, Timothy, you sure can. I wonder if it's just as easy to climb in?"

Timothy: "Yeah, I can. I got to put my leg over first." He climbs in the box, accidentally putting his foot on Janelle's shoulder.

Janelle: "Watch out, Timothy!"

Me: "Whoops! He accidentally hit your shoulder, huh?"

Janelle: "Yeah. Watch me hide in this corner." She does so, and almost gets stuck between the layers of foam. She finally gets herself out. "I almost got stuck!"

Me: "Yeah, you finally slipped your way out."

Jenny (who has crammed herself in more firmly, shrieks): "Help me, teacher. I can't get outta here!"

Me: "Uh oh! Now Jenny's stuck in there. (Jenny continues to twist and struggle.) Janelle, do you remember how you got out?"

Janelle: "Yeah! Here, Jenny, I'll help you." With Janelle pulling and Jenny pushing, Jenny manages to get out.

Me: "Good, you guys! She sure needed you, Janelle!"

Jenny: "Yeah, I was stuck! I woulda spent the night in there!" (She laughs.)

Or sometimes helping takes the form of one youngster's teaching another something.

Roe (aged 4 years, 8 months) is washing and drying some toy animals when Yvonne (aged 2 years, 3 months) walks up, takes up the other towel, and wants to play. Roe takes the towel away from Yvonne and looks at me.

Roe: "Will *you* dry?"

Me: "Yvonne looks like she really wants to play. Why don't you ask her to dry them for you?"

Roe is agreeable to the suggestion.

Roe: "Yvonne, will you dry?" (Yvonne nods her head "Yes." She begins to dry but is having difficulty.)

Roe: (snatching the towel away impatiently) "She's too slow. *You* dry."

Me: "I think you should give Yvonne a chance. Maybe you can show her how to do it."

Roe: "Here, Yvonne, do it this way."

Yvonne catches on quickly and squeals with delight.

Roe: "Wow, now she's waiting for me. I better hurry up."

Me: "You girls work well together. Thanks, Roe."

Soon all the toys are washed and dried.

Or it takes the form of both comfort and help.

At the swings two children were playing and unhooked the seats from the chains. Anathea (playing in the cornmeal) looked over and saw this. "They broke it!" she cried. She seemed really upset by it.

A friend in need.

Earon reached over and patted her on the back, saying, "It didn't break," and went on playing. Then he repeated this about three more times. "It didn't break, Anathea; it didn't break."

I said, "You're right, Earon, but can you tell Anathea what happened?"

"They didn't break it—they just took it off of there. See?" (He goes over and hooks them up.) Anathea smiled at him, and they both went back to playing in the cornmeal.

Note that it is necessary to handle these situations carefully in order to avoid the undesirable effect of comparing children with each other. For example, rather than saying, "Why don't you do it the way Alan does—he's a big boy," it is better to say, "Alan just learned how to zip his coat. Why don't you ask him to show you how it goes together?" Children are often generous about teaching such skills to each other as long as it does not take so much time that they lose patience.

Goal IV: Teach Children That Everyone Has Rights and That These Rights Are Respected by All

I made the point earlier that children have individual needs and that teachers should not hesitate to meet these on an individual basis; that is, they should not interpret fairness as meaning that everyone gets exactly the same thing. But children do, in general, have to conform to the same rules. This impartiality of rule enforcement will help children gradually understand that everyone is respected as having equal rights.

Teach Children That Rules Apply to Everyone

A good example of this may be seen in handling sharing problems. At the beginning of the year there always seem to be one or two children who seize possession rather than asking and waiting for turns. Of course, the teacher often has to restrain such a youngster from doing this. It is particularly important with this kind of child that the teacher also watch carefully and almost ostentatiously protect the seizer's rights when someone tries to take his trike away, so that he sees that everyone, himself as well as others, has his rights of possession protected. This is an effective way to teach fairness and to help the child see what the rule is and that it applies to every child. The message is, "You may not intrude on their rights, and they may not intrude on yours, either." As the year progresses and the child learns to know and apply these rules himself, he will become increasingly able to enforce them without the teacher's help and thus be able to stand more securely on his own in social interaction situations.

Teach Respect for Others' Rights by Honoring Personal Privacy

Children enjoy bringing things from home; it is a cheerful link between their families and the school. Since these items are their personal possessions, it should be their choice whether to share them or not. Even the teacher should ask, "May I see it?" before she reaches out to handle a personal possession.

When he does not choose to share something, the child should put it in his cubby. Keeping his possessions there provides an opportunity to teach privacy and personal rights if the rule is enforced that a child may go only in his own cubby, never in anyone else's without permission. Of course, there will be many transgressions of this rule, but the children will learn to honor this policy over a year's time, just as they will learn to stay out of the teacher's desk and out of the staff rest room if these rules are insisted on.

Goal V: Emphasize the Value of Cooperation and Compromise Rather Than Stressing Competition and Winning

Competition and winning are so much a part of American life that it hardly seems necessary to emphasize them with such young children, and yet many teachers do so because appealing to children's competitive instincts is such an easy way to get them to do what teachers want. It is particularly easy to employ competition as a manipulative device with 4- and 5-year-olds because rivalry increases around that time (Stott & Ball, 1957). Examples include, "Oh, look how well Joan's picking up the blocks; I bet you can't pick up as many as she can!" or "It's time for lunch, children. Whoever gets to the bathroom first can sit by me. Now, remember, no running!" The trouble with these strategies is that they reward children for triumphing over other children and neglect the chance to teach them the pleasure of accomplishing things together.

In Place of Fostering Competition, Model Cooperation and Helping Behavior Yourself

One effective way for the teacher to substitute cooperation for competition is to model it by helping the children herself. Thus when it is time to put away the blocks, the teacher warns in advance and then says, "It's time to put the blocks away. Come on, let's all pitch in. I guess I'll begin by picking up the biggest ones. Henry, would you like to drive the truck over here so we can load it up?" Henry may refuse, of course, but after a pause he will probably join in if the teacher continues to work with the group to complete the task, meanwhile thanking those who are helping.

Teach the Art of Compromise

Being able to compromise is another basic part of learning to cooperate. Four-year-olds love to strike bargains and are often able to appreciate the fact that everyone has gained some of what he wants when a fair bargain or agreement is reached. The following episode, which occurred at our children's center, is a good example of this.

> Jimmy has been pulling some blocks around the play area in the wagon. Finally, tiring of this, he asks the teacher to pull him instead. Just at this moment Alan arrives and wants the wagon. This is too much for Jimmy who, dog-in-the-manger style, suddenly decides he wants to pull it after all. He says, "No, Alan! You can't have it! I'm using the wagon. I'm not done. I want to pull it! Get off!" "My gosh, Jimmy," says the teacher. "Weren't you just saying you wanted a ride? Here's your chance. Weren't you just asking for someone to pull you?" She pauses to let this sink in. "Maybe if you let Alan have a turn pulling the wagon, he would give you the ride you want." She turns to Alan. "Would you do that, Alan?" She turns to Jimmy, "Would that be OK with you, Jimmy?"

Thus the teacher helped the boys strike a bargain whereby both got what they wanted.

As children become more socially experienced, the teacher could encourage the boys to think the situation through for themselves rather than intervening so directly herself. Perhaps she might say at that point, "Jimmy, Alan is telling you he really wants to use the wagon, too. Isn't there some way you can both get something good out of this?" If the boys cannot conceive of any solution, then she can go on to the more obvious approach outlined above.

Teach Children to Work Together

The teacher should also be on the lookout for opportunities where it takes two children (or more) to accomplish what they want. Perhaps one youngster has to pull on the handle while the other shoves the wagon of sand from behind, or one must steady the juicer while the other squeezes. When these circumstances arise, encourage the children to help each other, rather than hurrying too quickly to help them yourself (Adcock & Segal, 1983).

There are also a few pieces of play equipment that require cooperation for success, and a point should be made of acquiring these (Doescher & Sugawara, 1989). Double rocking horses, for example, just will not work if the children do not cooperate and coordinate their efforts; neither will tire swings that are hung horizontally. Some kinds of jump ropes also need at least two people participating for success, as does playing catch.

Goal VI: Help Children Discover the Pleasures of Friendship

Children become more and more interested in having friends as they grow older. By age 5 they are likely to spend more than half their playtime with other children (Valentine, 1956), and friendship bonds between particular children are generally much stronger at this age than they are in younger children (Gottman, 1983). By second grade it is almost intolerable to be without a friend.

As early as the preschool years friendships occur typically between children of the same sex (Hartup, 1989), and those friendships persist over longer periods of time than was previously thought. For example, some recent research by Howes (1988), which studied children in day care situations, reported that some friendships continued for as long as 3 years although most of the children in the study also made new friends, separated from old friends, and ended friendships during that same time.

Ways of demonstrating friendship pass through a number of developmental stages (Youniss, 1975)—moving from a 6-year-old's interpretation of showing friendship by means of sharing toys and material items through the stage of playing together as a primary indication and going on to showing friendship by offering psychological assistance, such as giving comfort when needed.

One list compiled by a group of 4-year-olds at the Institute included the following ways of showing friends they liked them: hug them, kiss them, play with them, have a party, celebrate Valentine's Day, run to them, mail them a letter, sing a song to them, tell a secret, give them a present, and let them spend the night.

Friendship depends on many variables, including similarity of age, sex, propinquity, and sociability, as well as the less readily analyzable qualities of personal attractiveness (Young & Cooper, 1944). There also appears to be considerable variation in the capacity and need for close friendships at the preschool age.

Rubin (1980) reports a study by Lee that was carried out in a day nursery and that found that some children were friendlier and better liked by other children even during the first 6 months of life (Lee, 1973). He reports another extensive study by Hartup et al. (1967) that found that the most popular, sought-after children in nursery school were the ones who most often paid attention to other children, praised them, showed affection, and willingly acceded to their requests. Children who frequently ignored others, refused to cooperate, ridiculed, blamed or threatened others were most likely to be disliked by their classmates. In short, for a child to be included and accepted, he must also include and accept. (p. 52)

It sometimes seems that the only friendships teachers are aware of are the ones they try to break up between older boys who egg each other on into trouble. Yet we must remember there are many desirable relationships, which should be noted and nurtured in the preschool. Having friends is important at every age.

Facilitate Friendliness by Using Reinforcement to Reduce Isolated Behavior

Social interaction between children can be increased by the judicious use of reinforcement. This is a particularly helpful technique to employ with shy, isolated children (Allen, Flekkoy, Sigsgaard, & Skard, 1964). Using this approach the teacher provides some kind of social dividend whenever the child approaches a group or interacts with them but withholds such recognition when the child withdraws and plays by himself. (It is hoped that over a period of time the pleasure the youngster finds in being part of the group will replace this more calculated reward.) Note that this approach is just the opposite of the pattern that often occurs where the teacher tends to "try to draw the child out" when he retires from the group, thereby rewarding with attention the very behavior it is desirable to extinguish.

This child is yearning to join the fun but is too shy unless the teacher lends some support.

Increase the Social Skills of Disliked Children

Another way to foster friendships among children is to teach less likable youngsters social skills that make them more acceptable to the other children.* For example, a child who has learned to ask for what he wants is generally more welcome than one who rushes in and grabs whatever appeals to him (Roopnarine & Honig, 1985).

This can sometimes be best accomplished on a one-to-one basis where children are "coached" by the teacher in more successful ways to behave. Sometimes, for example, it really clarifies things if the teacher simply points out, "You know, when you knock their blocks down, they don't like you. It makes Hank and Charley really mad, and then they won't let you play. Why don't you try building something near them next time? Then maybe they'll gradually let you join them and be your friends."

Particularly with 4-year-olds, simple small-group discussions of what works and what doesn't also help children learn techniques that foster friendly relations. It is, of course, important not to single out specific personalities during these discussions as being either "good" or "bad" examples.

Asher, Oden, and Gottman (1977) report two fascinating studies on the effect of teaching social skills by means of modeling (Evers & Schwarz, 1973; O'Connor, 1972), where a film demonstrating successful methods of entering a group was shown to young children. Observation of their behavior following this film revealed marked and continued improvement in their use of these strategies.

Although such films are not readily available, other ways of presenting models can be developed easily. I recently observed two teachers acting out such situations in brief, simple skits for their 4-year-olds at group time. The children were delighted and readily talked over the skits afterward. Remember when presenting such skits that it is important to avoid the temptation to parody specific personalities in the group.

Pair Children Together

Pairing children sometimes helps them make friends. Coming to school in a car pool or going home from school to play together can cement a friendship, as can doing a number of jobs together or sharing an interest in common. In the long run, though, it is up to the child to form the friendship; all the teacher can do is make such possibilities available to him.

Help Children When a Friend Departs

Sometimes teachers underestimate what it means to a child when a friend moves away, or makes a new friend and rejects the former one, or is transferred to another room. Children often feel quite despondent and adrift when this occurs.

---

*Please refer to the discussion of teaching children alternative ways of getting what they want in the chapter on aggression (chapter 10).

Indeed, in her study of friendships among children in day care, Howes (1988) found that "children who lost a high proportion of friends because the friends moved, and children who moved to new peer groups without familiar peers were less socially skilled than were children who stayed with friends" (p. 66).

When someone is transferring rooms or leaving school, everyone needs to be prepared for the change. This should include the child and his parents and the other children as well. When a child is transferring, we have often prepared everyone by inviting the child for a "visit" to the new room once or twice before making the total switch. And, if we have warning, we often serve a festive snack when a child is moving away. Allowing the departee to choose it adds to the fun.

As in working through any other kind of separation, the leaver's and the left-behinds' feelings of grief, apprehension, and sometimes anger need to be recognized and honored. There is no shame in feeling saddened when a friend has departed, and children should be allowed to mourn this without being ridiculed. They should also be assisted, in an unpushy way, to strike up a new friendship at the right moment.

As Rubin (1980) points out, rejection by a former crony hurts, too. Teachers of young children need to be on the lookout for these happenings, which occur all too frequently, and ease the ache when they can. Sometimes the break is only temporary, but sometimes one of the pair is simply ready to move on. When this happens, about all that can be done is acknowledge the child's feelings and encourage a new beginning with another friend or group.

Goal VII: Help Children Begin to Deal with the Problems of Peace and War

Are Young Children Aware of War?

The possibility of war, particularly nuclear war, is so repugnant to many of us that we shrink from considering it ourselves, much less confronting the possibility that children of nursery school age should trouble themselves about that terrible issue. Yet research indicates that children as young as 4 and 5 are all too aware of the nuclear threat. For example, when Goldenring and Doctor (1983) questioned over 900 students aged 11 through 19, more than half of them reported they had first heard about nuclear weapons between ages 5 and 10. Friedman (1984) found that 12% of the children in her study, which included youngsters aged 4 to 12, included references to nuclear weapons in their play and stories. We cannot assume, then, that young children are unaware of the menace.

What Should We Say to Children When They Have Such Concerns?

Young children translate concerns about war, as with any other fear, into their immediate lives, so their questions will be directly related to their own welfare and will focus on tangible threats such as bombs.

The most effective way to respond to such questions is to ask the children simple questions in reply to theirs in order to find out what they are afraid of. Then they can be reassured that the airplanes flying overhead are not going to drop bombs on their houses and that there will always be someone to take care of them (Carlsson-Paige & Levin, 1985)—statements we all devoutly hope are true! They should also be told that there are many grown-ups working hard to prevent war from happening and that, when they grow up, they can work for peace, too.

Besides Reassuring Children, What Else Can Early Childhood Teachers Do to Help Them Grow Up to Be Peace-Loving Citizens?

Working for peace is indeed a long-term goal to consider when discussing social development; but, in reality, it is not as farfetched as one might think once we realize that we spend considerable time every day teaching young children exactly that—to be peaceful and nonviolent. Every time we teach children to stand up for their own rights without hurting another child, every time we show them alternative ways of getting what they want, and every time we help them understand people from another culture, we are working toward the valuable goal of teaching them to be peaceful grown-ups.

We can work more directly toward this goal by making the concept of peace as concrete as possible by pointing out what it feels like. Carlsson-Paige and Levin (1985) suggest talking about feelings while listening to soothing music, for example, or contrasting parts of stories that are peaceful with parts where people are fighting. We can also commend children when they cooperate and thank them when they have helped someone else, thereby fostering positive (prosocial) interaction.

And, finally, when tempers *do* flare, we can use the methods suggested in the following chapters to help children bring their rage under control without harming other people.

SUMMARY

Social competence develops at a rapid rate during the years of early childhood. Children become socialized partly as a result of identifying with and emulating models they admire and partly as a consequence of reinforcement that encourages or suppresses various kinds of social behavior.

Although children begin to attain many social skills during this period, seven of them were selected in this chapter as being particularly important: developing empathy, learning to be generous, understanding that everyone has rights that must be respected, learning that it feels good to help other people, discovering the value of cooperation and compromise rather than stressing competition, discovering the joys of friendship, and learning the value of using words in place of war.

QUESTIONS AND ACTIVITIES

1. *Problem:* You are working as a teacher in a Head Start center. One of the volunteers is supervising the trike area and is firmly telling each child that he can ride his trike around the track three times and then must give a turn to the next child who is standing in line (there are several children standing there already, making plaintive noises about wanting turns). What would you do to handle this situation on both a short- and long-term basis?

2. During the next week, watch for situations in which a child could be helped to understand another person's feelings or point of view. Using the situations you observed, discuss possible ways that genuine feeling for another person could have been developed from these situations.

3. How much do *you* know about effective ways of entering a group? Make a list in class of strategies adults and children can employ for successful entrée.

4. Have you witnessed examples at your school of children seeking to comfort each other? Share the situation with the class, and explain what the comforter did to help the other child.

5. *Problem:* You agree with the author that children should have a special place of their own to keep their personal belongings while at school. Your school provides hooks for the children's hats and coats and a shelf above that for "storage." What would you suggest could be done to provide private places for each youngster?

SELF-CHECK QUESTIONS FOR REVIEW

Content-Related Questions

1. What are some typical social behaviors of 2-year-olds? How does the social behavior of 3-year-olds differ from that of 4-year-olds?

2. After reviewing the processes by which children become socialized, discuss what the implications are for teachers. Basing your comments on what is known about the process of socialization, explain how teachers can apply that knowledge to further socialize the young children in their care.

3. Review the seven social learning goals and then list some practical "pointers" you would give a new teacher about how each of those goals might be accomplished.

Integrative Questions

1. Review the equipment in the school where you are teaching or have taught and identify which things facilitate social interaction between children. Are there items, for example, that require two people using them at once to make them work effectively? Suggest additional activities you could offer that would be more successful if two or more children worked together to accomplish them.

2. The book discusses two theories about how children become socialized. What do the two theories have in common and how do they differ? Do these differences mean that only one of them is correct and the other wrong?

3. Propose two or three brief skits or episodes the staff might act out that demonstrate social situations and/or social problems for the children to discuss. For example, two people might act out a problem at the snack table where two children both want to get refills. Be sure to think of at least one situation that demonstrates positive social interaction.

4. The woodworking table is very popular this morning—everyone wants to hammer and saw. Carpentry is offered several times a week. Which of the following solutions to regulating participation would you favor? Be sure to explain the pros and cons for following each of the four policies. (a) Allow each

child to make one item and then let the next child have a turn. (b) Have the teacher keep a list and have the children sign up in order for turns. (c) Tell requesters the table is full right now and to please come back later. (d) Suggest to children as they finish that they alert waiters there is space for them.

5. Are there such relationships as desirable and undesirable friendships between children as young as 3, 4, and 5? Identify the differences between them from the teacher's point of view. What might be the advantages from the children's viewpoint of participating in undesirable relationships? Since friendships are important to even young children, should teachers try to "break up" friendships they consider to be undesirable?

REFERENCES FOR FURTHER READING

Overviews

Kohn, A. (1990). *The brighter side of human nature.* New York: Basic Books. Studies from a wide variety of academic disciplines are drawn on in this book to support the contention that humans are more caring and altruistic than pessimists assume.

Moore, S. G. (1982). Prosocial behavior in the early years: Parent and peer influences. In B. Spodek (Ed.), *Handbook of research in early childhood education.* New York: Free Press. Moore reviews research clearly and discusses the antecedents of altruistic behavior, how child-rearing practices can affect its development, and prosocial behavior as related to behavior in the peer group.

Fostering Helping Behaviors

Edwards, C. P., & Ramsey, P. G. (1986). *Promoting social and moral development in young children: Creative approaches for the classroom.* New York: Teachers College Press. Many interesting approaches to furthering social understanding in young children are included here as the authors demonstrate how cognitive developmental theory can be translated into classroom practice.

Katz, L. G., Evangelou, D., & Hartman, J. A. (1990). *The case for mixed-age grouping in early education.* Washington, DC: National Association for the Education of Young Children. The authors make a strong case for the virtues of encouraging cross-age helping behaviors between children.

Encouraging Friendships

Adcock, D., & Segal, M. (1983). *Making friends: Ways of encouraging social development in young children.* Englewood Cliffs, NJ: Prentice-Hall. Although focusing on friendship, Adcock and Segal also provide sagacious comments about helping children with different social styles get along comfortably with other children and with the teacher. *Highly recommended.*

Roopnarine, J. L., & Honig, A. S. (1985). The unpopular child. *Young Children, 40*(6), 59–64. In this readable review of research, the authors examine many factors that influence popularity.

Wolf, D. P. (Ed.). (1986). *Connecting: Friendship in the lives of children.* Redmond, WA: Exchange Press. Many practical suggestions are included for helping preschool children build friendship skills.

Fostering Cooperation in Play

Adcock, D., & Segal, M. (1983). *Play together, grow together.* Mount Rainier, MD: Gryphon House (Distributors). Interesting and unusual activities are proposed for many areas of the curriculum that have the potential for fostering cooperative play.

Sobel, J. (1983). *Everybody wins.* New York: Walker. This book is full of delightful ideas for cooperative, noncompetitive games suitable for nursery school or kindergarten. *Highly recommended.*

Working Toward Peace

Carlsson-Paige, N., & Levin, D. E. (1985). *Helping young children understand peace, war, and the nuclear threat.* Washington, DC: National Association for the Education of Young Children. In addition to an overview, the authors provide classroom suggestions and bibliographies—a sensible, age-appropriate approach.

McGinnis, K., & Oehlberg, B. (1988). *Starting out right: Nurturing young children as peacemakers.* Oak Park, IL: Meyer, Stone. A thoughtful presentation of ways of encouraging peaceful solutions to difficulties is presented here.

For the Advanced Student

Adler, P. A., & Adler, P. (1988). The carpool: A socializing adjunct to the educational experience. In G. Handel (Ed.), *Childhood socialization.* New York: Aldine De Gruyter. This delightful bit of research investigated the potential social learnings and contratemps available in the social life of the car pool. It deals with 5-year-olds and older.

Eisenberg, N., & Mussen, P. (1989). *The roots of prosocial behavior in children.* New York: Cambridge University Press. This well-written, fairly brief book sums up what is known about the development of prosocial behavior from a variety of aspects. *Highly recommended.*

Grusec, J. E., & Lytton, H. (1988). *Social development. History, theory, and research.* New York: Springer-Verlag. This is a thorough, comprehensive review of social development useful for advanced students.

Hartup, W. W., & Rubin, A. (Eds.). (1986). *Relationships and development.* Hillsdale, NJ: Lawrence Erlbaum. These articles cover many different aspects of relationships from attachment to new relationship styles.

Other Resources of Particular Interest

Concerned Educators Allied for a Safe Environment (CEASE). Peggy Shirmer, 17 Gerry St., Cambridge, MA 02138. This national network publishes a quarterly newsletter of interest.

CHAPTER 9

Helping Young Children Establish
Self-Discipline and Self-Control
But what if she won't do what I say?

Giving up coercive techniques to control children is the hardest task for many teachers. Giving up personal control sometimes feels to the teacher as though she is giving up responsibility. However, if child autonomy is to be fostered, the teacher has to give the child freedom to control himself. This is scary because it is hard to know whether children can [do this]. . . . Children accustomed to being regulated by adults do not know how to take responsibility for their actions at the first opportunity for autonomy. Developing children's autonomy takes time. The teacher's development of confidence in children's ability also takes time.

—R. DeVries and L. Kohlberg (1990)

Have you ever wondered . . .

How to help children control themselves instead of depending on other people to control them?

How to make it easier for children to behave in acceptable ways?

What to do when a child won't stop doing something she shouldn't be doing?

If you have, the material in the following pages will help you.

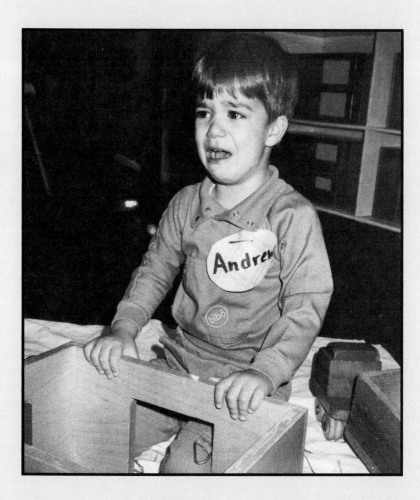

Because discipline worries beginning teachers the most, it is usually the subject they want to discuss first when they begin teaching. Sometimes this is because they fear physical aggression or that the children will not like them, but more frequently they fear losing control of the situation because they do not know what to do next. So when teachers say fervently that they want to discuss "discipline," what they usually have in mind is how to control the children or, as one forthright young student put it, "how to get the kids to do what I want."

TWO BASIC GOALS OF DISCIPLINE

Although "getting the kids to do what I want" is undeniably part of the package, should it be all that is encompassed by the concept of discipline? The teacher should also have in mind the higher goal of instilling inner self-controls in the child in place of teacher-maintained external ones. Therefore, every discipline situation not only should achieve a workable solution to the current crisis (and this will be discussed in the second part of the chapter) but also should seek to interiorize self-control.

ESTABLISHING INNER CONTROLS: EGO STRENGTH AND MORAL DEVELOPMENT

Why Does Self-Control Matter?

Self- rather than "other" control is desirable for a number of reasons: people who can control themselves are trustworthy and responsible. They can be counted on to do the "right" thing whether or not a police officer is standing on the corner watching to see if they run the red light. Because the control is internal, it is more consistent; and most valuably for mental health, the individual who is "inner-controlled" makes choices in his own behalf. This is the opposite of the neurotic personality who feels powerless, unable to control what happens to himself, and who sees himself as "done to" and in the power of others.

Granted that such internalization is desirable, the question that remains for early childhood teachers to answer is how can they begin to establish these inner controls in such young children. How can they teach them not only to *know* what is right but to *do* what is right? Teachers must realize that this is a long process taking many years, and it rests on the gradual development of ego strength and moral judgment. A strong ego enables the child to control her impulses, and moral judgment (telling right from wrong) enables her to decide which impulses she must control.

Building Ego Strength

Fraiberg (1977) describes the ego as being the part of the personality that has to do with the executive and cognitive functions of the individual and that also regulates the drives and appetites. Obviously it is this part of the personality we will want to strengthen in order to make it available to the child to help her control her impulses.

One way to do this is to *increase the child's feelings of mastery by giving her many opportunities for making decisions.* However, the choices offered must be appropriate and not too difficult. I recall a 4-year-old who was asked by her divorcing parents to decide which parent she wished to live with—an intolerably difficult choice for a child of that age to make.

On the other hand, the preschool day abounds with opportunities for decisions well within the ability of most 3- and 4-year-olds to handle. The catch is that *the teacher must be prepared to honor the choice once the child has made the decision.* Such questions as "Do you want dessert?" "Would you rather finger-paint or play with the blocks?" or "Would you like to pass the napkins today?" are examples of valid choices because it is all right if the child chooses to refuse. Unfortunately, many teachers use "Would you like . . . ?" or "Would you please . . . ?" or "OK?" as a polite camouflage for conveying an order. Thus they inquire, "Let's get on the bus, OK?" or "Would you like to put on your sweater?" Young children are likely to retort "No!" when asked such questions, and then the teacher is really stuck. It is better not to ask, "Let's get on the bus, OK?" if the child has to get on the bus anyway, but to try saying, "The bus is here, and it's time to go home. Where do you want to sit?" or "It's cold today. If you want to go out, you will need to put on your sweater." In short, honor choices when given, but give no choice when there is no valid opportunity to make one.

It is also important to see to it that the child experiences the consequences of her decisions. Perhaps the reader will recall the example in the chapter on routines where the child who elects to skip snack is not permitted to change her mind at the last minute. Abiding by decisions once they are made teaches youngsters to make responsible choices.

Increase the Child's Feelings of Being a Competent, Worthwhile Person

The feelings of self-esteem generated by competency also make the ego stronger. The child who thinks well of herself because she is competent is in a favorable position to assume command and control of herself because she sees herself as being effective and strong (Faber & Mazlish, 1980).

Unfortunately some children are noticed only when they do something wrong. This continual negative relationship with the teacher does not enhance their feelings of self-worth. Even the "worst" child in school does not misbehave all the time. A considerable part of her day is spent in acceptable activities. If her self-esteem and self-mastery are to remain intact, it is vital that she receive credit for her good behavior as well as control for her transgressions.

However, as we saw in the chapter on self-esteem, the most desirable source of self-worth stems not from the opinion of the teacher, but from the acquisition of competencies. These may range from being able to walk the balance beam to knowing effective strategies for worming one's way into a play group. It does not really matter what the competency is, as long as it contributes to the child's perception of herself as being an able person who is in command of herself.

Encouraging Moral Development: Fostering the Interiorization of Conscience

Another aspect of helping children establish inner controls has to do with the establishment of conscience and instilling a sense of what is right and wrong. Conscience (sometimes termed the *super-ego*) can be described as that inner voice that tells us what we should or should not do. Theoretical arguments continue over how this voice is instilled (Kagan & Lamb, 1987), but Hoffman's comprehensive reviews of research on this subject (1970, 1975), which have been further supported by Edwards (1980), indicate that growth of conscience is facilitated most strongly by the presence of two factors, both of which can be easily used by parents and teachers. One of these is the presence of affection and a nurturing relationship between the adult and the child—a condition that should generally pertain in school as well as in the home. This factor was identified as being present in about half the studies reviewed by Hoffman. The second factor, which appears to be even more potent since it was more

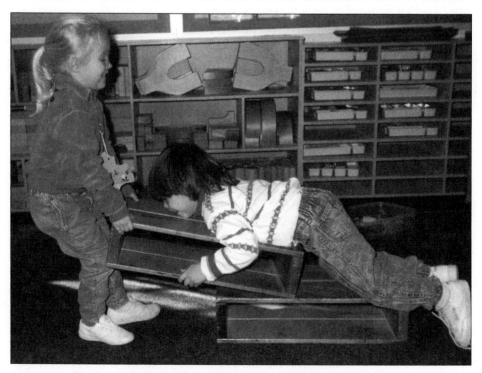

Keeping aggression under control is a sign of developing ego strength.

consistently present in the reported studies, is the use of what is termed "induction techniques" (Maccoby & Martin, 1983). In simple language this just means giving a child a reason why she should or should not do something. For example, one might say, "I can't let you hit Ginny with the block—it hurts too much" or "We always flush the toilet so it's fresh for the next person." Another more advanced example might be "We have to put the candy back. We didn't pay for it. We always have to give the clerk money when we take something. That's how people who work here get money to buy what *they* want." Surely such an explanation is preferable to the "You're a bad, naughty girl for stealing that candy" that is so frequently heard.

The examples of reasons given in the preceding paragraph have another quality that also appears to help children grow toward moral maturity. Each example gives the child what Bearison and Cassel (1975) term a "person-oriented" and Hoffman (1985) terms a "victim-oriented" reason for behavior. "Victim" here refers to the other person involved in the situation. Saying that "We flush the toilet because it leaves it fresh for the next person" rather than saying "Remember the rule, flush the toilet" encourages children to think of other people's well-being. In other words, it begins to teach them perspective taking—thinking of the other person and taking her point of view or perspective into consideration. Even though young children are not skillful at doing this, they can begin to learn such consideration. It is certainly a better approach than teaching blind obedience to a rule.

Moral Development Occurs in a Number of Stages

There is one more fascinating thing about the growth of conscience that the teacher needs to understand. It is that children and adults have very different ways of thinking about what is right and wrong (Maccoby, 1980). The works of Damon (1988), Kohlberg (1985), Piaget (1932), and Rest (1983) reveal that there is a developmental sequence to moral development just as there is a sequence in the development of reasoning. Ideas of what is "right" or "wrong" vary from culture to culture too (Shweder, Mahapatra, & Miller, 1987).

Progression from one stage to the next is a result of interplay between cognitive maturation and social experience (Damon, 1988). Although some research indicates that children who are on the verge of passing on to the next stage may be influenced by teaching (Turiel, 1973), in general such growth is thought to be the result of *con*struction by the child rather than direct *in*struction by the teacher. Nor should it be assumed that everyone attains the final level. Some adults remain at stage 1 or 2, and many at stage 4 (Kohlberg, 1985).

The interesting thing about the stage theory of moral development is that as a result of her moral developmental level the conscience of a child may tell her something is wrong when an adult's conscience tells him the same action is right. Examples of this will be presented later in this chapter. This developmental difference can certainly confuse teachers if they do not understand how young children view right and wrong and do not make allowances for their differing points of view.

Stages of Moral Development*

A. Preconventional level

Stage 1: Unquestioning obedience based on external power and compulsion. Right or wrong is what is rewarded or punished. Right is "following the rule." Rules are accepted unquestioningly. Child has not "decentered, and self-interest is a strong motivator in his decision making." Moral judgments are based on observable, physical consequences rather than on intentions of person.

Stage 2: Instrumental-relativist orientation. Right or wrong is what instrumentally satisfies own needs and sometimes the needs of others. "Back-scratching" kind of reciprocity is understood. One behaves well in order to get what one wants.

B. Conventional level

Stage 3: Right behavior is what pleases others. Behavior is often judged by the intention behind it. ("She means well."): good girl/bad girl idea of morals.

Stage 4: Law and order. Right behavior is doing one's duty, showing respect for authority, following rules because they are "right."

C. Postconventional, autonomous, or principled level

Stage 5: Social-contract legalistic orientation. Right is a matter of personal values, which have been examined and agreed on by the whole society. Laws are not absolute but subject to modification. The U.S. Constitution is an example of this level of moral development.

Stage 6: Universal ethical principle orientation. Right is defined by individual conscience in accord with self-chosen, ethical principles of justice, reciprocity and equality of human rights, and respect for dignity of human beings as individual people. (Golden Rule is an example of this.)[†]

Stages 1 and 2: Implications for teaching.   Young children define "right" as being what the rule says. A rule is right because a parent or teacher says it is right. This does not mean children necessarily obey the rule (Power & Reimer, 1978), but it does mean that they do not reason and question whether the rule itself is fair or just.

Nor do young children make allowances for what someone intended or meant to do (Maccoby, 1980). They render judgment only on the observable consequences. (This is similar to their reasoning in the realm of conservation of materials—seeing is believing.) As Piaget (1932) pointed out, children of preschool age conclude that the child who has broken more cups has done a greater wrong than the child who has broken only one, regardless of the reason for the breakage (that is, preschool children reason that the child who breaks several cups while helping her mother should be punished more than the child

---

*Based on Kohlberg (1976) and Turiel (1973).

†Kohlberg has stated he no longer differentiates clearly between stages 5 and 6 (1978).

who breaks a single cup while stealing cookies). Older children would, of course, reach a quite different conclusion, based on the fact that stealing itself is "bad," whereas an adult who had advanced to a still higher moral level might decide that the fact the child was starving negated the "sin" of theft because preserving human life is a greater good.

Understanding that young children take results rather than intentions into account may help the teacher comprehend the continuing resentment expressed by a child toward someone who has knocked her down, even after the teacher has explained it was an accident. Despite the teacher's interpretation, it remains difficult for her to grasp the transgressor's harmless intention when she is experiencing the actual result.

Four-year-olds approaching stage 2 are beginning to understand a very simple form of reciprocity as justice—"I do something for you, and you do something for me." The implication for teaching (and it is borne out by experience) is that this is a practical time to introduce the concept of bargaining as an alternative to simply demanding what one wants. An obvious example of this that I heard recently was a child who bargained, "Well—I'll let you sit in the cradle, but you can't 'waa-waa' all the time!" (A less obvious example occurred when a 5-year-old said to an importuning 3-year-old, "Well, OK. I'll tell you what—you *can* be the leader, but in *this* gang, leaders always go at the end of the line!")

Finally, Piaget and Kohlberg emphasize that the young child is centered on herself and that because of this egocentrism she has great difficulty imagining herself in the shoes of another. And yet, research also indicates that young children who are taught by parents and teachers using other-person-oriented rather than rule-oriented reasons for behavior tend to be more mature morally than are youngsters who are simply provided with arbitrary rules. This finding implies that young children must have at least a partial ability to take another person's point of view. Meanwhile, as debate and investigation continue about just how much children aged 3 and 4 are able to decenter, early childhood teachers are left with the desire to teach children to be sensitive to the way other people feel and to teach them to take those feelings into consideration (a very basic aspect of moral behavior).

The problem is, how to accomplish this. The answer is that the simpler the explanation is, the better. I have often heard well-meaning preschool teachers scold a child who has just tossed sand into another youngster's face by saying, "Stop that! How would *you* like that if *you* were her? What if *you* were Maggie and a little girl threw sand in *your* eyes? How would *you* feel then?" This "what if *you* were" approach is so complicated and involves so much role switching it leaves a 3- or 4-year-old bewildered.

The same lesson can be taught much more effectively by making a simple change in approach that is person oriented and related to the sand-thrower's own experience as well. This teacher might begin by saying "Stop that. Keep the sand down! Throwing sand hurts too much when it gets in Maggie's eyes. Remember when Jim threw sand in your eyes? Remember how that hurt? Well, that's how Maggie's eyes feel now." This "remember when" approach may not sound like a major difference, but it is much easier for children to understand, and it does help children learn to think about how their actions affect other people's feelings.

PRACTICAL THINGS TO DO TO MAKE IT EASIER FOR CHILDREN TO BEHAVE IN ACCEPTABLE WAYS

It is evident from the foregoing discussion that establishing ego strength and conscience in young children is a complex and lengthy task that can only be begun in the early years. While this is in process, the teacher must be willing to assume control when necessary, always bearing in mind the ultimate goal of helping children achieve responsibility for themselves. There are many practical ways to go about doing this, as well as some things teachers do that make discipline of any kind more difficult.

No one intentionally makes trouble for themselves by creating a poor environment; yet so many of the situations in the following list happen in centers and nursery schools from time to time that it seems appropriate (as well as fun) to begin by pointing them out.

1. Make the children wait a lot and expect them to sit quietly while they wait, preferably like little ladies and gentlemen with their hands in their laps and their feet on the floor.

2. Be inconsistent: let the children ride their trikes on the grass on days when you don't feel up to par, but take their trikes away when you're feeling better, because it's against the rules to ride on the grass.

3. Be unreasonable: never make allowances for children who are (a) tired, (b) hungry, (c) coming down with something, or (d) getting over something. It will also help ruin the day to have a great many arbitrary rules that are never explained although rigidly enforced.

4. Decide that the way to let children learn for themselves is never to intervene; pay no attention to the possibility that the younger, smaller children are being bullied and that some older ones are actually learning that "might makes right."

5. Be consistent: always punish the children by doing the same thing to them. For example, no matter what they do, make them sit in the office, or don't let them have dessert at lunch.

6. Give up halfway through a confrontation, and let the child run off. After all, you're not supposed to leave your work station.

7. Lose your temper and yell at the children. This will frighten them into behaving and will make you feel better.

8. Strike a child; pinch her or jerk her arm when no one is looking. This will also frighten her badly, but maybe she'll behave after that.

9. Ignore the problem; just send the troublemaker off to play with the new teacher. It will help him gain experience.

10. Talk too much. Confuse the child: moralize, shame, or embarrass her, or warn her that you're going to tell her mother! This will help her understand the consequences of her actions and set an example of verbal control for her.

When behaviors such as these are singled out, it is clear how undesirable such approaches are. Yet they are more common than one would wish them to be in many schools, probably because they reflect discipline practices many teachers experienced in their homes while growing up. However, if the following principles are put into practice, the need for these more unproductive methods will be reduced.

Positive Approaches to Discipline

Besides fostering ego strength and the development of conscience, there are two other fundamental things to do to help young children behave in acceptable ways and to improve the ease and quality of discipline and control in the group: (a) prevent discipline situations when it is possible to do so and (b) know what to do when a crisis occurs.

Ten Practical Ways to Stop Discipline Situations Before They Start

Reward behavior you want to see continued; don't reward behavior you wish to discourage.   Children (and adults) repeat behavior from which they obtain satisfaction. This reward does not necessarily come in the form of payoffs of chocolate chips or gold stars. Whether teachers realize it or not, they use rewards every time they say "thank you" or "that's a good job" or even when they smile at a child. The value of this technique, which is one form of behavior modification called *positive reinforcement,* has been well proven (Hilgard & Bower, 1966; Walker & Shea, 1991). There is no doubt that it is an effective way to deal with recurring discipline and behavior problems. Therefore, when undesirable behavior persists, it is a good idea to take a look at what the child is getting out of it. Preventing the payoff can help eliminate the behavior. It is also effective to note positive actions on the part of the children and to respond to them with pleasure, since this positive reward, combined with the pleasure inherent in successful accomplishment, is a potent reinforcer.

While on the subject of reinforcement, I want to comment that I agree with Caldwell (1977) that it is not effective to "extinguish" aggressive behavior in young children by simply ignoring it. In my experience such behavior does not subside when ignored—apparently because children interpret this laissez-faire attitude as permission. Not only that, one cannot overlook the fact that there are inherent gratifications (payoffs) in attacking other children; these range from simply seizing what is desired to enjoying hitting someone—if you are angry, hitting somebody feels pretty good. For these reasons, *it is important to take more assertive action and stop undesirable behavior* rather than let it slip past on the grounds that it will go away if no attention is paid to it.

Doing things together breeds positive social skills.

Be persistent.   When working with a child who repeats undesirable behavior, remember that, in addition to analyzing and preventing the payoff, it takes time to change behavior. Sometimes teachers try something for a day, or even just once or twice during a day, and expect such a short-term change to work miracles. When it doesn't, they give up. Don't give up! Be consistent and persistent. It often takes repeated experience for learning to take place, but children can and *will* learn if you stick to your guns!

Consistently position yourself so that you are able to see a large area of the room or play yard at the same time.   All too often beginning teachers focus on only a small group of children at a time. This is partly because it is less scary to do this and partly because many teaching lab situations unintentionally encourage this by assigning specific areas to students for supervision. But no matter what the underlying reason is for such behavior, it is wise to teach oneself to avoid the kind of "tunnel vision" this promotes.

Learning to position yourself close to a wall or fence, for example, means that you have a clear view of a larger area, just as sitting at a table so that you face most of the room makes it easier to scan the larger space (providing you remember to look up occasionally from what you are doing). Such scanning has been shown to be one of the qualities that differentiates good classroom managers from ineffective ones (Anderson, Evertson, & Brophy, 1979).

Teachers who circulate within the supervision area instead of remaining planted in one place are also more likely to be aware of what is going on. This awareness can help children avoid many unnecessary confrontations and misunderstandings by providing opportunities for timely interventions and positive teaching to take place instead of tears and fights.

When trouble repeats itself, analyze the situation and try changing it rather than nagging the child. When something happens over and over, in addition to checking up on payoffs, the teacher should also think about changing the situation instead of the child. For example, instead of telling a restless youngster to be quiet all the time, it might be better to let her leave after hearing one story, to ask a volunteer to read to her alone, or even to let her play quietly nearby during story time until she becomes more interested and can be drawn gradually into the group.

Emphasize the positive rather than the negative; always tell the child the correct thing to do. This habit can be formed with a little practice. When using positive directions, rather than saying "Don't get your feet wet" or "Stay out of that puddle," say "Walk around the puddle." Or say "Put the sand in the dump truck" rather than "Don't throw the sand." This technique is desirable not only because it reduces negative criticism, but also because it directs the child toward something she can do that is acceptable.

Warn ahead of time to make transitions easier. The teacher should anticipate transitions with the children a few minutes before the activity is due to change. He might say, "It's going to be lunchtime pretty soon. I wonder what we're going to have?" Or he might warn, "There's just time for one more painting. Then you can help me wash the brushes, and we'll have a story." Warning ahead gives the children time to wind up what they are doing. Sometimes just walking around the yard and commenting here and there that soon it will be time to go in will serve this purpose. It takes the abruptness out of the situation and makes compliance with routines much easier for the children.

Arrange the environment to promote positive interactions. Interest is continuing in studying the ecological relationship between children and their environments (Bronfenbrenner, 1979; Pence, 1988; Prescott, 1981; Smith & Connolly, 1980), and some of these findings about the interconnections are helpful to know about when planning ways to prevent discipline situations from occurring.

Rohe and Patterson (1974) found that a combination of many children in a small space (a high density of children) combined with few resources produced more aggression and more destructive and unoccupied behavior. In another study, Smith and Connolly (1980) found that reducing square footage per child to 15 square feet also produced more aggression, more parallel (rather than social) play, less rough and tumble play, and less running (and even walking) activity.

The conclusion from such studies seems obvious. If enough space is provided for the children to use, discipline problems will be reduced accordingly.*

---

*Note that these studies also have significant implications for licensing regulations.

The area illustrating this situation that comes most glaringly to my mind is the block area of many preschools. Although interest can run high in this activity, all too often blocks are cramped into a corner where there is no possibility for play to expand as interest dictates. Moreover, unless encouraged to carry blocks a little distance away from the storage shelves, children tend to crowd as near the source of supply as possible. This combination of restricted space plus the crowding near the shelves at the beginning of a project promotes territorial struggles and consequent discipline situations (Allen & Hart, 1984).

On the other hand, if the block area is planned so there is room to spread out when enthusiasm mounts and if children are taught to start their projects 2 feet away from the shelves, the likelihood of positive interaction in play is enhanced.

Another matter-of-fact thing to do about room arrangement that decreases the necessity to restrain and discipline the children is separating areas with high levels of activity from each other in order to provide protection. In one situation where I taught, only one large open area was available for block and large muscle activity. Noisy chaos was often the result in winter weather when children tried to use the same space for both activities at the same time. Students and staff dreaded working there.

With some rearranging, two widely separated areas were created. The result was that block play and the wonderful social-cognitive learnings that accompany it increased dramatically. The second area was then available for large muscle activities and for dance and group time. The entire tone of the group of 4-year-old children became calmer and more pleasant.

Attention to traffic patterns can also increase constructive participation and reduce problem behavior. When the large rooms frequently used in child care situations are broken up with dividers so that children are physically detoured around activity centers, the temptation to disrupt what other children are doing is reduced. Such dividers can be low bookcases, bulletin boards, or even a Japanese futon. Defining areas by using rugs for this purpose also helps guide children's feet away from trouble in a more subtle way.

A final facet of environmental planning that will help reduce the need for discipline is the provision of quiet places to which children can retreat when they feel the need for such refreshment. We adults know that constantly being with large numbers of people is tiring, but we tend to forget that it is tiring for children, too. Cozy corners for books, a quiet retreat with some simple manipulative activity, or simply an area to stretch out and do nothing in can meet this need and reduce the fatigue and irritability that so often lead to loss of self-control.

Have as few rules as possible, but make the ones you do have stick. Unless the teacher is watchful, rules will grow up like a thicket around each experience. But if situations are reviewed from time to time, unnecessary restrictions can be weeded out.

On the other hand, some rules are genuinely necessary, and their enforcement is desirable not only because research shows that establishing firm limits, coupled with warmth and a simple explanation of the reason behind the rule, enhances children's self-esteem (Coopersmith, 1967; Honig, 1985a, 1985b), but also (as we have seen earlier in the chapter) because it increases their ability to establish inner controls.

The problem is to decide, preferably in advance, which rules are really important. Students in particular seem to have trouble in this area—sometimes treating relatively minor infractions such as not saying "please" or "thank you" as though they were major transgressions, while dealing indecisively with more serious misbehavior such as tearing up picture books or running out the front door without an adult. In general, the most serious infractions of rules are those related to hurting other people, hurting oneself, or destroying another person's property. If a reason is not easy to come up with, it may be a sign that the rule is not important and could be abandoned.

Although we adults regard following rules as being important, there is another interesting way to think about them—that is, from the point of view of the child. In an amusing and enlightening analysis of that point of view, Corsaro (1988) selected several rules enforced in a nursery school he observed: running was OK outdoors but not inside; guns and shooting were not permitted; bad language was not permitted; and everyone had to participate in cleaning up.

Terming the children's evasion of these rules "the underlife of the nursery school," Corsaro (1988) identified common ploys such as pretending not to hear the clean-up time signal and continuing to play, or developing indoor games such as Policeman that required using guns and running to catch the bad people. He maintains that these responses of the children serve more than one purpose. Obviously, they *do* provide ways of getting around rules, but they also foster the children's ability to function in the culture of their peers. Although this bonhomie is inconvenient for the teacher, it is important to realize that being able to function in their peer group becomes of ever-increasing importance as the children grow older. Mildly "beating the system" at nursery school is one of the ways they learn to do this.

When supervising children, plan ahead. Try to anticipate the point where the children will lose interest or the play will fall apart and have alternatives ready to propose that will help the play continue to flourish. An insightful teacher might think, "Now, if I were she, what would I like to do next with those blocks and cars?" Perhaps it would be getting out the arches or the wood strips to make a garage, or maybe it would be constructing ramps for the cars to run down. Tactfully posing several possibilities to the children will serve to continue play and to lengthen concentration as well as keep the children happily occupied and out of trouble.

Keep the day interesting. To combat idleness, the center day needs variety—not only variety of pace to avoid the fatigue that leads to misbehavior, but also a variety of things to do to maintain interest and fun and to keep the children busy in productive ways. Accomplishing this requires planning and sensitivity, but it is well worth the investment of effort.

Ten Things to Do When a Crisis Occurs

Of course, the ideal to work toward even in crisis situations is to teach the children to solve their own problems, since in their adult life they will not always have a teacher present to arbitrate differences. The situations discussed in the following sections, however, are ones where it is evident that the child has to have help to control herself and to be able to take action that is socially acceptable. Even in these situations the focus should never be on the God-like powers of the teacher to bring about justice, but on development of the child's ability to do this for herself.

Be decisive; know when to step in and control misbehavior. Inexperienced teachers are often unsure of when they should interfere and when they should let children work the situation through between themselves. As I said earlier, the general rule of thumb is that children should not be allowed to hurt other people (either children or grown-ups), to hurt themselves, or to destroy property. This policy leaves considerable latitude for noninterference, but it also sets a clear line for intervention. An occasional teacher is particularly unsure about whether he should allow children to hit him or kick him as a means of "getting their feelings out." Children should not be allowed to attack adults any more than adults should attack children. Aside from the fact that it hurts and cannot help making the teacher angry, permitting such attacks makes the child feel guilty and uncomfortable. She really knows she should not be allowed to do it.

Taking time to recognize and respect a child's feelings is an essential step in maintaining good discipline.

The best way to prevent physical attack if it appears to be imminent is to hoist the child on the hip, with her head forward and her feet stuck out behind. This unglamorous pose, known as the *football carry,* works very well to stave off attack and permit the teacher to carry the child someplace if he has to. Although it is rarely necessary to resort to such measures, it helps to know what to do in a real emergency.

When trouble brews, take action yourself before the child does. Over and over again I have seen teachers sit on the sidelines and let a situation go from bad to worse until it explodes, and then step in to pick up the pieces. If the situation is one that will have to be stopped at some point, *it is much more effective to step in before trouble starts* rather than a minute after blood has been shed.

Prompt intervention makes it more probable that the teacher can use a rational approach with the children; this is a better environment for teaching any skill. Intervening before the fight occurs also prevents either child from receiving gratification from the attack. For example, stepping in before one child bites another takes preternatural quickness but is vital to do because biting feels so good to the biter that no amount of punishment afterward detracts sufficiently from the satisfying reward of sinking teeth into unresisting flesh.

Accept the fact that physical restraint may be necessary. We have already discussed using the football carry as an emergency means of fending off an attack by a child; but even when children are not attacking the teacher directly, it is often necessary in a crisis situation to move swiftly and take hold of a child before she can strike someone else again (Miller, 1984).

When doing this, it is important to be as gentle as possible and yet be firm enough that the child cannot slip away. Usually just catching an arm is enough, though sometimes it is necessary to put both arms around the obstreperous one. Unfortunately this often makes the child struggle harder against the restraint, but at least it prevents her from having the satisfaction of landing another blow on her victim. As soon as the child is calm enough to hear what is being said to her, it will help bring things under control if the teacher says something on the order of "As soon as you calm down, I can let go of you, and we can talk."

When a situation has deteriorated to the extent that physical restraint is needed, it is usually best to draw the child or children away from the group so that they do not continue to disrupt it. It is seldom necessary to take them out of the room, and it seems to me it is more desirable to remain where the other children can see that nothing too terrible happens to the offenders. Otherwise, anxious children fantasize too much about what was done to the fighters.

When Immediate Control *Is* Necessary, Follow the Six Steps for Teaching Children Self-Control

Since children do not always stop throwing sand or grabbing tricycles simply because the teacher tells them to or redirects them to another activity, it is necessary to know what to do when a child continues to misbehave. I call the approach I use the six learning steps in discipline: (a) warning the child, (b) removing her, (c) discussing feelings and rules, (d) waiting for her to decide when she is ready to return, (e) helping her return and be more successful, and (f) following through with "losing the privilege" when this is necessary.

Warn the child and redirect her if she will accept such redirection. For example, you might warn a youngster that if she continues to throw sand, she will lose the privilege of staying in the sandbox; then suggest a couple of interesting things she could do with the sand instead of throwing it. It is important to make the child understand *that her behavior is up to her*. It is *her* choice; but if she chooses to continue, you will see to it that you carry out your warning.

If necessary, remove child promptly and keep her with you. Warn only once. If she persists in doing what she has been told not to do, act calmly and promptly. Remove her and insist that she sit beside you, telling her she has lost the privilege of playing in the sand. This is much more valuable than just letting her run off. Having her sit beside you interrupts what she wants to do, is a mildly unpleasant consequence of her act, and prevents her substituting another activity she would enjoy.

Instead of keeping the child right beside the teacher, many teachers send the child off to sit in a "time-out" chair. Although this time-hallowed method is certainly an improvement over spanking or saying hurtful things, there are some drawbacks to its use that must be considered. Basically, what is happening when the time-out chair is used is that the child is sent to the corner—all that is lacking is the old-fashioned dunce cap. Sent off by herself, the child is emotionally abandoned. Besides that, teacher and child frequently become involved in secondary struggles when the child tries to sneak away and the teacher catches her. Finally, as Clewett (1988) points out, many time-out episodes go on way too long, either because it's such a relief to the teacher to have the child removed or because he forgets she's there. For all these reasons, despite its inconvenience, it is more desirable to keep the child nearby.

Discuss feelings and rules after a reasonable degree of calm has prevailed. This is a very important part of handling a discipline crisis. Even if the child is saying such things as "I hate you—you're mean! I'm going to tell my mother and I'm never coming back!" It is possible to recognize her feelings by replying, "You're real angry with me because I made you stop grabbing the trike. [Pause] But the rule here is that people can keep something 'til they're done with it." If more than one child is involved, it is vital to put each child's feelings into words for them as well as you can. The virtue of doing this is that when children know you understand what they feel, even though you don't agree, they don't have to keep *showing* you how they feel.

Once feelings have been aired and everyone is calmer, this is also a good time to state whatever rules apply and discuss alternative ways of solving the difficulty. If the child is mature enough, she should be able to contribute her own ideas as well as hearing what the teacher has to say.

Internalize responsibility; that is, have the child take the responsibility for herself of deciding when she is ready to return. At this step many teachers say something on the order of "Now you sit here with me until lunch is ready," thus shifting the responsibility for the child's behavior to their own shoulders instead of putting the child in command of herself. But if the long-term goal of internalizing self-control is to be reached, it is much wiser to say, "Now, tell me when you can control yourself, and then we will go back" or, more specifically, "When you think you can remember to keep the sand down, tell me, and then you can go back and play." Some children can actually say they are ready, but others will need help from the teacher who can ask them when they look ready, "Are you ready to go back now?" (Perhaps she nods or just looks ready.) "Good, your eyes tell me you are. What would you like to do for fun there?"

Finally, it *is important to go with the child and help her be successful* when she does go back, so that she has the experience of substituting acceptable for unacceptable behavior. It will probably be necessary to take a few minutes and get her really interested. Be sure to congratulate the child when she has settled down, perhaps saying, "Now, you're doing the right thing. I'm proud of you!"

What to do if the child repeats the behavior. Occasionally the teacher will come across a glibber customer who says hastily when removed from the sandbox, "I'll be good, I'll be good!" but then goes right back to throwing sand when she returns. At this point it is necessary to take firmer action. Have her sit beside you until she can think of something acceptable to do, but do not permit her to go back to the sandbox. You might say, "What you did [be explicit] shows me that you haven't decided to do the right thing; so you'll have to come and sit with me until you can think of somewhere else to play. You've lost the privilege of playing in the sandbox for now." Then when she decides, *go with her and take her to another teacher and tell him about her special need to get started on something productive.* Avoid sounding moralistic or "nasty-nice" while explaining the situation to the teacher because this will just prolong bad feelings.

Keep Your Own Emotions Under Control

One way children learn attitudes is by observing models (Bandura, 1986). Teachers need to control their own tempers, since by doing so they provide a model of self-control for the children to copy as well as because intense anger frightens children. Also, when discipline situations arise, it is not just one child and the teacher who are involved: every child in the room is covertly watching what is happening and drawing conclusions from it. Therefore, it is often valuable for the teacher to talk over what happened with various children afterward to help them deal with how they felt about it and to clarify and consolidate what they learned from it. For example, he might explain to a worried-looking 3-year-old, "Jacob was crying because he wanted that car, but Teddy had it first so Jacob had to let go. He was pretty upset, wasn't he? Did he scare you?"

Sometimes, of course, it is simpler to advocate self-control in the teacher than to achieve it. Things that can help teachers retain control include remembering that one is dealing with a child, deliberately keeping control of oneself, and acknowledging the feeling and saying to the child, "Let's wait just a minute until we're both a little calmer. I feel pretty upset about what you did." The biggest help, though, comes from analyzing scenes and upsets after they have occurred and planning how best to handle them the next time they happen. This experience and analysis builds skills and confidence, and confidence is the great strengthener of self-control. Children sense this assurance in the teacher just the way dogs know who loves or fears them, and children become less challenging and more at ease when they feel the teacher knows how to cope and has every intention of doing so.

Remember, You Don't Have to Make an Instantaneous Decision

Not only does admitting to a child that you need time to control your feelings help you regain control of them, it also models self-control and provides time to think about what to do next. In the heat of the moment it is so easy to make a decision about punishment that the adult regrets later because it is inappropriate or too severe. For example, a child who has tried the teacher's patience all morning may be shoved into a chair with the statement "You're gonna stay here 'til your mother comes, no matter what!" or a culprit who has smeared paint all over the sink will be told "Well, you just can't use any more paint this week!"

Once the physical action has been halted, it is not necessary to render instant justice in this manner. Waiting a minute and thinking before speaking gives the teacher time to remember that he is going to have to keep that child sitting in that chair for an entire hour or to decide it would be more effective to have the youngster wash the paint off the sink rather than deny her the privilege of using paints for 4 long days.

Remember, when one child is disciplined, many other children are watching, too.

Knowing Where Your Flash Points Are Is Helpful, Too

Different behaviors make different teachers (and parents) angry, and it is helpful to take time to analyze what your particular flash points are because this awareness can help you control your response to them.

Some examples of flash points students and staff provided recently included deliberate insolence, withdrawing and acting coy, intentionally hurting another child (particularly after the teacher has stopped the behavior a moment before), outright defiance, use of ''bad'' language, calculated ignoring of the teacher, and pouting or sulking and refusing to tell why.

No doubt all these behaviors are irritating to all teachers sometimes, but each of them had a special power to evoke anger in some particular member of our discussion group. The reasons that lie behind these specific vulnerabilities range from early upbringing to lack of knowing how to respond effectively to a particular child's style. Sometimes, however, a teacher has no idea why he is sensitive to a particular behavior. Although knowing the origin can be helpful, it is not essential to understand why you become specially angry when such behavior occurs. Just *knowing* that you are vulnerable can help enough because the knowing can be linked to reminding yourself to make a special effort to keep your temper under control and be fair and reasonable when a child behaves in that particular way.

Settling Fights

In the chapter on mental health considerable time was spent in explaining how to help children express their feelings verbally. Although this is fairly easy to accomplish when the teacher is dealing with only one child, it is considerably more difficult *but just as important* when dealing with more than one. When two children are involved, it is a wonderful opportunity to help both of them develop this social skill, and the teacher should urge them to talk things over and to tell each other what they want and how they feel. Telling each other how they feel and knowing these feelings have been heard often mean children are no longer driven to act them out, and the way is opened for compromise.

It is also essential that teachers avoid being trapped into rendering judgments about situations they have not seen. Four-year-olds are particularly prone to tattle about the misdeeds of others. A polite name for this is *prosocial aggression;* it is a natural if unappealing stage in the development of conscience. Unless the reported activity is truly dangerous, the best course of action in the case of tattling is for the teacher to encourage the child to return with him and settle the matter. He should avoid taking sides or the word of one child, because George Washingtons are remarkably scarce in nursery school. When it is a case of who had what first, it may be necessary, if a compromise cannot be reached, to take whatever it is away from both youngsters for a while until they calm down. Remember, it is often the child who is crying the loudest who began the fight, although she may appear to need comforting the most. The only thing to do in situations such as this is be fair and deal with both children in a firm but nonjudgmental way. Impartiality is the keynote.

Keeping sand down can be a problem.

When a fight develops, it can also be helpful to call a meeting of the children who are nearby to discuss ways of settling it. Some 3-year-olds and the majority of 4-year-olds are capable of offering practical remedies if the matter catches their interest. The point of such discussions is not to ask the witnesses who was to blame (remember, it takes two to make a fight) but to ask them for ideas and suggestions about how to arbitrate the difficulty. The fighters can often be prevailed upon to listen to what their peers have to suggest, and children often come up with surprisingly practical solutions, although these tend to be severe (Kohlberg, 1976; Turiel, 1973). It is fine experience for them to think about how to get along together and work out solutions based on real-life situations.

When a child has gone so far that she has hurt another youngster, she should be allowed to help remedy the injury. Perhaps she can put on the bandage or hold a cold towel on the bump. This constructive action helps her see the consequences of her act, relieve her guilty feelings, and show concern by doing something tangible. I do not believe children should be asked to say they are sorry. Often they are not sorry, and even if they are, I fear teaching the lesson that glib apologies make everything all right. Moreover, a replicated study by Irwin and Moore (1971) supports the idea that young children grasp the concept of restitution (doing something to right a "wrong") before they understand the true significance of apology, so making restitution by righting the wrong is a more developmentally appropriate approach.

Whenever Possible, Let the Punishment Fit the Crime

Preprimary teachers (and enlightened parents) avoid doling out punishment in its usual forms. Teachers do not spank children, shut them in closets, take away their television privileges, or deny them dessert because they have not been good. But they do *allow* another form of "punishment" to happen when it is appropriate. This is simply permitting the child to experience the natural consequences of her behavior (Samalin, 1990). Thus the child who refuses to come in for snack is permitted to miss the meal; the child who rebelliously tears a page from a book is expected to mend it; and the youngster who pulls all the blocks off the shelf must stay to help put them away. Even young children can appreciate the justice of a consequence that stems logically from the action. It is not necessary to be unpleasant or moralistic when any of these results transpire; it is the teacher's responsibility only to make certain that the child experiences the logical outcome of her behavior.

When the Encounter Is Over, Forgive and Forget— Don't Hold a Grudge

Inexperienced teachers sometimes dread confrontations because they fear that the child will be hostile afterward or actively dislike them for keeping their word and enforcing their authority. However, such confrontations almost invariably build a closer bond between the teacher and the child, who usually seeks him out and makes it evident that she likes him after such encounters. Teachers are often surprised by this commonplace result. What I want to suggest here is that, since children do not usually hold a grudge when disciplined fairly, teachers too should be willing to wipe the slate clean.

It is so important for a child's sense of self-esteem that she be seen in a generally positive light. If the teacher allows a couple of negative encounters to color his perception of the youngster so that she is seen as a "bad girl," it is difficult for her to overcome this image and establish a more positive relationship. For this reason, particularly with "difficult" children, teachers need to call upon all their reserves of generosity and maturity and make every effort to concentrate on the youngster's positive qualities.

Most Important, Notice When Children Do the Right Thing, and Comment Favorably

This entire chapter has been spent talking about preventing or coping with misbehavior. Fortunately most of the center day does not revolve around such episodes; many days go smoothly and the children get along happily. When the day is a good one, when the children are obviously making progress, when they mostly talk instead of hit each other, when they share generously and enjoy the opportunities to help each other, let them know that you are pleased with their good behavior. They will share your pleasure in their accomplishments, and this recognition will help perpetuate the growth and self-discipline they have displayed.

A Final Thought

There is no teacher (or parent, for that matter) in the world who handles every discipline situation perfectly! When one of those less-than-perfect situations happens between you and a child, it is all too easy to spend energy on feeling guilty or regretful about how things went. Rather than doing that, it is wiser to think over what happened and learn from it because every discipline situation provides opportunities for *two* people to learn something. When things have not turned out well, think about what the child learned and what you learned, and consider possible alternatives. Then resolve to use a different approach the next time a similar situation comes up. Perhaps it will be rearranging the environment, or perhaps stepping in sooner, or perhaps firmly seeing a struggle all the way through. Taking positive steps to analyze difficulties and improve your skills is infinitely more desirable than exhausting yourself over past mistakes.

SUMMARY

Discipline should be more than just "getting the kids to do what I want." The real goal should be the development of self-control within the children. This is accomplished, in part, by strengthening the ego and by fostering the beginning of conscience. Two ego-strengthening experiences often used by early childhood teachers are offering appropriate choices to children to give them practice in decision making and helping children feel masterful through becoming competent.

The growth of conscience is facilitated by the presence of warm, nurturing relationships between child and adult, as well as by the use of person-oriented induction (reason-giving), techniques; but the moral judgments rendered by the conscience are profoundly influenced by the stage of moral reasoning the child has attained. Progress from one stage to the next depends on cognitive maturation combined with social experience. From this interaction the child constructs the next step in moral growth.

There are many undesirable ways to control children, but there are also more desirable approaches that can be subsumed under the general heading of preventing discipline situations when possible and knowing what to do when a crisis occurs. When all these strategies fail and a child continues to misbehave, it is important to take her through all six of the steps in learning self-control: (a) warning her, (b) removing her from the activity while keeping her with the teacher, (c) acknowledging feelings and stating rules, (d) waiting for her to make the decision to return to the activity, (e) helping her return and be more successful, and (f) following through with losing the privilege when that becomes necessary. Consistent use of this approach will be effective in helping children gain control of themselves, thus helping them become socially acceptable human beings.

QUESTIONS AND ACTIVITIES

1. Give three examples of choices you could encourage the children to make for themselves the next time you teach.

2. Have you ever had the experience of deciding, theoretically, how you intended to handle misbehavior and then found yourself doing something different when the occasion actually came up? How do you account for this discrepancy?

3. *Problem:* A child is throwing sand in the sandbox, and you want her to stop. What should you say to put your statement in positive form rather than telling her what not to do, that is rather than saying, "Don't throw the sand"?

4. Select an activity, such as lunchtime, and list every rule, spoken and implicit, that you expect children to observe in this situation. Are there any that could be abandoned? Are there any that are really for the teacher's convenience rather than for the purpose of fostering the children's well-being?

5. Team up with another student and take 15-minute turns for an hour, keeping track of how many times you reinforced positive behavior of the children. Then, keep track of how many opportunities for such reinforcement you overlooked.

6. *Problem:* Elaine, who is 4½, is playing at the puzzle table and keeps slipping little pieces of puzzle in her pocket. No one except you sees her doing this. You have already told her twice to keep the puzzles on the table so the pieces won't get lost, but she continues to challenge you by slipping them in her pocket. What should you do next to handle this situation?

7. *Problem:* As you enter the room you see John and David hanging on to a truck, both shouting "I had it first" and "I can keep it until I'm done with it." How would you cope with this crisis?

8. *Problem:* Jeanette is angry with Margie because Margie has refused to put her doll in the back of the trike wagon. So Jeanette takes the trike and deliberately rides over the doll, crushing one of its arms. Margie begins to cry. The teacher says, "Oh, Jeanette! That's awful! How would you feel if you were Margie's doll, and she ran over you with her trike?" How would you approach this situation and what would you suggest saying to simplify this response and, possibly, build a feeling of empathy in Jeanette's heart for Margie?

SELF-CHECK QUESTIONS FOR REVIEW

Content-Related Questions

1. What are the two basic goals of discipline? In the long run, which is of greatest value?

2. Is it true that someone who possesses ego strength is conceited? Please explain your answer.

3. According to Hoffman's review of research, what are the two most important factors involved in interiorizing conscience?

4. Why are 4-year-olds likely to reason differently about a "crime" than 20-year-olds are?

5. List and explain several principles teachers can follow that will help prevent discipline situations from developing.

6. When a discipline crisis *does* occur, list at least six things the teacher should do to foster a positive outcome.

7. There are six learning steps children and teachers should go through when the children have done something they shouldn't. Explain these six steps.

Integrative Questions

1. The book discusses self- versus "other"-controlled behavior. Using a college-aged student as the example, how might that student behave who is "other controlled" compared to one who has established inner controls? Give an example of potential behavior

in a group social situation and one involving taking a class.

2. Give two examples of choices that are developmentally appropriate for a 4-year-old to make and two that would not be developmentally appropriate.

3. Review the list of ways *not* to reach the basic goals of good discipline (pages 218–219) and provide descriptions of actual situations that show how teachers sometimes enforce those undesirable policies.

4. Jerry and Austin are squabbling over a sprinkling can in the garden, each wanting to water the radishes with it. Finally Austin tips it over and pours water on Jerry's shoes, and Jerry begins to cry. He seizes a shovel and whacks Austin's hand with it. Using this situation as the example, explain how you would use the six learning steps to control the boys' behavior. Next, explain some longer-term actions you might take to make it less likely that behavior would happen again.

5. Do you agree with the positive social values for nonconforming that Corsaro (1988) suggests in the discussion of the "underlife" of the nursery school? Explain your reasons for agreeing or disagreeing.

REFERENCES FOR FURTHER READING

Overviews

Maccoby, E. E. (1980). *Social development, psychological growth and the parent-child relationship.* New York: Harcourt Brace Jovanovich. A clearly written, sensible book, *Social Development* combines research findings with experience. It offers useful information on moral development.

Helpful Discussions About Handling Discipline Situations

Clewett, A. S. (1988). Guidance and discipline: Teaching young children appropriate behavior. *Young Children, 43*(4), 26–35. This is a very practical article that discusses both philosophical and specific approaches to discipline.

Faber, A., & Mazlish, E. (1980). *How to talk so kids will listen, & listen so kids will talk.* New York: Avon Books. Although cited previously in chapter 5, this is such a good book about fostering self-discipline it deserves mentioning once again.

Marion, M. (1991). *Guidance of young children* (3rd ed.). Columbus, OH: Merrill. Marion's book is filled with a sound combination of research, theory, and practical advice on this subject.

Miller, D. F. (1990). *Positive child guidance.* Albany, NY: Delmar. Miller devotes this entire book to the subject of guidance and includes many practical suggestions for teachers.

Mitchell, G. (1982). *A very practical guide to discipline with young children.* Marshfield, MA: Telshare. Mitchell brings a world of experience to this useful book that discusses a general approach to discipline combined with discussions of typical problems.

Saifer, S. (1990). *Practical solutions to practically every problem: The early childhood teacher's manual.* St. Paul, MN: Toys 'n Things Press. My only problem with this book is where to place it in the references because it covers a wide range of problems such as gifted children, death, and biting, to name just a few. This is a good, useful book.

Moral Development

Damon, W. (1977). *The social world of the child.* San Francisco: Jossey-Bass. Kohlberg should surely be read for the value of his overall approach to stage theory, but teachers of young children will find the work of William Damon even more useful since his research, which is ingenious, concentrates on children aged 4 to 12.

Hetherington, E. M., & Parke, R. D. (1986). *Child psychology: A contemporary viewpoint.*

New York: McGraw-Hill. This is a generally excellent text that provides a good overview of theories of moral development.

Kohlberg, L. (1976). The development of children's orientations toward a moral order. Sequence in the development of moral thought. In P. B. Neubauer (Ed.), *The process of child development*. New York: Jason Aronson. Here is a lucid explanation of Kohlberg's six-stage theory of moral development, including good examples of the attitudes characterizing each stage.

Schulman, M., & Mekler, E. (1985). *Bringing up a moral child: A new approach for teaching your child to be kind, just, and responsible*. Reading, MA: Addison-Wesley. Writing in layman's language, Schulman and Mekler base their recommendations on research mingled with common sense.

For the Advanced Student

Bushell, D. (1982). The behavior analysis model for early education. In B. Spodek (Ed.), *Handbook of research in early childhood education*. New York: Free Press. Bushell provides a clear description of a purist approach to behavior modification. His chapter is replete with tables listing a variety of studies using behavior modification techniques.

Kagan, J., & Lamb, S. (1987). *The emergence of morality in young children*. Chicago: University of Chicago Press. The authors present several differing points of view about how morality develops.

Piaget, J. (1932). *The moral judgment of the child*. London: Routledge & Kegan Paul. A hallmark study of moral attitudes that forms the foundation for much of the later work in this area; easier reading than most works by this master.

Rest, J. R. (1983). Morality. In P. H. Mussen (Ed.), *Handbook of child psychology. Vol. III: Cognitive development* (4th ed.; J. H. Flavell & E. M. Markham, Eds.). New York: John Wiley & Sons. An extensive, clearly written review of research on morality is included here.

Shweder, R. A., Mahapatra, M., & Miller, J. G. (1987). Culture and moral development. In J. Kagan & S. Lamb (Eds.), *The emergence of morality in children*. Chicago: University of Chicago Press. This fascinating study contrasts Brahmin and Untouchable Indian ideas of morality with those of the American middle class.

Wolfgang, C. H., & Glickman, D. C. (1986). *Solving discipline problems: Strategies for classroom teachers* (2nd ed.). Boston: Allyn & Bacon. Seven theoretical approaches to discipline are outlined by the authors before they go on to discuss special problems such as helplessness, verbal aggression, and so forth. Written primarily for the teacher of older children.

CHAPTER 10

Aggression: What to Do About It*

We can structure our spaces at home and in the center, the schedule, diet, outings, frequency of visitors, and so on, to bring out the best in easily overwrought, easily exhausted babies and young children whose emotional and social systems quickly "short circuit" under stress. We can also structure our own lives to provide enough sleep, healthy food, time off, rewarding projects beyond the child, and other friends so that we can act with maximum maturity—can muster maximum patience and understanding. . . . All this is preventive discipline. Nonetheless, situations calling for limits to be set, standards to be established, and desired behaviors to be encouraged will arise with mobile infants, into-everything toddlers, and increasingly independent preschoolers. Therefore, we are continuously faced with the questions: Am I disciplining in a way that hurts or helps this child's self-esteem? Am I disciplining in a way that attempts to control (to disempower) the child or in a way that attempts to develop self-control in the child (personal empowerment)?
—P. Greenberg (1988)

Have you ever wondered . . .

> What to do about a child who is particularly aggressive?
>
> What to teach a youngster that would help him enter a group peacefully instead of by starting a fight?
>
> What you could substitute in place of direct aggression that might still relieve an angry child's pent-up feelings?

If you have, the material in the following pages will help you.

---

*Adapted from "Aggression: What to Do About It" by J. B. Hendrick, 1968, *Young Children*, 23(5), pp. 298–305.

Now that the general subject of discipline has been discussed, it is time to talk about dealing with aggressive behavior in particular. When we work with young children we must consider two kinds of aggression. The first, and by far the commonest kind of aggression, is *instrumental aggression.* This is aggression that occurs without basic hostile intent. For example, a child reaches over and takes away another child's felt-tip pen because he wants to draw, or a 2-year-old pushes another child aside so he can reach a book. While these actions may require arbitration and explanation and protection of the second child's rights by the teacher, they differ from the hostile types of aggression discussed in this chapter. *Hostile* aggressive behavior refers to "actions that are intended to cause injury or anxiety to others, including hitting, kicking, destroying property, quarreling, derogating others, attacking others verbally and resisting requests" (Mussen, Conger, & Kagan, 1969, p. 370). Montagu (1978) defines aggression even more succinctly as being "behavior designed to inflict pain or injury on others" (p. 6), and Tavris (1982) points out that aggression is the result of anger—anger being the feeling and aggression being the expression of that feeling.

At the preschool level we see examples of this kind of behavior manifested when children barge through the room leaving a bedlam of smashed blocks or ravished housekeeping corners behind them, or when they spend most of their time whooping wildly about being tigers or monsters, or when they deliberately seek to injure other children by destroying what they are doing, teasing them, or physically hurting them. Such aggression differs from ordinary rough-and-tumble play because it is marked by angry frowns and unwillingness to stop until someone has been really hurt (Kostelnik, Whiren, & Stein, 1986).

UNDESIRABLE WAYS TO COPE WITH AGGRESSION

Teachers and parents deal with acting-out behavior in both useful and not-so-useful ways. Some of the more undesirable methods of responding to such behavior follow.

The Authoritarian Teacher

At one extreme are teachers who are tightly controlling authoritarians. These teachers are similar to the authoritarian parents described by Baumrind (1989) in her studies of parenting styles. She describes authoritarian parents as intending to shape, control, and evaluate the way their children behave according to absolute standards of what is right. Such parents value obedience and favor taking punitive, forceful measures when children's behaviors conflict with those standards.

Authoritarian teachers also tend to respond to conflict between themselves and the children as if expressing their own aggressive tendencies, garbed in the

Not all aggression is hurtful.

disguise of authority and control, were the only way to cope with the problem. In forthright cases, schools dominated by such teachers are likely to be riddled with many rules generally determined by what is convenient for the teacher. Don't run! Don't make noise! Sit down! Line up! Be quiet! Don't easel paint with your fingers! Stay clean! Don't splash! Take turns! Tell him you're sorry!—and a thousand other tiresome injunctions are typical. Punishments used by such teachers are apt to be severe, occasionally to the point of being emotionally destructive or physically painful.

Sometimes beleaguered teachers feel that controls of this type are necessary because the classes are too large or too obstreperous for them to cope with any other way. Sometimes they believe that this kind of control is what the parents expect and that they had better conform to this expectation or the children will be withdrawn from school.

More than likely the real reason for their reaction runs deeper than this and has to do with strong patterns carrying over from their own childhood, when little tolerance and freedom were granted to them by the adults in their lives, and they were provided with very authoritarian models. The frustration, resulting hostility, and covert aggression instilled by this treatment are particularly likely to be rearoused when they are confronted by the challenge of a belligerent 4-year-old or balky 2-year-old. Transgressions are often dealt with by stringent punishments, and contests of will are highly probable if these teachers cross swords with a genuinely spirited child.

What of the aggressive child who exists in this tightly controlled environment? What is the effect of overcontrol on him? For a few youngsters the bright edge of creative expression is dulled. Some children cannot afford to risk nonconforming (which is the essence of creativity) under these circumstances, and so most of their energy is used up holding onto themselves and "doing the right thing." These children have had their spirits broken. They conform—but at what a price!

There are almost bound to be other defiant young souls who continue to challenge or sneak past such teachers. Common examples of such underground, continued aggression may range from quietly pulling the fur off the guinea pig to being unable to settle down for stories, or consistently destroying other children's accomplishments at the puzzle table or in the block corner. Other children internalize the angry feelings generated by authoritarian restrictions and become resistant and sullen; still others settle for becoming openly defiant.

In such schools a basic restlessness and tension seem to simmer in the air, and teachers work harder and harder to hold the line, an exhausting business for all concerned. They tend to operate on the assumption that stronger punishment will result in greater control of aggression, but this is not necessarily true. Evidence from research studies indicates that strong punishment, particularly physical punishment, can actually increase the amount of aggressive behavior (Maccoby & Martin, 1983). This finding holds particularly true for children who already show aggressive tendencies (Patterson, 1982). Such teachers also overlook the fact that there is a limit to how far they can go to enforce dicta. What will they do if matters persist in getting out of hand?

Unfortunately, the next step for some of these teachers is resorting to corporal punishment. Although hitting and otherwise physically terrorizing young children may seem unthinkable to many readers, the fact is that such treatment does occur. In fact, as recently as 1988 it was still sanctioned in the public school systems of 39 states (Viadero, 1988).

The evil results of such an approach are well summed up by Moore (1982):

> Any parenting technique will work some of the time, but as a general rule, using harsh punishment to curb high levels of aggression does not work. Highly punitive parents (and we might equally well substitute the word *teachers* for *parents* here) not only provide their children with aggressive interpersonal models to emulate but they also risk undermining their child's sense of personal worth, frustrating and embittering the child, and orienting the child toward his own misery rather than to the plight of another. (p. 74)

The Overpermissive Teacher

At the other disciplinary extreme are teachers who feel that "anything goes." Such teachers are often confused about the difference between freedom and license, and they fail to see that true freedom means the child may do as he wishes *only as long as he does not interfere with the rights and freedom of other people.* This extremely permissive teacher is fairly rare in children's centers because the pandemonium that occurs quickly makes parents uneasy. Apparently the results of this kind of mishandling are more obvious to the unprofessional eye than are the results of overcontrol.

In response to overpermissiveness the children may display behavior similar to the response for overcontrol (Olweus, 1980). They may destroy other children's accomplishments or unconcernedly take whatever appeals to them. Sometimes they seem driven to tyrannical desperation trying to find out where the limits are and just how far they must go before the teacher at last overcomes her apathy and stirs herself to action. A common example of children's behavior in these circumstances is defiant teasing and baiting of the teacher by being ostentatiously, provocatively "naughty."

What the children really learn in such overpermissive circumstances is that "might makes right." This is a vicious circle, since the aggressor is often rewarded by getting what he wants and so is more likely to behave just as aggressively next time. Indeed, research indicates that attendance at a "permissive" nursery school does increase aggressive behavior (Patterson, Littman, & Bricker, 1967), and additional research by Bandura and Walters (1963) indicates that the presence of a permissive adult generally facilitates the expression of aggression. Appel (1942) also found that when adults did not intervene in an aggressive encounter, the child who began the fight was successful about two-thirds of the time; but when an adult stepped in, the aggressor's success rate fell to about one-fourth of the time. Clearly an overly permissive attitude by teachers can promote the expression of aggression by allowing such behavior to be rewarded.

The Inconsistent Teacher

The third undesirable way to deal with aggressive behavior is to be inconsistent. Teachers may be inconsistent because they are unsure that it is really all right to control children, or they may be uncertain about how to control them, or they may be unaware that consistency is important; hence, they deal erratically with out-of-hand behavior, sometimes by enforcing a rule when they think they can make it stick and sometimes by sighing and letting the child run off or have his own way.

This approach creates deep unease in children and fosters attempts by them to manipulate, challenge, and bargain in order to gain special dispensations. Whining, nagging, wheedling, and implied threats by the youngsters are all likely to be prime ingredients in this environment. For example, a 4-year-old may threaten, "If you don't give me that trike right now, I'll have to cry very, very hard, and then I'll prob'ly throw up, and you will have to tell my mother!"

Inconsistent handling may sound merely weak; however, it may actually be the most undesirable approach of all, since it has been found to increase aggressiveness in the children (Hom & Hom, 1980; Parke & Slaby, 1983). The probable reason for this result is that the reward for aggressive behavior is intermittent rather than continuous. It has been effectively demonstrated that an intermittent reinforcement schedule is a powerful means of causing behavior to continue (Duer & Parke, 1970; Parke & Duer, 1972), particularly when there are additional payoffs involved such as having gotten what one wanted by grabbing it.

Conclusion

It is fairly easy to see that teachers who are overcontrolling (authoritarian) or undercontrolling (extremely permissive) or very inconsistent bring special difficulties upon themselves when dealing with aggressive behavior. It is less easy to determine what constitutes a reasonable balance between aggression and control and to decide how to handle this problem in an effective and healthy way. We want to harness and direct this energy, not abolish it (Kostelnik et al., 1986). Teachers often feel confused about how and where to draw the line. They think it is important to relish the burgeoning vitality of young children, and so they want to provide vigorous, free, large muscle play, and plenty of it. But most teachers do not think that large muscle activity should be permitted to be expressed in preschool as endless, aimless, wild running about or terrorization of the quieter children.

Many teachers can go along with the idea that the child has the right to destroy anything he has made so long as it is his own and not someone else's. However, they also believe that direct aggression in the form of throwing things at people, biting, hitting others with objects in hand, outright insolence, and defiance of basic rules are generally unacceptable.

The problem is how to permit the expression of these feelings in acceptable ways at school and in society. The remainder of this chapter provides some basic approaches that will help the teacher solve this problem.

DESIRABLE WAYS TO COPE WITH AGGRESSION

Assess the Underlying Causes of Aggression, and Ameliorate Them When Possible

First, it is helpful to remember that pronounced self-assertiveness is part of the developmental picture for 4-year-old boys and girls. Many boys show evidence of this by attempting feats of daring, being physically aggressive, and swaggering about with an air of braggadocio. Girls are more likely to express it by being bossy or tattling in a busybody way on the wrongdoings of other children. It is important to realize that this rather out-of-hand phase serves a healthy purpose for these youngsters, who are busy finding out who they are by asserting their individuality (it is somewhat like adolescence in this regard).

Additional evidence that aggression should not be regarded as "all bad" is furnished by Lord (1982), who cites studies that show that "preschool children who are more aggressive than average often are also more friendly, empathetic, and willing to share materials than other children" (p. 237). But she also stresses that this finding holds true only for preschoolers and not for aggressive children who are older than that.

Besides the influence of the developmental stage, native temperament may have a lot to do with the expression of aggression (Soderman, 1985). Some children can stand more frustration than others can without exploding (Block & Martin, 1955). Sex-linked characteristics also affect its expression (Dorwick, 1986). Maccoby and Jacklin (1974) summarize many studies indicating that in our culture more direct physical aggression is expressed by boys than by girls, and Feshbach and Feshbach (1972) have reported that girls are more likely to employ indirect means of expressing aggressive feelings. However, how much of this

An impasse like this presents rich opportunities for the teacher to help children work things through.

behavior is due to biological differences and how much to culturally instilled values has yet to be determined.

In extreme cases of aggression, particularly when it is combined with hyperactivity, the possibility of brain damage should be considered, since lack of impulse control may be indicative of such a condition. In these unusual circumstances medication can produce considerable improvement in such behavior for some acting-out youngsters.

Parental mishandling is the reason most frequently given by teachers as the cause of undue aggression in children; and it is true that rejection, particularly cold, permissive rejection by parents, is associated with aggressive behavior in children (Glueck & Glueck, 1950; McCord, McCord, & Howard, 1961; Patterson, DeBaryshe, & Ramsey, 1989). If this appears to be the case, the teacher should encourage the parents to seek counseling.

It is all too easy for teachers to slough off their responsibility for aggression in a child by raising their eyebrows and muttering, "He sure must have had a tough morning at home—what do you suppose she did to him this time?" But it is more practical to ask oneself how the school environment might also be contributing to the child's belligerent behavior, since this is the only area over which the teacher has any real control. Teachers should ask themselves, Am I teaching him alternative ways of getting what he wants or am I just stopping his aggressive behavior? How frustrating is the center environment for this child? Take a look at him and assess how he is relating to the program. At what time of day does he misbehave? With whom? What circumstances bring on an outburst? Does he receive more criticism than positive recognition from the staff? Does he have to sit too long at story hour? Does he consistently arrive hungry and so need an early snack? Is the program geared to tastes of little girls and female teachers and lacking in areas that hold a boy's interests?

Use Direct Control When Necessary, Then Teach the Child to Find Alternative Ways to Get What He Desires

There is nothing quite like the agonizing dread some beginning teachers experience because they fear they will be unable to control one or more children in their group. There is no denying that the problem of gaining confidence in control situations is one of the major hurdles students have to get over in the early days of their teaching. Reading about handling aggression will help to a degree, of course, but the truth is that to learn to cope with aggressive children, you have to get in there and cope! It does not work to shrink away or to let your master teacher do it for you. Sooner or later, every teacher must be willing to confront children and exercise direct control over them because doing this is an essential method of coping with children's aggressive behavior.

To recapitulate what was said in the previous chapter, a child must definitely be stopped from hurting himself or another person or destroying property. It is important that the teacher step in *before* the child has experienced the gratification of seizing what he wants or of hurting someone. This is particularly true if it is unlikely that the child he has attacked will retaliate. It is also important to intervene promptly because it allows teachers to act before they are angry themselves, and it is highly desirable to present a model of self-control for an aggressive child to imitate (Bandura, 1986).

Once the teacher has put a stop to the aggressive action, the next part of handling the problem is going through the six steps for learning self-control outlined in chapter 9. These include (a) warning and redirecting, (b) removing the child and keeping him beside you, (c) putting his feelings into words and discussing rules, (d) having him wait with you until he takes the responsibility of deciding to return, (e) getting him started on something that is all right for him to do, and (f) following through with "losing the privilege" when this is necessary.

With children who frequently attack other children, there is an additional part to the learning that must be included. Such youngsters need to learn there are other effective ways to get what they want besides hurting people (Asher, Renshaw, & Geraci, 1980).

Teach Children Alternative Ways of Getting What They Want

Perhaps the aggressor can be encouraged to ask the other child for a turn or if he can join the group. Although research by Corsaro (1981) as well as my own experience indicates that such requests are often met with an initial refusal, Corsaro (1981) also found that children who accepted such rejection and then began to play as the group was playing in an unobtrusive way beside them often were able to slip their way into the play without continued objection. So this might be an effective strategy to suggest to would-be intruders.

Sometimes encouraging the youngster to report his feelings to the other child will help; sometimes a substitute or similar satisfaction can be provided (perhaps a tricycle can be located); perhaps he can make a bargain ("I'll let you see my sore knee, if you'll let me be the patient"); sometimes a cooperative arrangement can be developed (the child might deliver blocks to the block builders in one of the trucks); sometimes a diversion can be created ("How about using the swing until Marie is done with the wagon?"); and sometimes the child just has to face the reality that he must wait until the other youngster is finished, or he has to accept the fact that he is rejected and find someone else to play with.

Whatever alternative is employed, the teacher should see that the child clearly understands that hurting others is not allowed but that this need not mean he must swallow his anger and knuckle under; instead there are a variety of both effective and acceptable alternative ways to get what he wants.

Permit Reasonable Deviations from the Rules

Despite the fact that consistency is important and should generally prevail as a policy, there are exceptions to this rule. We have all seen timid children at school and have rejoiced when they finally ventured to shove back and stand up for their rights. It is important for such children to express these aggressive feelings in some form and come out of their shell as a first step; learning control can come later. Teachers simply have to use their knowledge of the children and good judgment in these matters.

Teachers must also make allowances for children when they are under special stress. For example, standards should not be unreasonably high at 11:00 in the morning, since lower blood sugar levels at that time usually mean less self-control. This is the time to practice adroit avoidance of confrontations, since children cannot be expected to control themselves very well under such circumstances. The same thing holds true for children who are recovering from illnesses or experiencing family problems. They may require that special allowances be made for them until they have regained their emotional balance.

Reduce Frustrating Circumstances When Possible

Although controversy continues over whether aggression is an inherent trait (Lorenz, 1966) or a learned behavior (Bandura, 1986), there is considerable evidence that frustration makes the expression of aggression more likely (Otis & McCandless, 1955; Yarrow, 1948). Thus it makes sense to reduce aggression by reducing frustration where it is possible to do so.

Frustration usually occurs when the child wants something he cannot have, be it the teacher's attention, going outside to play, the new fire engine, or even the blue sponge at the snack table. It is not possible to remove all frustrating circumstances from the life of a child, and it would not be desirable to do so anyway, since this would mean that he never has a chance to learn to cope with these feelings. However, there are so many restrictions and frustrations in everyday life that we really do not have to be concerned over the possibility of living in an environment without frustration (Murphy, 1976).

As previously described, the most effective way to reduce frustration is to empower the child by helping him learn a variety of acceptable ways of getting what he wants. Another way to reduce frustration is to have a plentiful amount of play equipment available. The value of having sufficient equipment is borne out by a study done in England by Smith and Connolly (1980). They reported that the provision of plentiful equipment had several effects: although children tended to play by themselves more frequently or to play in small groups, there was also less aggression, less competition, and less chasing and running about.

This supports the idea that it is desirable to have several tricycles, three or four swings, and a number of toy trucks and cars, sandbox shovels, and hammers. Children cannot endure waiting very long, and enough play materials will reduce the agony of anticipation, which if unassuaged can lead to frustration and acting out.

Still another way to reduce frustration is to keep rules to a minimum. The enforcement of the many petty rules cited in the discussion of the authoritarian teacher is one of the quickest ways to build anger in children. Such rules often go hand in hand with unreasonably high expectations of behavior, such as insisting that young children stand in line, sit for extended periods while waiting for something to happen, or never raise their voices.

Finally, two other good frustration preventers, also previously mentioned, are (a) following the policy of warning in advance so that children have the chance to prepare themselves for making a transition to a new activity and (b) providing many opportunities for choices in order to reduce children's feelings of defiance by helping them feel they are masters of their environment.

Provide Substitute Opportunities for Socially Acceptable Expressions of Aggression

The cathartic (emotionally relieving) value of substituting socially acceptable but nonetheless aggressive activities has been questioned in recent years by some researchers who maintain that such activities do not drain off or relieve aggression but rather reinforce such behavior (Parke & Slaby, 1983). Their arguments are persuasive, and I can only comment that my own experience and that of other early childhood teachers continue to convince me that offering substitute ways of working off steam does have value, cathartic or not, when working with aggressive children and children who have strong needs for high levels of physical activity. Such activities are obviously emotionally satisfying to children; they are safe for those around them; and they provide chances to be assertive in a harmless way for youngsters too immature to resist the need to express aggression in some physical form.

These activities are best offered, however, *before* the child reaches the boiling point. It is generally unsatisfactory to march a youngster over to a

It's difficult sometimes to decide when it's rough-and-tumble and when someone's likely to get hurt.

punching bag after he has hit someone and say, "It's all right to sock this!" By the time this happens, or by the time he gets the boxing gloves on and the fight set up, a lot of the flavor has gone out of the experience. Not only that, it is better to offer acceptable aggressive activities as part of each day, as well as to make sure they are available when the teacher anticipates that the day will be especially tense either for an individual child who is upset or for the entire group (on Halloween, for example). Fortunately there are a great many activities that will help. Remember, though, that these activities are substitutes for what the child would really prefer to do. When offering someone a substitute experience, be as free with it as possible, and supply plenty of material, plenty of time, and as few restrictions as you can tolerate.

In general, any kind of large muscle activity that does not have to be tightly controlled is valuable. Jumping on old mattresses spread out on the grass or jumping off jungle gyms or boxes onto mattresses works off energy harmlessly and satisfies a need to be daring as well.

Swinging is particularly effective because the rhythm is soothing and because it isolates the child from his companions and calms him at the same time. If the teacher has time to do some friendly pushing, the one-to-one relationship is easing, too.

Trike riding, climbing, and sliding, or, as a matter of fact, anything that works off energy harmlessly helps.

Some preschool teachers buy play equipment too small or flimsy to take the vigorous activity of 4- and 5-year-old children. It is always better to invest in sturdy, large equipment that will stand up to hard use rather than to continually nag the children, "Don't shake the jungle gym, you'll break it" or "Not too high now!"

Activities that provide for vigorous use of the hands in an aggressive yet acceptable manner should also be included. If the teacher joins in with gusto from time to time and uses the material herself, the child will often participate with more spirit.

Beanbags are fine to use for this purpose, but rules should be established about where they are to be thrown. A large wall, maybe with a face on it, is best, and the more beanbags the better. It is no fun to have to stop and pick them up after every three throws. Thirty bags are about the right number.

Punching bags have some use, but it is hard for young children to coordinate really satisfying socks with the bag's tendency to rebound.

Inflatable clowns are somewhat useful, but there may be trouble with maintaining them in airtight condition.

Hammering and sawing and even smashing things, such as old egg cartons, orange crates, or piano cases, are appealing. Very young children can use knock-out benches for this same purpose.

Large quantities of dough (not tiny, unsatisfying dabs) are fine aggression expressers. We restrict the tools the children use with it (such as cookie cutters) and encourage the children to stand at the table so that they can work forcefully, using their hands to pound and squeeze and pinch and punish the dough to their heart's content.

In finger painting and other types of smearing techniques such as soap painting, emphasis should be placed on richness of color and lots of gooey paint base, be it liquid starch, wallpaper paste, or homemade, very thick, cooked starch.

Once in a while a particular child finds relief in tearing and crumpling paper or stomping on crumpled balls of it. Again, large amounts are better than small amounts.

Although cutting up fruits and vegetables requires considerable self-control (by child and teacher), for some children the controlled opportunity to use a knife can be helpful. It is best to start with things such as bananas, which are easy to cut and which do not wobble around. Mashing potatoes is another good outlet.

Noise is an excellent outlet for expressing aggression. The aggression-expressing possibilities of sheer noise (at least on the days when the teacher does not have a headache) should not be overlooked. It is wise to remember that noise has an infectious effect on the entire group and may accelerate activity too much. However, on the many occasions when things are in good order, I am all in favor of noise! Drums are an all-time, satisfying "best" for noise, but pounding on the piano is good, too. Real music and dancing can be added for those who enjoy it. Sitting on top of the slide and kicking heels hard makes a wonderful, satisfying noise. Yelling and playing loudly, and crying (the louder the better) also serve to express feelings harmlessly.

Opportunities for dramatic play can also help the child come to terms with aggressive feelings. Direct participation by dressing up and playing house will let youngsters work through situations that may be troubling them. Anyone who has ever watched an irate young "mama" wallop her "naughty" baby doll will understand the merit of providing this kind of play material as an aggression reliever. Dollhouse furniture and little dolls are useful, but more so for 4-year-olds than for 3-year-olds.

Sets of fairly large rubber wild animals and hand puppets lend themselves admirably to controlled aggressive play. Interestingly enough, the animal that produces the greatest amount of this play is not the lion or tiger, but the hippopotamus. I have concluded that it is the open mouth and all those teeth that brings this out. It makes me think how angry adults with toothy open mouths must appear to children, particularly since youngsters tend to look up and in!

The best thing for out-of-hand children to play with is water. It is deeply relaxing in any form. Washing doll clothes or plastic cars, playing with soap bubbles, or playing with water in the housekeeping area is beneficial. Even when squirted it does no lasting harm.

Whenever weather permits, the best thing of all is a running hose and lots of sand and mud. This combination has led to some of the calmest, happiest days we have ever had in our school, but pouring and playing with water in tubs or basins can also be satisfying. At home a warm bath can work miracles.

Finally, encouraging very overactive youngsters to take time out to go to the toilet often simmers things down considerably.

Additional Techniques to Help Reduce
the Amount of Aggressive Behavior

So much for the specifics. There are also some general techniques that the teacher may find helpful for handling aggression.

Provide kindly, one-to-one attention for acting-out children. A few minutes consistently invested every day with an aggressive child when he is doing positive things (that is, before he gets into difficulties) often works wonders.

Teach children to use words in place of teeth and fists. Once more I want to remind the reader of the value of teaching children to tell other youngsters what they want and what their feelings are, instead of physically showing them what they feel.* Even as simple a sentence as "I want that!" or "Give it here!" is a step up from snatching what is desired. Of course, the other child may well refuse, but the teacher can support the requester by saying, "I'm sure glad to hear you asking him instead of just grabbing it." Then she can go on to teach the next step. "Jennie says you can't have it now. Why don't you ask her if you can have it when she's done with it. Say, 'Jennie, can I have a turn when you're done?' I bet she'll let you have it then!"

A more mature child can be encouraged to ask, and then add, "I really want that trike!" or "Gosh, I wish you'd give it to me now!" Remember, these statements should *focus on what the child is feeling* and what he wants, not on calling the other child bad names or insulting him.

Stopping some activities before they start saves criticism and discipline later. I have learned, for example, to keep an eye out for "angry monster" games or a local variation on the same theme, referred to as "Golden Eagle" by some young friends of mine. When such a game gets too high pitched, the quickest way to bring it under control is to look for the ringleader and get him involved in something else that he particularly likes to do.

Our staff discourages gun play at our center. We believe that children can play at better things than killing each other, and it is also true that such play usually leads to overexcited running about. Therefore, when guns are brought to school, they are stored in the cubbies until time for the children to go home.

Be on the lookout for combinations of personalities that are currently poisonous, and do what you can to dilute them. Children who egg each other into trouble should not snack together or rest near each other, and other friendships for both children should be encouraged.

Finally, plan, plan, plan! Plan to provide interesting activities that children really like, and plan the daily program with specific children in mind. ("John is coming today; I'd better get out the hammers and saw.") The program must not make undue demands on their self-control and should include acceptable outlets for their energy. As a general principle, consistent opportunities that allow children to achieve mastery and competence in acceptable areas should be

---

*For a more in-depth discussion of this principle, please refer to chapter 5, "Fostering Mental Health in Young Children."

"He did it!" Tattling is a typical form of prosocial aggression in 4-year-olds.

provided. Every time a youngster can do something well, whether it's building blocks, doing meaningful work, creating a painting, or learning to pump on the swing, his aggression has been channeled into accomplishing something constructive.

SUMMARY

Aggressive behavior is defined in this chapter as action intended to cause injury or anxiety to others. This kind of behavior needs careful handling and guidance so that children are not forced to suppress such feelings completely but learn instead to channel these impulses into socially acceptable activities.

Three approaches to coping with aggression in young children are particularly undesirable, since they are all likely to increase aggressive responses from them. These include authoritarian, overpermissive, and inconsistent methods of dealing with such behavior.

On the more positive side, several approaches for working with acting-out children are effective in reducing and channeling such behavior. Among these are assessing the underlying causes of aggression and ameliorating them when possible, using direct control when necessary, and teaching the child to find alternative ways to get what he wants. In addition, permitting reasonable deviations from the rules in special cases and reducing frustrating circumstances when possible are helpful. Finally, substituting socially acceptable opportunities for expressing aggression can relieve the child's feelings without jeopardizing the safety and happiness of those around him.

Teachers who apply these principles when handling aggressive behavior will reduce tension within the child and themselves by pre-venting aggressive feelings from building up and will also help the child remain happier, more open, and more ready to welcome life with enthusiasm.

QUESTIONS AND ACTIVITIES

1. Everyone seems to have different "breaking points" in tolerating aggression. For example, one person sees red if a child is insolent, whereas another finds it more difficult to cope with a child who is cruel to animals or who deliberately hurts another child. Compare notes among the people in class about what they feel constitute acceptable ways to express aggression and where their breaking points are.

2. Keep an eye out during the coming week and observe and briefly record several situations where children or staff members appeared to be angry. Note what each individual did about this feeling. If the teacher was working with a child, what did she do to help the youngster recognize and express his feelings in an acceptable way?

3. Are there any "discipline" situations in your school that seem to recur? For example, are the children always being told not to run inside the building? Suggest several ways the situation could be changed instead of continuing to "teach the children to behave."

SELF-CHECK QUESTIONS FOR REVIEW

Content-Related Questions

1. Describe three styles of teaching that are likely to increase an aggressive response by some children.

2. Does aggression always stem from the same cause? If not, what are some things that tend to generate such behavior?

3. List several alternative approaches children can be taught that will help them get what they want without hurting other people.

4. Suppose that you have a high-energy, aggressive child in your group. Suggest several ways he or she could work off this energy without hurting other people.

Integrative Questions

1. Some reasons why a teacher might be too authoritarian are suggested in this chapter. What are some reasons that might lie behind the behavior of the teacher who is too permissive?

2. The book defines *instrumental* and *hostile aggression*. Give two examples of behavior that fit each kind of aggression.

3. If corporal punishment is such an undesirable way to discipline children, why do you think it is still allowed in the public schools of 39 states? Select a reason and provide an argument that might convince an advocate of corporal punishment who supports that reason to change his or her mind.

4. Four-year-old Sarah is reading a book, and Nancy tries to grab it. Sarah hits Nancy's hand, and when she tries again, Sarah pinches her very hard. Nancy begins to cry. You have worked through the first steps in the "Learning Self-Control" sequence and now Nancy is ready to return to Sarah. Suggest at least two alternatives you could propose to Nancy about how she might get a chance to look at the book she wants to see so badly. What alternatives might you suggest to Sarah about how to protect her rights without hitting or pinching?

REFERENCES FOR FURTHER READING

Reducing Aggression

Bullock, J. (1990). Understanding and altering aggression. In J. S. McKee (Ed.), *Early childhood education 90/91* (11th ed.). Guilford, CT: Dushkin. Bullock provides a concise practical article on this subject.

Kostelnik, M. J., Whiren, A. P., & Stein, L. C. (1986). Living with he-man: Managing superhero fantasy play. *Young Children, 41*(4), 3–9. The authors explain the considerable values of such play, suggest how to tell it apart from undesirable aggression, and conclude with recommendations for successful management.

Samalin, M., & Jablow, M. M. (1987). *Loving your child is not enough: Positive discipline that works.* New York: Viking Press. This is a good practical book about getting along peacefully with children written for parents, but helpful for teachers, too.

Soderman, A. K. (1985). Dealing with difficult young children. *Young Children, 40*(5), 15–20. Soderman discusses understanding children's behavior in relation to various temperamental characteristics.

Wichert, S. (1989). *Keeping the peace: Practicing cooperation and conflict resolution with preschoolers.* Philadelphia: New Society. Many wholesome, practical suggestions for helping children solve problems without violence are included here.

Corporal Punishment

Cryan, J. R. (1987). *The banning of corporal punishment in child care, school and other educative settings in the United States.* Wheaton, MD: The Association for Childhood Education International. For those who need ammunition in the fight against corporal punishment, this ACEI position paper is persuasive.

Hyman, I. A. (1990). *Reading, writing and the hickory stick: The appalling story of physical and psychological abuse in American schools.* Lexington, MA: Lexington Books. The title of this useful book is self-explanatory.

For the Advanced Student

Baumrind, D. (1989). Rearing competent children. In W. Damon (Ed.), *Child development today and tomorrow.* San Francisco; Jossey-Bass. In this valuable chapter, Baumrind reviews her decades of research concerning long-term effects on children of authoritative, authoritarian, permissive, and rejecting parental styles.

Parke, R. D., & Slaby, R. G. (1983). The development of aggression. In P. H. Mussen (Ed.), *Handbook of child psychology. Vol. IV: Socialization, personality, and social development* (4th ed., E. M. Hetherington, Ed.). New York: John Wiley & Sons. This article offers a definitive review of research related to aggression.

Patterson, G. R., Debaryshe, B. D., & Ramsey, E. (1989). A developmental perspective on antisocial behavior. *American Psychologist, 44*(2), 329–335. The authors review research that traces the development of antisocial behavior from infancy to adolescence.

Shantz, C. V. (1987). Conflicts between children. *Child Development, 58*(2), 283–305. In this summary of research Shantz includes valuable insights into what generates conflicts between young children and how they resolve them.

Additional Resources of Further Interest

The National Center for the Study of Corporal Punishment and Alternatives in the Schools, 253 Ritter South, Temple University, Philadelphia, PA 19122. The Center provides valuable references, research, and workshops about the evil results of corporal punishment.

CHAPTER 11

The Pleasures of Meaningful Work*

"It builds confidence in kids if adults trust them," JoAnne says. *"That's why I look for ways to give them real work to do, like getting the mail or taking messages to the other room."* One day the phone rang in the day-care center, and Henry, four years old, answered, spoke for a few minutes, and then hung up. JoAnne asked who it was, and Henry replied, *"It was Gigi, and she wanted to know if Cameron was up from his nap yet. I said he'd had a good nap, and she said she'd come by after she went running."* JoAnne beamed as Henry told her about the conversation.

—W. Ayers (1989)

Have you ever . . .

Thought that young children were too young to do anything really helpful at school?

Wondered just what kinds of things children might do that would be real work but not too hard for them?

Wondered how to get children to want to pitch in on work projects?

If you have, the material in the following pages will help you.

*Adapted from "The Pleasures of Meaningful Work for Young Children" by J. B. Hendrick, 1967, *Young Children*, 22(6), pp. 373–380.

D oes the idea of young children performing meaningful work sound ridiculous, impossible, or even repugnant? Apparently it does to many preschool teachers because it is an area rarely considered in textbooks on early childhood education,* even though we know it is vitally important for adults to have good feelings about their work. In *Childhood and Society* (1963) Erikson quotes Freud, when asked the question, "What should a normal person be able to do well?" as replying, "To love and to work." Maslow also supports the value of work in his comment: "This business of self-actualization via a commitment to an important job and to worthwhile work could also be said, then, to be the path to human happiness" (1965, p. 5).

But is early childhood too soon to begin laying the foundation for enjoying work? Pleasure in work cannot be expected to suddenly appear full blown as the child attains adulthood; at some point in human development it must begin to be nurtured and encouraged. Since work is such a fundamental part of our culture, teachers should start with children as young as age 3 or 4 to establish a wholesome conviction that work is rewarding and that it can be a significant way of giving meaning and satisfaction to life (Wenning & Wortis, 1988).

TEACHING CHILDREN TO DISLIKE WORK

We all know of people who face the working day as though it were a deadening burden, an oppression to be struggled through; this is nothing short of tragic. What happened to these people that caused them to feel like that? Some of our work-burdened adult friends must have been subjected to very negative training about work as they grew up. Let us picture what such a negative teaching model might be, bearing in mind that this model may exist at home as well as at school.

Suppose we begin by asking, How do you teach a 3- or 4-year-old child that work is to be loathed, shirked, and put off as long as possible? For people who have such an aim in mind, the following commandments should be followed faithfully to teach children to hate work—and what better time to begin than in the early, formative years?

1. Select the chores you dislike most yourself, such as picking up every one of the small blocks, and insist that each time a child uses such equipment she pick it all up immediately as soon as she has finished. Never offer to help her with such jobs, because this will make her too dependent on you. Bright children catch on to this quickly: "Oh, no! Let's not get those out, we'll just have to put them all away!"

2. Be sure that all work is tedious and long drawn out. Also insist that the child finish every task she begins on the grounds that this will teach her to be diligent.

3. Be sure that everyone always works at the same time because this is fair.

4. Provide no variety to the work; keep it dull. Expect each child to repeat the same portion to perfection, over and over, because repetition is valuable

---

*Montessori is a rare, welcome exception to this statement.

Children love the opportunity to take on grown-up roles.

habit training and preparation for later life, where a lot of things will be boring anyway.

5. Never allow enough time, and remind the child constantly that she should hurry. This will encourage her to stick to business.

6. Expect a great deal, and be very critical of any work a child attempts. This will teach her that high standards are important.

7. Tell the child exactly how to do the work; be rigid; be demanding; watch closely so that she doesn't make any mistakes, and be quick to call her attention to all errors so that she will learn to do it the "right" way. This will prevent her from forming bad habits.

8. Compare her achievements with the other children's; draw her attention to where she has failed and how she could do better by copying them. This will help her appreciate other children's strong points.

9. If a child does express interest in doing some helpful job, accept her help with condescending indulgence rather than with thanks and respect. After all, she's only a child.

10. Above all, act abused yourself. Talk to the other adults about how tired you are, how much work everything is, and grumble over the unfairness of it all. Be careful to do this in front of the children because it will teach them to appreciate you more and to look forward to becoming a grown-up working person.

TEACHING THE POSITIVE VALUES OF WORK

What if we want the children in our care to relish work, to find deep rewards in accomplishment, and to anticipate each day with at least mild pleasure because of the interest their jobs hold for them? Then we must not fall into the trap of assuming that work should consist only of doing what we do not like or do not want to do. We must be wary of thinking that work for young children can never be more than helping out in routine tidying up, and we must stop assuming, even tacitly, that the only work children are capable of is the routine, lengthy, repetitive kind of chore usually disliked by both teachers and children.

In place of such negative attitudes we must substitute an appreciation of the potential that meaningful work holds for young children's development and understand the kinds of work they are likely to find satisfying.

Work Allows the Child to Experience the Pleasure of Accomplishment Linked with Helping Other People

One of the most important values of work is that it provides children with the opportunity to experience achievement, which possesses obvious social value, since doing a job often results in accomplishing a task and helping other people at the same time. Thus the 4-year-old who has washed the dishes after making cookies or who has sawed off the sharp corners of the woodworking table experiences not only the glow of satisfaction that comes from honest labor but also feels good because she has contributed to the welfare of the group, particularly if the teacher points this out to her and remembers to say "thank you."

Work Increases the Reality of Role Playing

Another pleasure inherent in work grows out of young children's passion for imitating adults. When Joel repairs the seat of the rowboat "just the way my mom would," he gains insight into what it is like to be a grown-up. Perhaps he thinks, "This is the way grown-ups do things. I am just a little boy, but one day I, too, will be doing things like this all the time, and it's good to do them."

Role playing need not stop at the "family" level. In the past few years interest in career education has increased for children of all ages (Beach, 1986; Jalongo, 1989). Although information on career awareness and attitudes for children of preschool age remains very scanty, one trend is apparent. Leifer and Lesser (1976) cite two studies that reveal that even as early as preschool, girls show a more restricted number of career choices than boys. Girls saw themselves as parents, teachers, and nurses, whereas boys chose a wider range of occupations including such things as doctor, police officer, and firefighter. This finding was further supported by Beuf's study (1974), which showed that the vast majority of preschool children chose sex-stereotyped jobs for themselves. In addition, the study found that "all the girls could suggest occupations they might hold if they were boys, while many of the boys could not imagine what jobs they might hold if they were girls." The report of a conversation with one preschooler illustrates the boy's perplexity: He put his hands to his head and sighed, "A girl?" he asked. "A girl? Oh if I were a girl I'd have to grow up to be nothing" (Leifer & Lesser, 1976, p. 18).

That this attitude continues to persist is documented by a study of second-, fourth-, and sixth-grade girls who replied that they wished to be teachers and

Talk about the pleasure of accomplishment: Courtney worked and worked on washing these blocks prior to painting them.

nurses, although the investigator also found that girls whose mothers worked outside the home had a more liberal attitude toward breaking such traditional role stereotypes than did those whose mothers did not (Nemerowicz, 1979).

Nor have these limited stereotypes changed in the past decade. Even though the realities of family life are changing and so many more women now work outside the home, children continue to see the roles of mothers and fathers as being quite different. For example, a recent study of day-care- and kindergarten-aged children reported that mothers were perceived as doing most of the domestic work and custodial child care, and fathers were much more likely than mothers to be perceived as working for pay despite the fact that two-thirds of the mothers in the study were employed outside the home (Smith, Ballard, & Barham, 1989).

If the teacher wishes to conduct a nonsexist, nonracist classroom, the implications of these findings on career awareness are obvious. Even at the preschool level we should surely make a point of widening both boys' and girls' ideas of job possibilities that are becoming available for both men and women of all ethnic backgrounds.

Using work as a means of experiencing many careers can be done successfully even with very young children. I am thinking of such possibilities as helping the visiting nurse unpack tongue depressors and assemble the examination light, or raking up leaves for the gardener, or helping the delivery person store the milk cartons in the refrigerator. This kind of education takes considerable cooperation, briefing, and patience by the adults involved but can be very effective from time to time.

In addition, various work roles can be investigated by taking the children on field trips, particularly to places where their parents work (Beach, 1986; Wenning & Wortis, 1988). Having visitors come to school to show children what they do is also helpful. A special effort should be made to include people in nontraditional occupations and to make certain that people from a variety of ethnic groups are included. Parents and grandparents are wonderful resources for occupations—not only because of the variety of jobs they do themselves, but also because of their acquaintance in the community with other people on whom they can prevail to visit the school. It is always a good idea to talk with these visitors in advance. Explain carefully the kinds of things the children will understand and encourage them to wear their work clothes and bring their tools. Otherwise, visitors tend to talk too long at too advanced a level.

Work Presents Many Opportunities to Achieve Something Together

Although some jobs can be done alone, many simply require more than one person's contribution to be successful. One child can hold the dustpan while another sweeps or dry the dishes another has washed. Working together in this fashion has special merit because it presents such fine opportunities for learning the benefits of cooperative endeavor.

Work Also Presents Many Opportunities for Doing Something That Benefits the Group

If we want children to develop a sense of family and togetherness at school, a fine way to do this can come from doing helpful work for the good of the group. This may be as simple as passing the napkins at snack, or it can be as long and drawn out as our block washing, painting, and storing experience. The point I wish to make here is that, while the activities are satisfying in themselves as work projects, they can be made even more satisfying if teachers point out that what the child or group of children is doing helps the group in some way. It is a good thing for children to feel they can contribute to everyone's welfare. It makes them socially aware and helps them feel personally valuable as well.

Work Is an Ego Strengthener

The experience of success in work can strengthen the ego and build self-esteem. Every time a child accomplishes something tangible and sees the results turn out reasonably well, her image of herself as being a capable person is strengthened. This is particularly valuable for very retiring or very aggressive children (Wenning & Wortis, 1984).

At school one year our staff had a boy who had been rejected from kindergarten. At the age of 5 he was already convinced that he was helpless, worthless, and a menace, and he expressed this self-despair in the kindergarten room by throwing scissors, destroying other children's achievements, and refusing to try anything himself. When he joined us at nursery school, we all held our breath. Although the teachers worked on the problem from a number of angles, what appeared to do the most direct good for him was the staff's thinking of some specific simple jobs he could do to help them. I recall that the first one of these was smashing, and I mean *smashing*, an old piano box we no longer needed. It was a real help to us and a genuine relief and achievement for him. His self-image was rebuilt largely through this avenue of productive work. We are still using a beautiful tree in our insect cage that he made for us.

There is something to be said, too, for the value of work in reducing guilt feelings. I would much rather help a child "fix" something she has broken, clean up after a spill, or apply a Band-Aid to someone she has hurt than settle for "Say you're sorry!" It is valuable not only because a child should experience the actual consequence of her action through repairing the result, but also because it is a good way for her to learn that doing something "wrong" is not the end of the world and that one can often make amends.

INCORPORATING MEANINGFUL WORK INTO THE LIFE OF THE SCHOOL

Now that the reasons have been reviewed why work can be beneficial for young children, the question remains, just what kinds of jobs can they do? The

Any work involving water is the most fun.

following list constitutes some of the activities I have seen them participate in that were both productive and pleasurable. Most teachers will be able to supply many more examples from their own schools.

Washing dishes after cooking with them

Loading sand in a small wheelbarrow, carting it to the swing area, and shoveling it under the swings after a rainy day

Planting and weeding the garden

Fertilizing and watering the garden

Cutting flowers and arranging them

Cleaning the aquarium

Setting up the rabbit cage for a new baby rabbit

Feeding and cleaning the rabbit (which reminds me of one 3-year-old who looked at the rabbit droppings and informed me, soberly, "Dem's not raisins!")

Mixing paint

Washing the finger-painting tables

Cutting up fruits and vegetables for snacks

Helping set up the snack baskets

Fetching juice for the snack table

Doing all kinds of cooking (making butter, whole-wheat pizza, soup, vegetable dip, cranberry-orange relish; using a grinder is a special joy because children can carry out the work of assembling it as well as using it)

Carrying simple messages such as, "Mrs. Marquis needs some more clothespins"

Sanding and waxing blocks and then stapling different grades of sandpaper to them to make music blocks for our music corner

Sawing square corners off the tables to make them safer

Puttying up the holes in the much drilled-on woodworking table

Filling the holes in the edges of a new shelf with putty

Dyeing eggshells and crushing them for collage material

Nailing the seat more firmly into the boat when it works loose

Hammering nails back into the benches so that clothing is no longer snagged on them

Taking down bulletin board displays and helping put up new ones

Hosing off the sandy sidewalk

Mopping the housekeeping corner when the water play runs deep

Oiling tricycles when they begin to squeak

Using the flatbed ride-'em truck to load up and deliver the baskets of sand toys to the sand pile

Washing easel brushes (a favorite)

Shoveling snow

Pumping up the big inner tube to bounce on

These chores, which adults regard as rather run-of-the-mill, were all performed with interest and enthusiasm by the children. Their pleasure did not come mainly from satisfaction with the finished job. Children are more fortunate than that in their approach to work. They love the process as much as the product and do not drive relentlessly toward the single-minded attainment of the goal; their satisfaction is spread throughout the experience. Wouldn't it be ideal if this were also true for more adults in their own working lives?

Not All Work Experiences Are Successful

It may also be illuminating to talk about some of our failures as well as our successes, because, of course, some work projects do not turn out well.

The second year of the garden was one of these occasions. We gave the children some excellent shovels and talked about seeds, flowers, and worms, and they started to dig with a will—and quit almost as promptly. We couldn't

Most Work Requires Supervision

Almost all jobs require some supervision by the teacher. This is perhaps one reason children are not allowed to do more work at home as well as at school (until they are too old to want to do it, of course). Adults often feel it is easier on a short-term basis to do it themselves than to allow the time and exercise the patience it takes to let the child make the effort. The other common reason children are not allowed to help more is that adults underestimate their abilities. But think what such consistent underestimation does to the child's self-concept!

Take Time to Talk About How Hard the Children Are Working

Children love the sense of doing *real* work, and a fine way of sharing and deepening their pleasure is to talk about the fact they are working when they are involved in that kind of task. Making such comments as, "This sure *is* a big job!"

The opportunity to really fix the truck was deeply gratifying to this 3-year-old.

or "My gosh! You're *really* working hard on that" will not discourage them. Rather, it makes children feel grown-up and important to realize they are doing something really worthwhile.

The Teacher's Own Attitude Toward Work Is Significant

The teacher's attitude toward work can influence the way the child feels about it, since children acquire attitudes from models whom they care about. The teacher who willingly lends a hand if the job is onerous (picking up blocks again comes to mind) is setting a pattern for the future young mother who may one day offer her help with equal generosity to her own child. The teacher who enjoys his own job is helping convey the idea that work can be pleasurable as well as challenging. Finally, the teacher who expresses a genuine attitude of respect for the child's work helps her build good attitudes toward it even more directly. If the teacher reveres the child's power of concentration and refrains from interrupting her while she is working, if he values her suggestions about how to accomplish the task, and if he is quick to acknowledge her achievements, the child's pleasure in this kind of activity will be deepened, and she will be more likely to participate in working again when the opportunity arises.

SUMMARY

Although we would never wish to emphasize work in the nursery center to the extent that it minimizes the significance of play, work is a valuable experience to offer young children. It allows them to enjoy the pleasure of accomplishment linked with helping other people, it builds reality into role playing, it promotes an expanded awareness of job opportunities, it strengthens the ego, and it enhances self-esteem.

Many different jobs, ranging from preparing the snack to making simple repairs, are both interesting and not too difficult for children to perform. Their pleasure in these tasks can be increased if teachers keep them reasonably short and easy, provide tools that are effective, allow children to select jobs they prefer to do, and maintain a healthy attitude toward work themselves.

QUESTIONS AND ACTIVITIES

1. What is it about work that causes many people to think of it as a difficult, tiresome activity to be avoided if possible?

2. If you happen to be someone who feels that work is enjoyable, can you account for how you came to feel this way about it?

3. Why do you think real work is an appealing activity to young children?

4. Do you feel children should be paid for doing chores around the house, or should they be expected to do them because they are contributing members of the family unit?

5. Watch during this coming week for opportunities for children to participate in new kinds of work experiences they have not tried before. Be prepared to assess what made these experiences successful or unsuccessful.

SELF-CHECK QUESTIONS FOR REVIEW

Content-Related Questions

1. What did Freud reply when asked what a normal person should be able to do well?

2. List at least five things you could do that would help a child learn to *dislike* doing work.

3. Explain what benefits might accrue to a child involved in doing meaningful work.

4. List several possibilities for meaningful work that might be available at the school where you are teaching.

5. Imagine you are explaining to a new teacher how to go about making shoveling snow off the school sidewalk appealing to the children. What suggestions would you give to him?

Integrative Questions

1. In your opinion, would it be practical to rely on children to volunteer to help with work spontaneously as the opportunities arise, or is it fairer to have a list of jobs that must be done each day and assign the children to different ones at different times? How might the research by King on defining work and play affect your policies about assigning work?

2. The 3-year-olds in your group have played happily with the blocks all morning, but now it is time to put them away. Suggest three things you could do that would make participating in this work reasonably attractive to the children. Give two examples of what would be unreasonable expectations for accomplishing this work for 3-year-olds.

3. The children see you working as a teacher every day. If you were to use that role for career education, suggest how you might involve the children to make it real for them.

4. The author makes quite a point of the stereotyped ideas about work roles held by young children. Why is it valuable for teachers to realize that these attitudes continue to persist?

REFERENCES FOR FURTHER READING

Beach, B. (1986). Connecting preschoolers and the world of work. *Dimensions, 14*(3), 20–22. In this practical article Beach suggests a curriculum that helps preschoolers understand their parents' work.

Montessori, M. (1967). *The discovery of the child* (M. J. Costelloe, Trans.). Notre Dame, IN: Fides. The practical life activities recommended by Montessori (in this and other books describing her curriculum) remain one of the rare discussions of work that can be successfully performed by young children.

Wallinga, C. R., & Sweaney, A. L. (1985). A sense of real accomplishment: Young children as productive family members. *Young Children, 41*(1), 3–7. The authors describe a project centering on children doing work at home, but the list of suggestions for making work appealing apply equally well to work opportunities at school.

Wenning, J., & Wortis, S. (1984). *Made by human hands: A curriculum for teaching young children about work and working people.* Cambridge, MA: The Multicultural Project for Communication and Education. While mainly dwelling on understanding work done by others, *Made by Human Hands* does include a brief discussion of jobs children can do. Suggested teaching units and bibliographies are included.

Wenning, J., & Wortis, S. (1988). Work in the child care center: A curriculum about working people. *Day Care and Early Education, 15*(4), 20–25. The authors suggest many ways children can learn about the jobs adults do at the center and also suggest ways children themselves can participate in meaningful work.

Wilson, G. L. (1985). Teaching pre-schoolers about work—A complex task. *Interracial Books for Children: Bulletin, 16*(4), 9–14. Wilson discusses teaching about paid and unpaid work and helping children understand the relationship of work and money. A good nonsexist-nonracist bibliography of children's books is included.

For the Advanced Student

Jalongo, M. R. (1989). Career education: Review of research. *Childhood Education, 66*(2), 108–115. This review covers the subject of career education for children of all ages.

Lewko, J. H. (Ed.). (1987). How children and adolescents view the world of work. *New Directions for Child Development, 35* (Spring), 1–96. This issue of *New Directions* reports a number of research studies on how children above preschool age perceive work.

CHAPTER 12

Providing Cross-Cultural, Nonsexist Education

I hear the train a comin',
A comin' round the curve.
She's using all her steam and brakes
And straining every nerve.

Get on board, little children,
Get on board, little children,
Get on board, little children,
There's room for many-a-more.

The fare is cheap and all can go,
The rich and poor are there.
No second class aboard this train,
No difference in the fare!

Get on board, little children,
Get on board, little children—
Get on board, little children!
There's room for many-a-more!

Have you ever wondered . . .

> What to say when a youngster says to a Black child, "I won't sit by you—your skin is dirty"?
>
> What to tell a 4-year-old who asks where babies come from?
>
> What to do about name calling and racial insults?
>
> How to help children value everyone, no matter what their race or color or sex?

If you have, the material in the following pages will help you.

The wonderful lines of the old gospel tune,

> No second class aboard this train,
> No difference in the fare!

sum up what is meant by *equity in education* because in a well-presented cross-cultural, nonsexist curriculum there are no second-class children and surely no difference in what children must do or be in order to be allowed on the train with the other youngsters.

Perhaps the reader is thinking indignantly, "What does she mean! Of course there are no second-class children," but the truth is that sometimes teachers *do* treat some children as being second-class people.

EXAMPLES OF TEACHER PREJUDICE

Many examples of the way teacher prejudice shows through in relations between teachers and students are presented by Leacock (1982), who reviewed studies of teacher attitudes toward low- and middle-income children who were Black or White. She reported that teachers not only spoke less frequently about curriculum matters to the Black children but also made many more critical and negative remarks to them, with poor Black children receiving the brunt of the negative comments. This was true even when teachers were Black themselves and when little difference in behavior by the children could be noted.

Prejudice shows through in the different ways some nursery school teachers treat boys and girls. For example, Serbin, Connor, and Citron (1978) report that in one study boys were more likely to be reprimanded for aggression than girls were, that they received much more detailed instruction on how to solve problems then girls did, and that little girls had to be closer to the teacher than little boys did to be noticed by her.

Prejudice can also be expressed in more subtle ways. For example, when Hendrick and Stange (1990) analyzed the conversational behavior of children and their teachers at the snack table, she found that not only did 4-year-old boys interrupt the teacher more than the girls did, but also that teachers interrupted the girls far more often than they interrupted the boys.

Can we deny, with such evidence before us, that many of us, however inadvertently, are actually relegating some children to second-class status?

CAN SUCH ATTITUDES BE CHANGED?

Fortunately, the answer to this question is yes—at least to some degree. Although we must realize that attitudes and responses to groups, or individual representatives of certain groups, stem from long-ingrained habits and prejudices, research shows that teachers *can* change, and children can, too.

Changes in Teachers' Attitudes

In the follow-up study, Serbin and colleagues (1978) reported that after instruction and "consciousness raising," teachers were able to change their behavior and notice children of both sexes whether they were nearby or across the room—one of the results being that the little girls stopped hovering around the teacher so much and began to make fuller use of the room's opportunities. In her journal, *White Teacher*, Paley (1979) gives an encouraging description of how she grew and changed as she came to appreciate the value of cultural pluralism as an approach to teaching.

This willingness to grow and change is becoming ever more vital because the population of children in the schools is changing. Statistics from the 25 largest school districts in the United States support this claim (Washington & Oyemade, 1987). Whereas 1 in 10 children in 1950 was from a minority group; by 1970, 1 in 2 was of minority background; and currently minorities constitute the majority of schoolchildren in 23 out of 25 of the nation's largest cities.

Changes in Children's Attitudes

Guttentag and Bray (1976) demonstrated that children's attitudes about sex roles could be changed when they encouraged teachers to provide numerous examples of various career possibilities to kindergarteners. Following this experience the children saw women as capable of holding higher status jobs, saw fewer jobs as being restricted to one sex, and listed more jobs as being possible for women to hold than they had thought possible prior to that educational experience.

In an English study where the teachers were concerned about prejudice against the children of West Indian and Pakistani immigrants, Milner (1981) reported that the use of multiethnic materials in kindergarten and first grade had a somewhat positive effect on the English children (results almost reached statistical significance) but had a pronounced effect on the immigrant children, who had been ambivalent about the value of their racial identity. By the program's end more than half of these youngsters "had thoroughly identified themselves with their own racial group" (p. 10).

Spencer and Markstrom-Adams (1990) report an experiment with preschool children that used dolls and token reinforcers in an attempt to shift negative connotations toward the color black and Black people to more positive attitudes. Although both the Black and White experimenters were equally well trained, it turned out that "the white experimenter was more reinforcing of the child's acquisition of new pro-black color connotations, attitudes, and preferences" (p. 295). While interesting to note the difference in effectiveness of the experimenters that the authors ascribe to the difference in races, it is also important to note that it *was* possible to shift the children's attitudes to a more positive attitude.

Little girls need to be adventurous, too.

Suggestions for Controlling and Overcoming the Expression of Prejudice

Of course, none of us wants to be prejudiced, but studies such as the ones described force us to examine our consciences. We must also realize that different people are prejudiced against different things. Some teachers who are not concerned about skin color or ethnic background may find they have real difficulty accepting the lifestyles of some families they serve. They may feel ill at ease with unmarried couples or with vegetarians, or they may disapprove of how welfare recipients spend their money.

The problem for the teacher is that it is difficult to see things from another's point of view and to accept rather than wish to change the attitudes of someone with different values. Most teachers either consciously or unconsciously intend that families and children will move over to the teacher's side of the value scale. Thus teachers are likely to use the term *culturally deprived* to describe children who, though deprived of middle-class Anglo culture, actually possess a rich culture of their own.

For example, many teachers deplore the high noise levels and large numbers of people often present in the Black home environment, seeing it as being chaotic, but other researchers, looking at it from the Black perspective, see it as producing a stimulating environment that produces greater "verve" in Black children (Hale, 1986).

A wonderful quotation from Tolstoy that comes to mind sums it all up. "Everyone thinks of changing the world, but no one thinks of changing himself." If we could only learn to accept some differences as being just that, *differences*, without condemning them, it could be the beginning of changing ourselves and accepting a wider, more tolerant view of the world.

Sometimes, of course, people either cannot or do not wish to change their points of view, and the rest of us need to accept that! But, if they are teachers, they should at the very least make certain they practice some mental hygiene rules such as these suggestions quoted from Clark (1963, p. 107):

1. As a beginning, find ways to become acquainted with at least one person or family of each racial and cultural group in your community.

2. Extend common courtesies and titles of address to persons of all groups, regardless of sinful community customs, regardless of their position, and regardless of however strange it may seem at first.

3. Learn the difference between paternalism (that is, loving down, loving in "their place") and true . . . respect of one human being for another.

4. Keep a close check on your thoughts and feelings. Watch out for any tendency to blame whole groups of people for what individuals do.

5. When you hear rumors that reflect on any group, demand proof. Do not repeat lies.

6. Never use hateful terms that slur any group. Show disapproval when others use them.

7. Do not tell stories, however funny, that reflect on any group. Do not laugh at them.

8. As a present or future employee, welcome new workers without regard to race or creed. Make very sure the boss does not refuse to hire people of some group because he imagines you would resent it. If you are seeking a new job, inquire among organizations where no such distinctions are made.

9. Request a policy of non-discrimination where you spend your money. (Remember, business firms may discriminate in employment and in serving customers because they imagine this pleases you. Make sure they know that it does not.)

10. Where there is a choice, take your patronage where there is the most democracy in every way. And let the proprietor know why.

11. . . . When going with interracial groups to public places, always assume that you will be served. Many places will say "no" if you ask in advance, but will serve you when you come. It is good education for them to know you assume that they will serve you.

12. Watch out for the term "restricted." It generally means discrimination against someone.

Acquisition of knowledge about different ethnic groups and cultures can also foster understanding and acceptance and help the teacher overcome her own cultural deprivation. For example, the teacher who knows that owls are regarded as birds of ill omen and death by the Navajo will not include them in Halloween decorations, nor would a teacher visiting the home of a Japanese family refuse a cup of tea offered as a welcome.

It can be extraordinarily instructive to live for even a month on the amount of money allotted by the welfare department. Although some aspects of doing this are admittedly synthetic, finding out the ways people make do and manage to get by can increase the teacher's respect for their ingenuity as well as her understanding of their feelings of rage and helplessness. Finally, learning the language of the families and actually using it form the best cultural bridge of all, since the use of their language says to the families, "I'm really trying to meet you halfway."

Ethnic studies programs offer a wealth of information on particular cultures, and teachers should take such courses whenever they can. It will not only broaden their horizons but may also teach them how to avoid offending those whom they really want to help. Even just reading about the characteristics of various ethnic groups can help build appreciation and sensitivity to variations in cultural style. Personal interviews, which are assigned in some courses, are particularly valuable in overcoming stereotypes and building friendships.

DO YOUNG CHILDREN NOTICE ETHNIC AND GENDER DIFFERENCES?

It is evident from the studies cited that what teachers and parents do in this area of cross-cultural and nonsexist education can really make a difference—a difference for good or evil. But the question remains, Do young children really notice the ethnic or gender differences of other children? If not, perhaps they are too young to require instruction. Might it not be better to ignore these issues and practice "color blindness" rather than make children self-conscious about such differences when they are so young?

Although some teachers might still prefer to answer yes to these questions, research on the perception of differences in skin color shows that children as young as age 3 respond to the skin color of Blacks and Mexican-Americans (Katz, 1982; Morland, 1972; Parrillo, 1985). Beuf (1977) has reported that this is also true for preschool-age native American youngsters of Southwestern and Plains tribes. Moreover, the number of these differentiating responses increases markedly from age 3 to 5. A study by Derman-Sparks, Higa, and Sparks (1980) of the questions and comments by preschool children provides continuing evidence of their concern with and awareness of racial and cultural differences. These ranged from "Is Mexican my color?" to "I didn't know that babies came out Black."

Awareness of ethnic differences precedes the development of prejudice, so we must also ask, When do positive or negative *attitudes* toward ethnic differences begin to surface? After an extensive review of the literature, Aboud (1988) concludes:

> Ethnic attitudes are acquired by most children some time between the ages of 3 and 5 years. The age of 4 is probably a safe bet if one wanted to pick a single age at which children express negative reactions to certain ethnic members. Whether the negativity is directed toward their own or other ethnicities depends to a certain extent on the child's own ethnic membership. White children are consistently negative toward members of another group. Of the minority groups discussed here, only Native Indians were consistently more negative to their own group than to Whites. The other minority children—Blacks, Hispanics and Asians—were more heterogeneous in that some were initially more negative to their own ethnic members [than to Whites]. (p. 43)

Aboud goes on to say that as children approach age 7 and 8, there is an increasing tendency for all groups to assign the most preferred rating to children who come from their own ethnic background.

Awareness of sexual differences also begins as early as the age of 2 as any teacher of young children can attest, and children will comment freely on such differences unless suppressed (Greenberg, 1985; Gundersen, Meläs, & Skär, 1981). One has only to listen during any toilet period in a children's center to hear such remarks as "Why don't she have a hole in her pants?" or "Don't you use that thing to wet on me!"

These kinds of comments and questions from the children, as well as the more formal research already cited, make it clear that the children are indeed revealing a dawning awareness of ethnic and gender differences and developing feelings about these differences at a very early age. If we want them to learn at this same sensitive time that such differences are to be valued rather than scorned, that is, if we wish to combat the formation of bias and prejudice at the earliest possible moment, then we must conclude that early childhood is the time to begin.

WHAT DO CROSS-CULTURAL AND NONSEXIST EDUCATION HAVE IN COMMON?

Perhaps the reader has been startled at finding cross-cultural and nonsexist topics linked together in one chapter even though it is now clear that a common problem of bias ties them together.

They are linked together also because there are two underlying educational principles that apply to both subjects. One principle is that we want children to value their *unique* identity both in relation to their ethnic background and their gender. The other is that we want children to learn that people of all races and both sexes have many *needs and abilities in common*, and we must recognize these held-in-common needs and abilities and encourage their satisfaction if we want to enable all children to make use of their potential.

In the following pages these principles will be applied first to cross-cultural and then to nonsexist education.

Have to get that temperature set just right!

PRINCIPLES OF CROSS-CULTURAL EDUCATION

Encouraging Equity by Recognizing and Honoring Cultural Differences

It is particularly important that the teacher seek to honor each child for his cultural and ethnic uniqueness because this positive valuing has a profound effect on increasing self-esteem, and positive self-esteem is vital in maintaining good mental health. Such acceptance and honoring of diversity, sometimes termed *teaching cultural pluralism*, helps children learn that different does not mean inferior. The emphasis in the following pages is placed primarily on this *pluralistic education* because that appears to be the place where teachers need the most help.

Importance of Sensitivity

The policy of recognizing cultural differences and honoring them used to be the exception rather than the rule in public schools. Readers may recall the books used in their own elementary school days wherein pink and white children visited Grandpa's farm and pulled their puppy around in a shiny new wagon. Now the trend is in the other direction, and we are finally able to purchase at least a few books and learning materials that have true relevance to family life in a variety of cultures.

Although these materials are of value, the student should also realize that teaching about differences must be done with sensitivity. In their extensive study of children's views of foreign peoples, Lambert and Klineberg (1972) question the desirability of teaching that emphasizes that foreign people are different or peculiar. The desirability of emphasizing differences should also be questioned when teaching about friends and neighbors. We do not want young children to deduce from our presentations of varying cultural strengths and values that a child should be set apart because of variation in custom or behavior. It would defeat the entire purpose of cross-cultural education if we generated experiences where people felt they were being used or as though they were being mounted on the head of a pin and examined.

Instead the basic learning should be that everyone is worthwhile and that each child brings with him from his family special things that enrich the group and that are fun to share. In other words, we hope to teach that each child is special, not that each child is peculiar.*

Relate Cross-Cultural Learnings to the Here and Now

Just as other learnings are linked to reality, cross-cultural learnings should be linked to present experiences in which the children are actually involved. I don't know what leads otherwise sensible teachers to lose their heads and retreat to quaint pictures of little Dutch girls when they begin to talk about people of different cultures.

However, even when the people are real there can still be limited benefit in exposing young children to the concept of foreigners and foreign countries. An incident that happened in my own school comes to mind that illustrates this point. The Institute was visited by a delegation of Russian women touring the United States as part of the Peace Links group. Our families had, as usual, been informed of the impending visit, so on the following evening one of the fathers

---

*Since it is impossible to discuss each ethnic or cultural group in detail in a single chapter, in the following discussion I have used examples from as many individual cultures as possible. There is, of course, no one set of culture-based learning experiences universally appropriate to all early childhood programs, because each group of children has its own ethnically and socially unique composition (Ramsey, 1982). Teachers who want to provide culturally responsive environments for the children in their particular group will find it helpful to peruse the references included at the end of this chapter for more detailed information on specific cultures. Fortunately there are also some general principles that can be applied in almost all circumstances.

asked his little girl if she had enjoyed the visitors. "Oh, yes," she replied. "They were real nice grandmas!" "Ah," he said, "that's good, I'm glad you liked them. By the way, where did you say they came from?" "Oh," she replied, "they didn't say—" she paused, wrinkling her brow in thought, "but I think they were from some place out of town."

An interesting example of an effective way of helping children relate cross-cultural experiences to the here and now of their daily lives comes from some teachers at Pacific Oaks College who have been doing just that with considerable success. They are developing what is called "The Anti-Bias Curriculum" (Pacific Oaks College, 1989), and they define the purpose of that curriculum as being to "empower people to resist being oppressed or to resist oppressing others." The work includes dealing with concerns about bias against gender and handicaps as well as about racial prejudice.

Although space does not permit a review of all their ideas here, I want to provide a taste of what they suggest in the hope that interested readers will pursue the matter further on their own (Derman-Sparks & the ABC Task Force, 1989). The curriculum, which emerges from day-to-day life experiences at the school, stresses the importance of fostering direct, open communication with children that helps them become aware of racially oppressive beliefs and learn that they can begin to counter these beliefs with positive action.

The children are mixing cornstarch, water, and tempera to make "skin" gloves that match their skin color.

The teaching varies with the child's age, of course, in order for it to be developmentally appropriate. For example, they favor providing 2-year-olds with direct information about race, such as the fact that the brown color of skin does not wash off and is not dirty; whereas older 5-year-olds are encouraged to participate in more activist possibilities. These have included helping the children recognize examples of unfair practices and take action to correct them. One instance involved the youngsters writing to an adhesive bandage company advocating the development of bandages not geared to pinkie-white skins, and another involved painting over a wall near their school that had been covered with racist graffiti.

How much more meaningful it is to children to offer such down-to-earth experiences that are closely related to their own lives and that include activities they can do and enjoy rather than exposing the youngsters momentarily to people "from out of town"! The satisfaction they experience while participating in such activities can build a foundation of positive attitudes toward other cultures on which we can build more advanced concepts at a later date.

Provide a Cross-Cultural Link Between Home and School

The past 15 years have witnessed the publication of stories about Black, Indian, Mexican-American, and Asian children. Records and pictures are also available, but it is not necessary to depend on only commercial sources. Children often know rhymes and songs from their families, and the teacher can learn these with the parents' coaching and then help youngsters teach them to the group. Most homes have popular records or tape decks, but this is a resource frequently ignored by teachers who deem the music vulgar. However, many of the children's homes are saturated with blues or country music, and using such music in school can draw into movement and dance children who spurn less colorful songs about little duckies waddling around the fish pond.

Reaching the child by using his dominant language is even more important. Someone must be available in every preschool room who can understand what the child has to say and who can make friends with him in his own language. Even such simple courtesies as learning to pronounce the child's name as his family does rather than anglicizing it can make a difference. The subject of teaching English as a second language and the use of Black English is discussed more fully in chapter 16. I pause here only to emphasize that a bicultural or multicultural program is a farce if we deny the child the right to speak his native tongue or dialect. To be truly effective, cross-cultural programs must honor language as well as other traditions.

Serving familiar food is another excellent way to honor particular backgrounds and to help children feel at home. Sometimes a shy child who appears to be a poor eater is actually just overwhelmed by the strangeness of the food served to him. Food in some day care centers still seems to be planned with the best of nutritional intentions but with total disregard of local food patterns and customs. This situation can be remedied by asking parents for suggestions about appropriate food, by using recipes from ethnic cookbooks (see the references following chapter 3), and by employing a cook who comes from a culture similar to that of the majority of the children.* Children can also be encouraged to bring recipes from home that they can cook at school, or mothers or grandmothers may have time to come and participate in this way. As the children feel more at ease, it can also be fun to branch out and visit local markets and delicatessens that specialize in various ethnic foods. For example, even in a community as small as my own, we have a Chinese market, several Mexican-American tortilla factories, and German and Greek delicatessens. (Delicatessens are particularly good to visit because the food is ready, and it smells good and looks attractive.)

The special customs of the children must be considered, too. For example, we discovered the reason one Saudi Arabian child was not eating much lunch was because he had been taught that it is good manners to refuse food the first time it is offered!

Holidays and other special occasions are also good times for children to share various customs. I recall one event in our group when a young boy lit Hanukkah candles and explained their purpose and the custom of gift giving very clearly. (It was specially fortunate that he was able to do this because he had recently experienced a severe burn, and the prestige of lighting the candles helped him overcome his fear of fire as well as add enrichment to the life of our group.)

A note of caution should be inserted here about the need to increase our sensitivity to the way some people feel about certain holidays. For example, some Indian groups have come to feel increasingly angry about the stereotyped presentation of Indians during the Thanksgiving season. All too often Indians in these circumstances are presented as wearing feathers in their hair and dancing around, war whooping as they go, and their real contribution toward helping the Pilgrims, as well as the way the White people ultimately responded, is overlooked. For this reason some Indian groups have gone so far as to observe Thanksgiving as a time of mourning for the Wampanoag Indians—the people who helped the Pilgrims so generously during those early days and who have almost completely disappeared. (Derman-Sparks and the ABC Task Force, 1989; Ramsey, 1979).

The backgrounds of each child may be savored by the group in many additional ways. Dress-up clothes that reflect the occupations of various parents or national costumes, when they can be spared, contribute much to the life of the school. Stories brought from home, ethnically accurate and attractive dolls, and integrated pictures are also good choices. *Such cross-cultural materials should be available consistently rather than presented as isolated units.* Dolls, pictures, books, and music from many cultures should be deliberately, though apparently casually, woven into the fabric of every preschool day.

---

*Refer also to Table 3.4 for cultural food preferences of seven ethnic groups.

It is, of course, also necessary to take a continuing close look at the materials, particularly books, offered to the children to make certain they are not teaching undesirable attitudes. Just as we are making the effort to become sensitive to sexist books that perpetuate certain role models as acceptable for girls or boys, so must we also become more sensitive to racist themes and roles, and such slanted books abound.

For example, in a review of 66 children's books, mainly about Americans of Chinese and Japanese ancestry, the committee from the Asian American Children's Book Project concluded that all but two were "racist, sexist, and elitist" and that "the image of Asian Americans they present is grossly misleading" (1976, p. 3). Among the things the committee objected to were the emphasis on exotic festivals and ancient superstitions and the promotion of the myth that Asian Americans are a "model minority."

In a study of books about Puerto Rican children that evaluated trends from 1972 to 1982, Nieto (1983) reports the equally unsatisfactory finding that the quality of children's books about that country has not improved markedly since a survey completed in 1972 (Council on Interracial Books for Children, 1976). Flaws in current books include the inaccurate use of Spanish, little or no mention of racial oppression, and an overglorification of the United States and the joys it holds for Puerto Rican immigrants. Reviews of books on Central American themes repeat the same complaint: unfair misrepresentation of peoples and countries (Anderson & Beck, 1982).

Not only has the quality of books remained spotty, the actual number of books published about minority children is declining. For example, the number of in-print children's books about Blacks has declined from 950 titles in 1974 to 450 in 1984 (Banfield, 1985).

These comments and trends should alert teachers to the continuing necessity of reviewing the books we read to the children with great care. Appendix D offers some helpful guidelines to follow when selecting books about minority children. We need also to be aware that the supply is diminishing. Publishers print what the public will buy. If we want to have a continued supply of good quality books that represent the cultures of all the children we teach, we are going to have to write to publishers and make our desires known.

Suggestions That Foster Cross-Cultural Understanding
Going Beyond Foods, Books, and Holidays

What worries me about listing such ideas as the ones above is that so many teachers seem to think this is all there is to multicultural education, whereas it is actually only the beginning. We must realize that the basic purpose of providing multicultural experience is *not* to teach the children facts about Puerto Rico or Japan, or to prove to the community that the teacher is not prejudiced. *The purpose of multicultural curriculum is to attach positive feelings to multicultural experiences so that each child will feel included and valued and will also feel friendly and respectful toward people from other ethnic and cultural groups.*

When you get right down to it, all the multiethnic pictures and recipes and books in the world will not make much difference if teachers, in their hearts, cannot appreciate the strong points of each child and his family and help the other children appreciate them also.

Dealing with Racial Comments and Slurs at the Preschool Level

Preprimary teachers often ask me how they should reply when a 3- or 4-year-old comments on the difference in skin color of one of their classmates.

It seems to me there are two kinds of comments. The first is the kind of information-seeking question cited previously by Derman-Sparks and coworkers (1980): "Will it rub off?" or "How come her backs [of hands] are brown but her fronts are pink?"

Such comments should be welcomed (rather than brushed aside in an embarrassed way) because they provide opportunities to clear up confusions about skin color. Our Black head teacher has taught us all never to allow such opportunities to slip past. She is quick to explain and demonstrate that skin color does not wash off and that it is not dirty. She also points out that people may be different colors on the outside, but we are all the same color on the inside.

The second kind of comment, however, is more difficult to handle. When 4-year-old Sue yells at Jimmy, "That's my trike, you dirty nigger, get off!" it is easy for teachers to feel so upset and angry they lose sight of the probable reason such a young child resorts to such an ugly slur.

First of all it is necessary to remember that 3- and 4-year-olds do not comprehend the full extent of the insult—just as they rarely comprehend the true meaning of son-of-a-bitch. What they *do* know about these words is that they have a strong emotional power to hurt, and the children who are using these words use them because they *are* angry and they *do* intend to hurt. This means that the problem has to be dealt with in two parts.

Part one has to do with pointing out to *both* children the real reason Sue is angry. She is angry because she does not want Jimmy taking her trike, not because he is Black. It is important for Jimmy to understand this to protect his self-esteem. It is important for Sue to realize that it is not the color of the person taking her trike that matters, it is the fact she does not want *anyone* taking it at all. *She needs to learn to attach anger to its real cause rather than displacing it by substituting innocent or incorrect reasons.* This not only helps prevent the formation of prejudice but also is a basic principle of mental health everyone needs to learn and practice.

Following this clear labeling of the reason for the fight, coupled with a brief description of each child's feelings ("I can see you're angry, and I can see you don't want to wait"), the argument has to be settled just as any other fight would have to be. The second part of the problem must also be faced. No one likes having his feelings hurt, and name calling of any sort is intended to and does hurt feelings. Although the usual advice about such matters is that if "bad" language is ignored it will go away, experience in the real world of day care has taught me that sometimes ignoring such words works and sometimes it does not. It is also true that some name calling hurts worse than others, and when this is the case, it is necessary for the teacher to be quite firm and clear with children about what is acceptable and stop what is not.

These standards of acceptability vary from school to school. My own level of tolerance is that although I can ignore many insults and bathroom words, I will not tolerate racial or sexist insults to myself or to anyone else. So, after dealing with the social contretemps just described, I would take Sue aside for a quiet, firm talk about hurt feelings, reiterating the rule, "We do not use the word nigger because it hurts too much. When you're mad at Jimmy, hold onto the trike and tell him 'You can't have the trike—I'm using it now. You have to wait 'til I'm done,' *but we do not use the word nigger in our school.*"*

As the moment presents itself, I would also say again to Jimmy that Sue was mad at him because he grabbed her trike, and she wanted to get even by calling him "nigger." Next time he had better ask for the trike instead of just taking it. If she calls him "nigger" again, pay no attention, she just does not know any better yet.

It is important to understand that the problem of helping minority children deal with such attacks is a difficult one and could fill a book by itself. Wilson (1980) suggests many ways families can help Black children defend themselves against such attacks. She states that it is important for children to be able to respond with dignity and keep control of themselves. They might respond by saying, "Call me by my name!" or say, "Don't call me that again." She stresses that youngsters need a range of strategies that include everything from ignoring the taunt, to walking away and then returning with a reply, getting help from someone else, combining a response with getting help, and sharing the sadness at home, where she cautions parents that children should be allowed to cry about it if they feel like doing that and they should be comforted. In addition, it should be pointed out once again that providing the continuing countermeasure of building pride in ethnicity, which was discussed earlier in the chapter, is probably the strongest defense of all.

Show Respect for People of Differing Ethnic Origins by Employing Them as Teachers

Cross-cultural learning in the children's center should be based on real experiences with real people whenever possible. This means, for example, that when we talk about how to emphasize that Mexican people are effective human beings, it is just not satisfactory at such an early level to use the historical examples recommended in many Hispanic curriculum guides. Historical figures are so remote and intangible they do not mean much to preschoolers.

A much more effective way of teaching young children that people of all ethnic backgrounds are important is to employ them in positions of power. Many schools employ minority group members as aides. But this is far from

---

*I realize that in some circles of Black people "nigger" is no longer a derogatory term, but this is still untrue for the majority of the population.

enough. Children are quick to sense the power structure of the school, and they need to see people of all ethnic backgrounds are employed in the most respected positions as teachers and directors.

Unfortunately, Asian, Mexican, Indian, and Black preschool teachers are still relatively rare. Professional associations can and should help remedy this deficiency by encouraging their local colleges to recruit heavily among ethnic groups other than Anglo, and they can also help by offering scholarships to sustain such students through college. Even a modest book scholarship may mean the difference for some young people between going to a community college or working in the variety store.

Increase the Number and Variety of Children in the School Who Come from Various Ethnic and Cultural Groups

As I commented earlier, some full-day centers and Head Start–type groups are luckier in the assortment of children who come naturally to their doors than are middle-class schools. Such multiethnic contacts can introduce children at an early age to the values of an integrated society. It can teach the basic fact that James's face is not dirty because it is brown and can couple this learning with the fact that James is fun to play with because he is the best block builder in the school.

Suggestions for Recruiting Children for Middle-Class Nursery Schools

In *The Shortchanged Children of Suburbia,* Miel and Kiester (1967) comment on the "extraordinary effort [that] was required to bring about any encounter between a child of the suburbs and persons different from himself. . . . He is largely insulated from any chance introduction to a life different from his own" (p. 3). Twenty-five years later such insulation remains the case for many youngsters as "white flight" continues to the suburbs and more and more northeastern schools become racially segregated.

Some middle-class nursery schools who feel this isolation is undesirable try to achieve a better ethnic balance through recruitment. The teacher who attempts this should realize that families understandably resent being used as tokens or being included only because of their color or poverty. The slightest trace of condescension or patronage will give offense, and it requires tact and genuine warmth to achieve participation by all.

Middle-class schools may do best when recruiting if they find three or four mothers who can come at the same time and therefore lend each other moral support. The fact that some states now allow their welfare departments to purchase child care from any licensed center also makes recruitment easier. Sometimes the children of foreign students can be sought out and included.

Of course, the closer the school is to the children it serves, the more likely it is that families will participate. Why should a Mexican mother trek her child halfway across town for the dubious privilege of placing him in an all-white children's center? It is hardly reasonable to accuse people of being standoffish under such circumstances; yet I have heard this conclusion drawn when such an invitation was refused.

Involve and Honor All Parents When They Visit the Center

I recommended earlier that teachers should seek to acquaint themselves with various cultures by reading, taking courses, learning the language, and so forth, but I want to emphasize here that the most vigorous and lively source of ethnic learning is right on the school's doorstep, namely, the families themselves. In the long run, cooperative sharing of themselves and their skills will teach the teacher and the children the most about the personal strengths of family members. As a matter of fact, I do not see how one could conduct a multiethnic classroom without drawing on these resources.

Successful communication is vital.   The teacher who is unafraid of parents and who genuinely likes them will communicate this without saying anything at all; there is really no substitute for this underlying attitude of good will and concern for the children. All parents appreciate the teacher who has the child's welfare genuinely at heart, and this mutual interest in the child is the best base on which to build a solid teacher-parent relationship. Since listening is so much more important than talking, teachers should particularly cultivate that ability in themselves.

Other matter-of-fact things about communication can help when speaking with the foreign born. A friend of mine to whom English is a foreign language suggests that teachers speak slower (but not louder!) and without condescension when talking with parents who are learning English. Sometimes writing something down in English also helps since some parents read English better than they understand the spoken word.

It is also worthwhile to go to the trouble of having a translator handy when necessary. This may be another adult, but sometimes it can even be a 4- or 5-year-old who is bilingual. Notices sent home stand a much better chance of being read if they are written in the language of the home. Both languages should be printed side by side to avoid the implication that the one that comes first is better.

Welcome parent volunteers.   The problem with making parents feel at ease and glad to participate in the school program is that they are always a little out of their element in the beginning. I have often thought that it would be fair to require the teacher to visit and help out in the families' homes on a turnabout basis. If this were possible, it would certainly help teachers gain a better insight into how it feels to step into a strange situation where the possibility of making fools of themselves is quite likely.

Over and over I have witnessed teachers asking mothers to wipe off tables or help in the kitchen, or letting them simply stand around, smiling a lot, but knowing in their hearts their time is being wasted. Visitors may prefer simple tasks in the beginning because these are familiar, not threatening, and because

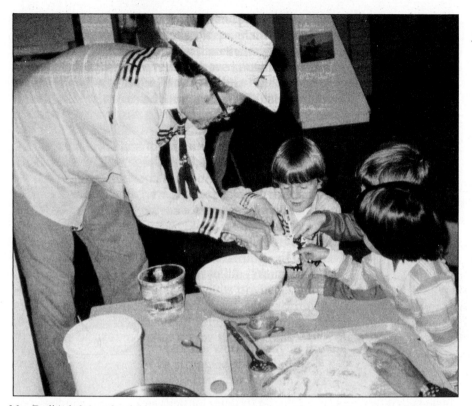

Mr. Duff is helping the children make fry bread. Contact with real Indian people can help children understand that they do not always wear feathers or dance around giving war whoops.

they do not want to make waves or antagonize the teacher. However, keeping them at such tasks is fundamentally denigrating, teaches the children that parents are not important at school, and deprives the children of the unique contribution such people can make if properly encouraged. For example, instead of setting up the tables for lunch, a mother might share with the children a book she has kept from her own childhood or bring pictures of her family's latest trip to India, or help the children make her child's favorite recipe or bring the baby for a visit and let the children help bathe him (this presents a specially nice opportunity to teach about the universal similarities of human beings). Last fall one of the fathers in our group who is a member of the Wichita tribe helped the children make an authentic (and tasty) squash and cornmeal dessert. The children were delighted.

Remember that the fundamental purpose of providing these experiences is to create emotionally positive situations for the children and the adults who are involved. For this reason the teacher should concentrate on doing everything possible to help visitors feel comfortable and successful. It takes considerable planning, but the results are worth it.

Although it is not fair to put parents on the spot and ask them to control a group of children they do not know, it can be genuine fun and very helpful to have parent volunteers come along on field trips where everyone can be together and where everyone takes some responsibility. Families who are poor may latch on to such opportunities to get out and do things, and field trips can be a refreshing change for mothers who are homebound otherwise. On trips where toddlers would be a burden, we have, from time to time, worked out arrangements whereby two mothers take over the little ones while others come on the trip, and then switch off child care the next trip.

Families can often provide ideas for excursions, too. The children at our center greatly enjoyed a visit to a communal organic garden one spring, and they also loved a trip to a pizza parlor owned by one of the families.

Make visitors welcome for meals.   One of the wisest policies of the Head Start program has been their welcoming, open attitude at mealtimes. I cannot recall working in a Head Start center where people were not spontaneously invited to share meals with the children, and it is true that breaking bread binds people together in basic friendliness. If possible, this is a good policy for all schools to follow. When finances cannot support this drain, visiting parents can order lunch a day in advance and pay a nominal fee to defray the cost.

Trust and use parent expertise on the advisory board.   All programs receiving federal funds are required to have advisory boards that must have at least 50% parent representation to be legal. But many schools use such boards as rubber stamps and present parents with programs and plans literally for approval rather than for consideration and modification—a policy that certainly does not make parents feel welcome or respected. A much better way to make plans is to trust the parents. It is unlikely they will suggest activities or policies detrimental to the children; and when differences arise, they can usually be settled by open discussion, which educates everyone.

Teachers who seek out parents' suggestions because they value their practical experience with their children will find that this approach reduces the parents' feelings of defensiveness when the teacher happens to be better educated or better paid. If meetings are held during times when child care is available, more board members are likely to attend. Attendance also increases when parent suggestions are actually used and when parents are thanked sincerely for coming.

Emphasizing the Similarities As Well As Valuing the Uniqueness of People

Children and families not only need to have their cultural uniqueness welcomed and valued, they also need to learn that all people have many things in common and that they are alike in some fundamental ways.

Teach the Commonality of Biological and Psychological Needs

One way to teach the similarities of all people is to emphasize the commonality of biological and psychological needs. Thus, when talking about the children's favorite food or what they traditionally eat for various holidays, the teacher can remind them that no matter what we like to eat best, everyone gets hungry and everyone likes to eat some things or can point out at the right moment that it feels good to everyone to stretch and yawn or to snuggle down in something warm and cozy.

The same principle can be taught in relation to emotions: everyone feels mad sometimes, everyone wants to belong to somebody, most people want to have friends, and most children feel a little lost when their mothers leave them at school.

In addition, the teacher can draw the children's attention to the fact that people often use individual, unique ways to reach a goal that most people enjoy. For example, Josie's father plays the guitar, while Heather's mother uses the zither; but they both use these different instruments for the pleasure of making music and singing together with the children.

Help Families Look Beyond Various Differences to Focus on Common Goals

Schools of various types can provide opportunities for friendships to form and thrive. Cooperatives are famous for doing this, of course, but it can also be accomplished in other groups. Advisory boards can draw families into projects that focus on the children and benefit everyone. This activity can take the form of a potluck dinner, with slides of what the children have been doing; it can be a series of discussions on topics chosen by the parents; it can be a workday combined with a picnic lunch where everyone pitches in to clean and paint and tidy up. (There is nothing like scrubbing a kitchen floor together to generate a common bond.) It makes little difference what is chosen, as long as it results in the realization of a common goal and creates opportunities for everyone to be together in a meaningful, friendly way.

Keep Working Toward the Basic Goals of Socialization That Teach Children to Consider the Rights and Needs of Everyone

Finally, the teacher should remember that working toward the goals of socialization discussed in chapter 8 will help children learn that everyone has the same basic rights and privileges and everyone is respected and treated fairly at school. The social goals most important to emphasize in relation to cross-cultural education are developing empathy for how other people feel, learning that everyone has rights that are respected by all, and gaining skill cooperating rather than achieving satisfaction by competing and winning over others. If these social skills are fostered, living in the group will be a good experience for all the children, and a healthy foundation will be laid for a more truly integrated society in the future.

CAN TEACHING ABOUT CULTURAL UNIQUENESS AND SIMILARITY OF NEEDS BE COMBINED?

There is at least one way to teach preschool children both concepts—that is, that people are enjoyably unique and that they have many similar needs in common at the same time. The staff at our day care center gradually evolved this approach after passing through two earlier stages.

During the first stage, in an effort to make experiences more real for the children, students and staff tended to bring in things from other cultures for the children to pass around and look at during group time, or the items were displayed on a table accompanied by books and pictures about the culture. This was, basically, a beginning attempt to honor cultural uniqueness. We now refer to this as "our museum period."

During the second stage we increased the here-and-now aspect by doing a lot of the sort of thing described in the first part of this chapter. We cooked ethnic foods together and enjoyed them, or we celebrated a holiday or made a piñata and talked about how there were many wonderful ways of satisfying hunger or having parties. We still continue to offer many of these stage 2 experiences during the week, and the children continue to appreciate them.

However, the staff remained unsatisfied with these approaches. It just did not seem to us that we were helping the children grasp the reality and value of other cultures and appreciate the common humanity that binds us all. With such young children we felt we needed to link things together in more explicit and literal ways.

To accomplish *this* goal we developed a stage 3 approach. In this current stage we are offering the children comparative experiences where they can actually try out what it is like to sleep in a Czechoslovakian feather bed, a Guatemalan hammock, and our child-sized "American" bed, and we make these comparative play experiences available for a week at a time.

In another example we set up a comparison between Japanese and Western eating styles. On the Japanese side the children took their shoes off upon entering, sat on low cushions, and used bowls and chopsticks as they partook of ramen noodles and Japanese cookies. (Our Japanese children were gratifyingly proficient with chopsticks!) On the Western side they wiped their shoes on a mat, sat on low chairs, used plates and bowls, and had noodle soup and wheat crackers. In the offing is an experience comparing the different methods by which mothers carry their babies around, and one of our students has just finished a comparison of Navajo and Anglo weaving where the children tried out a Navajo-style loom.

Experiences do not have to be this elaborate to get the point across. During a warm spring rain last year, one of the students brought a number of banana leaves (often used in Thailand when it rains), and the children delighted in using them and comparing them to their more familiar umbrellas. Another easy comparison to offer is a simple tasting experience. For example, it's interesting to compare French bread, tortillas, matzoh, and pita bread; or various cheeses; or fruits that come from different countries such as mangoes, oranges, and guavas.

Once again, remember that families can make invaluable contributions of advice and resources if you decide to attempt stage 3 activities, and it is most beneficial when these experiences are family related and are based on the cultural backgrounds of children in the group.

Please understand that these more concentrated experiences do not constitute our entire approach to cross-cultural education. If they did, that would be too much like reverting to "Japanese Day" or "Cinco de Mayo." We continue to make certain that multiethnic materials such as books, pictures, puzzles, and other equipment are used throughout the school on a matter-of-fact, daily basis. The purpose of the stage 3 activities is to accentuate the fact that there is more than one satisfactory way to meet a human need and, most important of all, that many of these ways are *fun*.

ENCOURAGING EQUITY BY PROVIDING A NONSEXIST EDUCATION AND HELPING CHILDREN VALUE THEIR OWN SEXUALITY

Today, when educational emphasis tends to be placed on the value of nonsexist education, it may be necessary to remind the reader that it is also important to teach children about reproduction and gender differences and to help them value their maleness or femaleness.

Even though many of us want to enable children of both sexes to step beyond the narrowly restricted ideas of sex roles and stereotypes that presently exist, we must be careful to help them value their basic sexuality as well because that is an important and deeply elemental part of every individual's personality. If children grow up with the idea that sexuality is unimportant or not valued, or, worse yet, that reproduction and sex are smutty topics to be snickered about and investigated in secret, we may have unwittingly undone much of what we hoped to accomplish by adding a nonsexist emphasis to teaching.

Teaching Simple Physiological Facts

The more open and matter of fact teachers and parents can be about differences in the anatomy of boys and girls, the more likely it is that children will not need to resort to "doctor" play or hiding in corners to investigate such differences "on the q.t." Open toileting has long been the rule in most preschool settings because, when children use the same toilets, secrecy about sexual differences and toilet practices is avoided. This policy also generates opportunities for the teacher to supply answers to things young children wonder about, such as explaining why boys urinate standing up whereas girls sit down. The teacher makes simple statements about these matters: "Yes, boys and girls are made differently. Boys have penises, and so they stand up to urinate. Girls have vulvas, so they sit down." If little girls still want to know why they cannot stand up, the teacher can invite them to try it. There is no substitute for learning by experience! Casualness and answering questions actually asked, rather than ones the teacher is nervously afraid the children will ask, should be the order of the day.

Sometimes it helps clarify matters if the adult replies to questions by asking the youngster what he thinks the answer is, since this can provide a clue to how complicated the adult explanation should be. Sometimes, though, such a return question embarrasses an older 4-year-old who is sophisticated enough to suspect he should not be asking about such things anyway, and questioning in return can cause him to stop asking. So it takes a delicate perception of the child to know whether to respond with a question or just answer as simply and clearly as possible. Of course, if you want to keep the line open for more questions, it is deadly to betray amusement at some of the naive answers you will receive.

Although the use of accurate words such as *penis* or *vagina* is more commonplace than it used to be, teachers and parents should note there is an interesting piece of research which points out that grown-ups are more likely to use explicit terms when referring to boy's genitalia than when talking about the genitalia of little girls. Koblinsky, Atkinson, and Davis (1980) surmise this is because boy's genitals are more visible. It seems that what we adults need to learn from this research is that we must make a special effort to remember to discuss the anatomy of little girls as well as that of little boys, even though that part of the anatomy is not as apparent.

Since every child's self-concept is intimately tied to her or his sense of sexual worth, we must be careful to teach that each sex has an important role to play in reproduction. When grown, girls have the opportunity to carry and bear children, and boys, when grown, help start the baby growing. Then mothers and fathers work together to care for the baby following its birth.

(Bear in mind when discussing the dual roles of parenting that it is necessary to think about the child's home situation. So many children in day care now come from single-parent homes that this has to be gently taken into account in such discussions so that the child does not feel "different" or peculiar because he has only one parent. And yet, it is these very children who may be least experienced with mother-father roles and who need most help in understanding the ideal mutuality of the parenting relationship. It takes a combination of sensitivity and matter of factness without sentimentality or pity to deal with this problem successfully.)

Once past the matter of simple anatomical differences, it is still the case that many adults dread questions about reproduction and because of their discomfort either evade them (just as they avoid discussing race) or give such confused or elaborate replies that the children are bewildered. Therefore it can be reassuring to learn that the kind of question most preschool children are likely to ask is, "Where did the baby come from?" "How will it get out?" This level of questioning, common to 3- to 5-year-olds, is termed the "geography level" by Bernstein in a delightful book called *The Flight of the Stork* (1978). Thinking of it as a "geography" question can make it reasonably unembarrassing to explain that a baby is growing inside the mother's uterus or that it will be born through a special hole women have between their legs, near where their urine comes out but not exactly the same place.

For the slightly older youngster who wants to know how the baby gets inside to start with, it is far better to tell him or her the truth rather than to talk about animals or seeds. This is because when children see animals mating, it really looks like fighting to them or they may note an expression of resigned submission on the part of the female animal—attitudes we would rather not have children associate with human intercourse. The problem with the "planting seeds" idea is that it encourages them to think too literally about this concept in terms of what they already know about gardening. I was told of one little girl who queried after such a discussion, "Well, what *I* want to know is, when you picked out that seed, did it have my picture on it?"

To avoid such misconceptions, I suggest that the teacher or parent explain that the mother and father start the baby growing in the mother by being very loving and close with each other and that when they are feeling this way, the father fits his penis inside the mother's vagina and a fluid passes into her that joins with the mother's egg and helps the baby start growing. I prefer this explanation because it is truthful and accurate and also because it mentions the role of warmth, caring, and mutual responsibility as being important parts of the experience.

Masturbation

Another aspect of helping children value their own sexuality has to do with dealing with masturbatory behavior so that children are not shamed by the teacher's reprimand and do not come to feel that their sexual impulses are unclean or "bad."

Research indicates that masturbation is commonplace in adult males and females (Kinsey, Pomeroy, & Martin, 1948; Kinsey, Pomeroy, Martin, & Gebhard, 1953), and it is in children, too. Although the extent of such behavior is unknown in children (Langfeldt, 1981), a Norwegian study found that 85% of the kindergarten teachers who were interviewed reported that some of the children in their classes engaged in masturbation, though only 24% of the teachers reported that such behavior happened "often" or "very often" (Gundersen et al., 1981).

The question that confronts teachers once they admit the frequency and normality of the behavior is what to do about it, since it is still true that masturbating is not acceptable public behavior. It seems wisest to take the child aside and explain to her or him that you realize such behavior feels good but that it is something people do only in private.

Meeting the Special Needs of Boys in the Preschool

Still another aspect of helping children value their own sexuality has to do with recognizing the boys' needs for high-physical-energy activities and meeting their needs for role models in the children's center. Although it is difficult to talk about this without having it misinterpreted as advocating sexist practices, experience has taught me it is necessary to remind women teachers how important it is to provide young boys with many experiences that fit their needs and that do not feminize them since the temptation is to approve of "female type" activities and reward those with positive attention. LaTorre (1979), for example, cites a study that noted that the four preschool teachers that were observed paid attention to (reinforced) boys' behavior "approximately 86 percent [of the time] when it followed involvement in feminine behaviors" (p. 91).

Boys' physical activity needs appear to differ from those of girls, at least at the present time. Research shows they tend to engage in more rough-and-tumble play than girls do (Johnson & Roopnarine, 1983) and that they are more aggressive than girls are after the age of 2 (Barfield, 1976; Maccoby & Jacklin, 1974). But women teachers tend to suppress this vigor and energy, since it is contrary to the teacher's own behavior patterns and also makes running a day care center more difficult. Although all children need opportunities for vigorous physical activity, boys *do* seem to need it specially, and we must provide for meeting that need. Their play requires large, sturdy equipment, plenty of space, and a teacher who genuinely welcomes such activity rather than regarding it as a threat to her ability to control the children.

Boys not only must be supplied with enough room to move and to let off steam but also must have the chance to form relationships with men who can serve as models for them. In an age when the divorce rate remains high and many unmarried women are electing to raise their children rather than surrender them for adoption, many children in day care centers come from single-parent, mother-centered homes. The effect on the boy's developing sense of masculinity of these mother-centered, father-absent homes is at present uncertain. Herzog and Sudia (1973), after an extensive review of research, sum up their findings when they say, "The findings reviewed do not provide clear-cut and conclusive answers to . . . questions about the sturdiness of the masculine identity of fatherless boys as compared with that of boys in two-parent homes" (p. 184). However, common sense cannot help encouraging one to believe that the presence of a father facilitates sex-role development (although there is also evidence that boys can develop normally without it). For this reason centers should do all they can to provide consistent contacts for boys with men who care about children. Girls too benefit from such experience, since it probably helps them develop concepts of masculinity and femininity, also.

Incidentally, one of the continuing and unfortunate examples of sexism in our society is the fact that few men are employed as early childhood teachers (Robinson, 1988). In 1989 the Child Care Employee Project reported that out of 1,300 child-care workers surveyed in five metropolitan areas, only 3% were male (Cohen, 1990). According to Robinson (1988), this is due in part to the perception that such work requires the nurturing qualities commonly attributed to females rather than to males, but it is also due to low pay combined with rising concerns about the potential for accusations of child abuse.

These difficulties mean that we will continue to need to use ingenuity in thinking of ways to include men as participants in the preschool day. High school and college men can often be employed as aides, and occasionally warmhearted fathers will volunteer to come regularly and spend time with the children. All of the contacts, though admittedly not as satisfactory as a father's continuing presence in the home, will help both boys and girls formulate their concepts of what it means to be a man or woman in our society and, ideally, will

FIGURE 12.1 Summary of sex comparisons

Physical

Anatomy: Females have a uterus, ovaries, a clitoris, and a vagina.
   Males have testes, a penis, and a scrotum. Males tend to be bigger and more muscular.
Processes: Females mature faster, have slower metabolism.
   Differences in sensation are unclear; females may be more sensitive to touch, pain, and visual stimuli. Hormonal production is cyclic in females after puberty (ovulation and menstruation); it is mostly continuous in males.
Brain organization: Females may have less localization of function than males and may be cognitive specialists.
Vulnerability: Males are more vulnerable to disease, physical disorders, and early death.
Activity level: There are no differences in the amount of activity, although differences in type of movements and activities are found.

Cognitive

Learning and memory: No difference.
Intelligence: No difference in level of intelligence.
   Verbal: Females tend to excel up to age 3 and after age 11.
   Quantitative: Males tend to excel after age 12.
   Visual-spatial: Males tend to excel after age 8.
   Analytic: No difference.
   Concept mastery: No difference.
Cognitive style: Differences are unclear.
Creativity: No difference with nonverbal material; females tend to excel with verbal material.

Personality and Temperament

Self description: Females are more people-oriented; males are more achievement-oriented.
Emotionality: No difference during childhood.
Fears: The evidence is contradictory; females report more fears.

help boys and girls grow up to be sturdy, attractive men and women themselves.

Suggestions for Providing a Nonsexist Curriculum

Are boys really better than girls at analyzing problems? Are girls better than boys at nurturing and comforting others? Although research indicates that the answer to these questions is no, many teachers continue to act as if these myths were true and plan their curriculum and treat children accordingly, thereby limiting and preventing children of both sexes from reaching their true potential (Halpern, 1986). Figure 12.1 provides a quick overview of comparisons of sexual similarities and differences.

Social Behavior

Communication patterns
  Verbal: Males dominate.
  Nonverbal: Males dominate; females may be more sensitive to cues.
Person-centered interactions
  Dependency: No difference depending on the definition used.
  Affiliation: No difference during childhood. After adolescence, females tend to be more interested in people.
  Empathy: No difference depending on the situation and the person.
  Nurturance: No difference depending on experience.
  Altruism: No difference depending on the situation and the person.
Power-centered interactions
  Aggression: Males tend to be more aggressive after age 2.
  Assertiveness: Differences are unclear; depends on the situation and the person.
  Dominance: Differences are unclear; males may be more dominant depending on the situation.
  Competition and cooperation: Differences are unclear; males may be more competitive depending on the situation.
  Compliance: No difference depending on the situation and person to whom compliance is required.

Sexual Behavior

Response: No difference; females are capable of multiple orgasms.
Interest: Males express more and have more experiences. Meaning of sex may be different for the two sexes.
Response to erotica: No difference.
Homosexuality: Reported more in males.
Masturbation: Reported more in males.

From *Sex-Role Stereotypes: Traditions and Alternatives*, by S. A. Basow. © 1980 by Wadsworth, Inc. Reprinted by permission of the publisher, Brooks/Cole Publishing Co., Monterey, CA.

On the other hand, I have just emphasized the importance of encouraging children to treasure their physical functions and sexual potential as being significant aspects of their identity. Does this "treasuring" mean that teachers should not change former approaches to teaching about sex roles and establishing sexual identities for the children? Of course not. But it *does* mean they should be thoughtful, careful, and not destructive about what they plan to do and that they should have a clear grasp of the difference between a nonsexist curriculum and one that attempts to deny or destroy the children's deep, basic valuing of their own sexuality.

One way ideas about sex roles can be changed for the better without undermining the child's pride in gender is by presenting an open curriculum that provides opportunities for both sexes to participate in all learning activities rather than restricting children to obsolete sex-role expectations. Teachers should work to develop wider competence and equal privileges for both sexes. Sprafkin, Serbin, Denir, and Connor (1983) recently demonstrated that providing 3½- to 4-year-old boys and *girls* with opportunities to practice with "boy preferred" toys such as blocks, dominoes, and building toys significantly improved the children's visual spatial ability—a skill on which boys typically score higher. This skill is fundamental to later achievements in such fields as architecture, mathematics, and engineering and so is one well worth fostering in children of both sexes.

Preschools are often the last chance children have to try out materials and activities that are contemptuously labeled in elementary school as "girl stuff" or "unfeminine." Surely activities such as woodworking and blocks should be freely available to girls, just as opportunities to enjoy dressing up or sewing should be available for boys. The chance to experience a full range of roles enriches the knowledge of each sex, does not produce sexual perverts, and, ideally, deepens understanding and empathy for the opposite sex.

Sprung and the Women's Action Alliance have produced a first-rate book (1975) replete with examples of how the nursery school curriculum can be presented so that all areas, whether it be blocks or the housekeeping corner, will attract both boys and girls. *Equal Their Chances* (Shapiro, Kramer, & Hunerberg, 1981) also offers many suggestions that could either be used with younger children directly or to raise the awareness of teachers who might otherwise use such phrases as "The girls can go first because . . ." when they could easily say, "This table can go first" if they take a minute to think before they speak.

It is, of course, important not only to offer wider opportunities to girls but also to offer them to boys. For example, opportunities for additional male roles should be included in homemaking such as scaled-to-comfortable-size men's clothing for workers of various kinds. These garments should be freely available for use by both sexes, and boys should be encouraged to join in formerly female-dominated activities, such as cooking and caring for children.

Teachers may encounter a bit more resistance from boys when such cross-gender activities are first proposed than they will from girls. This is because girls are less criticized by their peers when they engage in "masculine preferred" activities than boys are. Fagot's research (1977) indicates that even when teachers encourage boys to cook or engage in self-expressive art activity,

Everybody needs the chance to try everything.

other boys do criticize them for such behavior, so it is well to be on the lookout for such remarks by peers and discourage them when possible.

Greenberg (1985) presents a particularly interesting perspective on early childhood education. She points out that most of that curriculum stresses skills girls already possess but that boys often lack. These include emphasis on verbal activities (large group time, for example), small muscle activities (cutting, painting, etc.), and assistance in gaining impulse control. Participation in these activities, she maintains, is virtually obligatory.

On the other hand, much of the curriculum that might remediate deficiencies in little girls' education is left to "choice and chance." Participation in such activities as block play, and large muscle activities that might also aid in developing spatial awareness, are a matter of self-selection (as is selection of various science activities).

Basing her recommendations on research, Greenberg suggests teachers make a special effort to provide the following activities for girls:

1. Activities that require spatial exploration

2. Activities for practice in large muscle coordination and development of large motor skills (increase structured gym activities)

3. Equipment that enhances investigatory activity

4. Activities that permit learning from following directions

5. Tasks that require cooperative groups of three or more children for their accomplishment

6. Tasks that encourage distance from adults

7. Opportunities for experimenting with a wide range of future career options

Activities to be provided for boys include:

1. Activities that encourage listening, speaking, and conversing.

2. Activities for small muscle coordination.

3. Opportunities to learn from examples.

4. Opportunities that encourage responsibility for others and to others.

5. Opportunities for nurturing activities.

6. Activities for helping boys develop flexible, effective self-management skills.

All teachers should take a closer look at the materials they offer for educational activities (Scott & Schau, 1985). More nonsexist, multiracial materials in the way of puzzles and lotto games are becoming available; they can be found if one searches diligently through enough catalogs. The companies of which I am most aware at present who have made a real effort to produce them include Milton-Bradley, Instructo, and the Judy Company. The Women's Action Alliance also offers a catalog that includes nonsexist puzzles, pictures, and play people.[*] A book distributor, Gryphon House, makes a policy of only listing nonracist, nonsexist books for children.[†]

These materials are rarely sufficient for the needs of the preschool, however, so teachers should also expect to make many of their own items; the books by Sprung (1975) and Jenkins and Macdonald (1979) described in the references at the end of the chapter contain directions on how to do this.

One encouraging note is the trend in children's books revealed by a recent study of Caldecott Award winners (Collins, Ingoldsby, & Dellmann, 1984). (The Caldecott medal is awarded to the outstanding picture book of the year.) In contrast to a study of such winners carried out in 1972 (Weitzman, Eifler, Hokada, & Ross), which found that males in central roles outnumbered females in similar roles by 3½ to 1, the newer study found books that won the award in the past 10 years presented a more even balance of (about) 1½ males to every female. The same trend is apparent in basal readers where the percentage of major male characters decreased from 60% in the mid-1970s to 35% in the early 1980s (Britton & Lumpkin, 1983). Nonsexist book lists may be found in Jenkins and Macdonald (1979) and in reviews of new books that are consistently included in *Interracial Books for Children: Bulletin* and *The Multicultural Leader*.

---

*Women's Action Alliance, 370 Lexington Ave., Room 603, New York, NY 10017.

†Gryphon House, PO Box 217, Mount Rainier, MD 20822.

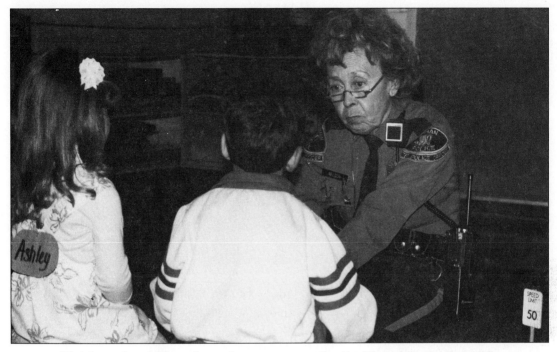

"But do you have babies and wear dresses on your mother time?" queried a skeptical Ashley.

Importance of Attitude and Modeling

More basic, however, than all the nonsexist curriculum in the world is the need to sensitize men and women to the negative consequences of unconsciously biased sexist teaching. What happens to the self-esteem of young boys who are criticized by female teachers for their high-energy, aggressive response to life? What effect does the constant use of such words as mail*man*, fire*man*, and police*man* have on young girls and their anticipation of future occupations?

Or, on a positive note, what do children conclude when they see their female teacher confidently using the electric drill to install a new blackboard or their male teacher matter-of-factly sewing a button on a child's shirt?

We do, indeed, have a long way to go in raising our awareness and control of the long-ingrained patterns of behavior and speech that perpetuate sexist and racist teaching, but we have come a long way, too. The danger to guard against is that complacency may permit us to become careless or to stop trying. Doing that opens the way to recapitulating the racist/sexist problem all over again.

SUMMARY

Since children as young as age 3 differentiate between people of differing skin color and gender, it is important to begin a program of cross-cultural, nonsexist education as early as possible so that they learn that *different*, be it a difference in sex or race or culture, does not mean *inferior*.

Teaching this principle of equity can be achieved in a number of ways. Fundamentally we want to emphasize that every individual has the unique, treasurable gift of individuality to share with others. Secondly, no matter how unique the individual is, each person has some basic common needs that can be satisfied in a variety of differing ways. And finally, every child of either sex or any color should be encouraged to explore the full range of his or her abilities and potential competencies.

Schools that incorporate such cross-cultural, nonsexist emphases in their programs help children learn to value the differences and similarities in themselves, their friends, and their teachers as being positive strengths. It is this positive valuing that lies at the heart of equity in education.

QUESTIONS AND ACTIVITIES

1. Have you been with a young child when he commented on differences in skin color or other differences related to ethnic group membership? What did he say, and what would be an effective way to reply to his comments or questions?

2. Do you feel it might be confusing or contradictory to teach children that people are alike and different at the same time?

3. *Problem:* You are a middle-class, White, well-meaning teacher, and you have just gotten a job working with a Head Start group where the children are predominantly first-generation Puerto Ricans. What will you do to make these children feel truly welcome? How can you utilize the rich cultural traditions of this minority group in your classroom? Suppose that you could not serve Puerto Rican food, use their native dances, or read books to the children about Puerto Rican children. What might be other valuable, though more subtle, ways to honor the cultural uniqueness of these youngsters? Are there ways *you* might change to match the groups you are serving more closely? Would changing yourself mean that you are losing your own cultural heritage?

4. *Problem:* A delegation of parents calls on you and says they want to discuss the racist policies of your school. In particular, they question the fact that all the teachers are white, and all the aides are minority people. They have called a meeting for this evening and invite you to attend. What would be a desirable way to deal with this situation? Be sure to consider short-term and long-term possibilities.

5. It is the beginning of the year, and there are many new parents in your group whom you hope to involve in participation. List some things you plan to do that will foster this participation. Also list some policies that would subtly discourage parents from wanting to come and be part of the life of the school.

6. Do you ever wonder if perhaps you are unconsciously behaving in a prejudiced way by paying more attention to children from certain ethnic groups and less to members of other groups? One way to check up on yourself is to ask a trusted colleague to keep track for various time periods of your contacts with the children over a week or more. All it takes is a list of the children's names and putting a check by each one for each contact made. If you wish to refine this strategy, plus and minus checks can be used depending on the kind of encounter, whether it is disciplinary,

showing positive interest, and so on. (A word of encouragement—this behavior is fairly easy to correct once the teacher is aware of it.)

7. Analyze the books in your center. Are there ones that present both boys and girls as effective, active people? Are there ones that appear to perpetuate stereotypes of little girl and little boy behavior? Are these necessarily undesirable?

8. *Problem:* You are working in a school that serves many single-parent families where mothers have primary care of the children. Many of the children, therefore, have relatively little experience with men. Suggest some practical plans that would help alleviate this deficit for the children you care for.

9. Take a few minutes and make two columns headed "What I Am Good at Doing" and "What I Am Not Good at Doing" and then analyze why you are either good or not good at those particular activities. If you answer, "Well, I never learned that," identify what prevented you from learning it, whatever it was.

10. Is it really the responsibility of schools to provide information about reproduction and gender differences? If you feel it is not, how would you handle such comments as "What happened to her wee wee—did they cut it off?" or (from a little boy) "When I grow up, I'm gonna have six children! There won't hardly be room in my stomach I'm gonna have so many!"

SELF-CHECK QUESTIONS FOR REVIEW

Content-Related Questions

1. When incorporating multicultural and nonsexist goals into the curriculum, what are the two fundamental principles we want children to learn?

2. Is the majority of the school population in 23 of the 25 largest school districts in the United States currently composed of White or minority group children?

3. Are preschool children too young to notice ethnic and gender differences? Cite some examples that support the accuracy of your answer.

4. Name five things you as an individual can do to control your own prejudices.

5. Are children's books about various ethnic groups improving in quality?

6. Are books representing sex-role stereotypes improving in quality?

7. Provide several examples of ways multicultural experiences could be consistently included in early childhood curriculum.

8. Provide several examples of ways nonsexist experiences could be consistently included in early childhood curriculum.

9. Why is encouraging pride in gender an important part of nonsexist education?

Integrative Questions

1. Could some of Clark's mental hygiene rules for overcoming prejudice apply also to sexism? Which ones apply most directly in your opinion? Can you produce examples where sexism has been expressed at the college level? At the preschool level?

2. Discuss the following quotation from William Blake's "The Little Black Boy." Are there racist implications in this verse? Are there antiprejudice implications? If so, what are they?

My mother bore me in the Southern wild,
And I am black, but oh my soul is white.
White as an angel is the English child.
But I am black, as if bereft of light.

And how would you interpret these final verses of the same poem?

. . . And thus I say to little English boy:
When I from dark and he from white cloud free,

And round the tent of God like lambs we
joy:
I'll shade him from the heat till he can bear
To lean in joy upon our father's knee
And then I'll stand and stroke his silver hair
And be like him and he will then love me.

3. Research shows that teachers interrupt girls
more frequently than they do boys. How do

you think this behavior might influence
girls' concepts of their sex roles? How might
the boys' sex-role concepts also be influenced?

4. List some principles that cross-cultural and
nonsexist education have in common.

REFERENCES FOR FURTHER READING

Overviews of Multicultural and/or Nonsexist Education

Banks, J. A. (1988). *Multiethnic education: Theory and practice* (2nd ed.). Boston: Allyn & Bacon. Banks, a distinguished authority in this area, concludes this analysis of multicultural education by listing 23 guidelines curriculum should follow to be truly multiethnic.

Derman-Sparks, L., & the ABC Task Force. (1989). *Anti-bias curriculum: Tools for empowering young children*. Washington, DC: National Association for the Education of Young Children. *Anti-Bias Curriculum* explains in practical terms how that approach can be integrated into the early childhood curriculum. *Highly recommended.*

Neugebauer, B. (Ed.). (1987). *Alike and different: Exploring our humanity with young children*. Redmond, WA: Exchange Press. *Alike and Different* covers usual and unusual aspects of living with differentness. Topics range from "foreign" children to giftedness and children with handicaps. Outstanding bibliography of children's books. *Highly recommended for the beginning student.*

Office of Bilingual Education, California State Department of Education. (1986). *Beyond language: Social and cultural factors in schooling language minority students*. Los Angeles: Evaluation and Dissemination and Assessment Center, University of California at Los Angeles. This book concentrates on ways teachers can help students maintain their cultural and linguistic heritage while achieving success in school. *Highly recommended.*

References That Deal with Cultural Characteristics

Chhim, S.-H. (1989). *Introduction to Cambodian culture*. San Diego: Multifunctional Resource Center, San Diego State University. The largest proportion of immigrants to the United States in recent years has come from Asia. So this book and the ones on Laotian and Vietnamese culture listed later here are both rare and particularly valuable.

Hale, J. E. (1986). *Black children: Their roots, culture, and learning style* (2nd ed.). Baltimore, MD: Johns Hopkins University Press. A wealth of information about the similarities and differences that exist between middle-class White and Black cultures is included. *Highly recommended.*

Luangpraeseut, K. (1989). *Laos culturally speaking*. San Diego: Multifunctional Resource Center, San Diego State University. This rich resource covers everything from history to culture.

Pepper, F. C. (1985). *Effective practices in Indian education: A teacher's monograph*. Portland, OR: Research and Development for Indian Education, Northwest Regional Educational Laboratory. Pepper provides some general information about working with Indian children (focuses on Indians from the Northwest) combined with specific recommendations for classroom management.

Powell, G. J. (Ed.). (1983). *The psychosocial development of minority group children*. New York: Brunner/Mazel. This book is a gold mine of information about many kinds of minorities—good reference about Hispanic youngsters.

Saracho, O. N., & Spodek, B. (Eds.). (1983). *Understanding the multicultural experience in early childhood education*. Washington, DC: National Association for the Education of Young Children. The authors provide cultural information about Native Americans, Asians, Hispanics, and Blacks. They discuss problems related to teaching but deal with curriculum only in passing.

Te, H. D. (1989). *Introduction to Vietnamese culture*. San Diego: Multifunctional Resource Center, San Diego State University. Te includes interesting material on names and nonverbal communication as well as history and culture.

Wardle, F. (1987). Are you sensitive to interracial children's needs? *Young Children, 42*(2), 53–59. Wardle provides a wealth of practical recommendations and resources on this rarely treated subject.

Development of Children's Racial Awareness

Katz, P. A. (1982). Development of children's racial awareness and intergroup attitudes. In L. G. Katz (Ed.), *Current topics in early childhood education* (Vol. 4). Norwood, NJ: Ablex. Katz traces the development of race awareness through eight overlapping stages. She also presents evidence that verbal expression of those differences begins around age 4, but that children do exhibit awareness of differences by age 3.

Resource and Activity Books About Cross-Cultural Education

There is a real need and place for publications of this sort, but I do wish to reiterate that *providing these kinds of environmental embellishments and activities should constitute only the beginning of true multicultural education.*

Cole, A., Haas, C., Heller, E., & Weinberger, B. (1978). *Children are children are children: An activity approach to exploring Brazil, France, Iran, Japan, Nigeria, and the U.S.S.R.* Boston: Little, Brown. Although the title largely explains the contents, it should be added that each section contains recipes, information on games, holidays, suggestions for activities (some of which could be done by preschoolers), general information on the country, a few commonly used words, and a map.

Kendall, F. E. (1983). *Diversity in the classroom: A multicultural approach to the education of young children*. New York: Teachers College Press. Kendall offers a good, readily available annotated list of books for young children.

McNeill, E., Schmidt, V., & Allen, J. (1981). *Cultural awareness for young children: Asian, Black, cowboy, Eskimo, Mexican, and Native American cultures*. Mount Rainier, MD: Gryphon House (Distributor). *Cultural Awareness* is distinguished by a good list of films, books, and magazines for children and adults. It divides the children's activities into family living, foods, creative activities, nature/science, language development, and special events.

Tannenbaum, L. (Ed.). *The New York cooking experience: A guide to classroom cooking with young children emphasizing ethnic foods and holiday celebrations*. Pamphlet begins with a discussion of what can be learned while cooking. It includes a diverse group of recipes and a list of ethnic holidays. Available from the Early Childhood Education Council of New York, 66 Leroy St., New York, NY 10014.

Identification of Racism and Sexism in Children's Books

Council on Interracial Books for Children. (1980). *Guidelines for selecting bias-free textbooks and storybooks*. New York: The Council. A handy reference, these guidelines cover sexism, racism, handicapism, ageism, and classism, providing discussions, examples of illustrations, and checklists helpful in identifying desirable and undesirable books. (No book lists included.)

Klein, G. (1985). *Reading into racism: Bias in children's literature and learning materials*. London: Routledge & Kegan Paul. A thoughtful book that documents the current situation, carefully considers such problems as censorship, and mentions other methods of dealing with racist literature.

Moore, R. B. (1985). Racism in the English language. In N. Colangelo, D. Dustin, & Foxley, C. H. (Eds.), *Multicultural nonsexist education: A human relations approach* (2nd ed.). Dubuque, IA: Kendall/Hunt. This essay exposes how bias against Blacks and Native Americans is reflected in our everyday language.

Relating to Parents of Differing Cultural Backgrounds

Lightfoot, S. L. (1978). *Worlds apart: Relationships between families and schools.* New York: Basic Books. Lightfoot discusses the delicate relationship between mothers and teachers, not hesitating to consider the matter of differing cultures and the potential difficulties such differences make possible.

Nedler, S. E., & McAfee, O. D. (1979). *Working with parents: Guidelines for early childhood and elementary teachers.* Belmont, CA: Wadsworth. This excellent book is full of ideas for generating parent involvement in the early childhood center. Very practical advice about conducting a group meeting is a highlight of this book.

Trohanis, P. L. (Ed.). (1978). *Early education in Spanish-speaking communities.* New York: Walker. Although this book actually focuses on working with Spanish-speaking parents of children who have handicaps, it has many practical suggestions about how to communicate and get along with any children or adults who speak another language. A helpful book.

Wardle, F. (1989). Children of mixed parentage: How can professionals help? *Children Today, 18*(4), 10–13. Wardle maintains that children from such marriages often experience pronounced prejudice and then offers a number of practical suggestions to remember when working with these families.

Bibliographies

Dickerson, G. D. (1990). *A guide to black children's books.* Maral Enterprises (PO Box 361, New York, NY 10028). This is an annual publication highly recommended by the Children's Defense Fund.

Jenkins, E. C., & Austin, M. C. (1987). *Literature for children about Asians and Asian Americans: Analysis and annotated bibliography with additional readings for adults.* Westport, CT: Greenwood Press. Title is self-explanatory.

Norton, D. E. (1990). Teaching multicultural literature in the reading curriculum. *The Reading Teacher, 44,* 28–40. This article deals mainly with elementary school reading but is included here because of an extensive discussion of books about Indian children.

Schon, I. (1988). Hispanic books. *Young Children, 43*(4), 81–85. This reference includes references for adults plus a list of books for young children that are written in Spanish.

Education About Sex

Arnstein, H. S. (1978). *What to tell your child: About birth, illness, death, divorce, and other family crises.* New York: Condor. This is a practical compendium of advice suitable for both parents and teachers. It covers the topics listed and updates a previous version done originally in collaboration with the Child Study Association of America.

Bernstein, A. (1978). *The flight of the stork.* New York: Delacorte Press. *The Flight of the Stork* describes Bernstein's research on what children know about reproduction at different stages of their growth. The author provides suggestions about what adult responses and information are appropriate for each developmental stage. A truly excellent and delightful book.

Koblinsky, S., Atkinson, J., & Davis, S. (1980). Sex education with young children. *Young Children, 36*(1), 21–31. This useful, sensible article suggests a number of practical guidelines for teaching young children about gender differences and sexuality.

Ratner, M., & Chamlin, S. (1987). *Straight talk: Sexuality education for parents and kids 4–7.* New York: Penguin Books. In this concise book Ratner and Chamlin provide clear, sensible advice. This would be a helpful addition to the teacher's and parent's library.

Sex Roles and Stereotypes

Fagot, B. I., & Kronsberg, S. J. (1982). Sex differences: Biological and social factors influencing the behavior of young boys and girls. In S. G. Moore & C. R. Cooper (Eds.), *The young child: Reviews of research* (Vol. 3). Washington, DC: National Association for the Education of Young Children. After reviewing three major theories that attempt to account for differences in sexual behavior, Fagot and Kronsberg trace the development of such differences through early childhood and conclude that "biological components of gender identity and sex-role behavior, while definitely of consequence, are relatively small by comparison with cultural influences" (p. 204).

Greenberg, S. (1985). Educational equity in early education environments. In S. S. Klein (Ed.), *Handbook for achieving sex equity through education*. Baltimore, MD: Johns Hopkins University Press. Greenberg summarizes research that identifies ways early childhood teachers perpetuate sex-role differences and then proposes ways to change such teaching. *Highly recommended.*

Robinson, B. E. (1988). Vanishing breed: Men in childcare programs. *Young Children, 43*(6), 54–58. Robinson documents the scarcity of male preschool teachers and provides a discussion of the causes of that unfortunate circumstance.

Resource Books for Nonsexist Activities

Jenkins, J. K., & Macdonald, P. (1979). *Growing up equal: Activities and resources for parents and teachers of young children*. Englewood Cliffs, NJ: Prentice-Hall. Although on the "cute" side, this book does have a number of activities that could encourage children to try out nonsexist activities. It also includes facts about sex-role development that are intended to dispel old sexist myths of various sorts.

Northwest Regional Educational Laboratory Center for Sex Equity. (1983). *Guide to nonsexist teaching activities*. (K–12). Phoenix: Oryx Press. This is a first-rate reference that includes films, textbooks, and bibliographies. *Highly recommended.*

Pogrebin, L. C. (1980). *Growing up free: Raising your child in the '80s*. New York: McGraw-Hill. A lengthy, well-written guide useful for teachers and parents in search of ideas about how to implement nonsexist attitudes in their families and themselves. Not an activity book.

Shapiro, J., Kramer, S., & Hunerberg, C. (1981). *Equal their chances: Children's activities for non-sexist learning*. Englewood Cliffs, NJ: Prentice-Hall. Written with elementary school teachers in mind, *Equal Their Chances* takes the curriculum of the school topic by topic and provides numerous examples of how nonsexist information could and should be incorporated into those studies. Enough of the ideas could be translated to the preprimary level that the book is worth examining.

Sprung, B. (1975). *Non-sexist education for young children: A practical guide*. New York: Citation Press. This paperback contains a wealth of practical ideas for conducting a nonsexist nursery school using five curriculum topics as examples. The best reference in the field.

For the Advanced Student

Aboud, F. (1988). *Children and prejudice*. New York: Basil Blackwell. Aboud provides well-summarized research reviews concerning the emergence and possible determinants of prejudice.

Acuña, J. E. (1987). *The development of thinking among Filipinos: Implications for public education*. Manila, Philippines: DeLaSalle University. The author concentrates on studies concerned with the discrepancies in academic achievement between differing groups of Filipino students. She includes suggestions for improving that situation.

Allport, G. W. (1979). *The nature of prejudice* (25th anniversary edition). Reading, MA: Addison-Wesley. This classic in the field of race relations provides a valuable foundation for understanding the nature of prejudice.

Beuf, A. H. (1977). *Red children in white America*. Philadelphia: University of Pennsylvania Press. I have included this book particularly because it contains the first study done on racial attitudes ever conducted with Native American children from the tribes of the Southwest and Plains.

Child Development. The entire April 1990 issue of this distinguished research publication is devoted to research concerning minority children.

Halpern, D. F. (1986). *Sex differences in cognitive abilities.* Hillsdale, NJ: Lawrence Erlbaum. Halpern presents a thorough research-based review of gender-related differences, including a thoughtful discussion of possible causes of such differences.

Koblinsky, S. A. (1983). *Sexuality education for parents of young children: A facilitator training manual.* Fayetteville, NY: Ed-U Press. Although as the title indicates this is primarily a training manual, the resources, attention to multiethnic families, and summary of facts about sexuality make this book an outstanding reference in the field. *Highly recommended.*

Low, V. (1982). *The unimpressible race: A century of educational struggle by the Chinese in San Francisco.* San Francisco: East/West. This book provides an example of how institutional racism can limit the development of young children, as well as a heartening example of how parents can overcome such racism.

Modgil, S., Verma, G. K., Mallick, K., & Modgil, C. (Eds.). (1986). *Multicultural education: The interminable debate.* London: Falmer Press. The authors review multicultural education from the English, Canadian, and Australian points of view. Useful reading that reminds us how widespread interest is in this subject.

Palmer, B. C. (1982). *Migrant education: An annotated bibliography.* Newark, DE: International Reading Association (800 Barksdale Rd., Newark, DE 19711). Since so many children of migrant families come from minority groups, it seemed wise to include this rare bibliographical resource in this chapter. It is carefully annotated and wide ranging. The scarcity of current references cited within its covers illustrates, once again, the general lack of concern for such youngsters in our society.

Shetlin, E. M. (1985). Racism and sexism: Similarities. In N. Colangelo, D. Dustin, & C. H. Foxley (Eds.), *Multicultural nonsexist education: A human relations approach* (2nd ed.). Dubuque, IA; Kendall/Hunt. In an amusing and penetrating analysis, Shetlin draws many parallels between the plight of women and minorities in our society.

Torrance, E. P. (1977). *Discovery and nurturance of giftedness in the culturally different.* Reston, VA: Council for Exceptional Children. Torrance admits this work lacks scientific rigor, yet it does provide useful insights and food for thought. One of the most helpful items is a sample checklist for signs of giftedness among the culturally different.

Journals and Newsletters of Particular Interest

The Black Child Advocate. 1463 Rhode Island Ave., NW, Washington, DC 20005. This is the quarterly newsletter of the National Black Child Development Institute. It focuses primarily on current legislation that could affect the lives of all children and Black children in particular.

Interracial Books for Children: Bulletin. Published by the Council on Interracial Books for Children, 1941 Broadway, New York, NY 10023. Each issue focuses on a particular topic, which might be handicapism, or raising children in a racist society, or Black children in picture books. It also contains film and book reviews that mince no words. An invaluable resource.

Multicultural Leader. Educational Materials and Services Center, 144 Railroad Ave., Suite 107, Edmonds, WA 98020. This publication includes reviews of research and books, plus articles of interest. *Highly recommended* because of its scope and diversity.

Siecus Report. Sex Information and Education Council of the United States, 80 Fifth Ave., New York, NY 10011. Affiliated with the Department of Health Education of the School of Education, Health, Nursing and Arts Professions of New York University, this newsletter provides an excellent way to keep up with various publications in the area of sex education. It contains articles, book reviews, and resources for further information. Liberal in point of view.

Spectrum. Newsletter of the Multiracial Americans of Southern California (12228 Venice Blvd., #452, Los Angeles, CA 90066) is of and about interracial families.

PART FIVE
Enhancing Creativity

CHAPTER 13

Fostering Creativity by Means of Self-Expressive Materials

The essence of the creative person is being in love with what one is doing.

—E. Paul Torrance (1988)

They [materials and activities] are food for learning in the nursery school, being displayed for children to choose like food in a cafeteria. Each is used only until the hunger for that particular kind is satisfied. (There are times, too, when none are selected: instead, a child may talk with others, rest, watch, dream, wander about in a vague state of relaxed sensory awareness, or carry on a vivid internal dialogue. Passivity and activity are necessary parts of the rhythm of living). . . . but again, as with food, if this process is to go on beneficially, there must be plenty of well-chosen materials from which to select.

—Eleanor Fitch Griffin (1982)

Have you ever wondered . . .

> What to reply when a child whines, "Draw me a horse"?
>
> How on earth you can vary easel painting today?
>
> How to explain to parents why your school doesn't send home pie plates with little faces glued on them?

If you have, the material in the following pages will help you.

Early childhood teachers have long valued creativity and sought to enhance it by fostering self-expression in the young children they care for. In the past we teachers have been particularly successful in presenting expressive materials and activities such as paint, clay, and dance in a manner that fosters unique personal responses from the children. But today we are coming to realize that artistic creativeness represents only one facet of creative endeavor and that there are additional aspects of creativity in play and in divergence and originality of thought that should be encouraged more fully. For this reason the discussion of creativity in this book does not stop with the presentation of expressive materials but extends, in two additional chapters, to play and to fostering originality in thought.

DEFINITION OF CREATIVITY

Defining creativity where young children are concerned is rather difficult, since the commonly accepted definitions include not only the requirement that the idea or product be novel but that it be related to reality and stand the test of being worthwhile, too (Tardiff & Sternberg, 1988). However, a definition by Smith (1966) suits our needs well, since it fits young children's creative abilities more aptly. He defines creativity as being the process of "sinking down taps into our past experiences and putting these selected experiences together into new patterns, new ideas or new products" (p. 43). May (1975) also describes it as "the process of bringing something new into being" (p. 39).

This "putting prior experiences together into something new" is a good description of what we hope young children will be able to do when they use self-expressive materials, play imaginatively, solve problems, or generate new ideas. It stresses originality and does not emphasize the quality of evaluation, which is less applicable to very young children, although even they can be encouraged to try out ideas, thereby going through reality testing and evaluation in an informal way.

The student should also understand that creativity is not limited to a few gifted Rembrandts and Einsteins, nor is it necessarily associated with high intelligence. The work of Getzels and Jackson (1962; 1987), Wallach and Kogan (1965), and Ward (1968) has demonstrated that high scores on creativity tests do not correlate strongly with high scores on academic tests of achievement or with high scores on standard measures of intelligence. Another finding of interest is a study by Margolin (1968), which indicates that teachers who deliberately foster uniqueness and originality of response in creative activities can actually increase the variety and diversity of such responses in young children.

These findings imply that we do not have to wait for that specifically gifted child to come along in order for creative behavior to take place in our groups. The ability to generate original ideas and to produce satisfying, freshly conceived products resides in many children; and since such behavior can be increased by appropriate responses from the teacher, it is worthwhile to learn how to do this.

IMPORTANCE OF CREATIVITY

The experience of being involved in creative activity satisfies people in ways that nothing else can, and the ability to be creative appears not only to reflect but also to foster emotional health (Singer & Singer, 1990). The act of creation enhances the child's feelings of self-esteem and self-worth. (The reader can test the validity of this statement by recalling the last time she or he produced something original—perhaps something as simple as a Christmas decoration or as complex as a set of bookshelves—and then recall the feeling of well-being that rose up inside when it was accomplished.) There *is* something about creating a unique product or idea that leaves people feeling good about themselves.

Creative experiences provide unparalleled opportunities for expressing emotions and, by gaining relief and understanding through such expression, for coming to terms with them (Brittain, 1979). Since they have this strong affective component, they provide a balance for the emphasis on intellectual development, which may overwhelm the rest of the program unless it is carefully managed.

While providing that balance, such activities also foster cognitive growth by providing endless opportunities for trying out ideas and putting them into practice, for seeing there are many alternative ways to solve problems, and for encouraging the use of symbols in place of "real" objects to represent ideas and feelings (Lowenfeld & Brittain, 1987; Weisberg, 1988). Incidental learning inevitably results from such experiences also. Clay changes its form when water is added; sand feels gritty between the toes; paint runs down the same way water does.

Finally, creative activities offer an excellent opportunity to individualize teaching. Materials and activities that depend on open-ended replies permit uniqueness and diversity to flourish and allow each child to be herself rather than requiring her to conform to closed-system, authority-centered learning.

STAGES OF DEVELOPMENT

One of the peak periods for creative self-expression in our culture occurs between the ages of 4 and 6 (Schirrmacher, 1988). This stage correlates well with Erikson's developmental stage for this age, which he identifies as the stage of initiative versus guilt. Erikson's stage is characterized by reaching out, exploring, and experimenting and also reflects an increase in creative behavior that is partially characterized by this same kind of activity.

As is true in other areas, children pass through general stages of development in the use of creative materials (Smart & Smart, 1972). First, *they explore the material itself* and investigate its properties. Two- and 3-year-olds, for instance, spend many satisfactory hours in what appears to be mainly manipulation and exploration of paints and brushes or in relishing the mixing of play dough, and they employ all their senses to do this. Who has not seen such a youngster meticulously painting her hands up to the elbow, or beheld another squeezing the sponge in the paint bucket, or a third looking thoughtfully into the distance as she licks the back of the play dough spoon?

Once the qualities of the material have been explored and some skill has been gained in its manipulation, the child is likely to move on to what is called the *nonrepresentational stage.* Paintings at this stage, for example, seem to have more design and intention behind them, but the content is not readily recognizable by anyone but the painter. Since painting at this stage is not always done with the intention of depicting something in particular, the teacher must beware of asking, "What is it?" lest such a question unintentionally put the child on a spot.

Ultimately the youngster reaches the pictorial or *representational stage,* where she quite deliberately sets out to reproduce or create something. She may paint a picture of herself, or the sun in the sky, or depict a fascinating event such as the toilet overflowing or going trick-or-treating. Some children attain this stage of representational art in preschool, but most children develop this ability during their year in kindergarten.

Brittain (1979), in a much more detailed study, has described similar stages for the evolution of drawing from scribbling. What is particularly interesting about Brittain's work is the finding that representations of a man done by a particular child at a particular age were very similar, no matter which medium the child employed—drawing, collage, or clay.

Implications for Preprimary Teachers

One implication to be drawn from these sequential stages of development is that teachers should permit children countless opportunities to experience and explore expressive materials, because this learning is fundamental to the creative experience. The full knowledge gained through such exploration extends the ways a child may use the material, thereby enriching her creative opportunities; and the freedom to explore is also likely to keep alive her interest and openness to the medium (Amabile, 1989).

The second developmental implication is that young children, when using expressive materials, should not be expected to produce a finished product. Some 4-year-olds will do this, of course; but since many will not, the expectation of some sort of recognizable result is not a reasonable creative goal to set for children in their early years.

GENERAL RECOMMENDATIONS ABOUT CREATIVITY

It is hoped the reader will apply to all three chapters on creativity the general comments made here about fostering the child's creativity with self-expressive materials.

Be Aware of the Value of Nonconforming Behavior and of "Unattractive" Personality Characteristics

Torrance (1962) has frequently emphasized that the kind of behavior teachers identify as desirable in children does not always coincide with characteristics associated with the creative personality. For instance, teachers who think they value uniqueness may find they do not like creative exploration as much as they thought they did when a youngster has spilled her milk because she tried holding the cup with her teeth.

Not only can this lack of conformity be inconvenient, but the teacher should also realize that some creative individuals possess character traits she may not care for. Torrance (1962) cites 84 characteristics that differentiate the more creative person from the less creative one. Some of the less attractive qualities include stubbornness, finding fault with things, appearing haughty and self-satisfied, and being discontented—qualities often disliked by teachers. Yet it is easy to see how stubbornness might be a valuable quality to possess when carrying through a new idea, or how finding fault and being discontented could result in questioning and analyzing a situation before coming up with suggestions for improving it. In all fairness, we must admit that we do not know at present if some of these less attractive attitudes lie at the root of creativity or if some of them are only the result of squelching and mishandling by teachers, peers, and families as the child matures. On the other hand, Torrance also found that creative children possessed many likable qualities, such as determination, curiosity, intuition, a willingness to take risks, a preference for complex ideas, and a sense of humor.

The purpose of pointing out these possible problems of living with creative children is not to discourage teachers from fostering such behavior, but to enlighten them so they will not subtly reject or discourage creative responses because they fail to recognize the positive side of such apparently undesirable behavior. Ideally, such understanding will result in increased acceptance and valuing of creative endeavor.

Acceptance is vitally important because it will encourage children to develop these abilities further and because it will help balance the rejection and isolation to which people who dare to be different are often subjected. As long as we have creative youngsters in our care, we must help guard against rejection by recognizing and supporting originality in thought and deed.

Cultivate Three Teaching Skills in Yourself

Each creative area requires a specific teaching skill for its facilitation. The cultivation of these skills is discussed at greater length in the appropriate chapter, but they are listed here to provide the reader with a quick overview.

In fostering creativity by means of expressive materials, the teacher should make ample materials freely available and encourage children to explore and use them as their impulses and feelings require. When seeking to facilitate play, the teacher needs to be able to move with the children's imaginative ideas and respond to them by providing materials and support that keep the play ongoing and creative. When developing original thinking, the teacher must reinforce the children's production of ideas by recognizing their value and by learning to ask questions that encourage the development of the children's thoughts.

Do Your Best to Maintain an Emotionally Healthy Climate

In the chapters on emotional health, handling routines, and discipline, considerable time was spent discussing ways to keep the center environment reasonable, consistent, and secure so that children will feel emotionally at ease. Such a stable, predictable climate is valuable for many reasons, but one of the outstanding ones is that it forms a sound base for the generation of creative activity, which in turn contributes to the development of emotional health. Children who feel secure are more likely to venture forth, try new experiences, and express themselves in creative ways than are children who are using up their energy by worrying or being frightened or anxious.

In addition, some research supports the idea that highly structured classrooms where preschool children are continually the focus of adult control and adult-designated activities appear to reduce the amount of imaginative play (Huston-Stein, Freidrick-Cofer, & Susman, 1977) and curiosity and inventiveness (Miller & Dyer, 1975). The use of structured play materials, such as puzzles and coloring books, has also been shown to reduce divergent, creative responses to problem solving (Pepler, 1986). These findings provide yet another reason teachers who wish to foster these creative traits should make certain there is an open structure to the program that provides many opportunities for children to think for themselves and to make choices and decisions within reasonable limits.

USE OF SELF-EXPRESSIVE MATERIALS TO FOSTER THE CREATIVE SELF

Expressive materials include such diverse media as painting, collage, dough and clay, woodworking, sewing, and dance. Although the materials themselves are different, some basic principles apply to all of them. (Suggested guidelines for use of specific materials are included later in the chapter.)

Value of Using Free-Form Materials

The most valuable quality that expressive materials have in common is that there is no right thing to do with them or one right way to use them; so in a real sense these materials are failure-proof for the child. As long as the child observes a few basic rules, such as keeping the sand down and seeing that the dough stays on the table and off the floor, there is no way she can make a mistake with them.

For this reason alone such materials are an invaluable addition to the curriculum.

There are additional reasons why expressive materials are indispensable. Psychologists and experienced teachers agree that these experiences provide many opportunities for children to express their feelings and come to terms with them (Seefeldt, 1987). It can be fascinating to watch the development of a shy child who may begin finger painting by using only the middle of her paper and then see her gradually come to fill her paper with rich colors and swooping strokes of joy as she gains confidence during her months at school. Since each child is free to do as she wishes, these materials also represent the ultimate in individualized curriculum. The youngster can express who she is and what she is as something within her urges her to do; she is able to suit the material to herself in an intensely personal way.

In addition, many values associated with creative materials lie in the social, sensory, and intellectual spheres. Children who are working side by side often develop a spirit of camaraderie. As a matter of fact, research by Torrance (1988) found that 5-year-olds were most willing to risk attempting difficult new tasks when working in pairs.

Using creative materials provides numerous opportunities for rich sensory input in that dough feels sticky and then firm; finger painting feels cool, gushy, and slippery; dance makes the child aware of her body as she moves in response to the music. Finally, the amount of factual information children acquire about the substances they are using contributes to their intellectual growth; red and yellow mixed together create orange; some woods are easier to saw than others; two smaller blocks equal one large one.

Although these social, sensory, and intellectual learnings are worthwhile, I still regard them as being like the frosting on the cake. The primary values of using expressive materials remain in the affective sphere. Expressive materials are fundamentally useful because they foster creativity, build self-esteem, and provide a safe, failure-proof experience. Most important, they can be the source of open-ended opportunities for the child to be herself and for her to express and work through her individual feelings and ideas.

Practical Ways to Encourage the Creative Aspect of Self-Expressive Materials

Interfere as Little as Possible

As I mentioned earlier, the most significant skill the teacher can cultivate in presenting self-expressive materials is the ability to let the child explore them as her impulses and feelings require, intervening only when needed. Brittain (1979), who studied various kinds of teacher interventions under such circumstances, found that the more instruction the teacher offered, the less involved the child was likely to be in the project. Teachers who stayed entirely on the sidelines also had children stay and paint for shorter periods of time. The children who stayed longest and who were judged most involved were ones

You can see both the restraint and the body language the student is using to help Katie cut the paper.

whose teachers "played the role of an interested adult . . . who gave support and intervened only when the child seemed hesitant about either his own powers or the next direction to take in the project" (p. 160).

Of course, allowing children to explore self-expressive materials as their impulses and feelings require does not mean they should be permitted to experiment with scissors by cutting the doll's hair off or that they should be allowed to smear clay all over the school chairs to "get their feelings out." It is as true here as in other situations that the teacher does not allow children to damage property or to do things that may hurt themselves or others.

However, although inexperienced teachers occasionally allow destructive things to happen in the name of freedom, experience has taught me that the reverse circumstance is more likely to occur. Many teachers unthinkingly limit and control the use of expressive materials more than is necessary. Thus they may refuse to permit a child to use the indoor blocks on the table "because we always use them on the floor," or they may insist she use only one paintbrush at a time despite the fact that using two at once makes such interesting lines and patterns. These ideas are essentially harmless ones and should be encouraged because of their originality.

Never Provide a Model for the Children to Copy

A copy is not an original. When I was a little girl in kindergarten, the "creative" experiences offered consisted mainly of making things just the way the teacher did. I particularly recall sewing around the edges of paper plates to make letter holders and cutting out paper flowers to glue on sticks. I suppose that what was creative about these activities was that we got to pick which flowers to cut out, and as I remember, we could choose any color of yarn to sew with. Whatever educational merit such activities possess, creativity is not among them. Yet some child care centers persist in offering such experiences in the name of creativity. If the teacher really wishes to foster originality and the child's self-expression rather than his own, he will avoid models and make-alike activities and will merely set the materials out and let the children go to it themselves.

Sometimes a child will attempt to lure the teacher into drawing something for her to copy by pleading, "Draw me a house" or "Draw me a man so I can color him." Rather than complying, the wise teacher meets this request by recognizing the child's deeper request, which is for a one-to-one relationship; so he meets this need by talking with her, meanwhile encouraging her to make the picture herself.

Understand and Respect the Child's Developmental Level

We spoke at the beginning of the chapter of the stages through which children's drawings pass as they become more mature. I am including here a developmental chart (Table 13.1) calling attention to the usual age at which children are able to copy various shapes, because some teachers do not understand that the ability to do this rests at least in part on maturation (Brittain, 1979) and so struggle endlessly to teach children at too early an age to draw squares and

TABLE 13.1   Drawing and writing movements*

Age (in years, months)	Behavior
0.1–1	Accidental and imitative scribbling.
1–1.6	Refinement of scribbles, vertical and horizontal lines, multiple line drawing, scribblings over visual stimuli.
2–3	Multiple loop drawing, spiral, crude circles. Simple diagrams evolve from scribblings by the end of the second year.
3	Figure reproduction to visually presented figures, circles, and crosses.
4	Laboriously reproduces squares, may attempt triangles but with little success.
4.6–5	Forms appear in combinations of two or more. Crude pictures appear (house, human form, sun). Can draw fair squares, crude rectangles and good circles, but has difficulty with triangles and diamonds.
6–7	Ability to draw geometric figures matures. By seven, can draw good circles, squares, rectangles, triangles and fair diamonds.

*Source: From *Perceptual-Motor Efficiency in Children: The Measurement and Improvement of Movement Attributes* (p. 85) by B. J. Cratty & M. M. Martin (1969). Philadelphia: Lea & Febiger, © 1969 by Lea & Febiger. Reprinted by permission.

triangles when everyone's energies could surely be better expended teaching and learning more important things.

Understand That It Is the Process Not the Product That Matters Most to the Young Child

We live in such a work-oriented, product-centered culture that sometimes we lose sight of the simple pleasure of doing something for its own sake. For young children, however, getting there is more than half the fun. They savor the process and live for the moment. Therefore, it is important not to hurry them toward finishing something or to overstress the final result. They *will* love to take their creations home, of course, and all such items should be carefully labeled, at least occasionally dated, and put in their cubbies so that this is possible, but the primary emphasis should remain on doing.

Allow Plenty of Time and Opportunity for the Child to Use Materials So That Her Experience Is Truly Satisfying

In the discussion about sharing I made the point that it is important for each child to have enough of an experience in order to be truly satisfied before giving up the place to someone else. This is particularly true when using expressive materials. One painting or one collage is just not enough. Children need the chance to work themselves into the experience and to develop their feelings and ideas as they go along. For this reason it is important to schedule time periods that allow for many children to move in and out of the expressive experience as their needs dictate. For real satisfaction this opportunity needs to be available for an hour or an hour and a half at a time.

Learn How to Make Comments That Enhance the Child's Creative Productivity

Making effective comments as the child creates will encourage her to continue and to involve herself ever more deeply in the activity (Kratochwill, Rush, & Kratochwill, 1980). But it can be risky, as well as embarrassing, to be trapped into commenting on what the child is making either by trying to guess what it is or by asking her to name it. As mentioned previously, children often do not deliberately set out to represent anything in particular, and even if they do intend a representation, it may defy recognition by anyone else. An additional drawback to requesting that creations be labeled is that it places emphasis on the product rather than on the creative, dynamic aspect of the experience.

It is more enhancing to comment on the pleasure the child is feeling as she works or to ask her if she would like to tell you about it. "You're having such a good time doing that!" or "My goodness, you've worked on that a long time! Would you like to tell me about it?" or "Do you need some more of . . . ?" These remarks show her that you are interested in and care for her, but they avoid the taint of passing judgment on the quality of what she has made or of emphasizing that the end is better than the means (Schirrmacher, 1986).

Grant the Child Who Is Dubious the Right to Refuse

Children benefit from the opportunity to stand and watch before they plunge into an activity more vigorously. Three-year-olds do a lot of this standing around, but older children who are shy or new to school may behave this way, too. This is a valid way to learn, and the teacher should respect the child who copes with new experiences in this manner. Usually after a few days she will want to try whatever it is she has been watching so intently.

A few children are extraordinarily concerned about getting painty or sticky. These youngsters are usually reassured if the teacher talks with the mother in their hearing and asks the mother to tell them that using paint and glue is all right at school. It can also help if "clean" materials, such as soap painting or snow, are offered as beginning messy activities. It should be made clear to such youngsters that there is water instantly available should they feel the need to wash their hands and that the apron will protect themselves and their clothes from undue contamination.

Some Comments on Expressive Materials Themselves

It is important to provide enough of whatever the children are using. There is nothing sadder than children making do with skimpy little fistfuls of dough when they need large, satisfying mounds to punch and squeeze. The same thing holds true for collage materials, woodworking, and painting. Children need

Painting objects is a lot of fun, too.

plenty of material to work with as well as the chance to make as many things as they wish.

Providing enough material for the children means that teachers must develop their scrounging and pack rat instincts to the ultimate degree. They not only must ferret out sources of free materials but also must find time and energy to pick them up regularly and produce a place to store them until they are needed. Parents can be helpful in collecting materials if the teacher takes the time to show them examples of what he needs. There are many sources of such materials in any community. (Appendix E is included to inspire the beginner.)

Variety in materials is also crucial. Creative activity should not be limited to easel painting and paper collage. The reader will find examples of variations suggested for materials, but I want to remind the reader to be quite clear there is a difference between the use of self-expressive materials and many craft-type projects advocated for preschool children, even when these materials do not require making something just like the model.

Sometimes teachers justify such activities on the grounds that they have to do this because the parents expect it, but I have never had a parent protest the looser, freer treasures their children have borne home once they understood our goals of preserving the creative, less directive approach. Day care centers are particularly likely to be seduced by such crafts because of the need to provide variety and stimulation for the children in order to sustain their interest. Unfortunately the emphasis with these items is usually on learning to manipulate the material and on how clever the teacher was to think of doing it. The attraction for the teacher of sheer novelty tends to obscure the tendency of such crafts (a) to be inappropriate to the age and skills of the children, (b) to require excessive teacher direction and control, (c) to fail to allow for adequate emotional self-expression and (d) to emphasize conformity rather than creativity.

It is difficult to see what real benefits children gain from string painting, for example. The string is dipped in paint and then placed between a folded piece of paper and pulled out. The results are fortuitous, and although the colors may be pretty, this activity is not likely to be satisfying to the child unless she manages to turn the process into finger painting—which frequent observation proves to be the common outcome unless the teacher prevents it! Fortunately there are several very good references currently available that list innumerable and appropriate ways to present basic materials that also keep in sight the fundamental values of self-expression (Bos, 1978; Cherry, 1972; Kohl, 1989; Pitcher, Feinburg, & Alexander, 1989).

Finally, creative materials that will be used together should be selected with an eye to beauty. For instance, rather than simply setting out a hodgepodge, the teacher should choose collage materials that contrast interestingly and attractively in texture and color. Pieces of orange onion bags could be offered along with bits of dark cork, white Styrofoam, beige burlap, and dry seed pods; a black or bright yellow mat would be a good choice as a collage base for these items. Finger-paint colors that make a beautiful third color should be selected. For example, magenta and yellow combine to form a gorgeous shade of orange, but purple and yellow turn out dull gray.

PRESENTATION OF SPECIFIC MATERIALS

I have selected only the more common materials for the outlines in the following pages,* but the reader can find additional suggestions in the references at the end of this chapter. I hope that these ideas will not be followed as gospel but will serve to inspire the teacher to develop and carry out his own and the children's creative ideas.

The suggestions for presentation of various materials in this and the following chapter have been written as individual, self-contained units so they may be abstracted and posted in various areas about the school should this be desired. For this reason I hope the reader will forgive a certain repetition in the descriptions of setting out and cleaning up.

Easel Painting

Easel painting is perhaps the one form of artistic endeavor offered by all children's centers, and it is an outstanding example of a creative material that is intensely satisfying to young children. In the fall, particularly with younger children and with newcomers, it is wise to begin with the basic experience of a few colors, one size of paintbrush, and the standard, *large-sized* paper; but as the year progresses and the children's skills increase, many interesting variations and degrees of complexity can be offered that will sustain interest and enhance the experience of easel painting for the more sophisticated young artists.

When looking at paintings or other expressive products, one can be tempted to play psychologist and read various interpretations into the children's work. Although it is perfectly all right to encourage a child to tell you about what she has painted if she wishes to do so, the interpretation of children's painting should be left to experts. Correct interpretation depends on a knowledge of the order in which paintings were produced, knowledge of the availability of colors, access to the case history, and a complete record of comments made by the child while the work was in progress. In addition, young children often overpaint, restructuring paintings two or three times as they work; this increases the likelihood of misinterpretation. Since all this information is required for understanding, it is easy to see why even professional psychologists may differ considerably about interpretations of such material, and it makes sense that teachers who have only a modicum of training in such matters should be circumspect about ascribing psychological meanings to children's art.

---

*I am indebted to the staff and students of the Santa Barbara City College Children's Center for their help in formulating the following outlines.

Easel painting is a perennial favorite of young children.

Suggested Variations

Offer a wide variety of colors, and ask children to select those they prefer; use a different size or shape of paper or one with a different texture, such as corrugated cardboard or "oatmeal" paper. You may want the children to experiment by learning how to mix a new color from the ones you have presented. Try using the same color paint on the same color paper or several shades of just one color. Different sizes of brushes or different kinds of bristles in the same color paint make a nice contrast. Thinner brushes encourage children to add more detail to their work. You might want to try painting to music, painting woodworking, painting the fence with water, using watercolors, having several children paint on one large sheet to make a mural, or painting on a flat surface instead of an easel. Printing and stamping, using paint and sponges, can also be an interesting although not extraordinarily successful experiment to try. Cookie cutters are really a more effective thing to use for stamping than sponges are.

A. Preparation
   1. Decide where to put the easels for the day. Painting is easiest to clean up if done outside, but in bad weather the easels can and should be moved indoors.

2. Assemble the equipment. This will include easels, easel clips, aprons, paint containers, brushes, large paper, paint, and a felt marker. You will also need clothespins, drying racks or a line, a sink or a bucket, towels, and a sponge.
3. Check the paint to make sure it is rich and bright, not watery, and neither too thick nor too thin. Decide, possibly with the children's help, on what colors to offer.

B. Procedure
1. If time permits, invite one or two children to help you mix the paint. (Sometimes this is done a day in advance, but it is always good to invite a child to help: mixing paint is interesting and educational.) Begin by shaking a generous quantity of powdered paint into the mixing container. Next, add water a little at a time, stirring constantly just as one does when making flour and water thickening for gravy. The paint should look rich and bright. It should spread easily, but not be a thin, water-looking gruel. If the paint was mixed the day before, be sure it is thoroughly stirred before pouring so that all the pigment is mixed back into the water. A dash of liquid detergent added to each container seems to help paint wash out of clothing more easily.
2. Several pieces of easel paper may be put up at one time; doing this makes getting a new sheet ready for use much faster.
3. Put just a small quantity of paint in each easel container. The paint may have to be replaced more frequently, but frequent replacement means the paint stays brighter, and small amounts mean less waste when it is spilled.
4. If necessary, invite children to come and paint, and help them put on the aprons to protect clothes. Remember to roll up sleeves firmly.
5. Write the child's name and the date on the back right-hand corner.
6. If it is windy, use additional easel clips at the bottom edges of the paper.
7. Encourage children to remember to replace brushes in the same color paint and to do their color mixing on the paper. Older 4-year-olds can learn to rinse brushes in between times.
8. Children may use their hands in the painting as long as they keep them off other children.
9. Hang pictures on drying racks, chain link fence, or clothesline.
10. Children should wash hands *before* removing their aprons. Use an outdoor sink or bucket for hand washing if possible. If children must wash in the bathroom, be sure to alert a nearby teacher to keep track of what is going on. Sometimes children also enjoy sponging off their aprons. If this is the case, rejoice.

C. Cleanup
1. Encourage children to help clean up. Washing paintbrushes is usually a richly enjoyed experience. Store brushes bristle end up to dry.
2. Put clean, unused paint back into the storage bottles and *ruthlessly discard spoiled, discolored paint*.

3. Replace all equipment in the correct storage places.
4. Roll and store dry paintings in the children's cubbies; the paintings should go home every day. If a painting is kept for room decoration, ask the child's permission before keeping it. If such permission is refused, be sure to respect that refusal.

Finger Painting

Finger painting is one of the most tension-relieving and delicious creative experiences available. The brilliance of the colors and the general gushiness that characterizes successful participation make it both appealing and relaxing. It is particularly valuable because it is so messy, beautiful, and free, and because it is a direct sensory experience for the children. It should be offered several times a week.

Suggested Variations

Children may paint directly on the table, using a whipped soap mixture, either white or tinted with food coloring. Ivory Snow is most useful for this purpose. Remember, the children will enjoy helping beat this up. (Adding some vinegar to the wash water will make cleanup easier.) They may also fingerpaint directly on the table and take prints of their painting by pressing a piece of newsprint down on it. These prints are often stunning. Shaving cream offers another attractive way to vary finger painting. Painting can be done on textured papers, or different recipes can be used for variation in texture. Using cooked laundry starch or cornstarch in place of the liquid variety is always interesting because different thicknesses can be concocted, and it is also more economical.

Cornstarch finger paint

Dissolve ½ cup cornstarch in 1 cup of cold water and pour mixture into 3 cups boiling water, stir constantly until shiny and translucent. Allow to cool and use as a finger-paint base, or ladle into jars and stir in tempera or food coloring.

If a thicker mixture is desired, be sure to add glycerine to reduce stickiness. Adding a little glycerine or talcum powder makes painting particularly slick. Scents such as oil of cloves may be used to add fragrance. Starch bases can be refrigerated and then offered as a contrast to warmed starch—perhaps one kind for each hand.

A. Preparation
1. Decide what kind of finger painting you will offer. There are many satisfying variations available (Hendrick, 1990).
2. Finger painting should look rich and bright. This means that plenty of paint and starch must be used.
3. Assemble all equipment before you start. Once begun, this activity is so beloved by children that the teacher will find it difficult to obtain even a moment to fetch something forgotten. Needed equipment will include *oilcloth* or *plastic* aprons (paint soaks right through old shirts if a child leans

Joe has a wonderful ability to let himself experience paint fully.

against the table, and most of them do), finger-paint paper or a good quality butcher paper, a felt pen for names, starch, tempera paint (it is possible to buy ready-mixed finger paint, but this is likely to cost more), plastic-covered tables, something to hang the paintings on, clothespins, buckets of soapy water, sponges, and towels.

    4. When weather permits, set up outside; cleanup is infinitely easier there.

B. Procedure

    1. Finger painting is more successful when children stand up. Standing enables them to use their large arm muscles more freely, reach the entire paper without straining, and really see what they are doing.

    2. Roll up sleeves and take coats or sweaters off. Even liberal mothers may balk at a child coated with fingerpaint from head to toe. Put on aprons.

    3. Allow each child to do as many paintings as she wishes, and let her return for as many as she desires.

    4. Finger paint is usually mixed right on the paper as the child works. Pour about 3 or 4 tablespoons of liquid starch on the paper. Shake powdered paint onto the starch. Ask children to tell you which colors they want, but do not let them shake it themselves; they often waste it.

5. Offer one, two, or three colors of tempera placed on different paper areas so that the children can combine them. Unless you have some special purpose in mind, pick colors that combine to make an attractive additional color.

6. Hang up finished paintings. Offer the child a chance to make another one.

7. Show children how to rub their hands with the sponges in the bucket *before* they remove their aprons. (Many children will spend additional time squeezing the colored soapy bucket water through the sponge— another fine sensory experience.)

8. If the day is windy or the room drafty, sponging the table lightly with water before putting the paper down will keep it from blowing away.

C. Cleanup

1. Invite some children to help clean up. (The use of soapy water and sponges will attract helpers.) Wash off table, aprons, and so forth. Be sure to wash the edges of tables.

2. Return all supplies to correct storage places.

3. Roll up dried paintings and place in cubbies.

Collage and Assemblage

Collage is particularly useful because it fosters an appreciation of the way different materials look when arranged together, thereby emphasizing the elements of design and composition. If offered as recommended below, it also provides opportunities for deliberating over selections and making choices and provides many exposures to a wide variety of materials, which may range from cotton balls to shells and wood shavings. Also included might be bright bits of ribbon and yarn, coarse netting, sponge, tin foil, corks, and packing materials. Collage or assemblage lends itself nicely to carrying out nursery school themes or other matters of interest to the children. Using natural materials in this kind of work adds potential beauty and interest to the activity. For example, shells, seaweed, and sand are nice to use as collage ingredients after a trip to the beach. The teacher should remember that the intent is not to have the child make a picture of where she has been or copy what the teacher has made; the intent is to encourage the appreciation of contrast in texture and color and to foster pleasure in creating a design based on these differences.

Suggested Variations

Almost anything can be used as collage material, and it is pitiful to limit it to cutouts from magazines. This is one area where the good scroungers are in their element. Carpet scraps, pumpkin seeds, buttons, fur, and textured papers are all attractive ingredients. *Because food is so short in the world, our center no longer uses such items as macaroni, peas, and rice as collage materials.* The experience can be varied by using different mats and bases: large pieces of old bark, heavy

Collage encourages children to be aware of design as a component of self-expression.

cardboard, or pieces of wood too hard to saw make interesting foundations. Food coloring can be used to tint the glue, or tempera can be added if a stronger, brighter-colored glue base is desired. The variety can be endless and the satisfaction great!

An excellent way to recycle cardboard containers involves gluing boxes and cartons together to create interesting structures. These are particularly appealing if a mixture of cylinders and square shapes are provided. The advertisements add color and appeal, and children love painting over these once the glue has dried.

A. Preparation
  1. Plan what materials to use, both background mats and collage substances. Many things may be used as a base. Cardboard, construction paper, or large pieces of bark are ideal. *Avoid using paper plates and cottage cheese lids as bases because they are too small and skimpy and do not give the children sufficient scope to work.* Select materials for contrast, variety, and beauty. Choose materials that will be aesthetically pleasing when used together.
  2. Plan to use *two* tables for collage: a work table covered with newspaper and a "choosing table" from which the children will make their selections. If you set the materials out on colored paper or in attractive containers, they will be more appealing and also easier to keep sorted and neat.
  3. If the collage items are heavy, use undiluted white glue, such as Elmer's, which may be purchased by the gallon for economy. If light items such as

feathers, fabrics, or paper are used, dilute the glue with starch or a *little* water.

4. Offer scissors or clippers to encourage children to modify the shape of materials to suit themselves.
5. Assemble aprons, glue brushes, white glue and containers, felt-tip pens, and collage materials.

B. Procedure
1. Give each child an apron. Roll up sleeves.
2. Encourage the child to take a collage tray and go to the choosing table. Gradually teach children to think about their choices: would that be interesting to use? How would this feel? What would go well with what?
3. On returning to the work table, give each child a brush and glue container (with very little glue in it at a time; children need to learn that glue is not paint), or allow the child to dip each item lightly in a saucer of glue.
4. Collage takes patience and perseverance. Many younger children will spend only a little time at it, but most older children will spend 15 or 20 minutes or longer if deeply interested.
5. Unless monitored carefully, it is easy for the choosing table to become an unsorted mess of rumpled materials. Keep it neat and good looking to facilitate judging and selection by the children.
6. Collages have to dry flat. Glue takes a long time to dry, so select a drying place that will be out of the way.

C. Cleanup
1. Children may help wash glue brushes; warm water will make this easier.
2. Return undiluted glue to the bottle and diluted glue to the thinned-glue container. Remember to wipe off the neck of the bottle!
3. Wipe off furniture that has glue on it.
4. Put dried collages in cubbies.

Dough and Clay

Dough and clay are alike because they both offer opportunities to be creative while using a three-dimensional medium. They also provide particularly satisfying opportunities to release aggression harmlessly by hitting, punching, and squeezing. In addition, these materials allow the child to enjoy smearing and general messiness, activities that many psychologists value because they feel it provides a sublimated substitute for handling feces. (Whether or not the reader agrees with this theory or is repelled by it, they will certainly find, if they listen, that children often do talk with relish of "pooh pooh" while they work with this kind of material.) For all these reasons, *dough and clay should usually be presented without cookie cutters, rolling pins, or other clutter*, since these accessories detract from the more desirable virtues of thumping and whacking, as well as from making original creations.

Besides these general benefits, mixing dough helps the child learn about the transformation of materials and changes in texture. It also provides opportunities to learn facts about measuring and blending.

It is interesting to note that recent research has identified developmental stages in the use of clay just as such stages have been found in the use of other materials. Brittain (1979) comments that 2-year-olds beat, pull, and mush clay, while a child of 3 forms it into balls and rolls it into snakes. Shotwell and colleagues (1979) identify the progression as moving from "product awareness" at 12 months to "elementary shaping" by age 3.

Suggested Variations

Allow the dough or clay objects made by the children to harden, and then paint and shellac them, or dip painted clay objects in melted paraffin to give a "finish." *Occasionally* use dough and clay with accessories such as dull knives for smoothing it or cookie cutters and rolling pins to alter form. Offer chilled dough as a contrast to the room temperature variety. Cookie and bread recipes are also dough experiences. Vary the dough experience by changing the recipe. The following are two of the best.*

Play dough

3 cups flour, ¼ cup salt, 6 tablespoons oil, enough dry tempera to color it, and about ¾ to 1 cup water. Encourage children to measure amounts of salt and flour and mix them together with the dry tempera. Add tempera before adding water. If using food coloring, mix a 3-ounce bottle with the water before combining it with the salt and flour. Combine oil with ¾ cup water and add to dry ingredients. Mix with fingers, adding as much water as necessary to make a workable, but not sticky dough.

Many basic recipes do not include oil, but using it makes dough softer and more pliable. It also makes it slightly greasy, and this helps protect skin from the effects of the salt. Dry tempera gives the brightest colors, but food coloring may be used instead if desired. Advantages of this recipe are that it can be totally made by the children, since it requires no cooking, and it is made from ingredients usually on hand that are inexpensive. This dough stores in the refrigerator fairly well. It gets sticky, but this can be corrected by adding more flour. This is a good, standard, all-purpose, reusable dough.

The following dough is lighter and more plastic than the first one. Feels lovely. It thickens as boiling water is poured in and cools rapidly so that children can finish mixing. It keeps exceptionally well in the refrigerator; oil does not settle out, and it does not become sticky; a paragon among doughs! Beautiful to use at Christmas if colored with white tempera.

Basic play dough II

Combine 3 cups self-rising flour, 1 cup salt, 5 tablespoons alum (purchase at drug store) and 1 tablespoon dry tempera. Boil 1 and ¾ cups water, add ⅓ cup oil to it, and pour over flour mixture, stirring rapidly. Use.

---

*From *Total Learning: Developmental Curriculum for the Young Child* (3rd ed.) by J. Hendrick, 1990, Columbus, OH: Merrill.

A. Preparation
   1. Cover tables with oilcloth for quick cleanup later on. Keeping a special piece of oilcloth just for clay saves work, since it can be dried, shaken off, and put away for another day without wiping. Masonite boards or plastic-topped boards can also be used handily.
   2. Assemble materials: clay or dough, aprons, oilcloth, cleanup buckets, and towels. (Do not allow children to wash their hands in the sink; this is the quickest way to clog the plumbing.) If mixing dough, assemble ingredients and equipment according to the requirements of the recipe. Offer small pans of water for moistening hands only if children are using clay.

B. Procedure
   1. Put on aprons and help children roll up sleeves.
   2. Give each child a *large* lump of clay or dough. It is important to offer plenty.
   3. Use the materials to foster children's imagination and creativity: clay and dough often generate a lot of playful talk among the children. Avoid making models for them to copy. Emphasize squeezing, rolling, and patting.
   4. Supervise the children's handwashing before removing their aprons.
   5. Clay and dough products are usually not saved but are just returned to the storage container.
   6. Mixing dough:
      a. Always plan this event so the children can participate in making the dough, because this is an additional valuable learning experience and great fun.
      b. Talk about the procedure while it is going on. Ask them, "What's happening? What do you see? How does it taste? How has it changed? How does it feel?"
      c. When making dough, make at least two batches at once in two separate dishpans. This avoids overcrowding and jostling among the children.

C. Cleanup
   1. Cleanup from these activities takes quite a while, so begin early enough that the children have time to help, too.
   2. Sponge off aprons and anything else that needs it.
   3. Replace leftover ingredients in containers. Clay must be stored in tightly sealed containers. Make a depression in each large ball of clay with your thumb and fill with water—this is an old potter's trick that will keep clay moist until used again. Dough should be stored in the refrigerator.
   4. Flush the buckets of water down the toilet to avoid clogging drains.

Woodworking

Woodworking is a challenging and satisfying experience that should be available to the children at least two or three times every week. It requires unceasing supervision from the teacher, not so much because of possible hammered fingers or minor cuts from the saw, but because an occasional child may impulsively throw a hammer and injure someone. Although rare, this can happen in the twinkling of an eye, and the teacher must be alert so that he steps in before this occurs. *Never leave a carpentry table unsupervised.* The teacher should alleviate frustration by assisting children who are having difficulty getting the nail started or the groove made for the saw.

It is essential that the school purchase good-quality tools for the children to use. Tinny little hammers and toy saws are worthless. Adult tools, such as short plumbers' saws, regular hammers (not tack hammers, because their heads are too small), and braces and bits can all be used satisfactorily by boys and girls. Two real vises that can be fastened securely at either end of the woodworking table are essential to hold wood while the children saw through it. A sturdy, indestructible table is a necessity.

One of woodworking's best qualities is the opportunity it offers for doing real work. Children can assist in fixing things while using tools or can make a variety of simple items that *they have thought up.* These often include airplanes, boats, or just pieces of wood hammered together.

Note the substantial table and adult-sized hammer being used. Using real tools is an important part of fostering success when offering woodworking.

I particularly like offering carpentry because it is so easy to increase the challenge and difficulty of the experience as the year moves along. Children can begin with simple hammering, go on to using the saw, and finally enjoy the brace and bit. During the year they can learn many kinds of tool-related skills, and they can learn how to select the right tool for the right job. Carpentry is also an excellent way to develop eye-hand coordination. (But beware of the canny youngster who says, "Now, you hold the nail while I hit it!")

Finally, woodworking is a splendid way to harness intense energy and to sublimate anger. Hammering and sawing, in particular, are effective relievers of feelings.

Suggested Variations

Allow the children to take apart the brace and bit and the vise to find out how they work. Have a number of various-sized bits available for making different-sized holes, and purchase dowels that will fit these holes when cut into pieces. Furnish different accessories for variety: bottle caps, film container lids, and jar lids make good wheels or decorations. String or roving cotton twisted among the nails is interesting. Unusual wood scraps that come from cabinet shops are nice. Wood gluing in place of nailing appeals to some youngsters and is a quicker form of wood construction. Many children enjoy going on to paint whatever they have made; this works well if done under another teacher's supervision at a separate table. Children will enjoy using a wide array of nails, ranging from flat, broad-headed roofing nails to tiny little finishing nails, which for some reason they often like to hammer in all around the edges of boards. Sandpaper is occasionally interesting, particularly if there are several grades of it available for comparison. An occasional child will also enjoy measuring and sawing to fit, although this activity is more typical of older children. Very young children will do best if soft plasterboard or even large pieces of Styrofoam packing are offered rather than wood.

A. Preparation
    1. Check the wood supply in advance. You may need to visit a cabinet or frame shop or a construction site to ask for free scraps if your supply is low. Teach yourself to tell hardwoods from softwoods. Plywood and hardwoods are good for gluing but are usually too frustrating for children to use in woodworking.
    2. Decide whether to use any accessories, such as spools or bottle caps, for added interest.
    3. Assemble wood, tools, supplies, and a pencil for labeling products.
    4. Arrange tools and materials so that they are easy for children to reach. Make the arrangement attractive. Encourage children to select what they need and to replace what they do not use. Keep rearranging materials if the area becomes disorganized.

B. Procedure
    1. Decide how many children you will be able to supervise at one time. For safety's sake you will probably need to limit yourself to three or four

children at once. *Encourage children to work on separate sides of the table to spread them out.*

2. Help children when necessary; teach them to treat tools with respect and to use them safely.
3. Be alert to interaction between children. Self-control at this age is not highly developed: *intervene swiftly when necessary.*
4. Be sure to encourage children who persevere in particularly difficult tasks, such as sawing through a large board or making a nail go all the way through two pieces of wood.
5. Remember to label finished products.

C. Cleanup
   1. Replace tools and wood scraps in correct storage area.
   2. Put finished work in cubbies.

Sewing

Sewing is not often offered in the preschool, and yet it is interesting to some children, boys as well as girls. Besides the obvious value of developing eye-hand coordination, it also offers good opportunities to experiment and to be creative. Occasionally it can be an opportunity for accomplishing meaningful work and can also provide a chance to experience the satisfaction of role playing a "motherly" activity.

Suggested Variations

You may want to try sewing on Styrofoam meat trays or sewing through plastic berry baskets; these have the advantage of being stiff and light to hold. An occasional adept 4- or 5-year-old will enjoy sewing top and side seams on simple doll clothes. Sometimes children enjoy sewing large buttons to material. Children may enjoy appliquéing cutouts loosely to burlap to create wall decorations for home or school. An old variation to sewing, which is fun but not really creative, is the punched cardboard sewing cards and laces enjoyed by youngsters since the turn of the century.

A. Preparation
   1. Choose a loosely woven fabric as the material for sewing. Cheap dishcloths are colorful and ideal for this purpose. Thick or heavy fabric will be too difficult for the children to get the needle through.
   2. Assemble the equipment: yarn or thick cotton string; fabric; large, dull embroidery needles; scissors; and embroidery hoops. Offer a choice of different colors of yarn and materials if possible. Make sure the scissors will really cut the fabric.
   3. You might prethread some needles in advance. It helps to knot the thread onto the needle if it constantly slips out, provided that the material is coarse enough, or to use double threads knotted together at the ends to prevent them from being pulled out of the needle.

B. Procedure
1. Choose a fairly small group of children to work with—four or five children at a time.
2. Be prepared for stuck fingers, some frustration, and a lot of requests for help, especially the first few times. Some children are disappointed with their technique but do not end up sewing for them because they want it to look a certain way. Encourage them to do it their own way and be pleased with their experiments.
3. Embroidery hoops help a lot, although children tend to sew over the edges of them. Rather than constantly criticizing this tendency, you can have them snip the yarn later for an interesting fringed effect. Children will also gradually learn to sew in and out rather than up and over as they become acquainted with the material, but it takes a while to grasp this concept.
4. Safety pin the child's name to her work.
C. Cleanup
1. Put the sewing materials away; never leave needles lying about.
2. Place finished work in cubbies.

Dancing and Creative Movement

Dancing has great potential for self-expression because it stimulates the child's imagination and offers many opportunities for emotional release. Moving to music can involve the child's entire body and draw satisfying expressions of emotion and pleasure from her that other creative experiences cannot tap.

There seem to be two extremes in presenting dance experiences that are not creative. In one, the teacher conceives the dance entirely beforehand and then puts the children through the paces. Folk dances, though desirable for cultural ethnic reasons, are examples of this. This is simply providing a model for the children to copy. At the other extreme the teacher puts on some music and sits passively by while expecting the children to generate the entire experience for themselves. Children usually require more stimulation than this from the teacher to get a dance experience going. Beginning teachers often feel self-conscious about participating, but dancing with the children is essential for success. Taking a couple of modern dance classes in college frequently helps students feel more at ease with this medium.

Suggested Variations

Accessories add a great deal to dancing and are helpful materials to use to get dance started. Scarves, long streamers, and balloons help focus the child's awareness away from herself and so reduce her self-consciousness at the beginning. Ethnic dance materials offer a rich resource for dance. Folk dance records and other rhythmic songs and melodies are delightful resources to draw on. Using percussion instruments can also vary the experience. Dancing outdoors often attracts children who shun this activity in a more enclosed

Following the children's suggestions encourages them to be more creative.

setting. Remember to include dance activities that appeal to boys as well as to girls. Moving like submarines, airplanes, seals, or bears helps take the stigma out of the dance for boys, who may have already decided dancing is "sissy."

A. Preparation
   1. Decide what kind of music to use and familiarize yourself with its possibilities.
      a. It is ideal to have a pianist available who can improvise as the teacher and children request, but this is by no means essential. Records or percussion instruments are also satisfactory.
      b. Familiarize yourself fully with records that are available. Choose two or three that offer a good range of rhythms and emotional expression.
      c. Do not overlook the possibilities offered by popular music. It has the virtues of being familiar and rhythmic, and it offers a wide variety of emotional moods as well.
   2. Clear the largest room available of chairs, tables, and so forth.
   3. Arrange to avoid interruptions. It is fatal to the experience for the teacher to answer the phone or to stop and settle a fight on the playground.

B. Procedure
   1. Avoid having other activities going on in the room at the same time, although some children will need to putter around the edges watching

before they join in. Accomplished teachers often feel comfortable having children drift in and out of the group, but beginners may find that a more secluded atmosphere where children may leave as they desire but where newcomers may not intrude is helpful. Do not try to have all the children in school participate at once.

2. *The most important skill to develop in dance is the ability to be sensitive to individual responses and ideas as the children generate them and to encourage these as they come along.*

3. It is necessary for the teacher to move freely along with the children. Sometimes it helps to ask other adults to stay away while you are leading a dance activity to avoid self-consciousness. Sometimes a teacher feels more secure with another adult present.

4. It is good to have in mind a general plan that contains some ideas about ways to begin and also things to try that will vary the activity. Always have more activities in mind that you could possibly use. It is better to be safe than sorry, but remember to use the children's suggestions whenever possible. It is essential to offer relaxing experiences and to alternate vigorous with quieter ones to avoid overstimulation and chaos. Children enjoy showing all the ways they can think of to be kittens or the ways they can get across the floor on their tummies, or as they become more practiced and at ease, ways of moving as the music makes them feel.

C. Cleanup
   1. Warn the children, as the end nears, that the time is drawing to a close.
   2. At the end, involve the group in some kind of quiet response to the music so that they have themselves under reasonable control as they leave the room.
   3. Help them put on their shoes and socks if these have been taken off.
   4. Return the room to its usual order.

Using Rhythm Instruments

There are other ways to respond to music besides dancing, and participating with rhythm instruments is one of them. This activity is both somewhat creative and somewhat an exercise in conformity, since children may respond imaginatively and individually with their instruments while doing something together at the same time. Basically, participating in a musical experience will introduce children to the pleasures and delights of sound, rhythms, and melodies. If well handled, it should also teach children to care for instruments as objects of beauty and value and should help them learn to listen to music and respond in a discriminating way.

Suggested Variations

Improvisations with musical instruments are a delight. Children can be encouraged to use them as the music makes them feel—to play soft or loud, fast or slow, together, or a few at a time. They can also make some simple instruments of their own, such as sand blocks and shakers (Hunter & Judson, 1977). Moving to music while using instruments (typically, marching) can also be a satisfying way of integrating this experience into a larger activity.

A. Preparation
1. Familiarize yourself with the music you will present. Listen to the records or practice on the instrument you intend to use yourself.
2. Select the instruments for the children to use.
3. Plan to start with a small group of children and a small number of instruments at first. You can always add more things later when you know how many children you can comfortably supervise.

B. Procedure
1. Instruments are not toys and must be supervised to prevent abuse when used. It will help if you plan in advance details such as where the children will put them when they are finished and how they will get another instrument. Decide on a reasonable procedure that will allow you to relax and not worry about the possibility of a child's stepping through a tambourine that was left on the floor.
2. Insist on these few basic guidelines: Drums and tambourines are to be hit with the hand only. (Drum heads do not stand up under steady pounding from sticks. Hit the rhythm sticks together if stick hitting is desired.) Allow one maraca to a child. Maracas crack easily when hit together.
3. Be prepared to get right into the music with the children and become involved. Your enthusiasm will communicate itself and make the experience special.

C. Cleanup
1. Warn ahead.
2. Put records back and return instruments to their area, arranging them so they look attractive and orderly.

SUMMARY

Early childhood teachers have always valued the creative part of the child's self and have sought to enhance its development by fostering the use of self-expressive materials. Today we also seek to foster creativity in additional ways, which include generating creative play and encouraging originality of thought.

To accomplish these goals, there are three teaching skills teachers should cultivate in themselves. When presenting self-expressive materials, they must cultivate their ability to let children explore and use them as their impulses and feelings require. When seeking to facilitate play, they must learn to move with the children's imaginative ideas and support

them. When working to develop originality in thought, they must be able to recognize the value of the children's ideas and to ask questions that will encourage further development of ideas.

Creativity is particularly valuable because it increases the child's feelings of self-esteem, facilitates self-expression and the expression of emotion, provides a vital balance for the cognitive part of the program (while also promoting its growth), and helps teachers individualize their curriculum.

Teachers can foster creativity by understanding and accepting the creative child and by maintaining in their groups an environment that helps children feel secure so they become willing to risk and venture. When presenting self-expressive materials for the children's use, teachers should avoid making models for them to copy, emphasize the process rather than the product, allow plenty of time and opportunity for the child to use the material, learn to make

enhancing comments, and give reluctant children the right to refuse to participate. But the most important thing to do is to make the materials freely available and let the children explore them as their impulses and interests dictate.

QUESTIONS AND ACTIVITIES

1. If copying a model is really inhibiting to the development of creative self-expression, why do you think so many teachers persist in having children copy projects "just the way the teacher made it"?

2. Do you think of yourself as being artistic, or are you the sort of person who "can't even hold a paintbrush right side up"? What attitudes in your previous teachers do you feel contributed to your feelings of confidence or lack of confidence in this area?

3. *Problem:* Chester, who is 3 years old, is still new at school and has been watching the finger painting with considerable interest. At last he engages himself in this activity, only to discover to his horror that the purple paint has soaked right through his cotton smock onto his tee shirt. He is very con-

cerned about this, particularly when the teacher is unable to wash all the paint out of the shirt, and his mother is genuinely angry when she picks him up that afternoon. How would you cope with this situation?

4. *Problem:* Irene is painting at the easel and gradually begins to spread paint off the paper onto the easel itself, then to paint her hands and arms up to the elbows, and then to flick drops of paint onto a neighboring child and her painting. Should the teacher intervene and control any or all of this behavior, or should it be allowed to continue?

5. The variations of self-expressive activities listed at the end of each section represent only a few numerous possibilities. What other activities have people in the class witnessed that could be added to these lists?

SELF-CHECK QUESTIONS FOR REVIEW

Content-Related Questions

1. Is it true that a person must be very intelligent in order to have creative ideas?

2. Identify several values the experience of creativity offers to the growing child.

3. List and define the stages children pass through when using a material that has creative potential.

4. Self-expressive materials are one avenue open to children for creative self-expression. What are the other two? What special skill is required of the teacher in relation to each of those avenues?

5. Discuss four or more practical suggestions for encouraging the creative use of the self-

expressive materials that are introduced in the chapter.

6. Select one of the self-expressive materials discussed in the chapter and pretend you are explaining to a newcomer how to present it effectively. What advice would you give him? Be sure to include some suggestions for ways he could vary the experience.

Integrative Questions

1. A 4-year-old girl has just hammered together two pieces of wood and proudly announced she has made an airplane. In addition to noting the creative value of that experience, explain how woodworking

might also benefit her physical, emotional, and cognitive selves. How might the experience also be made to benefit her social self?

2. It is the policy of some schools to allow each child to make just one painting or piece of wood gluing so that all the children have a chance to do the activity every time it is presented. What are the pros and cons of this approach in relation to fostering creativity?

3. The preschool teacher in the next room has had her 3-year-olds make caterpillars out of styrofoam egg cartons and pipe cleaners.

Each child was allowed to decide whether to use purple or red pipe cleaners for the legs and yellow or pink ones for the antennae. Her next project is showing the children how to glue artificial flowers onto pipe cleaner stems and stick them into balls of clay for Mother's Day. Evaluate these projects in terms of their potential creative benefit for the children. Be sure to explain why you think these projects would or would not enhance the children's creative selves.

REFERENCES FOR FURTHER READING

Overviews

Amabile, T. (1989). *Growing up creative: Nurturing a lifetime of creativity*. New York: Crown. This delightful book is full of sensible recommendations of ways parents and teachers can foster creativity in children. *Highly recommended.*

Belliston, L., & Belliston, M. (1982). *How to raise a more creative child*. Allen, TX: Argus Communications. This is a really good book about what to do or not to do to foster creative self-expression. The information is presented as a series of axioms, with discussion and a specific, practical list of do's for each one. *Highly recommended.*

Schirrmacher, R. (1988). *Art and creative development for young children*. Albany, NY: Delmar. Schirrmacher provides a comprehensive discussion of what creativity is. This is more than an activity book although it includes a rich resource of activities for two- and three-dimensional creative self-expressive activities.

Striker, S. (1986). *Please touch: How to stimulate your child's creative development*. New York: Simon & Schuster. Though written for parents, *Please Touch* is useful for beginning teachers, too, because of its clear discussions about, defense of, and practical suggestions for fostering various creative activities. *Highly recommended.*

Safety

Peltz, P. A., & Rossol, M. S. (1984). *Children's art supplies can be toxic*. New York: Center for Occupational Hazards. An unusual and useful pamphlet that identifies various dangerous materials. It also includes a lengthy list of safety-approved art materials with their trade names. Available from The Center, 5 Beekman St., New York, NY 10038.

Money Savers

Sunderlin, S., & Gray, N. (Eds.) (1967). *Bits & pieces: Imaginative uses for children's learning*. Wheaton, MD: Association for Childhood Education International. This is such a good pamphlet that it is still in print. There are many suggestions for scroungers and pack rats here that relate to all areas of the curriculum, not just to art activities. A fine way to save money.

Presentation of Self-expressive Materials*

Bos, B. (1978). *Please don't move the muffin tins: A hands-off guide to art for the young child*. Carmichael, CA: the burton gallery. Nicely illus-

---

*As I browsed through a considerable number of activity books that purported to present creative activities for children, I became increasingly depressed over the utter lack of creativity in evidence. Over and over these so-called creative activities were, in reality, tightly structured craft ideas that left almost nothing for the children to contribute in the way of their ideas or feelings. I encourage readers to look carefully at the values reflected in such activities before pawning them off on children as being creative.

trated, *Don't Move the Muffin Tins* has many practical suggestions, including a discussion of "traps" or pitfalls when presenting basic expressive materials. It draws a nice distinction between craft and art.

Chenfeld, M. B. (1983). *Creative activities for young children.* New York: Harcourt Brace Jovanovich. This is a very good book in which Chenfeld divides activities according to such topics as bodies and people we meet. She then suggests creative activities, including art, movement, and discussion activities, that could be related to the topic. Excellent bibliographies for children and adults complete each chapter.

Cherry, C. (1972). *Creative art for the developing child: A teacher's handbook for early childhood education.* Belmont, CA: Fearon. Cherry's books are always filled with practical suggestions offered by an experienced teacher, and this one on art is no exception.

Hendrick, J. (1990). *Total learning: Developmental curriculum for the young child* (3rd ed.). Columbus, OH: Merrill. The chapter "Freeing Children to be Creative" offers numerous recipes for doughs and finger painting.

Lasky, L., & Mukerji, R. (1980). *Art: Basic for young children.* Washington, DC: National Association for the Education of Young Children. This is one of the better books because it discusses the values of art activities and provides many suggestions and variations for them. The instructions are helpfully detailed and practical. Lists of "found" materials also are included.

Pitcher, E. G., Feinburg, S. G., & Alexander, D. A. (1989). *Helping young children learn* (5th ed.). Columbus, OH: Merrill. The authors cover the majority of creative experiences and deal with other aspects of curriculum as well. This is primarily a how-to book filled with practical, factual information and curriculum ideas based on brief discussions of theory.

Painting

Smith, N. R. (1983). *Experience and art: Teaching children to paint.* New York: Teachers College. The title of this book is somewhat mislead-

ing, since Smith's intention is not so much teaching as enabling children of various ages to use paints with satisfaction.

Clay

Hagen, J., Lewis, H., & Smilansky, S. (1988). *Clay in the classroom: Helping children develop cognitive and affective skills for learning.* New York: Peter Lang. The authors describe a research project that used three methods of instruction about modeling clay. The chapter "Clay in Your Classroom" is a gold mine of information on the practical aspects of presenting clay to young children.

Kohl, M. F. (1989). *Mudworks: Creative clay, dough, and modeling experiences.* Bellingham, WA: Bright Ring. A tremendous variety of mixtures are included together with estimates of appropriate age, palatability, and variations.

Woodworking

Skeen, P., Garner, A. P., & Cartwright, S. (1984). *Woodworking for young children.* Washington, DC: National Association for the Education of Young Children. At last, a truly practical book about woodworking for teachers and young children. This book deals with everything from how to tell softwoods from hardwoods to describing how tools should be used and how to straighten a nail. It also contains suggestions for helping children become effective young woodworkers. *Highly recommended.*

Music and Dance

Andress, B. (1980). *Music experiences in early childhood.* New York: Holt, Rinehart & Winston. Andress has provided a wide-ranging book that features simple arrangements of music, brief instructions on how to play various instruments, and many ideas for activities involving singing, sounds, and movement.

Bayless, K. M., & Ramsey, M. E. (1987). *Music: A way of life for the young child* (3rd ed.). Columbus, OH: Merrill. This is *the* outstanding book on music for young children. Replete with simple arrangements, it covers toddlers, children of nursery school age, and handicapped youngsters and also offers a rare chapter on including music for and about children from differing cultures. The resource lists are outstanding. Not to be missed.

Cherry, C. (1971). *Creative movement for the developing child: A nursery school handbook for non-musicians* (rev. ed.). Belmont, CA: Fearon. Cherry bases her approach to dance on creative movement. The material is simply presented, and all the suggested activities can be accompanied by familiar tunes and improvised words, which are included in the text.

Morningstar, M. (1986). *Growing with dance: Developing through creative dance from ages two to six.* Heriot Bay, Canada: Windborne. Of particular value because the activities are arranged according to developmental stage, this book combines those suggestions with practical and theoretical information about dance.

Stinson, S. (1988). *Dance for young children: Finding the magic in movement.* Reston, VA: American Alliance for Health, Physical Education, Recreation, and Dance. This is another practical book filled with ideas for themes and the presentation of dance material. Has good resource lists.

Methods of Evaluating the Creative Environment

Harms, T., & Clifford, R. M. (1980). *Early childhood environmental rating scale.* New York: Teachers College Press. Although it is not exactly a book, I want to call the reader's attention to this scale, because it offers a valuable way of assessing the presence of creative activities in early childhood settings.

For the Advanced Student

Albert, R. S. (Ed.). (1983). *Genius and eminence: The social psychology of creativity and exceptional achievement.* Elmsford, NY: Pergamon Press. A fascinating collection of articles on genius and creativity (not always the same thing). A good book to browse through.

Amabile, T. M. (1983). *The social psychology of creativity.* New York: Springer-Verlag. This is a rare book in a new field in which the author substantiates her premises with research. A useful resource for the serious student on this subject.

Biber, B. (1984). *Early education and psychological development.* New Haven, CT: Yale University Press. In the chapter "Drawing as Expression of Thinking and Feeling" Biber combines insights of 50 years ago with present ones in this discussion of the evolution of children's drawing.

Gardner, H. (1980). *Artful scribbles: The significance of children's drawings.* New York: Basic Books. Gardner carefully considers the relationship between drawing, development, and the other "evolving capacities" of the child. A readable, interesting, provocative book, profusely illustrated.

Rubin, J. A. (1984). *Child art therapy: Understanding and helping children grow through art* (2nd ed). New York: Van Nostrand Reinhold. The material focuses mainly on older children. Interesting reading.

Sternberg, R. J. (Ed.). (1988). *The nature of creativity: Contemporary psychological perspectives.* Cambridge: Cambridge University Press. This collection of articles presents a variety of approaches, definitions, and research studies concerned with this topic.

Wohl, A., & Kaufman, B. (1983). *Silent screams and hidden cries: An interpretation of artwork by children from violent homes.* New York: Brunner/Mazel. A valuable but depressing introduction to the subject of art therapy as it relates to abused children.

CHAPTER 14

Fostering Creativity in Play

Widespread misunderstanding of children's play has resulted in a growing tendency to replace vibrant, enchanting, natural and magical playscapes with overly slick, technology-inspired, manufactured structures. Further, the child's life is growing increasingly structured and centered upon the achievement ethic in the mistaken notion that what adults think is good for adults is also good for children. Overly anxious parents and misguided bureaucrats are robbing children of their right to play and, consequently, their sense of wonder and enchantment.

—James Talbot & Joe L. Frost (1989)

Have you ever wondered . . .

Whether play is as important as some people claim it is?

How to encourage play without dominating it?

Why some teachers think blocks are so important?

If you have, the material in the following pages will help you.

W hen the first edition of *The Whole Child* went to press in 1975 there was only a handful of citations available concerned with research and the value of play. Seventeen years later it is a happy fact that citations dealing with theory, research, and practice related to children's play abound (Bergen, 1988; Fein & Rivkin, 1986; Frost & Sunderlin, 1985; Singer & Singer, 1990; Smilansky & Shefatya, 1990).

And yet, despite increasing evidence that play is the serious business of young children and that the opportunity to play freely is vital to their healthy development, early childhood teachers find that many administrators and parents continue to misunderstand and underestimate the importance of play in the lives of children.

It is difficult to say why some adults have undervalued play to such a degree. Perhaps it is a throwback to our Puritan ethic, which is suspicious of pleasure and self-enjoyment. Unfortunately, as people advance through our educational system, they seem to conclude that any activity that generates delight must be viewed with suspicion—learning can only be gained at the expense of suffering. But play is just the opposite of this. It is a pleasurable, absorbing activity indulged in for its own sake. The live-for-the-moment aspect of it, combined with the fact that play arises spontaneously from within the child and is not teacher determined, lends an air of frivolity to it that has led some work-oriented persons to assume it is not worthwhile.

Whatever the reason for that point of view, teachers of young children must be prepared all their lives to explain and defend the value of basing large parts of their curriculum on play. For this reason, the following pages include an extensive analysis of the many contributions that play makes to the development of the whole child.

PURPOSES OF PLAY

A variety of reasons why play is valuable for young children are given here because preprimary teachers must be prepared to defend and explain the worthwhile character of this activity to people who still attack it as being a trivial waste of time, time that they contend would be better spent "really learning something."

Play Fosters Physical Development

Play fulfills a wide variety of purposes in the life of the child. On a very simple level it promotes the development of sensorimotor skills (Kaplan-Sanoff, Brewster, Stillwell, & Bergen, 1988). Children spend hours perfecting such abilities and increasing the level of difficulty to make the task ever more challenging. Anyone who has lived with a 1-year-old will recall the tireless persistence with which he pursues the acquisition of basic physical skills. In older children we often think of this repetitious physical activity as the central aspect of play, since it is evident on playgrounds where we see children swinging, climbing, or playing ball with fervor; but actually, physical motor development represents only one purpose that play fulfills.

Play Fosters Intellectual Development

Piaget (1962) maintains that imaginative play is one of the purest forms of symbolic thought available to the young child, and its use permits the child to assimilate reality in terms of his own interests and prior knowledge of the world. Thus it is evident that imaginative, symbolic play contributes strongly to the child's intellectual development. Indeed, some investigators maintain that symbolic play is a necessary precursor of the development of language (Athey, 1987; Greenfield & Smith, 1976).

Play also offers opportunities for the child to acquire information that lays the foundation for additional learning. For example, through manipulating blocks he learns the concept of equivalence (two small blocks equal one larger one) (Cartwright, 1988). Through playing with water he acquires knowledge of volume, which leads ultimately to developing the concept of reversibility.

The pioneering work of Smilansky (1968) has offered additional support for the importance of play in relation to mental development. She points out that sociodramatic play develops the child's ability to abstract essential qualities of a social role and also to generalize role concepts to a greater degree.

Saltz and Johnson (1977) found that 3-year-olds who received training in either thematic fantasy play or sociodramatic play performed significantly better on some tests of intellectual functioning than did the children who only discussed fantasies (in this case, fairy tales) or who were not particularly encouraged to participate in fantasy or role playing.

Language has also been found to be stimulated when children engage in dramatic play. Pellegrini (1986) found this to be particularly true in the housekeeping corner where children tended to use more explicit, descriptive language in their play than they did when using blocks. For example, they used such phrases as "a very sick doll" or "a big, bad needle" in contrast to using *this*, *that*, and *those* when pointing to various blocks. (Could this be true because teachers do not teach children names for various sizes and shapes of blocks? We have no way of knowing.)

Research on the use of blocks as a means of representation (symbolization) further supports the value of play as an avenue for cognitive development. Work by Reifel (1982) and Reifel and Greenfield (1982) demonstrating the developmental progression of complexity in symbolic play and by Goodson (1982) in her study of how children perceive the way models of blocks could be duplicated are only two of a number of examples of how play and thought are intertwined and of the kinds of intellectual learnings that develop during children's play.

FIGURE 14.1   Children play: Children learn

If a child is to develop competencies in reading, writing, and mathematics, it is necessary to develop:
  Visual memory
  Auditory memory
  Language acquisition
  Classification
  Hand-eye coordination
  Body image
  Spatial orientation

In order to develop these abilities, a child needs experiences with:

Configurations	Arranging objects in sequence
Figure-ground relationships	Organizing objects in ascending
Shapes	and descending order
Patterns	Classification
Spatial relationships	Verbal communication
Matching (shape, size, color)	Measurement
Whole-part relationships	Solving problems

These concepts and skills can be acquired as a child has time and space to initiate activities with such open-ended materials as:

Blocks	Dough
Cubes	Clay
Pegs	Water
Finger paint	Sand
Brush paint	Wood

Thus, the basic concepts and skills for reading, writing, and mathematics are learned as children . . .

PLAY

Source: From Swedlow, R. (1986). Chart: Children play: Children learn (p. 33). In J. S. McKee (Ed.), *Play: Working Partner of Growth* (pp. 29–34). Wheaton, MD: Reprinted by permission of R. Swedlow and the *Association for Childhood Education International*, 11141 Georgia Ave., Ste. 200, Wheaton, MD. © 1986 by the Association.

The extensive relationship between play and cognitive learning is well summarized by Swedlow in Figure 14.1.

Play Enhances Social Development

In addition, there is a strong social component to certain kinds of play (Garvey, 1977). Here again the methodological analysis provided by Smilansky and Shefatya (1990) is helpful. They speak of dramatic and sociodramatic play, differentiating between the two partially on the basis of the number of children

Consider the planning and social skills that were required in order for the fours to complete this building.

involved in the activity. Dramatic play involves imitation and may be carried out alone, but the more advanced sociodramatic play entails verbal communication and interaction with two or more people, as well as imitative role playing, make-believe in regard to objects, actions, and situations, and persistence in the play over a period of time.

Sociodramatic play also helps the child learn to put himself in another's place (Rubin & Howe, 1986), thereby fostering the growth of empathy and consideration of others. It helps him define social roles: he learns by experiment what it is like to be the baby or the mother or the doctor or nurse. And it provides countless opportunities for acquiring social skills: how to enter a group and be accepted by them, how to balance power and bargain with other children so that everyone gets satisfaction from the play, and how to work out the social give and take that is the key to successful group interaction.

Play Contains Rich Emotional Values

The emotional value of play has been better accepted and understood than the intellectual or social value, since therapists have long employed play as a medium for the expression and relief of feelings (Axline, 1969; Schaefer & O'Connor, 1983). Children may be observed almost any place in the nursery center expressing their feelings about doctors by administering shots with relish or their jealousy of a new baby by walloping a doll, but play is not necessarily limited to the expression of negative feelings. The same doll that only a moment previously was being punished may next be seen being crooned to sleep in the rocking chair (Curry & Bergen, 1988).

Omwake cites an additional emotional value of play (Moffitt & Omwake, no date). She points out that play offers "relief from the pressure to behave in unchildlike ways." In our society so much is expected of children, and the emphasis on arranged learning can be so intense that play becomes indispensable as a balance to pressures to conform to adult standards that may otherwise become intolerable.

Finally, play offers the child an opportunity to achieve mastery of his environment. When he plays, he is in command. He establishes the conditions of the experience by using his imagination, and he exercises his powers of choice and decision as the play progresses. The attendant opportunities for pretended and actual mastery foster the growth of ego strength in young children.

Play Develops the Creative Aspect of the Child's Personality

Play, which arises from within, expresses the child's personal, unique response to the environment. It is inherently a self-expressive activity that draws richly on the child's powers of imagination. Since imaginative play is also likely to contain elements of novelty, the creative aspect of this activity is readily apparent. Evidence is also accumulating that links opportunities for free play with the ability to solve problems more easily following such experiences (Sutton-Smith & Roberts, 1981).

The freedom to experiment creatively with behavior in the low-risk situations typical of play is one of the virtues mentioned by Bruner (1974), who points out that play provides a situation where the consequences of one's actions are minimized and where there are many opportunities to try out combinations of behavior that under other circumstances could never be attempted. In addition, Sutton-Smith (1971) points out that play increases the child's repertoire of responses. Divergent thinking is characterized by the ability to produce more than one answer, and it is evident that play provides opportunities to develop alternative ways of reacting to similar situations (Pepler, 1986). For example, when the children pretend that a fierce dog is breaking into their house, some may respond by screaming in mock terror, others by rushing to shut the door, and still others by attacking the "dog" or throwing water on him. The work of Lieberman (1968) provides added indications that playfulness and divergent thinking are related—though which comes first remains to be determined.

Another researcher interested in "pretend play" is Garvey (1977, 1979). She points out various ways children signal to each other that they are embarking on "pretend" play or have stopped pretending. These include *negation* ("Well, you're just Jon. You can't be a monster while we eat lunch"), *enactment of a role* (crying affectedly like a baby, for example), or *stating the role or transformation that is taking place*. ("This is the operating table—lie down, baby, so I can cut you up!")

In young children creative play is expressed primarily in two ways: through the unusual use of familiar materials and equipment (chapter 15) and through role playing and imaginative play.

Conclusion

No matter what value the theoretician perceives in play, the fact remains that it is common to all cultures and that it is the lifeblood of childhood. Thus Russians may offer hollow blocks while reasoning that their size promotes cooperation, whereas Americans may offer them on the grounds that their cumbersome qualities develop feelings of mastery. But the children continue to use blocks with satisfaction regardless of adult rationalizations, just as they continue to play house on the windswept tundra of the North and in the Wendy corners of the British Infant School.

DEVELOPMENTAL STAGES OF PLAY

As is true in so many other areas, children's play progresses through a series of stages. There are two particularly well-known ways of identifying these, and a combination of the two is often used by researchers (Bergen, 1988), because they concentrate on differing aspects of the activity.

The first of these has its roots in Piaget (1962). In this theory, play is divided into stages according to the way children use play materials. Thus, play begins at the *functional* level (simple, repetitive, exploratory activity—as simple as a baby playing with her toes or a 2-year-old squeezing dough through his fists). The next stage is *constructive* play (activity that has some purpose or goal, such as pouring water to fill a bucket), which develops into *dramatic play* (play involving "pretend" circumstances), and finally proceeds to the stage of *games with rules*.

It is the two middle levels of play, constructive and dramatic, that are of most interest to preschool teachers. According to Butler, Gotts, and Quisenberry (1978), constructive play is most frequently seen in children aged 2 to 4 years, and it is characterized by children learning the uses of simple or manageable play materials and then employing them to satisfy their own purposes. For example, a child might learn how to string beads and then make a necklace for himself. Dramatic play increases in frequency as children mature, and the golden age of sociodramatic role playing develops between ages 4 and 7, although we see the beginnings of this play in much younger children. It is at this level that we see children assigning roles ranging from "teacher" to "baby" to "dog biter" to themselves and others around them.

The second commonly used system for identifying stages of play is one developed by Parten (1932, 1933), which divides play according to the kind of social interaction that is taking place between children. In this system of classification play develops from *solitary* through *parallel* play (playing beside but not with another child); to *associative* play (playing together); and, ultimately, to *cooperative* play (playing together with role assigning and planning).

This division into steps is not a mutually exclusive one, however. While acknowledging that solitary play happens more frequently with younger children, research by Rubin (1977) provides evidence that there are varying levels of sophistication in solitary play. That is, while some of that kind of play takes place at the functional level, some of it, as anyone can attest who has watched a 4-year-old playing alone with a dollhouse, uses a great deal of imaginative language, role assigning, and story telling at a more mature, dramatic play level (Strom, 1981). Therefore, the teacher should not assume that solitary play by older preschoolers is generally regressive and undesirable. It is particularly important to recognize the value of such individual playful preoccupation in day care centers where children are almost relentlessly in contact with other people all day long. Children need the opportunities to think and develop their ideas through play by themselves as well as while in the company of other children, and they need opportunities for privacy too. Of course, if solitary play continues too long or is the only kind of play indulged in by a 4-year-old, it should be cause for concern, but some of this less social play is to be expected and even encouraged for most children attending preschool.

Parallel play also continues to have its uses even after group play has developed, and it is often used by 3-year-olds as a method of entering a group, the children first playing alongside and then with the group as they work their way into the stream of activities. Perhaps teachers could deliberately utilize this strategy with 3-year-olds, encouraging them to play beside the other youngsters as a stepping stone to more direct social encounters.

Educational Implications

Although preschool teachers are likely to see functional, constructive, and dramatic play, they will rarely come across the final stage—games with rules—because this kind of play is the prerogative of older children. The child care center teacher should realize that organized, competitive games are developmentally inappropriate as well as uncreative for young children. Activities such as relay races, dodge ball, and kick the can are loved by second and third graders but do not belong in centers for younger children.

While hoping to foster originality and imagination in young children's play, we must realize that not every idea generated by the children will be new, no matter how supportive and encouraging the atmosphere of the school. Children's inspirations will be like flashes—touches here and there, embedded in a foundation of previously played activities. There will always be a lot of "old" mixed in with a little "new."

Finally, the teacher should be prepared for the somewhat chaotic quality of creative play, since it is impossible to organize inspiration before it happens. But this chaos can be productive, and the teacher can maintain reasonable order by picking up unused materials and returning them to their place and by seeing that the play does not deteriorate into aimless running about.

FACTORS LIKELY TO FACILITATE CREATIVE PLAY

Teachers Should Avoid Dominating the Play

As is true with self-expressive materials, teachers should do their best to avoid dominating the play experience and seek instead to foster children's abilities to express themselves in their own unique ways. Such teachers help children base their play on their own inspirations because they are convinced youngsters can be trusted to play productively without undue intervention and manipulation.

Some teachers are so eager to use play as a medium for teaching that they cannot resist overmanipulating it in order to provide a "good learning experience." For example, I recently visited a teacher who had taken the children to the fire station for a visit. The next day, overwhelmed by the temptation to use play as an avenue for teaching, she set out all the hats, hoses, ladders, and pedal trucks she could muster, and as the children walked in the door, she pounced on them, announcing, "Boys and girls, I have the most wonderful idea. Remember when we went to the fire station yesterday? Well, why don't we play that here today? Jerry, you can be the chief. Now, who wants to hold the hose?"

Children may learn a good deal about fire engines this way, and if this is the real purpose, very well. However, the spontaneous, creative quality of the play will be greatly reduced by the teacher's using this approach. It is generally better to wait until the children express an interest and then ask them how you can help and what they need.

On the other hand, there are other circumstances where the teacher must assume a more direct, intervening role since, as mentioned earlier, some children come to the center with poorly developed play skills. This approach

Teacher interest can really encourage children's satisfaction in playing together.

was first investigated by Smilansky (1968) when she investigated differing methods teachers might use to stimulate increased sociodramatic play between children who came from families of the poor. In her more recent work Smilansky has continued to be a strong advocate of deliberate intervention. In *Facilitating Play* (1990) Smilansky and Shefatya cite a number of studies where such intervention has produced rich dividends for these children, ranging from increased receptive and expressive language skills, higher intellectual competence, and more innovation and imaginativeness, to reduced aggression, better impulse control, and better emotional and social adjustment. Because of these benefits, sociodramatic, make-believe play should be included as a vital element in every preschool and kindergarten day, and during such play teachers should help the children gain skills rather than focusing on content or subject matter.

Butler and associates (1978) describe this approach well when they advise that "you become an active participant in the play by making suggestions, comments, demonstrating activities or using other means relevant to the situation" (p. 68).

The problem with recommending consistent intervention in some children's play is that this can be tricky advice to give beginning teachers, since many beginners have great difficulty maintaining the subtle blend of authority and playfulness required to sustain this role. Instead, they either overmanage and overwhelm the children or reduce themselves to "being a pal"— approaches not at all what those authors had in mind. It is vital to remember that even when teaching children with special educational needs, *the purpose is not to dominate but to stimulate play.* The teacher should make interventions accordingly, stepping in only when necessary and withdrawing whenever possible. The following suggestions are intended to illustrate some effective ways of doing this.

Some Practical Ways to Stimulate and Extend Play

I think about play as being like pulling taffy—the more it is stretched and extended, the better the result! To be most helpful to the children it is important to pay attention to what they are playing and to think a little ahead of what is happening so that the teacher can encourage the play to continue *before* it languishes.

One way to do this is to ask the children what will happen next. For example, if they are playing "going to the market," the teacher might ask, "Now you've got all those big bags of groceries, I wonder how you're going to get them home?" Or "I see you've bought a lot of soup and crackers—does your family have a pussycat, or an elephant? What do you suppose they'd like to eat?"

Suggesting additional roles for bystanders to fill can also extend play. Perhaps there's a child on the sidelines yearning to join the others at the airplane/rocket site. A question such as "Gee, how's that airplane going to fly without any gas?" (Pause.) "Perhaps Aahmed could use that hose and help you" or "I see you all have such full grocery carts—where could that checker be?"

It is also very important to provide enough time for play to develop. When Johnsen and Peckover (1988) compared the kinds of play that took place between children during 15- and 30-minute play intervals, they found that the amount of group play, constructive play, and dramatic play increased substantially in the later portion of the 30-minute sessions. As they commented, it takes time for children to recruit other players, conceive and assign roles, and get the play under way. It seems to me that the play arena where this requirement of plenty of time is most apparent is the block corner where construction requires much satisfying time before other sorts of playful interaction can begin.

And, finally, never forget the value of enriching and extending the play by use of language—putting what the children are doing into words. Doing this while the play is going on, recapitulating it in large group, and recalling

The children loved seeing their teacher receive her allergy shot. It sparked a lot of reminiscences as well as stimulating productive play after the nurse departed.

yesterday's play at the start of the next self-select period will delight the children as well as increase their own ability to think about what they are doing or have accomplished already.

Teachers Should Encourage Divergence of Ideas

As in creative thought, the teacher seeks to remain open to originality of ideas in the children's play and to do everything possible to reinforce their production of imaginative ideas by giving them the satisfaction of trying the ideas out. For this reason the use of equipment is not overrestricted, and children are encouraged to use familiar equipment in original and unusual ways. Play materials are kept accessible so they are instantly available when the children require them.

Teachers Should Cast Themselves in the Role of Assistant to the Child

Fostering creative play demands that teachers add another skill to their repertoire: the ability to move with the child's play and support it as it develops. This does not mean that they play with the children as their peer, any more than it means they should sit on the sidelines being thankful that the children are busy and not in trouble. Rather, teachers who are skilled in generating creative play sense what will enhance the play and remain ready to offer suggestions that might sustain or extend it should this become necessary. Such teachers cast themselves in the role of supporter or facilitator of the child; they imagine themselves inside his skin and see the child's play from that point of view. This gives them an empathic understanding that enables them to serve his play needs well. Sometimes this insight is expressed by as simple a thing as going to the shed and getting out a variety of ropes, chains, and hooks for a construction project. Sometimes it is evident on a more subtle level as the decision is quietly made to delay snack in order that play may build to a satisfying climax.

Some of this empathic ability may go back to remembering what it was like to be a child oneself, and some of it may be related to opening oneself to sensing the child and taking time to "hear" him. It is a skill well worth cultivating because it makes possible the perception of the child's play in terms of what he intends. This enables the teacher to nurture the play by sensitively offering the right help at the right moment.

Putting the child in command of the play situation is valuable not only because it fosters his creative ability but also because it strengthens his feelings of mastery. When the teacher becomes his assistant and helper and defers to his judgment, the child is freed to determine what will happen next in his play. He exercises his ability to make choices and decisions. As mentioned previously, Erikson maintains that becoming autonomous and taking the initiative are fundamental tasks of early childhood. Creative play presents one of the best opportunities available for developing these strengths.

A Rich Background of Actual Life Experience Is Fundamental to Developing Creative Play

Children build on the foundation of real experience in their play. The more solid and rich the background of experience that children accumulate, the more varied the play will become. Field trips, holidays, and experiences with many ethnic groups, as well as things brought into the school in the way of science experiments, books, and visitors, will increase the base of experience upon which they can build their play (Woodard, 1986). There is no substitute for this background. In addition, play is thought to serve the function of clarifying and integrating such experiences (Piaget, 1962) as the child gains a greater understanding of reality through his recapitulation of it in make-believe.

Equipment Plays an Important Role in Facilitating Play

The Teacher Should Buy Equipment That Encourages the Use of Imagination

The kinds of equipment the teacher provides have a considerable influence on the play that results. Research indicates that children younger than age 3 benefit from the use of realistic play props when involving themselves in pretend play (McLoyd, 1986). Then, as the children mature and as their ability to represent reality through imagination increases, it becomes more desirable to offer them less realistic items to play with (Elder & Pederson, 1978). Thus a young 2½-year-old may play house more freely, using actual cups and saucers, whereas a 4-year-old may simply pretend he is holding a cup in his hand with equal satisfaction.

Of course, I am not advocating that 3- and 4-year-olds should never have realistic playthings to enjoy. We all know that dolls, dress-ups, and little rubber animals are beloved at that age and act as powerful enhancers of play. I just mean that teachers should not go overboard on supplying every little thing. Some things are best left to the child's imagination.

Where larger pieces of equipment are concerned, however, teachers can make their money go further and enhance the potential variety of play experiences for the children by buying equipment that can be used in a variety of ways and that is not overly realistic (Chaillé & Young, 1980; Pepler, 1986). Boards, blocks, and ladders, for example, lend themselves to a hundred possibilities, but a plywood train tends to be used mostly as a plywood train. A good question to ask before investing a lot of money is, How many ways could the children use this? If there are three or four rather different possibilities, it is a good indication that the children will use their imaginations to think of many more.

The Teacher Should Select a Wide Variety of Basic Kinds of Equipment

There also needs to be good range and balance to the sorts of equipment selected. This means that careful attention must be paid to all areas of curriculum, both indoors and outdoors. For example, puzzles should be chosen not only with a varying number of pieces in mind but also in terms of different kinds of puzzles: Have they informative pictures in the frame behind the pieces? Are they printed on both sides to make them more complicated? Are they the three-dimensional kind? And outdoor, wheeled equipment should not be limited to only trikes and wagons. Instead, scooters, an Irish mail, and a wheelbarrow should be included.

Although equipment does and should vary from school to school, it is also helpful to refer to a basic list from time to time as a source of ideas and inspirations. One of the best is *Selecting Educational Equipment and Materials for School and Home* (Moyer, 1986). This reference is particularly useful for new centers because it sets priorities for purchases according to essential first-year items, suggests second- and third-year additions, and extends from infant through upper elementary levels.

The Teacher Should Change Equipment Frequently

Changing accessories in the basic play areas such as the housekeeping area and the block corner will attract different children, keep life fresh and interesting for them, and encourage them to play creatively. Adding boys' clothes or an old razor (minus the blade, of course) or bringing the guinea pig for a visit might break the monotony in the housekeeping corner. Using trains, rubber animals, dollhouse furniture, or the cubical counting blocks could provide variety in the block area. Moving play equipment to a new location is another fine way to vary play and foster creativity. Boys, for example, are more likely to play house if the stove and refrigerator are out on the grass or if the house is made of hollow blocks for a change. Different locations attract different customers.

The Teacher Should Rearrange Equipment Frequently and Recombine It in Appealing and Complex Ways

Besides moving equipment to new places, it is also valuable to consider how it can be recombined. What if we moved the mattress to the base of the low wall? Would this attract (and protect) the 2-year-olds while they teeter along its edge or jump freely from it? What if the refrigerator box was moved near the climbing gym with boards, ladders, and sawhorses provided nearby? What if the pots and pans from the sandbox were included in this play? Or perhaps we might move the refrigerator carton over to the sandbox. What would happen then?

A helpful concept to understand here is the one presented by Kritchevsky and Prescott (1977). They pointed out that *simple* play units such as swings or tricycles have low absorbing power; that is, each item soaks up only one child at a time for play. When two kinds of materials or equipment are combined, such

Providing real-life experiences also enriches play: We had a rash of fire fighting after the fire truck left.

as when digging equipment is added to the sandbox, the play unit becomes *complex.* This has stronger absorptive power for children than the simple units do. Better yet are the *super play units.* These units, which combine three or more kinds of equipment and materials at once (for example, sand, digging tools, and water), do an even more effective job of drawing groups of children into cooperative play for extended periods of time. Evidently, if we wish to draw children into interactive, creative play, we should do all we can to concoct these super units for their delight.

Of course, teachers do not have to produce all the ideas for recombining equipment and enriching play. If the children are encouraged and their ideas supported, they will contribute many fruitful ideas for such elaborations and recombinations on their own, thus providing an additional outlet for their creative ideas.

The Teacher Should Store Equipment in Convenient, Easy-to-Reach Places

Besides purchasing equipment that will stimulate imagination and changing and recombining it to keep the play fresh and interesting, the teacher must also arrange adequate storage for these materials. This is often the place that nursery centers scrimp, but good storage will keep equipment available and save the

The combination of crowding and chaos makes it hard for children to enjoy the blocks.

teacher's sanity as well. Storage can actually make or break a play situation, so it is well worth the time, effort, and money involved to solve this problem adequately. Material should be conveniently arranged so that it can be reached easily, and, of course, it should be returned to the same place after use to expedite locating it the next time it is needed. Labeled shelves, racks, hooks, and storage closets that are large enough all help. In addition, storage should be located close at hand so the teacher may continue to provide supervision while getting something out that the children have requested.

Play Areas Should Be Safe and Attractive

The general appearance and presentation of the play areas will inspire (or discourage) children to play there. All areas should be set up at the beginning of the day in a fresh, appealing way. New touches should be added here and there to spark interest and avoid dull repetition.

Play is also better encouraged if materials are not allowed to degenerate into a shambles during playtime. No one wants to wade through a welter of costumes on the floor or build in a chaos of blocks dumped and abandoned in that corner. Attractiveness fosters attraction, and the teacher is the person who bears the primary responsibility for creating and maintaining appealing play areas.

Moreover, when things are left scattered about, they not only lose their appeal, they also become navigational hazards. Children (and sometimes teachers) rarely watch their feet as they hasten from one area to another, and loose pegs, little cars, and beads on the floor increase the likelihood that someone may fall and strike his head on the corner of a chair or table.

A Final Thought

One last reminder: children need plenty of freedom, time, and materials if they are to become maximally involved in imaginative play. They need the freedom to move from one activity to another as their tastes dictate, they need uninterrupted time to build a play situation through to its satisfying completion, and they need enough materials to furnish a challenge and provide a feeling of sufficiency. Making these resources available is a good way to say to a child in tangible terms that there is enough of what he needs in the world and that he need not scheme and plot to get his fair share.

SPECIFIC ACTIVITIES TO ENCOURAGE CREATIVITY IN PLAY*

Creative Dramatic Play—"Just Pretending"

Creative dramatic play such as dress-up and housekeeping is usually social and imaginative in nature, and its value as a vehicle for imagination cannot be overemphasized. Not only does it provide many opportunities for divergent ideas to come forth, but according to Singer and Singer (1990) such make-believe activity has many additional benefits besides. Among these are findings that children who use more imaginative play are measurably happier, their verbalization is richer in such things as metaphors and descriptive statements, and the amount of actual physical aggression is decreased.

Pretend play always involves more than one child at a time and contains a lot of role assigning and role assuming ("Now, you be the mother and I'll be . . ."). Three-year-olds tend to play a simple version of "house," but 4-year-olds love to embellish the premises with dogs, cartoon characters, naughty children, and interesting domestic catastrophies. All these activities develop the use of language, since the children will discuss and describe among themselves what is happening ("Let's get the babies and pretend they've been in that mud again."). Teachers should encourage this use of imaginative language whenever possible.

Dress-ups and props can enhance the play, but having unstructured materials available that may be used in many ways is even more desirable

---

*I am indebted to the staff and students at the Santa Barbara Community College Children's Center for their assistance in developing the outlines on the following pages.

Using what comes to hand helps keep play spontaneous.

because it helps the children be inventive and use their imaginations. Thus a scarf may become a hat, an apron, a blanket, or even a child's wished-for long hair.

Suggested Variations

Some teachers enjoy assembling play kits for the children. This is all right as long as the teacher resists the tendency to supply every little thing or to offer such specific equipment that there is no room left for developing a creative use for a familiar material. It is essential to vary dress-up clothes and housekeeping accessories regularly. Using different hats and costumes, different pans, empty food packages, or a milk bottle holder and bottles can kindle new interest. Dress-up clothes for both sexes should be provided. Hats, vests, and old firefighters' jackets and boots will find favor with boys, but both sexes should be encouraged to try all kinds of garments. Ethnic costumes are a nice variation and often enhance the image of the child who lends them, but be sure these are not valuable, treasured mementos. Doctor play is always popular, partly because it represents thinly veiled concerns about sexual differences and partly because it offers invaluable chances for children to play out their fear of doctors, shots, and being hurt. The teacher should be available for interpretation and control when such play takes place. Additional variations that have found favor in our school include a modest amount of paraphernalia donated by a local fast food chain,

obsolete typewriters and other business equipment, wedding veils and bou-
quets, backpacks and camping gear, and, always, cowboy/girl accessories such
as an old saddle and plenty of boots.

A. Preparation
1. Be attuned to the interests of the children. Has something happened in
the life of the group that could be played through? Perhaps a child has
had his tonsils out or the children went to see a car being lubricated. Have
a few props available that may enhance this play if it develops.
2. Think back to yesterday's play: could it be drawn over and continued with
satisfaction today? Is there a little something extra that might be added to
sustain interest?
3. Arrange materials attractively. If dress-ups are offered, hang them neatly
in view, or set out play accessories in an appealing way. Make sure the
clothing is clean and not torn and that buttons and fastenings are in place
and that a variety of clothing for both sexes is available.
4. Hold one or two possibilities in reserve to offer in case play begins to lag
(perhaps an old piece of rope to hitch the wagon to the trike in case the
children decide to lubricate a trailer truck).

B. Procedure
1. Sit nearby, or, while working in the general area, keep an eye on the
role-playing activity.
2. Stay alert; step in with a facilitating suggestion *before* the play deteriorates
into a hassle, but be prepared for the children to refuse your idea if they
wish.
3. The teacher's role is facilitation of the play, not participation as a peer.
However, sometimes it is necessary to be more involved at first and then
withdraw gradually.
4. Be sensitive to the children's needs as they materialize. *It is better to supply
helpful equipment on the spot as requested* rather than tell the children you will
"get it tomorrow; it's put away now."
5. Ask the children for ideas. For example, if they request train tickets or say
they need eggs to scramble, ask them what they could use for that
purpose. Encourage them to concoct solutions and produce creative
problem-solving ideas.
6. Help them give direction and focus to their play by asking them
occasionally what they plan to do next. "Now that your children are up
from nap, I wonder what they're going to do next?"
7. Remember that too obvious an interest in the play or amused comments
to other adults will make the children ill at ease and self-conscious,
thereby destroying some of their pleasure in the activity.
8. Tidy up unobtrusively whenever possible in order to keep the area
attractive. (This advice should not be construed as advocating compulsive
neatness but is intended to encourage the teacher to pick clothes up off the
floor and return unused, scattered equipment to the appropriate play
area.)

C. Cleanup
  1. Warn the children in advance that it is almost time for the play to draw to a close.
  2. Encourage them to restore order and to take satisfaction in arranging the materials for the next time. This is also a good time to chat with them about what they did and what fun they had.
  3. Remove any torn, soiled, or broken materials for repair or discard them.
  4. Put away accessories not intended for use during the next play period.

Blocks

Blocks, ranging from Froebel's "gifts" to the big hollow blocks designed by Hill, are one of the timeless, classic play materials that have withstood the many comings and goings of ideologies and theories of early childhood education. No matter what theory of learning is espoused by which educator, children have continued to play with blocks with concentrated devotion.

The sheer variety of kinds of blocks available for use in the preprimary school rooms attests to their appeal. These range from large hollow ones through unit blocks to the so-called cubical counting blocks (which have so many other wonderful uses besides counting!). In addition, there are a number of well-designed types of interlocking blocks available that foster the development of fine muscle abilities.

The quantity of blocks available is also an important point to consider. There is no such thing as having too many. This conclusion has been supported by Bender (1978), who found that increasing the supply of hollow blocks from 20 to 70 tripled the number of children participating, generated a great deal more conversation and role playing, reduced fighting significantly, and increased the amount of problem solving.

Unfortunately, because of their initial expense, many schools stint on this kind of equipment, but there are ways around that problem. Initially, cardboard blocks can serve as a reasonable substitute for the more expensive hollow ones, or someone with an electric saw can make an inexpensive but copious set of unit blocks from pine until the school can begin acquiring the longer lasting maple variety. Then, every year, additional blocks should be included without fail in the equipment budget.

Infants begin to stack objects (a primitive block-building skill) almost as soon as they are able to sit up, and children continue to use blocks with satisfaction throughout elementary school years if given this opportunity. Blocks provide endless opportunities for the development of emerging perceptual-motor skills. Stacking, reaching, grasping, lifting, shoving, carrying, and balancing are only a few of the countless motor skills practiced in block play.

Possibilities for emotional satisfactions abound as well. What teacher has not seen a shy child build himself a corral and seek safety within it, or a pent-up child send blocks toppling down, or two little girls construct block houses and establish families firmly within their confines?

Blocks lend themselves readily to achieving large effects quickly, thereby building ego-expanding structures of considerable height and large dimensions, which help the child feel strong and masterful, as well as providing opportunities for him to be creative.

Blocks provide unparalleled opportunities for understanding visual-spatial relationships (Reifel, 1984). What does a structure look like when viewed from one side and then the other, or when seen from above or peered up at from underneath? They also provide opportunities for developing insight into mathematics and physics as the children struggle with cause-and-effect relationships when unbalanced towers topple down or roofs remain in place.

Blocks are also strong in their contribution to the child's learning the intellectual operations basic to Piagetian theory. They offer many opportunities for the child to grasp the principle that operations are reversible (when a tower falls, it returns to a prior form). They may be used to demonstrate conservation (four blocks can be piled into a variety of shapes and yet retain their quality of "fourness"), and they provide additional opportunities to demonstrate the principle of transitivity (four short blocks equal two longer ones, which in turn equal one very long one).

Finally, blocks foster the development of creative play. By nature they are unstructured and may be used to build anything that suits the child's fancy (Cartwright, 1988, 1990). Older children enjoy planning such structures in advance, but younger ones will content themselves with the experience of stacking and balancing for its own sake and perhaps assign a useful function to the construction at a later point in the building.

Suggested Variations

Accessories that may be offered to stimulate block play are legion and can add a lot of attractiveness to the area. However, teachers should not overlook the value and delight inherent in presenting block play with blocks alone. (I make this point because, from time to time, I have seen students at the Institute become so dependent on accessories that they lose sight of the value of block construction combined with imagination and almost stifle the children with too many props.)

When accessories *are* used, the touches of color they can lend add beauty as well as stimulation to the play. Dollhouse furniture and rug samples, small rubber animals, and miniature people are all successful accoutrements. Variations in blocks themselves, such as gothic arches, flat "roofing" blocks, spools, and cubical counting blocks, add embellishment. Not all the blocks should be offered all the time; it is sound to save the arches, switches, or triangular blocks and ramps and offer them as interesting variations when the more common varieties begin to pall. The Skaneateles train is an incomparable block accessory; tracks and additional cars should be purchased every year, since it seems to be impossible to own enough of these materials. It is also fun to build pens for the rats and guinea pigs with blocks, although this requires careful supervision from the teacher for the animals' protection. Cars, trucks, derricks, boats, and airplanes are also delightful to use with block materials.

Outside, the addition of boards, sawhorses, ladders, and old bedspreads and parachutes will extend large block play in a satisfactory way. Large, sturdy boxes and cement pipes are additional accessories that make good combination units with blocks, and wagons and wheelbarrows are handy for carrying blocks about and delivering them to many locations in the yard.

It is also fascinating to combine large and small blocks indoors. Older children often enjoy using the small blocks as trimming on large block constructions, and some creative and interesting structures can result from this merging of materials. If large blocks are moved close to where dramatic play is taking place, children will often incorporate them into the play in a way that facilitates and enlarges that activity. Moreover, Kinsman and Berk (1979) found that when these materials were combined (by simply removing a barrier that had been between them), sex-typed house and block play was reduced. Younger 4- and 3-year-olds in particular interacted more frequently with children of the opposite sex when this was done.

A. Preparation
  1. Make sure the blocks are well sorted and neatly arranged.
  2. Try to include accessories that are related to current curriculum interests; for example, it may stimulate play to offer some boats after a visit to the harbor.
  3. Recall what the children were interested in the previous day when they played with blocks, and be sure to have these materials (and a possible embellishment) readily available should they be called for again.
  4. Be sensitive to the expressed interests and requests of the children as they draw near the blocks; the best accessory is the one they request.
  5. Children may be attracted if the teacher builds some small, interesting structure to begin with (the old principle of the nest egg under the chicken); but this creation should be offered as a stimulus, not as a model intended for emulation.
  6. Avoid setting out every accessory the school owns. This usually results in a clutter, which ultimately discourages participation.
  7. Outdoors a good supply of large hollow boxes should be set out to begin with. Children should be encouraged to get out the rest as needed. There is no point in owning a beautiful supply of outdoor blocks if they remain unused in the shed.

B. Procedure
  1. Settle yourself nearby on a low chair. *The teacher's presence is one of the best incentives to block play.*
  2. Teach the children to select blocks and carry them somewhat away from the shelves or storage shed so that everyone can easily reach more of them as building continues.
  3. Be an interested observer of the children's block play, but be ready to redirect children or offer suggestions to extend the activity according to their interests should the need arise. Avoid taking over the play; make sure it remains the children's activity.

4. Remember that children need time to play with their block structures after they have built them. Children appreciate having the privilege of leaving such things up during nap or overnight if it is possible to arrange this.

5. Remember to stress that block buildings belong to the children who did the work. Children may knock down their own structures but may not destroy the work of other children unless they have the owner's consent. Dumping all the blocks onto the floor and running off or throwing blocks should be prevented. Children who sweep blocks off the shelves need to stay and help pick them up.

6. Drawing diagrams of the children's constructions from time to time increases the child's interest and satisfaction in this activity. If a carbon copy is made, one copy can go home and the other be retained in the child's folder as part of his developmental record. Be sure to date it and note the child's companions and comments.

7. Mathematical relationships such as equality and seriated relationships should be casually drawn to the children's attention as the occasion warrants.

8. Tidy up as needed to keep the play area attractive and to make room for further building.

C. Cleanup

1. Some teachers discourage the use of blocks because they dislike picking them up, but this problem can be somewhat alleviated by encouraging the children to help, too. However, it is not desirable to enforce the rule, "You have to put away every block you got out before you leave the block corner." Since many children will not participate under these conditions, enforcement of this rule can spoil play. Teachers will obtain the best cooperation from the children if they warn enough ahead of time so children have time to wind up their play and if they pitch in with them and everyone puts the blocks away together at the end of the morning.

2. Always categorize blocks neatly when putting them away, and shelve them with the long side in view so their size is readily apparent. *Never store blocks by dumping them into a bin or tub;* it is impossible for children to find needed sizes in such a welter, and it knocks corners off the blocks as well.

3. Return extra accessories to the block closet and arrange the remaining ones so they make attractive, colorful accents in the room.

Water Play

Water play is one of the freest, finest play opportunities we can offer children. Although inexperienced teachers often dread it because they fear the children may become too wild or overstimulated, the opposite of this behavior is usually the case. Water play is absorbing and soothing; children will stay with it a long time and come away refreshed and relaxed if it is well presented. It is also valuable because it offers children many opportunities to work through conflicts resulting from the demands of toilet training (there is no better present for a newly trained 2-year-old than a sprinkling can!), it provides relief from pressures and tensions, and it stimulates social play. Sometimes children will play companionably with others while using water, though they remain isolated the rest of the day.

Activities such as pouring and measuring help develop eye-hand coordination. Children also acquire intellectual concepts having to do with estimating quantity (how much will the cup really hold?), with Piagetian conservation (but it looks like more in the tall bottle!), and with physical properties of water (what became of the water when we poured it on the hot sidewalk?). A particularly good pamphlet, *Mud, Sand and Water,* which makes useful supplementary reading on this subject, is included in the references at the end of the chapter.

Water play should be offered several times a week to provide maximum satisfaction for the children. In winter a large indoor bathroom with a drain in the floor is an invaluable asset. When water play is set up in such a location, spills run off quickly. Water can be offered in deep dishpans or sinks but is best offered in larger containers, such as galvanized laundry tubs, water tables, concrete-mixing tubs made of plastic, or even wading pools. At the Institute we put the containers at floor level when possible because this keeps the children's clothes drier as they kneel and play.

Suggested Variations

Too many schools limit this kind of play to hand washing or dabbling in the sink. Although these activities are certainly better than not having water available at all, they stop far short of what children really require for this experience. Many variations can be employed for a change, although basic water play always remains a favorite. Running water from the hose is a fine thing to offer, though it is, of course, a warm weather activity. Water can be used in conjunction with a sandbox or mud pit with real pleasure. Apartments and manicured suburban gardens deprive children of the opportunity to play with such concoctions.

In addition, water can be offered to use in sinking, floating, pouring, and quantifying experiments. Unbreakable bottles and containers, as well as various sizes of sieves and funnels, can be saved for this purpose. Ice is a fascinating variation to offer, or washing activities with dolls, doll clothes, preschool furniture, cars, or tricycles can be presented. Scrubbing vegetables, watering the garden, and washing dishes should not be overlooked as additional variations, which have the added appeal of participating in meaningful work. Making a variety of pipes and joints available for assembling and using with water is fascinating to children and teaches them some valuable concepts about cause and effect. Adding sponges, soap, or a little color will also change the appeal of the water and create additional interest.

A. Preparation
   1. Decide what kind of water play you want to offer and what kind of water you wish to use (soapy, colored, clear, hot, or cold).

Rice can help substitute for sand in rainy weather.

2. Assemble additional equipment and accessories for play.
3. Be sure to include oilcloth or plastic aprons, deep containers for the water, sponges, and towels.

B. Procedure

1. Make any rules or guidelines clear to the children *before* they begin. Children cannot be allowed to run around in soaked shoes or clothing when it is cold. It is better to explain the temperature of the day and also the limits of the experience before someone impulsively gets drenched.
2. The children will enjoy helping fill the tubs and setting out the equipment.
3. Put on aprons and roll sleeves up as far as possible. Remove shoes and do what you can to minimize the problem of getting wet, but be prepared for the fact that considerable dampness is the inevitable accompaniment of water play.
4. Expect some incidental splashing, but control deliberate splashing unless the weather is warm. You may give a splasher a second chance; but if a child persists, then the privilege of participating must be surrendered for a while.

Sand and water go together like ham and eggs.

5. While the children are playing, talk about pouring, measuring, or whatever you have planned as the focus of the activity with the children.
6. Listen carefully to the children's comments and ideas, and change and provide equipment accordingly.

C. Cleanup
1. Children may help bail out water tubs or tip them over on the grass at the end of the play.
2. A nice let's-find-out lesson can be built around the use of a siphon when emptying the tub, and cause and effect demonstrated by simply removing the plug from the table!
3. If rags are at hand, many children like to help dry buckets and toys.
4. Replace all equipment in proper storage areas.
5. Wipe aprons and change wet clothes.

Mud and Sand

Mud and sand have wonderful, messy, unstructured qualities that make them among the most popular creative play materials in preschool. They offer rich tactile sensory experiences and provide emotional relief as well: messing and slopping through water and sand or mud are relaxing and are thought by some psychologists to provide relief from the stringent toilet training demands of our society. These materials also facilitate a lot of social interaction. Older children play imaginatively and cooperatively with each other while digging tunnels, constructing roads, and carrying on "bake-offs"; but sand and mud are also rewarding for younger children to use, and they often settle down to this activity in a particularly absorbed and satisfied way. In short, the chance to mix, stir, pour, measure, mold, and squish sand and mud is an indispensable component of the curriculum.

Since this experience is often restricted at home, it is particularly important to offer it consistently at the center, where it can be planned in advance and where it is relatively easy to clean up. It is good planning to locate the sandbox as far from the school door as possible, in the hope that some of the sand will shake off clothes on the way inside, and it is also sound to check pants cuffs when the play has been especially vigorous, to reduce the likelihood of dumping the whole sandbox on the carpet. The sandbox should have a wide border around it so that children may sit on it and stay warm and dry when the weather is chilly. A waterproof chest beside it will make storage of commonly used equipment easier; plastic laundry baskets also make good containers because they allow the sand to fall back into the sandbox.

Mud is different from sand, and the school should provide chances for the children to play in both these materials. A mud hole and the opportunity to dig deep pits and trudge around in mud are interesting to children, so a place in the yard should be set aside for this purpose. (If the holes are deep, it will be necessary to fence them off for safety's sake.) Children will dig astonishingly deep pits if given room, good tools, time, and opportunity, and the satisfaction of doing this work is plain to see on their faces.

Suggested Variations

It is a shame to leave the same old buckets and shovels in the sandbox day after day when there are so many interesting variations that may be employed. All kinds of baking and cooking utensils make excellent substitutes and may be readily and cheaply acquired at rummage sales. Toy trucks and cars are nice to add too, particularly if they are wood or sturdy plastic, since metal ones rust and deteriorate alarmingly fast if used outside. Sturdy tools of various kinds are good to use. (Remember that when digging large holes, children need real shovels or clamming shovels—often sold in "surplus" or sporting goods stores—just as they need real hammers and saws at the woodworking table.)

Adding water to sand and mud is the best accessory of all. It can be offered in deep galvanized washtubs or buckets or as running water from hoses (having two hoses available at once will reduce fighting and competition considerably). Many children will enjoy having temporary low tables, constructed from sawhorses and planks, added to the sandbox. Such tables are particularly helpful to provide when the weather is cold and children should not get chilled.

Substitutes for sand and water may be offered when the real thing is unavailable. Cornmeal is good for pouring and measuring and may be presented in deep tubs or a sand table indoors, but the reader should realize that cornmeal makes floors slippery. Cleanup is easier if a small, battery-operated vacuum is

Delicious!

kept nearby. Some schools also use rice or dried peas or wheat as a substitute in cold weather.

Gardening is another useful variation of digging and working with mud. Since digging is the best, most involved part of gardening from the children's point of view, several weeks of this experience should be offered to the children *before* seeds are planted. The other part of gardening that young children enjoy the most is watering. Although this can be done with a hose that has a sprinkling head attached, it is easier to control if sprinkling cans and a big tub of water for filling them are provided instead. This allows the children to water to their heart's content without washing the seeds away or creating undue runoff.

A. Preparation
   1. Consider various possibilities for sand and mud play in terms of the weather and time available. If the day is warm, water is a valuable addition to this experience.
   2. Make sure the sand is at least damp so that it holds its form well when patted and molded. It may be necessary to sprinkle it a little.
   3. In hot weather, if the area is not shaded, set up beach umbrellas or large Japanese parasols to provide cool oases for the play.
   4. In cold weather, encourage the children to sit on the edge of the sandbox to keep knees and seats of pants warm and dry.

5. Have some sandbox accessories set out as the children arrive, but be alert to special requests and ideas from the children. It is excellent policy to change equipment according to their expressed needs.

B. Procedure
1. Stay nearby and keep a careful eye on what is happening. Children will occasionally throw sand and will need to be controlled from time to time. Shovel users need lots of space and must learn to be careful of other people's toes and noses.
2. Think of additional ideas you might suggest to continue the play if the children's interest lags.
3. If the day is warm and water is being used freely, have the children roll up their pants and take their shoes off.
4. Encourage children to keep the sand in the box and mud in the pit so it will be there for play next time.
5. If sturdy shovels are being used for digging, make sure there is plenty of space between children and that they have shoes on so that shovel edges will not cut their feet.
6. Foster the use of imagination and language whenever possible by playfully chatting with the children about what they are doing.

C. Cleanup
1. Warn the children that it will soon be time to finish their play.
2. Solicit their help in gathering up the play equipment and putting it away.
3. If the day is warm, hose off the area to get rid of the sand and mud, or sweep up the extra sand and return it to the box.
4. Help the children brush each other off, and shake out cuffs of pants and sweaters.
5. Put away accessories that will not be used during the next play period.

SUMMARY

Play serves many valuable purposes in the life of the child. It provides occasions for intense practice of sensorimotor skills; the symbolic nature of imaginative play fosters development of the intellect and generates increased understanding of events; play facilitates role playing and develops social skills; it furnishes opportunities to work through emotional problems and to experience the relief of acting like a child instead of an adult; and it provides many occasions for children to be creative by using their imaginations and abilities to think in divergent ways.

Teachers who wish to foster the creative aspects of play will seek to extend but avoid dominating it and will encourage children to try out original ways of using materials. They will purchase, plan, and arrange equipment so that creativity will be enhanced. But, above all, teachers who wish to foster creativity in play will cast themselves in the role of assistant to the children, seeking to move with and support their play as it develops and to serve their play needs to the best of the teachers' ability.

QUESTIONS AND ACTIVITIES

1. *Problem:* Suppose a parent comes to you, after touring the school, and says dubiously, "Well, it looks nice enough here, and I can see the children are happy; but don't they ever learn anything? Don't they ever do anything but play around here?" How would you reply?

2. Take time to make a brief record of the play of several children during the coming week. Can you find evidence in these observations that play is used symbolically by children to translate experience into a deeper understanding of events? Did you find evidence that children employ play to express emotions and work these through? Did you observe any instances where the children generated new, divergent solutions to problems by trying them out in play?

3. What is the difference between overcontrolling play and acting in a supportive, fostering role that encourages it to develop in greater depth? Role play the same play situation, demonstrating differences between these two approaches.

4. *Problem:* It is wintertime, and you live in a northern city. The children play outdoors at your school, but water play cannot be offered outside for most of the year because it is too cold. Identify several ways it could be offered on a regular basis indoors.

5. Survey the play yard of your school. List the different play units around which activity occurs. Are there some that appear to generate more imaginative activities than others? Identify what properties these units possess in common. How are they alike?

6. Put all the housekeeping equipment away for a change, and offer only hollow blocks in its place and some props, such as pots and pans and dolls. Observe what happens to the children's play under these circumstances.

7. Try duplicating Bender's (1978) research by increasing the number of blocks available for the children to use (you may have to consolidate the supply of blocks from two or three rooms to accomplish this). What kinds of play did you see increase as a result of such consolidation? Did fighting increase or decrease? Do you think the results are valuable enough that it would be worthwhile to have more blocks less of the time and pool the blocks permanently in this fashion?

SELF-CHECK QUESTIONS FOR REVIEW

Content-Related Questions

1. Explain how play helps each of the five selves of the child (physical, intellectual, emotional, social, and creative) develop.

2. List and describe the four developmental stages of play as identified by Butler, Rubin, and Piaget, and then list and describe the four stages of play identified by Parten. What is the difference between the two systems of classification?

3. What are three ways teachers can encourage creativity in play?

4. Describe how equipment may influence the play of children. Be sure to give several examples to illustrate your answer.

5. Pretend that you are escorting a visiting parent around your center and compose an answer to her question, "Why do you have such a large block corner? Aren't they an awful lot of trouble to pick up all the time?" Be sure you explain the educational benefits of this material.

6. Now, explain to that same parent why you make a point of offering water, sand, and mud play to the children.

7. Is it ever appropriate for teachers to intervene in children's dramatic play? Explain why doing this is or is not a desirable approach for teachers to use.

8. Name two practical ways teachers can extend play and cause it to persist.

Integrative Questions

1. The chapter opens with a quotation about "overly slick, technology-inspired, manufactured structures." Give an example of a piece of play equipment that meets this definition and then suggest a more natural, child-appropriate piece of equipment that could be used instead.

2. Imagine that a number of children are playing about families in the housekeeping corner. Suggest some possible ways that play could contribute to the development of each of the child's five selves.

3. A group of children are playing outdoors with the tricycles and have lined them all up and are playing "train." Suggest two possibilities you might propose to them that could extend their play. Be sure to put these suggestions into the sentences you would use if you were actually speaking to the children.

4. If you intended to dominate rather than extend their play, show how you would change your sentences to be more intrusive and overwhelming.

5. Explain how you could turn a simple play unit such a climbing gym into a complex unit. Then explain what you might add to make it become a superunit.

6. The 4-year-olds in your school have just returned from taking a bus ride.

   Possibility 1: Next day the teacher sets a number of chairs up just like the bus and has a bus driver's cap set out. She also has prepared some cut up green paper for bus money.

   Possibility 2: Next day the teacher sets out on the children's bulletin board by the entry a number of Polaroid photos of yesterday's trip and encourages the children to notice and comment on these as they arrive. Later on she sees a couple of children trying to fasten the wagon on to one of the trikes because they want to make a bus.

   Explain which one of these situations is likely to generate more creative play by the children and provide reasons to support your answer.

REFERENCES FOR FURTHER READING

Overviews

Bergen, D. (Ed.). (1988). *Play as a medium for learning and development: A handbook of theory and practice.* Portsmouth, NH: Heinemann. For a good overview of the values of play written in readable form by well-known specialists in the field, this book is hard to beat. *Highly recommended.*

Frost, J. L., & Sunderlin, S. (Eds.). (1985). *When children play: Proceedings of the International Conference on Play and Play Environments.* Wheaton, MD: Association for Childhood Education International. This wide-ranging collection of articles is crammed with useful information that is research based but practically oriented.

Hughes, F. P. (1991). *Children, play, and development.* Boston: Allyn & Bacon. Hughes provides an overview of play including chapters on play therapy, gender variations, and theoretical foundations.

Johnson, J. E., Christie, J. F., & Yawkey, T. D. (1987). *Play and early childhood development.* Glenview, IL: Scott, Foresman. The authors present a comprehensive analysis of factors affecting play. The material is well founded in research yet remains readable. *Highly recommended.*

Practical Advice on Generating Various Kinds of Play

Cartwright, S. (1988). Play can be the building blocks of learning. *Young Children, 43*(5), 44–47. This analysis of the pleasure of building with unit blocks includes an appealing list of learning goals associated with that activity.

Cartwright, S. (1990). Learning with large blocks. *Young Children, 45*(3), 38–41. Cartwright presents a practical discussion of how to offer large blocks most effectively in the curriculum.

Frost, J. L., & Klein, B. L. (1979). *Children's play and playgrounds.* Boston: Allyn & Bacon. A substantial book about play and how to enhance it out of doors. Profusely illustrated and practical. One of a kind.

Hill, D. M. (1977). *Mud, sand and water.* Washington, DC: National Association for the Education of Young Children. A rewritten version of an old favorite, this useful analysis emphasizes the virtues of using these materials for play and learning.

Hirsch, E. S. (Ed.). (1984). *The block book.* Washington, DC: National Association for the Education of Young Children. *The Block Book* is the most comprehensive discussion of block play presently available. It does a satisfactory job of covering this subject in a helpful, thorough manner.

Provenzo, E. F., Jr., & Brett, A. (1983). *The complete block book.* Syracuse, NY: Syracuse University Press. Lavishly illustrated, *The Complete Block Book* covers the history of blocks in the curriculum, as well as their potential uses.

Somerset, G. (1987). *Vital play in early childhood.* Auckland: New Zealand Playcentre Federation Incorporated (Box 67-085, Mt. Eden, Auckland). *Vital Play* is filled with explanations about why play is valuable and how to present self-expressive and dramatic play material effectively.

For the Advanced Student

Fein, F., & Rivkin, M. (Eds.). (1986). *The young child at play: Reviews of research* (Vol. 4). Washington, DC: National Association for the Education of Young Children. This review offers study after study documenting the value and impact of play on children's development.

Görlitz, D., & Wohlwill, J. F. (Eds.). (1987). *Curiosity, imagination, and play.* Hillsdale, NJ: Lawrence Erlbaum. The editors present a mix of European and American authors who are interested in carrying out research about play and its relationship to developing curiosity and imagination. A difficult but valuable reference.

Hartley, R. E., Frank, L. K., & Goldenson, R. M. (1962). *Understanding children's play.* New York: Columbia University Press. This old but invaluable book discusses the virtues of specific play materials and what each contributes to the healthy development of young children. A classic!

Kelly-Byrne, D. (1989). *A child's play life: An ethnographic study.* New York: Teachers College Press. This revealing ethnographic study is based on a series of play episodes that took place between the investigator and a 7-year-old girl in a naturalistic setting. An interesting list of aptitudes and attitudes the author feels is necessary for adults involved in children's play is included.

Pettit, F. H., & Pettit, R. M. (1978). *Mexican folk toys, festival decorations and ritual objects.* New York: Hastings House. For an intriguing look at the colorful toys of another country's children, I suggest you examine this book. Full of pictures, it is fun to see the similarities and differences in play these toys imply.

Piaget, J. (1962). *Play, dreams and imitation in childhood.* New York: W. W. Norton. In his classic description, Piaget discusses how children assimilate knowledge of the world around them by means of imitation and the use of symbolic play; rather difficult but interesting reading.

Rubin, K. H., Fein, G. G., & Vandenberg, B. (1983). Play. In P. H. Mussen (Ed.), *Handbook of child psychology,* E. M. Hetherington (Ed.), *Volume IV: Socialization, personality, and social development.* New York: John Wiley & Sons. This is the most recent, comprehensive review on the subject of play. It is an invaluable starting point for serious students of the subject.

Smilansky, S., & Shefatya, L. (1990). *Facilitating play: A medium for promoting cognitive, socioemotional and academic development in young children*. Gaithersburg, MD: Psychosocial & Educational Publications. Includes a detailed description of the 1968 Israeli experiment plus a review of other relevant play intervention studies and the Smilansky Scale for Evaluation of Dramatic and Sociodramatic Play.

CHAPTER 15

Fostering Creativity in Thought

Against the ruin of the world, there is only one defense—the creative act.

—Kenneth Rexroth

In these ways, and hundreds of other ways, life has changed dramatically since 1950—all because, in one way or another, somebody had an idea—all because somebody was creative. Certainly, the production of something creative involves much more than simply the having of wonderful ideas. But it is the having of wonderful ideas that distinguishes creativity from the other things that people do, and it is upon this that the progress of civilization rests.

—Teresa Amabile (1987)

Have you ever wondered . . .

> How to avoid asking questions the children just answer yes or no to?
>
> Whether it is all right for a child to ride backward on a trike?
>
> How to get children started telling stories?

If you have, the material in the following pages will help you.

Smith's definition of creativity as "the process of sinking down taps into our past experiences and putting these selected experiences together into new patterns, new ideas or new products" (1966, p. 4) applies to thought, as well as to play and the use of expressive materials. The ability to put prior experiences together to form new ideas is crucial in developing creative thinking, although building on past knowledge can produce unexpected results sometimes. I recall hearing of two young friends who were eating lunch together when the following dialogue took place.

> Henry: "Well, you know, Andrew, I'm black! I'm black all over—from my head right down to inside my shoes!"
> There is a pause while this information is digested in silence by his friend Andrew.
> Henry continues, "But that's OK! Cuz my Mother says, 'Black is beautiful!'"
> Andrew continues to eye Henry speculatively while Henry somewhat complacently spoons up his Jell-O. There is silence around the table.
> "Well," says Andrew, putting down his spoon and looking thoughtfully at Henry, "I guess being black's OK, all right—it's OK with *me*—but you know, Henry, if you wuz green, you could hide in the trees!"

Using prior information as Andrew did to produce new solutions is just one kind of creative thinking. Children are also thinking creatively when they produce more than one answer to a question, or conceive of new uses for familiar materials, or generate uniquely descriptive language and self-expressive stories. To do these things, they need a wealth of experience to draw upon, and they need the help and expertise of the teacher to encourage them (Leipzig, 1989).

Although preschool teachers have long maintained that the development of creative thinking in children is desirable, the work of Guilford has drawn fresh attention to the value of thinking that emphasizes a many-answers approach. Guilford terms this ability *divergent thinking* and contrasts it with *convergent thinking*. He maintains that the critical difference between these mental operations is that in convergent thinking the kind of response is completely specified (that is, there is only one correct answer), whereas in divergent thinking more than one solution or answer is possible (1981).

Convergent thinking is elicited by such questions as, What color is this? Can you tell me the name of this shape? What must we always do before we cross the street? There is nothing wrong with this kind of mental activity; children need to have a variety of commonly known facts at their fingertips. But teaching that stops at the fact-asking level fails to develop the creative aspect of the child's mental ability. Children who are trained like robots to produce facts when the right button is pushed are unlikely to grow up to produce the new ideas desperately needed in science, medicine, and human relationships.

Unfortunately, most teaching is still geared to convergent, one-answer learning. Zimmerman and Bergan (1971) found that even as early as first grade there was what they termed "an inordinate emphasis placed on factual knowledge questions." They reported that only about 2% of the questions asked

"I'm the invisible man," chortled Grady Kent.

by first-grade teachers were structured to draw forth divergent replies. Honig has also studied question-asking behavior and reports similar discouraging findings. The children she studied averaged around 27 months of age, and of the nearly 800 questions she observed asked by caregivers, "15% were requests, 4% were reproofs, and 81% were true questions" (1982a, p. 64). This sounds encouraging until one reads that only 20% of those questions were divergent and that fewer than 1% offered these young children any choices!

But just because this has been true of teaching in the past does not mean it must continue. The following examples of ways to generate creativity in thought may encourage teachers to produce more divergent thinking in the children in their groups. Doing this is fun, it is interesting, and it can be exciting for both children and teachers when it is presented in the right manner. All it takes is practice.

THINGS TO REMEMBER ABOUT CREATIVE THINKING

The Number of Original Ideas Can Be Increased If the Teacher Recognizes Their Value and Responds to Them in a Positive Way

It is easy to go on doing things the same old way or to establish a set of procedures that have become so sanctified by custom that no one considers deviating from the established formula. But an open-minded teacher who keeps on the lookout for spontaneous ideas and suggestions will find he can frequently go along with variations in approach and changes in procedure when they are suggested by the children. The teacher who is willing to let the children put their ideas into practice offers strong positive reinforcement for this behavior, which will nourish creative talent in the children, and he will find himself blessed with ever more interesting, fresh contributions from the youngsters in his group.

For example, I remember the time we offered a cooking project that involved slicing bananas for Jell-O. The inexperienced young student in charge felt she could watch only two children working with paring knives at once and therefore sensibly limited the activity to two children at a time. A third little boy hung around and watched, badly wanting to have a chance with the bananas; but the student truthfully explained she was so new that she felt she just couldn't supervise more than two knives at once. Then he said to her, ''I tell you what—I could use one of the scissors for the bananas. I know how to do that. I *never* cut myself with scissors.'' She immediately saw the value of his suggestion and let him snip up as many pieces as he liked.

Another independently minded 2½-year-old was going through a streak of wanting to get into the swing by herself. Since she was short and the swing was high, she struggled and wriggled, doggedly refusing assistance. Finally, she rushed away and returned with a large hollow block, which she put under the swing and used successfully as a mounting block.

Ideas That Turn Out to Be Unsuccessful Are Also a Valuable Learning Experience

Of course, creative ideas and experiments do not always work; and adults, who have a much better grasp of cause and effect, as well as more experience than children have, can often foresee problems and difficulties associated with ideas produced by young thinkers. But if the situation is reasonably safe, the children should be allowed to try out their ideas even if the adult knows they will not work. Children are entitled to the right to fail, as well as to the right to succeed. The sensitive teacher will be matter-of-fact and low-keyed about such ineffective trials. He might say, ''I'm sorry that didn't work out just right, but I'm proud of you for trying it,'' or simply, ''I can see you're really disgusted. Can I help?'' or, ''Well, it was worth trying—otherwise, how would we know it doesn't work?''

Children can learn a lot from experiencing failures, just as they learn from successes. Sometimes they can modify the idea and make success more likely next time. More important than that, they can learn to cope with the experience of failure if they undergo it in a generous, noncritical atmosphere.

Language Should Be Used Along with More Tangible Means of Trying Out Ideas

Although there are perils in overintellectualizing the role of question asking, language is of genuine importance in the development of ideas. Language is a great facilitator of thought, and language and cognition are closely linked. Therefore it is vital to couple experience with talk and to discuss what the children learned when the experience is completed, but remember, conversation must not be allowed to take the place of actual involvement with real things.

FOSTER CREATIVE THINKING BY ASKING QUESTIONS THAT ENCOURAGE CHILDREN TO DEVELOP THEIR OWN IDEAS

Although some youngsters solve problems and create interesting ideas without outside help, in general the teacher needs to take an active role in stimulating creative thought. The most effective way to do this is by asking the children questions that help them think up their own answers.

The value of such questions should not be underestimated. Piaget maintained that they exercise a vital influence on cognitive development (1977), and he particularly favored questions that point out contradictions of what the child already knows or that cause children to think about something from another point of view (Lay-Dopyera & Dopyera, 1987). This is exactly what is required when children are asked to come up with creative solutions and possibilities.

Wait for Answers and Ask Only a Few Questions

One of the most important things about asking questions is learning to *wait* for an answer. This is surprisingly hard to do. Many teachers ask excellent questions but then plunge right ahead and answer them themselves. In one study of "wait time," Rowe (1974) found that teachers only waited, on the average, *1 second* before doing this. Perhaps this is because teachers are afraid of silence or of the child's failing. But children, like adults, need time to collect their thoughts and formulate their replies. Pausing allows them to do this.

Another thing to beware of is asking too many questions. The plaintive little song by Hap Palmer puts this neatly when he inquires,

Questions, questions, askin' me endlessly
How many more must I answer today?
Questions, questions, don't drive me crazy, please,
How much more can I say?*

In our zeal to help children think we must remember that most young children are not highly verbal, and they do not enjoy long, drawn-out intellectual dialogues. To prevent questions from becoming burdensome, it is best to weave them into general discussions while the actual experience is going on, as well as to provide all possible opportunities for children to promptly put their suggestions into practice.

Stimulate the Inquiry Process by Helping Children Think Up Answers for Themselves

To develop creative thinking, teachers must also learn to deal sensitively with questions the children ask them. And, of course, they ask questions endlessly. Teachers have to learn that it is *not* their primary function to provide answers. Of course, children are entitled to information when they cannot figure things out for themselves, but often a child can satisfy her curiosity by providing her own answer if the teacher does not rush in and furnish the fact immediately. This is another instance where it is necessary to pause and think before replying.

I recall a child's asking one of the students, "What makes the wind blow?" Instead of saying, "It's due to the weather," he replied, "That's a good question, Jeannie—we can really feel that old wind today, can't we? Can you make it yourself?" And they were off on a long discussion of ways to produce wind. These included blowing with your mouth, flying a kite (a little confused, but still a related idea!), running fast, getting Daddy to drive fast in the car, riding behind a bus, letting leaves fall, making fans, and squirting a bicycle pump. Eventually this all led to the conclusion that pushing on the air makes it move and makes wind blow.

Sort Out Different Kinds of Questions: Fact and Thought Questions

We have already noted that all questions are not alike because some elicit convergent and others divergent replies. This is easiest to understand if one thinks of questions related to mental development as being of three kinds: (a) *fact questions,* which request the child to reply with one right answer; (b) *figuring-out questions,* which require the child to apply a concept in order to arrive at one or more right answers; and (c) *creative questions,* which elicit an original idea or solution from the youngster.

---

*From "Feelin' Free," a record by Hap Palmer made for Educational Activities, Freeport, NY, AR 516. There are also some nice creative questions on this same record.

The question: "How can we make both scales say the same thing?"

The simplest, and regrettably the most frequently used question, the *fact* question, can usually be spotted because it (a) requests information ("Do you make cookies in the oven or in the broiler?" "You're right! It *is* a rabbit. What else do you know about rabbits?"), (b) requests labeling or naming ("Let's see, I have some things in this bag and I wonder if you can tell me what they are?"), or (c) requests the child to recall something from memory ("How about telling us what happened when you went to the pet store? Did you buy rabbit food?"). All these questions are "closed" or convergent questions since they anticipate simple, correct-answer replies.

Figuring-out questions, which will be dealt with mainly in the following chapter, are a big step up from fact questions, but are still in the final analysis going to produce right (convergent) answers. They are more advanced than fact questions because, in order to answer the question, the child must be able to apply a concept to a situation and reason out the reply. For example, to select the pictures that are just the same (playing lotto, for instance), a youngster must understand the concept of sameness and then be able to apply it by matching the pictures that are identical. Or if asked how birds are not the same as butterflies, she must analyze what is the same about them and what is different. Even though there would be a number of differences to identify, and though more analysis and insight is involved, the final result is the production of closed-end, correct answers.

Creative questions, on the other hand, foster the production of original, divergent ideas and solutions. They are termed "open ended" because the questioner does not know what the answer will turn out to be (Lay-Dopyera & Dopyera, 1987). Questions likely to draw forth such kinds of replies are phrased like these: What could you do about it? How could we fix it? I wonder if there's another way? How else could you do that? What's your opinion? Just suppose that . . . then what? What would happen if . . . ?

Thinking of such open questions can be difficult at first since our own educations have placed so much emphasis on asking and answering fact questions, but it *is* possible to form the habit of doing this. In addition to learning to use the stock questions listed above, it also helps to think up several questions in advance to pose to the children. How could we make the ball bounce higher? What if Little Blue (the parakeet) loses all her feathers? I've sprained my ankle—have you any ideas how I can get downstairs? These are all examples of questions thought out in advance that would encourage the children to do some creative thinking in return.

Encourage the Child or the Group to Produce More Than One Answer

Since in divergent thinking more than one correct answer is possible, teachers need to learn how to encourage children to propose more than one possible solution to a problem.

Making sure the child's ideas are not criticized will help generate many answers, whereas the negative experience of criticism will make sensitive children clam up and refuse to take the risk of confiding a second thought (Kline, 1988). If the goal is to encourage children to mention their ideas, it makes simple good sense to welcome the suggestions and ask for more rather than to submit each one to instant critical appraisal or, worse yet, amused laughter.

The kinds of questions that often lead children to generate more ideas related to creative problem solving are sometimes called "what else?" and "what if?" questions (Campbell & Arnold, 1988). Questions such as "What else could you do?" or "Is there another way?" will stimulate many suggestions from the children. For example, Aline and Franklin, both 4-year-olds, are trying to get the rat cage open to feed him. As they work, the teacher jokes with them a little and asks them, "I wonder what we'd do if the gate were really stuck and we *couldn't* get it open. How could we feed the rat then?" "We could poke it through the lines [bars]," says Franklin. "Sure we could—that's a good idea, Franklin—but let's suppose we couldn't get it through the bars; what then?" "We could teach him to reach out," says Franklin. "Yes, he likes to reach; but if he couldn't do that, what then?'' There is a long silence while the children consider. ''But he *can*,'' answers practical Franklin. ''But let's imagine, just pretend for fun, that he can't. Could we feed him another way, or would he just get hungry?'' Suddenly Aline brightens visibly and says, ''We could slide the tray out and feed him from the cellar!'' (She means from underneath.) ''Yes, we could,'' says the teacher. ''My goodness, Franklin, you and Aline sure have a lot of ideas. I guess we'll be able to feed our rat after all,'' and the children laugh with him.

This kind of elementary brainstorming can be done quite successfully with preschool children in a playful way. It encourages them to see that questions can have a number of right answers and to develop the habit of looking for more than one solution to a problem.

''What if?'' questions encourage even freer and more creative answers than ''what else?'' questions do. Sometimes with older 4- and 5-year-olds this approach can be presented as a guessing game during group or lunch time. A

John is surely using some familiar equipment in an unusual way! He announced to us that these were his snowshoes.

problem can be postulated, such as "What if we didn't have any blankets at nap; how could we keep warm?" Then all kinds of possibilities can be suggested. (One of our little boys said, "Grow fur.") Four-year-olds often delight in thinking up nonsensical solutions whose funniness adds delight to this process and exercises their sense of humor as well.

Asking the children to consider a nonsensical possibility using a variation of "what if?" questions provides good practice and lots of fun, too. This *just supposing* approach stimulates many imaginative replies.

For example, one might ask the children to just suppose that something were true, and then consider what would happen as a result. Just suppose that bean vines never stopped growing, dogs could talk to cats, mice had wings, you were only as big as your thumb, or that your wishes would come true. It is clear that some of the most interesting fairy and folktales such as "Jack and the Beanstalk," "Tom Thumb," and "Why the Sea Is Salt" are based on exactly these kinds of interesting, fantastical possibilities.

When two of our 4-year-olds, Caroline and Katie, were asked what they would wish for if their wishes could come true they composed the following poem.

> I wish it could be snowy every day, and I could play in it
> I wish I had a long dress with a matching hat and purse
> I wish I was a big person
> I wish I had a house you could go out on the roof of
> I wish I had a crystal star

On a more mundane level, I recall one of my own children wishing thoughtfully one day that she was one of the big people at nursery school so then, said she, "I could eat snack indoors and kick all the little kids in the stomach!"

PERMIT THE CHILD TO EXPLORE NEW WAYS TO USE EQUIPMENT, AND PROVIDE OPPORTUNITIES TO TRY OUT UNCONVENTIONAL IDEAS

Dealing with questions for which there is more than one right answer is just one example of creative thinking. Children can also be encouraged to develop creative thought by allowing them to use equipment in fresh and unconventional ways. They look at a familiar thing in a new way and perceive new possibilities in it. This is a fine way to develop originality, and one of the easiest and most productive approaches to use with young children.

Sometimes such uses can be quite ingenious. An acquaintance told me an interesting instance of such an unconventional idea. His little boy was going through the stage of flipping light switches on, something he could just manage to do by standing on tiptoe and shoving up on the switch. The trouble was that he was too short to pull the switch down again, so his father always had to walk over and turn the light off for him. This went on for several days; and finally, as

There's more than one right way to paint a picture.

he said, "I reached my limit—I'd had it. He flipped the switch, and I was just too tired to get up and turn it off. I was really mad. So I said to him, 'All right Joey, I've warned you and you did it anyway. Now *you* think up some way to turn it off, and you do it before I count to 10. No! you can't drag the chair over there; that scratches the floor.' And so," he continued, "I began to count one, two, three, four. Well, he just stood there for a minute and looked at the light and looked at me. Then he ran over to me, took my steel measuring tape out of my pocket, and hurried over to the switch. He extended the tape up to reach it, hooked the little metal lip over the switch, and pulled it down. I gotta hand it to that kid! Don't you think that was smart? After all, he's only 3!"

This incident is a particularly felicitous example of using familiar equipment in an original way, but teachers can have this kind of original thinking happen at preschool too if they do not overrestrict children and equipment. Many things children want to try out are unconventional but not seriously dangerous. I have seen various children try the following things, which though unusual, were reasonably safe.

1. A child turned a dump truck upside down and pushed it along, making train noises.

2. Another one extended the slide by hooking a board to the end of it. Then, finding that it slid off and dumped her on her bottom, she talked her crony into bracing it at the end to keep it from slipping.

3. Another youngster used the half-moon plywood blocks to make a cradle for her doll.

None of these ideas worked perfectly or were earthshakingly different, but all of them had two cardinal advantages: they were original ideas that came from within the children, and they required a generous amount of imagination to make them be completely satisfactory.

And from another culture come these delightful examples collected by Spar and McAfee:

> On the Navajo reservation when I was little, I tended my grandfather's sheep. I would search out areas where I could find soft clay. I would shape figures of men and women and sheep with the clay. I would find sand and press it in my hand and shape it into a small hogan. I pushed my finger into the side to make a door and stuck a small twig in the top to make a chimney. The clay figures of

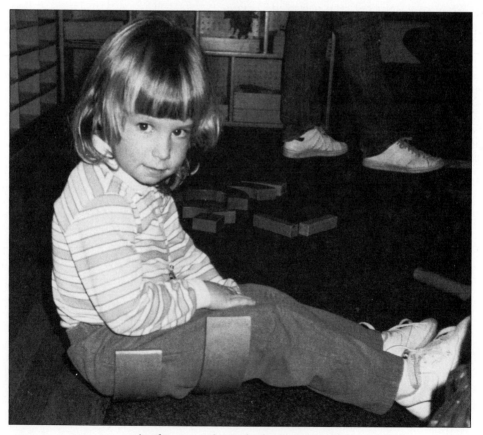

Another unusual use of a familiar material.

the sheep went in a small twig corral near the hogan, and the people would fit into the hogan.

There were many different colors of sandstone near our home. I spent hours pulverizing the sand and layering it in soft colors in an old canning jar.

We made corncob dolls. The ear of corn was the doll, the silk was the hair, and the leaves were draped around the corn as clothes.

We would fill the small milk-cartons our older brothers and sisters brought home from school with mud mixed with dried straw to make adobe brick. We built dollhouses with small tree twigs or branches.

We played a lot with mud and water, constructing roads, ditches, rivers and canals.

We molded mud-pies in empty flat cans.*

FOSTER THE DEVELOPMENT OF IMAGINATIVE, SELF-EXPRESSIVE STORY TELLING

As we saw in the chapter on creative play, children often play out situations that are developed from their past experience but that are not literal representations of events as they actually occurred. This part fact–part fantasy condition is also true when young children are encouraged to tell stories. In order for the teachers to know what to expect in the stories of children of various ages, it is helpful if they understand children's developmental trends.

Pitcher and Prelinger (1963) have studied over 300 stories told by children aged 2 to about 6 years. They found that as the children matured, their stories included an increasing utilization and mastery of space, a less clear differentiation of main characters, more happenings that affect the characters, and a significant increase in the use of fantasy and imagination. Therefore, when pursuing creative stories with preschool-aged children, the teacher should be prepared for considerable literalness in stories by younger children and a greater use of fantasy and imagination by older ones. But since the stories are personal descriptions and reflections of the children's feelings and perceptions, they may also be considered self-expressive and hence creative.

The following two examples of dictated stores are both factual and quite expressive of feelings.

The Doctor and the Nurse

Marice

When I got the cast off, we used an electric saw and I had something on my ears. The saw was very sharp and looked just like the sun.

The thing I had on my ears was round. I couldn't hear the electric saw, but the other doctors could. It played music very loud, as loud as the saw.

---

*From McAfee, O. (1976). To make or buy. In M. D. Cohen & S. Hadley (Eds.), *Selecting educational equipment and materials for home and school*, p. 27. Wheaton, MD: Association for Childhood Education International. Reprinted by permission of Oralie McAfee and the Association for Childhood Education International, 11141 Georgia Ave., Ste. 200, Wheaton, MD. © 1976 by the Association.

The doctor held my hand because he didn't think I could walk by myself. He's not a very good doctor, and I don't like him either—the first doctor I'm talking about.

The nurse clipped the cast off. She went out after that. I needed my privacy, anyways.

My House Story

Angelique

This first page will be about my dog. His name is Toulouse. Sometimes I can't play with him because he goes to dog school. At dog school, somebody makes him fetch sticks and makes him beg. Then he comes home and he shows me what he has learned. I also have a cat. His name is Goya, named after a painter. We always name our animals after painters.

Providing materials when requested allows children to be spontaneously creative. This little girl needed to make a hat right now!

Now about my grandmother and grandfather. My grandmother goes to Weight Watchers. They weigh her there without her shoes on.

Now about my grandfather. He drives a car. It's a red Datsun wagon pickup.

My house is white with a white picket fence. My grandma, grandpa, mommy, and me all live in the house.

My grandfather went to the hospital the day before yesterday. He had his operation yesterday. I don't like to have him in the hospital. He's not here to read me a bedtime story.

I miss him.

These stories mattered a lot to the children who wrote them. At that time the teachers were using little handmade books for recording the stories so that the children were free to illustrate them if they wished. This provided an additional way to work off their feelings and be creative. But it is not necessary to make story telling that elaborate an occasion. Taking the story down as the child dictates it often provides sufficient encouragement for the young storyteller. Pitcher collected her stories by waiting until a child was either sitting quietly by herself or playing alone and then by saying, "Tell me a story. What would your story be about?" This is a good way to get started. Of course, children sometimes do not want to participate. In this case the teacher just says, "Well, I expect you'll want to do it another time. I'll ask you then."

As with other creative materials, the teacher should scrupulously avoid suggesting what the story should be about or what might happen next. But it does encourage the creator to ask, "Then what happened? Then what did she do?" or "Do you want to tell me anything else?" These questions will help sweep the child along into the narrative.

Creative stories can also be stimulated by providing hand puppets (Burn, 1989) or flannel board materials, which can be set out for the children to use as they feel the need or used at group time for this purpose. Rubber dolls and toy animals offer another medium for imaginative stories and play. Creative stories can also be stimulated by providing pictures, which may be used as starting points for discussion.

SUMMARY

Creativity does not have to be limited to the use of self-expressive materials, such as paint and clay, or to creative play. It also includes the realm of creative thought.

Teachers can do three specific things to enhance creative mental ability in young children: they can (a) encourage children to produce more than one solution to a problem by asking well-phrased questions, (b) permit them to explore new ways to use equipment and try out unconventional ideas, and (c) foster their ability to create imaginative, self-expressive stories.

It is particularly important that teachers reinforce such activities by responding to them positively and that they form the habit of asking questions that encourage original and various replies.

QUESTIONS AND ACTIVITIES

1. The next time you have to solve some sort of problem, take a few minutes and just for fun list all the ways, both silly and practical, that the problem might be solved. Try not to evaluate the merit of the ideas as you produce them, but just play around with many possibilities. Then evaluate them. Is there a fresh one included that might be a good, new, though perhaps unconventional way to solve the situation?

2. *Problem:* You have in your room a little girl about 3 years old who asks a lot of questions. For example, she might ask, "Why are we going in now?" When dutifully provided with the reasons, she then asks, "But why do we have to do that?" When answered, she asks, "But why?" If you were her teacher, would you think this type of inquiry should be encouraged? How would you handle it?

3. Isn't it a waste of time to let children try things out that obviously won't work? Might it not be better just to lead a discussion with them about the proposed solutions rather than going to all the trouble of actually trying something out only to experience failure?

4. Observe the children during the next week and report back to the class the unconventional ways you saw them using equipment. What role did imagination play in their activities? How practical were their substitutions and solutions? How satisfying?

5. Make up blank paper "books" and invite the children to dictate stories to you on any relevant subject. Many youngsters will relish adding illustrations to these tales if encouraged to do so.

SELF-CHECK QUESTIONS FOR REVIEW

Content-Related Questions

1. Explain what the difference is between *divergent* and *convergent* thinking and why each is an important aspect of thought.

2. What are three principles to remember about creative thinking?

3. There are a number of important strategies to use when asking questions that encourage children to think. List several of these and be able to explain why each is valuable.

4. Give some examples from your own experience of how children have used equipment in new, unconventional ways. Why is it worthwhile to permit or even encourage such behavior?

5. Asking questions and permitting the use of materials in unconventional ways are two ways of fostering creativity in thought. What is the third way? How might you include

possibilities for using that third way in the curriculum?

Integrative Questions

1. Select a learning experience based on a scientific subject (ants, for instance), and make up a list of questions on this subject that will require convergent, fact-based answers. Now modify the questions so they will be more likely to require children to do some creative thinking in order to answer them.

2. You are teaching the first year in a 3-year-old classroom. You would like to add dishes to the housekeeping area, but there is no money for new ones. Propose three "What else could you use instead of new ones?" solutions.

3. The author suggests that using "what if?" and "what else?" questions help generate

creative problem skills in young children. What different skills do each of the two types of questions require the children to use when answering them?

4. Sort the following questions into their appropriate categories.

"What did you watch on television last night?"

After reading the book, *If You Give a Mouse a Cookie* (Numeroff, 1987): "Well, according to this story, *is* it a good idea to give a mouse a cookie?"

"It looks like there are only two pieces of cheese left, but everyone wants them. What do you think we should do?"

"But what if Peter hadn't caught the wolf, what then?"

"Who remembers the name of the little monkey in this book?"

Finally, add another example of your own to each category.

REFERENCES FOR FURTHER READING

Overviews

Goffin, S. G., & Tull, C. (1984). Ideas! Creating possibilities for problem solving. *Dimensions, 12*(2), 15–19. This is a very good article that explains strategies for problem solving appropriate for each age.

Kline, P. (1988). *The everyday genius: Restoring children's natural joy of learning—and yours too.* Arlington, VA: Great Ocean. This refreshing book stresses the healthy integration of learning and reminds us of the overall value of having faith in the inherent willingness and ability of children to learn.

Neugebauer, B. (Ed.). (1989). *The wonder of it: Exploring how the world works.* Redmond, WA: Exchange Press. The focus of this book is on approaching science effectively with young children, but it also offers a general, valuable approach to developing thinking.

Paley, V. (1981). *Wally's stories.* Cambridge, MA: Harvard University Press. This delightful book illustrates how Paley encouraged her kindergartners to propose creative, imaginary solutions to problems posed in stories and discussion.

Asking Good Questions

Campbell, K. C., & Arnold, F. D. (1988). Stimulating thinking and communicating skills. *Dimensions, 16*(2), 11–13. The article features a developmentally based series of types of questions, moving from "what is?" to "what else?" and "what if?"

DeBono, E. (1972). *Children solve problems.* London: Penguin Press. This is a delightful book filled with many proposed questions, such as "If you were a zookeeper and wanted to find out how heavy an elephant was, how would you do it?"

Sigel, I. E., & Saunders, R. (1979). An inquiry into inquiry: Question asking as an instructional model. In L. G. Katz (Ed.), *Current topics in early childhood education* (Vol. 2). Norwood, NJ: Ablex. This chapter presents a list (with examples) of all sorts of questions teachers ask or *should* ask. *Highly recommended.*

Sprung, B., Forschl, M., & Campbell, P. B. (1985). *What will happen if . . . ? Young children and the scientific method.* New York: Educational Equity Concepts (Gryphon House, distributor). The authors single out a few topics and illustrate how they might be used to teach the scientific method. Outstanding because of its nonsexist, age-appropriate emphasis.

Creative Story Telling

Lewis, C. (1979). *A big bite of the world: Children's creative writing.* Englewood Cliffs, NJ: Prentice-Hall. Lewis begins her book with a chapter of sagacious comments and charming examples of the way 3-, 4-, and 5-year-old children express their creative ideas and perception of the world through language. She also provides ideas about how to help them do more of this.

For the Advanced Student

DeVries, R., & Kohlberg, L. (1987). *Constructivist early education: Overview and comparison with other programs.* Washington, DC: National Association for the Education of Young Children. The authors take Piagetian and Bank Street approaches one step further and emphasize the importance of active learning, the value of cognitive conflict, and the virtue of figuring out (constructing) knowledge for oneself.

Duckworth, E. (1987). *"The having of wonderful ideas" and other essays on teaching and learning.* New York: Teachers College Press. It's good to have this essay and other stimulating ones back in print. *Highly recommended.*

Suchman, J. R. (1961). Inquiry training: Building skills for autonomous discovery. *Merrill-Palmer Quarterly, 7,* 147–169. This is the article that "began it all" in the area of inquiry training. The strategies recommended are much too advanced to employ with preschool children, but the first three pages are filled with sage comments (such as "More basic than the attainment of concepts is the ability to inquire and discover these autonomously") that make searching out this article worthwhile.

Von Oech, R. (1983). *A whack on the side of the head: How to unlock your mind for innovation.* New York: Warner Books. Definitely for grown-ups, this is another helpful book with techniques that could release the reader to produce more creative ideas.

Watson, J. D. (1968). *The double helix: Being a personal account of the discovery of the structure of DNA.* New York: Atheneum. All the excitement, disappointment, satisfaction, intuition, and tenacity associated with this supremely difficult kind of creative mental effort come through clearly in this fascinating book. Watson and Crick were about 25 years old when they won the Nobel Prize for their discovery.

PART SIX

Developing Language Skills and Mental Ability

CHAPTER 16

Fostering the Development of Language Skills

Learning a native language is an accomplishment within the grasp of any toddler, yet discovering how children do it has eluded generations of philosophers!
—Jerome Bruner (1978)

Have you ever wondered . . .

What are some practical things teachers can do to foster language development?

How to encourage children to talk with you and with other children?

Whether or not you should insist a Mexican-American child speak English at school?

If you have, the material in the following pages will help you.

I n the past few years we have become increasingly aware of the value of developing language skills in early childhood, and almost without exception the newer, research-based schools have included a language component in their curriculum. This emphasis is the result of research findings that indicate that a close relationship exists between language competence and cognitive development (Bruner, 1978), that differences exist between the speech of middle- and lower-class children (Bernstein, 1960; Durkin, 1982; Olson, Bayles, & Bates, 1986), and that children acquire most of their language skills, though not most of their vocabulary, by age 4 or 5 at the latest (Menyuk, 1963). As preschoolers pass the age of 3, ego-enhancing boasting statements show an abrupt increase, and children begin to use more joining and collaborative statements, as well as simply talking more with their peers. Also, around age 4 and 5, children go on to even more highly socialized speech than this—speech that takes the needs of the listener more into account. For example, 4- and 5-year-olds use more "because" sentences that give the listener reasons or explanations for their behavior (Schachter, Kirshner, Klips, Friedricks, & Sanders, 1974).

Whether one sees language as being separate from thought, as did Piaget (Piaget & Inhelder, 1969), or ultimately bound together (Vygotsky, 1978), there is still general agreement that the development of language abilities goes hand in hand with the development of mental ability (Moshman, Glover, & Bruning, 1987). For this reason we devote considerable attention to methods of fostering language development as we study the child's intellectual self.

Petty and Starkey (1967) have defined language as a learned, arbitrary, structured system of sounds and sequences of sounds that includes a system of socially shared meanings. But this is a bare-boned definition indeed for preschool teachers, who must come to grips with the problem of how to foster language development to maximize the child's potential for both comprehension and expression. To bring this about, teachers must understand how the ability to use language is acquired and how it develops; above all, they must determine what they can do in the children's center to foster its growth.

HOW LANGUAGE IS ACQUIRED

Knowledge about language acquisition is increasing rapidly, and it behooves preprimary teachers to know as much as possible about the process so they may apply this knowledge when teaching language skills. At the present time we have considerable information on what happens and when it happens. But since we still do not understand completely how it happens, it is necessary to employ several theories that are, at best, only partial explanations of the process.

The current point of view about language acquisition that is most helpful for the early childhood teacher to assume is the one presented by Genishi and Dyson (1984). They maintain that language is acquired through a process that combines the effects of heredity (the inborn potential of the child—what the child *may* become) with the effects of the environment (what the child *does* become). It is this interaction between nature and nurture that enables children to learn to talk. This is a helpful way to think about language acquisition because it makes use of both of the two most prominent theories.

The first of these theories is the environmentalist (nurture) theory. This theory stresses the importance of imitation, modeling, and reinforcement in language acquisition.

Role of Imitation and Modeling

Brown and Bellugi's (1964) early investigations presented the theory that imitation is one primary means of speech acquisition. In their study of two children nicknamed Adam and Eve, they provided evidence that some of the early sentences used by the children were obviously imitations of the mother's speech. But imitation works in two directions. The investigators also found that much of the maternal speech consisted of imitation and expansion of the infant's speech—the mother preserving the infant's word order but adding auxiliary words. For example, when Eve said, "Mommy sandwich," the mother replied, "Mommy'll have a sandwich." This building directly on what the child knows is enough to gladden the heart of any educator.

Bandura (1977) championed the value of learning language by means of imitation, which he termed "modeling" or "observational learning." Work by Hamilton and Stewart (1977) also demonstrated that children in preschools added to their vocabulary by copying the language of other children—a fact that is not news to any nursery school teacher who has seen a whirlwind of profanity sweep through the 4-year-olds in her school.

Role of Reinforcement

But the question remains, What causes children to imitate their mothers or to imitate other people who are important to them? Perhaps the most satisfactory explanation can be found in learning theory, which is based on the principle that people tend to repeat acts from which they gain satisfaction. Children probably imitate because their imitation is rewarded with parental pleasure and warmth as well as with getting other things they want.

Thus the process of language acquisition begins with imitation, perhaps first by the mother, who stimulates the infant to repeat random vocalizations. When this repetition is reinforced in turn by parental response, the baby persists in the behavior. This process finally results in verbal labels becoming attached to important things in the environment, such as *Mama, bye-bye,* and *baw* (bottle). After a number of these labels have been acquired, the child gradually pairs them together (Braine, 1963) and then begins to place them in sequences.

Role of Nature

The second theory, sometimes termed the *nativist* theory, maintains that children learn to talk because human beings possess a natural, innate ability for developing language. These theorists argue that there is more to the ability to learn language than parrotlike imitation and reinforcement. This is the ability children have to put language together from what they hear said around them. In English, for example, they learn to form plurals by adding *s* to the end of the names of objects and deduce that adding *ed* means that something happened in the past. Their initial overgeneralization as they apply these rules is what produces such amusing (to adult ears) words as *sheeps, goed,* and *breaked* (Schachter & Strage, 1982).

Slobin (1975) presents interesting supporting evidence that this ability to abstract rules and process language really is part of the acquisition process. His report looks at children in more than 40 cultures. He wanted to see if there were common strategies for developing rules that were employed by children who came from widely differing backgrounds. He found that there were indeed common strategies or operating principles the children used without, of course, putting them into explicit sentences. Examples of these child-developed strategies might be "pay attention to the ends of words," "pay attention to the order of words and morphemes," and "avoid rearrangements (of words)."

What we do not understand at the present time is the means by which children are able to ascertain and generalize such rules as these. Debate continues in this area (Chomsky, 1987; Genishi, 1987; Pflaum, 1986), and that question remains to tantalize future researchers.

Contributions by Adults to the Child's Acquisition of Language

Perhaps after even this brief review the reader is shaking her head over the complexity of the task of language acquisition. If so, it may be comforting to learn that adults make the child's work somewhat easier for her by using a special form or style of language when they speak to infants and very young children. Although this has been called *Motherese*, in actuality this adjustment of form is used by most adults and even older children when talking with little ones (D'Odorico & Franco, 1985). The style includes such characteristics as using a higher pitch and a wider range of pitch, speaking more slowly and distinctly, repeating words and phrases, using limited vocabulary, and "coining" words such as "goney-gone" and "tum tum." Adults also tend to expand the briefer utterances of children and, most interesting of all, adjust the level of communication difficulty to the child's increasing level of understanding as the youngster matures (George & Tomasello, 1984/85).

Maternal responsiveness—that is, how much attention mothers paid to their 1- and 2-year-old's attempts at talking—also makes a significant difference in the size of the youngster's vocabulary. The more responsive the mother is, the greater the child's number of words (Olson et al., 1986). Surely this implies that teachers, also, should be careful to be attentive when children want to talk with them.

Contributions of Linguistics

From the practical point of view of the early childhood teacher, the most valuable contribution of linguistics so far is the information it is providing on the order in which various grammatical structures develop in the speech of children. Although linguistic theory is too advanced and complicated a subject to be presented in detail here, two examples of the kinds of information this science is producing may help the beginning student gain an appreciation of the importance of this approach. For a more extensive treatment of linguistics, the reader is referred to Lindfors (1987).

One early example of applied linguistics is the classic study by Menyuk (1963), who used the grammatical theory developed by Chomsky, a linguistic theorist in transformational grammar, to study the language of young children. Menyuk studied 3- and 6-year-olds and found there were few examples of restricted children's grammar at this level. Surprisingly, most of the children's speech was similar to that of adults, and the children had gained a remarkable proficiency in structuring language correctly even by age 3. This is important information for the preschool teacher to possess, since it implies that we need to stress the development of language function skills earlier than age 4—the point at which many preschool compensatory programs now begin. Obviously, if grammatical structure has been largely acquired by this time, we should be building language skills in children between 18 months and 3½ years old to be maximally effective.

In another study, Cazden (1970) also used transformational grammar to analyze the way children learn to pose questions. Briefly, she found that children first form questions by using inflection. Following that, questions become the yes-no kind, which depend on interchanging only two phrases. For example, "The boy can drive a car" would change to "Can the boy drive a car?" Next, children learn to perform a more difficult transformation, the "wh" question—"When can the boy drive a car?"—which involves two transformations. The next step involves forming negative questions: "Won't he be able to drive the car?" Finally comes the use of tag questions: "It's all right if he drives the car, isn't it?"

As more of these studies become available, it will be possible to outline sequential steps for many forms of grammatical structures. Then, following an analysis of a child's present level of ability, the teacher will be able to refer to these "maps" and know what step should be selected next for him and plan her teaching accordingly.

Contributions of Sociolinguistics to the Understanding of Language Development

Some researchers are becoming increasingly dissatisfied with the emphasis on the significance of grammatical structure in the development of speech and are stressing the interactional importance of the social and developmental aspects of language acquisition (Bloom, 1975; Bruner, 1975; Snow, 1989).

They point out that the child can say the same thing (that is, the grammatical structure can be identical) and yet mean quite different things depending on the *social context* (the circumstances) in which he says it. For instance, a 1½-year-old may say "Mine!" very emphatically, meaning Give it to me right now! or I won't let you have it! or even At last I've got it! (Ferrara, 1985).

Another growing edge in language acquisition is the interest in the interrelationship and interdependency between language and stages of mental development. Edmonds (1976) and Sinclair (1971), for example, maintain that children cannot generate their first words until they have attained the Piagetian stage of object permanence. Young children must be aware that an object has a separate, independent existence before they are able to use language, and conveniently language then enables them to represent these objects even when they are absent.

Finally, Bruner has been engaged in observing mothers and children, and he emphasizes the importance of interactive communication between them as a primary influence on how babies learn to talk (1975, 1978). He speaks with admiration of the sensitive "fine tuning" of the mother to the abilities and developmental level of the child. Bruner points out that learning to carry on a conversation between mother and baby is probably the earliest form of turn taking learned by youngsters. He also takes the position that children learn to talk not primarily because they are "reinforced" for this behavior but "in order to get things done with words" (1978, p. 49).

Conclusion

And so the debate on how the miracle of language comes about continues—with, it seems, an ever-widening range of things that affect its acquisition being considered. It is an exciting, fast-growing area of study and research that is particularly interesting because it has attracted the attention of people from a variety of academic disciplines who, by their diversity of approaches, have greatly increased the richness of our understanding (Ingram, 1989).

One asks at this point, have we reached the place where these studies offer sufficient explanations of how language is acquired? Surely the foregoing explanations are sensible and useful as far as they go, but the fact remains that although we are in the process of acquiring linguistic maps, and although we are fairly certain that imitation, reinforcement, and rule abstracting play an important role in the acquisition of these forms, and although we acknowledge that context and development and social interaction are important influences, we still cannot explain the fundamental magic of what happens in the child's mind that enables him to substitute symbol for object and to assemble these symbols into sentences he has never heard.

DEVELOPMENTAL MILESTONES

In addition to understanding that grammatical structure develops according to predictable rules, teachers should become acquainted with additional developmental milestones so that they can identify children who show marked developmental lags and also so that they may have a clear idea of what is reasonable to aim for when establishing goals for language development. The teacher may find Table 16.1, developed by Masland for the National Institute of Neurological Diseases and Stroke (1969), quite helpful; but remember that the checkpoints represent averages, and children who are developing well may often be either ahead or behind the suggested time listed. The lag should be considered serious enough to warrant concern if the child is more than a few months behind on a particular measure.

Another quick rule of thumb for checking language development is sentence length, still thought to be one of the best indicators of verbal maturity. In general, sentence length increases as the child grows older. Schachter and Strage (1982) outline a pattern for the development of language in Table 16.2.

When assessing language competence, the teachers in our center have also found it helpful to determine whether English or some other language, typically Spanish, is the child's dominant language and also to determine whether he appears to possess what I term "the habit of verbalness." For whatever reason, be it temperament, age, level of intelligence, cultural pattern, or socioeconomic status, it is evident to our center teachers that some children use language to meet their needs more frequently than others do. We always try to note this behavior and use the techniques described in the following section to encourage less verbally oriented children to increase their language abilities while attending the center.

METHODS USED FOR INCREASING LANGUAGE COMPETENCE IN YOUNG CHILDREN

As one might expect, methods of teaching language skills are closely linked to the philosophy of the teachers involved, and at present there is much controversy about how preprimary teachers should teach language. Approaches range from programs that stress drill and pattern repetition (DISTAR, 1969) to those that use structured sequences of questions (Blank, Rose, & Berlin, 1978; Lavatelli, 1973) to programs that emphasize improvisation and story telling (BECP, 1973; Hohmann, Banet, & Weikart, 1979).

It is not within the scope of this book to go into detail about these individual programs. In summary, the majority of the programs listed above have the effect of significantly increasing IQ scores and scores on the Illinois Test of Psycholinguistic Abilities or the Peabody Picture Vocabulary Test. The great diversity of the curricula makes it evident that a variety of approaches can succeed in teaching language to children.

I prefer an approach that seeks to develop fluency and the child's ability to use language to verbalize concepts and express thought. This approach, characterized by Bartlett (1981) as being based on instructional dialogue, is illustrated by curricula developed by Bank Street College (1968); Hohmann, Banet, and Weikart (1979); and many others. These programs have the advantage of providing teachers a framework for what they should teach next; yet they also allow enough scope that the child, as well as the adult, is free to initiate conversation. Moreover, such an approach lends itself well to helping

TABLE 16.1 Milestones in the development of language ability in young children*

Average Age	Question	Average Behavior
3–6 months	What does he do when you talk to him? Does he react to your voice even when he cannot see you?	He awakens or quiets to the sound of his mother's voice. He typically turns eyes and head in the direction of the source of sound.
7–10 months	When he cannot see what is happening, what does he do when he hears familiar footsteps . . . the dog barking . . . the telephone ringing . . . candy paper rattling . . . someone's voice . . . his own name?	He turns his head and shoulders toward familiar sounds, even when he cannot see what is happening. Such sounds do not have to be loud to cause him to respond.
11–15 months	Can he point to or find familiar objects or people when he is asked to? *Example:* "Where is Jimmy?" "Find the ball." Does he respond differently to different sounds? Does he enjoy listening to some sounds and imitating them?	He shows his understanding of some words by appropriate behavior; for example, he points to or looks at familiar objects or people, on request. He jabbers in response to a human voice, is apt to cry when there is thunder, or may frown when he is scolded. Imitation indicates that he can hear the sounds and match them with his own sound production.
1½ years	Can he point to parts of his body when you ask him to? *Example:* "Show me your eyes." "Show me your nose." How many understandable words does he use—words you are sure *really* mean something?	Some children begin to identify parts of the body. He should be able to show his nose or eyes. He should be using a few single words. They are not complete or pronounced perfectly but are clearly meaningful.
2 years	Can he follow simple verbal commands when you are careful not to give him any help, such as looking at the object or pointing in the right direction? *Example:* "Johnny, get your hat and give it to Daddy." "Debby, bring me your ball." Does he enjoy being read to? Does he point out pictures of familiar objects in a book when asked to? *Example:* "Show me the baby." "Where's the rabbit?" Does he use the names of familiar people and things such as *Mommy, milk, ball,* and *hat?* What does he call himself?	He should be able to follow a few simple commands without visual clues. Most 2-year-olds enjoy being "read to" and shown simple pictures in a book or magazine, and will point out pictures when you ask them to. He should be using a variety of everyday words heard in his home and neighborhood. He refers to himself by name.

Average Age	Question	Average Behavior
2 years (cont.)	Is he beginning to show interest in the sound of radio or TV commercials?	Many 2-year-olds do show such interest by word or action.
	Is he putting a few words together to make little "sentences"? *Example:* "Go bye-bye car." "Milk all gone."	These "sentences" are not usually complete or grammatically correct.
2½ years	Does he know a few rhymes or songs? Does he enjoy hearing them?	Many children can say or sing short rhymes or songs and enjoy listening to records or to mother singing.
	What does he do when the ice cream man's bell rings, out of his sight, or when a car door or house door closes at a time when someone in the family usually comes home?	If a child has good hearing, and these are events that bring him pleasure, he usually reacts to the sound by running to look or telling someone what he hears.
3 years	Can he show that he understands the meaning of some words besides the names of things? *Example:* "Make the car go." "Give me your ball." "Put the block in your pocket." "Find the big doll."	He should be able to understand and use some simple verbs, pronouns, prepositions, and adjectives, such as *go, me, in,* and *big.*
	Can he find you when you call him from another room?	He should be able to locate the source of a sound.
	Does he sometimes use complete sentences?	He should be using complete sentences some of the time.
4 years	Can he tell about events that have happened recently?	He should be able to give a connected account of some recent experiences.
	Can he carry out two directions, one after the other? *Example:* "Bobby, find Susie and tell her dinner's ready."	He should be able to carry out a sequence of two or three simple directions.
5 years	Do neighbors and others outside the family understand most of what he says?	His speech should be intelligible, although some sounds may still be mispronounced.
	Can he carry on a conversation with other children or familiar grown-ups?	Most children of this age can carry on a conversation if the vocabulary is within their experience.
	Does he begin a sentence with "I" instead of "me," "he" instead of "him"?	He should use some pronouns correctly.
	Is his grammar almost as good as his parents'?	Most of the time, it should match the patterns of grammar used by the adults of his family and neighborhood.

*Source: From *Learning to Talk: Speech, Hearing and Language Problems in the Pre-school Child* by the National Institute of Neurological Diseases and Stroke (1969). Washington, DC: U.S. Department of Health, Education, and Welfare.

TABLE 16.2   Development of language*

Age in Months	Characteristics of Vocalization and Language
4	Coos and chuckles.
6–9	Babbles; duplicates common sounds; produces sounds such as "ma" or "da."
12–18	A small number of words; follows simple commands and responds to no; uses expressive jargon.
18–21	From about 20 words at 18 months to about 200 words at 21; points to many more objects; comprehends simple questions; forms 2-word phrases.
24–27	Vocabulary of 300 to 400 words; has 2- or 3-word phrases; uses prepositions and pronouns.
30–33	Fastest increase in vocabulary; three- to four-word sentences are common; word order, phrase structure, and grammatical agreement approximate the language of surroundings, but many utterances are unlike anything an adult would say.
36–39	Vocabulary of 1000 words or more; well-formed sentences using complex grammatical rules, although certain rules have not yet been fully mastered; grammatical mistakes are much less frequent; about 90 percent comprehensible.

*Source: From "Adults' Talk and Children's Language Development" by F. F. Schachter and A. A. Strage. In S. G. Moore and C. R. Cooper (Eds.), *The Young Child: Reviews of Research* (Vol. 3), p. 83. (Adapted from Lenneberg [1966]). Reprinted by permission. © 1982, National Association for the Education of Young Children, 1834 Connecticut Ave., NW, Washington, DC 20009.

children bridge the gap between oral and written language and take those first steps toward emerging literacy that will be discussed in the next chapter.

BASIC WAYS TO FOSTER LANGUAGE DEVELOPMENT

I. Listen to the Children

Many adults, particularly women and most particularly nervous women teachers, are so busy talking themselves that they drown the children out. But children learn to talk by being heard. Paying attention to what they say and listening both to the surface content and to the message underneath offer the most valuable inducements to children to continue making the effort to communicate.

Of course, it is not always easy to understand what they have to say. If a comment is unintelligible, it is all right to ask a child to repeat it; and if the message is still unclear, it may be necessary to admit this and say, "I'm sorry, I just can't tell what you're saying. Could you show me what you mean?" At least this is honest communication and shows children that the teacher is really interested and is trying.

Jennifer clearly has the language situation well in hand!

II. Give the Children Something Real to Talk About

Children's talk should be based on solid, real, lived-through experience. Sometimes inexperienced teachers want to begin at the other end and set up group experiences wherein the children are supposed to discuss planting seeds or thinking about what will sink and float before they have been exposed to the experience itself. This means they are expected to use words that have few actual associations for them and talk about something vague and relatively meaningless. No wonder their attention wanders. It is much more satisfactory to provide the opportunity to live through the experience and to talk about what is happening while it is going on as well as after it has been completed. At this point the child can really associate "sink" with "things that go down" and "sprout" with the pale green tip that poked its nose out of the bean.

Note also that talk and questioning are advocated as an accompaniment to experience (Mattick, 1981). In former years, some teachers of young children seemed to assume that mere exposure to interesting materials in the presence of a warm adult would automatically produce growth in language and mental ability. The work of Blank and Solomon (1968, 1969) has shown that unfocused attention in a rich environment is *not* enough. Children develop language best when required to use words to express concepts and thoughts about what is happening, has happened, or will happen; it is this kind of activity that produces the greatest gains.

III. Encourage Conversation Between Children

As interest in the influence of social interaction on the development of speech increases, more attention is being paid to the importance of encouraging children to talk to each other. Of course, Piaget (1983) has long advocated such "discourse" and exchanges of opinion as an effective means of facilitating the acquisition of knowledge, but presently the value of conversation between children as a facilitator of language development itself is receiving attention (Garvey, 1984; McTear, 1985).

Encouraging children to talk to each other has many benefits, ranging from teaching them to use words to negotiate disagreements in place of physical attack to providing them with effective ways of entering a group. Besides these obvious advantages, talking together can help them put ideas into words, increase their abilities to use language in order to explain to someone else what is happening, repeat an interesting experience, or make cheerful social contact with another youngster.

Most important of all, such encounters help persuade them that talking is satisfying and important—a valuable attitude to inculcate as a foundation for later interest in other language skills related to literacy.

For these reasons, the teacher should avoid making herself the constant center of attention, whether the situation is dramatic play or participating at the lunch table. Instead, it is important to think of oneself as seeking to increase the amount of talk *among the children whenever possible.* Such comments as "That's really interesting. Why don't you tell Blake about that?" or "Maybe Beth would say 'Woof, woof' if you asked her" provide openings for the children to relate to each other and focus attention on the relationship between them rather than keeping attention focused on the teacher.

IV. Encourage Conversation and Dialogue Between Teachers and Children

There is much more to language development than teaching the child to name colors or objects on demand, although learning the names of things has undeniable value. The skills involved in discussion and conversation are vital too, and the ability to conduct such dialogues develops rapidly throughout the preschool period (Garvey, 1984).

To develop these conversational interchanges, teachers must relax and stop seeing their role as one of instructor and admonisher. *Always supplying a fact or rendering an opinion in reply to a child's comment kills conversation very quickly.* Cazden (1972) quotes a perfect example of this. As she points out, the more frequent the prohibition in an adult's talk, the less the children reply.

Tape plays

> Teacher: Oh, you tease, Tom, what are you telling Winston?
> Tom: I tellin' him my brother Gary a bad, bad boy.
> Teacher: O, now that ain't nice.

After an analysis and discussion on this tape recording, the same teacher returns to the child, and the following conversation ensues.

> Teacher: Tom, what was you tellin' Winston this mornin' when you playin' with the ball?
> Tom: I tole him Gary my brother.
> Teacher: You like Gary?
> Tom: Yeah, I lahk him, but he bad.
> Teacher: Why's dat?
> Tom: 'Cus he walked up and set with his friend when they was singin' 'bout Jesus and the preacher was preachin'.
> Teacher: Who whipped him?
> Tom: Daddy—he tuk him outside and whupped him with a red belt.
> Teacher: Did Gary cry?
> Tom: Oh, yeah, he got tears in his eyes. Mama wiped his eyes with a rag when he come back in. Then he popped his fingers. That boy can't never be quiet.*

The example brings out another important point to remember when building conversation. *Teachers should seek to prolong the interchange whenever they can.* Tossing the conversational ball back and forth is a sound way to build fluency and also to establish the habit of being verbal.

The value of the one-to-one situation cannot be overestimated in this regard. It is not necessary to put this off and wait for a special moment; indeed this is impossible to do if the teacher wants to talk specially with every child every day. Instead of waiting the teacher can seize many little interludes to generate friendly talk between herself and a child or between two children. One of the teachers in our center maintains that some of her best opportunities for such chatting occur while she is helping children go to the toilet. Another capitalizes on brief moments while putting on shoes or while greeting children as they arrive at school.

---

*Adapted with permission of Macmillan Publishing Company from *The Devil Has Slippery Shoes: A Biased Biography of the Child Development Group of Mississippi* by Polly Greenberg. © 1970 by Polly Greenberg.

"Here, you take it!" says Andrew. "It's your mother!"

Teachers should monitor themselves regularly to make certain they are not talking mainly to the most verbal children, since at least one research study shows that teachers talk most to children who are the best talkers to start with (Monaghan, 1974). Some youngsters have a knack for striking up conversations with adults, whereas others do not. It is the children who lack this ability who are often overlooked and who, therefore, receive the least practice in an area where they need it the most. If teachers will make a checklist of the children's names and review it faithfully, they will be able to recall which youngsters they have talked with and which they have not and then make a particular effort to include the ones who have been passed over in conversation.

Of course, a reasonable ratio of adults to children makes it more likely there will be time for such friendly encounters, but a good ratio is not the only thing that matters. Some English research indicates that quality of conversation between child and adult is also increased if there are not too many very young children (children under the age of 3) included in the group. Stability of staff (that is, low staff turnover) also increased the quality of interaction, as did staff feeling of autonomy (when staff was supervised very closely, they tended to be more aware of needing to please the supervisor than of the value of generating meaningful conversation with the children) (Tizard, Mortimore, & Burchell, 1972). Since all these qualities stem from good management and job satisfaction of the employees, it is evident that preprimary schools that wish to foster language and its accompanying opportunity for mental development must pay close attention to solving these management problems.

Besides these one-to-one conversations, there are two classic, larger group opportunities that occur each day in the center where it is particularly possible to generate conversation. These occur at the snack or lunch table and during group time.

Developing Conversation at Mealtimes

Gone are the days when children were expected to be seen and not heard at meals or when they had to clear their plates before they were allowed to talk. There are several practical ways the teacher can encourage conversation during meals.

Keep lunch and snack groups as small as possible. It is worthwhile to keep the mealtime group down to five or six children if possible. Anyone who has ever sat at a banquet table knows how difficult it is to get conversation going under such circumstances, and yet an occasional children's center persists in seating 12 or 15 children all around one table. This kills interchange, as well as making supervision difficult.

Adults need to plan their activities so they are free to sit with the children during meals. Surprisingly often when I have visited day care centers at mealtime, I have seen staff roaming restlessly around, passing food, running back and forth to the kitchen, or leaning on counters, arms folded, simply waiting passively for the children to eat but not being part of the group at all. Good advance planning on food delivery should make it possible for staff to sit with the children, and a clearer understanding of the potential educational value of such participation should make them willing to do so. Sitting with the children fosters the feeling of family time that young children need and also encourages the relaxed chatting that makes mealtime a pleasure.

On the other hand, it is wise to avoid putting two adults together at one table. The temptation to carry on a grown-up conversation over the heads of the children can be too great when two adults eat lunch together. It is better to add more tables when more adults are present, thereby seizing this golden opportunity to reduce group size and making it more likely that individual children will join in the talk.

Think of good conversation starters. Such questions as, "Did you see anything good on TV last night?" "What would you like for Christmas?" or "How's that kitty of yours?" will lead the children into talking about things that really interest them and that they can all share together. It is also fun to talk about brothers and sisters, new clothes, birthdays, what their parent's first name is, what they call their grandfather, or what they did over the weekend. In addition, their memories can be developed by asking them if they can remember what they had for lunch yesterday or what they saw on the way to school.

It takes tact to ensure that one ardent talker does not monopolize the conversation under these circumstances. The teacher may need to make a deliberate effort to draw all the children into the discussion lest someone be consistently drowned out. But in the space of the half hour or so that lunch requires, there is really ample opportunity for everyone to converse.

Don't let the children get by with pointing to food they wish to have passed or with saying "I want that." Conversation, as such, is highly desirable to develop at the lunch table, but mealtime also provides many opportunities to build the children's vocabulary and concepts. All too often teachers permit pointing and saying "give me" to pass for language. This is just not enough. Children, particularly children from low-income families, need to acquire commonly used vocabulary, and mealtime is an effective place to teach this. It is easy for the teacher to make sure that the child says the real name of the food he is requesting and then give it to him promptly. There is no quicker way to teach him that talking pays off!

If the child does not know the word, the teacher can say, "This red stuff is called Jell-O. Now you can tell *me*." When he does, she should give it to him right away and tell him, "Good for you! You said the real name." Sometimes, however, the child refuses to reply. It is best to pass over such a response lightly

When adults are interested, children are interested, too.

without making a major issue of it, perhaps saying, "Well, maybe you'll want to tell me it's Jell-O next time."

Mealtimes are also good opportunities to teach certain concepts. For example, the teacher might start by talking about the food: "What are we having today? Did any of you look in the kitchen to see what dessert is?" She might then go on to ask, "What does this meat taste like? Is it hard or soft? Hot or cold? Tough or tender? Can you think of anything else that's like that?"

A word of warning is in order here. Mealtimes should remain basically social occasions where verbal fluency and fun are the keynote, not opportunities for continuous dull inquisitions. Vocabulary and concept building should not be allowed to dominate the occasion, and such a delightful event as lunch should never be permitted to degenerate into a boring mechanical drill where the talk centers on naming each food and discussing where it came from.

V. Use Questions and Answers That Generate Speech and Develop Language

Once again, the value of questions must be highlighted as we discuss effective ways of encouraging the development of language.

Ask Questions That Require More Than One-Word Answers

In chapter 15 I mentioned the desirability of asking questions that are open ended because doing this encourages children to see there is more than one answer to many questions. Asking these kinds of questions has an additional virtue we should think about in this chapter, too, because they also foster language development by promoting conversation. Rogers, Perrin, and Waller (1987) conducted a series of observations of a teacher named Cathy that illustrates the value of doing this. This teacher had a particularly good relationship with the children in her care. When the researchers analyzed the reasons for this, they concluded she was adept at asking the children what she termed "true questions." These were questions where she didn't have a preconceived answer in mind. (The opposite of a "true question" is a "known-answer" or fact question.)

For example, in one instance when the children had been building with bristle blocks the following conversation took place:

> Adam: There's the chimney, see?
> Cathy: Oh-h-h. Do you have a woodstove in there? Or a fireplace?
> Adam: Uh-huh, a woodstove.
> Cathy: A woodstove.
> Adam: That's where the smoke comes out. Where my mom and dad live.
> Cathy: The what? (She leans closer to Adam.)
> Adam: It's our house.
> Cathy: Oh-h, and you built it for them, huh?
> Adam: Uh-huh, and we are living in it.
> Cathy: You're a good thing to have around. Does Nora live there, too?

(Rogers et al., 1987, p. 21)

Clearly, there was no way Cathy could have known the answers in advance to the questions she asked—they reflect her genuine interest in what Adam was doing and what he had to say about it. That interest is an important element in generating true conversation.

When Replying to a Child's Questions or Statement, Elaborate

After the work of Brown and Bellugi (1964) revealed that parents spend a good deal of their time reconstructing and expanding the limited sentences used by their young children, some teachers concluded that this technique of expansion would naturally be the most effective way to teach enriched language to all young children. Thus when a child commented, "Train, bye-bye," the teacher would dutifully reply, "Yes, the train is going bye-bye." It now appears that this technique may be most effective with children about 18 months to 3 years old. Cazden's work (1972) with developing vocabulary seems to indicate that expansion is not as effective as providing enriching replies when working with 4-year-olds. This would mean that rather than replying "Yes, the train goes bye-bye," the teacher would respond to an "older" child by saying, "Yes, the

Drawing children's attention to things and asking questions about them is a useful way to stimulate putting ideas into words.

engine is pulling the train out of the station. Goodbye, train. Goodbye, people." When working with older preschoolers, this kind of enrichment is superior to simple expansion in fostering language progress.

VI. When Necessary, Seek Professional Assistance Promptly

Every once in a while a teacher will come across a child who speaks rarely, if at all, or one who has a pronounced speech problem. These disabilities are discussed in more detail at the end of this chapter, but I want to emphasize here as a basic principle that it is important to seek professional help for these children promptly. Too often both teacher and parent let the year pass, hoping the child will somehow outgrow his difficulty. Although this does happen occasionally, it is generally wiser to refer such youngsters for professional help after 2 or 3 months at most. Children who have pronounced developmental lags or other speech disorders and who do not show signs of improvement by that time generally need consultation from a qualified speech therapist or psychologist, and a referral is definitely in order.

LANGUAGE AND DIALECTICAL DIFFERENCES

Which Language Should the Teacher Encourage?

In the chapter on cross-cultural education, a good deal of time was spent discussing ways to honor the cultural background the child brings with him from his home. Although there is no finer way to do this than by welcoming and encouraging him to use his native language or dialect at school, teachers are often torn in two directions on this question. On one hand, they want to make the child welcome and facilitate his learning in every possible way. This makes the use of his dominant language essential. On the other hand, the teacher cannot help looking ahead and knowing that as schools function today, each youngster will soon move on to elementary school, where he will have to speak Standard English, the dominant language of the middle-class world (Trueba, 1990).

It is quite a dilemma. Somehow the teacher who provides the first school experience for such children must stand with a foot on either side of the stream. To be maximally effective, she should be bilingual herself, as well as knowledgeable about dialectical differences that exist between herself and the children in her care. Failing this, she should at least see that the assistant teacher possesses these strengths.

It is also vital for the teacher who forms this bridge to acquaint herself with research that indicates that Black children who come from city ghettos speak a form of non-Standard English whose value, before the work of Labov (1970), went largely unassessed and unappreciated. For example, White teachers often bemoan the lack of language skills of their Black students and yet are in total ignorance of verbal games such as "the dozens," which are played on street

corners and depend on the ability to concoct elaborate and very funny insults—obviously a language-based skill of a high order (Folb, 1980; Heath, 1989). Moreover, middle-class teachers are often unable to grasp even the most common argot used by the Black families they serve. This ignorance causes them to look down on the verbal abilities of the children. The books by Folb (1980) and Smitherman (1977) described in the References for Further Reading provide much information and actual examples of Ebonics (the term currently used in place of the former "Black English"). As our understanding about it grows, it is becoming evident that its grammar has definite rules and that there is real sophistication to its structure (Brasch, 1981; Labov, 1970; Smitherman, 1977). Indeed some theorists are already asserting that the variation in language that exists between social classes or ethnic groups may ultimately turn out to be more a question of difference than defect or deficit (Pflaum, 1986; Wiggins, 1976).

The best recommendation appears to be that the teacher should respect the Black child's lect* just as she respects the Mexican or Puerto Rican child's Spanish yet, while doing this, also make it possible for him to learn Standard English, because many Black parents as well as teachers agree it is a valuable tool for the child to possess (Cazden, 1981; Dyson & Genishi, 1984).

This ability to switch from one form of English or even from one style of address to another is termed *code switching* (Gleason, 1981). It may turn out that the most desirable thing somehow to teach children is facility in being able to shift from one lect to the other as the situation warrants, just as speakers of Spanish, German, or French learn to code-switch from that language to English to make themselves understood. While acquiring this skill, it is hoped that the child has the opportunity to learn Standard English in an atmosphere that values and appreciates his already present linguistic strengths rather than in one that smacks of condescension and noblesse oblige.

At present, the effects of learning two languages at approximately the same time remain difficult to assess and continue to be debated (Imhoff, 1990). Early research studies that concluded bilingualism had a negative effect on language and possibly mental development were confounded by the presence of additional variables that affect learning and behavior such as poverty. When such a mixture of possible causes is present, it is next to impossible to sort the effects of one from another.

Current, more sophisticated studies suggest that when the effects of poverty are controlled, bilingualism is not a deterrent to development. As Hakuta and Garcia (1989) document, *"all other things being equal,* higher degrees of bilingualism are associated with higher levels of cognitive attainment" (p. 375). Evidently learning a second language is not hampered by possession of the first language (McLaughlin, 1987). Indeed, some research indicates that the acquisition rate for a second language is closely related to the proficiency level of the native language. The more proficient the child is in his first language, the quicker he will be able to learn the second one (Cummings, 1984).

---

*The word *lect* is currently the term preferred by many students in place of *dialect*.

Another debate that is continuing centers on how best to teach non-English-speaking children as they enter school (Garcia, 1990; Imhoff, 1990). Common sense argues against the folly of insisting that children try to learn important new concepts in a language they are only beginning to acquire. Imagine having to learn geometry by means of first-year French, which you are learning simultaneously—that's the stuff nightmares are made of. Yet, in essence, we expect this degree of expertise from a young semi-bilingual child when we teach him "all the important things" only in his second language (Areñas, 1978; Gonzalez-Mena, 1976). Children who are coming to school for the first time are undergoing a complicated enough set of adjustments without the teacher's expecting them to function entirely in a new language at the same time.

Probably the best we can do at present, since children are expected to speak English in grade school and beyond, is to follow the bilingual model wherein young children are taught concepts first in their dominant language and then in English. This approach has been shown to be successful in a number of studies involving concept training or learning to read (Garcia & August, 1988; Macnamara, 1966; Nedler & Sebera, 1971; Orata, 1953). It has been effective with children speaking a variety of languages and ranging in cultural background from Mexican-American to Irish. Moreover, it has the virtue of helping maintain the child's ability to remain bilingual rather than pushing toward proficiency only in English.

What to Do When You Do Not Speak a Child's Language

While it's all very well and good to discuss bilingual education on a remote level, the problem that ordinarily confronts the preschool teacher is the young child who arrives at school unable to speak any English at all. This problem is not going to go away. In 1990 there were approximately 35,000,000 people who spoke a language other than English at home, and 11,000,000 of these were schoolchildren (Trueba, 1990).

Somehow, a bridge of understanding must be built between that child and the teacher. I never think about this situation without recalling the sage advice of my former head teacher, Clevonease Johnson. At that center we had many youngsters who came to us from Vietnam and Cambodia. There they would stand, alone and bewildered, struggling not to cry as their parent and the interpreter walked out the door.

Although it wasn't possible for the teacher to acquire the child's language (at one time Clevonease would have had to have known eight languages to meet that standard), there were two phrases she said it was essential for her to know, and she never allowed the interpreter to leave without writing these down in phonetic English. The first was "Your mother will be back soon," and the second was "Do you need to go to the bathroom?" With these phrases tucked in her pocket, combined with warm smiles and many gestures, Clev felt she could handle anything!

Actually, of course, there were many additional language-related strategies we found useful to employ when working with a child who spoke another language, and several suggestions are included below. Even more valuable than these strategies, however, is the overall attitude toward cultural differences that must prevail in the center. There is no substitute for providing the newcomer with the warm welcome and appreciation of his background advocated in chapter 12, "Providing Cross-Cultural, Nonsexist Education."

1. First of all, remember to talk to the child. Sometimes teachers give up speaking to him just because the child does not respond. However, it's obvious if he isn't spoken to in English, he won't have much of a chance to learn it.

2. Encourage the child to say something right from the start if he is comfortable doing this, but remember that many children require a considerable "wait period" before they are ready to venture in an unfamiliar tongue (Sholtys, 1989). This hesitancy can sometimes be overcome if other children are encouraged to talk freely to the newcomer. Children are less shy talking with each other than with the teacher.

3. When possible, pair the child with another youngster who speaks the same language. This can help him feel he has someone to turn to when feeling blocked.

4. When speaking to the child, keep your voice natural and not too loud. Talking louder does not help children understand any better, and sometimes it makes them think you are angry with them.

5. Use the child's name when you speak to him, and take care to pronounce it as accurately as you can. Never deny the child his identity by giving him an "American" name instead (Morrow, 1989).

6. If you can pick up a few basic, frequently used words in the child's language it will be helpful—words like *outside*, *jacket*, and *lunch*. Activity words like *blocks* and *tricycle* will help a lot in smoothing the child's way.

7. Be visually expressive. Use gestures, smiles, encouraging looks, and friendliness to help the child understand and feel at ease.

8. Demonstrate what you mean as you speak. For example, ask, "Would you like to paint?" Then pick up the brush, gesture toward the paper, and repeat, "Would you like to paint?"

9. Link language to objects and real experience whenever possible. Teach nouns and verbs first; they are some of the most meaningful and useful words (except for *yes!* and *no!*).

10. Don't try to teach too many words at once, and be careful to repeat words many times until they become familiar.

11. Offer some short, easily repeated rhymes and songs each day so the child can join in with the group without being self-conscious about speaking out on his own.

12. Be careful not to overwhelm the child with attention. Too much pressure is as bad as no attention at all.

13. Encourage other children to include the newcomer in their play. Explain that he needs special help; encourage them to name things for him as they use them.

14. And, finally, be aware yourself of how limited *you* feel because you speak only one or perhaps two languages. Encourage the child's parents to help him retain his ability to be (ultimately) bilingual. In this way he will always retain the advantage we might lack—the advantage of being able to communicate in two languages.

Make It Clear to the Families That You Value the Child's Native Language and Cultural Background

In the following discussion I use Spanish for the sake of brevity, but Navajo, French, Vietnamese, or any other language could be used to make the same points.

The most important thing for children to learn about school is that it is a place where they feel welcome and comfortable. Including songs and stories in Spanish, using multiethnic pictures, and observing Mexican customs honor the family by using the language and customs of the home at school. Asking children for the Spanish equivalents of English words will help clarify that there are two languages and, if done with respect and enthusiasm, point up the fact that the Spanish-speaking child has a special ability and skill.

It is also valuable to form close bonds of mutual concern with the parents of the children (Areñas, 1978; Bowman, 1990). Not all parents want their children to continue to learn in Spanish. This attitude varies a good deal from family to family; and teachers should discuss this subject with them, help them weigh the pros and cons, and respect their preferences in every way they can. Most families are realistic about the value of learning English and are almost too eager to have their children gain this skill. It may even be necessary to explain why Spanish is being included as a major component in the curriculum. Other families, rarer in number, will welcome the bicultural emphasis to such an extent that they may be reluctant to include English at all.

Sometimes school values in language development run counter to deep-seated cultural values in the home. For example, it may be necessary to explain to parents the positive relationship between language competence and the maximum development of intelligence. Such explanations may encourage families to overcome their traditional view that children should be seen and not heard, and the parents may make greater efforts to encourage their children to talk more at home.

Sometimes, of course, it is the teacher rather than the family who needs to make the cultural adjustment. Some teachers, for instance, in their eagerness to promote verbalness in the children fall into the habit of allowing them to interrupt adult conversations whenever they please. This is frowned on in Mexican-American homes. In such cases the teacher would do well to change her policy and encourage participation by the children while seeing to it that they continue to observe the basic good manners taught by their own culture.

When Teaching Bilingual Children, Do Not Attribute All Verbal, Expressive, and Comprehension Difficulties to Bilingualism

Many children who come to school speaking only a little English are quite fluent in their mother tongue, and for them the transition to English is not too difficult. *It is very important to distinguish between these youngsters and those who do not talk very much in either language.* These nontalkers are the ones who need all the help they can get in developing the habit of verbalness. For such youngsters the goal is to increase fluency and participation in whichever language they feel more at ease; teaching English to them is of secondary importance to gaining fluency and the habit of talking (Dyson & Genishi, 1984).

CHILDREN WHO HAVE SPECIAL DISABILITIES OF SPEECH AND HEARING

Several kinds of speech and hearing disabilities are seen quite commonly in the nursery school classroom. Indeed, the teacher may find that she is the first person to be aware that the child has a speech problem, since the parent may be too accustomed to it to notice or too inexperienced to identify it as deviating markedly from normal speech. The four problems the teacher is most likely to come across are articulation disorders, delayed speech, hearing disorders, and stuttering.

With all these conditions, if the difficulty is pronounced or continues without positive change for 2 or 3 months after the child enters the center, the teacher should talk the problem over with the parents. Such referrals usually require both time (for the parents to become used to the idea that their child needs extra help) and tact (so that they do not feel blamed or accused of neglecting him). (For more on how to make a successful referral, please refer to chapter 21.)

There are a number of appropriate referral resources for such children. Colleges and universities often maintain speech and hearing clinics supervised by highly trained professionals. Moreover, there is often little or no cost involved because the clinics also serve as training experiences for beginning speech clinicians. Children's hospitals usually have speech clinicians on their staffs, and public schools almost always have a speech therapist available. These people are always glad to suggest appropriate referrals for speech therapy if the youngster does not qualify for help directly from the hospital or school.

Children with Disorders of Articulation

The teacher's problem with articulation disorders is deciding which ones are serious and which should be overlooked. To make this decision, the most important thing the teacher must know is that children do not acquire accuracy in pronouncing certain sounds until they are in the first or second grade. The information included in Figure 16.1 will be helpful in determining whether a

FIGURE 16.1 Average age estimates and upper age limits of customary consonant production. The solid bar corresponding to each sound starts at the median age of customary articulation; it stops at an age level at which 90% of all children are customarily producing the sound.

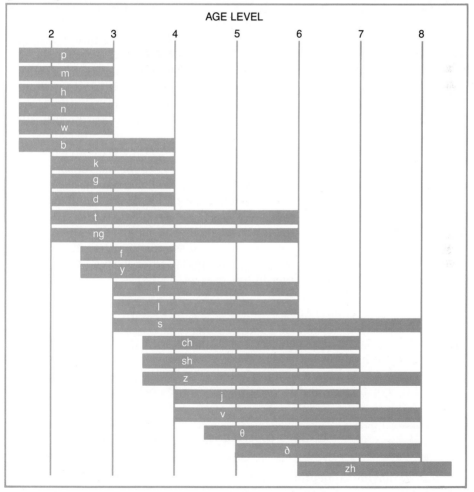

From "When Are Speech Sounds Learned?" by E. K. Sander, 1972, *Journal of Speech and Hearing Disorders, 37*(1), p. 62. © 1972 by the American Speech and Hearing Association. Reprinted by permission.

child who is mispronouncing certain sounds should be referred to a speech pathologist for help. At the preschool level, therefore, there will be many distortions, substitutions, and omissions that can be treated with a combination of auditory training and benign neglect. *However, referral is warranted when the child's speech is generally unintelligible and the child is older than 3 or 3½,* since it is likely that he will need special help from a professionally trained clinician to learn to speak more plainly. The only unfortunate outcome of such a referral is that the therapist might decide the child does not need special help after all. This can be mildly embarrassing to the teacher, but it is better that she take this risk if the child's speech seems seriously impaired than let his poor speech habits continue until he reaches kindergarten.

Besides knowing when to refer and when to overlook the articulation disorder, the teacher should realize that there is a lot more to correcting an articulation problem than just reminding the child, "Don't say 'wed,' say 'red'." Traditional speech therapists usually proceed by (a) using auditory discrimination games to help the child hear the error and tell it apart from other sounds, (b) eliminating the cause of the disorder if possible (for example, encouraging the parents to raise their speech standards at home so that the child no longer gets by with infantile speech patterns), (c) teaching him to make the correct sound by itself, and (d) finally incorporating it into familiar words (Secord, 1985; Van Riper & Emerick, 1984).

The problem with this kind of specific work is getting it to carry over into everyday speech (Kirk & Gallagher, 1989). This is where the nursery school teacher can be the most help—not by nagging the child but by encouraging conversation. During such talk an occasional puzzled look of not understanding what the child is saying followed by pleased comprehension if he repeats the word more clearly will encourage better articulation habits. Of course, all the children will benefit from consistent auditory discrimination activities included in group time, just as they will from the many other means of developing language ability discussed earlier in this chapter.

Children with Delayed Speech

Although articulation disorders are encountered with greater frequency, the teacher is more likely to notice the child who does not talk or who talks very little. Such youngsters are often referred to nursery schools and children's centers by pediatricians and in certain cases can be helped effectively by that teacher.

Causes of Delayed Speech

Causes of delayed speech are myriad and range from the child's being hard of hearing to having a neuromuscular disorder such as cerebral palsy. Low intelligence is another common cause of delayed speech, and negativism or extreme shyness also takes its toll. Lack of sufficient environmental stimulation or low parental expectations may also mean that a child has not developed to his full verbal potential.

In such cases the teacher needs to take a keen, continuing look at the child to try and determine what lies behind the lack of speech. Making a home visit can help ascertain whether he just does not talk at school or whether his nonverbal behavior is consistent in all situations.

It is often difficult or impossible for someone who is not specially trained to spot the cause of lags in speech development. Contrary to general opinion, children who are slow learners do not necessarily look different from their peers. I have known several instances where mildly or even moderately retarded youngsters were denied help and appropriate teaching because the cardinal symptom of delayed speech went unquestioned by an inexperienced teacher because the child "looked normal." The services of a competent psychologist can be enlisted to identify the slow learner if the child is referred to her. Neuromuscular disorders do not always manifest themselves in obvious ways either; so when such a condition appears to be a likely possibility, a referral to the child's pediatrician is a sound approach to take.

Children who restrict themselves from talking because they are overwhelmed by the newness of school or who do not talk because they appear to have been deprived of sufficient speech stimulation at home are the ones with the brightest prognosis. In these cases the teacher can gently draw them forth and elicit more speech by responding positively to their venturings. Many of these children will make a heartening gain in fluency during the year or two they spend at the center if the methods described in the previous section on developing language skills are applied to them.

Children with Disorders of Hearing

Another useful way teachers can help the children in their care is to be on the lookout for those who do not hear well. This is a surprisingly common disorder, yet it often goes by unnoticed.

Studies show that as many as *one out of every three young children suffer from some form of hearing loss* (Brooks, 1978; Denk-Glass, Laber, & Brewer, 1982). Ironically the most common kind of loss, a conductive hearing loss resulting from trouble in the middle ear and often due to infection, is not usually picked up in screening tests so that many youngsters who "have had their hearing tested" slip through the testing screen with this disability not identified. This is particularly unfortunate because middle-ear-type losses account for about 90% of all hearing losses in children and are also most amenable to cure or correction once detected. For these reasons it is important to educate parents that they should request a test for conductive hearing loss called a tympanometric test as well as a pure tone audiometer test when having their children's hearing evaluated.

A child with the following behaviors or conditions should alert the teacher to the possibility that he may be hard of hearing. The teacher should be on the lookout for:

1. The child who does not talk.

2. The child who watches you intently but often "just doesn't seem to understand."

3. The child who does not respond or turn around when the teacher speaks to him in a normal tone of voice from behind him.

4. The child who consistently pays little attention during the story hour or who always wants to sit right up in front of the teacher.

5. The child whose speech is indistinct and difficult to understand, most particularly if high-frequency sounds such as "f" and "s" are missing from his speech.

6. The child who talks more softly or loudly than most of the children.

7. The child whose attention you have to catch by touching him on the shoulder.

8. The child who often asks you to repeat sentences for him or says "Huh?" a lot.

9. The child who has a perpetual cold, runny nose, frequent earaches, or who usually breathes through his mouth.

10. The child who consistently ignores you unless you get right down and look him in the eye as you talk to him.

11. Any child who has recently recovered from measles, meningitis, scarlet fever, or from a severe head injury.

Such youngsters are prime candidates for audiometric testing. Of course, it is also true that children talk indistinctly, want to sit close to the teacher, or fail to pay attention for reasons other than hearing loss. But *particularly if more than one of these symptoms describe his usual behavior,* the possibility of a hearing deficit would be worth investigating. Referrals may be made to an otolaryngologist (a doctor who treats ear and throat disorders) or to the child's pediatrician, who will send him to the best place to receive help.

Hearing losses can result from many causes. The most commonplace one is due to transitory ear and/or throat infections. Sometimes the loss can be remedied through surgery; but if the loss is permanent, continued professional guidance will be necessary. Although hearing aids do not alleviate all forms of deafness, they can be effective in many cases. Hearing aids combined with speech therapy and auditory training are helpful for many children suffering from loss of hearing.

Children Who Stutter

Although we do know that an easy, unself-conscious form of repetitive speech is often observed in children of nursery school age, we do not yet understand why this should be the case. This first stage of repetitive speech differs markedly from the strained, emotion-laden hesitancies and repetitions of the confirmed stutterer and is more than likely liable to vanish if teachers and family do not react to it with concern and tension.

Teachers can play an effective role in helping parents deal with their concern over this potential problem. First, they should encourage them to relax and not to direct attention to the behavior. This includes *not* saying to the child, "Now, just slow down; I'll wait 'til you're ready," or "Don't talk so fast," or "Your ideas just get ahead of your tongue; take it easy" (Gottwald, Goldbach, & Isack, 1985). They should also reassure the family by explaining that this behavior is common in young children who are undergoing the stress of learning to talk. The goal here is to encourage parents to relax and reduce stressful situations in the home so that the child will not become concerned about his speech.

Since stuttering increases when the child is undergoing stress, it can be helpful to avoid hurrying him when possible, to allow plenty of time for him to speak, to speak a little slowly when carrying on conversations with him, and to avoid putting him on the spot by asking direct questions or urging him to talk in front of others during group time.

It is also wise to inquire of the family if something is currently making life more difficult for him at home. Do what you can to relieve that situation. Examples of stressful events could include a visit from a critical grandparent, adjusting to a new baby-sitter, moving, the arrival of a baby, holding the child to unreasonably high standards of behavior, or a death or divorce in the family. Tension-relieving activities such as dramatic play, water play, and various forms of sublimated aggressive activities can be provided that may reduce some of the child's tensions and attendant stuttering.

As with other speech disorders, it is also necessary to have some rule of thumb for referral when working with a child who stutters. At the preprimary level it seems wise to refer the family for further help if they are reacting strongly to the behavior and are unable to control their signs of concern, if they seem unable to reduce the tension-generating situations without outside help, or if the stuttering persists.

SUMMARY

The development of language skills in pre-school children has become of cardinal interest to their teachers as evidence mounts that linguistic competence and mental ability go hand in hand.

Children appear to acquire language in part through the process of imitation, in part by means of reinforcement, and in part through internalized rule construction. The science of linguistics is also providing the teacher with valuable maps of the order in which linguistic structures are acquired. At the present time, however, we still cannot provide an adequate explanation of how children learn to form novel sentences. This remains one of the tantalizing mysteries of human development. But we do know that the growth of language occurs in a predictable, orderly sequence.

Teachers of young children can do many things to facilitate children's language acquisition:

1. They listen carefully to what children have to say.

2. They provide a meaningful base of experience to talk about.

3. They encourage conversation between children.

4. They talk with children themselves.

5. They use questions to generate speech and develop language.

6. When necessary, they seek professional assistance for children who require it.

In this chapter the question of bilingualism in the preschool was also discussed, and some suggestions were included about teaching English as a second language.

Finally, four common disorders of speech and hearing were identified: disorders of articulation, delayed speech, deficient hearing, and stuttering. Recommendations were made for classroom treatment and remediation of these disorders, and suggestions for referral were included.

QUESTIONS AND ACTIVITIES

1. Identify some factors in the school where you teach that encourage the development of conversation between children and adults. What are some things that discourage conversation between them?

2. List some additional conversation starters you have found useful in getting young children involved in talking with the teacher or with other children.

3. Role play a story hour where the teacher seems to do everything possible to prevent the children from talking.

4. *Problem:* A mother calls and says her pediatrician has suggested that she place Silas in nursery school because he has been a little slow in learning to talk. As you become acquainted with Silas, it does appear to you that his speech is slow to develop. He is 3 years old and still communicates mainly by grunting, nodding his head, or pointing when he wants something. List some possible reasons why his speech might be developing so slowly. How would you go about determining which cause is the most likely one? Propose a course of action that would be most appropriate for each probable cause.

5. Do you feel that teachers have the right to change something as personal to the child as his lect or dominant language? Under what circumstances do you think doing this is warranted or unwarranted?

6. Do you advocate setting up schools that use only the child's native tongue or lect? What would be the strong points of doing this? What might be the drawbacks?

SELF-CHECK QUESTIONS FOR REVIEW

Content-Related Questions

1. What are the names of the two groups of theories that are included in the nature/nurture theory presented by Genishi and Dyson? How does each of them explain how children acquire language?

2. About how many words should a child have at his command by the age of 1? By the age of 2?

3. Give some examples of what a teacher might say to encourage conversation between children.

4. List some important principles the teacher should remember for encouraging conversation between herself and the children.

5. Suppose you had a child in your room who did not speak any English. How could you help him feel comfortable and gradually learn a second language?

6. What are the four most common types of speech and language disorders in young children, and what might be the symptoms for each of these that the teacher should look for?

7. Should teachers and parents always be concerned when children repeat words several times when speaking?

Integrative Questions

1. Does the nature or nurture theory offer more hope to a teacher who has a 3-year-old child in her class who isn't talking yet? Explain why you have selected whichever theory you chose.

2. You have decided to present a week that uses babies as its theme or focus. Provide several examples of ways you could make the topic real and involving for 2-year-olds. How would you keep it real but change it to the appropriate developmental level for 4-year-olds?

3. A friend has brought a female goat to visit your group of 4-year-olds at school and is milking her. Sarah Lee says, "The milk's splashing!" Give an example of what you would reply that would expand that comment. Next, give an example of a reply that would enrich and extend it.

4. The teacher in the room next door says to you, "Well, I certainly admire you for taking that Spanish class so you can talk to Miguel and Angelica, but if I were you I wouldn't bother. After all, this is America, and if they want to be American they'd better learn to talk English! You go on speaking Spanish to them it'll just slow them down." What would be your response to her?

REFERENCES FOR FURTHER READING

Overviews

Genishi, C., & Dyson, A. H. (1984). *Language assessment in the early years.* Norwood, NJ: Ablex. The title of this book is misleading because it includes so much more than recommendations for assessment. There are descriptions of research on language acquisition, as well as discussions of language in relation to families and preschool settings.

Lindfors, J. W. (1987). *Children's language and learning* (2nd ed.). Englewood Cliffs, NJ: Prentice-Hall. This is an excellent, readable presentation of an important subject. *Highly recommended.*

Moshman, D., Glover, J. A., & Bruning, R. H. (1987). *Developmental psychology: A topical approach.* Boston: Little, Brown. A clear yet concise overview of language theory and development is presented by the authors.

Fostering Conversation

Bos, B. (1983). *Before the basics: Creating conversations with children.* Roseville, CA: Turn the Page Press. Bos's book is an utter delight! It is mostly about generating happy, wholesome relationships with children through the medium of music, conversation, and movement.

Rogers, D. L., Perrin, M. S., & Waller, C. B. (1987). Enhancing the development of language and thought through conversations with young children. *Journal of Research in Childhood Education, 2*(1), 17–29. The authors provide a clear analysis with examples of ways one teacher fostered the growth of language and conversation.

Bilingual and Multilectical Information

Folb, E. A. (1980). *Runnin' down some lines: The language and culture of Black teenagers.* Cambridge, MA: Harvard University Press. This book would be particularly useful for teachers dealing with young parents of Black children.

Grosjean, F. (1982). *Life with two languages: An introduction to bilingualism.* Cambridge, MA: Harvard University Press. Ever wondered what it would be like to use two or more languages? This book covers all sorts of issues related to this ability. Useful and insightful.

Interracial Books for Children: Bulletin. (1986). *Bilingual education and equity* (entire issue). Reading this issue is the best and quickest way to acquire information about the status and political problems of bilingual education in the United States.

Morrow, R. D. (1989). What's in a name: In particular, a Southeast Asian name. *Young Children, 44*(6), 20–23. Factual advice on respecting and using correct family names of children from Vietnamese, Cambodian, Laotian and Hmong cultures is included. Very helpful.

Smitherman, G. (1977). *Talkin' and testifyin': The language of Black America*. Boston: Houghton Mifflin. This book is filled with many examples of Black English and also with discussion of the rules of Black grammar.

Speech and Language Disorders

Dumtschin, J. U. (1988). Recognize language development and delay in early childhood. *Young Children, 43*(3), 16–24. Dumtschin offers guidelines for determining developmental language delay and suggests practical ways teachers can help remediate delayed speech through the appropriate use of conversation.

Oyer, H. J., Crowe, B., & Haas, W. (1987). *Speech, language and hearing disorders: A guide for the teacher*. Boston: College Hill. This is a clear, quick-reading, concise book that offers practical recommendations for what the classroom teacher can do to facilitate good language habits. *Highly recommended.*

Van Riper, C., and Emerick, L. (1984). *Speech correction: Principles and methods* (7th ed.). Englewood Cliffs, NJ: Prentice-Hall. A classic text, Van Riper and Emerick's work is filled with suggestions of activities that may be used to correct a wide variety of speech problems.

For the Advanced Student

Allen, H. B., & Linn, M. D. (Eds.). (1986). *Dialect and language variation*. New York: Academic Press. For an up-to-date review of research related to dialects and language variations, this book is helpful because it includes information on Mexican-American and American Indian English as well as Ebonics.

Escobedo, T. H. (Ed.). (1983). *Early childhood bilingual education: A Hispanic perspective*. New York: Teachers College Press. The authors of articles in this book present research to substantiate their practical recommendations for instructing the child who speaks Spanish and English.

Garvey, C. (1984). *Children's talk*. Cambridge, MA: Harvard University Press. Garvey considers many aspects of children's talk such as conversational turn taking and using talk to facilitate social interaction.

Genishi, C. (1987). Acquiring oral language and communicative competence. In C. Seefeldt (Ed.), *The early childhood curriculum: A review of current research*. New York: Teachers College Press. This is a brief, useful review of current research.

Heath, S. B. (1989). Oral and literate traditions among Black Americans living in poverty. *American Psychologist, 44*(2), 367–373. Heath discusses special difficulties and stresses that schools should capitalize on Black children's strengths including their "positive transfer of adaptability, keen interpretive talents, and group collaboration" (p. 372).

McTear, M. (1985). *Children's conversations*. New York: Basil Blackwell. McTear recounts research in the new field of discourse analysis.

Ramirez, A. G. (1985). *Bilingualism through schooling: Cross-cultural education for minority and majority students*. Albany: State University of New York Press. The author emphasizes the benefits of bilingual education for language-majority students. Includes many research findings and resources.

CHAPTER 17

Fostering the Emergence of Literacy

Children are provided many opportunities to see how reading and writing are useful before they are instructed in letter names, sounds, and word identification. Basic skills develop when they are meaningful to children. An abundance of these types of activities is provided to develop language and literacy through meaningful experience: listening to and reading stories and poems; taking field trips; dictating stories; seeing classroom charts and other print in use; participating in dramatic play and other experiences requiring communication; talking informally with other children and adults; and experimenting with writing by drawing, copying, and inventing their own spelling.

—S. Bredekamp (1987)

Have you ever wondered . . .

What to say to parents when they suggest you teach the 4-year-olds to read?

What people are talking about when they mention *emergent literacy*?

How you can get wiggly Matilda to hold still during group time?

If you have, the material on the following pages will help you.

A current concern of many preprimary teachers is the pressure some parents and school districts are putting on them to present a highly structured reading program in the preschool.

Rather than just deploring the effects such pressure would have on the children because such expectations are developmentally inappropriate, as the opening quotation makes clear, it is wiser to understand what it is parents (and, hence, school districts) want, and then to understand how to reassure them while protecting the children from unreasonable expectations.

Parents are not ogres; they simply want what's best for their children. They see the world as a difficult place to grow up in; they see technology advancing at a frightening pace; and they want their children to be successful, competent grown-ups who can cope with that world. They know that intellectual competence is one of the keys to effective functioning in that world, and they think of the ABCs and numbers, reading and arithmetic, as being the cognitive skills that will provide their children with that competence. After all, this is what they were taught when they went to school, so it is only reasonable that they think of education as consisting of that kind of instruction.

What teachers should do is conduct a careful educational campaign with the children's parents to inform them about what the children are learning at the center. The teachers should explain that what they are doing *is* appropriate for the children's age and developmental stage and will pave the way for learning to read more easily later on.

Part of this information will, inevitably, involve explaining how children learn from play and also explaining all the benefits children derive from being involved in such preschool activities as blocks, sand, and water. But it should also include clear-cut descriptions of the various thinking and reasoning skills that are incorporated into the curriculum each day, accompanied by explanations of how these abilities underlie later competence in school. These skills are discussed in detail in chapters 18 and 19.

In addition to these explanations, the teacher needs to add information about all the language development activities that are part and parcel of a good preschool curriculum. He needs to emphasize that these activities construct the foundation on which reading is later built. (Please refer to chapter 16.) These range from learning new words to telling a coherent story about what happened on the way to school. They include using language in conversation or using it to make the child's desires known, as well as learning that books can be a source of fascinating pleasure at group time.

Activities such as these form the foundation for later reading and writing. Parents need to understand that learning to read is a lengthy process, and much preparation and maturation must take place before it can be accomplished successfully (Fields, Spangler & Lee, 1991; Schickedanz, 1986). Once parents realize that the teacher knows what he is doing and that he is "really teaching the children something" that will form a solid foundation for later learning at the elementary school level, they generally stop asking about reading per se and become supportive of what is provided at the preschool level.

> WAYS TO TELL OUR
> FRIENDS WE LIKE THEM,
> 1. Hug Them
> 2. Kiss Them
> 3. Play with them
> 4. Have a party
> 5. Valentine's Day
> 6. Run to them
> 7. Mail them a letter
> 8. Sing a Song
> 9. Tell a secret
> 10. Tell them
> 11. Tell a secret
>   I LOVE YOU.
> 12. Give Them a present
> 13. LET THEM SPEND THE
>   NIGHT

Children can do their part in creating a print-rich environment.

DOES FOSTERING LITERACY MEAN TEACHING READING?

From one point of view, it is unnecessary to discuss implementing literacy in the preschool classroom because children have been doing it for years, anyway! Every time a child singles out his name tag and puts it on, or finds the book he has been hunting for, or supplies the phrase the gingerbread boy says as he runs from his potential captors, or counts the number of spoonfuls needed in a recipe, he is using literacy-related skills. Every time he substitutes a pretend spoon for a real one, or tells what's happening in a picture, or uses language in any form, then, too, he is engaged in emerging literacy activities because all of these activities and hundreds like them are examples of the array of skills that underlie the ultimate skills of reading and writing.

This understanding of what constitutes true literacy makes it clear that its development entails far more than learning skills such as handwriting, decoding the printed word, and spelling. As McLane and McNamee (1990) point out, "Literacy development consists of mastering a complex set of attitudes, expectations, feelings, behaviors, and skills related to the written language. This collection of attitudes and skills constitutes what has been called 'emergent literacy'" (p. 4).

And yet the idea of fostering reading and writing skills continues to make many preschool teachers feel uncomfortable and concerned (Gibson, 1989). This resistance is not without reason. As the guardians of children's rights to be children and to learn in developmentally appropriate ways and at suitable levels, we teachers of very young children have had to resist the pressures of inappropriate expectations and methods and watered-down elementary curriculum for more years than we like to remember. If literacy means teaching the ABCs and phonics to 3- and 4-year-olds, then we must continue our resistance (Manning, Manning, & Kamii, 1988).

However, *emergent literacy* does not advocate such approaches. It does *not* mean that we are going to teach the children to read—far from it. Research has shown time and time again that the arts of reading and writing (for the two must go together) rely on the prior acquisition of a great many foundation skills—skills that teachers of young children have been encouraging children to develop for many years. Table 17.1 lists many of those activities that are basic to helping children develop literacy. Note that all of them down through scribbling in item 5 are frequently part of the preschool curriculum.

TABLE 17.1 Literacy basics*

1. A print-rich environment Adults who read and write Contextualized print Being read to Dictation experiences Exposure to quality literature	**5.** Pressure-free experimentation with writing Drawing Scribbling Nonphonetic writing Invented spelling
2. Oral language development	**6.** Pressure-free exploration of reading
3. First-hand experiences with topics of interest	Reading from memory Reading with context clues
4. Symbolic representation experiences Dramatic play Drawing and painting Music and dance	Matching print to oral language

*From *Let's begin reading right: Developmentally appropriate beginning literacy* (2nd ed.), p. 38, by M. V. Fields, K. S. Spangler, and D. M. Lee (1991). Columbus, OH: Merrill. Used by permission.

SOME FUNDAMENTAL PRINCIPLES TO KEEP IN MIND

The majority of the basics listed in Table 17.1 have been discussed in previous chapters, so only the most fundamental principles will be reviewed here.

Teachers Should Make It Plain
They Value the Wonderful World of Books

This can be done as the teacher clearly enjoys the good book she is reading aloud as much as the children do. There is no substitute for this enthusiasm.

It is also shown in more subtle ways by the quality of the books available to the children and by the care that people take of them. Books belong in people's laps or enjoyed in the rocking chair—not left on the floor to be trampled. Old favorites are promptly mended and torn pages carefully taped with the children's help.

Teachers Should Emphasize How Useful
the Written Word Can Be

For example, the shared experience of writing a note to the janitor asking her to leave up their block construction can make this usefulness obvious to the block builders. Empowering children by encouraging them to follow an illustrated recipe on their own provides the satisfaction of accomplishment for independent 4-year-olds. "You didn't even have to tell me nothin'!" chortled one of the Institute youngsters the other day. "I read it all!"—and he had. Labeling containers and activity areas also helps tie together the idea that written words stand for real objects.

Even Very Young Children Can and Should Be Involved
in Producing the Written Word

Perhaps the children can share with the teacher the experience of turning language into written text by dictating stories, letters, or ideas for the teacher to write down. Doing this emphasizes the relationship between reading and writing.

They can chant along with the teacher, "I think I can, I think I can, I think I can" as she reads the beloved *Little Engine That Could* (Piper, 1980). They can listen as the teacher reads aloud to them the note she is sending home to their family, and they can mail their letters at the post office before Valentine's Day. If attractive writing materials are assembled in a convenient spot, they can elaborate on their scribbles and use old envelopes to enclose the messages.

Although these literacy activities and others like them should be spread throughout the curriculum, just as *whole language* is integrated into the curriculum of many elementary schools, there is one particular experience during the day that provides an outstanding opportunity to foster emergent literacy. This is the experience of group time.

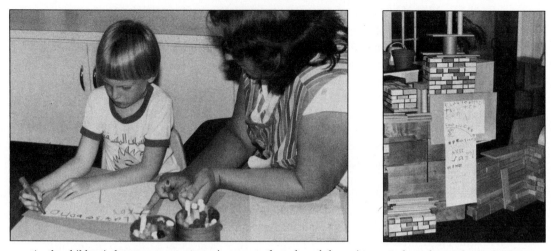

As the children's language competence increases, the value of the written word can be emphasized. This is a step toward teaching reading that is developmentally appropriate. Here Cené is helping a 5-year-old spell out a sign telling the janitor to leave his block structure up for the potluck dinner.

SUGGESTIONS FOR PRESENTING A LANGUAGE-RICH GROUP-TIME EXPERIENCE

A well-planned group time can be a high spot of the day for teachers and children, or it can become a dreaded encounter between them as the children thrash about and the teacher struggles to maintain a semblance of order.

Successful group times depend on careful advance planning by the teacher that takes into consideration such things as including enough variety, making certain the material is interesting, providing opportunities for the children to interact with the teacher, and knowing how to pace activities so they sustain the children's interest. The primary goal, of course, is to provide wonderfully enriching opportunities for the use of language and the development of emergent literacy.

Include a Variety of Activities

Unfortunately, a survey by McAfee (1985) reveals that only one out of every three teachers actually took the trouble to plan for group time at all! The same study showed that out of 14 potential activities mentioned by teachers as being likely ingredients for group time, only a handful were actually included. Of these, the ones most frequently presented were books and music-related items.

Although books are an essential ingredient of group time, it is a pity to restrict this potentially rich language experience to only a book and a song when there are so many other interesting language-related things for the group to do together. Poetry (only mentioned three times by teachers in the McAfee study as a possibility); fingerplays; auditory discrimination skills; and chances for discussions that involve problem solving, thinking, and reasoning skills are additional activities that merit inclusion. The inclusion of reading material that is nonsexist and multicultural is a must.

Some Specific Suggestions About Materials to Include

Do Include a Book and Poetry

The selection of a fine children's book is often the best place to begin when planning the time together, and there are many good lists of such books available (Shelton, Montgomery, & Hatcher, 1989; Sutherland, 1986). Poetry should be offered on a daily basis (Arbuthnot & Root, 1968). (Incidentally, the only way I have ever been able to use poetry successfully has been to make a poetry file. This entails duplicating a large variety of poems from various books, mounting them on stiff cardboard to preserve them and keep them from getting lost, and then filing them according to topic. This arrangement has meant that when we suddenly need a poem about rain, all we have to do is look under that topic heading in the file and pull out a number of poems on that subject.)

Music and Fingerplays Are Important, Too

Singing has its merits because it fosters language, memory, musical development, and pleasure. It takes a good deal of repetition for children to learn a new song; teachers should be prepared to sing one or two verses with them three or four times, then repeat the same song for several group times so that children can learn them well enough to sing them with verve (Bayless & Ramsey, 1987).

Jalongo and Collins (1985) remind us that children of different ages respond differently to songs presented by the teacher. By age 2 to 3, children can sing an average of five different notes, join in on certain phrases of familiar songs, and show interest in records and rhythm instruments. By age 3 to 4, children have better voice control and mastery of song lyrics. They are able to combine creative drama with singing and possess basic musical concepts such as loud-soft and fast-slow. By age 4 to 5, children can sing an average of 10 different musical notes as well as sing complete songs from memory. At that age they form the concepts of high-low and long-short tones.

Fingerplays are another fine ingredient to include during groups. Again experience has taught me that 2- and 3-year-olds are likely to be able to do just the actions at first and then later will add the words. But you should not be discouraged. If you persevere long enough, they will eventually be able to put words and actions together, which they do love to do.

Auditory Training Should Also Be Provided

A well-planned group time includes at least two additional kinds of activities besides those previously listed. The first of these is some activity that provides for auditory training and discrimination. Sometimes this can be included as part

Sharing books together shares joy and delight as well.

of a fingerplay or poem, and sometimes it needs to be a special activity. Children need work on learning to tell sounds apart or telling when they are the same, and group time provides a fine chance to have practice in this skill. It is a valuable activity because it is an important step toward attaining literacy and also because it helps children learn to discriminate between sounds and speak more clearly.

Perhaps during a song they could sing as loud as they can and then as soft as they can; or listen to high and low notes on the autoharp, standing up when they hear a high one, and sitting down when they hear a low one; or perhaps half the children can clap their hands when they hear the sound "eee" and the other half listen for "iii."

Some other examples of activities include matching the sounds of shakers, some of which have been filled with sand, some with beans, and some with rice; everyone shutting their eyes and opening them when a particular sound is heard; listening for words left out of familiar nursery rhymes; or having the children signal when they hear sentences that do not make sense, such as "When I went to the market, I bought a camelope"—a game that appeals strongly to 4-year-olds.

Most speech correction texts (Van Riper & Emerick, 1984; Wiig & Semel, 1976) contain many suggestions for such activities that may be adapted for preschool children. Appendix F lists some ideas, too.

Group Time Is an Ideal Time to Provide Practice in Cognitive Skills

The second kind of activity that is rarely included but that should be is one that provides practice in thinking and reasoning (activities that are described in more detail in chapters 18 and 19). These include matching, grouping, temporal ordering, seriation, pairing common relations, or providing a cause-and-effect experience. Offering these activities during group assures that all the children are receiving practice in these vital skills.

Group Time Should Provide Multiracial, Nonsexist Subject Matter

There are two additional ingredients that should also be woven into group time. Every group should contain some multiethnic or nonsexist material, or both, and conversely should not contain material that is sexist or racist. This means that the teacher will have to make a careful appraisal of the material in songs, books, and poetry before presenting them and either discard those that possess objectionable material or draw it to the children's attention and discuss it.

For example, should the teacher choose to read a book about going to the hospital where all the doctors are white males and the nurses white females, a discussion should ensue about whether there are women doctors and male nurses and whether only white people can work at such jobs. (Please refer to chapter 12, "Providing Cross-Cultural, Nonsexist Education," for additional suggestions.)

Management Suggestions to Help Group Time Go More Smoothly

It Is Always Wise to Plan More Activities Than You Are Likely to Use

Particularly for inexperienced teachers, it is difficult to know in advance which activities will go well and which will not. It is also difficult to estimate the amount of time a particular activity will absorb. So, it is better to be safe and have extra reserves than to be caught short and run out of things to do.

Make Certain the Children Talk, Too

Include opportunities for children to respond to the teacher. During group time children should be encouraged to think, reason, and guess (hypothesize) about what is being discussed. "What would you do if you were Peter and Mr. MacGregor chased you into the potting shed?" "What *is* a potting shed, anyway?" "Do you think Peter was really sick when he got home?" "Was that the best punishment his mother could do, to put him to bed without dinner?" "What does *your* mother do when you're naughty?" and so forth. These opportunities for discussion are an invaluable part of the group experience.

Table 17.2 presents an example of one student's plan and evaluation of a group time for 4-year-olds. The theme of the week was family living.

TABLE 17.2 Plan and evaluation of a group time for 4-year-olds with the theme "family living"

Area	Materials	Reason for Inclusion	Was It Used?	Evaluation
Story	Radlaver, E. *Father Is Big* (Bowman Publishing, 1967)	Many children today do not have a father figure. This book was not sexist; it just stated fact. Example: "His hand feels big around mine." There were actual photos that gave realistic quality.	Yes	The children seemed to enjoy the book. I got lots of comments about "my daddy." However, there seemed to be some competition as to whose daddy was biggest. This might have been bad for a child without a father. So, next time, to avoid any negative side effects, I would have used another book to read aloud (about daddies) and left this book out for individual utilization.
Poetry and fingerplays	Fingerplay: Grandmother's Glasses.	This provided a good way to include the third generation in my large group. This fingerplay also incorporated poetry (rhyming words) and gave the children some form of a guided activity since they were to make the actions follow the words of the fingerplay.	Yes	The children were familiar with this fingerplay, and I received some advice on "how to do it." So, although I intended this activity to be teacher directed, the children felt free to give suggestions. I thought that this was good. Next time, I would probably do this fingerplay two times in a row—as one time went so quickly, and the children did enjoy themselves.
Auditory training	Tape recorder. Identify sound of family members on a tape recorder. Example: baby, mom, dad, child, dog,	It would be interesting to see if the children could identify different family members' voices. The household sounds tape	No	I did not use this activity, but if I did I would try to steer the activity in a nonsexist way. Example: "Daddies can wash dishes too."

	and older person. Also could include some household sounds. Example: washing dishes, raking leaves, TV, doorbell. Ask the children, "Who is making these noises?"	could lead to good discussions of whose jobs are whose responsibilities; also, to find out if the children help at home. Would hope to encourage nonsexist ways of thinking.		
Song	"This Is the Way," (sung to Mulberry Bush)	I wanted to get the children to realize all the duties that go into making a household work. I also wanted to have more movement in the large group time.	Yes	This activity did not work well. I started a verse and demonstrated the actions, but I found that some of the children just sat and watched me. So I encouraged them to get up and asked them how we would move to the next verse—raking leaves. This helped a little bit, but still not all the children had stood up before I started. Also I might ask individual children to move to each verse, or ask them to suggest work that members of their family do around the house.
Cognitive game	Pictures of families or members of family cut from magazines. Asked the children, "What do you think is happening here?"	I wanted to hear the children's suggestions about what was going on in the pictures. I thought that this activity might give good insight into what the children's families were like. I tried to include nonsexist and multiethnic pictures.	Yes	This activity went much better than I had expected. The children seemed really interested in looking at the pictures, and I got lots of feedback. Next time, however, I would allow more time—as I feel that I quit while the children were still interested.

TABLE 17.2 *continued*

Area	Materials	Reason for Inclusion	Was It Used?	Evaluation
Discussion	See ideas for topics throughout outline.	Wanted children to realize that there are many kinds of families and all are equally good. I wanted some feedback, would mostly try to give information, new terms, etc., would hope to increase the children's positive feelings about their own families.	No	I did not include this activity because I felt it would take too much time, and I wanted to include the other areas.
Multiethnic and nonsexist area	I would probably normally end the large group session by having some "stereotyped" activities that both boys and girls could use (woodshop area, cooking area, housekeeping, etc.) and encourage everyone to use those activities.	I would use this activity in hope of encouraging the children to be involved in nonsexist type play. Also, I think, that sometimes teachers "forget" to incorporate this into everyday activities.	No	Since this was not possible on this particular day, I tried to incorporate nonsexist and multiethnic material in all my other activities. Example: In a picture I showed a father cooking with his son and talked about how everyone can be a good cook.

*Source: Courtesy Erika Miller, Institute of Child Development, University of Oklahoma, Norman.

Make Certain the Material Is Interesting

Part of the secret of doing this is to read the material first yourself. If you don't think it's interesting, it's a sure thing that the children won't either. It helps a lot to select books the children genuinely enjoy. Unfortunately the world abounds in dull books designed to improve children's minds but not lift their spirits. However, when books of such charm as *Mary Betty Lizzie McNutt's Birthday* (Bond, 1983), of such humor as *Gregory the Terrible Eater* (Sharmat, 1980) and *Silly Goose* (Kent, 1983), and of such sound social values as *A Chair for My Mother* (Williams, 1982) and *The Goat in the Rug* (Blood & Link, 1980) exist, there's really no excuse for boredom. The teacher who selects stories like these will enjoy them right along with the children, and they will arouse much comment and discussion from everyone. Remember, when a book is dull and the children are not interested, it is not necessary to read grimly through to its end; it is better to simply set it aside and go on to a more attractive choice.

Think, too, about how to present material so that it captures their attention. Using visual aids such as flannel boards helps, as does simply telling

Telling a story makes a nice change from reading one.

a story (Trelease, 1989). I have seen children absolutely enraptured by this activity, and telling stories lets the teacher look at the children all the time and be more responsive to them as they listen. Using a hand puppet also increases appeal.

Read with verve and enthusiasm. Remember, using different voices for different characters when reading *The Three Bears* (Galdone, 1985), suiting your tone of voice to the mood of the material (for example, sounding anxious and wistful when being the little bird that enquires "Are *you* my mother?") (Eastman, 1960), or building suspense during *The Three Billy Goats Gruff* (Galdone, 1981) as the children wait for the troll to appear all contribute to the fun for everyone.

Keep the Tempo of Group Time Upbeat

"Pace" has a lot to do with sustaining interest. If things move along well and the teacher does not drag things out, children pay better attention. This is the reason it is deadly in a preschool group to go all around in the circle and have each child say something. When this happens, attention lags among the other youngsters and restlessness rises like a tide. Far better to include children spontaneously as the opportunity presents itself—a few adding suggestions to the story, others putting figures on the flannel board, and the entire group participating in a fingerplay.

Opportunities for the group to move around a bit also provide a needed change of pace. Singing a song where children get up and down answers the need for large muscle activity, just as fingerplays about the "eensy weensy spider" harness the energy inherent in wiggly fingers.

Assess the difficulty of what the children will be learning and present anything that is new or potentially difficult to understand early in group while the children are still feeling rested. A new mental ability activity, for instance, should follow the opening songs rather than coming at the very end of the time together.

Some Advice About Starting and Stopping

Start as soon as the children begin to gather, and quit while you're ahead. It is not necessary to wait until all the children have arrived to begin group activities. The children who have come promptly need something to do rather than just sit and wait for stragglers. A good action song or fingerplay is a fine way to begin. It catches the group's attention and involves them immediately, and it is easy for latecomers to join in unobtrusively while this is going on. If such late arrivals are welcomed with a quick smile rather than a reproachful look, they will want to arrive more quickly next time.

Closing a group time well is equally important. Some teachers do this by always ending with the same song to give the children a sense of finishing or completion. Others just anticipate its ending by saying something like "Well, we certainly did a lot of interesting things in group today, didn't we?" and then summarizing what was done. Still others just move smoothly into some sort of dismissal routine: "Everyone who is wearing blue jeans can go first today, or everyone who has spotted socks, or who has freckles, or who ate oatmeal for breakfast." Children enjoy this sort of thing, and it has the advantage of not sending the entire herd off at once in a thundering way.

The most important points about finishing group time are that the children have a clear idea of what they are expected to do next and also that group time ends before the youngsters are so exhausted that the experience has degenerated into a struggle to maintain order. Finishing a group time while the children are still interested and attentive makes it more likely they will want to return because they recall group time as being a satisfying experience they enjoyed.

What to Do About Undesirable Behavior

The McAfee (1985) survey also points out that, when teachers were asked to explain why certain group times or activities were not successful, they cited conditions that were beyond their control 75% of the time. These included such things as the children's developmental levels, their emotional or behavioral problems, home background, and classroom conditions, such as too large a group or too wide an age span. It is certainly true that all of these conditions can and do cause problems. What is distressing is that so few of the teachers saw themselves as generating some of the difficulties. Yet teachers *can* control some of the aforementioned variables.

For example, it is quite possible and valuable to suit the material to the age of the children. The younger the children, the shorter the books, poetry, and songs should be and the more opportunities should be provided for moving around. Whatever the age of the children, the teacher must remain sensitive to the group—tuned in—so she can sense when a shift of material is necessary to hold their attention. Of course, no group is completely attentive at any time. Even during a very high-interest activity, McAfee reported there were several children who were not attentive. So another thing to remember is not to expect perfection from children who are, after all, very young.

To obtain maximum benefit from such experiences, groups should be kept as small as possible. Larger groups almost always produce behavior problems because of lack of involvement and inattention. What typically happens is that assistant teachers spend their time admonishing some children, patting others on the back, and holding still other unwilling participants on their laps. When a second teacher is available, it is much better to split the group in half so that each staff member works with a smaller number of children. Under these circumstances there can be a better balance between teacher-dominated activities and conversation and discussions, and the children will pay closer attention and develop their language skills more richly.

But these recommendations do not deal with the problem of what to do about the child who is punching his neighbor, rolling over and over on the floor, or continually drifting away from the group to play in the housekeeping area.

There are a number of ways of dealing with this situation. Making certain the material is interesting is the first thing to consider. Sometimes it is effective to have the acting-out youngster sit beside you as you read, turning the pages or doing other helpful things. Sometimes it is enough just to separate him from his boon companion. Sometimes calling the child by name and drawing his attention back to what the group is doing is helpful, although I avoid doing this as a reproach. Sometimes the behavior can be overlooked. And, as a final resort, sometimes the child loses the privilege of staying in the group and must be sent away. The problem with this method is that an adult really has to go with him to prevent him from getting into further mischief.

Remember, almost all children who misbehave at the beginning of the year can learn to conform to the requirements of the group if provided with patient teaching. Hold them only to reasonable expectations. Be persistent and don't give up hope. It can be helpful to talk with the youngster privately at some time other than group, *pointing out when he has done well,* and arranging with him in advance that he does not have to stay the entire time. Perhaps he will just try to stay for the first song and poem, or for the story, and then, *before he loses control* he can go off with the staff member and do something quiet until group time is over. The time in the group can be gradually extended as the child's ability to control his behavior increases.

When a child has consistent difficulties enjoying group time, we should take a careful look at possible reasons within the child for this behavior because, if most of the children are enjoying the activity, there may be some special reason that this particular child is not. Some possibilities to consider when this is the case include hearing and vision difficulties. These are common but frequently overlooked reasons for inattentiveness. The other common reason is immaturity. If the material being presented is above the child's level, he won't pay attention. Any of these conditions require sensitive discussion with the family as well as special diagnosis by an appropriate professional person. (For a discussion of how to make an effective referral, please refer to the chapters on exceptionality and parenting.)

USING THE COMPUTER AS A METHOD OF PRESCHOOL INSTRUCTION

The preschool world seems to be divided into two distinct camps on the issue of computers in the classroom, and the subject has so little research to support either pro or con that much of what is said remains in the realm of opinion (Brady & Hill, 1986; Waldrop, 1989).

Those who favor the introduction of that technological marvel suggest that it possesses many virtues. Among these are that computer-based activities are self-pacing and encourage independent work, that they can be fun, that they prepare children for later literacy, and that they prevent children from becoming "computer shy." Such enthusiasts are quick to provide examples of ways computer-based activities can be used to foster creativity and provide for social interaction (Beaty & Tucker, 1987; Davidson, 1989).

Those who are less certain of the benefits argue in return that computers are very expensive in relation to their educational value for young children, that many programs are little more than electronic workbooks, and that the push-button, creative "painting" experiences touted by supporters are so far from the pleasures experienced by actually splashing paint on paper, there are no grounds for comparison. This, perhaps, is the most telling argument of all (Kreuger, Karger, & Barwick, 1989). Computers *are* removed from direct experience. They are, by nature, a highly symbolic, visually based activity. As such, their value in the education of young children is bound to be somewhat limited. We must not allow them to preempt time best used for other activities (as television is now preempting real-life experiences at home). And yet my guess is that computers will find their niche in the preschool classroom as time goes on and as more appropriate programs are written for computers and as teachers of young children are trained how to present them effectively by linking them closely to real experience.

SUMMARY

The current approach to preparing children for learning the later skills of reading and writing is termed *emergent literacy.* This term includes the underlying skills related to developing all aspects of language, both written and oral.

Because many other aspects of language development have been discussed in previous chapters, chapter 17 emphasizes that teachers should make it plain they value good books, stress the usefulness of the written word, and involve the children in producing written language.

Group time presents a particularly rich opportunity for fostering emergent literacy, and the chapter concludes with a number of practical suggestions for making that experience satisfying for both children and teachers.

QUESTIONS AND ACTIVITIES

1. *Problem:* The mother of a child in your group glows as she tells you her 3-year-old is so smart—she knows all her ABCs and her father is drilling her every night with flash cards to help her learn to read. What, if anything, do you think you should do about this?

2. Role play a story hour where the teacher seems to do everything possible to prevent the children from talking.

3. For the sake of variety and to extend your language-building skills with the children, resolve not to use books at all during group time for a month! What will you offer instead that will enhance the language abilities of the children?

SELF-CHECK QUESTIONS FOR REVIEW

Content-Related Questions

1. Give three examples of emergent literacy activities a 3-year-old might participate in with pleasure.

2. What are three fundamental principles for developing literacy that teachers should keep in mind?

3. Name three additional kinds of language activities besides songs and stories that should be regularly included in group time.

4. You have a beginning student teacher working with you in your class of 3-year-olds. She reads to them in a steady monotone, never looking up and never smiling. What advice would you give her that would help her hold the children's attention?

5. Discuss some possible ways teachers could reduce misbehavior during group time.

Integrative Questions

1. The teacher next door who works with 4-year-olds complains to you that she has a terrible time during group because the children keep interrupting her. Explain why you would or would not agree that this is undesirable behavior on the children's part.

2. Picture in your mind's eye one of the books you most enjoy reading to children, and propose three questions based on that book that would promote discussion between you and them.

3. Then, using that book as the central idea or theme, suggest a poem, an auditory discrimination activity, and a nonsexist or multicultural idea you could use along with the book during a group time for 3- or 4-year-olds.

REFERENCES FOR FURTHER READING

Overviews

Fields, M. V., Spangler, K., & Lee, D. M. (1991). *Let's begin reading right* (2nd ed.). Columbus, OH: Merrill. This book discusses the underpinnings of literacy and then discusses the development of reading and writing with older youngsters. *Highly recommended.*

Schickedanz, J. A. (1986). *More than the ABCs: The early stages of reading and writing.* Washington, DC: National Association for the Education of Young Children. Schickedanz traces reading from the infant's first encounter with books through storybooks and the beginning of writing. She offers many developmentally appropriate suggestions for fostering literacy in young children.

Strickland, D. S., & Morrow, L. M. (Eds.). (1989). *Emerging literacy: Young children learn to read and write.* Newark, DE: International Reading Association. These useful articles by well-known authorities are filled with practical suggestions.

Enjoying Books and Presenting Effective Group Times

Glazer, J. I. (1991). *Literature for young children* (3rd ed.). Columbus, OH: Merrill. This book works particularly well for students using *The Whole Child* because some of it is divided into chapters dealing with literature and the social self, the intellectual self, etc.

Jalongo, M. R. (1988). *Young children and picture books: Literature from infancy to six.* Washington, DC: National Association for the Education of Young Children. The joy of really good picture books is captured here. The author explains how to select quality books and how to present them so effectively that children will fall in love with them and with reading, too. *Highly recommended.*

Raines, S. C., & Canady, R. J. (1989). *Story s-t-r-e-t-c-h-e-r-s: Activities to expand children's favorite books.* Mount Rainier, MD: Gryphon House. In addition to providing a wonderful selection of really *good* books, Raines and Canady offer extensive ideas of ways to tie them to other activity areas. *Highly recommended.*

Teale, W. H., & Martinez, M. G. (1988). Getting on the right road to reading: Bringing books and young children together in the classroom. *Young Children, 44*(1), 10–15. Many practical, research-supported ideas are included in this discussion of linking children and books.

Trelease, J. (1989). *The new read-aloud handbook.* New York: Penguin Books. A sensible, easy-to-read paperback that is filled with good advice for parents and teachers on enjoying books with children. Excellent bibliography.

Zeece, P. D., & Corr, M. (1989). Group time treasures: Implications for learning. *Day Care and Early Education, 17*(1), 32–34. The authors identify some basic values of group time and include practical suggestions about presentation as well.

Poetry and Fingerplays

Andrews, J. H. (1988). Poetry: Tool of the classroom magician. *Young Children, 43*(4), 17–24. Practical and inspiring ways to integrate poetry into the life of the school are presented.

Arbuthnot, M. H., & Root, S. L. (1968). *Time for poetry* (3rd ed.). Glenview, IL: Scott, Foresman. This book is a treasure. It is filled with poetry (most of which can be used at the preschool level) arranged by topic, and it also contains a valuable chapter on sharing poetry with children.

Dowell, R. I. (1987). *Move over, Mother Goose: Finger plays, action verses, & funny rhymes.* Mount Rainier, MD: Gryphon House. This nice mix of materials is divided into topics such as animals, family, and so forth.

Prelutsky, C. (Ed.). (1986). *Read aloud rhymes for the very young.* New York: Alfred A. Knopf. Delightfully illustrated, these poems *are* simple. They are also arranged somewhat according to subject.

Helpful Bibliographies

Child Study Children's Book Committee. (1988). *Children's books of the year.* (Available from Bank Street College, 610 W. 112th St., New York, NY 10025.) The Committee annually provides an annotated, trustworthy source of excellent books. It lists the best choices of the year selected from several thousand possibilities.

Schon, I. (1986). *Basic collection of children's books in Spanish.* Metuchen, NJ: Scarecrow Press. Title is self-explanatory.

Shelton, H., Montgomery, P., & Hatcher, B. (1989). *Bibliography of books for children, 1989 edition.* Wheaton, MD: Association for Childhood Education International. Title is self-explanatory.

Using Computers with Preschool Children

Davidson, J. I. (1989) *Children & computers together in the early childhood classroom.* Albany, NY: Delmar. Davidson makes the useful assumption the reader knows *nothing* about computers and provides step-by-step instructions. Very helpful for those who need the information.

Haugland, S. W., & Shade, D. D. (1990). *Developmental evaluations of software for young children.* Albany, NY: Delmar. The authors use a clearly defined scale to rate numerous programs and conclude that only a handful are developmentally appropriate. An indispensable resource for anyone intending to use computers with young children.

Additional Resources of Particular Interest

The Children's Book Council, 568 Broadway, New York, NY 10012. This wonderful nonprofit organization sponsors Children's Book Week and is an excellent source of posters and resources. A one-time fee entitles you to issues of the informative *Calendar* forever. *Highly recommended.*

CHAPTER 18

Developing Thinking and Reasoning Skills: Part I

The best school, after all, for the world of childhood is not the school where children know the most answers, but the school where children ask the most questions.

—John Coe (1987)

Have you ever wondered . . .

> If there wasn't a better way to develop thinking skills than teaching children the names of colors and shapes?
>
> Why working on cognitive skills always seems so boring?
>
> How to tie children's interests and important cognitive abilities together?

If you have, the material in the following pages will help you.

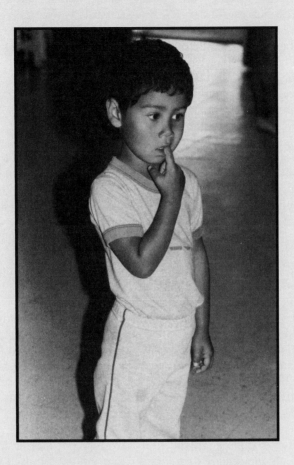

I have left the analytical thinking and reasoning aspect of the child's self until last for several reasons. For one thing, this kind of learning prospers best when the child is physically healthy, emotionally stable, and socially competent, so it was logical to discuss these aspects first. Creativity was discussed following that, not only because it is an educational value highly esteemed by early childhood teachers, but also because it deserves special emphasis since it is such an important element of mental development.

Indeed, the idea that intuitive, creative, synthesizing thought is as valuable as analytical thought has gained increasing respectability in recent years, thanks to the work of such neuropsychologists as Ornstein (1977, 1978) and Lee, Ornstein, Galin, Deikman, and Tart (1976), who have been studying the differing cognitive styles or ways of knowing of the left and right sides (hemispheres) of the brain. (According to these findings the left hemisphere specializes in dealing with things that occur in sequence, such as logical, analytical reasoning and language-based activities; whereas the right hemisphere deals more with all-at-once, non-language-based perceptions often described as intuitive, insightful ways of knowing.) Their work has helped emphasize that both ways of knowing (Annett, 1985), though different, are valuable. This is a point with which I heartily concur, and before continuing I wish to remind readers that although this chapter deals primarily with "left brain" functions, considerable attention has already been devoted to "right brain" functions in the chapters on creativity.

The other reason I left the discussion of the cognitive-analytical self until last is that working with the cognitive aspect of the child's self seems to bring out the worst in some teachers. By putting these chapters toward the end of the book, I hope that readers have absorbed enough of its basic philosophy to be armed against the tendency to reduce intellectual learning to a series of isolated activities and drills or to assume that the fundamental intent in developing cognitive-analytical ability should be the acceleration of the child to the point of precocity.

Rather than focusing intellectual learning on academic exercises or struggling to push adequately developing children beyond their peers, the true goal of cognitive development should be to give each youngster ample opportunity to achieve levels reasonable for her age and commensurate with her ability. In my opinion this is best accomplished by providing a balanced program that keeps children in contact with their feelings, encourages original ideas and problem solving, fosters the use of language, and provides practice in certain reasoning and thinking skills. Such opportunities are helpful for all children, but they are vital for children from lower economic groups who tend to lag behind middle-class children in this area (Honig, 1982a).

SELECTING VALUES AND PRIORITIES IN THE COGNITIVE REALM

To help all children realize their true potential, teachers have to get their values straight on what they want to emphasize in the area of cognitive development (and many preprimary teachers are very confused about this). Getting these values straight requires careful thinking about priorities (what it is important for children to learn). Once decisions about this have been made, it also requires clear understanding of how to offer instruction that will honor these priorities and foster the development of certain fundamental mental abilities.

As you rank priorities, it is most helpful to consider them in terms of their relative merit. For example, is it more important that the child experience joy and verve when learning or that she learn to sit quietly and not interrupt the teacher? Is it more significant that she speak fluently and spontaneously, or that she speak Standard English? Is it more valuable to know the names of the colors or be able to figure out how to capture a runaway duckling?

It is not that any of these values are reprehensible or should not receive attention when teachers plan their cognitive curriculum; it is a question of deciding which goals should receive *primary* emphasis, because the teacher who elects to foster joy and verve is likely to employ a different teaching style from one who feels that quietly paying attention is vital to classroom success.

Thus we must begin by asking ourselves what are the most important things we want children to learn in the cognitive sphere, which goals should have first priority. Then we can go on to consider some additional points that are significant but secondary in value to those discussed next.

Priority I: Maintain the Child's Sense of Wonder and Curiosity

As teachers of young children know, most youngsters come to school wondering about many things. They want to know where the water goes when

A sense of curiosity is an important part of motivating learning.

the toilet flushes, why the dog died, and what makes their stomach gurgle. Lewis (1979) catches the essence of this when she says,

> Children in the preschool years constantly show us that they do not take our ordinary world for granted. They wonder about anything and everything, trying to figure out reasons, answers, and inner workings. A four-year-old is walking to school with his teacher one day in the autumn: "What is on the top of those trees that makes the leaves fall down?" he asks. A three-year-old produces a definition for herself: "Tomorrow is the day we sleep for." A four-year-old suddenly announces out of nowhere while he sits quietly eating at the lunch table: "There are nineteen people in this room and the nineteenth is the turtle." (p. 13)

The age of 4 is particularly appealing in this respect. Four-year-olds are avid gatherers of facts and are interested in everything. For this reason it is a delight to build a cognitive curriculum for them. But 3-year-olds are seeking and questioning also. They are more concerned with the manipulation of materials and with finding out what everyday things and people close to them are like. This kind of investigation, although different in focus from that of the 4-year-olds, may also be used to make a rich contribution to mental development.

The most obvious way to maintain the children's sense of curiosity is by encouraging them to continue to ask questions and helping them find out the answers. But underlying the willingness to encourage investigation lies something deeper: the ability to support the child's drive toward venturing and independence—to capitalize, in other words, on her passing through the stage of autonomy described by Erikson (1963). Autonomy and the willingness to venture flourishes best in a climate where there is a balance of reasonableness, choice, trust, protection, spontaneity, moderate control, and challenge. Given both security and encouragement, children feel they have a firm base from which to explore when the impulse moves them to do so (Bradbard & Endsley, 1982).

Sometimes rather than sustaining and encouraging curiosity, the teacher finds it necessary to reawaken it. Deci and Ryan (1982) link such disinterested unawakened behavior to the concept of learned helplessness (Garber & Seligman, 1980; Seligman, 1975), where individuals have become hopeless and helpless because they feel that what they do cannot affect what happens in the environment. Therefore, one of Deci and Ryan's recommendations for generating the energy it takes to wonder and question is to encourage children to see themselves as powerful, effective people. As chapter 6 reminds us, the development of this positive sense of self is directly related to the child's sense of self-esteem (Curry & Johnson, 1990).

The teacher can also help by presenting materials that are fascinating and by modeling curiosity and wonder as well. Asking simple questions about cause and effect or wondering together what will happen next often captures children's interest and starts them observing, wondering, and thinking for themselves. Thus the teacher might discuss with the children whether the mother rabbit will do anything to get ready for her babies now that she is growing so fat and full of them, or he might ask the children whether they think it would be better to keep the ice in the sun or shade until time to make the ice cream and why they think so.

Given this attention from the teacher combined with a stronger concept of self, children who have not previously done so will soon begin to come alive and question and wonder for themselves. Then the teacher can encourage them and lead them on to further investigation and thinking.

Priority II: Let Cognitive Learning Be a Source of Genuine Pleasure

If we agree with the behaviorists that people tend to repeat activity that is rewarded in some way, it follows that we should do everything in our power to attach pleasure to cognitive learning. We want children to want to think and learn, and they are more likely to continue to do so if they experience pleasure while they are involved in learning. Therefore, the second most important priority that we should consider when planning a cognitive curriculum is presenting it so that it is a genuine source of pleasure to the child. This can be accomplished in a number of ways.

Sustain Interest by Making Curriculum Content Relevant

In these days of "relevant curriculum" it has become almost a truism to say that a good curriculum for any age is based on the student's interests and that it teaches her what she wants to know. A curriculum that does not accomplish this goal breeds disinterested, dissatisfied learners, no matter how old they are (DeVries & Kohlberg, 1990). Yet even preschool teachers often lay out a year's curriculum in advance, formulated at best on knowledge of what other children in previous years have cared about. Thus a schedule will show that in September the school will be building experiences around the family, in December on holidays, and in the spring on baby animals. Although this approach has a certain value, the danger of such extremely long-range planning is that teachers may become so tied to it that they are unable to respond to the interests of the children who are now in their room, thereby deadening some of their pleasure and motivation for learning. This does not mean that the curriculum will be completely unpredictable; it does mean that the subject matter should be drawn from the current interests of the group.

The teacher's responsibility is to use the children's interests in two ways: he supplies the children with information and vocabulary about subjects that matter to them, and he also employs the material as a medium for teaching a number of basic skills he feels they need to acquire. For example, almost any topic of interest to children, whether it be animal homes or changes in the weather, can be used to provide interesting facts, to foster proficiency in language, and to develop such thinking and reasoning skills as grouping, ordering, or learning about simple cause-and-effect relationships.

Keep It Age Appropriate

Nothing is more disheartening to a youngster than being confronted with material that is too difficult. To foster pleasure in learning it is necessary to match the child's learning opportunities with her developmental level. This means that learning opportunities must be challenging but not so difficult they are beyond the child's grasp.

On the other hand, they should be challenging enough that the bright 4-year-olds in the class are not bored by too much repetition at the same ability level all year. Teachers have to know what level of learning can reasonably be expected at various developmental stages so that they expect neither too much nor too little.

The exciting work done by Forman and Hill (1980) demonstrates countless ways equipment can be simply built or modified that causes children to question and figure out reasons why things happen. Their research is a current example of how challenging, curiosity-arousing curriculum can be developed. The fact that these investigators are also sensitive to the developmental levels and consequent levels of understanding of their young charges makes their work of even greater value.

Keep It Real

Cognitive learning should be based on actual experience and experience that makes the child an active participant (Piaget & Inhelder, 1967; Williams & Kamii, 1986). DeVries and Kohlberg (1990) provide some useful criteria to apply as tests of true involvement.

Criteria of Good Physical-Knowledge Activities*

The constructivist rationale and objectives emphasizing action lead to four criteria for good physical-knowledge activities. These were conceptualized with activities in mind that involve the movement of objects.

1. *The child must be able to produce the phenomenon by his own action.* As stated above, the essence of physical-knowledge activities is the child's action on objects and his observation of the object's reaction. The phenomenon selected must therefore be something the child can produce by his own action. The movement of a piece of Kleenex in reaction to the child's blowing or sucking on it through a straw meets this criterion. The movement of objects caused by a magnet, on the other hand, is an example of a phenomenon that is produced only indirectly by the child's action and primarily by magnetic attraction. This does not imply that magnets should be omitted from a classroom. It does imply that we should recognize the educational limitations of experimenting with magnets.

2. *The child must be able to vary his action.* When the variations in the child's action result in corresponding variations of the object's reaction, the child has

---

*From *Constructivist early education: Overview and comparison with other programs*, pp. 92–93, by R. DeVries and L. Kohlberg (1990). Washington, DC: National Association for the Education of Young Children. Used by permission.

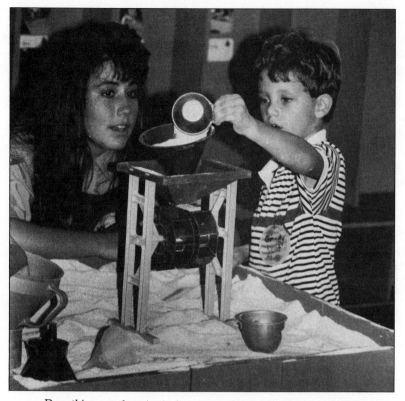

Does this meet the criteria for a good physical-knowledge activity?

the opportunity to structure these regularities. In a pool game, for example, if the child misses the target by hitting a ball too far to the left, he can adjust the next attempt accordingly. In a pinball-type game, by contrast, the child's action is limited to pulling a lever, and there is very little variation possible in how he releases the lever. The child thus cannot significantly affect the outcome. Without a direct correspondence between the variations in actions and reactions, a phenomenon offers little opportunity for structuring.

3. *The reaction of the object must be observable.* If the child cannot observe a reaction to his actions on objects, there is no content for him to structure. For example, an opaque tube in waterplay prevents observation of the water inside, and provides less material for structuring than a transparent tube.

4. *The reaction of the object must be immediate.* Correspondences are much easier to establish when the object's reaction is immediate. For example, when a child rolls a ball toward a target, she can immediately observe whether the target is hit or not, and if so, how it specifically reacts. In contrast, the reaction of a plant to water is not immediately observable, and its action on the water is only indirectly the result of the child's action. This does not imply that growing plants should be omitted from the classroom. In light of the immediacy criterion, sprouting beans on wet paper towels is a better activity to promote such understanding than watering a houseplant.

Keep It Brief and Unstressful

Thinking is hard work. The episodes should be brief enough that the children do not feel strained from working too long. It is always better to stop before stress and boredom set in, since stopping at the right moment makes it more likely the child will want to return the next time.

The teacher must learn to recognize common signs of stress in children because these behaviors are an indication that it is past time to stop or that the activity needs to be modified to a more attractive and appropriate level. These signs include thumb sucking, wiggling, inattention, restlessness, hair twisting, constantly trying to change the subject, asking to leave or just departing, picking fights, and creating disturbances (Chandler, 1982; Honig, 1986a).

Enjoy the Experience with the Children

The final way to sustain the child's pleasure in learning is to enjoy it with her. Cognitive learning does not have to be a sober-sided, no-nonsense business. It is a fine place for one-to-one experiences that include humor and fun when the teacher enjoys the activity along with the children. Teachers who are able to share their joy in learning with the youngsters in their care make a valuable contribution to their satisfaction.

Priority III: Bind Cognitive Learning to Affective Experience Whenever Possible

Other emotions in addition to pleasure are bound to be involved in cognitive learning, since such learning does not take place in an emotional vacuum. Feelings and social experience should be a fundamental part of cognitive learning. *Good education recognizes, accepts, and deals with feelings as they arise;* it does not ignore them or push them aside until later because now it is time to learn about baby animals or study the weather. *The same principle holds true for social skills. Many opportunities for understanding and getting along with others will arise during experiences that are primarily intellectual. These moments should be capitalized on as they occur.*

Priority IV: Teach Children Thinking and Reasoning Skills Geared to Their Correct Developmental Level Rather Than How to Read Before They Are Ready to Do So

Because cognitive learning is tied so tightly to reading and writing in some people's minds, it is important to remind the reader once more of all the emergent literacy skills young children need to attain before they are able to read and write on their own. Many of these, as will be demonstrated in this chapter, involve thinking and reasoning skills. The preschool years must provide many opportunities to practice them combined with time enough for maturation to take place if we truly want to foster a future generation of readers.

Priority V: Accompany Cognitive Learning with Language Whenever Possible

The word *accompany* is crucial here because language should be part of rather than precede cognitive learning. One of the most common errors of beginning teachers seems to be that they forget this principle when they approach cognitive development, and the first thing they do is begin a new experience with a formal discussion. As noted in the chapter on creative thought, a discussion about growing things is largely worthless for children who need to have experience with real beans and earth and water and sunlight before they can talk meaningfully about how plants develop.

On the other hand, mere experience has also been shown to be insufficient (Blank & Solomon, 1968, 1969). Teachers play a vital role in concept and mental development because it is they who blend language with experience, adding a word the children cannot supply themselves or asking a thought-provoking question that leads them to think something through more clearly. It is this deliberate interweaving that enriches the meaning of both experience and language for young children and increases the likelihood of mental activity and development.

Priority VI: Develop Children's Reasoning Skills in Addition to Teaching Facts and Names for Things

As studies of the questions asked by teachers substantiate (Honig & Wittmer, 1982; Zimmerman & Bergan, 1971), even in the early grades many teachers still see their role as that of fact provider and extractor. But with factual knowledge increasing at a phenomenal rate, it appears that learning time is better spent on developing underlying concept-formation abilities and processes for dealing with facts rather than emphasizing mainly facts themselves.

In the past the problem with developing these abilities in children was that teachers felt unsure of what the processes involved. Since they were uncertain, they tended to teach colors and names of shapes because they knew that at least children could pass certain tests if they possessed this particular information. Thanks to Piaget, however, we are now beginning to have a more adequate grasp of what some of these concept formation skills are; therefore, the task of building a cognitive curriculum is not so difficult or mysterious as we once surmised.

CONSTRUCTING THE COGNITIVE CURRICULUM

Now that we have reviewed the priorities for maintaining and fostering curiosity (keeping learning pleasurable, linking feelings and language to cognitive learning, gearing learning to the correct developmental level, and including reasoning along with learning facts), the next step is to learn how to actually

"But what makes the water come out?"

develop a curriculum that will be fun, interesting, and age appropriate. This curriculum also needs to provide many opportunities for children to practice thinking and reasoning skills.

It is easiest to think of this kind of curriculum as having three steps. First, there is the basic foundation on which the other two steps rest. It consists of the topic the teacher picks to provide a thread of consistency to the curriculum. (In elementary school this is sometimes called a *unit*, but units tend to be so fact oriented I would prefer to avoid that term and call it the *focus* or *theme*.) It is terribly important that the topic be interesting to the children, so it is best to choose one based on their current interests.

The second step of the cognitive curriculum includes the facts about the topic the teacher and children find out together. As we shall see later, Piaget termed this *physical* knowledge, and it consists of all sorts of information about all sorts of things.

Step III provides all the opportunities for children to think and reason. That's crucial, of course, but Steps I and II are just as vital because Step III is only successful if the children are interested in the subject and if they have some facts to use as a basis for practicing their thinking skills.

At the preschool level, these thinking skills include being able to tell whether things are the same or different, deciding which items belong in the same group or are closely related, arranging objects in order, and understanding simple cause-and-effect relationships.

The First Step: Identifying What Interests the Children and Choosing That Topic as a Focus for the Curriculum

The best way to find out what the children are interested in is to observe their play. They may be interested in trucks and tunnels and cars out in the sandbox, or they may be on a baking spree in the same area. Or perhaps one of the girls has had a high fever and lost some of her hair, and the children are concerned and interested in hair as a result, or perhaps a subdivision is being built next door to the school, or maybe several mothers are expecting babies. These are the kinds of interests that are quite directly revealed in the dramatic play of children (remember, dramatic play happens all over the school, not just in the housekeeping corner), and it is this sort of topic with its rich relevance to the children's lives that is best chosen for expansion in curriculum. The advantages are numerous: the curriculum will surely be related to the children's interests; using the children's ideas enhances their feeling of being valued; such a topic almost always includes the home in some way; and, for all these reasons, the children are almost bound to enjoy it. (Remember what we said about the value of making learning pleasurable?)

The children's interests are also wonderful sources for those quick, spontaneous learning situations that arise each day. The teacher who quickly fits a caterpillar poem to a fuzzy visitor or produces the hospital kit for a potential tonsil patient increases his own pleasure in teaching as well as the satisfaction of the children in being at school.

The real problem with spontaneity, or excessive reliance on spur-of-the-moment curriculum, is that the children may gain only small pepperings of factual knowledge on a multitude of subjects and lack an overall sense of integration and direction in what they learn. In addition, it may mean that some valuable opportunities for practice of more specific reasoning abilities are not provided, since the fortuitous nature of these curriculum "happenings" makes advance planning impossible. Improvisation in developing Step III thinking and reasoning curriculum can be difficult for all but the most experienced teacher.

The Second Step: Developing the Factual Part of the Curriculum

Once a genuine interest of the children has been identified, it is time to advance to Step II of the curriculum. Most teachers of young children are good at

Learning about the cycle of life via a rotting pumpkin is a good example of expanding the factual aspect of the curriculum. What would need to be discussed to develop the same activity into a thinking and reasoning experience?

developing this level. Step II typically involves teaching interesting facts to children and is also likely to involve reading books, setting out interesting displays, singing songs, taking field trips, and having many experience-based learning opportunities centered on a particular topic. I think of this as *horizontal* curriculum because it seems to me to spread out flatly into widening circles of information and participation from the basic interest areas, rather the way dropping a stone into a quiet pool creates ripples of water moving outward from it. A "focus" in curriculum provides the energy for waves of interest to spread out from it in various directions while remaining centered about the subject at the same time.

Thus, if children are studying birds, many different experiences involving every avenue of the senses are provided. These might include hatching out a chicken, making suet bird feeders, bringing in old nests to examine, making deviled eggs, raising a baby duck, keeping parakeets, or visiting an aviary. The list of possibilities is endless. The experiences are typically accompanied by language that identifies and labels different aspects of the experience. For example, the children may learn a number of words, such as *feathers, wings, hatch, droppings, sea gulls,* and *robins.* Many schools also add books, songs, pictures, and poetry, which widen the experience and, happily, encourage the use of symbolic representations as well.

This fact-oriented curriculum provides the children with an excellent opportunity for reality-based experiences about what birds are actually like and is indispensable, as anyone who has ever felt the underside of a setting hen knows. Words alone can never equal the adventure of slipping a hand between the eggs and the warm softness of that irritable chicken.

Additional advantages of this broadening development of subject matter include the fact that teachers can select the next experience in accordance with the children's interest as it develops from the previous one (Katz & Chard, 1989). For example, a teacher might go on to investigating things that fly by visiting the airport, building kites, and blowing up balloons with some youngsters, or by visiting the myna bird at the zoo and bringing a parrot to school for other children who have become interested in how birds talk. Thus the strengths of Step II, the factual curriculum, are that it is relevant to the real interests of the children (unless teachers become carried away with their own interests and enthusiasm and lose sight of the children's concerns), is based on actual experience, results in the acquisition of facts and information, can be used to develop language ability, and is also satisfying to teachers, because it draws on their own creative powers to present experiences that are attractive, integrated, and varied.

With all these virtues it is easy to understand why many teachers stop at this point and do not go on to Step III, which has to do with fostering less familiar conceptual abilities. *But children need more than the opportunity to acquire the rich experience and vocabulary that Step II curriculum provides; they also need the chance to do some thinking.* For this reason the third aspect of curriculum development must not be overlooked.

The Third Step: Developing the Reasoning/Thinking Part of the Curriculum

The third step in the development of cognitive curriculum is termed *vertical* because it builds from the tangible, indispensable, experiential foundations provided by the horizontal curriculum of Step II and uses those facts and experiences as a means of practicing skills. *At this level the subject matter is just the medium through which the skills are taught:* it becomes the means to an intellectual end.

For example,* one of the more useful mental abilities for young children to develop is the ability to sort groups according to a common property. This is the earliest form of classification and an important precursor to mathematical and other reasoning skills. To provide practice in this, the teacher might give the children little models of birds and other animals to sort, or older preschoolers could be asked in a playful, riddlelike way to begin to define what a bird is and what it is not. "Are kites birds? Oh, they aren't! How do you know? Well, then, what about airplanes—are they birds?" Or if he wanted the children to practice

---

*Ways of presenting such experiences are discussed in much greater detail later in the chapter; these examples are only for the purpose of illustration.

temporal sequencing (the order in which events occur in time), he might use pictures taken while the chicks hatched and ask the children to tell the story of what happened while arranging these in order. Or he could help the children understand cause and effect by comparing a raw egg with a poached one and then encouraging them to propose and test out possible reasons for the hardening and propose additional ways they might make an egg hard.

In all these examples the subject matter (birds, chicks, and eggs) is really used as the means of providing practice in thinking and reasoning skills rather than just for the purpose of teaching facts about it. Unfortunately, many nursery school teachers do not understand the value of this kind of instruction and settle for teaching only factual information. This is regrettable, because facts can change and the amount of available information is growing by such leaps and bounds that none of us can keep up. Besides that, many children from low-income homes do not receive exposure to this kind of mental activity at home. For all these reasons it is really valuable for the teacher to provide children with opportunities to develop mental abilities that enable them to *deal* with the facts, rather than just stuffing them full of information.

The inclusion of Step III reasoning and thinking learning at the preschool level is not difficult once it is understood, but it does require careful planning by the teacher, and this rests in turn on a clear knowledge of what he is doing and what conceptual skills he is seeking to enhance. It also requires that he participate actively with the children, since it is necessary not only to develop learning materials but also to talk with the children while they are using the materials and to ask them questions that encourage them to think. As Kamii (1973) so aptly puts it, "The art is to ask the right question at the right time so the learner can build his own knowledge" (p. 203). It is this building of one's own knowledge that lies at the heart of what is spoken of as *constructivist education.* Children of preprimary age need this assistance in order to focus clearly on the task at hand.

SUMMARY

There are, then, three steps to include when building a cognitive curriculum for preschool children. The first and vital step is to choose subjects that are of particular interest to the children being taught. The second step, the development of a factual information base, deals with expanding the child's informational horizon, increasing her labeling vocabulary, and so forth. The third step, the development of thinking and reasoning skills, uses the materials, facts, and experience acquired in Step II but uses them for a different purpose. The purpose of Step III, the thinking and reasoning curriculum, is to provide opportunities for children to practice and develop such mental abilities as basic grouping and classification skills, the concept of temporal ordering, and the ability to reason about cause and effect.

A well-rounded cognitive curriculum requires that teachers appreciate and include all three of these curriculum steps when they plan their educational program.

QUESTIONS AND ACTIVITIES

1. What are some of the pros and cons of stressing intellectual development at the preschool level? Can you suggest a model for such learning that you feel would have undesirable side effects?

2. Do you agree that pleasure should be the inevitable accompaniment to learning? Can you think of occasions where this has been true of your educational experience and cases where it has not been true? Analyze the circumstances that made the learning pleasurable or burdensome.

3. Might it be possible that preprimary teachers are depriving children of the right to learn the things that would help them succeed best in elementary school when we stress play, creativity, and mental health rather than emphasizing such skills as learning the alphabet and counting? What might be the case for placing greater emphasis on academic learning at the preschool level?

SELF-CHECK QUESTIONS FOR REVIEW

Content-Related Questions

1. What are some ingredients of a school climate that are likely to encourage the growth of autonomy and the willingness to venture?

2. Describe some things teachers can do that will help cognitive learning be a source of genuine pleasure to the children.

3. Does work on cognitive learning mean that the teacher should ignore what is going on emotionally and socially between the children?

4. What are the three steps involved in constructing the cognitive area of curriculum, and why is each step an important element to include?

Integrative Questions

1. One of the 3-year-olds in your room notices some bird tracks in the snow when the children go out to play. Suggest some spontaneous activities you could do with her that would encourage her to interact with the snow herself and investigate further how the bird tracks were made. Now demonstrate that you understand the difference DeVries and Kohlberg make between active involvement and more passive interest by suggesting a couple of things you could do where the child did not take action herself.

2. On that same snowy day, the children are fascinated with the snow itself because it's the first snow of winter. What are some activities you could do with them that would provide some learning while remaining real fun for the children? Be sure to identify what the children would be learning and why you think they will enjoy the experiences.

3. Select a spontaneous interest a child has brought up in the group you teach, and suggest some Step II activities that could add to the child's information base about that subject.

REFERENCES FOR FURTHER READING

Building Desirable Attitudes Toward Learning

Ashton-Warner, S. (1965). *Teacher*. New York: Bantam Books. Sylvia Ashton-Warner gives an exciting description of the way she approached teaching and learning and made these activities truly relevant to the lives of her young Maori students.

Bradbard, M. R., & Endsley, R. C. (1982). How can teachers develop young children's curiosity? In J. F. Brown (Ed.), *Curriculum planning for young children*. Washington, DC: National Association for the Education of Young Children. An excellent review of research is included here with implications for teachers following each portion of the review.

Development of the Brain

Brierley, J. (1987). *Give me a child until he is seven*. New York: Falmer Press. In this very good book Brierley explains what is known about principles of brain physiology and development. The author includes discussions about the educational implications of this information for teachers of young children. *Highly recommended.*

Healey, J. M. (1987). *Your child's growing mind: A parent's guide to learning from birth to adolescence*. Garden City, NY: Doubleday. This sensible book discusses everything from how the brain develops to lateralization and learning to read.

Encouraging Children to Explore Their World

Crabtree, B. (1982). *Challenges for children: Discovering science together*. Auckland: New Zealand Playcentre Federation (PO Box 67-085, Auckland, New Zealand). This is a delightful book that is well worth sending for. It includes lots of practical, inexpensive, intriguing ideas for children to explore.

Harlan, J. D. (1988). *Science experiences for the early childhood years* (4th ed.). Columbus, OH: Merrill. I recommend this book as being a particularly rich source of curriculum-related ideas, including music, fingerplays, lists of children's books, creative ideas, and examples of "thinking games." Helpful for developing Step II activities.

Katz, L., & Chard, S. C. (1989). *Engaging children's minds: The project approach*. Norwood, NJ: Ablex. Among many useful topics discussed is the discussion of "webbing," which demonstrates how interest in one subject can lead to further ones. An excellent example of how to build Step II curriculum.

McIntyre, M. (1984). *Early childhood and science*. Washington, DC: National Science Teachers Association. This is a collection of brief articles about all sorts of possible science experiences and how to present them. The presentation is low key and age appropriate. *Highly recommended.*

For the Advanced Student

Deci, E. L., & Ryan, R. M. (1982). *Curiosity and self-directed learning: The role of motivation in education*. In L. G. Katz (Ed.), *Current topics in early childhood education* (Vol. 4). Norwood, NJ: Ablex. Deci and Ryan are primarily concerned with the role of intrinsic motivation. They hypothesize that children who are intrinsically motivated because of interest, rather than extrinsically motivated because of external rewards, will be more curious, self-motivated learners.

DeVries, R., & Kohlberg, L. (1990). *Constructivist early education: Overview and comparison with other programs*. Washington, DC: National Association for the Education of Young Children. The authors emphasize the importance of active learning, the value of cognitive conflict, and the virtue of figuring out (constructing) knowledge for oneself.

CHAPTER 19

Developing Thinking and Reasoning Skills: Part II

In classrooms that encourage natural, spontaneous, lively, intense curiosity in an environment of interesting and challenging materials, children will gain experiences needed for developing both linguistic and mathematical concepts. For example, by using dough, they may experience that which is alike *(one dough ball is like another). In using sand, they understand things that are* not alike *(wet sand is not like dry sand). The environment can yield other experiences: objects that are* patterned *(a brick wall is patterned, children's chants are patterned): events that follow a* sequence *(story comes after snack);* parts *and* wholes *(cutting apples, oranges, and bananas for salad); things that have* direction *(a pulley lifts the pail up); objects that have* size, weight, texture.

—Nancy Balaban (1984)

Have you ever wondered . . .

Why studying Piaget is so important?

What specific mental abilities could be worked on at the preschool level that would build a foundation for later success in primary school?

How to include practice in these abilities and keep it fun, too?

If you have, the material in the following pages will help you.

S ince the third step in the construction of cognitive curriculum is the most poorly understood by many teachers, this chapter concentrates on this aspect. However, the reader should bear in mind that the following material is only the last of three steps in such planning and that the other two are also important.

As I have indicated from time to time, teachers who have yearned to teach more than the names of colors or go beyond teaching such limited concepts as "The ball is on the table" versus "The ball is under the table" have had considerable difficulty identifying just what mental abilities they should select when working with young children. Fortunately, in the past few years some of this problem has been resolved by the work of Jean Piaget.

BASIC CONCEPTS OF PIAGETIAN PSYCHOLOGY

Although it is not within the scope of this book to attempt a comprehensive summary of Piaget's work, any discussion of the thought processes of young children must begin with at least a brief review of his work, since he devoted a lifetime to studying the mental development and characteristics of young children (Piaget, 1926, 1930, 1950, 1962, 1963, 1965, 1983; Piaget & Inhelder, 1967, 1969). He was primarily interested in how people come to know what they know—the origins of knowledge—and his work has important implications for teachers who are interested in the cognitive development of the children in their care.

Many of Piaget's ideas are bound to sound both familiar and comfortable to the contemporary student, since a good deal of what he said for 60 years has been practiced in nursery centers during the same period and is similar in part to the philosophy of Dewey and Montessori (because of its emphasis on the value of experience). For a variety of reasons, however, his work passed largely unnoticed in the United States until the 1960s, and it is only since then that it has been deliberately implemented in the preschool classroom by such investigators as Almy (Almy et al., 1966), DeVries (DeVries & Kohlberg, 1990), Forman and Hill (1980), Kamii (1975, 1982, 1985), Lavatelli (1970a, 1970b), Saunders and Bingham-Newman (1984), and Weikart (Hohmann, Banet, & Weikart, 1979).

Although his own realm of investigation was primarily in the cognitive area, Piaget agreed that affective, social, and cognitive components go hand in hand (Piaget, 1981; Wadsworth, 1989). Since these components are interdependent, it is evident that a school where good mental health policies are practiced and where sound social learning is encouraged will also be one where mental growth is more likely to occur (Weber, 1984).

Piagetian Categories of Knowledge

Piaget theorized that children acquire three kinds of knowledge as they grow. *Social-conventional knowledge* is the first kind. This is information that society has agreed on and that is often learned through direct social transmission. For example, English-speaking people agree that the word *table* stands for a large flat object with four legs. Rules that define what acceptable behavior is provide another example of socially transmitted knowledge.

The second kind of knowledge is *physical knowledge.* It is information children gain by acting on objects in the real world. Information about the quality of things and what they do are examples of physical knowledge.

The third kind of knowledge is less tangible because it cannot be directly observed. It is knowledge that is developed (constructed) in the mind of the child as she thinks about objects. Piaget calls this *logico-mathematical knowledge.* The development of logico-mathematical thought, which we might also think of as being the ability to reason, ultimately enables children to develop ideas of relationships between objects. When they can grasp what it is that items in a group have in common, for instance, they are able to assign a common name to that group, thereby classifying or grouping the things together. For example, they might divide a set of pictures, sorting them into things you can wear and things you eat and name the groups clothing and food. As Kamii (1985) points out, this idea of a common property exists only in the mind. It is not inherent in the pictures themselves; it is an *idea*, not a physical property. It is important to remember that reasoning knowledge is closely tied to physical knowledge since reasoning usually requires a foundation of factual information, but it also differs from factual information.

This division of knowledge into external, factual knowledge and knowledge that results from reasoning should sound familiar since it closely parallels our previous discussions of fact and thought questions and Step II factual and Step III thinking and reasoning learning.

It is this gradual development of Step III logico-mathematical ability that frees children from being tied to concrete experience because it enables them to think with symbols and deal with abstractions. It takes many years for children to reach that level of maturity, however. In order to attain it, Piaget and colleagues identified a series of stages through which they must pass as they develop. These stages are outlined in Table 19.1.

Research conducted over a period of more than 60 years convinced Piaget that the order of the stages through which children progress cannot be changed, although the age at which the stage occurs may vary. He demonstrated this convincingly in his detailed reports of investigations he conducted in which he presented problems to children and then asked them questions about their answers.

Piagetian Stages of Development

Of greatest interest to early childhood teachers is the preoperational stage that extends roughly from age 2 to age 7. During this stage children make the profound transition from depending on the way things appear to depending on logic and reasoning when making a decision. They become able to keep two ideas in their minds at once. In other words, children acquire the ability to think

TABLE 19.1 Summary of the Piagetian model

Basic Stages in Developing the Ability to Think Logically	Behavior Commonly Associated with the Stage
Sensorimotor Stage (0–2 years)* Understanding the present and real	Composed of six substages that move from reflex to intentional activity, involving cause-effect behavior Involves direct interactions with the environment
Preoperational Stage (2–7 years) Symbolic representation of the present and real Preparation for understanding concrete operations (this is a tremendous period of transition)	Overt action is transformed into mental action. Child uses signifiers: mental images, imitation, symbolic play, drawing, language to deal with experience Understands verbal communication Uses play to assimilate reality into herself Believes what she sees; is "locked into" the perceptual world Sees things from her own point of view, only one way at a time ("centering") and is learning to decanter Thinking is not reversible. Intensely curious about the world Busy laying foundations for understanding at the later concrete operations stage, which involves grasping concepts of *conservation, transitivity, classification, seriation,* and *reversibility*
Concrete Operational Stage (7–11 years) Attainment of and organization of concrete operations Learns to apply logical thought to concrete problems	Has probably acquired the following concepts: *conservation, reversibility, transitivity, seriation,* and *classification;* that is, now believes that length, mass, weight, and number remain constant; understands relational terms such as *larger than* and *smaller than;* is able to arrange items in order from greatest amount to least amount; can group things according to more than one principle; can manipulate things in her mind, but these things are real objects. Becomes interested in following rules; games are important.
Formal Operational Stage (11–15 years) Hypothesis-making and testing possible Masters logical reasoning	Age of abstract thinking; logical reasoning Able to consider alternative possibilities and solutions Can consider "fanciful," hypothetical possibilities as a basis for theoretical problem solving; abstract thinking, can make logical deductions and generalizations; can think about thinking

*Note that the ages represent the *average* age of acquisition. This means that there is considerable variability in the time different children acquire the ability.

Beginning seriation requires the understanding of size relationships.

back to the original starting point and at the same time compare it in their minds to a current situation. Piaget calls this mental operation *reversibility*, and it is a good example of what is meant when we say the child is freed from concrete experience, since she performs this logico-mathematical reasoning process in her mind (Weber, 1984).

But young children who are in the preoperational stage do not possess this ability. Because they cannot consider two possibilities at once, they are unable to *conserve*; that is, they do not understand that quantity stays the same despite a change in appearance. This is because they cannot keep one idea in their minds while considering a second one. Thus they are likely to believe that a taller jar contains more water than a shorter jar does, even though they had previously been shown that the quantity was the same before pouring. For preoperational children, seeing is believing (Resnick, 1989).

At this stage, also, children may have difficulty shifting objects into more than one kind of category (sorting according to size and then shifting to color, for example), taking two attributes into account at the same time, (sorting large pink circles and pink squares, small blue circles and blue squares into separate categories), or arranging a long series of graduated cylinders in regularly ascending order. Adults, however, no longer have difficulty grasping these concepts. This difference in the way children and adults think illustrates an important Piagetian principle—the thinking of children and adults differs in kind from each other. Children reason differently from the way adults do.

Additional Basic Concepts of Value

Although Piaget has been criticized on such grounds as inconsistency of theory, obscure terminology, and poor scientific rigor, and although his work is consistently subjected to further critical evaluation and testing (Gardner, 1986; Siegel & Brainerd, 1978; Thomas, 1985), there is little doubt that despite these weaknesses he made many significant contributions to our understanding of the growth of children's mental abilities. Among these contributions is the idea that mental development is a dynamic process that results from the interaction of the child with her environment. The child acts on her own world, and by means of interaction with it she constructs her own knowledge (DeVries & Kohlberg, 1990). This is why Piaget favored the saying that construction is superior to instruction (Thomas, 1985). This close observer of children maintained that they use language and play to represent reality, and for this reason he emphasized the extraordinary value of play as a basic avenue through which young children learn (1932). Finally, he stressed the importance of actual involvement of children with materials (as compared to observation and teacher explanation) and the significance of experience as a medium for learning.

At present, it appears that in addition to his general theoretical ideas, his identification of significant cognitive concepts and the steps and means by which they develop may be the most helpful contribution he has made to our understanding of the cognitive self. It is this understanding that makes it possible for teachers to generate a curriculum for stimulating the growth of cognitive abilities rather than merely teaching children an endless array of facts.

From a Piagetian Perspective, What Can Teachers Do to Help Children Develop Fully at Each Cognitive Stage?

Of course, it is neither desirable nor even possible to accelerate children markedly through the stages of cognitive development. This practice of overpressure is called *hothousing* and robs children of their childhood (Elkind, 1987; Sigel, 1987). What teachers should do instead is assist children to develop richly and fully at each stage, thereby paving the way for successful attainment of the next stage at the appropriate time.

Piaget maintained there are four factors that work together to promote cognitive growth. These are *maturation, experience, socialization,* and *equilibration.* The thinking teacher can make a helpful contribution to each of these factors as he leads children through the day.

For example, physical maturation underlies cognitive maturation, and the good health practices followed by children's centers can make a definite contribution to physical development by providing the sound nutrition, rest, and physical activity so necessary for the child's growing body to thrive.

Second, the provision of real experience with the physical world so stressed by Piaget is an essential cornerstone of early childhood education (Williams & Kamii, 1986). These experiences should include many opportunities for children to arrange things in order, to return things to their prior state, and to group them according to their common properties *as well as the chance to talk about why they have put them in particular configurations.* Opportunities for exploring other relationships such as cause and effect, as well as the basic skill of telling same from different, should also be included. (The remainder of this chapter presents many examples of ways such experiences may be integrated into the daily life of the school.)

Socialization, too, is something most early childhood teachers know a good deal about. Here, however, there is a special point that requires emphasis when discussing cognition from a Piagetian point of view. Whereas preschool teachers often think of socialization as lying in the realm of teaching children how to get along together or teaching them language (a profoundly useful social skill), Piaget thought of socialization as having another important facet. He maintained that interaction between children, particularly discussion, which he termed *argument,* is of extraordinary importance. It is through such exchanges of ideas that children test and modify what they think. And these modifications of what they think lead to the fourth factor that influences cognitive growth— equilibration.

Equilibration is the mechanism that brings maturation, experience, and social interaction into balance. It is the mechanism by which the child regulates her ideas (Wadsworth, 1989) and "puts things all together."

So if the teacher wishes to strengthen cognitive growth, in addition to providing optimum opportunities for physical maturation and real experience, he should also encourage dialog *among* the children (as well as carrying out discussions between himself and the children). The results will be that children figure out more things for themselves. This enables them to coordinate their existing knowledge with their newly acquired knowledge by exercising the faculty of equilibration.

Thus, when the children complain that it's no fun to swing because their feet drag on the ground, instead of obligingly shortening the swing, he might ask the children to propose what might be done to change that situation. Could they make their legs shorter? Could they stand up in the swing instead? Could someone push them so they could hold their legs out straight? Or . . . ? Children can think up and debate many possibilities once provided with the chance to do so. Such discussions and proposed solutions enable children to construct knowledge for themselves, construction that is so much more valuable than instruction.

WHY CHOOSE THESE PARTICULAR MENTAL ABILITY SKILLS?

The abilities selected for discussion in the following pages were chosen because they provide children with a valuable foundation for success in elementary school.

Piaget argued that the gradual development of such abilities underlies progression from the preoperational stage to that of concrete operations, wherein children become capable of more advanced logico-mathematical reasoning; but there are also some more ordinary ways these skills provide valuable foundations for later successful functioning. Table 19.2 provides an analysis of some of these.

It is useful for teachers to keep this information well in mind so that when parents want to know what the children are learning that will help them in school, the teacher can give clear, well-informed explanations. For example, matching (being able to tell whether things are the same or different) is an important prerequisite for being able to read. If one cannot tell the difference between *d* and *b*, how can one tell the difference between *dog* and *bog?* Grouping (identifying the common property of several nonidentical items) underlies the concept of class inclusion, which is necessary for understanding set theory. Grouping is also an essential element of such sciences as botany, where classification is very important. Seriation (arranging things in regular, graduated order) gives real meaning to enumeration. Finally, common relations (the ability to identify pairs of items associated together) helps children learn to draw analogies. This fascinating ability to move from one known relationship to a second by perceiving parallels in the two sets involves transferring ideas and making such new linkages. It is surely an indispensable element in creative thought.

Each of these concepts develops over time by building on lower-level concepts. One teacher presents this explanation of progression as follows:

> Thus, grouping begins with an understanding of the concepts of same and dif-ferent and the ability to match identical objects, followed by the ability to see similarities across different objects. Gradually children develop the awareness that one object may belong to several possible groups (red, round, and big) and thus can begin to understand matrices (for example, arranging objects in rows by color and in columns by shape). Not until elementary school do they fully comprehend hierarchical classification (dogs and cats are animals; animals, peo-ple and trees are living things) and class inclusion (all dogs are animals, but not all animals are dogs).

TABLE 19.2 Links between basic mental abilities and later school-related skills

Ability	Value
Matching: Can identify which things are the same and which things are different Basic question: Can you find the pair that is exactly the same?	The ability to discriminate is crucial to development of other mental abilities. An important aspect of gaining literacy: discriminate between letters (such as m and w). Promotes understanding of equality. Encourages skill in figure/ground perception (separating a significant figure from the background).
Grouping: Can identify common property that forms a group or class Basic question: Can you show me the things that belong to the same family?	Fosters mathematical understanding: set theory and equivalency. Children must discriminate, reason, analyze, and select in order to formulate groups. Regrouping encourages flexibility of thought. Depending on manner of presentation, may foster divergent thinking—more than one way to group items. Requires use of accommodation and assimilation. Classification is a basic unit of life sciences: allows people to organize knowledge.
Common relations: Can identify common property or relationship between a nonidentical pair Basic question: Which thing goes most closely with what other thing?	Fosters mathematical understanding: one-to-one correspondence. Fosters diversity of understanding concepts: many kinds of pairs (opposites, cause-effect, congruent). Can teach use of analogies and riddles.
Cause and effect: Can determine what makes something else happen: a special case of common relations Basic question: What makes something else happen?	Basis for scientific investigations. Conveys sense of order of world. Conveys sense of individual's ability to be effective: act on his world and produce results, make things happen. Encourages use of prediction and generation of hypotheses. Introduces child to elementary understanding of the scientific method.
Seriation: Can identify what comes next in a graduated series Basic question: What comes next?	Fosters mathematical understanding. Relationship between quantities: counting (enumeration) with understanding, one-to-one correspondence, equivalency, estimation. If teacher presents series going from left to right, fosters basic reading skill.
Temporal ordering: Can identify logical order of events occurring in time Basic question: What comes next?	Fosters mathematical understanding. Conveys a sense of order and a sense of time and its effect. Relationship between things: cause-and-effect and other relationships. Prediction. Requires memory: what happened first, then what happened?
Conservation: Can understand that a substance can return to its prior state and that quantity is not affected by mere changes in appearance Basic question: Are they still the same quantity?	Idea of constancy (reversibility) is fundamental as a foundation for logical reasoning, basic for scientific understanding; it is also the basis for mathematical calculations involving length, volume, area, and so forth.

Making comparisons (with a little play along the side) is a fundamental reasoning skill.

Seriation requires, first of all, an understanding of absolute size (big and small), followed by relative size concepts and the ability to compare sizes (this is bigger than that). As with grouping, children must learn that an object can have multiple size designations (bigger than some things and smaller than others). This leads to the ability to seriate, first by trial and error and with a few objects, and then without hesitation, with any number of objects. Awareness of these developmental progressions can help a teacher assess where children are in their thinking and what activities would be appropriate for them.*

Practice in these abilities entails the use of and practice in some additional mental skills which must be so generally employed that they apply to all the abilities. These are listed here rather than being repeated in Table 19.2. They include the ability to pay attention, observe carefully, make comparisons, and use symbols (representations) in place of actual objects. The symbols might consist of models, pictures, language, or simply imaginary items as is done in play (Dyson, 1990). A base of factual knowledge is also needed, as was pointed

*I wish to thank Jean Phinney of California State University at Los Angeles for contributing this explanation of developmental progressions.

out previously in the discussion of Step II factual learning. Memory skills are also called into action, as is the ability to generalize.

I want to stress once again, however, that the purpose of including the following material on developing reasoning skills is not to foster precocity in young children. It is included because experience has taught me that hardly any preprimary teachers possess a framework that identifies significant mental abilities or explains how to go about fostering these skills in young children. Although teachers may use a few lotto games that give practice in matching or grouping, or talk from time to time about the order in which something has happened, offering these activities seems to be haphazard and fortuitous rather than part of a deliberate, coordinated plan. This *may* be all right for middle-class children who seem to absorb skills through their pores, but it is unforgivable for the large group of preschool youngsters who, though possessing other strengths, apparently lack experience with these aspects of learning in their daily lives. Quite literally, teachers need to get their own heads together on the subject of cognitive development so that they can systematically and regularly provide opportunities for practice of these mental abilities at a developmentally appropriate level. (Incidentally, all the activities suggested in the following sections have been used over and over with preschool age children in our center and at the Institute of Child Development as well as by students in other preschools, so we know they are not too difficult.*) It is my hope that regular exposure to these kinds of activities will furnish all children with beginning thinking and reasoning skills that will stand them in good stead as they move on to the next stage of intellectual development.

Note that the following descriptions of activities include suggestions for children who are less advanced as well as ones for those who are more mature. They also stress that a diversity of experiences should be offered, including large muscle activities. All too often this kind of education is limited to small muscle, tabletop experiences, which is most unfortunate.

THINKING AND REASONING SKILLS THAT SHOULD BE INCLUDED IN STEP III CURRICULUM

Matching

Matching is the ability to perceive that two items are *identical*, and it depends on the child's grasping the concept of sameness and differentness. At our center we have found that this is one of the easier concepts for young children to acquire. Even 2- and 3-year-olds will work at this occupation with interest and diligence if the materials are attractive and not too detailed.

---

*For a more detailed discussion of research projects dealing with teaching some of these abilities, see Hendrick (1973) or Safford (1978). The research of Meeker, Sexton, and Richardson (1970) also contains many specific examples of teaching strategies, although these focus on elementary-aged children.

Many commercial materials are available that may be used to provide practice in matching. These range from simple, obvious pictures with few details to quite elaborate discrimination tasks that contain a great deal of detail and subtle differences. Lotto and bingo games are probably the most prevalent examples of such materials. But matching should not be limited to these kinds of activities. Younger children can grasp this concept by matching buttons (a perennial favorite), matching animal stamps or stickers, or playing simple picture dominoes. Fabric swatches and wallpaper samples are also fun to use for this purpose and can be surprisingly difficult. Incidentally, putting blocks back so that all of one kind go in the same place is a matching *not* grouping exercise, because the blocks are identical.

Matching experiences need not be limited to the sense of vision, of course. Children will also enjoy matching by touch (for texture and thickness), by hearing (duplicating simple sounds, rhythms, or melodies), and by taste and smell (it is interesting to cut up a variety of white fruits and vegetables, for instance, and ask the children to taste bits of them and find the ones that are the same). Imitation can also be thought of as an attempt to match actions; shadow or mirror dancing, "Follow the Leader," and "Simon Says" may be employed for this purpose. Large muscle activities may be further incorporated by setting out two or three pictures and choosing a youngster to walk over to match one of them with the picture in her hand. (She then has the privilege of picking the next child to do this.) Children who are proficient at pumping may be asked if they can match the arc of their swings with that of the child beside them.

When asking children to complete a match, the teacher should use sentences such as "Show me the one that matches" or "Find me one that's just the same" rather than "Show me two that are just alike," since an occasional child is misled by the term *alike* and will blithely select something to show the teacher, saying, "Here, I like this one best!" Once she has acquired this verbal misconception of what the teacher means, it can be difficult to get her to change her mind; so talking about *same* rather than *alike* is the more effective choice of language.

As the child becomes more skilled, matching tasks may be increased in difficulty by making the matches more complex and difficult to analyze. This is usually accomplished by increasing the number of details that must be inspected in each picture and also by increasing the number of items to be compared. Ultimately the material shifts from depending on pictorially meaningful content to more symbolic form. This leads, finally, to using the symbols of the alphabet and numbers.

I use the word *grouping* here in place of *classification* to remind the reader that we are discussing an elementary form of the more sophisticated skill described by Piaget (1965) wherein older children can form hierarchical classes or classify items according to a number of properties at the same time. Preschool children perform at a simpler level than classification, but 4- and 5-year-olds in particular are able to sort objects or pictures into categories meaningful to them. For example, I recall what happened when we were using companion animals as our focus for the week and invited the children to bring their pets to visit. When I asked Millie what kind of dog she had brought, she paused for a moment in thought and then replied, "Well, she's half collie—and half female."

Other examples of meaningful categorizing range from placing dollhouse furniture into rooms according to their function (kitchen equipment in the kitchen, for example) to sorting shells according to whether they are clams or mussels or pectins, rough or smooth, large or small. Teachers encourage categorizing every time they ask children, "Are airplanes birds? Why not?" or say "Show me all the buttons that belong together." In these instances the child is being asked to determine what it is that various items have in common—to determine the common property that defines the class—and then she is usually expected to decide whether an additional item also possesses this property and can be included.

In essence there are three ways to present such material. First, the child can be confronted with an assembled group and asked to choose things to add to it (perhaps it is pictures of clothing such as a sweater, dress, and shirt, and the additional pictures might be a doll, a pair of pants, and an ice cream cone). Second, she can be presented with an assembled group and asked to remove items that do not belong. ("Everyone who isn't wearing a plaid top, sit down.") Finally, she can be given a melange of articles or pictures and asked to sort them according to whatever criteria *she* establishes. *This third kind of presentation permits more divergent thinking* than the first two do and has the additional advantage of making regrouping according to different criteria more feasible.

Four-year-olds are rarely able to put their reasons for forming such groups into words at the beginning of the learning experience, although they can indicate by the sorting activity itself that they do perceive common properties. At our center we have found that many of them gradually learn to explain why particular items go together as they practice, or they become able to name the class or group they have in mind (Hendrick, 1973). Thus a child who is inarticulate in the fall may by spring put a toy frog, turtle, and fish together and be able to tell us that she did this because they all like water or because "they're swimmey things."

Even though many children will at first be unable to put the reason for grouping particular things together into words, the category may be obvious to the onlooker. If a child is unable to formulate a reply after she has assembled a group, the teacher can help by saying, "Hmmmm, it looks to me as though you are putting all the red ones here and the blue ones here. Is that what you're doing?" This assists the child in translating her actions into words.

It is wise to encourage the child to determine the categories for herself whenever possible. If the teacher hands a child a box of little animals and tells her to "pick out all the red ones" or to "pick out all the ones we saw at the zoo," he has done most of the thinking for her before she goes to work. But if he says, "Show me which ones you think belong together" and follows this with, "Why do they go

Using a "secret" box can add a lot of fun to mental ability activities.

together?" the child must do more of the thinking for herself. This is quite different from and more valuable than expecting the child to "discover" the category the teacher has thought up.

Of course, it is not necessary to limit "grouping" activities to small muscle experiences. Every time children are asked to show how many different ways they can run or to choose what equipment they need to play house with in the sandbox, they are essentially thinking of things that fit a particular category or class just as they are determining categories when the teacher asks them, "Do you think the wheelbarrow should be kept with the wagons and scooters or with the garden equipment?" Additional practice is also provided by asking older 4- and young 5-year-olds to select three or four children from the group who are wearing something similar—boots, perhaps, or plaid clothing—and then have the rest of the children guess what it is they have in common.

Piaget has noted that younger children will change categories as they sort. This is a natural phenomenon and does not mean they are unintelligent. Maturation combined with opportunities to practice and talk about grouping will help the children learn to maintain consistent criteria.

Occasionally teachers become confused and attempt to teach grouping by using identical items for this purpose. Although being able to pick out things that are exactly the same and to tell them apart from those that are different is a useful literacy skill, it is not grouping; it is simple matching. *To teach grouping it is necessary to use materials that possess common properties but are not identical.*

The easiest form of grouping is sorting that requires simple responses to a prominent sensory quality such as color (Lavatelli, 1970a, 1970b). Some children at the center will need to begin at this level, but this is only the beginning. The task may be made more difficult by asking the children to think of a way the materials can be regrouped, by using more complex materials, by increasing the emphasis on verbalization, or by asking them to group materials according to several properties at the same time.

Perceiving Common Relations

The basic skill required in developing this concept is the ability to identify and pair items that are usually associated together but that are *not* identical. The activity of perceiving common relations is similar to grouping because it depends on the identification of a common property or bond. It differs from grouping because it involves *pairing* such items rather than working with larger numbers of them. It is useful to cultivate because it probably forms the basis for the later understanding and formulation of analogies (ring is to finger as belt is to . . . waist, buckle, or sash?). Since these combinations are usually culturally based (salt and pepper, shoes and socks, hat and head), it is important to know the home backgrounds of the children in order to be able to develop pairs likely to be familiar to them.

Opposites can also be included in this activity, since there is also a true relationship between them. Thus, hot can be contrasted with cold, up with down, and thick with thin.

We have found that 3- and 4-year-olds enjoy practicing this conceptual task a great deal. It has the kind of appeal that riddles generally have, and the children relish pairing up an assortment of items that are either presented all together in a box or in more gamelike form where several items are set out and their related members are drawn out of a bag one by one. There are some commercial materials on the market that are useful for this purpose, such as two-piece puzzles linking animals with their homes, or occupations with appropriate tools. (We call these *congruent relationships*.) It is also helpful to acquire many pairs of real objects or models of them that belong together and to keep a reserve of these handy to be brought out from time to time for the fun of it.

When the teacher is working with those combinations, it is usually effective for him to ask the child to pick out the thing that *goes most closely* with

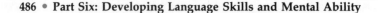

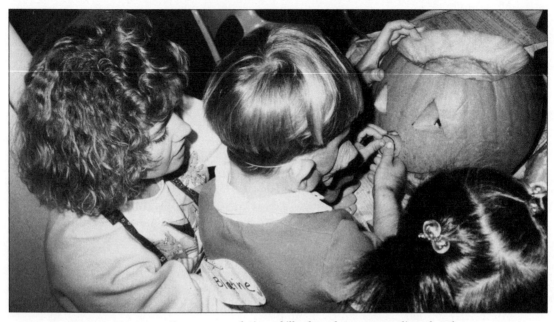

Opportunities to practice common relations skills abound once you realize what they are.

a selected item or that *belongs best* with it. This is language that the children understand and that is clear enough for them to be able to follow the directions.

Perceiving common relations may be made more difficult for more mature children by including less familiar combinations, by increasing the number of choices, or by setting up true analogies in which the child has to ascertain the quality common to both pairs of items.

Understanding the Relationship Between Simple Cause and Effect

Although it takes children a long time to develop clear ideas of physical casuality (Piaget, 1930), they can begin to acquire this concept while attending the center. Indeed, good discipline often depends on teaching exactly this kind of relationship between action and outcome, since letting the punishment fit the crime usually results in allowing the child to experience the logical consequence of her behavior. Thus the child who pulls all the blocks off the shelf is expected to help restack them, and the youngster who dumps her milk on the table must get the sponge and wipe it up herself.

In addition to understanding cause and effect in terms of social conse-quences, 4-year-olds can often handle cause-related questions that are phrased as "What would happen if . . . ?" or "What do you think made something happen?" These questions are sound to use because they do not require children to apply or explain scientific principles that lie beyond their understanding but depend instead on what they can see happen with their own eyes or on what they can deduce from their own experience.

Following are some examples of successful questions:

1. What will happen if we add some sugar to the dough?
2. What will happen to your shoes if you go out in the rain without your boots on?
3. How come John dropped the hot pan so quickly?
4. What made the kittens mew when mama cat got up?
5. What made the egg get hard?

Finding the answers to these questions can be accomplished by setting up simple experiments to identify the most probable cause. These experiments enable the children to try out suggested causes, compare results, and then draw conclusions about the most likely reason for something's happening, thereby introducing them to the scientific method.

For example, to determine what makes plants grow, the children might think of possibilities such as roots, water, and sunshine and then think of ways they could find out if their ideas are correct. They might think of cutting the roots off a marigold or of putting one plant in the dark and another in the sun while watering both. Or they might try growing plants with and without water.

Asking "What made those bubbles?" helps children think about cause-and-effect relationships.

Of course, doing experiments like this may involve wasting and breaking or destroying some things, but the teacher really cannot allow a misguided idea of thrift to stand in the way of letting the children figure something out. Four-year-olds in particular enjoy carrying out this kind of investigation, although they will need help figuring out how to set up the experiment. Remember it is much more valuable for children to propose possibilities, make predictions, and try them out than for teachers to guide them to thinking of possibilities the teachers have thought up already.

Teaching about simple cause-and-effect relations presents one of the most interesting educational opportunities available to the preprimary teacher, and both natural history and physical science offer rich possibilities that can be used for this purpose. For this reason, several references on science for young children are listed at the end of this chapter.

Of course, cause-and-effect experiences need not be elaborate, full-blown experiments. Here is a partial list of simple cause-and-effect experiences identified by students in various classes: using a squirt gun, flashlight, or garlic press (with dough or clay); blowing soap bubbles; turning on a light; blowing up a balloon and pricking it with a pin; using all sorts of windup toys such as hopping frogs, little cars, and paddle boats; blowing a whistle; using grinders and graters; making butter; scales (weighing heavy and light things for contrast); listening to children's hearts after they have been sitting, walking, or running; using a bank made like a doghouse (when a penny goes in the front, the dog comes out and grabs the money); turning a kaleidoscope; painting the sidewalk with water in sun and shade; striking a match; mixing paint to obtain different colors; pushing a button to make the clown move; and stretching rubber bands between various nails on a board, different tensions producing different pitched sounds.

Any of these experiences can generate good learning opportunities if the teacher encourages the children to do some predicting in advance or to explain in simple terms to each other what made the action happen.

Ordering

Ordering means arranging objects or events in logical order. The two kinds of ordering that appear to be most useful are arranging a variety of items according to a graduated scale (spatial ordering, the beginning of Piagetian seriation) and arranging events as they occur in time (temporal ordering). The basic question the child must be able to answer when dealing with either of these concepts is "What comes next?" There are many interesting activities that require a child to answer this question and to infer the logical order of either a spatial or temporal series.

Seriation

For example, almost any kind of item that comes in graduated sizes may be used for the purpose of teaching spatial, or seriated, ordering: various sizes of bolts and nuts, sets of measuring cups or spoons, nested mixing bowls, and empty tin cans of assorted sizes. There are also many commercial materials made for the purpose of practicing seriation. Montessori cylinders are excellent for this purpose, and an examination of equipment catalogs will reveal many additional possibilities, ranging from nesting blocks to flannel board materials. Hardwood blocks, of course, present classic opportunities for becoming acquainted with the relationship between their varying lengths as well as for studying the regular relationships of equivalency that occur in block construction, since blocks may vary in length but generally are of the same width and depth.

I also favor including variations on seriation that teach gradations in quality. Grades of sandpaper can be provided so that children have opportunities to arrange them in order from rough to smooth; flavors can be provided that range from sweet to sour; tone bells can be arranged from high to low. Large muscle experiences that will draw the children's attention to graduated sizes might include having the children arrange themselves from shortest to tallest. (This can be fun to do if everyone lies down side by side and their height is marked on a big roll of paper and then the same paper is used again later in the year to measure their growth.) Or they can be given a set of four or five boxes and allowed to throw beanbags into them when they have been arranged in correct order.

The easiest kinds of seriation problems are ones where the youngster is asked to choose which items should be added to a chain of two or three in order to continue an upward or downward trend (Siegel, 1972). Preschool children manage well using three, four, and even five and six items at a time as they become more experienced. Very young children often grasp this principle best if it is presented in terms of "This is the daddy, and this is the mother; now show me what comes next." The activity may be made more difficult by increasing the number of objects to be arranged, and even more difficult by asking the child to arrange a series and then giving her one or two items that must be inserted somewhere in the middle to make the series more complete. Finally, the challenge can be increased even more by asking the child to arrange two sets of objects in corresponding order or, more difficult yet, in contrasting order, for example, going from low to high for one set and high to low on a parallel set. This is *very* difficult! Nuts and bolts make particularly nice items to use for this purpose, as do padlocks and various sized keys and paper dolls with appropriately sized clothing.

Temporal Ordering

Recalling or anticipating the order of events as they occur in time is called temporal ordering. A child can be asked to recount the order in which she got up that morning: "First you got up, and then you went to the bathroom, and then . . ." Flannel board stories are another fine way to help children visualize the order in which things happen, and some social occasions also make excellent topics for discussion and pictures. Birthday parties, for example, often run quite true to form: first the guests arrive, then the birthday child opens her presents, and so forth. Recipes, also, can be set out with the ingredients arranged in the order in which they will be needed. Many of these orderly events can be played

What mental ability is Matthew practicing?

through as well as discussed—recapitulation through play is a most valuable way to rehearse the order in which events take place. Growth sequences based on human, plant, and animal development fit in here very naturally as a topic of study, as does the excellent series of sequenced puzzles generally available.

   Although even 2-year-olds are keenly aware of the order in which daily events occur and are sticklers for maintaining that order, as many a mother will attest, older preschoolers also need continuing practice with this concept. The level of difficulty for these more sophisticated children can be increased by adding more episodes to each event, asking the child to arrange a series of pictures and then to interpolate additional ones after the series has been formulated, asking her to arrange the events in reverse, or asking a child to consider what might happen if something occurred out of order ("What if you got in the bathtub and then took your clothes off?" To which one child replied, "Nothing, as long as I don't turn the water on!") Asking children to plan an activity step by step in advance also provides practice in temporal ordering. I recall doing some serious planning with one group about how to proceed with giving my springer spaniel a bath. All went well until Lady shook herself vigorously. "We didn't plan on that!" said one 4-year-old, looking with disgust at her dripping clothes.

Conserving

Perhaps no mental ability has come under more investigation than the ability to conserve quantity (Moore & Harris, 1978). When a child possesses this ability, she is able to recognize that the amount of the substance remains the same despite changes in its appearance. When she is too young to be able to conserve (typically in our culture before age 6 or 7), the child is deceived by appearances into reasoning that the quantity has increased or decreased because a change in shape has made the material look like more or less. For instance, two glasses of water that have been judged equivalent will then be judged unequal when one is poured into a squat, low dish and another into a tall, thin cylinder, and the two are compared again, or two balls of clay previously demonstrated to be the same amount will be judged different in quantity when one has been mashed flat or divided into many little balls.

Considerable interest has centered on the question of whether children can be taught this skill before the time they would typically acquire it, but the findings have been mixed and appear to be affected by a number of factors. For example, Inhelder (1968) reports that the amount children improve in their ability to conserve is always related to their prior level of development. Bruner (1966) reports that modifying the way materials are presented affects the children's answers to conservation problems. The age of acquisition of most conservation skills has also been shown to vary according to culture. Reporting on a survey of cross-cultural studies, Ashton (1975), for example, concluded that "acquisition of most conservation skills is delayed in non-Western cultures" (p. 481). Generally it appears that children who are on the verge of comprehending conservation may be pushed on to the next step in this process if they receive adequate instruction. The value of doing this, of course, remains open to debate.

Acceleration, however, is less important than making sure the child has ample opportunity to develop richly and fully at every level as she passes through it. This opportunity is particularly significant for children who come from lower socioeconomic levels, since evidence is mounting that such youngsters often lag behind their middle-class peers in developing such abilities (Almy et al., 1966; Golden, Bridger, & Montare, 1974; Sigel & McBane, 1967) and that additional experience and opportunities to practice may help them catch up.

Therefore, preprimary teachers should see to it that the children in their groups have many occasions to try out and experiment with the results of pouring liquids back and forth into various-shaped containers in order to learn that shape does not alter quantity. Blocks present outstanding opportunities to demonstrate conservation of mass, since it is relatively simple to see that a tower of four contains the same number of units as does a two-by-two stack. Clay and dough also lend themselves well to providing opportunities for youngsters to acquire this concept. In short, any material, whether liquid or solid, that can be divided and put together again may be used to investigate the principle of conservation.

It is also worthwhile to provide opportunities for measuring to demonstrate equality or inequality. Scales are useful in this regard, and yardsticks and measuring tapes are also valuable. Or children can create their own units of measure, using cutouts of feet or paper clips or Popsicle sticks. However, the teacher must realize that despite these aids, children who are too immature to grasp the principle of conservation will continue to insist that what their eyes tell them to be true is true.

The teacher's role in this area lies in providing many opportunities for the children to manipulate materials and experiment with changing their forms and with returning them to their prior state (reversing the reaction). In addition to supplying experiences, they should make a point of talking with the children and drawing their attention to the unchanging nature of quantity as they manipulate the materials. This is also an excellent time to build related vocabulary, such as *more than, less than,* and *equal to.* Finally, besides talking with the children themselves, teachers should foster discussion and "argument" among the children about the nature of conservation, since research (Murray, 1972; Smedslund, 1966) supports Piaget's contention (1926) that such interaction between children will help them reach correct conclusions.

It is unlikely that children of prekindergarten age will do more than begin to grasp the principle of conservation, but it may be of interest to know how problems could be increased in difficulty should they do so. Conservation problems can be made more difficult by making the contrasts in form more extreme, that is, by making the cylinder taller and thinner or the balls of clay more numerous. (This principle is easy to remember if the reader recalls that even adults can be seduced into believing that tall, thin cereal boxes are a better buy than thick, squat ones of the same weight.) The more pronounced the apparent contrast is between the two quantities, the more likely it is that the child will be misled by appearance and forget that the quantity is actually equal.

PROVISION OF OPPORTUNITIES FOR PRACTICING CONCEPT FORMATION SKILLS

Develop Needed Materials

There are two ways to obtain materials to use for teaching these reasoning skills. The easiest, most expensive, and most obvious way is to rely on commercially developed tabletop activities. There are many such materials available, particularly in the areas of matching and seriation. The trouble with them is that they often are not related closely to curriculum topics, and they generally use only pictures as the medium of instruction. (Montessori materials are a welcome exception to this trend.) Their advantage is that they are readily available and

This memory game gives children more sophisticated practice in matching and is fun besides.

convenient and can be self-selected and monitored by the children. The most significant danger to guard against is offering only commercially developed activities for concept development. This results in too narrow and dull a presentation to be fully effective.

The second way to introduce opportunities for this kind of concept development is to embed them directly in the curriculum. This is likely to be more work for the teacher, who will have to develop materials for the children's use but it is also more satisfying because it gives him a chance to be creative and to use a much wider variety of materials and activities. Best of all, teacher-developed experiences mean that Step III reasoning activities can be directly related to and coordinated with the topics that have interested the children. It is not difficult to generate such ideas; the plan that follows this section provides an example of how this can be done using the subject of water. Interested readers would also benefit from reading *Workjobs* (Baratta-Lorton, 1972), *Constructive Play* (Forman & Hill, 1980), *Piagetian Perspectives for Preschoolers* (Saunders & Bingham-Newman, 1984), *Young Children in Action* (Hohmann et al., 1979), or *The Piaget Handbook for Teachers and Parents* (Peterson & Felton-Collins, 1986).

Provide Consistent Opportunities for Practice

It is necessary to provide repeated opportunities for experience and practice (Hendrick, 1973). One or two chances to practice grouping, matching, or ordering are not sufficient. To understand these concepts fully and richly, children need to practice them consistently, using many materials and moving from simpler to more difficult activities as their skills increase.

Above All, Make Certain the Activities Are Fun

Every year the students in my college classes devise and construct a great many activities to stimulate mental development, and every year I am struck by the attractiveness of these materials. Indeed, if children are passing the door, it is all we can do to shoo them out while we are discussing what the teachers have made. Teachers seem to have a much better basic grasp of how to devise appealing materials than most manufacturers do. The teacher-made activities are so much more colorful, and they reflect a real familiarity with what young children really care about.

Pleasure is also increased for the children when the activities are at the right developmental level. The satisfaction of meeting the challenge of an activity that is just a little bit but not too much harder than what the child has already mastered is obviously gratifying. Throughout the previous discussion, suggestions have been included showing how the levels of difficulty of various abilities can be increased, so strategies will only be summarized here that might be used with any of the abilities to increase the challenge. These include adding more choices, asking if there is another way to do it, asking the children to put what they are doing into words, using a different sensory mode in place of vision (such as using only touch or only hearing), using memory, asking children to tell you something in reverse order, or using items that are less familiar. A word of caution—we have had children in the center, usually 5-year-olds, who enjoyed being challenged in all these ways; however, the key word here is *enjoyed*. The purpose is not to make things so difficult that children sweat and struggle over them. The foregoing list is included merely to provide an idea of possibilities to go on to.

Another caution I want to add is the undesirability of resorting to competition and comparison to generate "fun." Setting up activities with the aim of seeing who can do something quickest or "best" takes a lot of fun out of it for the losers. It is fairly easy to substitute something like suspense in place of competition to sustain interest. Suspense strategies can be as simple as having children pull things out of a mystery bag and then decide where they should go, or asking them to choose from one hand or the other when the teacher holds two things behind his back.

Here are some additional activities that one student developed for matching "games" that were fun for the children.*

---

*Activities courtesy Mary Anderson, class of 1979, Santa Barbara City College, CA.

Instead of choosing a cognitive game from the Center, I decided to make an original one. The idea is based on a game my grandmother used to give me to play. She would take the buttons from her button box and ask me to "help" her by sorting them into the compartments of her sewing tray. I was always so proud that I had been able to "help."

My cognitive game is simple to make. You simply cut an egg carton in half (either plastic or cardboard). The six cups are used as the compartments, and the lid (with the cut end closed with a strip of cardboard and tape) is the tray that holds the assortment to be sorted. For my game I have chosen a kitchen assortment of shapes and sizes of macaroni and spaghettis. These objects can be dyed with a little food coloring if color is desired. For younger children you might glue one of each thing in the bottom of each cup; for the older children this is not necessary. I have made six of these for group time. Each child receives his own individual game to work on by sorting the items into the cups.

Then to make it more fun, the teacher can use it as a group game. She can put several of each item into a "feely" box and have each child put his hand in and pick up one item and identify it in the box before he pulls it out. He can identify it by picking up a matching item from his own tray to show they are the same.

Another fun way to play this game, which the older children like especially, is to have them do the sorting with their eyes closed. Simply tell them which item they are to sort out from the others in their tray and have them do it by feel only.

Another way to use this game is to have a child choose one of the items (by turning her back) and to enclose it in her fist and pass it into the fist of the next child. That child then tries to identify it without looking (by choosing an identical item from his tray).

This cognitive game is simple to make and costs nothing. It develops the mental skill of matching as well as giving practice in haptic shape identification and can also be used for size ordering (as when the teacher asks "Which is the largest?" or "Which is the smallest macaroni?"). It can also be used to help develop receptive skills such as listening and comprehending what directions were given and following through on these, and it helps develop fine muscle control and eye-hand coordination.

SAMPLE LESSON PLAN BASED ON THE WATER UNIT

Some Things to Remember*

One of the most important things to remember about making a lesson plan is that it *is* only a plan. This means that it should be flexible and capable of adjusting to circumstances when something special comes along. Perhaps overnight the weather has turned cold. Then the teacher should take advantage of the skim ice on the puddles and integrate that into the curriculum. Or perhaps a youngster has brought her pet chameleon with her, and the children are so

---

*Please refer to chapter 2, "What Makes a Good Day for Children?" as a reminder of additional ingredients of a good day.

Look at all the things for children to do on this "Let's Find Out" table. (The worms are mostly plastic fishing lures.)

fascinated that it would be a sin not to get out the lizard books and colored cloth and forget about your carefully planned sound-jar demonstration til tomorrow.

Balance is also important to remember. This refers to a balance of quiet and active activities, a balance of interest that provides for the concerns and needs of all the children in the group, and a balance that includes educational opportunities for all five selves. The lesson plan on the following pages lists only the activities that *require special planning.* As do most teachers in their plans, *it takes for granted the inclusion of typical, basic foundation activities such as sand play, blocks, and an array of manipulative materials.*

To be effective, curriculum needs to suit the developmental level of the children and also take their cultural backgrounds into consideration. (Please recall that this unit was planned for older 3- and 4-year-olds and that there happened to be two Finnish children and four Japanese youngsters in the group. The remaining children were Anglo.)

As you review the daily plan, note the way Steps I, II, and III of cognitive learning are incorporated. The interests of the children are taken into account because the curriculum is based on something they care about, namely, water. Many opportunities for Step II, factual learning, are included: Sun melts snow, thick paint is harder to spread and brighter than thin paint is, and toilet water is stored in the tank behind the toilet.

Step III, thinking and reasoning skills, is identified throughout the plan, and, in addition, the Let's Find Out table also lists many opportunities to practice them. These include filling a cup with crushed ice and another equally full of water and asking the children to predict if the cups will still be filled to the

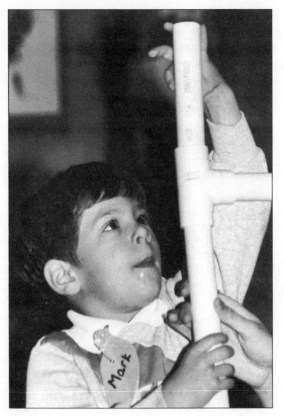

"And as soon as I get these here pipes together the water will come out, and we'll have a shower!" chortles Mark.

same level when the ice melts (matching), and, if not, how they could make them become the same level (cause-effect); using a set of teacher-made pictures of items that can be used for pouring, squirting, or just holding water and asking children to sort these according to function (grouping); arranging the sound-jars from low to high tones (seriation); and encouraging children to make up a second set of jars by pouring water into additional ones, attempting to achieve the same sound (matching).

Cause-and-effect learning is added to Let's Find Out as children bring in the plant cuttings, putting some in water while leaving others dry. The water play table provides endless opportunities for children to pour and repour water into various containers, comparing how the same amount of water looks when poured into differently shaped vessels (conservation). From time to time the teacher supervising Let's Find Out and water tables will ask the children questions intended to draw their attention to what is happening and asking them to draw conclusions about their observations.

Because the lesson plan outlines just one day, a quick synopsis of some special activities of the day before and a projection for the following day are included along with the detailed lesson plan (Table 19.3). (For additional ideas

TABLE 19.3   Lesson plan: full-day program*

Time	Activities	Self	Value to Child (Highlights)
7:00–7:30	Teachers arrive and set up.		Advance set-up is invaluable for everyone's peace of mind
7:30	Children begin arriving.	Emotional	Teacher welcomes each child individually; helps with separation; reconfirms caring, concerned relationship with youngsters
	Self-select activities		
	Plumbing equipment available to assemble (no water)	Cognitive Physical	Recapitulates prior day's experience with pipes and joints, etc.; eye-hand coordination
	New small plastic blocks	Physical Social	Eye-hand coordination; gives some children chance to use new material before crowd arrives—takes pressure off having to share too much, too soon
	Puzzles and additional manipulative materials	Cognitive Physical	Part-whole relations; eye-hand coordination
	Housekeeping	Social-Emotional	Get along with other children; play out feelings; some creative ideas may occur.
	Dampen seeds and leave others dry.	Social Cognitive	Opportunity to help the group; part of cause-and-effect project begun the day before
8:30	*Breakfast* available for those who want it; other activities continue.	Physical Social-Emotional	Nourishment; chance for friendly, intimate time with teacher, talking and sharing
9:00–9:15	*Transition*	Social	Children learn to start and stop; conform to group; help group by tidying up
9:15–9:35	*Group time* Discuss plans for afternoon field trip; how will group decide who goes to sauna and who goes to Japanese bath.	Emotional Social	Advance preparation to reduce anxiety; practice in group decision making; developing and expressing ideas

*This lesson plan takes the inclusion of typical foundation activities for granted. For the purpose of emphasis and clarity, it lists only the special activities planned for the day.

Time	Activities	Self	Value to Child (Highlights)
	Read "The Snowy Day."	Cognitive Social	Fact and cause and effect (sun melts snow); multiethnic (all kinds of people like to make snowmen); language development
	Sing "There's a Hole in the Bucket, Dear Liza."	Cognitive Social	Temporal ordering; language; minority folk song; cultural heritage
	Introduce sound-jars to be used at Let's Find Out table	Cognitive	Seriation; cause and effect (different amounts of water make different sounds when container is struck); teach *safe* use of glass containers
	Review Stevenson poem	Cognitive	Memory; language; cultural heritage; teaches part of water cycle
9:35–9:45	*Transition*		
9:45–11:45	*Outside: self-select activities*		
	Plumbing equipment in sandbox with running water from hose	Cognitive Social	Continue and develop yesterday's experience; cause and effect; children work together to solve problems (project may lead ultimately to bringing water over to garden)
	Large muscle equipment	Physical	Emphasize jumping, hanging, swinging, and climbing
	Tricycles	Social Physical	Cooperative play; alternating body movements
	Large hollow blocks/boards	Creative	Creative dramatic play; develop ideas through social interaction
	Cut pairs of plant pieces; take indoors to Let's Find Out table; put some in water, some not in water	Cognitive	Fact: plants need water; cause-and-effect learning
	Indoors: self-select activities		
	Blocks with boat accessories; small plastic blocks	Cognitive Creative	Many kinds of intellectual learning; representation of reality; creative play

TABLE 19.3 *continued*

Time	Activities	Self	Value to Child (Highlights)
	Easel painting using thick and thin paint	Creative Cognitive	Self-expression; cause and effect; how is paint same and different?
	Sound-jars	Cognitive	Experiment with cause and effect; matching; seriation
	Dramatic play Bathing babies	Social	Social, interactive play; ties in with field trips in afternoon
	Let's Find Out table combined with water table	Cognitive	Matching, grouping, seriation, cause/effect, conservation (see previous discussion)
11:40–12:00	*Transition:* inspect how toilet works for children who were interested in plumbing equipment	Cognitive Emotional	How things work; what becomes of urine and bowel movements; may reassure some children who fear flushing
12:00–12:35/ 45	*Lunch* (including fresh fruit juice sherbet)	Physical Social Cognitive	Good nutrition; social, "family" time; language development; what happens to sherbet when it melts? Can we turn it back into sherbet?
12:45–1:00	*Transition*	Physical	Toilet; get ready to care for body by resting
1:00–2:30	*Nap*	Physical Emotional Social	Relaxation-sleep; depending on skill with which nap is handled, a myriad of social and emotional learnings are possible.
2:30–3:00	*Get up; snack*—only fruit served—light snack because of bath field trip	Physical	Good nutrition combined with advanced planning for possible slight physiological stress
3:00–4:30	*Field trip* to Japanese or Finnish bath (sauna) (Parent volunteers help drive.)	Social Cognitive Physical	Multiethnic: people meet the same need in differing ways; unisex bathing; facts about different ways people bathe; bathing and getting clean feels good.
4:30–5:30	*Children return,* play quietly with manipulative materials. *One teacher has very relaxed group time.* Some children leave early because their parents drove on the field trip	Physical Cognitive Emotional	Chance to relax; be leisurely; talk over experience; anticipate next day's activities; look forward to more learning and fun; provides sense of completion for day

about using water as a topic, refer to Gruber [1978], Hill [1977], James & Granovetter, [1987], and Leigh & Emerson [1985].)

Lesson Plan

Activities the previous day. Pipes and joints were introduced; children used them outdoors and ran water through assembled pipes. Children planted seeds in pots and discussed what makes plants grow. Group decision was made to water some pots and leave others dry to see if plants would sprout without water. Discussion also took place about different ways people take baths (pictures included); upcoming field trip was discussed. Stevenson poem about river used during story time. Carpentry was offered as one of the creative activities. Dance and movement experience also included, with some raindrop music used as part of that experience.

Probable activities for the following day. Check plants for wilting, and seeds for possible sprouting. Share pictures from book *Paddle to the Sea* (Holling, no date) (use only pictures; text too difficult) along with Stevenson poem. Children will make ice cream. Try various ways to make ice melt fast. Include discussion and sharing between groups who went to different bathing experiences. Offer baby doll bathing again, possibly with Japanese and Finnish accessories. On walk, pry open manhole cover, look at sewer pipes under the street.

SUMMARY

Piaget made many significant contributions to our understanding of cognition. Among these are his identification of various categories of knowledge and stages of intellectual development. He maintained that mental development is a dynamic process that results from the child's actions on her environment, that play is an important avenue of learning, and that children construct their own knowledge base.

The chapter concludes with detailed discussions of some basic thinking and reasoning skills that form the foundation for later, more sophisticated cognitive abilities. These include matching, grouping, perceiving common relations, temporal and seriated ordering, conservation, and understanding elementary cause-and-effect relationships. A daily schedule illustrating how these skills might be incorporated into the curriculum is found at the end of the chapter.

QUESTIONS AND ACTIVITIES

1. Pick up on a current interest of the children in your group and propose some thinking and reasoning activities that could be based on that interest.

2. Concoct activities that fit the various mental abilities, such as ordering and grouping, and try them out with the children. Then add variations to the activities that make them easier or more difficult in order to suit the needs of individual children in the group. Set aside some shelves in your school where these materials can be accumulated.

3. Review the activities in the school where you teach and identify the ones that foster literacy skills that lead to reading later on.

SELF-CHECK QUESTIONS FOR REVIEW

Content-Related Questions

1. Piaget identified three kinds of knowledge involved in children's thought. What are they? How are they related to what is termed Step II and Step III knowledge?

2. List at least four important ideas Piaget contributed to cognitive education.

3. From a Piagetian point of view, explain what teachers can do to assist the cognitive development of young children.

4. This chapter discusses seven thinking and reasoning skills. Explain how these are related to later school-related skills.

5. Identify each of the reasoning skills, define it, and provide examples of how it could be included in the curriculum.

Integrative Questions

1. Cite a rule about social behavior that would be an example of social-conventional knowledge and one that would be an example of physical knowledge.

2. Explain why *matching* and *perceiving common relations* are examples of logico-mathematical knowledge.

3. Which of the following mental abilities is most likely to foster mathematical understanding—(a) matching, (b) seriation, or (c) cause and effect? Explain why you selected the answer you did.

4. How are *common relations* and *grouping* the same? And how do they differ?

5. How do *matching* and *grouping* differ?

6. What is the *scientific method*, and how is *cause-and-effect* reasoning related to it?

REFERENCES FOR FURTHER READING

Overviews

Greenberg, P. (1990). Ideas that work: Why not academic preschool? Part I. *Young Children, 45*(2), 70–80. This impassioned article vividly contrasts two points of view about the nature of education and instruction. *Highly recommended.*

Malkus, U. C., Feldman, D. H., & Gardner, H. (1988). Dimensions of mind in early childhood. In A. D. Pellegrini (Ed.), *Psychological bases for early education.* New York: John Wiley & Sons. This clearly written article is a good introduction to Gardner's theory of multiple intelligences and some implications of that theory for education. *Highly recommended.*

Sigel, I. (1987). Does hothousing rob children of their childhood? *Early Childhood Research Quarterly, 2*(3), 211–225. Sigel presents valuable arguments against this practice.

Understanding Piaget

Kamii, C. (1985). *Young children reinvent arithmetic: Implications of Piaget's theory.* New York: Teachers College Press. Although most of this book is devoted to first grade and beyond, Kamii also includes a clear description of the three kinds of knowledge and an explanation of why logico-mathematical knowledge and autonomy are so important.

Peterson, R., & Felton-Collins, V. C. (1986). *The Piaget handbook for teachers and parents: Children in the age of discovery, preschool–third grade.* New York: Teachers College Press. I wish I'd found this book years ago! It offers clear descriptions of some basic Piagetian principles combined with suggestions of practice activities.

Wadsworth, B. J. (1989). *Piaget's theory of cognitive and affective development* (4th ed.). New York: Longman. A good, clearly written introduction to Piaget that also deals with implications for teaching.

Curriculum Suggestions for Thinking and Reasoning Skills

Baratta-Lorton, M. (1972). *Workjobs: Activity-centered learning for early childhood education.* Menlo Park, CA: Addison-Wesley. Photographs accompany every suggested activity, showing how a wide variety of cognitive materials can be made by the teacher. Also included are ideas for presentations of the materials and recommendations for follow-up discussions.

Cratty, B. J. (1973). *Intelligence in action: Physical activities for enhancing intellectual abilities.* Englewood Cliffs, NJ: Prentice-Hall. The suggestions included in this book are helpful because they remind us that cognitive learning can and should be implemented by the use of large muscle skills as well as by means of more typical intellectual activities.

Hohmann, M., Banet, B., & Weikart, D. (1979). *Young children in action: A manual for preschool educators.* Ypsilanti, MI: High/Scope Educational Research Foundation. An outgrowth of one of the early experimental programs known as the Perry Preschool Project, this book discusses the presentation of curriculum from the Piagetian point of view.

Saunders, R., & Bingham-Newman, A. M. (1984). *Piagetian perspectives for preschools: A thinking book for teachers.* Englewood Cliffs, NJ: Prentice-Hall. This book offers many excellent ways to implement Piagetian principles throughout the classroom.

Sparling, J., & Lewis, I. (1984). *Learning games for threes and fours.* New York: Walker. The authors break learning games into activities appropriate for four stages of development. The activities cover many mental abilities and sound like genuine fun. Developmental checklists are also included. *Highly recommended.*

Suskind, D., & Kittel, J. (1989). Clocks, cameras, and chatter, chatter, chatter: Activity boxes as curriculum. *Young Children, 44*(2), 46–50. Many practical examples of collections of items suitable for grouping activities are included here.

For the Advanced Student

Bullinger, A., & Chatillon, J. F. (1983). Recent theory and research of the Genevan School. In P. H. Mussen (Ed.), *Handbook of child psychology* (4th ed.), J. H. Flavell & E. M. Markham (Eds.), Vol. III: *Cognitive development.* New York: John Wiley & Sons.

Gardner, H. (1986). Notes on cognitive development: Recent trends, new directions. In S. L. Friedman, K. A. Klivington, & R. W. Peterson (Eds.), *The brain, cognition, and education.* New York: Academic Press. Gardner presents an interesting, readable review of past, present, and future trends in the study of cognitive development.

Piaget, J. (1983). Piaget's theory. In P. H. Mussen (Ed.), *Handbook of child psychology* (4th ed.), W. Kessen (Ed.), *Vol. 1: History, theory, and methods.* New York: John Wiley & Sons. This work by the master himself is a reprint from *Carmichael's Manual of Child Psychology,* 1970 edition. A classic.

Resnick, L. B. (1989). Developing mathematical knowledge. *American Psychologist, 44*(2), 162–169. In this interesting article Resnick cites relevant current research about counting, adding, subtracting, and so forth. Included is a discussion of children's "invented mathematics."

Shulman, V. L., Restaino-Baumann, L. C. R., & Butler, L. (Eds.). (1985). *The future of Piagetian theory: The neo-Piagetians.* New York: Plenum Press.

Thomas, R. M. (1985). *Comparing theories of child development* (2nd ed.). Belmont, CA: Wadsworth. This invaluable book discusses a range of theories, including that of Piaget. Highly recommended for its clarity and comprehensiveness.

PART SEVEN
Working with Special Situations

CHAPTER 20

What Parents Need*

*The concept of a mutual relationship existing between parents and teachers with the central bond of interest being the child must prevail. In this concept, no room exists for blame. Nearly all parents and teachers are trying to do their best. The problem is to find how to do better, not to blame each other. The child must not be the frayed center of a tug-of-war. Parenting and teaching must be perceived as mutually interdependent. A child who sees his or her mother and teacher as friends is indeed fortunate. This means that we must develop a system of com*munication *between home and school that is clear, reliable, honest, ongoing; a system that speaks with authority by parent, as well as teacher; a system that is known and understood by the child to be in* his *or* her *best interest. We cannot afford tangled messages or unused lines.*

—Mary Lane (1975)

Have you ever wondered . . .

> Why a mother seems to avoid talking with you?
>
> How to open a discussion with parents about a problem their child is having?
>
> How to deal with your disappointment when parents refused your advice?

If you have, the material in the following pages will help you.

---

*Adapted from "What Mothers Need" by J. B. Hendrick, 1970, *Young Children,* 25, pp. 109–114.

No matter how dedicated and meticulous we are about establishing a good life for the child at school, teachers must never forget that the most significant part of the environment of the young child lies outside the school. Quite wholesomely and rightly, there is a much more profound influence in the child's life—his home and the members of his family (Anthony & Pollock, 1985). Because this is true, it makes good sense, if we hope to establish the best total environment for the child, to include his family as an important part of the preprimary experience (Powell, 1989; Swick, 1987).*

There are a number of formal and informal ways to build these links between home and school. The current interest at the elementary and secondary level in developing parent advisory boards and encouraging parent participation in the classroom (Snider, 1990) offers interesting confirmation of principles that early childhood teachers have championed for many years (Greenberg, 1989; Taylor, 1981). Such involvement ranges from making home visits (Powell, 1990) to inviting parents to volunteer in the classroom (Allen & Carlson, 1989) or asking them to serve on the parent board (Berger, 1991). All these avenues encourage interchange and communication between families and teachers if well done. One teacher-parent skill lies at the heart of them all—the ability to talk together in a sincere, nonthreatening way.

PROBLEMS THAT INTERFERE WITH GOOD COMMUNICATION

Despite the important advantages of keeping communication open, many parents and teachers do not get along comfortably together. (Galinsky, 1988). The teacher may dread the parents' criticisms ("Why does Joe have paint on his shirt again?") or feel financially at their mercy because displeased parents may take their child out of the center. Moreover, the teacher may blame the parents for the child's shortcomings; this is bound to interfere with a good relationship between them.

In these times when more than half of all mothers with preschool-aged children work outside the home (Children's Defense Fund, 1989), the additional burdens of fatigue and guilt that such added responsibilities may entail take an additional toll on parent energies (McCartney & Phillips, 1988). The results can be that, although the parents remain as loving and concerned as ever, the time for contact between school and home is diminished. Indeed, one survey found that one-third of the parents didn't enter the day care center at all when delivering their children for care (Powell, 1978).

When parents *do* have contact, they, like the teachers, feel vulnerable to criticism. After all, their child, who is an extension of themselves, is on view. First-time parents particularly can be quite frightened of the teacher's opinion, and all parents yearn to know that the teacher likes their child and that he is

---

*For additional material on parents' participation in the school, please refer to chapter 12, "Providing Cross-Cultural, Nonsexist Education."

doing well. The relationship is doubly touchy because a parent, particularly the mother, may be seeking validation of her own worth as a person by ascertaining that the teacher approves of her offspring. She is all too ready to believe the teacher (and also to feel threatened and angry) if blame is implied.

Parents may also fear that if they speak frankly and mention something they do not like about the school or about what their child is doing there, they will antagonize the teacher. They may worry about the possibility of reprisals against the child when they are not there. This is comparable to the parent who fears complaining to hospital personnel lest they discriminate against the child. The fact that most professional people are more mature than this may not affect the parent's innate caution in this matter.

Besides being vulnerable to criticism and wishing to protect her child, the mother may dread being displaced by the teacher in the child's affections. Separation involves mixed feelings for her. On one hand, she deeply wants to wean her child: she is tired of changing his pants and tying his shoes and never going anywhere alone. But, at the same time, something inside her resents having the teacher take over. To add to her confusion, the mother may also be struggling with guilty feelings over the relief she feels at being able to parcel her child out for a few days a week. Surely, if she were a "good mother," she wouldn't feel so elated at the thought of going shopping by herself! So she worries about what the teacher would think of her if the teacher only knew.

For both parents and teacher there remain all the past experiences and previous relationships with other teachers and parents that set the tone of what each expects of the other. In addition to pleasant memories, there are emotionally powerful ones of the principal's office, staying after school, authoritarian teachers and militant, unreasonable parents that lie at the back of consciousness and plague parents and teachers during their initial contacts. It is no wonder then, with all these things conspiring to build walls between families and teachers, that we must invest some effort and understanding if we wish to establish a more rewarding relationship between the adults who are so important in the life of the young child.

SUGGESTIONS FOR ESTABLISHING A GOOD RELATIONSHIP BETWEEN PARENT AND TEACHER

Surely there must be some way to establish a bond that leads to problem solving rather than to defense building. The question is, how can the teacher go about doing this?

Probably the most essential ingredient in a more satisfactory relationship between teacher and parent is that the teacher have the child's welfare truly at heart and that she be genuinely concerned about him. My experience has been that when parents believe this to be true—which means, of course, that it has to *be* true and not just something the teacher *wishes* were true—when parents really sense the teacher's goodwill, they will forgive teachers their inadvertent transgressions, and the relationship will warm up as trust develops.

Informal contacts as families come and go build comfortable relations between teachers and parents.

Genuine concern and caring can be expressed in a variety of ways. Faithful caretaking is one way. The teacher takes pains to see that everything the child has made is valued by being put in his cubby for him to take home, his belongings are kept track of, his nose is wiped when it needs it, and, although he may not be the pristinely clean youngster at the end of the day that he was upon arrival, he is tidied up and has had his face washed before his parent picks him up. The teacher also shows that she cares by carefully enforcing the health and safety regulations and by planning a curriculum that is interesting, varied, and suited to the needs of individual children.

Another way for the teacher to show concern is by expressing genuine interest in each child to his parent. For example, it is always sound practice to comment on something the youngster has enjoyed that day. It may be the friendly statement that "Helen really loves our new bunny; she fed him and watched him half the morning," or it might be "I think Jerry is making friends with our new boy, Todd; they spent a lot of time with the trains in the block corner today." These comments assure the parent that the child has had attention from the teacher and that she is aware of him as an individual rather than as just one of the troop.

Still another kind of caring can be indicated on a more subtle level by letting the parent know that the teacher is on the child's side *but not on the child's side as opposed to the family's.* Occasionally teachers fall into the fantasy of thinking, "If only I could take that child home with me for a week and give him a steady, loving environment." Or sometimes a child will say in a rush of affection, "Oh, I wish *you* were my mother!" To avoid an emotionally confusing and difficult situation for the child, it is important that the teacher clarify her role. She can handle this by gently replying, "We *are* having fun, and I like you, too; but, of course, you already have a mother—I'm not your mother, I'm your *teacher*. I take care of you at school, and your mother takes care of you at home." This avoids rivalry and makes a friendly alliance between mother and teacher more likely.

It is also difficult to be on the family's side if the teacher blames the parent for all the child's problems. The disapproval, even if unspoken, cannot help being sensed by parents. In any situation where I feel critical of a parent, I have found it helpful to remember what Leonhard (1963) recommends: "Ask yourself, if *I* were that mother, with that set of problems and that background, could I do any better with that child?"

Another thing to remember is that, as any parent of more than one child knows, children are born with different temperaments. No matter what fathers and mothers do, children are different to start with and remain so, no matter what the environment. Therefore it is ridiculous to hold the parent accountable for all the child's shortcomings.

Thus we see that the teacher can put parents at ease by letting them know that she is concerned about the child, that she is on both the child's and parents' sides, and that she does not feel that everything the child does is the family's fault. After all, parents, like teachers, also want what is best for their children. A sense of common, shared concern is worth working for, because once parents feel its existence, they are freer to work with the teacher on the child's behalf.

Of course, sometimes, despite our best intentions, a relationship with a parent may not be so harmonious. When this happens it can be helpful to know how to handle such encounters.

BUT WHAT IF THE RELATIONSHIP IS NOT GOOD?

It is inevitable that, from time to time, there will be parents who make teachers so angry it is almost impossible to resist the temptation to lose one's temper in return—a response that usually just makes things worse. Fortunately, there are alternative ways of coping with angry feelings that can help teachers (and other people) retain control of themselves and the situation—an important skill for a professional person to acquire.

The Preamble: What To Do Before the Situation Arises

A good place to begin is by knowing one's own points of vulnerability. I picture these points as being a series of red buttons people can push—red buttons that, when pushed, make me see red, too! Different things make different people angry. For some teachers it's the bossy, domineering parent, while for others it is the parent who is always late or who sends her child to school with a deep cough and runny nose.

Whatever the buttons are, it is helpful to identify them in advance because once they are identified it is possible to summon up the extra reserves of self-control that are needed when someone begins to push one.

Coping with the Initial Encounter: What to Do When That Button Is Pressed

Surviving an encounter with an angry parent is really a three-part process. It includes the immediate first encounter, what happens afterward, and the final resolution of the situation.

For the sake of an example, let's take an angry complainer, because teachers do have to deal with such people from time to time. The usual response to complaints is to give in to the impulse to defend and explain. However, this is not what complainers want. They want to complain and have the teacher apologize and do what they wish. Now, sometimes an apology is justified, but sometimes it is not! Either way, the teacher is likely to feel angry in return.

Rather than jumping right in with a defensive reply, the more effective thing to do is to wait a minute before responding. These precious seconds provide valuable lead time that allows an opportunity to recognize the anger inside oneself and to consider the reply.

Next, instead of defending or explaining, take time to rephrase what the complainer is saying, adding a description of her feelings. This is exactly the same strategy that was advocated in the chapter on emotional health and again in the one on discipline. There is no more effective way of dealing with strong feelings than using this response.

Admittedly, it can be even harder to remember to do this with a grown-up than with a child because grown-ups are so much more threatening than children are, but it does work like magic. For example, you might say, "You don't want me to . . ." or "You're upset because I . . ."

After the person has calmed down, it may be appropriate to explain your side of the situation or it may not. Many times, when a matter of policy is in question ("You mean you lost his mittens again?" or "If you let that kid bite Ann once more, I'm calling licensing"), the wisest thing to do is refer it to the director, or at least say you'll need to discuss it with the person in charge.* This is called "referring it to a committee," and it serves the invaluable purpose of spreading the responsibility for the decision around as well as providing a cooling-off period.

For the bravest and most secure teachers there is another way to cope with the initial encounter. After listening and rephrasing an attack, some people are comfortable enough to put their own honest feelings into words. "I'm feeling

---

*Student teachers should *always* follow this procedure.

Parents (and teachers) can feel this angry, too.

pretty upset (angry, frightened, worried) right now about what you've said. I don't know what to say. Let me think it over, and I'll get back to you." This kind of self-disclosure is too risky for some people to attempt, but it is an effective way of dealing with feelings for those who feel able to try it.

In the following anecdote, Docia Zavitkovsky (1990) provides us with an example of how such self-disclosure can be effective.

> There is always the element of the unpredictable at first. My first presentation to the Santa Monica Board of Education is a good example. I remember it as though it happened yesterday.
>
> It was budget time and I was asked to come and explain to the Board why more money was needed to operate the Children's Centers. The staff and I had worked long and hard compiling the necessary material, so I felt relaxed and confident that all would go well.
>
> When I arrived at the Board Room, every seat was occupied . . . and when my name was called, I walked to the front of the room and instantly be-

came aware that seven pairs of eyes were looking at me intently and expectantly. I suddenly had butterflies in my middle, a quiver in my voice, and a slight trembling of the legs. I took a deep breath and said the first thing that came to mind: "I like and respect each of you as individuals, but collectively you scare me to pieces." There were smiles and chuckles from Board members and then each one went out of his/her way to put me at ease. They nodded with approval, asked good questions, and, after some discussion, said they couldn't see why additional funds could not be made available.

Somehow these seven people no longer seemed formidable. Though in the future they might not agree with me on some issue or vote favorably for a request, they were human beings and they were interested, concerned, and friendly. It is amazing how one's perception changes when fear and anxiety are acknowledged and eliminated, and a situation takes on realistic proportions. (p. 62)*

What to Do After the Complainer Departs

The problem with controlling anger as I have suggested is that it doesn't always melt away after the attacker has left. A common way teachers deal with this residue is by justifying themselves to other people, describing the situation (perhaps slanted a trifle in their favor!), and explaining why they were right, thereby getting other people to take their side of the argument. Or they take revenge by undercutting the attacker, saying bad things about her so that the staff or director is turned against the parent.

A third, equally undesirable way of unloading anger is to pick on some hapless victim who cannot defend himself. This is called *displacement*. For example, parents yell at children when they fear confronting a spouse, or teachers may pick on children when they're afraid of a grown-up.

But is there a better way—one that doesn't require us to swallow our anger and that does no harm to other people? There is. And it is simple and available to everyone. All it requires is a good friend with a listening, uncritical ear.

Everyone needs someone to talk with—someone who is confident enough in us that they can listen while we express our feelings without arguing with us or telling us we shouldn't feel that way. Someone who knows we can draw the line between talking about what we would like to do for revenge and actually doing it. This opportunity to ventilate feelings in a safe place is a wonderful luxury that can lead eventually to forming constructive solutions to whatever problem exists.

It is also helpful to think through the best case/worst case scenarios during that discussion. Facing up to what would be the worst thing that could happen when you speak with the parent again and what would be the best thing that might happen will reduce anxiety a great deal and increase confidence when the meeting actually takes place.

---

*Reprinted with permission of Exchange Press, Inc., publisher of *Child Care Information Exchange* (a bimonthly management magazine for owners and directors), PO Box 2890, Redmond, WA 98073–9977.

The Return Engagement

A benefit of waiting and then returning to discuss an emotion-laden problem is that the other person has had time to calm down, too. They may even be a little ashamed about how they behaved so it may be necessary to save their face.

It can also be helpful to include a third person in the discussion, particularly if the problem has been "referred to a committee." Many times this person is the director or someone else who can support both teacher and parent.

This is the point at which various alternatives for solving the problem can be proposed, so it is a good idea to have several such possibilities in mind that are acceptable to the teacher and school and that allow the parent the opportunity to participate in the final solution, also.

Whatever that solution turns out to be, if the teacher has listened, rephrased, dealt with her own anger in safe surroundings, and offered explanations or solutions, it is probable that the parent will see the teacher as a reasonable person. The teacher will have the comfort of knowing she has done nothing that she need be ashamed of at a later date.

MAINTAINING GOOD RELATIONSHIPS: KEEPING THE LINES OF COMMUNICATION OPEN

Fortunately, most relationships with parents do not involve such difficult encounters. For these parents, too, it is important to keep communication lines open. Thus it is necessary for the teacher to be accessible in two senses of the word. First, she must be accessible because she cares about the child; second, she must be physically available when the parent is around the school. In some schools, availability can be hard to come by. The teacher may be occupied with setting up as the children arrive and able to give the parent only a passing word, or at the end of the day she may be so harrassed that she has no time or energy to talk.

It is possible and even desirable to arrange the schedule so that one teacher is free to greet parents the first and last 15 minutes of the day or during peak arrival and departure times. If she is free from other responsibilities at that time, she can see each parent for countless casual meetings and can build relationships of friendliness and trust more easily. The sheer informality of this encounter robs it of a good deal of threat. Chatting right by the gate, the parents know that they can hasten away if the conversation takes too threatening a turn. In addition, they are likely to see the teacher in a variety of moods and predicaments, which increases the teacher's humanity.

This repeated, consistent contact is far superior to relying solely on the more formal and frightening "conference" that may occur once or twice a semester. After a comfortable, everyday relationship is well established, an occasional conference with a longer uninterrupted opportunity to talk can be used to better advantage.

COUNSELING WITH PARENTS

Once lines of communication are open, the question remains, What do we do then?

When people talk together, many levels of relating can exist between them. During the year all these levels can be used by the teacher, depending on the situation.

The simplest level is a verbal or written message where the teacher may say to the parent, "This is what we did in school today" or "Samantha learned to ride the scooter today." On this level, at least the parents know that the teacher wants them to know what is happening at school. Most new relationships have to start about here.

On another level the teacher acts as the supportive information provider and general comforter. In this guise she interprets the child's behavior to the parent on the basis of her extensive experience with other children. For example, the simple information that many 4-year-olds relish "disgraceful" language can be a great relief to a family secretly tormented by the worry that they suddenly have a pervert on their hands.

At yet another level the parent-teacher relationship has more of a counseling flavor to it. This is guidance, but not guidance in the sense that the teacher tells the parents what to do. Guidance means that the teacher works with the parents in terms of conscious motivation and behavior to help them discover what may be causing various behavior problems in the child and to help them figure out how to cope with them.

My impression is that teachers who have had special training are more likely to have the aplomb to attempt this third level. However, all teachers could increase their skills and do no harm and probably considerable good by offering themselves in a guidance role to parents in need of help, especially if they concentrate on listening rather than prescribing. The truth is that even when parents ask for help, they usually know the answer already. They are simply having difficulty applying it.

Excluding the occasional special situation where more professional help is required, what parents need in order to work out a difficulty is the chance to talk out how they feel and evaluate whether a tentative solution is right for them and their unique child. Tremendous comfort comes to a distressed family when they are given the opportunity to air a problem with someone who can listen attentively and who is not too shaken by the confession that Jennifer and Mary have been sitting behind the back fence doing you know what! Allowing them to express their feelings of shame, or occasionally even anguish, over their child's behavior is a positive good to offer parents in a counseling situation.

It is also true that teachers who have known literally hundreds of youngsters do have a broader background of experience than most parents. It seems only right to pool this knowledge with the family's, as long as the teacher's alternatives are offered in such a way that they feel free to accept or reject them. Parents will be able to use the teacher's range of knowledge most easily if the teacher points out to them that no matter how much she knows in general about children, she will *never* know as much about the individual child as the parent does.

Instead of providing instant answers to all problems posed by parents, the teacher will find it more useful to ask questions instead, such as "Why don't you tell me what you've tried already?" or "What are your thoughts about what to do next?" When a mother comes to say that her child has begun "misbehaving" in some new way (perhaps he is fighting a great deal with his sister or has begun having nightmares), the best question to ask is "I wonder if you could tell me what else happened about the same time?" The typical response is "Well, nothing much. Let me see, now, I guess that was about the time my in-laws came to visit, and, oh yes, his little dog was run over, and . . ." By this means the mother gains useful insight into what has upset her child and usually can formulate a plan about what she might do to help him get on an even keel again (Koulouras, Porter, & Senter, 1986).

Another cornerstone of good counseling is patience. It seems to be human nature that we want instant results, but change often takes a long time. I used to despair when I made a suggestion that the parent ignored. I was most concerned on the occasions when I referred the family to a specialist, and the parent declined to act on the referral. My implicit assumption was that if the family did not do it then, they never would. Happily, I have found this to be a false assumption. To be sure, parents may not be ready this year to face the problem of Jeffrey's temper tantrums and hyperactivity, but they have at least heard that the possibility of a problem exists, and the next professional person who approaches them may have greater success because the ground has been prepared.

Nowadays I am more wary of the person who agrees completely and instantly with my suggestions. Usually there is not very much movement in these cases. The chance to think out, backtrack, consider various solutions, and take time to get used to an idea is indispensable in a guidance situation.

PRACTICAL POINTERS ABOUT CONDUCTING A PARENT CONFERENCE

Getting ready for the conference is as important as the conference itself, since neither teachers nor parents want to waste time just chatting. Preparation may involve accumulating a series of quick observations or developmental checklists if these are used by the school. Some teachers also take pictures of significant events or activities the youngster has participated in and find that sharing these at the beginning of the conference starts conversation off on a friendly note.

In addition to these tangible documents, it helps focus the conference to think through the points to be covered before beginning, but, at the same time, it's important to remember that a conference is just that. It is an opportunity to *confer*. So, while making plans on what to cover, it is also necessary to allow plenty of time and opportunity for parents to talk and to raise concerns of their own.

As obvious as it may sound, a conference consists of three parts: a beginning, a middle, and an end. It is a good idea during that time to convey a sense of this structure as things move along.

In particular, it is helpful to *set a clear time limit at the beginning* so the teacher and parent can pace themselves. This avoids a sense of rejection when the teacher suddenly jumps up like the white rabbit in *Alice* and says she must hurry away! Perhaps you might say, "I'm so glad we have this half hour to talk together, I've been looking forward to it," or "It's wonderful you're so prompt—that gives us our whole 45 minutes for discussion," or (over the phone) "That'll be fine if you come at two; that should allow us to finish by the time the children are due to go home."

Avoid Interruptions

Of course, avoiding interruptions is easier said than done sometimes, but parents resent the teacher's or director's taking a phone call during a conference. Doing this not only interrupts the flow of talk but also infringes on the parents' rightful time, and parents of young children are often paying a baby-sitter for the privilege of attending. So it is best to find a place to talk that cuts intrusions

Sharing pictures of the child at school can provide a warm and informal opening to a conference.

to the minimum. It might be outside in an undisturbed corner of the play yard during nap, or it might be in the teacher's office, or even the parent's car will do in a pinch. The essentials are privacy and quiet. The child, of course, should not be present (Bjorklund & Burger, 1987).

Some Ways to Begin

In addition to the common pleasantries about weather and being busy, there are ways of opening a conference that can get things off to a businesslike and not too threatening start. For example, one of the best therapists I ever knew often began conferences with the friendly question, "Well, what's new?"

Sometimes it works well to begin with a quick explanation of what you want to talk about. "Dave tells me you're moving soon, and I thought, if you like, we might do a little talking about how to help him adjust to the change." Or you might mention a concern expressed by the parent at a previous meeting. "I remember last time we were talking about Janie's stuttering. How's that coming along now?"

An even *better* way to begin is to encourage parents to express their concerns first. "Have you special things in mind you want to talk over about Brian?" (Even though their initial response may be, "Well, no, not really," this kind of early opening question often enables parents to bring something up later in the conference they were too shy to mention at first.) More frequently the parent will leap at this chance and start right in with a genuine concern, often phrased as a return question. "Well, I was wondering how he's . . ." It is gratifying how often this concern is related to that of the teacher also.

During the Conference, Stay as Relaxed as Possible

Take time to really listen to what the parent says. (A good way to monitor yourself about this is to check whether during conversations you are usually busy formulating a reply in your own mind. If you find yourself doing this habitually, it is probably an indication that you should focus your attention more completely on the speaker and take it easier on your response.) If you think of the conference as being a time for the parent to do most of the talking, it will help you at least to share the time more equally.

It is all right to admit to a parent that you are not sure about something. A parent asked me last week whether her youngster was acting "mopey" at snack time. I had no idea since I am never with that child at that time, but it was easy to promise to find out and get back to her, and then to ask, "Are you wondering about that for some special reason?" This led to a helpful talk about this 4-year-old's sulkiness and belligerence at home because her grandfather, who had recently moved in with the family, was insisting she eat everything on her plate. (Ultimately I anticipate offering some appropriate referrals or activities that will facilitate the grandfather's making friends in his new community and, perhaps, recommending a little family therapy to help them get their shifting roles straight under these new circumstances.)

Drawing the Conference to a Close

As time to close draws near, there are a number of ways of signaling this. (Remember, the wise teacher has mentioned the potential limit in the beginning in some tactful fashion.) These ending signals range from shifting a little in your chair to (in desperate circumstances where past experience has indicated that a parent is insensitive to time limits) having someone primed to interrupt in a casual way.

It is always worthwhile to sum up what has been said as part of the closing process. "I am really glad we had a chance to talk. Even though William is getting along so well, it never hurts to touch base, does it? I'll remember what you said about the allergy tests. We'll make sure he gets water instead of milk and that the other children understand and don't tease him about it." Or "I'm sure sorry to hear your family's going through that. We're here when there's something we can do to help. Give me a ring on the phone any time, and meanwhile, we'll do those special things with Jennifer we worked out today and let you know how they turn out."

What to Do After the Conference

For one thing, it is vital to follow up on any promises or plans you and the parents have made together. For the teacher who has spoken with 15 families, it can be all too easy to forget something or to defer doing it because she is so busy; but for the parents who have only that one particular conference to recall, it is much easier to remember! If you wish to maintain a condition of trust between you and the families you serve, it is necessary that you remember, too. This is one reason why it is valuable to make notes immediately following the conference. They can serve as a reminder of promises and plans that should be carried out.

Notes also provide useful take-off points for the next conference. I have even known them to be valuable in court, when the teacher was asked to document that a parent had demonstrated a faithful interest in the well-being of her child by attending a series of conferences during the year.

Finally, Remember That Information Shared by Parents During a Conference Is Confidential

It is unethical as well as unwise to repeat what was said in private to anyone else unless that person (the director, perhaps, or another teacher who works with the child) has a genuine need to know that information. Indeed, if you foresee the need to share such material with another person, it is a good idea to ask the parents first. That way you do not risk violating their trust.

LIMITS TO GUIDANCE WORK

When planning and carrying out conferences, we must also recognize that some behavior and developmental problems are beyond the teacher's ability, training, and time to handle. It is vital to be clear about where to draw the line and how far to go in guidance work. My rule of thumb is "When in doubt, refer." If the situation looks serious or does not respond to matter-of-fact remedies, it is time to suggest a specialist. In general it is too risky and takes more advanced training than a typical preschool teacher possesses to draw implications and offer interpretations to parents about deeper, more complex reasons for behavior. Fortunately there are highly trained, skilled specialists on whom we can rely to solve serious problems, so let's leave Oedipus and his troublesome kin to our psychiatric cohorts.

SUMMARY

Sensible caution and referral to an expert are advisable under some circumstances, but teachers can offer a lot of help and work in many ways with parents to bring about a happier life for their children. To do this, it is first necessary to overcome various problems that make communication between parents and teachers difficult. One of the most effective things teachers can do is make it plain to the parent that they have the welfare of the child at heart and that they want to join with the family to help the child. Teachers can also take care to be available when the parent wants to talk, and they can provide the opportunity for many easygoing, casual contacts.

Once the lines of communication are open, teachers can offer help by serving as friendly listeners who assist the parent in assessing the nature of the difficulty and in proposing alternatives until they find the one best suited for parent and child. Teachers who assume this guidance function offer parents what they need the most—an accepting attitude, an open ear, and a warm heart.

QUESTIONS AND ACTIVITIES

1. Have the class split into groups of two. One person in each pair should select a problem or difficulty to discuss while the other person listens. The only restriction on the listener is that, before making any other reply, she must first restate in her own words what she hears the speaker saying; that is, her primary task is to be open to the feelings and import of the communication. Then shift roles and have the speaker practice this sort of listening and responding.

2. Select children in your group who appear to require special diagnostic help of some description. List the reasons for your conclusion that they need help. With another student, practice how you might broach the subject of referral with the family. It is helpful to practice this with a "parent" who is resistant, one who is overly agreeable, and one who is obviously upset about your suggestion.

3. If you have children of your own, have you ever been summoned to school to discuss a problem? How did you feel about being asked to come in and do this?

4. *Problem:* You are now head teacher in a class of 3-year-olds. One afternoon a mother is half an hour late picking her child up. When you ask why she is late she snarls, "None of your damn business" and yanks her child out the door. How would you handle this situation?

SELF-CHECK QUESTIONS FOR REVIEW

Content-Related Questions

1. What are some reasons parents and teachers sometimes feel ill at ease with each other?

2. Give some practical examples of ways the teacher can show parents that she really cares about their child.

3. List and describe the three-part process involved in dealing with an angry parent.

4. What do parents really need in a parent conference?

5. List some practical pointers for conducting a successful conference.

Integrative Questions

1. How might the feelings of mothers who work outside the home and mothers who do not be similar when placing their 3-year-old in child care?

2. Teddy, a 4-year-old boy in your group, has taken to pinching children when they sit next to him, tearing pages out of books when you aren't looking, and doing other destructive things. You are quite concerned and ask his mother if she could come to a conference with you. Give three examples of things you would say to this parent during the conference that would blame her for her son's behavior. Be sure to use actual quotations.

3. Now that she's really mad at you, suggest an angry sentence or two she would reply. Then, for each of her sentences, phrase a response that would describe her feelings to her.

4. Now, suggest some approaches you could use instead that would *not* blame Teddy's mother for his behavior.

REFERENCES FOR FURTHER READING

Overviews

Allen, J., & Carlson, K. (1989). Volunteers in the classroom: Guidelines for orientation. *Day Care and Early Education, 17*(1), 4–6. The authors provide 18 guidelines for volunteers to follow in the classroom.

Berger, E. H. (1991). *Parents as partners in education: The school and home working together* (3rd ed.). Columbus, OH: Merrill. A solid, comprehensive coverage of this subject is offered by this textbook. *Highly recommended.*

Greenberg, P. (1989). Ideas that work with young children: Parents as partners in young children's development and education. A new American fad? Why does it matter? *Young Children, 44*(4), 61–75. Greenberg includes many clearly stated reasons for possible lacks of communication plus practical suggestions of how to involve parents more fully.

Hamner, T. J., & Turner, P. H. (1985). *Parenting in contemporary society*. Englewood Cliffs, NJ: Prentice-Hall. This good, general textbook provides an overall survey of parenting in the United States. It includes material on families from various ethnic groups and an outstanding list of resources for parents. *Highly recommended.*

Taylor, K. W. (1981). *Parents and children learn together* (3rd ed.). New York: Teachers College Press. This classic discussion of teacher-parent interaction remains one of the best in the field.

Talking with Parents

Koulouras, K., Porter, M. L., & Senter, S. A. (1986). Making the most of parent conferences. *Child Care Information Exchange, 50,* 3–6. These authors provide sensible advice about conducting a comfortable parent conference.

Morgan, E. (1989). Talking with parents when concerns come up. *Young Children, 44*(2), 52–56. Morgan contributes some practical ideas of ways to foster communication with parents.

Rotter, J. C., Robinson, E. H., & Fey, M. A. (1987). *Parent-teacher conferencing* (2nd ed.). Washington, DC: National Education Association. This pamphlet includes many examples of sample questions, tips related to conferencing, and sensible advice. *Highly recommended.*

Beyond the Conference

Clay, J. W. (1990). Working with lesbian and gay parents and their children. *Young Children, 45*(3), 31–35. Clay provides a helpful discussion and some valuable references on this subject.

Coner-Edwards, A. F., & Spurlock, J. (1988). *Black families in crisis: The middle-class.* New York: Brunner/Mazel. The chapter by Benoit on child advocacy in the schools is particularly relevant. There are also helpful chapters on counseling.

Herrera, J. F., & Wooden, S. L. (1988). Some thoughts about effective parent-school communication. *Young Children, 43*(6), 78–80. The unfortunate outcome of what happens when communication fails to work because of cultural misunderstandings in a Hispanic-Anglo situation is detailed here. *Highly recommended.*

Swick, K. J. (1989) Understanding and relating to transformed families. *Dimensions, 17*(4), 8–11. Special situations related to single, foster, teen, and stepparent families and some ways teachers can assist them are reviewed here.

Anger

Gaylin, W. (1984). *The rage within: Anger in modern life.* New York: Simon & Schuster. Gaylin presents an interesting and readable commentary on anger.

Tavris, C. (1982). *Anger: The misunderstood emotion.* New York: Simon & Schuster. Tavris makes the point that anger can be valuable once we learn to harness it and use it effectively.

For the Advanced Student

Maccoby, E. E., & Martin, J. A. (1983). Socialization in the context of the family. Parent-child interaction. In P. H. Mussen (Ed.), *Handbook of child psychology* (4th ed.), E. M. Hetherington (Ed.), *Vol. IV: Socialization, personality, and social development.* New York: John Wiley & Sons. This is an extensive review of research that explores how parents and children influence each other as development takes place.

McBride, B. A. (1989). Interaction, accessibility, and responsibility: A view of father involvement and how to encourage it. *Young Children, 44*(5), 13–19. The article describes a 12-week program involving fathers and their children in school and a discussion group.

Powell, D. R. (1989). *Families and early childhood programs.* Washington, DC: National Association for the Education of Young Children. Powell presents a research-based discussion of these relationships from children's, parents', and teachers' points of view.

Powell, D. (1990). Home visiting in the early years: Policy and program design decisions. *Young Children, 45*(6), 65–69. Powell provides an overview of various philosophies concerning home visiting.

Other Resources of Special Interest

Child Care Information Exchange, (PO Box 2890 Redmond, WA 98073–9977). *CCIE* invariably contains a wealth of useful information on child care practices and management. It is listed here because it often includes practical information on working with parents.

CHAPTER 21
Working with Exceptional Children

The principle that the child is a whole human being ought to be the foundation stone and directing force for all our efforts in behalf of children. A child—or an adult for that matter—is not synonymous with the handicap he or she might have. . . . The particular needs for instruction and intervention tend to focus attention on the treatment of the handicapping condition, often to the exclusion of the child who has the handicap. It is just at this juncture, however, that we must reinforce what is surely intuitively true to use and reassert the principle that the child is a whole human being with needs, desires, concerns, and a unique personality that also requires attention and development.

—Edward Zigler (1984)

Have you ever wondered . . .

About a child who might need special help but were unsure what to say to the parent about it?

How to tell if a child really needed help from a psychologist?

What to do with that exceptionally bright little girl who acts so bored when she comes to school?

If you knew enough about a handicap to admit a child with that condition to your class?

If you have, the material in the following pages will help you.

Although all children have special educational needs at one point or another in their lives, some children require specialized attention more consistently. This group includes a wide assortment of youngsters, ranging from those who are physically handicapped to those who are emotionally disturbed or who are experiencing intellectual development that lags behind or is markedly ahead of their peers. In short the category of exceptionality covers children who deviate in at least one respect far enough from the typical that they are noticeable in the group because of this deviation.

It is estimated that from 10 to 12% of all children fall within this category in the United States. Meisels and Anastasiow (1982) list the frequency of such difficulties in the following order, beginning with the most frequently occurring problem: speech impairment, learning disabilities, mental retardation, emotional disturbance, crippling conditions and other health impairments, loss of hearing, visual impairment, deafness, and multiple handicaps.

Despite the efforts of such federal programs as Child Find and the work of pediatricians and other health personnel, it is still the case that the children's center teacher is often the first person to suspect a child may have a handicap requiring special attention. That is the reason this chapter is included in the text. It is important to realize, however, that the subject of exceptionality is huge, and so only an introduction can be offered here. I hope it will pave the way to further reading and education in this important area.

LIVING AND WORKING WITH EXCEPTIONAL CHILDREN AT THE CENTER: GETTING STARTED

Including Exceptional Children

When the first edition of this book was released, it was the only book on early education that contained a chapter on working with the young exceptional child. Since that time, happily, things have improved, and now there are several books dealing exclusively with the early education of the handicapped (see References for Further Reading at the end of this chapter). Impetus to produce and disseminate information about these youngsters was added when Congress passed Public Law (PL) 94-142 in 1975. At that time the law mandated service to older children with handicaps but left service to preschoolers to the discretion of the states.

More than 10 years later, the original legislation was amended by PL 99-457. This law opened the door for expanded, mandated, multidisciplinary services for preschool children and their families. Handicapping conditions included in the legislation are children diagnosed as autistic, emotionally disturbed, learning disabled, mentally retarded, deaf, hard of hearing, speech impaired, visually impaired, orthopedically impaired, or health impaired or multiply handicapped. PL 99-457 also makes available a program for infants and toddlers through age 2 who have developmental delays or who have a high probability of developmental delays (Meisels & Shonkoff, 1990). It particularly emphasizes the involvement of families working along with their children.

The basic provisions of PL 94-142 also required by PL 99-457 include (a) a free public education must be available to all children with handicaps, (b) each child shall be provided with an individualized educational program (an IEP) that is reviewed at appropriate intervals, and (c) each child shall be educated in the least restrictive environment. Provisions are also included for parental input and protest opportunities to assure that the intentions of the law are carried out in fact (Gallagher, 1990).

A Further Word About IEPs

Individualized education programs merit special discussion here because many of us who have children with handicaps in our classrooms will participate in the construction of these individualized programs.

PL 99-457 requires that every child who meets the criteria for inclusion in its services be equipped with an IEP and that it be regularly reviewed. This plan identifies what skills the child should acquire and determines what constitutes the "least restrictive environment" for his schooling.

It is important to understand that the formation of an IEP must be preceded by a careful collection of information about the child. This is accomplished by a number of people, including the youngster's teacher and whatever specialists are deemed necessary such as psychologists, speech therapists, physicians, and social workers. Following this assessment process a meeting is scheduled wherein the information is presented to whomever will be teaching the child, at least one of her parents, a representative of the school district, the child herself if this is appropriate, and, if it is a first meeting, a member of the assessment team. During this conference, all information is pooled and a plan (the IEP) is developed that outlines the most important learning goals and objectives for the child.

This overall plan then serves in turn as the foundation for a more detailed instructional plan that the teacher puts into daily practice. (For a detailed description of this process, see Cook, Tessier, & Armbruster, 1987.) Follow-up meetings are scheduled to revise and update the IEP as needed.

Although this may sound like a good deal of paperwork (and this is true—it is!), the clear intention of the law is to benefit children who have special needs and to protect their rights to a free, public education—a right sorely abused in prior times. It also has the virtue of protecting the family's right to privacy and their right to participate actively in planning what is best for their child's well-being and future.

Determining Which Children Should Be Admitted

The words *least restrictive environment* are important ones to understand when thinking about PL 99-457. They do not mean that every child must be admitted to the ordinary classroom. Some children will flourish best in such settings combined with additional support services. Others require more intensive efforts and more specialized settings.

The truth is that long before Congress passed the law, many nursery schools made it a point to welcome exceptional children into their groups (Moor, 1960; Northcott, 1970), and their inclusion has usually worked out quite satisfactorily. The individualized curriculum characteristic of nursery schools and children's centers in this country makes it relatively easy to incorporate a child and her IEP into the life of the school. Indeed, one would hope that every youngster in that school already has at least an informal IEP developed for her and carried in the back of the teacher's mind.

Of course, preprimary centers, while strong in offering a range of developmental activities, are likely to be weak in providing the highly specialized educational strategies some children with handicaps require. For this reason, special instruction for part of the day combined with half-day attendance at a regular preschool often turns out to be the most desirable arrangement, providing this does not prove to be too exhausting for the child.

It must also be admitted, however, that occasional exceptional children will not be able to fit into that environment at all. The staff thus needs to handle potential placements carefully in order to maximize the possibility of success and provide emotional protection for the family, the child, and themselves in case the placement is not successful.

It Is Important to Make It Clear to the Family That the Staff Has Great Goodwill but Also Has Certain Limitations and Will Not Be Able to Work Miracles

Few early childhood teachers have much training in working with exceptional children. In addition, it is likely that during the year they will not be able to devote a large amount of extra time to studying this subject. On the other hand, they do know a great deal about working with children in general and will bring to this particular child the benefit of these insights and practical, matter-of-fact treatment that emphasizes the normal rather than the exceptional.

The Staff Will Have to Come to Terms with How Much Extra Effort the Child Will Require Them to Expend Every Day

It is one thing to accept a mentally retarded child in a flush of helpfulness and sympathy, but it may turn out to be quite another when her pants have to be changed three or four times a morning. Some emotionally disturbed children may also require an inordinate amount of time and attention. The difficulty is that the staff has obligations to all the children, and the time required to work with an exceptional child may eventually deprive the other youngsters of their due share of energy and concern.

Fortunately, the examples given above are the exception rather than the rule, but the possibility of overtaxing the staff must be taken into consideration

Even temporary handicaps like this eye patch can make children self-conscious.

when discussing an admission. However, experience has taught me that most exceptional children can and should be gathered in. Usually the amount of special care is considerable during the first few weeks but gradually declines as the child and staff make the adjustment.

It Will Be Necessary for the Staff to Examine Their Feelings About Why They Wish to Accept the Child

It is all too easy to succumb to a rescue fantasy and decide that what the handicapped youngster really needs is plenty of love and she will be all right. This is, of course, untrue. Children, whether exceptional or ordinary, require a great many other talents from their teachers besides the ability to express affection, and teachers should not delude themselves that affection can overcome all problems. If they intend to work with the child effectively, they must plan on learning the best ways to help her in addition to loving her.

Recommended Admission Procedures

Once these potential hazards have been thought through and a positive decision to accept the youngster has been reached, the staff and family should embark on a trial period that is as flexible and open-minded as possible.

Many Seemingly Insurmountable Problems Can Be Solved During the Trial Period if the Staff and Family Are Creatively Minded

For example, a child who cannot negotiate a flight of stairs and who is too heavy to be lifted can come to the center if her father builds a ramp over the stairs. A child who requires a good deal of extra physical care may be able to attend if she is accompanied in the beginning by her mother or, if the parent needs relief, by an aide who tends to the extra chores until the child becomes more self-sufficient (Jones, 1977; Safford, 1989).

There Are Several Ways to Ease Entry Pangs

The regular practice of asking the parent to stay with the child until she has made friends should be followed when welcoming handicapped children into the group. Research has shown that this policy is of special importance for young retarded children (Kessler et al., 1968).

A chat with the child's physician may also reassure the teacher and provide any special guidelines that may be necessary for handling the youngster. Children with heart conditions, for instance, occasionally require special treatment but sometimes arrive with firm instructions to let the child alone so she can pace herself.

Sometimes it also helps to begin with a short day and gradually extend the time the child attends as her skills and toleration of the group increase. The shorter day means that she can go home while she is still experiencing success and has not been overwhelmed with fatigue. It may be easiest if the child arrives in the middle of the morning and leaves when the other children do, since this means she does not have to depart when everyone else is still having a good time.

Many Disabilities Will Pass Unnoticed by the Other Children in the Group, but Some Will Require Explanation

The explanations need not be elaborate. They should avoid the condescension of pity and should stress matter-of-fact suggestions about how to get along with the child who is being asked about (Derman-Sparks et al., 1989). It may be necessary, for example, to help the children understand that a particular child uses her ears and hands in place of her eyes since she cannot see, to coach them to stand in front of a child who is hard of hearing and catch her attention before speaking to her, or to explain that another youngster has to stay outside the sandbox because the grit gets in her braces.

When our school recently included a child who had severe emotional problems, we found it helped the children and us a lot to discuss together what we could do to help him. It was heartening to see how our 4-year-olds, who were at first nonplussed by Stewart's behavior, came to ignore it in time and to brush off his panicky attacks. This was followed by a gradual shift to telling him he should "Stop it!" (which he often did, with staff assistance), and finally a gentle kind of pushing back and dogpiling took place while the children coached him about what to say. I recall one child's saying, "Tell me to stop—*tell* me to stop and I will!" There is no denying the therapy the child was undergoing

Providing an extra set of crutches helped Jennifer understand John's problem when he was admitted to school.

concurrently had a very significant effect on his growth and development, but some of the credit must also go to the staff and children who worked together to understand, accept, and help Stewart.

GENERAL RECOMMENDATIONS FOR WORKING WITH EXCEPTIONAL CHILDREN

See Through the Exceptional to the Typical in Every Child

It can be easy to become so caught up in the differences of an exceptional child that the teacher loses sight of the fact that she is largely like the other children in the group and should be treated as much like them as possible. Feeling sorry for a child weakens her character and ultimately does her a terrible disservice. Many exceptional children have too many allowances made for them out of pity, misguided good intentions, and inexperience—and sometimes, where parents are concerned, as a consequence of guilt. The outcome is that the child may become a demanding and rather unpleasant person to have around. In other words, she becomes just plain spoiled.

Consistency, reasonable expectations, and sound policies are, if anything, *more important* to employ when dealing with exceptional children than when dealing with typical children. Teachers should feel comfortable about drawing on their common sense and considerable experience, but they should also be able to turn freely to experts for consultation when they feel puzzled and uncertain about how to proceed.

Try to Steer a Middle Course, Neither Overprotecting nor Overexpecting

The most common pitfall in working with an exceptional child is becoming so concerned for her safety and well-being that the child is stifled and deprived of the opportunity to be as normal as she might be were she not overprotected. In general, the teacher should proceed on the assumption that the child should be encouraged to participate in every activity, with modifications provided only when necessary to ensure success. Thus a child who is behind her peers in intellectual development should be expected to participate in story hour but may enjoy it most if she sits with the youngest group.

On the other hand, some parents and teachers set their expectations unreasonably high and are unwilling to make any exceptions for the child with a handicap. This causes unnecessary strain and even despair for the youngster. Teachers can be helpful here by pointing out what is reasonable to expect of 3- or 4-year-old children in general and helping the parents understand what a reasonable expectation would be for their particular youngster. It is often helpful with such families to note each step as the child attains it and discuss what the next stage of development will be so that the parent can see progress coming bit by bit. This may reduce the feeling of desperate driving toward a difficult distant goal.

Be Realistic

It is important to see the child as she is and to avoid false promises and unrealistic reassurances when talking with parents or the child herself. Everyone yearns for an exceptional child to "make it," and sometimes this yearning leads to unwitting self-deceptions, which can do the family and child a disservice by delaying acceptance of the disability or by encouraging them to make inadequate future plans. I once watched as a blind preschooler said to her teacher, "I can tell by feeling things with my hands what they are like; but when I grow up, then I will be able to see the colors, too, won't I?" The teacher replied, with tears in his eyes, "Yes, then everything will be all right."

Acceptance of the child's limitations as well as capitalization on her strengths is the balance to strive for and to model for the family. Some children will in time overcome a disability entirely, but others will not be able to do this. Helping the parents and the child accept this fact, as well as accepting it oneself, is difficult to do but valuable.

Keep Regular Records of the Child's Development

Since progress with all children, including exceptional ones, occurs a little at a time, it is easy to feel discouraged from time to time and lose sight of how far the youngster has come. If teachers keep regular written records, however brief, an occasional review of that material can be encouraging.

It is particularly important to keep records on an exceptional youngster so that they may be summarized and referred to at the next IEP meeting or passed on to her next teacher to acquaint him with her interests and progress. The records should cover whatever incidents seem particularly important to the child, indications of growth or slipping backward, special interests and tastes, effective educational approaches, and significant information contributed by the parents, physician, and other support personnel.

Occasionally the teacher may be asked to participate in an in-depth study of an emotionally disturbed youngster and may want to make more detailed written observations to be used in discussion and consultation. Although time-consuming, this kind of study can be helpful and revealing. The teacher can refer to references at the end of the chapter for models and suggestions about how to carry out such observations successfully.

Remain in Constant Contact with the Family

All parents are concerned about their children and need consistent contact with teachers, but parents of children who have special problems require this even more, and so do the teachers who have welcomed such youngsters to their group.

Parents can help the teacher with many details about child management. It may be as simple as explaining the easiest way to slip the arm of a cerebral palsied child into her snowsuit or an offer of special equipment for pedals for a spina bifida child who is dying to ride the tricycle. Moreover, parents are often the go-between between specialist and teacher, relaying information from one to the other.

Parents often hang on the teacher's words about how their handicapped child is getting along at school. For this reason teachers should choose their words with care while remaining sincere and truthful. As many opportunities as possible should be created for quick, friendly chats. Even notes sent home can help, but chatting is really to be preferred because of the direct person-to-person encounter it provides.

THE PRESCHOOL TEACHER AS A SCREENING AGENT

In addition to accepting children with previously diagnosed difficulties into the center, there is another very important service preprimary teachers can provide. This is screening children already in their care for physical, emotional, and mental behavior that may indicate a serious underlying difficulty (Bower, 1981). It is a mistaken notion that such difficulties are always first noticed in the physician's office. Doctors see children for brief periods of time, often under conditions quite stressful to the child. In addition they can be hampered by parents who either raise questions about insignificant symptoms or who resist being told anything about their youngsters that may be upsetting. When physicians are caught in this kind of situation, it is only to be expected that occasional difficulties slip past without notice. These comments are not intended to imply that a highly trained medical specialist knows less than early childhood teachers do. Rather, teachers should keep their eyes open because they have the advantage of seeing the child in a natural setting for extended periods of time, and they have seen many youngsters of similar age and background. Thus it is possible that they may become aware of difficulties that should be drawn to the attention of the physician or psychologist.

The sooner such potential handicaps are identified, the sooner they may be ameliorated and further formation of undesirable habit patterns and emotional reactions reduced (Caldwell, 1973). Sometimes early diagnosis means that a condition can be cleared up entirely (as when a child's hearing is restored following a tonsillectomy-adenoidectomy), and sometimes the effect of the condition can only be mitigated (as is often the case with mentally retarded youngsters). But *nothing* can be done until the child is identified as needing assistance and a referral has been successfully carried out. These are points at which the teacher's help is crucial since he is the person most likely to provide day-by-day linkage between the family and the services that can help them.

REFERRING CHILDREN FOR SPECIAL HELP

Calling the Difficulty to the Parents' Attention

Calling a parent's attention to a special problem requires delicacy and tact on the part of the teacher, since it is all too easy for the parents to feel that they are being attacked or criticized and that they have failed to be good parents. This is particularly true if the teacher must raise the issue of a pronounced behavior problem. However, the teacher can do several things to reduce the strength of this understandable defensive reaction.

If Teachers Listen Carefully While Conversing with the Parents, They May Find That the Parents Themselves Are Raising the Problem Very Tentatively

For example, the mother may ask nervously, "How did she do today?" or comment, "He's just like his older brother. Doesn't he ever sit still?" Many a teacher responds to such questions by just as nervously reassuring the parent, saying brightly, "Oh, he did just fine!" (while thinking wryly to himself, "Just fine, that is, if you don't count biting John, destroying Emily's block tower, and refusing to come to story time.") Rather than being falsely reassuring, the teacher could use the opening the parent has provided by responding, "I'm glad you asked. She *is* having some difficulties at school. I'm beginning to think it's time to put our heads together and come up with some special ways to help her."

It Takes Time to Bring About a Referral

It is best to raise problems gradually with parents over a period of time because it takes a while for families to accustom themselves to the fact that their child may need special help. Even such an apparently simple thing as having an eye examination may loom as either a financial or emotional threat to particular families, and teachers should not expect acceptance and compliance with their recommendations just because they have finally worked their courage up to the point of mentioning a difficulty.

The Teacher Should Have the Reasons Why the Child Needs Special Help Clearly in Mind Before Raising the Issue with the Parent

This recommendation is not intended to mean that teachers should confront parents with a long, unhappy list of grievances against the child, but that they should be prepared to provide examples of the problem while explaining gently and clearly to the family the reason for their concern.

For example, while examining photographs I had taken for this book, the staff and I were surprised to notice that one of the children was looking at a seriation game with her eyes consistently close to the material. It was helpful to use these snapshots with the family when suggesting that they have her eyes examined.

Usually, of course, one does not have something as concrete as a picture to share, but episodes or examples of the problem can be described almost as well and are essential to have in mind when discussing such difficulties with parents.

It Is Not the Teacher's Place to Diagnose

A particular behavior can have many different causes. For example, failure to pay attention in story hour may be the consequence of a hearing loss, inappropriate reading material, borderline intelligence, fatigue, poor eyesight, or simply needing to go to the toilet. The teacher's role is to recognize that a difficulty exists, do all he can to mitigate it in the group, inform the parent, and suggest a referral to an expert professional person for diagnosis and treatment when necessary.

Therefore, when he confers with the parent, he should discuss the symptoms and express his concern but avoid giving the impression that he knows for certain what the real cause of the problem may be. Instead, he should ally himself with the parent in a joint quest to find the answer together.

Finding the Appropriate Referral Source

Teachers need to acquaint themselves with referral sources available in their community, since it is both senseless and cruel to raise a problem with parents and have no suggestions about where they can go for help. Some communities publish a directory that lists such services, but teachers will often find they must locate them by calling the public health nurse, asking friendly pediatricians, checking with local children's hospitals, county medical societies, and mental health clinics, and by generally keeping their ears open and getting to know people in their community who have contacts in these areas. If possible, it is always desirable to list three referral possibilities so that the family has the opportunity to select the one they feel suits them best.

Observing Professional Ethics

I have already pointed out that the teacher should not assume the role of diagnostician. However, he often possesses information that is of value to the specialist to whom the child is referred. It can be a temptation to pick up the telephone and call this person without pausing to ask the parent's permission, but this is a violation of professional ethics. The teacher must obtain the parent's consent before he talks to the specialist. Some professional people even require that this permission be in writing before any information is exchanged. After permission is obtained, exchanges of information and suggestions from the specialist can be extraordinarily helpful and should be used whenever the opportunity presents itself.

Also, when dealing with a special case, the teacher may be tempted to discuss it with people who are not entitled to know about it, because it is so interesting and perhaps makes the teacher feel important. This gossiping is an unforgivable violation of the family's privacy, and the desire to do this must never be indulged in.

IDENTIFYING AND HELPING CHILDREN WHO HAVE PHYSICAL HANDICAPS

Some Physical Conditions and Symptoms of Which the Teacher Should Be Aware

Speech and Hearing Problems

Various speech difficulties and symptoms of possible hearing impairment have already been reviewed in the chapter on language, so it will only be noted here that speech and hearing problems are among the physical disorders that occur most frequently in childhood (Tureen & Tureen, 1986). Speech difficulties are likely to be noticed, but hearing loss may be overlooked as a possible cause of misbehavior, inattention, or lack of responsiveness. However, once hearing loss is suspected, it is a relatively simple matter to refer the child to an otolaryngologist for examination. Since such losses may be due to infection, they can and should be treated promptly.

Difficulties of Vision

Another physical disability that may pass unnoticed but that occurs frequently is an inability to see clearly. The incidence of visual defects may run as high as one in four or five children of elementary school age (Reynolds & Birch, 1988). Although actual statistics on the incidence of vision defects in preschoolers could not be located, it seems probable that the incidence would be about the same. This means that in a group of 15 preprimary children there may be as many as three or four youngsters who have some kind of difficulty with their eyes.

The presence of the following symptoms should alert the teacher to the possibility that the child needs to have her eyes examined (Kirk, 1972):

1. Strabismus (crossed eyes); nystagmus (involuntary, rapid movement of the eyeball)
2. How the child uses his eyes; tilting his head, holding objects close to his eyes, rubbing his eyes, squinting, displaying sensitivity to bright lights, and rolling his eyes
3. Inattention to visual objects or visual tasks such as looking at pictures or reading
4. Awkwardness in games requiring eye-hand coordination
5. Avoidance of tasks that require close eye work

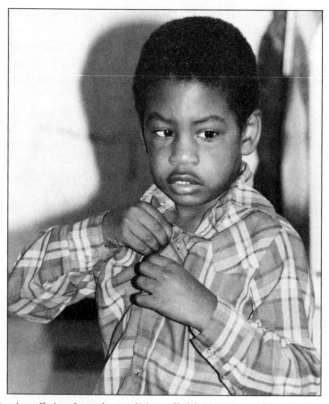

This youngster is suffering from the condition called lazy eye or amblyopia. He usually wears glasses to help correct the condition.

6. Affinity for tasks that require distance vision
7. Any complaints about inability to see
8. Lack of normal curiosity in regard to visually appealing objects

In addition to such symptoms, physiological ones include reddened or crusty eyelids, watery eyes, eyes that are discharging, and recurring styes (Cartwright, Cartwright, & Ward, 1981).

One defect of vision in particular requires treatment during early child-hood, since later attempts at correction are not so effective (Rosenthal, 1981). This is *amblyopia*, sometimes called *lazy eye*, a condition in which one eye is weaker than the other because of a muscle imbalance (Harley, 1973). Common signs of this condition include squinting with one eye or tilting the head to one side in order to see better. Since early treatment of this condition is important, *if there is any possible way to incorporate visual screening tests into the school program it should be done.* Sometimes local ophthalmological or optometric societies will sponsor this service; sometimes a public health nurse can be prevailed upon, or an interested civic group will employ a trained nurse to visit centers and nursery schools and conduct such tests.

Screening is best done at school rather than at a central clinic because coverage of children attending the school is likely to be more complete and the environment in which testing takes place is familiar to the children, so they will be more at ease. Giving the children practice before the actual examination day in holding the "E" according to instructions will facilitate testing and help save the examiner's sanity. Central clinics should also be offered as a service to children who do not attend school.

It is important to remember that a screening test does only that—it screens for some of the more obvious vision disabilities. For this reason, even though a youngster may have "passed" the screening test with flying colors, if she continues to have difficulties she should be referred for further testing. Of course, when the screening test *does* pick up a possible problem, that youngster should be referred to an ophthalmologist or qualified optometrist for diagnosis and follow-up also.

Hyperactivity

Nowadays the term *hyperactivity* has been supplanted by a newer, more comprehensive term, *attention deficit disorder*, otherwise known as *ADD* (Routh, 1986). The difference between terms is that ADD includes attention-related disorders that do not include hyperactivity as a symptom. Teachers are likely to find these terms used interchangeably by specialists to describe children who have particular difficulty staying with an activity and concentrating on it for a reasonable period of time. They may also find that parents and some teachers misuse the terms to describe every active, vigorous child.

The following criteria developed by a psychiatrist (Wender, 1973) who specializes in this condition are useful to apply when trying to determine whether a child should be referred for medical evaluation and possible treatment.

1. Restlessness—the child appears to be a bundle of energy. The mother may come to feel that she can't take her eyes off him for a minute without his climbing on the refrigerator or running into the street. At nursery school, the child may be incessantly in motion except that he seems able to settle down when given one-to-one attention.

2. The child is easily distracted and has a short attention span. In nursery school he may rush from activity to activity and then seem at a loss for what to do. He may do as the teacher asks but forget quickly and revert to his former behavior.

3. The child demands attention insatiably—monopolizes conversations, teases, badgers, repeats annoying activities. May be emotionally unresponsive or undemonstrative.

4. Shows a weaker-than-average ability to control his impulses. Hard for him to wait, he may become upset rapidly, has many temper tantrums, acts on the spur of the moment—often with poor judgment. Parents may complain that the child is incontinent.

5. About half of these children exhibit difficulties in the coordination of fine muscle activities such as using scissors, coloring and so forth, or with problems of balance.

6. The child may have various kinds of interpersonal problems including resistance to social demands from parents and teachers, excessive independence, and a troublesome tendency to dominate the children he plays with, which makes him unlikable.

7. He may have various emotional problems including swings of mood, becoming excessively excited over pleasant activities, sometimes appearing to be insensitive to pain, demonstrating a low tolerance to frustration and overreaction to it when frustrated, and low self-esteem.

8. Some of these children have real difficulty tolerating change.*

Of course, most young children exhibit these kinds of behaviors from time to time. What sets the truly hyperactive child apart is the *intensity* and *consistency* of the behavior. Some, though not all, of these behaviors may appear to subside by adolescence, but the years of stress and the unhappy side effects of this condition have usually taken a painful toll by then (Routh, 1986). The most adequate referral is one made to a child psychiatrist or a pediatrician conversant with behavior problems, since medication can be a factor in successful management of this condition (Wender, 1973).

The value of medication is being increasingly questioned, however, because of the presence of undesirable side effects and dubious long-term treatment results (Hallahan & Kauffman, 1986; Weiss & Hechtman, 1986).

A child psychologist or social worker can also make a helpful contribution since behavior modification techniques may be helpful to use with some of these youngsters (Bailey & Wolery, 1984).

Convulsive Seizures

The condition that does respond well to medication is epilepsy. Indeed the *generalized tonic clonic seizures* (formerly termed *grand mal* seizures) in which the individual loses consciousness are now rarely witnessed in children's centers. Unless a major convulsive seizure occurs for the first time at school, teachers usually need not worry about referring such children, since it is almost certain that they are already under treatment by their physician. They should, however, report seizures to the family. If an attack occurs at school, the Epilepsy Foundation of America recommends that the following procedure be carried out:

1. Remain calm. Students will assume the same emotional reaction as their teacher. The seizure itself is painless to the child.

2. Do not try to restrain the child. Nothing can be done to stop a seizure once it has begun; it must run its course.

3. Clear the area around the student so that he does not injure himself on hard objects. Try not to interfere with his movements in any way.

*From *The Hyperactive Child: A Handbook for Parents* by Paul H. Wender, MD. © 1973 by Paul H. Wender. Used by permission of Crown Publishers, Inc.

4. Do not force anything between his teeth. If his mouth is already open, a soft object like a handkerchief may be placed between his side teeth.

5. It generally is not necessary to call a doctor unless the attack is immediately followed by another major seizure or if the seizure lasts more than 10 minutes.

6. When the seizure is over, let the child rest if he needs to.*

The teacher will also need to explain to the other children, who may be either curious or distressed, what happened. The explanation should be simple and matter of fact to make it as easy as possible for the child to return to the group with little comment.

Epilepsy is not contagious, and people who have this condition are not mentally ill or mentally retarded (Kirk & Gallagher, 1989). The seizures are the result of disturbances to the nervous system due to inappropriate electrical activity within the brain, but the causes of such activity are largely unknown at this time. Stress and fatigue may increase the probability of a seizure, but erratic use of prescribed medication is the most common cause of difficulty (Lectenberg, 1984).

The teacher needs to be more alert to the much milder form of convulsion, formerly called *petit mal* but now called *generalized absence* (pronounced to rhyme with *Alphonse*). It is important to pay particular attention to this kind of lighter seizure because it sometimes escapes the notice of the family, to whom it may seem to be a case of daydreaming or inattention.

According to Seibel (1981) such seizures are characterized by short staring spells, momentary suspension of activity, blinking of the eyes, slight twitching, or dropping, or rhythmic nodding of the head. Seizures of this type may last a few seconds, usually no longer than 30 seconds. The child will maintain her position but may drop items held in the hand. The frequency of such seizures varies from one or two a month to as many as several hundred a day (p. 138). It is worthwhile to identify this behavior and refer the child for treatment to a pediatrician or neurologist because the probability of successful control by means of medication is high. Lectenberg (1984) estimates that probably 75 percent of all patients afflicted with convulsive seizures experience good control when given medication.

Excessive Awkwardness

The teacher should also notice children who are exceptionally clumsy. These are youngsters who, even though allowance has been made for their youthful age, are much more poorly coordinated than their peers. They may fall over their feet, run into things, knock things over, have trouble with climbing and balancing (and are often apprehensive about engaging in these activities), run consistently on their toes, or be unable to accomplish ordinary fine muscle tasks. This kind of behavior should not be "laughed off." Instead it should be drawn

---

*From "Epilepsy," published by the Epilepsy Foundation of America, 4351 Garden City Dr., Landover, MD 20785.

to the attention of the parent and referral to the pediatrician suggested. There are numerous causes for such symptoms, and many are amenable to treatment but only if they are identified (Arnheim & Sinclair, 1979).

Sickle-Cell Anemia

I have included a discussion of sickle-cell anemia because it is both painful and serious for some children, and most teachers don't know much about it. It is a serious, chronic, inherited condition that occurs mainly among Black people (Shirah & Brennan, 1990). It also occurs in some other populations; for example, some Greek youngsters and those of Italian (primarily Sicilian) stock can also be afflicted (Carter, 1983).

Because it confers immunity for certain types of malaria, possession of this condition has been a biological advantage for some African peoples, but in the United States where malaria is not prevalent, the advantages are far outweighed by the disadvantages.

Teachers should understand there is a difference between having the sickle-cell trait and being afflicted with sickle-cell anemia. Those who carry the trait as part of their genetic heritage do not necessarily experience this condition. Possession of the trait is harmless. It is only when a child inherits the trait from both parents that it becomes dominant and that the anemia develops. In the United States it is estimated that 1 in 600 Black children is born with sickle-cell anemia (Sickle Cell Disease Association, 1987).

This serious disorder is not infectious and cannot be "caught." It is incurable at present and causes much pain and misery, but it *can* be treated. As in other anemias, the child may lack energy and tire easily. When people have this condition, their red blood cells become sickle-shaped rather than round (hence the name), and painful episodes occur when these red cells stiffen because of lack of oxygen and stack up in small blood vessels. The plugging up of capillaries then deprives surrounding cellular tissues of oxygen. This is termed a *vaso-occlusive crisis*, and it may occur in various parts of the body. Depending on where it happens, the individual may have severe abdominal pain or an enlarged spleen, or the brain, liver, kidneys, or lungs may be affected. Children under age 3 are particularly likely to experience swollen hands and feet. Young children suffering from this condition are often characterized by a barrel-shaped chest, enlarged, protruding abdomen, and thin arms and legs (Lin-Fu, 1978). Sometimes, for unknown reasons, production of red blood cells stops altogether (aplastic crisis). Symptoms of this include increased lethargy, rapid heart rate, weakness, fainting, and paleness of the lining of the eyelids (Leavitt, 1981). (*If this occurs at school, the family and the doctor should be notified because this condition requires immediate medical attention.*)

Children who have been diagnosed as suffering from sickle-cell anemia must be under regular care by their physician. The teacher can help by encouraging families to keep medical appointments and by carefully carrying out the doctor's recommendations at school. These may include prohibiting vigorous exercise, since lowered oxygen levels increase the likelihood of a vaso-occlusive attack. Such youngsters tend to drink more water than most children do and so may need to urinate more frequently. Careful, early attention should also be paid to cold symptoms because these youngsters are very vulnerable to pneumonia and influenza (Shirah & Brennan, 1990).

Because the condition is inherited, parents sometimes ask advice on whether they should have more children. This question is a ticklish one to answer and is best referred to their physician for discussion.

Other Physical Problems

In general the teacher should watch for pronounced changes in the physical appearance of the child and, in particular, should take notice of children who are excessively pale or who convey a general air of exhaustion or lassitude. These conditions often develop so gradually that parents are unaware of the change. It is especially important to watch a child with care during the week or two after she has returned from a serious illness, such as measles, chicken pox, scarlet fever, or meningitis, since occasional potentially serious problems develop following such infections.

Guidelines for Working with Physically Handicapped Children

Since physical disabilities range from blindness to cerebral palsy, it is, of course, impossible to discuss each condition in detail here. The references at the end of the chapter provide further information on particular problems.

The suggestions already included apply to these children. A physically handicapped youngster should be treated as typically as possible, and she should be neither overprotected nor underprotected. Conferences with her physician, physical therapist, or other specialist can help the staff ascertain the degree of protection that is necessary.

The teacher who bears these guidelines in mind and who approaches each situation pragmatically will find it relatively simple to deal with children who have physical handicaps. Also, parents are often gold mines of practical advice about how to help the child effectively, and their information, combined with the fresh point of view provided by the center staff, can usually solve problems if they arise.

IDENTIFYING AND HELPING CHILDREN WHO HAVE EMOTIONAL DIFFICULTIES

Signs of Emotional Disturbance That Indicate a Referral Is Needed

Deciding when referral for emotional disturbance is warranted and when it is unnecessary can be a difficult problem, because symptoms of emotional upset are common during early childhood (Bower, 1981). One study, for example, found that the average child of nursery school age manifested between four and six "behavior" problems and that they seemed to appear and disappear over a period of time (Macfarlane, 1943). A good nursery center environment can accomplish wonders with children who are emotionally upset, and many physicians routinely refer children who are having emotional difficulties to nursery schools or centers because they have witnessed many happy results from such referrals.

There may come a time, however, when the staff begins to question whether the center environment, no matter how therapeutic, can offer sufficient help to a particular youngster. Perhaps after a reasonable period for adjustment and learning, she persists in "blowing her stack" over relatively inconsequential matters, or perhaps she insists on spending most of each morning hidden within the housekeeping corner or even crouched beneath a table. These behaviors, to name only two of a much wider list of possibilities, should arouse feelings of concern in the staff, since they are examples of behavior that (a) is too extreme, (b) happens too often, and (c) persists too long.

The teacher should also apply a fourth criterion when considering the necessity of a referral: whether the number and variety of symptoms manifested by the child at any one period is excessive. We have seen that signs of upset are common and often disappear either spontaneously or as a result of adequate handling by parents and teachers. Occasionally, though, a child will exhibit several reactions at the same time. She may begin to wet her bed again, be unable to fall asleep easily, insist on always having her blanket with her, cry a great deal, and refuse to play. When a cluster of these behaviors occur together, it is time for the staff to admit their limitations of time and training and to encourage the family to seek the advice of a qualified psychologist or psychiatrist.

Early Infantile Autism: A Special Case

From time to time the preschool teacher is still likely to come across children who seem truly out of the ordinary. A family may enroll a youngster who can generally be described in the following terms: she pays scant attention to other children or adults and seems emotionally distant and uninvolved; it is difficult or impossible to get her to look the person who is speaking to her in the eye; she may become very distressed when asked to change from one activity to another (for example, she may fly into a panic when asked to stop swinging and go inside for snack); her speech may be minimal or nonexistent; she may repeat phrases in a meaningless way and she may show a marked interest in things that spin or twirl, such as a tricycle wheel, which she may sit by and spin absorbedly, or a spoon, which she will twirl with great skill (Howlin, 1986; Kanner, 1944). When several of these symptoms occur together, the youngster may be suffering from infantile autism. This condition is rare, occurring in approximately 1 out of 2,000 people (Ciaranello, 1988).

With such unusual symptoms, it may be surprising that the teacher may be the first person who realizes how unusual this combination of behaviors is. (In my 25 years of working with children, I have come across seven such youngsters—none previously identified as unusual except by their concerned parents, and sometimes not even by them.) Treatment is difficult, and *these youngsters need highly professional help as soon as they can get it.* Therefore, the family should be urged to seek help from a child psychiatrist or psychologist promptly.

Parents and teachers wonder a good deal about the causes of this condition because the behavior can be so bizarre. Although included here in the category of emotional disturbance, research now indicates that the underlying cause of infantile autism is a disruption in the development of the brain. This has been traced to a variety of factors. Among these are rubella or other viral infections during pregnancy, PKU, genetically regulated disturbances, and many additional, yet to be ascertained physiological insults (Ciaranello, 1988). This is valuable information to remember because it takes away a lot of the mystery and the possible tendency to blame parents. However, much more remains to be learned about this unusual condition, and working with autistic children continues to be an exceedingly difficult challenge for their parents and teachers (Rutter & Garmezy, 1983).

Guidelines for Working with Emotionally Disturbed Children

Even though teachers may not have a chronically disturbed youngster in their school, it is certain they will have to deal with children who are at least temporarily upset from time to time. These upsets may be as minor as occasional emotional outbursts or as major as a child who weeps frantically when she comes to school, refuses to eat anything, and is unable to lose herself in play.

As we discussed in chapter 7, adults often discount the effect of important family crises on young children, either assuming that the children do not understand or that they simply are not aware of what is going on; but this is far from the real truth. Children are sensitive to the emotional climate of the home; and although they may draw incorrect conclusions about the reasons for the unhappiness, they are almost always aware that something is going on and are likely to respond with a variety of coping mechanisms.

There are many causes of such disturbances, including hospitalization of the child or of a family member, desertion by one of the parents, a death in the family, divorce, the birth of a sibling, moving from one home to another, a mother going to work, a father losing his job, chronic alcoholism, or involvement with drugs. Even something as relatively innocuous as a long visit from a grandparent can be upsetting to the child if it becomes an occasion for disturbances in routine or for dissension.*

The teacher should watch for any pronounced change in children's behavior, as well as signs of withdrawal, inability to give or receive affection,

---

*For a more detailed discussion of handling specific crisis situations, the reader is referred to chapter 7, "Tender Topics: Helping Children Master Emotional Crises."

reduced ability to play either by themselves or with other children, reduced interest in conversation, aggressive acting out, marked preoccupation with a particular activity or topic, and extreme emotional responses, such as bursting into tears or temper tantrums. He should also notice the usual signs of tension commonly seen in young children who are upset: whining, bed wetting, increased fretfulness and irritability, hair twisting, thumb sucking, stuttering, an increased dependence on security symbols such as blankets or toy animals, and so forth.

Teachers should realize that these behaviors are not reprehensible and that it is not desirable for them to concentrate their energy on removing them from the child's repertoire. They *are* signals that the child is suffering from some kind of stress either at home or school and that this should be looked into and mitigated.

Short-Term Techniques

First, a note of caution is in order. When a child who has been getting along well at school suddenly falls apart, it is always best to consider whether the upset could be due to physical illness. Many an inexperienced teacher has spent a sleepless night over such a child only to have her mother call and report chicken pox the next morning.

Make a special point of offering tension-relieving activities to the youngster who is upset. The best of these is water play in a relaxed atmosphere where the child can have her clothing well protected or can change afterward into something dry. Mud, dough, and soft clay can also be helpful, as are the sublimated activities listed in the chapter on aggression (chapter 10).

Relax standards somewhat in order to take stress off the child. This does not mean that anything goes; it does mean that the teacher should ease the child's way through the day with only the more important demands enforced. In other words, he should take the pressure off where he can without creating additional insecurity by letting the child get away with murder.

Talk things over with the family and work with them to identify what may be generating the upset in the child. Discussing a child's emotional problems requires a delicate touch to avoid the impression the teacher is prying into personal matters that are none of his business, but the insight gained from such discussions can provide valuable information that can enable the teacher to draw the child out and express in play or words what is troubling her. Increased understanding of the cause will help the teacher be more tolerant of the child's behavior. He may also be able to offer some helpful counseling resources for the family to explore or may sometimes offer help himself by listening and assisting the parents in clarifying alternative ways to solve the difficulty.

Help the child work through her feelings by furnishing opportunities to use dolls, puppets, and dramatic play to express her concern. For example, a child who has been through a term of hospitalization may delight in using a doctor's kit and administering shots to dolls or other children with spirited malevolence.

The opportunity to play out feelings harmlessly is worthwhile for children. Believe it or not, this is not real rage—just an intense game of "monster."

When such play is combined with the teacher's perceptive comments that recognize how frightened and angry the child is, this activity can do a world of good.

Long-Term Techniques with More Severely Disturbed Youngsters

There are a few fortunate communities that offer special preschool experiences for children categorized as chronically disturbed. However, because such opportunities are still rare and because many disturbed children profit from inclusion in at least half-day school, it is desirable for preprimary teachers to offer this special service whenever they feel they can manage it. Apart from treating psychotic children, who generally require a specialized environment that allows more one-to-one contact combined with special expertise, there is nothing particularly mysterious about providing care for more severely disturbed youngsters. What it really takes to make such a placement turn out successfully is common sense, patience, a steady temperament, determination, faith in oneself, and faith that the child and her family will be able to change.

Treat the chronically disturbed child as much like the other children as possible, and use his strengths to bring him into the life of the group.   In my school one boy who was unable to talk with either children or adults loved using the large pushbroom and spent many hours sweeping sand off the tricycle track. The first words he ever used at school grew out of this participation when, after weeks of sweeping, he yelled at one of the children who had bumped into his broom, "You just stay outta my way or I'll pop you one!" Once the sound barrier was broken, this youngster became increasingly verbal and was able to move on to kindergarten with reasonable success.

Anticipate that progress will be uneven.   Chronically disturbed children may move ahead in an encouraging way and then suddenly backslide. This should not be cause for despair. If she progressed once, she will do it again, and probably faster the second time. It is, of course, desirable to identify and ameliorate the reason for the regression if this can be discerned.

Provide support for those who are working with the child.   The staff members who make the decision to include a severely disturbed child will also require many opportunities to meet together and discuss the child's behavior. This is important so that consistency can be maintained in the way she is handled, so that everyone's insights and information can be pooled together, and so that group decisions on what should be done next can be made.

Working with such youngsters requires stamina and the ability to take a long-term perspective. It also requires enough staff so that someone can be spared as needed when the child flies off the handle. At the end of an exhausting day a touch of humor, but never in the sense of ridicule or denigration of the child, can help staff maintain perspective and provide the sense of camaraderie needed when people are under stress.

Draw on the advice of specialists and encourage the family to continue to do this.   A disturbed child often comes to school because she has been referred by a specialist. A regular arrangement for calling and reporting progress to the expert, invitations to him to come and visit the school, and perhaps some written reports during the year should be part of the teacher's professional obligation when he agrees to enroll a chronically disturbed youngster. Needless to say, the specialists who make such referrals should be willing to discharge their responsibilities by guiding the teacher when he requires their help.

IDENTIFYING AND HELPING CHILDREN WHO HAVE DELAYED OR ADVANCED MENTAL ABILITY

Children with Developmental Lags

All teachers of young children need to know enough about developmental sequences and the ages at which behavioral milestones can be anticipated that they can tell when a child is developing normally or when she is lagging markedly behind her peers or is quite advanced for her age. Lists of developmental standards have been included in many chapters in this book, not with the intention of urging developmental conformity, but in the hope that they will help the teacher be tolerant of behaviors characteristic of various ages and also alert to children who are developing so far out of phase that they require special help. Appendix C also provides a chart of developmental guidelines.

Many preprimary teachers do not recognize retardation when they see it. Being unaware of retardation can be an advantage in a way, since it means that a child is not stuck with a stereotyped reaction to her condition or burdened with an undesirable label (Seltzer & Seltzer, 1983). On the other hand, it may also mean that an undiagnosed, slow-learning 4-year-old who is actually operating at a 2½-year-old level may be expected to sit with the other 4-year-olds for long stories she does not comprehend or may be criticized and disciplined for refusing to share equipment when actually she is behaving in a way typical of her developmental but not chronological age. An adequate diagnosis would enable the teacher to match his expectations to the child's real level of ability.

Behavior that should be cause for concern includes a widespread pattern of delayed development that is a year or more behind the typical in physical, social, and intellectual areas. Such lags are usually accompanied by speech that is obviously immature for the child's chronological age.

Causes of slow development are numerous, ranging from chromosomal disorders to pseudoretardation induced by an insufficiently stimulating environment, and it is often impossible even for specialists to determine why the child is developing slowly. For example, Weiss and Weisz (1986) state that "at present there are several hundred known causes of mental retardation; many professionals, however, believe this to be only a fraction of the total number of actual causes" (p. 357).

The simplicity and adaptability of the preschool curriculum mean that many mildly or moderately retarded children can fit comfortably into that environment. Some, of course, require more special educational services. Since truly retarded children do not outgrow their condition or ultimately catch up with their more fortunate peers, it is necessary for teachers and parents to come to a realistic understanding of what can be expected of them. Knowledgeable specialists can provide many helpful suggestions about how to maximize learning for these youngsters.

Pseudoretarded Children

Although heredity appears to control the range of intelligence of each individual, environment has been shown also to have an effect on how well individuals develop (Edgerton, 1979; Meisels & Anastasiow, 1982). There is general agreement that cognitive development can be depressed by the adverse environmental circumstances often associated with poverty. However, the extent of this pseudoretardation and the ability of education to remedy it are still the subject of debate (Weiss & Weisz, 1986; Zigler & Balla, 1982).

Since the middle 1960s, infant and preschool education has been characterized by the development of many programs intended to overcome retardation due to environmental insult. Some results of these attempts have been disappointing (Cicerelli et al., 1969), but some programs have reported heartening successes in achieving this goal, as was discussed in chapter 2 (Begab, Haywood, & Garber, 1981; Gray et al., 1982; Heber, Garber, Harrington, Hoffman, & Fallender, 1972; Lazar & Darlington, 1982; Schweinhart et al., 1986).

Characteristics of Pseudoretarded Children

Children who come from the lower socioeconomic class have many characteristics and needs that are common to all children, but many of them also have some characteristics that reduce the likelihood of their succeeding in a middle-class school. Teachers who wish to work with them need to take these characteristics into account when planning educational programs in order to help the children develop maximally.

Many of the children will have poorer health than middle-class children do, since they receive little medical care after they stop attending well-baby clinics around the age of 2 years. Poor diet (both prenatally and postnatally) also contributes to less than optimum conditions for fostering growth (Dobbing, 1987). Many poor children who also come from a culturally different background are behind in their ability to use Standard English, although they may be fluent in a dialect such as Black English or another language such as Spanish (Golden et al., 1974); and some lack verbal ability in any language. Children from families of the poor characteristically score lower on verbal tests than middle-class children (Bruner, 1970; Deutsch, 1971; L'Abate & Curtis, 1975). They may lack experiences that are common among middle-class children. (For example, in my own community we found that many of the children had never been to the beach or to a supermarket, even though they lived within walking distance of both.) These youngsters often appear more action oriented than given to reflective thought. When they are confronted with standard measures of intelligence, such as the Stanford-Binet or the Peabody Picture Vocabulary Test, they usually score, for many reasons, below the average performance of their middle-class peers (Loehlin, Lindzey, & Spuhler, 1975; Reese & Lipsitt, 1970).

Unfortunately, these kinds of reports may cause the teacher to overlook the positive strengths of such children, strengths that middle-class children may not possess. For example, children from poor families may be able to cope with various human failings, make money stretch, or get along with intrusive adults from welfare or law enforcement agencies with an aplomb that a middle-class child could not manage. There can also be a self-reliance, sense of humor, and a kind of wise cynicism expressed even by 4-year-olds, which may make a sentimental teacher's heart ache but which should also arouse his admiration if he realizes how effective such attitudes are as coping mechanisms.

Most of the literature on working with children from the lower socioeconomic class makes it sound difficult and possibly frightening to the beginning teacher, but there are cogent reasons why many teachers who become involved in a Head Start or other compensatory program vow never to return to teaching middle-class children. This decision may partly be due to ego gratification related to noblesse oblige, but some of it is also due to the pleasure of seeing children flourish and go on to a better school experience as a result of their years in preschool care.

It takes considerable energy, perseverance, and skill to help young "economically disadvantaged" children supplement their home educations with material that will enable them to fit into the middle-class school. A number of successful programs have demonstrated that this can be done. (For an extensive list of such programs refer to Begab et al., 1981.) It behooves teachers who work with such youngsters to acquaint themselves with a variety of these programs, select a model that fits their own tastes and predilections, make a consistent plan based on the model, and carry it out with determination.

Guidelines for Working with Mentally Retarded Children

Mental retardation is defined as "subaverage intellectual functioning, which originates during the developmental period and is associated with impairment of adaptive behavior" (Heber, 1961). The severity of the condition varies widely: mildly or moderately retarded children are the best prospects for inclusion in children's centers. The mildly retarded child will probably fit so easily into a program serving a heterogeneous age group that no special recommendations are necessary other than reminding the teacher to see the child in terms of her actual developmental level rather than her chronological age.

The moderately retarded child will also often fit comfortably into the heterogeneous center, but many teachers find it helpful to have a clear understanding of the most worthwhile educational goals for these children and also to understand some simple principles for teaching them most effectively.

Basic learning goals for a moderately retarded preschool youngster should center on (a) helping her to be as independent as possible, which includes learning simple self-help skills as well as learning to help other people by doing simple tasks; (b) helping the child develop language skills; and (c) helping her learn to get along with other children in an acceptable way.

These goals are really no different from ones that are part of the regular curriculum. The only differences are that the retarded child will be farther behind other children of her age and that she will need a simpler manner of instruction. Children who learn slowly should not be confused with a lot of talk and shadings of meaning. *They need concrete examples, definite rules, and consistent reinforcement of desired behavior.* In general, the bywords with these children are keep it concrete, keep it simple, keep it fun, and be patient.

Some specific suggestions may also help the teacher:

1. As much as possible, treat the child as you would treat all children in the group, but exercise common sense so that you expect neither too much nor too little.

2. Know the developmental steps so that you understand what she should learn next as she progresses.

3. Remember that retarded children learn best what they repeat frequently. Be prepared to go over a simple rule or task many times until the child has it firmly in mind. (This need for patient repetition is one of the things inexperienced teachers may find most irritating, particularly when the child has appeared to grasp the idea just the day before. Don't give up hope; if the teaching is simple and concrete enough, she will eventually learn.)

4. Pick out behavior to teach that the child can use all her life; that is, try to teach ways of behaving that will be appropriate for an older as well as a younger child to use. For example, don't let her run and kiss everyone she meets, since this will not be acceptable when she is just a little older. She has enough to do without having to unlearn old behavior.

5. Take it easy. Give short directions, one point at a time.

6. Allow sufficient time for her to accomplish a selected task. Complex things take longer; simpler things take less time.

7. Encourage the child to be persistent by keeping tasks simple and satisfying. This will encourage her to finish what she starts.

8. Remember that independence is an important goal. Make sure the child is not being overprotected.

9. Teach one thing at a time. For instance, teach her to feed herself, then to use a napkin, then to pour her milk.

10. Provide lots of concrete experience that uses as many of the senses as possible.

11. Don't rely on talking as the primary means of instruction. Show the child what you mean whenever possible.

12. Encourage the development of speech. Wait for at least some form of verbal reply whenever possible. Gently increase the demand for a "quality" response as her skills increase.

13. *Remember that retarded children are just as sensitive to the emotional climate around them as ordinary children are.* Therefore, never talk about a child in front of her. It is likely that she will at least pick up the feeling of what you are saying, and this may hurt her feelings badly.

14. Show the child you are pleased with her and that you like her.

15. After a fair trial at learning something new, if she cannot seem to learn it, drop the activity without recrimination. Try it again in a few months; she may be ready to learn it by then.

There is much to be said for the value of step-by-step, prescriptive teaching for retarded children in particular. This requires careful identification of the present level of the child's skills as well as knowledge of the appropriate next step. There are several programs available that outline these steps in detail (Johnson & Werner, 1975; Meyer Children's Rehabilitation Institute, 1974; Portage Project, 1976). Teachers who have developmentally delayed children in their group should refer to these materials frequently as well as obtain suggestions from the other specialists working with the youngster. This step-by-step approach is most successful if it is combined with the use of behavior modification techniques. The deliberate, systematic application of these principles, wherein behavior is either rewarded or not rewarded in a definite way, is of proven value with retarded children.

Intellectually Gifted Children

Although the child who is slow to learn and the child who is pseudoretarded have received special attention for several decades, it is only during the past few years that intellectually gifted preschoolers have received much attention at all. At present there are a handful of special programs that cater to their needs, but it is still true that they are overlooked or ignored in most preschool settings (Wolfle, 1989). Why this should be the case is hard to understand. Surely such promising children deserve the interest and support of their teachers. Perhaps they are overlooked because many of them fit smoothly into the center's curriculum (although it may present insufficient challenges for them), or perhaps most preschool teachers are uncertain about what kinds of behavior indicate outstanding mental ability and thus fail to identify the children.

A child with exceptional mental ability usually exhibits a general pattern of advanced skills, but not always. Sometimes the pattern is quite spotty or its manifestations may vary from day to day (Whitmore, 1986).

In general, a gifted child may exhibit some or all of the following skills: she learns quickly and easily; her language is more elaborate and extended than that of other children of the same age, and her vocabulary is likely to be large; her attention span may be longer if her interest is aroused; she grasps ideas easily; she probably possesses an exceptional amount of general information, which is characterized not only by more variety but also by greater detail. Gifted preschoolers like to pursue reasons for things, talk about cause-and-effect relationships, and compare and draw conclusions. They are particularly sensitive to social values and behavior of those around them. They are often almost insatiably interested in special subjects that appeal to them. Some of them already know how to read. They may prefer the company of older children or adults.

Children who are handicapped and those who come from minority groups tend to be overlooked to an even greater extent as possibly being gifted children (Karnes & Johnson, 1989; Strom, Johnson, & Strom, 1990).

Chicano children, according to Bernal (1978), may be identified as gifted when they acquire English readily, demonstrate leadership skills (though this may be done in a subtle way), enjoy venturing and taking risks carefully, keep themselves busy (particularly by using imaginative play), assume responsibilities often the prerogative of older children, and know how to get along smoothly in the community in which they live. Additional characteristics described by Torrance (1977) that apply to various ethnic-cultural minorities include being able to express feelings through story telling, movement, and self-expressive activities, being able to improvise, use rich imagery in informal talk, conceptualize problems in practical terms, have original ideas, adapt quickly to change, and be persistent in problem solving.

Teachers who do not build their curriculum and increase its complexity sufficiently during the year may find that gifted children become increasingly restless and gradually get into difficulties because they have lost interest in what is happening at school. Teachers who meet this challenge and deal with it satisfactorily modify the curriculum so that it meets the needs of these youngsters by adding more difficult and interesting learning activities. Some suggestions for accomplishing this are offered later in the chapter.

Teaching Mentally Gifted Preschool Children

Although there have been many interesting investigations of intellectual giftedness and education, ranging from Terman and coauthors (1925) to Marland (1972), these have focused on older children and adults, and the possibility of educating intellectually gifted preschool children is just beginning to receive the attention it deserves (Karnes & Johnson, 1989; Neisworth, 1986; Reis, 1989; Whitmore, 1986). Yet it is obvious that children of exceptional mental ability must be present in this portion of the population since they exist at an older age. (In 1973, Martinson estimated that 3% of the older school population is intellectually gifted.) However, it is still the case that when I raise the question of making special provision for such youngsters at the preschool level, many of my students and teaching colleagues appear bewildered at this possibility.*

Perhaps this is because we have fought a battle against undue intellectual pressure in the nursery school for so long that we forget that gifted children thrive when provided with additional stimulation and that we may be cheating them when we deprive them of it. Of course, gifted children should not be treated as precocious little adults or worshipped because of their special talents, but they should be provided with stimulating things to learn while at the same time keeping their social and emotional life as natural and easy as possible.

The provision of an enriched curriculum does not necessarily mean that the teacher must teach the child to read, although about 25% of gifted children already know how to read before they enter kindergarten (Cassidy & Vukelich, 1980). I will never forget my surprise when one of the bright lights in my school wandered into my office, picked up a plain bound book from my desk and commented, "Hmmmmm, this looks interesting—*All about Dinosaurs.* Can I borrow this?" (I let him.)

What the teacher *can* do is to make sure such children have plenty of opportunities to pursue subjects that interest them in as much depth as they desire. It is important to avoid the trap of thinking to oneself, "Oh, well, *they*

---

*Giftedness, of course, is expressed in many different forms (Karnes & Johnson, 1989), such as in the self-expressive giftedness of creative artists or the physical giftedness of talented athletes. Because ways of fostering such aspects of the child's abilities have been covered in previous chapters, this discussion will be limited to the giftedness of the intellectually superior preschooler.

wouldn't be able to do *that.*" It is astonishing what gifted children can do if they are provided with encouragement and materials. For example, I once had two young students, a boy and a girl, who were interested in the weather. They went from this to an interest in temperature and how heat makes thermometers work. Of course, all the children were interested in this subject to an extent, but these two youngsters, who later proved to be gifted, were truly absorbed. Their investigations included breaking open a thermometer to discover what it was made of, collecting different kinds of thermometers to see if they all worked the same way and if they all measured the same kinds of things, and even working out a number scale with drawings to show the range of temperatures measured by different instruments.

Intellectually gifted preschool children often love discussion that focuses on "What would happen if . . ." or "How could we. . . ." These questions require creative reasoning as well as transforming old information into new solutions. Asking them to evaluate the potential results of these ideas, if done sensitively so they do not feel crushed, will give them even wider scope for their talents.

Gifted children will also relish the more difficult activities suggested in the chapter on mental development, since these activities can be adjusted to their level of ability and thus sustain their interest. Perhaps a few examples of some specific ways of enriching curriculum for them will best illustrate how to accomplish this.*

Investigate how things work, either finding out by close observation or by taking them apart and reassembling them.   A music box, a vacuum cleaner and all its parts, a Christmas tree stand, a flashlight, an old bicycle, and so forth can be offered.

Build additional language skills.   Make a time to read books to the child that are longer and have more detail in them than picture books do. After story time, have a special discussion with her. Encourage her to expound on the stories that were just read—were they true? Has she ever had a similar or opposite experience? What did she like or dislike about the story? What would she have done differently if it had been her? Encourage the child to do most of the talking, and try to introduce new vocabulary. Select several pictures from the picture file, and ask the child to link them together by telling you a story about them—or allow her to select the pictures.

Offer more complex materials or advanced information.   A good example of this is the use of more difficult puzzles. Cube puzzles can be used to reproduce particular patterns, or jigsaw puzzles can be offered rather than only the framed wooden ones typical of nursery school. On a library trip take the child to the older children's section and help her find books on a particular subject she cares about.

---

*My thanks to nursery school majors from the classes of 1976, 1977, and 1978 at Santa Barbara City College for these suggestions.

Offer enriched curriculum in the area of science.   Be prepared to allow for expanded scientific activities. For example, provide vinegar for testing for limestone in various materials such as tiles, building materials, and so forth. Or explore the concept of time. The child could learn to identify specific hours on the clock and take responsibility for telling the teacher when it is snack time. Talk about ways of keeping track of time—perhaps help her make a simple sundial with a stick, letting the child mark the spot where the shadow falls when it is group time or time to go home. See if that spot stays at the same place over several weeks. Encourage the child to seek out people who speak different languages to tell her the names of different times of day in their own tongue. Visit a clock shop and write down for her all the kinds of clocks she sees there.

Note that language activities are particularly dear to mentally gifted preschoolers. They enjoy more advanced stories than average children do and also can put their superior ability to work by concocting tales of their own that are almost invariably complex, detailed, and advanced in vocabulary. An interesting example of this is the book *Barbara* (McCurdy, 1966), which begins with the writings of an intensely gifted 4-year-old and continues through her young adulthood. Discussion and conversation should be employed at every opportunity to allow these children to put their ideas into words and to test them out against the ideas of other people.

Above all, the use of instructional methods that foster problem solving and encourage development of creative ideas should be employed. How can everyday items be put to new uses? How can old problems be solved in new ways? Here, once again, the value of asking pertinent questions and providing rich opportunities for children to propose answers and test them out, to see if they are correct, must be emphasized. I refer the reader to chapter 15, "Fostering Creativity in Thought," for suggestions on how to go about doing this.

SUMMARY

Teachers who work with an exceptional preschool child must seek all the information they can on her particular condition if they really want to be effective teachers. This chapter can do no more than scratch the surface.

There are increasing numbers of courses in exceptionality being offered by schools of education, as in-service training, and by university extension units as the general trend toward including exceptional children in regular public school classes gains ground. In addition to these courses, books are also available, and many are listed in the references at the end of this chapter. Unfortunately the education of very young exceptional children is still only sparsely covered in the literature, but the Head Start mandate combined with Public Law 99-457 is gradually changing this situation for the better.

Preprimary teachers have two main responsibilities they owe to exceptional children. First, they must serve as screening agents and help identify possible problems (physical, emotional, or mental) that have escaped the attention of the physician. Following identification of a difficulty, teachers should attempt to effect a referral to the appropriate specialist.

Second, they must do all they can to integrate children with special problems into their group. This requires careful assessment before admission and flexibility of adjustment following entrance to school. It is vital that they treat the exceptional child as typically as possible and encourage her independence without demanding skills that lie beyond her ability. Specific suggestions for working with physically handicapped, emotionally disturbed, mentally retarded, and intellectually gifted preschool children conclude the chapter.

QUESTIONS AND ACTIVITIES

1. Do you feel it is generally wise to suggest medication as a means of controlling hyperactivity in children? Why or why not?

2. This chapter makes a strong case for the early identification of potentially handicapping disorders. What are the real disadvantages of labeling children as being different? What are some ways to obtain help for such youngsters without stigmatizing them at the same time?

3. What do you feel accounts for the fact that very intelligent children are often overlooked at the preschool level? Might the provision of a special curriculum for them result in precocity and overintellectualization, thereby spoiling their childhood?

4. *Problem:* Your staff has carefully interviewed and evaluated a severely handicapped youngster whose family has requested admission to school and has reluctantly decided that she cannot be accepted. How could this decision be relayed most effectively and humanely to the family?

5. *Problem:* You have a 4½-year-old girl attending your school who is mentally retarded and functions at about the 2½-year-old level. She hangs around the housekeeping corner and the blocks a lot, but the children push her aside. One of them, in particular, makes a point of saying, "She can't play here. Her nose is snotty, and she talks dumb." (There is more than a modicum of truth in this.) What to do?

6. *Problem:* You have a 4-year-old boy in your group who has a heart condition. In addition to looking somewhat pale, he is not supposed to exert himself by climbing or other vigorous exercise, which, of course, he yearns to do. He is well liked by the other children, who invite him frequently to climb around and play with them. What to do?

SELF-CHECK QUESTIONS FOR REVIEW

Content-Related Questions

1. What is one of the most important services preprimary teachers can provide for young children?

2. List some symptoms that should alert the teacher to the possibility that a child might need to have her eyes examined.

3. What is it, basically, that sets the hyperactive child apart from other young children?

4. If a child had a *generalized tonic clonic seizure* in your room, what would you do to help her? What about the other children?

5. What is sickle-cell anemia? Is it contagious? What does the teacher need to know about when to call the physician? What symptoms should he be aware of?

6. What are the guidelines for deciding when to refer a child who seems to be emotionally disturbed for outside help? What behaviors might signal that the child has possible autistic tendencies? What are some guidelines for working with emotionally disturbed children?

7. What kinds of behaviors might alert a teacher to the possibility that a child could be developing more slowly than normal? And what are some practical things to remember when teaching such a child?

8. Describe some behaviors that might signal to a teacher that a 4-year-old is intellectually gifted? Suggest some ways the teacher could adjust the curriculum to meet the needs of that youngster.

9. Explain some important steps in making a referral when a child has a special problem.

10. What are Public Laws 94-142 and 99-457? How do they affect the welfare of exceptional children?

11. Discuss important points to remember when deciding whether to enroll a child with a handicap in your children's center.

12. What are some general principles for working with exceptional children?

Integrative Questions

1. How do PL 94-142 and PL 99-457 differ, and how are they the same?

2. The book states that teachers should "see through the exceptional to the typical in every child." Explain how doing this could be an antidote for either expecting too much or too little from the youngster with a handicap.

3. It is important for teachers and parents of all children to remain in close contact. Using the example of a handicap, give an example of something a parent might share with the teacher that would be helpful. Now, give an example of something the teacher could share with the parent. Be as specific as possible.

4. *Problem:* Jody, a 2½-year-old, has been in the next-door teacher's classroom for 3 months and does not talk at all. At lunch the teacher tells you that she arranged a conference with the parents to tell them she thinks that Jody is mentally retarded. Analyze all the elements of this situation and explain why you would or would not agree that she has done the right thing.

5. Many people are confused about the difference between children who are termed *mentally ill* (emotionally disturbed) and those termed *mentally retarded*. Explain the similarities and differences between these conditions.

REFERENCES FOR FURTHER READING

Overviews

Kirk, S. A., & Gallagher, J. J. (1989). *Educating exceptional children* (6th ed.). Boston: MA: Houghton Mifflin. This is an excellent, wide-ranging, standard introduction to the field of exceptionality.

Musselwhite, C. R. (1986). *Adaptive play for special needs children: Strategies to enhance communication and learning.* San Diego, CA: College-Hill Press. It's a pleasure to read this book, which outlines a great many pleasurable, natural activities that can be used to enhance the development of children with special problems. *Highly recommended.*

Special Needs Children in the Early Childhood Classroom

Cook, R. E., Tessier, A., & Armbruster, V. B. (1987). *Adapting early childhood curricula: Suggestions for meeting special needs* (2nd ed.). Columbus, OH: Merrill. This textbook provides a rich resource of references and carefully assembled tables of information. It presents a description of what is generally accepted as sound preschool teaching and combines that advice and philosophy with general information about teaching children with special needs. *Highly recommended.*

Derman-Sparks, L., & the ABC Task Force. (1989). *Anti-bias curriculum: Tools for empowering young children.* Washington, DC: National Association for the Education of Young Children. Bias, of course, occurs against children with handicaps as well as in other situations. Derman-Sparks provides a practical approach to dealing with this problem at the preschool level.

Froschl, M., Colón, L., Rubin, E., & Sprung, B. (1984). *Including all of us: An early curriculum about disability.* New York: Educational Equity Concepts (114 East 32nd St., New York, NY 10016). This book, based on Project Inclusive, offers many suggestions of ways to incorporate understanding about disabilities into the preschool curriculum.

Safford, P. (1989). *Integrated teaching in early childhood: Starting in the mainstream.* White Plains, NY: Longman. Safford provides information about particular handicapping conditions and specific recommendations about how teachers of young children can help. This is a *useful* book.

Helping Teachers Deal with Their Feelings

Heitz, T. (1989). How do I help Jacob? *Young Children, 45*(1), 11–15. Heitz shares many of the qualms as well as the satisfactions of welcoming a physically handicapped child to her classroom.

Working with Particular Handicaps

Barker, P. A. (1979). *Basic child psychiatry* (3rd ed.). Baltimore: University Park Press. Barker's book is a plain-talking, sensible volume that discusses specific emotional disorders at both the neurotic and psychotic level. Although written for beginning psychiatrists, it is basic enough to be of considerable use to teachers who need a source for quick, basic information on various kinds of emotional disturbances.

Bleck, E. E., & Nagel, D. A. (1981). *Physically handicapped children: A medical atlas for teachers* (2nd ed.). New York: Grune & Stratton. This is an indispensable reference containing simple, clear descriptions and diagrams of physical disabilities, ranging from heart defects to muscular dystrophy and sickle-cell anemia. Most chapters include what the teacher should do in the classroom to help children afflicted with these conditions.

Ciaranello, R. D. (1988, Summer). Autism: The prison of self. *The Stanford Magazine*, pp. 18–21. This is the best, most concise summary of current information about autism and its causes I have seen.

Corn, A. L., & Martinez, I. (No date). *When you have a visually handicapped child in your classroom: Suggestions for teachers.* New York: American Foundation for the Blind (15 West 16th St., New York, NY 10011). Although much of this information applies best to elementary school, this is still a useful pamphlet for teachers who may be gathering a blind or partially sighted youngster into their group.

Edgerton, R. B. (1979). *Mental retardation.* Cambridge, MA: Harvard University Press. This is another in the series *The Developing Child.* As is characteristic of this series, the book is well written, combining descriptions of significant research with discussions of its implications. For a quick, authoritative, readable introduction to mental retardation, this would be hard to beat.

Lectenberg, R. (1984). *Epilepsy and the family.* Cambridge, MA: Harvard University Press. The discussion of epilepsy in childhood is particularly helpful in this good overall treatment of the subject.

Routh, D. K. (1986). Attention deficit disorder. In R. T. Brown & C. R. Reynolds (Eds.), *Psychological perspectives on childhood exceptionality.* New York: John Wiley & Sons. This is an excellent article on a difficult subject.

Strom, R., Johnson, A., & Strom, S. (1990). Talented children in minority families. *International Journal of Early Childhood, 22*(2), 39–48. The authors describe some alternative procedures used to identify gifted Hispanic and Anglo children and also analyze the particular parental strengths of their Hispanic and Anglo parents.

Wolfle, J. (1989). The gifted preschooler: Developmentally different, but still 3 or 4 years old. *Young Children, 44*(3), 41–48. The author deplores the lack of attention to these youngsters and suggests ways to identify them informally together with some approaches to instruction.

For the Advanced Student

Brown, R. T., and Reynolds, C. R. (1986). *Psychological perspectives on childhood exceptionality: A handbook.* New York: John Wiley & Sons. Information on general issues related to exceptionality and on specific handicaps. *Highly recommended.*

Cohen, D. J., & Donnellan, A. M. (Eds.). (1987). *Handbook of autism and pervasive developmental disorders.* New York: John Wiley & Sons. For those readers who are intensely interested in the subject, this over-700-page volume provides a gold mine of information.

Colangelo, N., & Davis, G. A. (Eds.). (1991). *Handbook of gifted education.* Boston: Allyn & Bacon. This fascinating book covers such diverse aspects of giftedness as creativity, counseling parents, young gifted children, and teaching children to think.

Edelstein, B. A., & Michelson, L. (Eds.). (1986). *Handbook of prevention.* New York: Plenum Press. How rare it is to read about prevention instead of treatment. The book covers everything from the prevention of psychopathology to dental decay.

Greenberg, P. (1988). Ideas that work with young children. *Young Children, 43*(5), 60–68. This article touches on various kinds of difficulties and discusses what the responsibilities of the teacher are in coping with them.

Karnes, M. B., & Johnson, L. J. (1989). Training for staff, parents, and volunteers working with gifted young children, especially those with disabilities and from low-income homes. *Young Children, 44*(3), 49–56. This article describes the RAPYHT model (Retrieval and Acceleration of Promising Young Handicapped and Talented) and how it was adjusted for the Head Start program. The model emphasizes developing convergent, divergent, and evaluative thinking.

Neisworth, J. T. (Ed.). (1986). *Topics in early childhood education: gifted preschoolers.* Austin, TX: Pro-Ed, 6-1. The issue covers a wide range of concerns including identification, instruction, and working with parents.

Rutter, M., & Garmezy, N. (1983). Developmental psychopathology. In P. H. Mussen (Ed.), *Handbook of child psychology* (4th ed.), E. M. Hetherington (Ed.), *Vol. IV, Socialization, personality, and social development.* New York: John Wiley & Sons. This chapter provides a first-class overview of what is presently known about autism, hyperactivity, and many other special difficulties.

Other Resources of Particular Interest

The Council for Exceptional Children (1920 Association Dr., Reston, VA 22091-1589). This organization is a good source of information on various facets of exceptionality.

Interracial Books for Children: Bulletin. 1841 Broadway, New York, NY 10023. The publishers of this bulletin are also sensitive to prejudice against handicapped children.

PART EIGHT

What Lies Ahead?

CHAPTER 22

Recent Trends
in Early Childhood Education

The moral test of government is how it treats those who are in the dawn of life, the children; those who are in the twilight of life, the aged; and those who are in the shadows of life, the sick, the needy, and the handicapped.

—Hubert H. Humphrey (1977)

Have you ever wondered . . .

Whether you would like to be a child advocate?

Whether there would be a need for someone with your training when you graduated from an early childhood program?

What are the newest trends in child care?

If you have, the material in the following pages will help you.

We live in the midst of change, and it is interesting to reflect, as this book draws to a close, on what trends we may be dealing with in the future because, after all, a beginning textbook is only that—a beginning. The teacher who has mastered the fundamentals must always look ahead to see what to turn to next. So it is important to pause and consider what trends are developing and to ask ourselves what concerns we will be facing in the coming years.

Of course, many of these issues have already been reviewed in this volume. Such things as cross-cultural, nonsexist education, child abuse, the development of a code of ethics, the role of cognitive development, and the inclusion of the exceptional child will continue to concern us in the coming decade just as building emotional health, fostering creativity, following sound routines, and building healthy bodies will remain eternally important. But we must also be aware of the shifts in emphasis and new trends that are now taking place.

CURRENT TRENDS THAT WILL BENEFIT YOUNG CHILDREN

Since the last edition of this book was published in 1988, there have been encouraging signs of progress in a number of areas benefitting young children, their families, and the people who care for them outside the home.

Increased Recognition of Developmentally Appropriate Curriculum

The publication of *Developmentally Appropriate Practice in Early Childhood Programs Serving Children from Birth Through Age 8* (Bredekamp, 1987) provided early childhood educators with an explicit set of guidelines matching recommended educational practice to children's developmental levels. The fact that, as of spring 1991, it had sold more than 160,000 copies plus over 1,000,000 brochures about it attests both to its influence and merit. *Developmentally Appropriate Practice* has already proven its worth in the ongoing struggle over appropriate kindergarten practice. It will be increasingly useful in interpreting what constitutes appropriate instruction for younger children as the trend toward including preschool classes in public schools accelerates (Hollifield, 1989).

More and More Early Childhood Facilities Accredited by the National Academy of Early Childhood Programs

As of December 1990, 1,393 centers had been accredited according to national standards, and 4,100 more were in the process of self-study leading to accreditation (National Academy of Early Childhood Programs, 1991).*

---

*For further information about accreditation, contact the National Academy of Early Childhood Programs, 1834 Connecticut Ave., NW, Washington, DC 20009; telephone 1-800-424-2460.

Increased Support and Recognition for the Head Start Program

The year 1990 witnessed Head Start's 25th anniversary (*Young Children*, 1990). That celebration reminded us of the cornerstones of the program: comprehensive educational and social services to needy children and their families, community-embedded programs, parent participation, and mainstreaming (Lombardi, 1990). In 1990 Head Start anticipated serving 488,470 children in 24,000 classrooms (Project Head Start, 1990). Although this seems like a lot of children, at present it includes only 25% of those qualifying for that service. The encouraging news is that recent funding increases reflect the intention of Congress to provide sufficient monies so that, by 1994, all eligible children can be included in the program (*CDF Reports*, 1990).

Continuation and Redefinition of the Child Development Associate Program

The CDA is a nationally available teaching certificate based on demonstrated teaching competencies. In many states it represents the first step on the ladder of professional development for early childhood caregivers (Council for Early Childhood Professional Recognition, 1990).* The CDA program helps assure the delivery of quality to the consistently expanding number of children that Head Start serves.

The Passage of Public Law 99-457 Is Another Encouraging Trend

Since the impact of PL 99-457 was discussed in the chapter on exceptionality, I will only remind the reader in this chapter of how helpful it will be in providing increased services to preschool children with special needs.

The Child Care and Development Block Grant Will Significantly Assist Poor Children and Their Families in the United States

The Block Grant squeaked through Congress as part of the budget reconciliation process in 1990. It authorized $2.5 billion for the states to use over the next 3 years to help low-income families pay for child care and to improve the quality of child care services (*CDF Reports*, 1990).

---

*For further information about CDA, contact the Council for Early Childhood Professional Recognition, 1718 Connecticut Ave., NW, 500, Washington, DC 20009; or call 1-800-424-4310.

THE CHILD ADVOCACY MOVEMENT

During the past 10 years as the political fortunes of young children have waxed and waned on the national and state level, people who care about them have gained a new skill (Goffin & Lombardi, 1988; Jensen & Chevalier, 1990). We have learned how to speak out for children in order to protect programs such as WIC (a maternal/child nutrition program) (Jensen, 1990) and Head Start from being slashed from the budget.

In order to be most effective, a number of child advocacy groups have formed. These are growing in strength as time goes on, and the need for them has become increasingly obvious as budgets are slashed and services cut.

Perhaps the best evidence of how effective that advocacy effort has become is to quote from the previous edition of *The Whole Child* published in 1988. It said, "One newly formed advocacy group, the Alliance for Better Child Care, intends to begin a long-term effort directed toward developing and supporting a comprehensive federal child care bill. It is probable that this coalition will generate an important new trend in the coming years" (p. 501). It is precisely the efforts of that coalition that produced the ABC bill (Act for Better Child Care), which was largely incorporated in the Block Grant discussed previously.

One of the best-known child advocacy organizations is the Children's Defense Fund.* The Fund publishes a timely newsletter, *CDF Reports*, that contains information on various issues affecting children as well as lists of the Fund's other publications.

There are a number of additional, more specialized advocacy groups of which the reader also should be aware. Their concerns range from improving the quality of children's television[†] to providing input from minority groups into the decision-making process.[‡] Still other organizations are pressing for better family day care,[§] to alleviate child abuse,[‖] or to improve the wholesomeness of our food and our knowledge of good nutrition.[¶]

In addition to these groups, there are the professional organizations such as the National Association for the Education of Young Children (NAEYC), the Day Care and Child Development Council of America, the Association for Childhood Education International, the Southern Association for Children Under Six, and the Child Welfare League of America. These groups have had an interest in the well-being of children for many years and are more and more active in advocacy. (For addresses of these organizations, see Appendix G.)

Besides continuing to act individually in accordance with their special areas of concern, many of these advocacy groups are also creating "networks"—

---

*Children's Defense Fund, 122 C St. NW, Washington, DC 20001

†Action for Children's Television, 46 Austin St., Newtonville, MA 02160

‡Black Child Development Institute, 1463 Rhode Island Ave., N.W., Washington, DC 20005

§The Children's Foundation, 725 15th St. NW, #505, Washington, DC 20005

‖National Committee for Prevention of Child Abuse, 332 S. Michigan Ave., Suite 950, Chicago, IL 60604

¶Center for Science in the Public Interest, 1875 Connecticut Ave., Suite 300, NW, Washington, DC, 20009-5728

coalitions that seek by combining powers to bring even stronger force and expertise to bear for the benefit of children. Many of these networks are forming on an informal basis at the local and state level, and a heartening aspect of this movement is the intention of these groups to be, as they put it, "in on the takeoffs instead of the crash landings" (that is, to stress prevention and the enactment of effective legislation rather than eternally trying to clean up results after a disaster).

So it is evident that much effective advocacy work is taking place and that groups are gaining expertise and effectiveness as time goes on. People realize that the time is past when parents and teachers of young children can afford to remain ignorant of what is happening in Washington or in various state capitals across the nation. Fortunately, many organizations are now including this information in their publications. For example, *Young Children*, which is the official publication of the National Association for the Education of Young Children, regularly carries a "Washington Update" column.

The difficulty with many advocacy efforts is that politically naive people often assume that because they have succeeded in winning on an issue once, they have won on that issue forever. When the same question comes up again in the next session of the legislature, they feel tired and disillusioned. They ask themselves, "What's the use?" and then they surrender.

Sophisticated advocates, on the other hand, realize that political life is a series of skirmishes and that winning one battle does not mean they have won the war. Instead, they are prepared to continue the fight with vigor—every year, with every legislature. They seize every opportunity to get to know every one who has influence and to educate them about the values and necessity of providing quality care for young children, *and while they may have to compromise sometimes, they never give up.* This persistence is going to be increasingly important in the coming years as the United States struggles under the burden of war costs incurred in the Persian Gulf and the rising national debt.

INCREASED NEED FOR SERVICES TO YOUNG CHILDREN

Is the Need for Child Care Increasing?

Since the early 1970s the proportion of mothers working outside the home has shifted from 29% in 1970 to 51% in 1988 (Hofferth, 1989). The most dramatic change has been in the proportion of mothers working outside the home who have children under 1 year of age, which increased by 65% between 1975 and 1987 (Hofferth, 1989). Projections estimate that by 1995 two-thirds of the projected total population of preschool children will have mothers in the labor force (Hofferth & Phillips, 1987). These dramatic facts indicate just how badly additional child care, particularly infant care and afterschool care, is needed and will continue to be needed in the years to come.

In order to meet this need, the number of workers in prekindergarten and kindergarten programs almost doubled between 1972 and 1984 (NAEYC, 1985).

It is estimated that between 1982 and 1995, employment in programs for young children will increase by as much as 40% (U.S. Department of Labor, 1984), so it is clear that jobs in this field will be plentiful. But there is another side to this apparently rosy employment picture: it is that a great many people in the child care profession leave it each year. The Child Care Employee Project (1988) reports that many communities are finding that between 40 to 60% of their teachers leave their jobs annually. This high turnover is due primarily to the currently unsolved problem of low wages and inadequate benefits for too many of the people who work in this field (NAEYC, 1990).

INCREASED CONCERN ABOUT LOW WAGES

Everyone deplores these low salaries but the question, "What can be done to improve the situation?" still lacks satisfactory answers.

When parents pay the cost of child care, as is the usual case in the United States, they are caught between two pressures. They want good care for their children, but they also have many demands made on their incomes. Parents therefore often choose the least expensive and most conveniently located program. But the fact is that in child care, just as with other services, you generally get what you pay for. Centers that charge minimum fees can only pay minimum wages, and staff who work for minimum wages may also have minimum training and suffer from low morale as well. The problem is a serious one, but some partial remedies are already available, and others are in the offing.

One part of the solution is a long-term effort. Our profession is already working to educate the public (and parents in particular) about the components of good child care and what those components cost. The largest expense of most programs is wages. Many parents would never consider working for minimum wages themselves, and they certainly want what is best for their children. These parents are often shocked to learn that their children's teachers work for little more than minimum wage and have few benefits, if any. Parents need to know that high-quality care requires competent people and that qualified people are entitled to a wage equivalent to salaries paid for other jobs requiring comparable levels of skills and training.

Unions are also entering the arena, and it may well be that in time union membership will be one of the most effective ways to raise wages and benefits to a more satisfactory level.*

Industry- and government-supported programs also exist; their staff salaries and benefits are often more competitive with other fields, and their program standards are generally also higher.

As more and more states come to recognize the value of education for children younger than age 5, more and more of them are offering at least some

---

*Daycare and Human Service Local District 65, UAW, 636 Beacon St., Boston, MA 02215.

programs for those youngsters. A recent report by the National Governor's Association and the Center for Policy Research (1987) and one by the National Research Council (Hayes, Palmer, & Zaslow, 1990) are encouraging indications that this trend will continue. Because publically supported programs are subsidized by the state, they also will provide more adequate salaries for teachers who work in those settings. We need to be aware when proposals for such programs come before our legislators and be prepared to let them know that we support them for the children's sake as well as our own.

The second part of the remedy is for us to be more courageous in standing up for ourselves. The problem of too low wages for too many of us is not going to go away unless *we* do something about it. As members of a growing profession, we cannot sit back and expect someone else to do it all for us.

Steps are already being taken by such organizations as the National Association for the Education of Young Children, the Children's Defense Fund, and the Child Care Employees Project, all of which are disseminating information about the salary issue. The current emphasis from NAEYC is summed up in the words "quality, compensation, and affordability." If quality is to be obtained, adequate compensation must be found for the teachers of young children. This must be accomplished while making sure the service remains within the financial reach of the families requiring care. It is encouraging to note that the Child Care and Development Block Grant also recognizes this serious problem and provides funds to the states that may be used to address the problem. It is up to us in the field to make certain these provisions are put in place.

QUALITY CARE FOR INFANTS AND TODDLERS REMAINS IN GREAT DEMAND

We have only to review the statistics concerning the increasing number of women working outside the home to realize that the need to provide care for very young children is not going to disappear.

Most of the need for infant/toddler care appears to be met by family day care arrangements within the neighborhood or by family members (Hayes et al., 1990). However, an increasing acceptance of *group* infant-toddler care arrangements is reflected by the publication of a number of books in this area (Leavitt & Eheart, 1985; Musick & Householder, 1986; Weiser, 1982; Wilson, 1990).

Although it is heartening to examine these books and see that expert advice is being made available to practitioners in this field, we must never forget that the younger the child, the more vulnerable he is to environmental insult and the less able he is to protect himself from malign conditions or from overstimulation (Bromwich, 1977). Nor can we depend on the possibility that parents are always good judges of child care or infant care situations. I hear frequent tales of parents in my own community who simply call and enroll their youngsters in nursery schools and children's centers without asking anything beyond the price and who express surprise when invited to visit.

Some states still do not license children's centers at all, and many who do, either do not license infant care or provide no educational standards for infant caregivers (Adams, 1990). Even in those states where licensing is in effect, quality of care provided varies widely.

If these circumstances are true of preschool care, it is not likely that they are also true of infant care? Yet poor infant care may have even more serious consequences for development than poor preschool care does. *For this reason, infant care should still be regarded with caution and championed as a cause only if strong safeguards are built into the program and knowledgeable people are on hand to provide continuing supervision, guidance, and encouragement for the staff.*

INCREASED FLEXIBILITY AND VARIETY IN CHILD CARE ALTERNATIVES

The pressing need for child care has produced a number of alternatives from which parents may choose. *Family day care* is most frequently selected at this time, particularly for children below age 3. The majority of these homes are not licensed or inspected in any way. Quality varies accordingly. The encouraging note is that some providers are banding together and making sincere, practical efforts to improve such care by advocating and supporting relevant courses in community colleges and extension programs and by attending workshops provided by their member organizations.

For-Profit Day Care Systems Continue to Grow

It is interesting to note that the United States appears to be the only nation in the world where private enterprise has entered the child care field. Prior to 1989, analysis of the 50 largest private organizations showed that they were increasing the number of their centers by 8 to 10% per year. However, in 1989 and 1990 this rate of growth decreased dramatically to less than 2% (Neugebauer, 1991). This decrease was due to a number of factors, including the recession, overbuilding in certain cities, and increased difficulty in locating financial backing. However, smaller chains continue to prosper, so it is likely that for-profit centers will remain a part of the U.S. child care scene in the years to come.

Still another alternative attempt to meet the need for child care is exemplified by *employer-related child care.* Sometimes such care is provided right where the parent works and even is subsidized by management (Polito, 1989). Hospitals, for example, have become increasingly interested in such services, seeing them as an effective way to help stabilize their nursing population (Perry, 1978). Sometimes vouchers are provided for child care of the parent's own choosing, or a referral service is maintained. Occasionally companies contract with an agency or for-profit system to furnish care.

The increasing number of young women of high school age who are having and keeping their babies has also resulted in the provision by some school districts of *child care on high school campuses* (Honig, 1982b). Provision of such care carries a number of benefits along with it—among them, the opportunity for mothers to remain close to their babies while continuing their education and the opportunity to provide support and child development information to them, too, so they can do a better job of caring for the children they have elected to keep.

On-base child care for military families has grown phenomenally in the past 15 years as it has gradually come to be recognized by the military services that providing child care is a stabilizing influence on families and helpful in eking out military pay. Presently the Pentagon operates 554 centers on more than 400 bases worldwide, and it spent $101 million on its child care programs in fiscal year 1985 (Day Care Special Report, 1986), so it is evident that it is making a large, continuing commitment to this service.

Of particular interest to students is the trend toward offering *child care on campuses*—a movement that extends from the university (Corrigan, 1984; Day, 1984) to the community college level. Offering child care is a popular cause with most students. Good services for children can come about as a result of this enthusiasm if early childhood personnel on campus are willing to make friends with sponsors of these movements and help them learn about what quality child care entails.

Still another pattern of service is the move toward *educating children in the home itself* (Berger, 1991; Gray et al., 1982; Honig, 1982b). Many home tutoring programs are based on the idea of a weekly visitor who brings materials for the children to use but who also focuses on drawing the mother in so that she gradually adds to her personal repertoire ideas and activities that enhance her youngster's growth. For example, when the mother herself understands how important it is to develop language competence in young children and also understands in simple, practical ways how she can foster this ability in her children, a positive, continuing influence has been built into her children's lives. The long-term benefits of this approach to the family are obvious.

The newest entry into the field of child care is, in reality, a very old-fashioned one. It is the institution of the *nanny*, long used by well-to-do people in Europe as a means of providing supervised child care in the home. At present there are a few colleges providing such training, but most nannies are trained by their placement service or by nanny schools. Some families have found this service to be a real boon, but, for the majority, it is too expensive.

INCREASED FLEXIBILITY AND CHANGES IN APPROACHES TO TEACHER TRAINING

Accompanying increased demands for flexibility in patterns of care is an interest in new patterns of teacher training (Spodek & Saracho, 1990). Community colleges have often led the way in this regard by enabling students to reduce expenses by living at home while taking classes. Four-year colleges are paying increased attention to training for kindergarten teachers that stresses an early childhood philosophy.

The Child Development Associate Program continues to provide training for some early childhood teachers, primarily those involved in the Head Start Program. The CDA is a competency-based program currently administered by the National Association for the Education of Young Children that equips the participant with a credential based on national rather than state standards. It combines on-the-job experience with course work often provided through community colleges. While engaged in these activities, the applicant builds a portfolio that shows how she or he has accomplished the goals of the program. When this work is completed and approved by an impartial committee, the CDA certificate is awarded (Council for Early Childhood Professional Recognition, 1990).

All levels of education are exploring the use of television as a means of offering high-quality educational programs to be viewed at home and taken for unit credit. Packaged programs of taped lectures and discussions are more readily available also.

THE DEVELOPMENT OF ADDITIONAL PREKINDERGARTEN PROGRAMS FOR 4-YEAR-OLDS

In 1988, 28 states provided such programs for at least some of the children (Day, 1988). This trend is encouraging since it means more children may be educated in a desirable way, and, at least in some of those states, will receive comprehensive health and social services as well.

The concern expressed by many early childhood educators, however, is that public schools will force these young children into an educative model that is developmentally inappropriate for their age. Fortunately, the majority of the programs now in place require teachers to have some type of early childhood certification (Morada, 1986), but early childhood advocates must remain vigilant lest administrators transfer unqualified elementary teachers into that program because they are tenured (Warger, 1988).

Obviously there are many issues involved in allowing 4-year-olds in the public school, among them standards, funding, and which children qualify for service (Kagan & Zigler, 1988). It is likely that these issues will have to be solved state by state as the decade progresses. The Developmental Guidelines published by the National Association for the Education of Young Children (Bredekamp, 1987) combined with other publications, such as *Right from the Start* (National Association of State Boards of Education, 1988) and *Focus on the First Sixty Months* (National Governor's Association and the Center for Policy Research, 1987), provide valuable resources for those of us working with legislators to define what constitutes wholesome and appropriate education for these young children.

RECOGNITION OF THE NEED FOR BETTER RESEARCH

Studies in the area of early childhood have not been as numerous as one might wish, nor do they offer the comfort of replication. Moreover, the existing studies have often been characterized by small sample size and, in some of the earlier studies, by naive design. Longitudinal studies are still in short supply.

Many fields remain to be explored (Seefeldt, 1987). We need to learn more about children who are functioning well and what benign circumstances in their lives have made this possible. Experts from diverse fields need to look over the walls of their specific disciplines and talk with each other. For example, early childhood and child development specialists should be talking intensively and frequently with individuals concerned about the special education of preschool children, and these groups should be pooling their knowledge for the benefit of those youngsters.

Finally, there is a need for systematic exploration of topics so that we will not have to depend on hunt-and-peck results that must be fitted into a larger pattern of needed knowledge like pieces of a jigsaw puzzle.

Yet with all these problems we are on firmer ground today with research than we have been in the past. More areas are being investigated, and designs and statistical methods are increasing in sophistication and rigor. The addition of our research journals, the *Early Childhood Research Quarterly* and the *Journal of Research in Childhood Education,* are promising indications that both the quality and quantity of research in the area of early childhood are increasing. (Refer to Appendix G for the journal addresses.)

UNSOLVED PROBLEMS AND NEW TRENDS DEMAND ATTENTION

While rejoicing over the strides made in helping young children during the past few years, we must remember that much remains to be done in the United States to assure children's welfare. Our infant mortality rate remains among the highest of the more advanced nations (Children's Defense Fund, 1989). One of every five children in the United States lives in poverty (Chafel, 1990). The AIDS crisis continues to grow and, with it, the need to care for children afflicted with that condition (Hutchings, 1988; Rudigier, Crocker, & Cohen, 1990). And so-called "crack babies," infants victimized by the cocaine addiction of their mothers, are becoming ever more frequent (Gittler & McPherson, 1990). The plight of homeless children and their families is also becoming more evident (Kozol, 1990).

These situations present terrible problems for our society to confront—problems that require concerted effort to solve. We early childhood teachers must do our part by advocating what the children need. They cannot do it for themselves.

TWO GUIDELINES TO REMEMBER

With so much to do and so many problems to solve, the reader may well wonder if there are any general principles to keep in mind that will help in making decisions for that uncertain and sometimes clouded future that lies before us. There are two, at least, that are helpful to remember.

First, there is the continuing need for teachers to remain open to new ideas and continued growth. We must beware of becoming trapped in congealing philosophy. Katz said it well in 1974 and it is just as true today: "We must proceed—having enough skepticism to keep on learning, but with enough confidence to keep on acting." If I could leave readers with only one thought, it would be, "Never hesitate to question, but do not allow doubt to paralyze your ability to act."

The second guideline to remember is "When in doubt about the value of a decision, put the child's welfare first." In the press of other concerns, whether it be legislation, teacher training, or the search for a "perfect" educational model, there is a real risk that in the struggle we will lose sight of the most important person of all—that young, vulnerable individual filled with fascinat-

That small, vulnerable individual we call "the preschool child" . . .

ing complexities and bewildering contradictions whom we have named "the preschool child."

It is, after all, this child's well-being that we must put ahead of every other concern in early childhood education. So when policies are made or compromises suggested that cause us concern, then we must unhesitatingly apply the yardstick of what will be of maximum benefit to him as we make the decisions that affect his future.

QUESTIONS AND ACTIVITIES

1. By the time you read this chapter on trends, even newer ones will be arising. What additional ones are you aware of that have developed in the field of early childhood education?

2. Are there any activities in your local community that reflect the child advocacy movement? Share with the class how these gained impetus and whether the advocacy activities appear to be producing positive changes in the lives of children.

3. Some people feel that the growth of day care and other early childhood programs is a threat to the home life of the child and will contribute to the destruction of family life by weakening bonds between its members. Explain why you do or do not agree with this point of view.

4. Many women now champion the cause of infant care outside the home as one of women's fundamental rights. If you were asked to be on a panel to discuss the desirability of infant care for very young children, what position would you take? Be sure to state your reasons for your point of view.

5. *Problem:* You have two young children of your own and, like many other students, you need child care badly in order to continue your education. The licensing restrictions for child care are clearly defined and enforced in your state and require such things as a fenced yard, a toilet for every seven children, 35 square feet of indoor and 75 square feet of outdoor space for every child, and some units of early childhood education for the teachers. You are desperately interested in starting a day care center, but these restrictions obviously increase the cost and difficulty of beginning it. Under these circumstances, do you feel it would be all right for the center to "just begin" and go underground? What might the alternatives be to doing this?

SELF-CHECK QUESTIONS FOR REVIEW

Content-Related Questions

1. List several trends that are currently benefiting young children in the United States.

2. What are some very serious problems that remain to be addressed?

3. What is one of the serious mistakes naive advocates for young children often make?

4. Do more women with young children work outside the home, or do more of them stay at home with their youngsters?

5. Is the demand for people working in the prekindergarten and kindergarten field likely to increase? And, if so, by what percentage?

6. List some possible ways salaries for preprimary staff could be increased.

7. List some alternative kinds of child care and tell a few facts about each kind.

8. What is a CDA credential and how is it obtained?

9. Many people are concerned about the possibility of adding 4-year-olds to public schools. What is the primary reason for such concern?

10. Give some examples that indicate that the quality of research about young children is improving.

11. What are the basic guidelines to remember as teachers continue to work toward quality care for all preschool children?

Integrative Questions

1. Compare the potential pros and cons of teaching a 4-year-old class in a public school versus teaching the same group in a non-public school such as a church-sponsored one.

2. How are quality child care and adequate compensation linked together?

3. You are a mother working outside the home and have a 6-week-old baby. What might be the advantages of placing the baby in a family day care home? And what might be the disadvantages?

4. You still have that 6-week-old baby and are still working outside the home. What might be the advantages of placing your baby in a child care center? What might be the disadvantages of doing this?

REFERENCES FOR FURTHER READING

Overviews

Hayes, C. D., Palmer, J. L., & Zaslow, M. J. (Eds.). (1990). *Who cares for America's children? Child care policy for the 1990s*. Washington, DC: National Academy Press. This indispensable volume sums up in clear prose much of what is known about what exists and what should exist in quality care for young children.

Hollifield, J. (1989). Trends in early childhood and elementary education. In J. Hollifield et al., *Children learning in groups and other trends in elementary and early childhood education* (#204). Urbana, IL: ERIC Clearinghouse on Elementary and Early Childhood Education. This paper presents a clear-sighted analysis of reasons the "trickle-down" and proacademic preschool pressures exist.

Hymes, J. L., Jr. (1990). *Early childhood education: The year in review: A look at 1989*. Washington, DC: National Association for the Education of Young Children. Hymes authors this review each year. It is the only way I know of to keep abreast of what has *just* happened in the field of early child care and teacher training. *Highly recommended*.

Guidelines for Quality Care for Young Children

Bredekamp, S. (Ed.). (1987). *Developmentally appropriate practice*. Washington, DC: National Association for the Education of Young Children. This invaluable publication defines what constitutes developmentally appropriate educational practices for children from birth to age 5. It is particularly useful because it also provides examples of what constitutes *inappropriate* practice.

National Association for the Education of Young Children (1984). *Accreditation criteria & procedures of the National Academy of Early Childhood Programs*. Washington, DC: The Association. The accreditation guide provides a list of standards that explicitly spells out the ingredients of a sound child care program. *An indispensable resource*.

Child Advocacy

Goffin, S. G., & Lombardi, J. (1988). *Speaking out: Early childhood advocacy*. Washington, DC: National Association for the Education of Young Children. Lots of down-to-earth examples of advocacy are included here that demonstrate how easy it is for everyone to become involved. Also contains useful resources.

Haycock, K., & Alston, D. (1990). *An advocate's guide to improving education.* Washington, DC: Children's Defense Fund. The authors stress the need for wide community-based support and provide a careful plan showing how to organize community action for networking.

Jensen, M. S., & Chevalier, Z. W. (Eds.). (1990). *Issues and advocacy in early education.* Boston: Allyn & Bacon. This unusual book presents issues and then suggests exercises for practice in advocacy. *Highly recommended.*

Schorr, L. B., & Schorr, D. (1988). *Within our reach: Breaking the cycle of disadvantage.* New York: Doubleday. The Schorrs review what is known about the potential positive effects of early education and other supportive services, and they make a good case for extending them. *Highly recommended.*

Information on Salary Concerns

The following publications all address various aspects of how to raise salaries and benefits. Titles are self-explanatory.

Boyer, M., Gerst, C., & Eastwood, S. (Eds.). *Between a rock and a hard place: Raising rates to raise wages.* Minneapolis: Child Care Workers Alliance (301 E. 38th St., Minneapolis, MN 55409).

Marx, E., & Zinsser, C. (1990). *Raising child care salaries and benefits: An evaluation of the New York State salary enhancement legislation.* New York: Bank Street College (610 W. 112th St., New York, NY 10025).

Morin, J. (1989). *Taking action: A proposal for improving compensation in the early childhood field through employee activism.* Madison: Wisconsin Early Childhood Association.

Willer, B. A. (1988). *The growing crisis in child care: Quality, compensation, and affordability in early childhood programs.* Washington, DC: National Association for the Education of Young Children.

Willer, B. A. (1990). *Reaching the full cost of quality in early childhood programs.* Washington, DC: National Association for the Education of Young Children.

Resources for Current Information

CDF Reports, Children's Defense Fund, 122 C Street, NW, Washington, DC 20001. This publication focuses on child advocacy information and also offers current lists of CDF's other publications.

Education Week: American Education Newspaper of Record. Editorial Projects in Education, 1255 23rd St., Washington, DC 20036. An overall newspaper-type publication that always has something of interest for the early childhood educator. Features useful compilations of statistical information as its centerfold. A very good value for the money.

Report on Preschool Education. Capitol Publications, 1300 N. 17th St., Arlington, VA 22209. Expensive but useful.

For the Advanced Student

General Accounting Office. (1990). *Early childhood education: What are the costs of high-quality programs?* (GAO/HRD-90-43BR). Washington, DC: U.S. Government Printing Office. This pamphlet gives the results of a study that used NAEYC-accredited programs to determine the true cost of quality care—a valuable reference.

Jorde-Bloom, P. (1988). *A great place to work: Improving conditions for staff in young children's programs.* Washington, DC: National Association for the Education of Young Children. The author discusses practical ways to improve job satisfaction besides raising wages.

Kagan, S. L. (1989). Early child care and education: Tackling the tough issues. *Phi Delta Kappan, 70*(6), 433–439. Kagan provides an overview of basic problems of inequity, discontinuity, and fragmentation that plague the delivery of child care services to children who need them. *Highly recommended.*

Warger, C. (1988). *A resource guide to public school early childhood programs.* Alexandria, VA: Association for Supervision and Curriculum Development. This book includes a particularly useful chart of child care services available state by state.

Appendices

APPENDIX A

The National Association for the Education of Young Children: Code of Ethical Conduct*

PREAMBLE

NAEYC recognizes that many daily decisions required of those who work with young children are of a moral and ethical nature. The NAEYC Code of Ethical Conduct offers guidelines for responsible behavior and sets forth a common basis for resolving the principal ethical dilemmas encountered in early childhood education. The primary focus is on daily practice with children and their families in programs for children from birth to 8 years of age: preschools, child care centers, family day care homes, kindergartens, and primary classrooms. Many of the provisions also apply to specialists who do not work directly with children, including program administrators, parent educators, college professors, and child care licensing specialists.

Standards of ethical behavior in early childhood education are based on commitment to core values that are deeply rooted in the history of our field. We have committed ourselves to:

- Appreciating childhood as a unique and valuable stage of the human life cycle
- Basing our work with children on knowledge of child development
- Appreciating and supporting the close ties between the child and family
- Recognizing that children are best understood in the context of family, culture, and society
- Respecting the dignity, worth, and uniqueness of each individual (child, family member, and colleague)
- Helping children and adults achieve their full potential in the context of relationships that are based on trust, respect, and positive regard

The Code sets forth a conception of our professional responsibilities in four sections, each addressing an arena of professional relationships: 1) children, 2) families, 3) colleagues, and 4) community and society. Each section includes an introduction to the primary responsibilities of the early childhood practitioner in that arena, a set of ideals pointing in the direction of exemplary professional practice, and a set of principles defining practices that are required, prohibited, and permitted.

*This Code of Ethical Conduct and Statement of Commitment was prepared under the auspices of the Ethics Commission of the National Association for the Education of Young Children. The Commission members were Stephanie Feeney (Chairperson), Bettye Caldwell, Sally Cartwright, Carrie Cheek, Josué Cruz, Jr., Anne G. Dorsey, Dorothy M. Hill, Lilian G. Katz, Pamm Mattick, Shirley A. Norris, and Sue Spayth Riley.
Reprinted with permission from the National Association for the Education of Young Children, © 1989.

The ideals reflect the aspirations of practitioners. The principles are intended to guide conduct and assist practitioners in resolving ethical dilemmas encountered in the field. There is not necessarily a corresponding principle for each ideal. Both ideals and principles are intended to direct practitioners to those questions which, when responsibly answered, will provide the basis for conscientious decision making. While the Code provides specific direction for addressing some ethical dilemmas, many others will require the practitioner to combine the guidance of the Code with sound professional judgment.

The ideals and principles in this Code present a shared conception of professional responsibility that affirms our commitment to the core values of our field. The Code publicly acknowledges the responsibilities that we in the field have assumed and in so doing supports ethical behavior in our work. Practitioners who face ethical dilemmas are urged to seek guidance in the applicable parts of this Code and in the spirit that informs the whole.

SECTION I: ETHICAL RESPONSIBILITIES TO CHILDREN

Childhood is a unique and valuable stage in the life cycle. Our paramount responsibility is to provide safe, healthy, nurturing, and responsive settings for children. We are committed to supporting children's development by cherishing individual differences, by helping them learn to live and work cooperatively, and by promoting their self-esteem.

Ideals

I-1.1 To be familiar with the knowledge base of early childhood education and to keep current through continuing education and in-service training.

I-1.2 To base program practices upon current knowledge in the field of child development and related disciplines and upon particular knowledge of each child.

I-1.3 To recognize and respect the uniqueness and the potential of each child.

I-1.4 To appreciate the special vulnerability of children.

I-1.5 To create and maintain safe and healthy settings that foster children's social, emotional, intellectual, and physical development and that respect their dignity and their contributions.

I-1.6 To support the right of children with special needs to participate, consistent with their ability, in regular early childhood programs.

Principles

P-1.1 Above all, we shall not harm children. We shall not participate in practices that are disrespectful, degrading, dangerous, exploitative, intimidating, psychologically damaging, or physically harmful to children. *This principle has precedence over all others in this Code.*

P-1.2 We shall not participate in practices that discriminate against children by denying benefits, giving special advantages, or excluding them from programs or activities on the basis of their race, religion, sex, national origin, or the status, behavior, or beliefs of their parents. (This principle does not apply to programs that have a lawful mandate to provide services to a particular population of children.)

P-1.3 We shall involve all of those with relevant knowledge (including staff and parents) in decisions concerning a child.

P-1.4 When, after appropriate efforts have been made with a child and the family, the child still does not appear to be benefitting from a program, we shall communicate our concern to the family in a positive way and offer them assistance in finding a more suitable setting.

P-1.5 We shall be familiar with the symptoms of child abuse and neglect and know community procedures for addressing them.

P-1.6 When we have evidence of child abuse or neglect, we shall report the evidence to the appropriate community agency and follow up to ensure that appropriate action has been taken. When possible, parents will be informed that the referral has been made.

P-1.7 When another person tells us of their suspicion that a child is being abused or neglected but we lack evidence, we shall assist that person in taking appropriate action to protect the child.

P-1.8 When a child protective agency fails to provide adequate protection for abused or neglected children, we acknowledge a collective ethical responsibility to work toward improvement of these services.

SECTION II: ETHICAL RESPONSIBILITIES TO FAMILIES

Families are of primary importance in children's development. (The term *family* may include others, besides parents, who are responsibly involved with the child.) Because the family and the early childhood educator have a common interest in the child's welfare, we acknowledge a primary responsibility to bring about collaboration between the home and school in ways that enhance the child's development.

Ideals

I-2.1 To develop relationships of mutual trust with the families we serve.

I-2.2 To acknowledge and build upon strengths and competencies as we support families in their task of nurturing children.

I-2.3 To respect the dignity of each family and its culture, customs, and beliefs.

I-2.4 To respect families' childrearing values and their right to make decisions for their children.

I-2.5 To interpret each child's progress to parents within the framework of a developmental perspective and to help families understand and appreciate the value of developmentally appropriate early childhood programs.

I-2.6 To help family members improve their understanding of their children and to enhance their skills as parents.

I-2.7 To participate in building support networks for families by providing them with opportunities to interact with program staff and families.

Principles

P-2.1 We shall not deny family members access to their child's classroom or program setting.

P-2.2 We shall inform families of program philosophy, policies, and personnel qualifications, and explain why we teach as we do.

P-2.3 We shall inform families of and, when appropriate, involve them in policy decisions.

P-2.4 We shall inform families of and, when appropriate, involve them in significant decisions affecting their child.

P-2.5 We shall inform the family of accidents involving their child, of risks such as exposures to contagious disease that may result in infection, and of events that might result in psychological damage.

P-2.6 We shall not permit or participate in research that could in any way hinder the education or development of the children in our programs. Families shall be fully informed of any proposed research projects involving their children and shall have the opportunity to give or withhold consent.

P-2.7 We shall not engage in or support exploitation of families. We shall not use our relationship with a family for private advantage or personal gain, or enter into relationships with family members that might impair our effectiveness in working with children.

P-2.8 We shall develop written policies for the protection of confidentiality and the disclosure of children's records. The policy documents shall be made available to all program personnel and families. Disclosure of children's records beyond family members, program personnel, and consultants having an obligation of confidentiality shall require familial consent (except in cases of abuse or neglect).

P-2.9 We shall maintain confidentiality and shall respect the family's right to privacy, refraining from disclosure of confidential information and intrusion into family life. However, when we are concerned about a child's welfare, it is permissible to reveal confidential information to agencies and individuals who may be able to act in the child's interest.

P-2.10   In cases where family members are in conflict we shall work openly, sharing our observations of the child, to help all parties involved make informed decisions. We shall refrain from becoming an advocate for one party.

P-2.11   We shall be familiar with and appropriately use community resources and professional services that support families. After a referral has been made, we shall follow up to ensure that services have been adequately provided.

SECTION III: ETHICAL RESPONSIBILITIES TO COLLEAGUES

In a caring, cooperative work place human dignity is respected, professional satisfaction is promoted, and positive relationships are modeled. Our primary responsibility in this arena is to establish and maintain settings and relationships that support productive work and meet professional needs.

A—RESPONSIBILITIES TO CO-WORKERS

Ideals

I-3A.1   To establish and maintain relationships of trust and cooperation with co-workers.

I-3A.2   To share resources and information with co-workers.

I-3A.3   To support co-workers in meeting their professional needs and in their professional development.

I-3A.4   To accord co-workers due recognition of professional achievement.

Principles

P-3A.1   When we have concern about the professional behavior of a co-worker, we shall first let that person know of our concern and attempt to resolve the matter collegially.

P-3A.2   We shall exercise care in expressing views regarding the personal attributes or professional conduct of co-workers. Statements should be based on firsthand knowledge and relevant to the interests of children and programs.

B—RESPONSIBILITIES TO EMPLOYERS

Ideals

I-3B.1   To assist the program in providing the highest quality of service.

I-3B.2   To maintain loyalty to the program and uphold its reputation.

Principles

P-3B.1   When we do not agree with program policies, we shall first attempt to effect change through constructive action within the organization.

P-3B.2   We shall speak or act on behalf of an organization only when authorized. We shall take care to note when we are speaking for the organization and when we are expressing a personal judgment.

C—RESPONSIBILITIES TO EMPLOYEES

Ideals

I-3C.1   To promote policies and working conditions that foster competence, well-being, and self-esteem in staff members.

I-3C.2   To create a climate of trust and candor that will enable staff to speak and act in the best interests of children, families, and the field of early childhood education.

I-3C.3   To strive to secure an adequate livelihood for those who work with or on behalf of young children.

Principles

P-3C.1   In decisions concerning children and programs, we shall appropriately utilize the training, experience, and expertise of staff members.

P-3C.2   We shall provide staff members with working conditions that permit them to carry out their responsibilities, timely and nonthreatening evaluation procedures, written grievance procedures, constructive feedback, and opportunities for continuing professional development and advancement.

P-3C.3   We shall develop and maintain comprehensive written personnel policies that define program standards and, when applicable, that specify the extent to which employees are accountable for their conduct outside the work place. These policies shall be given to new staff members and shall be available for review by all staff members.

P-3C.4   Employees who do not meet program standards shall be informed of areas of concern and, when possible, assisted in improving their performance.

P-3C.5   Employees who are dismissed shall be informed of the reasons for their termination. When a dismissal is for cause, justification must be based on evidence of inadequate or inappropriate behavior that is accurately documented, current, and available for the employee to review.

P-3C.6   In making evaluations and recommendations, judgments shall be based on fact and relevant to the interests of children and programs.

P-3C.7   Hiring and promotion shall be based solely on a person's record of accomplishment and ability to carry out the responsibilities of the position.

P-3C.8   In hiring, promotion, and provision of training, we shall not participate in any form of discrimination based on race, religion, sex, national origin, handicap, age, or sexual preference. We shall be familiar with laws and regulations that pertain to employment discrimination.

SECTION IV: ETHICAL RESPONSIBILITIES TO COMMUNITY AND SOCIETY

Early childhood programs operate within a context of an immediate community made up of families and other institutions concerned with children's welfare. Our responsibilities to the community are to provide programs that meet its needs and to cooperate with agencies and professions that share responsibility for children. Because the large society has a measure of responsibility for the welfare and protection of children, and because of our specialized expertise in child development, we acknowledge an obligation to serve as a voice for children everywhere.

Ideals

I-4.1   To provide the community with high-quality, culturally sensitive programs and services.

I-4.2   To promote cooperation among agencies and professions concerned with the welfare of young children, their families, and their teachers.

I-4.3   To work, through education, research, and advocacy, toward an environmentally safe world in which all children are adequately fed, sheltered, and nurtured.

I-4.4   To work, through education, research, and advocacy, toward a society in which all young children have access to quality programs.

I-4.5   To promote knowledge and understanding of young children and their needs. To work toward greater social acknowledgment of children's rights and greater social acceptance of responsibility for their well-being.

I-4.6   To support policies and laws that promote the well-being of children and families. To oppose those that impair their well-being. To cooperate with other individuals and groups in these efforts.

I-4.7   To further the professional development of the field of early childhood education and to strengthen its commitment to realizing its core values as reflected in this Code.

Principles

P-4.1   We shall communicate openly and truthfully about the nature and extent of services that we provide.

P-4.2   We shall not accept or continue to work in positions for which we are personally unsuited or professionally unqualified. We shall not offer services that we do not have the competence, qualifications, or resources to provide.

P-4.3   We shall be objective and accurate in reporting the knowledge upon which we base our program practices.

P-4.4 We shall cooperate with other professionals who work with children and their families.

P-4.5 We shall not hire or recommend for employment any person who is unsuited for a position with respect to competence, qualifications, or character.

P-4.6 We shall report the unethical or incompetent behavior of a colleague to a supervisor when informal resolution is not effective.

P-4.7 We shall be familiar with laws and regulations that serve to protect the children in our programs.

P-4.8 We shall not participate in practices which are in violation of laws and regulations that protect the children in our programs.

P-4.9 When we have evidence that an early childhood program is violating laws or regulations protecting children, we shall report it to persons responsible for the program. If compliance is not accomplished within a reasonable time, we will report the violation to appropriate authorities who can be expected to remedy the situation.

P-4.10 When we have evidence that an agency or a professional charged with providing services to children, families, or teachers is failing to meet its obligations, we acknowledge a collective ethical responsibility to report the problem to appropriate authorities or to the public.

P-4.11 When a program violates or requires its employees to violate this Code, it is permissible, after fair assessment of the evidence, to disclose the identity of that program.

APPENDIX B

Communicable Disease Chart for Schools*

Incubation and Symptoms	Methods of Spread
Chicken pox (varicella) *Incubation:* 2–3 weeks, usually 13–17 days *Symptoms:* Skin rash often consisting of small blisters, which leave a scab. Eruption comes in crops. There may be pimples, blisters, and scabs all present at the same time.	Direct contact, droplet, or airborne spread of secretions of respiratory tract of an infected person or indirectly with articles freshly soiled with discharges from such persons.
Common cold *Incubation:* 12–72 hours, usually 24 hours *Symptoms:* Irritated throat, watery discharge from nose and eyes, sneezing, chilliness, and general body discomfort	Direct contact with an infected person or indirectly by contact with articles freshly soiled by discharges of nose and throat of infected person.
Flu (influenza) *Incubation:* 1–3 days *Symptoms:* Abrupt onset of fever, chills, headache and sore muscles. Runny nose, sore throat, and cough are common.	Direct contact with an infected person or indirectly by contact with articles freshly soiled by discharges of nose and throat of the infected person, possibly airborne in crowded areas.
German measles (rubella) (3-day measles) *Incubation:* 14–21 days, usually 16–18 days *Symptoms:* Skin rash and mild fever. Glands at back of head, behind ear, and along back of neck are often enlarged. Some infections may occur without evident rash.	Direct contact with an infected person or indirectly by contact with articles freshly soiled by discharges of nose and throat of the infected person.

*Courtesy the Ohio Department of Health, Bureau of Preventive Medicine, Columbus, OH.

Note. References: American Academy of Pediatrics; Report on the Committee on Infectious Diseases (18th ed.), 1977, Evanston, IL; *Control of Communicable Diseases in Man* (12th ed.) by Abram S. Berenson (Ed.), 1975, Washington, DC: American Public Health Association.

Minimum Control Measures	Other Information
Period of communicability: Communicable at least 5 days before blisters appear and until all scabs are crusted *Control:* Exclude from school until all scabs are crusted.	Children with certain chronic diseases, like leukemia, are at extreme high risk for complications.
Period of communicability: 24 hours before onset of symptoms until 5 days after onset. (However, period may vary.) *Control:* Exclude from school until all symptoms are gone.	
Period of communicability: Probably shortly before onset of symptoms and at least 3 days after onset of symptoms *Control:* Exclude from school until symptoms are gone.	Routine immunization is not recommended for children.
Period of communicability: Most highly communicable from 7 days before and at least 4 days after the onset of rash *Control:* Exclude from school for at least four days after the onset of symptoms	Immunization of all children entering school is required by law. The disease, while mild in children, is very serious for unborn babies if it is contracted by a pregnant woman.

Communicable disease chart for schools *continued*

Incubation and Symptoms	Methods of Spread
Hepatitis A (infectious) *Incubation:* 10–50 days, average 25–30 days. *Symptoms:* Usually abrupt onset with loss of appetite, fever, abdominal discomfort, nausea, and fatigue. Jaundice may follow in a few days.	Person to person contact, presumably in the majority of cases by fecal contamination; may be spread by ingestion of fecally contaminated water and food
Hepatitis B (serum) *Incubation:* 45–160 days, average 60–90 days. *Symptoms:* Usually inapparent onset with loss of appetite, vague abdominal discomfort, nausea, vomiting; often progresses to jaundice. Fever may be absent.	Chiefly through blood or blood products by inoculation or ingestion of blood from an infected person. Contaminated needles and syringes are important vehicles of spread. Also may be spread through contamination of wounds or lacerations.
Impetigo *Incubation:* 2–5 days, occasionally longer *Symptoms:* Blisterlike lesions that later develop into crusted puslike sores that are irregular in outline.	Direct contact with draining sores.
Head lice (pediculosis) *Incubation:* The eggs of lice may hatch in 1 week, and sexual maturity is reached in approximately two weeks. *Symptoms:* Irritation and itching of scalp or body; presence of small light gray insects or their eggs (nits) that are attached to the base of hairs.	Direct contact with an infested person and indirectly by contact with their *personal* belongings, especially clothing and headgear.
Measles (rubeola) *Incubation:* 8–13 days, usually 10 days. *Symptoms:* Acute highly communicable disease with fever, runny eyes and nose, cough, followed by a dark red elevated rash that occurs in patches.	Direct contact with secretions of nose, throat, and urine of infected persons; indirectly airborne and by articles freshly soiled with secretions of nose and throat.
Meningitis (bacterial) *Incubation:* 1–7 days. *Symptoms:* Acute disease with sudden onset of fever, intense headache. Behavioral changes may occur including irritability or sluggishness.	Direct contact with secretions of nose and throat of infected persons or carriers.

Minimum Control Measures	Other Information
Period of communicability: Most highly communicable during the last half of the incubation period and continuing for approximately 1 week after jaundice *Control:* Exclude from school until at least 7 days after onset of jaundice. Student should be under physician's care.	Consult the local health department for help in controlling the disease within the school. Adequate sanitation facilities are necessary in reducing the spread of this disease. An adequate supply of soap and paper towels is essential. Students should wash their hands after each toilet use and before meals. Observe cafeteria personnel for symptoms of the disease and give particular attention to handwashing practices of all food handlers. Gamma globulin is usually *not* recommended for classroom contacts.
Period of communicability: Most highly communicable during latter part of incubation period and during acute illness *Control:* Exclude from school until symptoms are gone. Students should be under a physician's care.	Notify your local health department.
Period of communicability: From onset of symptoms until sores are healed *Control:* Exclude from school until adequately treated and sores are no longer draining.	Early detection and adequate treatment are important in preventing spread. Infected individual should use separate towels and wash cloths. All persons with lesions should avoid contact with newborn babies.
Period of communicability: While lice remain alive on the infested person or in his clothing and until eggs (nits) have been destroyed *Control:* Exclude from school until disinfestation is accomplished.	The local health department should be notified of any occurrence of lice. When a student is found with head lice, all family members should be inspected and those infested should be treated.
Period of communicability: From onset of symptoms until a few days after rash appears *Control:* Exclude from school until at least 4 days after the rash appears.	Immunization of all children entering school is required by law. Notify the local health department if a case occurs in the school. One of the most readily transmitted communicable diseases.
Period of communicability: No longer than 24 hours after initiation of antibiotic therapy *Control:* Exclude from school until adequately treated. Student must be under a physician's care.	Notify the local health department if a case occurs in the school. Antibiotic therapy may be necessary for intimate contacts. Classroom contacts are usually *not* candidates for antibiotic therapy.

Communicable disease chart for schools *continued*

Incubation and Symptoms	Methods of Spread
Meningitis (aseptic-viral) *Incubation:* Varies with causative agent *Symptoms:* Acute disease with sudden onset of fever, intense headache, nausea, forceful vomiting, and stiff neck. Behavioral changes may occur including irritability and sluggishness.	Varies with causative agent.
Mononucleosis *Incubation:* 2–8 weeks. *Symptoms:* Fever, sore throat, swollen lymph glands.	Direct contact with saliva of infected person.
Mumps *Incubation:* 12–26 days, commonly 18 days *Symptoms:* Usually fever followed by painful swelling under the jaw or in front of the ear.	Direct contact with saliva of infected person, or indirectly by contact with articles freshly soiled with discharges of such persons
Ringworm (scalp, skin, and feet) *Incubation:* Unknown *Symptoms:* 　*Scalp:* Scaly patches of temporary baldness. Infected hairs are brittle and break easily. 　*Skin:* Flat, inflamed ringlike sores that may itch or burn 　*Feet:* Scaling or cracking of the skin, especially between the toes, or blisters containing a thin watery fluid.	Directly by contact with infected person or animals or indirectly by contact with articles and surfaces contaminated by such infected persons or animals.
Scabies (itch) *Incubation:* First infestation in 4–6 weeks; reinfestation symptoms may occur in a few days. *Symptoms:* Small raised areas of skin containing fluid or tiny burrows under the skin resembling a line that appear frequently on finger webs, under side of wrists, elbows, armpits, thighs, and belt line. Itching is intense, especially at night.	Direct contact with sores and, to a limited extent, from undergarments or bedding freshly contaminated by infected persons.
Scarlet fever and strep throat (streptococcal) *Incubation:* 1–3 days but may be longer *Symptoms:* 　*Strep throat:* Fever, sore and red throat, pus spots on the back of the throat, tender and swollen glands of the neck 　*Scarlet fever:* All symptoms that occur with strep throat as well as strawberry tongue and rash of the skin and inside of mouth. High fever, nausea, and vomiting may occur.	Direct or intimate contact with infected person or carrier; rarely by indirect contact through transfer by objects or hands. Casual contact rarely leads to infection. Explosive outbreaks of strep throat may follow drinking of contaminated milk or eating contaminated food.

Minimum Control Measures	Other Information
Period of communicability: Varies with causative agent *Control:* Exclude from school during fever period. Student must be under a physician's care.	It is important to determine whether meningitis is aseptic or bacterial since the symptoms are essentially the same. Aseptic meningitis is a much less serious disease.
Need not be excluded from school under ordinary circumstances.	Not highly communicable.
Period of communicability: 48 hours before onset of swelling and up to 9 days after swelling occurs. *Control:* Exclude from school for at least 9 days after swelling occurs.	Immunization against mumps is available. The disease may have serious complications in adults.
Period of communicability: As long as sores are present *Control:* Exclusion from school is necessary for ringworm of the scalp and skin until treatment has begun.	Preventive measures are largely hygienic. All household contacts, pet, and farm animals should be examined and treated if infected. Scalp ringworm is seldom, if ever, found in adults.
Period of communicability: Until student and household contacts have been adequately treated (usually requires one treatment) *Control:* Exclude from school until student and household contacts have been treated adequately. (Single infection in a family is uncommon.)	Disinfection of the general environment is not necessary. After treatment of student and family, *no* waiting period for reentry is necessary.
Period of communicability: With adequate treatment, communicability is eliminated within 24 hours. *Control:* Exclude from school until 24 hours after treatment is started.	Early diagnosis and medical treatment are essential in the care of the student and in the prevention of serious complications.

Incubation and Symptoms	Methods of Spread

Venereal diseases (gonorrhea, syphilis, herpes simplex)
Incubation:
Gonorrhea: 3–9 days.
Syphilis: 10–90 days.
Herpes simplex II: Up to 2 weeks.
Symptoms:

Gonorrhea: Early symptoms in the male are a thick yellow discharge from the sex organs appearing 3–9 days after exposure, and a painful burning sensation during urination. The same symptoms may also appear in the female but often are so mild that they are unnoticed.

Gonorrhea: Direct personal contact—usually through sexual intercourse

Symptoms:

Syphilis: May include a sore that develops at the site the organism enters the body; a rash, unexplained and prolonged sore throat, fever, and headache.

Syphilis: Direct personal contact—usually through sexual intercourse.

Herpes simplex II: Very painful sores or blisters on or around the sex organs.

Herpes simplex II: Direct personal contact—usually through sexual intercourse.

Whooping cough (pertussis)
Incubation: 7–21 days, usually 10 days.
Symptoms: Begins with cough which is worse at night. Symptoms may at first be very mild. Characteristic "whooping" develops in about 2 weeks, and spells of coughing sometimes end with vomiting.

Direct contact with discharges of an infected person, or indirectly by contact with articles freshly soiled by discharges of infected persons.

Tuberculosis
Very few students have been found to be infected with tuberculosis.
Skin testing policies for tuberculosis testing in students are determined by local health departments.

Animal bites
1. The community should be made aware of the potential dangers of animal bites.
2. Preventive vaccination of owned dogs and control of all stray dogs should be encouraged.
3. All biting animals should be confined for a 10-day observation period.
4. All unprovoked attacks by wildlife should be considered as potential exposures to rabies.
5. All animal bites should be reported to the local health department so that an investigation of the case may be made.

Period of communicability:
  Gonorrhea: Communicable until treated (up to 8 months).

The control of the venereal diseases is the responsibility of the physician and the health department. Information must be held in the utmost confidence in order to successfully control these diseases.

Period of communicability:
  Syphilis: As long as early symptoms are present (up to 3 years).

  Herpes simplex II: Most contagious when blisters are moist; however, may remain communicable for several weeks.
Control: Herpes, gonorrhea and syphilis— there is no reason for restricting attendance except in the specific recommendation of the health department or family physician.
Period of communicability: From 7 days after exposure to 3 weeks after onset of "whooping" in untreated children, or 5–7 days after treatment is started.

Pelvic inflammatory disease (PID) is a serious complication of gonorrhea and requires medical treatment.

Immunization is required by law for entrance into school.

If an animal bite occurs:
1. Confine biting animal if possible.
2. Try to obtain as complete a description as possible if the animal escapes.
3. Give first aid immediately by copious flushing of wound with water or soap or detergent with water.
4. Refer for medical treatment by or under direction of physician.
5. Report all animal bites to the local health department serving the area where the bite occurred.
6. Work with animal control officials to keep dogs off school grounds as much as possible.

In health instruction classes:
1. Teach the proper conduct toward animals to avoid being bitten.
2. Emphasize the dangers in handling stray dogs, cats, and wild animals.
3. Stress the necessity of students reporting bites of all animals, especially bats.
4. Encourage immunization of pets.

APPENDIX C

Chart of Normal Development:
Infancy to 6 Years of Age*

The chart of normal development on the next few pages presents children's achievements from infancy to 6 years of age in five areas:

Motor skills (gross and fine motor)

Cognitive skills

Self-help skills

Social skills

Communication skills (understanding and speaking language)

In each skill area, the age at which each milestone is reached *on the average* is also presented. This information is useful if you have a child in your class who you suspect is seriously delayed in one or more skill areas.

However, it is important to remember that these milestones are only average. From the moment of birth, each child is a distinct individual and develops in his or her unique manner. No two children have ever reached all the same developmental milestones at the exact same ages. The examples that follow show what we mean.

By nine months of age Gi Lin had spent much of her time scooting around on her hands and tummy, making no effort to crawl. After about a week of pulling herself up on chairs and table legs, she let go and started to walk on her own. Gi Lin skipped the crawling stage entirely and scarcely said more than a few sounds until she was 15 months old. But she walked with ease and skill by 9½ months.

Marcus learned to crawl on all fours very early, and continued crawling until he was nearly 18 months old, when he started to walk. However, he said single words and used two-word phrases meaningfully before his first birthday. A talking, crawling baby is quite a sight!

Molly worried her parents by saying scarcely a word, although she managed to make her needs known with sounds and gestures. Shortly after her second birthday, Molly suddenly began talking in two- to four-word phrases and sentences. She was never again a quiet child.

All three children were healthy and normal. By the time they were three years old, there were no major differences among them in walking or talking. They had simply developed in their own ways and at their own rates. Some

*From *Mainstreaming Preschoolers: Children with Health Impairments* by A. Healy, P. McAreavey, C. S. Von-Hippel, and S. H. Jones, 1978, Washington, DC: U.S. Department of Health, Education, and Welfare, Office of Human Development Services, Administration for Children, Youth and Families, Head Start Bureau.

children seem to concentrate on one thing at a time—learning to crawl, to walk, or to talk. Other children develop across areas at a more even rate.

As you read the chart of normal development, remember that children don't read child development books. They don't know they're supposed to be able to point out Daddy when they are a year old or copy a circle in their third year. And even if they could read these baby books, they probably wouldn't follow them! Age-related developmental milestones are obtained by averaging out what many children do at various ages. No child is "average" in all areas. Each child is a unique person.

One final word of caution. As children grow, their abilities are shaped by the opportunities they have for learning. For example, although many 5-year-olds can repeat songs and rhymes, the child who has not heard songs and rhymes many times cannot be expected to repeat them. All areas of development and learning are influenced by the child's experiences as well as by the abilities they are born with.

0–12 Months	12–24 Months	24–36 Months	36–48 Months	48–60 Months	60–72 Months
MOTOR SKILLS **Gross motor skills** Sits without support Crawls Pulls self to standing and stands unaided Walks with aid Rolls a ball in imitation of adult	Walks alone Walks backward Picks up toys from floor without falling Pulls toy, pushes toy Seats self in child's chair Walks up and down stairs (hand-held) Moves to music	Runs forward well Jumps in place, two feet together Stands on one foot, with aid Walks on tiptoe Kicks ball forward	Runs around obstacles Walks on a line Balances on one foot for 5 to 10 seconds Hops on one foot Pushes, pulls, steers wheeled toys Rides (that is, steers and pedals) tricycle Uses slide without assistance Jumps over 15 cm (6") high object, landing on both feet together Throws ball overhand Catches ball bounced to him or her	Walks backward toe-heel Jumps forward 10 times, without falling Walks up and down stairs alone, alternating feet Turns somersault	Runs lightly on toes Walks on balance beam Can cover 2 m (6'6") hopping Skips on alternate feet Jumps rope Skates

599

Chart of normal development *continued*

0–12 Months	12–24 Months	24–36 Months	36–48 Months	48–60 Months	60–72 Months
Fine motor skills					
Reaches, grasps, puts object in mouth	Builds tower of three small blocks	Strings four large beads	Builds tower of nine small blocks	Cuts on line continuously	Cuts out simple shapes
Picks things up with thumb and one finger (pincer grasp)	Puts four rings on stick	Turns pages singly	Drives nails and pegs	Copies cross	Copies triangle
Transfers object from one hand to other hand	Places five pegs in pegboard	Snips with scissors	Copies circle	Copies square	Traces diamond
Drops and picks up toy	Turns pages two or three at a time	Holds crayon with thumb and fingers, not fist	Imitates cross	Prints a few capital letters	Copies first name
	Scribbles	Uses one hand consistently in most activities	Manipulates clay materials (for example, rolls balls, snakes, cookies)		Prints numerals 1 to 5
	Turns knobs	Imitates circular, vertical, horizontal strokes			Colors within lines
	Throws small ball	Paints with some wrist action; makes dots, lines, circular strokes			Has adult grasp of pencil
	Paints with whole arm movement, shifts hands, makes strokes	Rolls, pounds, squeezes, and pulls clay			Has handedness well established (that is, child is left- or right-handed)
					Pastes and glues appropriately
COMMUNICATION SKILLS					
Understanding language					
Responds to speech by looking at speaker	Responds correctly when asked *where* (when question is accompanied by gesture)	Points to pictures of common objects when they are named	Begins to understand sentences involving time concepts (for example, *We are going to the zoo tomorrow*)	Follows three unrelated commands in proper order	Demonstrates preacademic skills
Responds differently to aspects of speaker's voice (for example, friendly or unfriendly, male or female)	Understands prepositions *on, in,* and *under*	Can identify objects when told their use	Understands size comparatives such as *big* and *bigger*	Understands comparatives like *pretty, prettier,* and *prettiest*	
Turns to source of sound	Follows request to bring familiar object from an-	Understands question forms *what* and *where*	Understands rela-	Listens to long stories but often misinterprets the facts	
		Understands negatives *no, not,*			

600

Responds with gesture to *hi*, *bye-bye*, and *up* when these words are accompanied by appropriate gesture

Stops ongoing action when told *no* (when negative is accompanied by appropriate gesture and tone)

Attempts to imitate sounds

Spoken language

Makes cry and noncrying sounds

Repeats some vowel and consonant sounds (babbles) when alone or spoken to

Interacts with others by vocalizing after adult

Communicates meaning through intonation

Attempts to imitate sounds

---

other room

Understands simple phrases with key words (for example: *Open the door. Get the ball.*)

Follows a series of two simple but related directions

Says first meaningful word

Uses single words plus a gesture to ask for objects

Says successive single words to describe an event

Refers to self by name

Uses *my* or *mine* to indicate possession

Has vocabulary of about 50 words for important people, common objects, and the existence, nonexistence, and recurrence of objects and

---

can't, and *don't*

Enjoys listening to simple storybooks and requests them again

Joins vocabulary words together in two-word phrases

Gives first and last name

Asks *what* and *where* questions

Makes negative statements (for example, *Can't open it*)

Shows frustration at not being understood

---

tionships expressed by *if-then* or *because* sentences

Carries out a series of two to four related directions

Understands when told *Let's pretend*

Talks in sentences of three or more words, which take the form agent-action-object (*I see the ball*) or agent-action-location (*Daddy sit on chair*)

Tells about past experiences

Uses *s* on nouns to indicate plurals

Uses *ed* on verbs to indicate past tense

Refers to self using pronouns *I* or *me*

Repeats at least one nursery rhyme and can

Incorporates verbal directions into play activities

Understands sequencing of events when told them (for example, *First we have to go to the store, then we can make the cake and tomorrow we will eat it.*)

Asks *when*, *how*, and *why* questions

Uses models like *can*, *will*, *shall*, *should*, and *might*

Joins sentences together (for example, *I like chocolate chip cookies and milk.*)

Talks about causality by using *because* and *so*

Tells the content of a story but may confuse facts

There are few obvious differences between child's grammar and adult's grammar

Still needs to learn such things as subject-verb agreement, and some irregular past tense verbs

Can take appropriate turns in a conversation

Gives and receives information

Communicates well with family, friends, or strangers

Chart of normal development *continued*

0–12 Months	12–24 Months	24–36 Months	36–48 Months	48–60 Months	60–72 Months
COMMUNICATION SKILLS Understanding language *continued*					
	events (for example, *more* and *all gone*)		sing a song Speech is understandable to strangers, but there are still some sound errors.		Retells story from picture book with reasonable accuracy
COGNITIVE SKILLS					Names some letters and numerals
Follows moving object with eyes	Imitates actions and words of adults	Responds to simple directions (for example, *Give me the ball and the block. Get your shoes and socks.*)	Recognizes and matches six colors	Plays with words (creates own rhyming words; says or makes up words having similar sounds)	Rote counts to 10
Recognizes differences among people; responds to strangers by crying or staring	Responds to words or commands with appropriate action (for example, *Stop that. Get down.*)	Selects and looks at picture books, names pictured objects, and identifies several objects within one picture	Intentionally stacks blocks or rings in order of size	Points to and names four to six colors	Sorts objects by single characteristics (for example, by color, by shape, or size if the difference is obvious)
Responds to and imitates facial expressions of others	Is able to match two similar objects	Matches and uses associated objects meaningfully (for example, given cup, saucer, and bead, puts cup and saucer together)	Draws somewhat recognizable picture that is meaningful to child, if not to adult; names and briefly explains picture	Matches pictures of familiar objects (for example, shoe, sock, foot; apple, orange, banana)	Is beginning to use accurately time concepts of *tomorrow* and *yesterday*
Responds to very simple directions (for example, raises arms when someone says *Come* and turns head when asked *Where is Daddy?*)	Looks at storybook pictures with an adult, naming or pointing to familiar objects on request (for example, *What is that? Point to the baby.*).	Stacks rings on peg in order of	Asks questions for information (*why* and *how* questions requiring simple answers)	Draws a person with two to six recognizable parts, such as head, arms, legs; can name or match drawn parts to own body	Uses classroom tools (such as scissors and paints) meaningfully and purfully and pur-
Imitates gestures and actions (for example, shakes head no, plays	Recognizes difference between *you* and *me*		Knows own age Knows own last name Has short attention span		

peek-a-boo, waves bye-bye) Puts small objects in and out of container with intention

Has very limited attention span Accomplishes primary learning through own exploration

size Recognizes self in mirror, saying *baby* or own name Can talk briefly about what he or she is doing Imitates adult actions (for example, housekeeping play) Has limited attention span; learning is through exploration and adult direction (as in reading of picture stories) Is beginning to understand functional concepts of familiar objects (for example, that a spoon is used for eating) and part-whole concepts (for example, parts of the body)

Learns through observing and imitating adults, and by adult instruction and explanation; is very easily distracted Has increased understanding of concepts of the functions and groupings of objects (for example, can put doll house furniture in correct rooms), and part-whole (for example, can identify pictures of hand and foot as parts of body) Begins to be aware of past and present (for example, *Yesterday we went to the park. Today we go to the library.*)

Draws, names, and describes recognizable picture Rote counts to 5, imitating adults Knows own street and town Has more extended attention span; learns through observing and listening to adults as well as through exploration; is easily distracted Has increased understanding of concepts of function, time, part-whole relationships; function or use of objects may be stated in addition to names of objects Time concepts are expanding. The child can talk about yesterday or last week (a long time ago), about today, and about what will happen tomorrow.

posefully Begins to relate clock time to daily schedule Attention span increases noticeably; learns through adult instruction; when interested, can ignore distractions. Concepts of function increase as well as understanding of why things happen. Time concepts are expanding into an understanding of the future in terms of major events (for example, *Christmas will come after two weekends.*).

Chart of normal development *continued*

	0–12 Months	12–24 Months	24–36 Months	36–48 Months	48–60 Months	60–72 Months
SELF-HELP SKILLS	Feeds self cracker	Uses spoon, spilling little	Uses spoon, little spilling	Pours well from small pitcher	Cuts easy foods with a knife (for example, hamburger patty, tomato slice)	Dresses self completely
	Holds cup with two hands; drinks with assistance	Drinks from cup, one hand, unassisted	Gets drink from fountain or faucet unassisted	Spreads soft butter with knife		Ties bow
	Holds out arms and legs while being dressed	Chews food	Opens door by turning handle	Buttons and unbuttons large buttons	Laces shoes	Brushes teeth unassisted
		Removes shoes, socks, pants, sweater	Takes off coat	Washes hands unassisted		Crosses street safely
		Unzips large zipper	Puts on coat with assistance	Blows nose when reminded		
		Indicates toilet needs	Washes and dries hands with assistance			
SOCIAL SKILLS	Smiles spontaneously	Recognizes self in mirror or picture	Plays near other children	Joins in play with other children; begins to interact	Plays and interacts with other children	Chooses own friend(s)
	Responds differently to strangers than to familiar people	Refers to self by name	Watches other children, joins briefly in their play	Shares toys; takes turns with assistance	Dramatic play is closer to reality, with attention paid to detail, time, and space	Plays simple table games
	Pays attention to own name	Plays by self, initiates own play	Defends own possessions	Begins dramatic play, acting out whole scenes (for example, traveling, playing house, pretending to be animals)	Plays dress-up	Plays competitive games
	Responds to *no*	Imitates adult behaviors in play	Begins to play house		Shows interest in exploring sex differences	Engages with other children in cooperative play involving group decisions, role assignments, fair play
	Copies simple actions of others	Helps put things away	Symbolically uses objects, self in play			
			Participates in simple group activity (for example, sings, claps, dances)			
			Knows gender identity			

APPENDIX D

10 Quick Ways to Analyze Children's Books for Racism and Sexism*

Both in school and out, young children are exposed to racist and sexist attitudes. These attitudes—expressed over and over in books and in other media—gradually distort their perceptions until stereotypes and myths about minorities and women are accepted as reality. It is difficult for a librarian or teacher to convince children to question society's attitudes. But if a child can be shown how to detect racism and sexism in a book, the child can proceed to transfer the perception to wider areas. The following 10 guidelines are offered as a starting point in evaluating children's books from this perspective.

1. CHECK THE ILLUSTRATIONS

Look for stereotypes. A stereotype is an oversimplified generalization about a particular group, race, or sex, which usually carries derogatory implications. Some infamous (overt) stereotypes of Blacks are the happy-go-lucky watermelon-eating Sambo and the fat, eye-rolling "mammy"; of Chicanos, the sombrero-wearing

peon or fiesta-loving, macho bandito; of Asian Americans, the inscrutable, slant-eyed "Oriental"; of Native Americans, the naked savage or "primitive" craftsman and his squaw; of Puerto Ricans, the switchblade-toting teenage gang member; of women, the completely domesticated mother, the demure, doll-loving little girl, or the wicked stepmother. While you may not always find stereotypes in the blatant forms described, look for variations which in any way demean or ridicule characters because of their race or sex.

Look for tokenism. If there are non-White characters in the illustrations, do they look just like Whites except for being tinted or colored in? Do all minority faces look stereotypically alike, or are they depicted as genuine individuals with distinctive features?

Who's doing what? Do the illustrations depict minorities in subservient and passive roles or in leadership and action roles? Are males the active "doers" and females the inactive observers?

2. CHECK THE STORY LINE

The Civil Rights Movement has led publishers to weed out many insulting passages, particularly from stories with Black themes, but the attitudes still find expression in less obvious ways. The following checklist suggests some of the subtle (covert) forms of bias to watch for.

*Reprinted with permission from the *Bulletin* of the Council on Interracial Books for Children, Inc., 1841 Broadway, New York, NY 10023. The Council also publishes the *Bulletin* (eight issues a year), which reviews new children's books for the human and antihuman messages they convey.

Standard for success. Does it take "White" behavior standards for a minority person to "get ahead"? Is "making it" in the dominant White society projected as the only ideal? to gain acceptance and approval, do non-White persons have to exhibit extraordinary qualities—excel in sports, get A's, etc.? In friendships between White and non-White children, is it the non-white who does most of the understanding and forgiving?

Resolution of problems. How are problems presented, conceived, and resolved in the story? Are minority people considered to be "the problem"? Are the oppressions faced by minorities and women represented as casually related to an unjust society? Are the reasons for poverty and oppression explained, or are they accepted as inevitable? Does the story line encourage passive acceptance or active resistance? Is a particular problem that is faced by a minority person resolved through the benevolent intervention of a White person?

Role of women. Are the achievements of girls and women based on their own initiative and intelligence, or are they due to their good looks or to their relationship with boys? Are sex roles incidental or critical to characterization and plot? Could the same story be told if the sex roles were reversed?

3. LOOK AT THE LIFESTYLES

Are minority persons and their setting depicted in such a way that they contrast unfavorably with the unstated norm of White middle-class suburbia? If the minority group in question is depicted as "different," are negative value judgments implied? Are minorities depicted exclusively in ghettos, barrios, or migrant camps? If the illustrations and text attempt to depict another culture, do they go beyond oversimplifications and offer genuine insights into another lifestyle? Look for inaccuracy and inappropriateness in the depiction of other cultures. Watch for instances of the "quaint-natives-in-costume" syndrome (most noticeable

in areas like costume and custom, but extending to behavior and personality traits as well).

4. WEIGH THE RELATIONSHIPS BETWEEN PEOPLE

Do the Whites in the story possess the power, take the leadership, and make the important decisions? Do non-Whites and females function in essentially supporting roles?

How are family relationships depicted? In Black families, is the mother always dominant? In Hispanic families, are there always lots and lots of children? If the family is separated, are societal conditions—unemployment, poverty—cited among the reasons for the separation?

5. NOTE THE HEROES AND HEROINES

For many years, books showed only "safe" minority heroes and heroines—those who avoided serious conflict with the White establishment of their time. Minority groups today are insisting on the right to define their own heroes and heroines based on their own concepts and struggles for justice.

When minority heroes and heroines do appear, are they admired for the same qualities that have made White heroes and heroines famous or because what they have done has benefitted White people? Ask this question: Whose interest is a particular figure really serving?

6. CONSIDER THE EFFECTS ON A CHILD'S SELF-IMAGE

Are norms established that limit the child's aspirations and self-concepts? What effect can it have on Black children to be continuously bombarded with images of the color white as the ultimate in beauty, cleanliness, virtue, etc., and the color black as evil, dirty, menacing, etc.? Does the book counteract or reinforce this positive association with the color white and negative association with black?

What happens to a girl's self-image when she reads that boys perform all of the brave and important deeds? What about a girl's self-esteem if she is not "fair" of skin and slim of body?

In a particular story, is there one or more persons with whom a minority child can readily identify to a positive and constructive end?

7. CONSIDER THE AUTHOR'S OR ILLUSTRATOR'S BACKGROUND

Analyze the biographical material on the jacket flap or the back of the book. If a story deals with a minority theme, what qualifies the author or illustrator to deal with the subject? If the author and illustrator are not members of the minority being written about, is there anything in their background that would specifically recommend them as the creators of this book?

Similarly, a book that deals with the feelings and insights of women should be more carefully examined if it is written by a man—unless the book's avowed purpose is to present a strictly male perspective.

8. CHECK OUT THE AUTHOR'S PERSPECTIVE

No author can be wholly objective. All authors write out of a cultural as well as a personal context. Children's books in the past have traditionally come from authors who are White and who are members of the middle class, with

one result being that a single ethnocentric perspective has dominated American children's literature. With the book in question, look carefully to determine whether the direction of the author's perspective substantially weakens or strengthens the value of his/her written book. Are omissions and distortions central to the overall character or "message" of the book?

9. WATCH FOR LOADED WORDS

A word is loaded when it has insulting overtones. Examples of loaded adjectives (usually racist) are savage, primitive, conniving, lazy, superstitious, treacherous, wily, crafty, inscrutable, docile, and backward.

Look for sexist language and adjectives that exclude or ridicule women. Look for use of the male pronoun to refer to both males and females. While the generic use of the word "man" was accepted in the past, its use today is outmoded. The following examples show how sexist language can be avoided: ancestors instead of forefathers; chairperson instead of chairman; community instead of brotherhood; firefighters instead of firemen; manufactured instead of manmade; the human family instead of the family of man.

10. LOOK AT THE COPYRIGHT DATE

Books on minority themes—usually hastily conceived—suddenly began appearing in the mid-1960s. There followed a growing number of "minority experience" books to meet the new market demand, but most of these were still written by White authors, edited by White editors, and published by White publishers. They therefore reflected a White point of view. Only in the late 1960s and early 1970s did the children's book world begin to even remotely reflect the realities of a multi-racial society. And it has just begun to reflect feminists' concerns.

The copyright dates, therefore, can be a clue as to how likely the book is to be overtly racist or sexist, although a recent copyright date, of course, is no guarantee of a book's relevance or sensitivity. The copyright date only means the year the book was published. It usually takes a minimum of one year—and often much more than that—from the time a manuscript is submitted to the publisher to the time it is actually printed and put on the market. This time lag meant very little in the past, but in a time of rapid change and changing consciousness, when children's book publishing is attempting to be "relevant," it is becoming increasingly significant.

APPENDIX E

A Beginning List of Free and Recyclable Materials*

Material	Sources	Suggested Uses
Cardboard rolls	Gift-wrapping section of department stores for empty ribbon rolls; paper towel and toilet paper rolls	Tape two together beside each other, add string, and use as binoculars. Put beans, rice, etc., inside, tape closed, and use as shakers. Use as a base for puppets, by adding decorative scraps of material. Tape several together lengthwise and use as tunnels for small vehicles. Punch holes 2 in. apart, secure wax paper over one end with a rubber band, and you have a flute.
Wood shavings and scraps	Building scrap piles, carpentry shops	
Material remnants	Interior design stores, upholsterers, clothing manufacturers	
Suede and leather scraps	Leather goods stores	

*Source: Some materials and sources suggested by the Principles and Practices class, 1972, of Santa Barbara City College, CA; other materials and suggested uses from the resource sheet "Recycling for Fun: Creating Toys and Activities for Children from 'Beautiful Junk' " by the Canadian Child Day Care Federation and the Canadian Association of Toy Libraries and Parent Resource Centres.

A beginning list of free and recyclable materials *continued*

Material	Sources	Suggested Uses
Pieces of styrofoam	Throwaways from drug stores, 5 & 10s, radio and TV stores	Buy a supply of plastic colored golf tees, to be hammered easily into styrofoam chunks—a perfect activity for beginning carpenters. Poke sticks, straws, etc., into styrofoam chunks to make a 3-D collage.
Computer paper used on one side, or cards	Almost anywhere computers are used	
Used envelopes	Offices, schools, junk mail	Use large envelopes for safe storage of special projects. Cut the bottom corners off old envelopes and decorate each as a different finger puppet.
Small boxes	Dime stores, hearing-aid stores, department and stationery stores	Stuff with newspaper and tape shut to make building blocks. Cut ⅔ of one side of a flat box (e.g., pudding box), decorate, and fill with scrap paper cut to fit, to make an ideal notepaper holder.
Large boxes	Appliance stores, supermarkets, department stores	Decorate boxes for use as a "Treasure Box" to store artistic creations. Tie boxes together to make a train; large boxes also can turn into houses, cars, boats, etc. Use a series of large boxes for making an obstacle course or continuous tunnel.
Plastic lids and containers	Home throwaways	Cut shapes in the lids to use as shape sorters (make shapes from other household "junk"). Use different size containers for stacking and nesting toys. Add a wooden spoon to a large empty container, with lid, to make a perfect drum.

Material	Sources	Suggested Uses
Meat trays and aluminum pie plates	Home throwaways	Cut interesting shapes in lids and use as stencils for painting or coloring. Use as a base for paintings and collages, Christmas ornaments, or table decorations. Put them in the bathtub or swimming pool to use as boats in water play. Equip older children with a dull needle and yarn to sew color patterns on meat trays.
Milk cartons	Home throwaways	Cut an opening in one side, hang it up, and use as a bird feeder. Cut the top off, add a handle, and decorate with ribbon for a springtime basket.
Egg cartons	Home throwaways	Sort small objects into each egg pocket by size, texture, color, etc. Fill each egg pocket with earth, plant seeds (e.g., beans), and watch them grow. Decorate individual egg pockets and hang upside down for simple but effective bells. In the springtime, use separate egg pockets to house chicks made out of cotton balls painted yellow. Cut lengthwise and add paint and pipe cleaner legs for a cute caterpillar.
Wide-mouth jars	Home throwaways, recycling centers	Make a mini-terrarium by layering charcoal, potting soil, and humus, dampening the soil, and adding small plants; put the lid in place, but open weekly if too much moisture builds up.

A beginning list of free and recyclable materials *continued*

Material	Sources	Suggested Uses
		Glue a 3-D scene to the lid, fill jar with water and sparkles, put lid on, and turn upside down.
Pebbles, leaves, cones, feathers, seed pods, etc.	These natural materials abound; bird refuge for unusual feathers.	Make collages. Decorate other items.
Wallpaper sample books	Wallpaper stores	Decorate play areas or dollhouses.
Rug scraps	Carpet and department stores	Decorate dollhouses.
Burlap	Horse-boarding barns	Various art projects
Ticker tape and newsprint rolls and ends	Local newspaper office	
5-gallon ice cream containers	Drive-ins and ice cream stores	
Art papers of various sizes and colors	Print shops	
1- or 2-day animal loans	Local pet shops	

APPENDIX F

Activities to Develop Auditory Discrimination*

Have the children put their heads down on the table. Display on a nearby shelf or table various instruments: xylophone, cymbals, tambourine, bells, and so forth. While they have their heads down, play one instrument. Children can take turns making the sounds for others to identify.

I was in the kitchen at the sink, and D. was standing at the kitchen gate. He was swinging the gate back and forth so that it would bang against the stopper. As it got louder and louder I was about to tell him to stop when I decided to use this situation for auditory discrimination. We were promptly joined by two other children. First we listened to how loud the gate could bang shut. Then I asked them if they could make it very quiet so that there was not any noise. We did these two opposites several times. Then we started very quietly and got louder and louder and louder. We tried this with our feet stamping on the floor and also clapping our hands. First we did it loud then quiet, then quiet and louder, and then as loud as we could.

Under the table I made different sounds and asked the children to identify them. I used a bell, sandpaper rubbed together, two blocks hit together, scissors opening and closing, and

tearing paper. Then I asked one child to make his own sound and let the rest of the children guess what it was.

Using one sound, have the children shut their eyes while you move about the room, and ask the children to point to where you are. Then let the children be the sound makers.

Record on a tape recorder familiar sounds such as a car starting, water running, a train, a door shutting, a refrigerator door opening or closing, or a toilet flushing (if you use this last one, do it at the end, as it tends to break up the group). Stop at each sound and have the children identify it. For older children play a series of sounds, and see how many they can remember.

I put several things in a box, one at a time, and had the children listen to the sounds: a tennis ball, toothbrush, piece of metal, and a comb. Then I put the box behind my back, put one of the objects in the box, brought it in front of me and rattled it. The children guessed what made the noise.

With my children we listened to the sounds around us when we were outside. We heard the leaves blowing, other children yelling, a car going by, and sand falling. It was fun and made the children really aware of the sounds around them.

I used a triangle with a wooden stick and a metal one. The children listened while I showed them the sticks; then I had them close their eyes and tell me which stick I had used.

*Suggested by the Language and Cognitive Development classes, 1973, 1976, and 1978, of Santa Barbara City College.

613

Using a xylophone, strike a middle note, then play other notes and ask the children if the new note is higher or lower than the middle one. Also, for degree of loudness, strike the notes hard or lightly and ask the children if the sound is loud or soft.

Material. Cans with tops, small nails, rice, beans, salt. I made up two cans of each material. I had all the cans on the table and went around and asked the children to pick one and shake it. Then I asked them to try and find one that sounded exactly the same. Then we opened the cans to see if the cans really did contain the same ingredient. The children enjoyed playing this and wanted to have many turns.

Material. Six bottles, same size; one spoon; water. Take two bottles and put the same volume of water in them, then two other bottles with the same volume of water, and finally two more. I covered the bottles with Contact paper so the children would not see how much water each bottle held. Taking turns, the children tried to pick out sounds that matched by hitting the bottle with the spoon. If we were in doubt that the tones matched, we poured the water out and measured it.

In a small group, have one child turn his back and then have the teacher or a selected child point to someone in the group who says something. The child with his back turned guesses who has spoken; then the speaker takes his turn guessing, and the former guesser picks the next speaker.

I let each child draw out an animal picture from the "secret" box, and then they listened to me while I made various animal noises. They brought me the picture when they heard the noise that belonged to their animal. For variety, we played a tape recording of the sounds and had each child wave his card in the air when he heard "his" sound.

An activity for 4-year-olds that fosters auditory discrimination is to take different flannel board pictures in which the words rhyme, for instance, *cat/hat, mouse/house, rug/bug,* and so on. Either put up a few at a time and ask children to pair the ones that rhyme, or have groups of three pictured words and ask the children to remove the one that doesn't rhyme.

For older 4-year-olds, have children stand in a circle and close their eyes. One child moves around the outside of the circle several times and then stops behind one of the children, who guesses whether the child was hopping, jumping, tiptoeing, and so forth.

APPENDIX G

Educational Organizations, Newsletters, and Journals Associated with Early Childhood

EDUCATIONAL ORGANIZATIONS

AAHPER
American Alliance for Health, Physical Education, and Recreation
1201 16th St., NW
Washington, DC 20036

ACEI
Association for Childhood Education International
11141 Georgia Ave., Suite 200
Wheaton, MD 20902

ACT
Action for Children's Television
46 Austin St.
Newtonville, MA 02160

ACYF
Administration for Children, Youth and Families
PO Box 1182
Washington, DC 20013

American Montessori Society
175 Fifth Ave.
New York, NY 10010

Canadian Association for Young Children/
L'Association canadienne pour les jeunes enfants
36 Bessemer Court, #3
Concord, Ontario L4K 2T1 Canada

Canadian Child Day Care Federation/
Federation canadienne des services de garde à l'enfance
120 Holland, Ste. 401
Ottawa, Ontario K1Y 0X6 Canada

Canadian Day Care Advocacy Association/
Association canadienne pour la promotion des services de garde à l'enfance
323 Chapel St.
Ottawa, Ontario K1N 7Z2 Canada

CEC
Council for Exceptional Children
1920 Association Dr.
Reston, VA 22091

Children's Defense Fund
122 C St., NW
Washington, DC 20001

CWLA
Child Welfare League of America, Inc.
440 First St., NW, Suite 310
Washington, DC 20001-2085

DCCDCA
Day Care and Child Development Council of
    America
1401 K St., NW
Washington, DC 20005

ERIC/ECE
Educational Resources Information Center on
    Early Childhood Education
805 W. Pennsylvania Ave.
Urbana, IL 61801

International Montessori Society
912 Thayer Ave.
Silver Spring, MD 20910

NAEYC
National Association for the Education of
    Young Children
1834 Connecticut Ave., NW
Washington, DC 20009
(1-800-424-8777)

National Committee for the Prevention of Child
    Abuse
332 S. Michigan Ave., Suite 950
Chicago, IL 60604-4357

OMEP
Organisation Mondiale pour l'Éducation Pré-
    scolaire
School of Education
Indiana State University
Terre Haute, IN 47809

SACUS
Southern Association for Children Under Six
PO Box 5403
Brady Station
Little Rock, AR 72215

NEWSLETTERS

The Black Child Advocate
Black Child Development Institute
1463 Rhode Island Ave., NW
Washington, DC 20005

Child Health Alert
PO Box 338
Newton Highlands, MA 02161

ERIC/ECE Newsletter
805 W. Pennsylvania Ave.
Urbana, IL 61801

*Nurturing News: A Forum for Male Early Child-
    hood Educators*
187 Caselli Ave.
San Francisco, CA 94114

Report on Preschool Education
Capitol Publications, Inc.
2430 Pennsylvania Ave., NW, Suite G-12
Washington, DC 20037

Today's Child
Roosevelt, NJ 08555

JOURNALS

American Journal of Orthopsychiatry
American Orthopsychiatric Association
19 West 44th St., Suite 1616
New York, NY 10036

Beginnings
PO Box 2890
Redmond, WA 98073

Canadian Children
Child Studies Centre
University of British Columbia
Vancouver, British Columbia V6T 1Z5 Canada

*The Canadian Journal of Research in Early Child-
    hood Education*
Department of Education
Concordia University
1455 de Maisonneauve West
Montréal, Québec H3G 1M8X Canada

Child Care Information Exchange
PO Box 2890
Redmond, WA 98073

Child Development
Society for Research in Child Development
University of Chicago Press
5801 Ellis Ave.
Chicago, IL 60637

Childhood Education
ACEI
11141 Georgia Ave., Suite 200
Wheaton, MD 20902

Children Today
Office of Human Development Services
Superintendent of Documents
U.S. Government Printing Office
Washington, DC 20402

Day Care and Early Education
Human Sciences Press
72 Fifth Ave.
New York, NY 10011

Developmental Psychology
American Psychological Association
1200 17th St., NW
Washington, DC 20036

Dimensions
Southern Association for Children Under Six
PO Box 5403, Brady Station
Little Rock, AR 72215

Early Childhood Research Quarterly
National Association for the Education of
    Young Children
Ablex Publishing Company
355 Chestnut St.
Norwood, NJ 07648

Exceptional Children
Council for Exceptional Children
1920 Association Dr.
Reston, VA 22091

Interracial Books for Children Bulletin
1841 Broadway
New York, NY 10023

Journal of Children in Contemporary Society
Haworth Press
28 E. 22nd St.
New York, NY 10010

Journal of Research in Childhood Education
Association for Childhood Education Inter-
    national
11141 Georgia Ave., Suite 200
Wheaton, MD 20902

*Merrill-Palmer Quarterly of Behavior and De-
velopment*
Wayne State University Press
Detroit, MI 48202

Nutrition Action
Center for Science in the Public Interest
1875 Connecticut Ave. NW, Suite 300
Washington, DC 20009-5728

Young Children
NAEYC
1834 Connecticut Ave., NW
Washington, DC 20009

REFERENCES

Aboud, F. (1988). *Children and prejudice.* NY: Basil Blackwell.

Adams, G. C. (1990). *Who knows how safe? The status of state efforts to ensure quality child care.* Washington, DC: Children's Defense Fund.

Adcock, D., & Segal, M. (1983). *Play together, grow together.* Mount Rainier, MD: Gryphon House (Distributor).

Ainsworth, M., Blehar, M., Water, E., & Wall, S. (1978). *Patterns of attachment.* Hillsdale, NJ: Lawrence Erlbaum.

Allen, J., & Carlson, K. (1989). Volunteers in the classroom: Guidelines for orientation. *Day Care and Early Education, 17*(1), 4–6.

Allen, K. E., & Hart, B. (1984). *The early years: Arrangements for learning.* Englewood Cliffs, NJ: Prentice-Hall.

Allen, K. E., & Marotz, L. (1990). *Developmental profiles: Birth to six.* Albany, NY: Delmar.

Allen, Lady of Hurtwood. (1968). *Planning for play.* Cambridge, MA: MIT Press.

Allen, Lady of Hurtwood, Flekkoy, M. S., Sigsgaard, J., & Skard, A. G. (1964). *Space for play: The youngest children.* Copenhagen: World Organization for Early Childhood Education.

Almy, M., Chittenden, E., & Miller, P. (1966). *Young children's thinking.* New York: Teachers College Press.

American Public Health Association/American Academy of Pediatrics (1988). *Survey of selected state and municipal licensing regulations for out-of-home child care programs.* Washington, DC: The Association and Academy.

Anderson, L., Evertson, D. M., & Brophy, J. E. (1979). An experimental study of effective teaching in first-grade reading groups. *Elementary School Journal, 79,* 193–223.

Anderson, N., & Beck, R. (1982). School books get poor marks: An analysis of children's materials about Central America. *Interracial Books for Children: Bulletin, 13*(2 & 3).

Annett, M. (1985). *Left, right hand and brain: The right shift theory.* Hillsdale, NJ: Lawrence Erlbaum.

Anthony, E. J., & Cohler, B. J. (Eds.). (1987). *The invulnerable child.* New York: Guilford Press.

Anthony, E. J., & Pollock, G. H. (1985). *Parental influences in health and disease.* Boston: Little, Brown.

Appel, M. H. (1942). Aggressive behavior of nursery school children and adult procedures in dealing with such behavior. *Journal of Experimental Education, 11,* 185–199.

Arbuthnot, M. H., & Root, S. L. (1968). *Time for poetry* (3rd ed.). Glenview, IL: Scott, Foresman.

Areñas, S. (1978). Bilingual/bicultural programs for preschool children. *Children Today, 7*(4), 2–6.

Arnheim, D. D., & Sinclair, W. A. (1979). *The clumsy child: A program of motor therapy.* St. Louis, MO: Mosby.

Arnstein, H. W. (1978). *What to tell your child: About birth, illness, death, divorce, and other family crises.* New York: Condor.

Aronowitz, V., & Turner, S. (1989). *Healthwise quantity cookbook.* Washington, DC: Center for Science in the Public Interest.

Aronson, S. S. (1986). Exclusion criteria for ill children in child care. *Child Care Information Exchange, 49,* 13–16.

Aronson, S. S. (1988). Health update: Preventing heart disease begins in childhood. *Child Care Information Exchange, 63,* 41–43.

Asher, S. R., Oden, S. L., & Gottman, J. M. (1977). Children's friendships in school settings. In L. G. Katz (Ed.), *Current topics in early childhood education* (Vol. 1). Norwood, NJ: Ablex.

Asher, S. R., Renshaw, P. D., & Geraci, R. L. (1980). Children's friendships and social competence. *International Journal of Psycholinguistics, 7,* 27–39.

Asher, S. R., Renshaw, P. D., & Hymel, S. (1982). Peer relations and the development of social skills. In S. G. Moore & C. R. Cooper (Eds.), *The young child: Reviews of research* (Vol. 3). Washington, DC: National Association for the Education of Young Children.

Ashton, P. T. (1975). Cross-cultural Piagetian research: An experimental perspective. *Harvard Educational Review, 45*(4), 475–506.

Asian American Children's Book Project. (1976). How children's books distort the Asian American image. *The Council on Interracial Books for Children: Bulletin, 7*(2 & 3).

Athey, I. (1987). The relationship of play to cognitive, language and moral development. In D. Bergen (Ed.), *Play as a medium for learning and development: A handbook of theory and practice.* Portsmouth, NH: Heinemann.

Atkins, E., & Rubin, E. (1976). *Part-time father: A guide for the divorced father.* New York: Vanguard Press.

Axline, V. (1969). *Play therapy* (rev. ed.). New York: Ballantine.

Ayers, W. (1989). *The good preschool teacher: Six teachers reflect on their lives.* New York: Teachers College Press.

Bagley, C., Verma, G. K., Mallick, K., & Young, L. (1979). *Personality, self-esteem and prejudice.* Westmead, Farnborough, Hants, England: Saxon House.

Bailey, D. B., & Wolery, M. (1984). *Teaching infants and preschoolers with handicaps.* Columbus, OH: Merrill.

Balaban, N. (1984). What do young children teach themselves? In *Early childhood: Reconsidering the essentials: A collection of papers.* New York: Bank Street College.

Balaban, N. (1985). *Starting school: From separation to independence.* New York: Teachers College Press.

Balaban, N. (1989). Trust: Just a matter of time. In J. S. McKee & K. M. Paciorek. *Early childhood: 89/90.* Guilford, CT: Dushkin.

Ball, D. W., Newman, J. M., & Scheuren, W. J. (1984). Teachers' generalized expectations of children of divorce. *Psychological Reports, 54,* 347–353.

Bandura, A. (1977). *Social learning theory.* Englewood Cliffs, NJ: Prentice-Hall.

Bandura, A. (1986). *The social foundation of thought and action: A social cognitive theory.* Englewood Cliffs, NJ: Prentice-Hall.

Bandura, A., & Huston, A. C. (1961). Identification as a process of incidental learning. *Journal of Abnormal Social Psychology, 63,* 311–318.

Bandura, A., & Walters, R. H. (1963). Aggression. In H. W. Stevenson (Ed.), *Child psychology (62nd Yearbook of the National Society for the Study of Education).* Chicago: University of Chicago Press.

Banfield, B. (1985). Books on African American themes: A recommended book list. *Interracial Books for Children: Bulletin, 16*(7), 4–8.

Bank Street College. (1968). *Early childhood discovery materials.* New York: Macmillan.

Baratta-Lorton, M. (1972). *Workjobs: Activity-centered learning for early childhood education.* Menlo Park, CA: Addison-Wesley.

Barfield, A. (1976). Biological influence on sex differences in behavior. In M. S. Teitelbaum (Ed.), *Sex differences: Social and biological perspectives.* New York: Anchor.

Bar-Tal, D., & Raviv, A. (1982). A cognitive-learning model of helping behavior development: Possible implications and applications. In N. Eisenberg (Ed.), *The development of prosocial behavior.* New York: Academic Press.

Bartlett, E. J. (1981). Selecting preschool language programs. In C. B. Cazden (Ed.), *Language in early childhood* (rev. ed.). Washington, DC: National Association for the Education of Young Children.

Basow, S. A. (1980). *Sex-role stereotypes: Traditions and alternatives.* Monterey, CA: Brooks/Cole.

Baumrind, D. (1989). Rearing competent children. In W. Damon (Ed.), *Child development today and tomorrow.* San Francisco: Jossey-Bass.

Bayless, K. M., & Ransey, M. E. (1987). *Music: A way of life for the young child* (3rd ed.). Columbus, OH: Merrill.

Beach, B. (1986). Connecting preschoolers and the world of work. *Dimensions, 14*(3), 20–22.

Bearison, D. J., & Cassel, T. Z. (1975). Cognitive decentration and social codes: Communication effectiveness in young children from differing family contexts. *Developmental Psychology, 11,* 732–737.

BECP. Nedler, S. (1973). *Bilingual early childhood program.* Austin, TX: Southwest Educational Development.

Begab, M. J., Haywood, H. C., & Garber, H. L. (Eds.). (1981). *Psychosocial influences in retarded performance: Vol. II. Strategies for improving competence.* Baltimore, MD: University Park Press.

Bender, J. (1978). Large hollow blocks: Relationship of quantity to block building behaviors. *Young Children, 33*(6), 17–23.

Benzwie, T. (1987). *A moving experience: Dance for lovers of children and the child within.* Tucson, AZ: Zephyr.

Bergen, D. (1988). *Play as a medium for learning and development: A handbook of theory and practice.* Portsmouth, NH: Heinemann.

Berger, E. H. (1991). *Parents as partners in education: The school and home working together* (3rd ed.). Columbus, OH: Merrill.

Berk, L. E. (1976). How well do classroom practices reflect teacher goals? *Young Children, 32*(1), 64–81.

Bernal, E. M. (1978). The identification of gifted Chicano children. In A. Y. Baldwin, G. H. Gear, & L. J. Lucito (Eds.), *Educational planning for the gifted.* Reston, VA: Council for Exceptional Children.

Bernstein, A. (1978). *The flight of the stork.* New York: Delacorte.

Bernstein, B. (1960). Language and social class. *British Journal of Sociology, 11,* 271–276.

Berrueta-Clement, J. T., Schweinhart, L. J., Barnett, W. S., Epstein, A. S., & Weikart, D. P. (1984). *Changed lives: The effects of the Perry Preschool Program on youths through age 19.* Ypsilanti, MI: High/Scope Educational Research Foundation.

Beuf, A. H. (1977). *Red children in white America.* Philadelphia: University of Pennsylvania Press.

Biber, R. (1981). The evolution of the developmental-interaction view. In E. K. Shapiro & E. Weber (Eds.), *Cognitive and affective growth: Developmental interaction.* Hillsdale, NJ: Lawrence Erlbaum.

Biber, B. (1984). *Early education and psychological development.* New Haven, CT: Yale University Press.

Birch, L. L. (1980a). Effects of peer models' food choices and eating behaviors on preschooler's food preferences. *Child Development, 51,* 489–496.

Birch, L. L. (1980b). Experiential determinants of children's food preferences. In L. Katz (Ed.), *Current topics in early childhood education* (Vol. III). Norwood, NJ: Ablex.

Bjorklund, G., & Berger, C. (1987). Making conferences work for parents, teachers, and children. *Young Children, 41*(2), 26–31.

Blank, M., & Solomon, F. A. (1968). Tutorial language program to develop abstract thinking in socially disadvantaged preschool children. *Child Development, 39,* 379–390.

Blank, M., & Solomon, F. (1969). How shall the disadvantaged child be taught? *Child Development, 40,* 48–61.

Block, J., & Martin, B. (1955). Predicting the behavior of children under frustration. *Journal of Abnormal Social Psychology, 51,* 281–285.

Blood, C. L., & Link, M. (1980). *The goat in the rug.* New York: Four Winds Press.

Bloom, B. (1964). *Stability and change in human characteristics.* New York: John Wiley & Sons.

Bloom, L. (1975). Language development review. In F. D. Horowitz (Ed.), *Review of child development research* (Vol. IV). Chicago: University of Chicago Press.

Bond, F. (1983). *Mary Betty Lizzie McNutt's birthday.* New York: Thomas Y. Crowell.

Bos, B. (1978). *Don't move the muffin tins: A hands-off guide to art for the young child.* Carmichael, CA: the burton gallery.

Bos, B. (1983). *Before the basics: Creating conversations with children.* Roseville, CA: Turn the Page Press.

Bower, E. M. (1981). *Early identification of emotionally handicapped children in school* (3rd ed.). Springfield, IL: Charles C. Thomas.

Bowlby, J. (1973). *Attachment and loss: Separation* (Vols. I and II). New York: Basic Books.

Bowlby, J. (1980). *Loss: Sadness and depression.* New York: Basic Books.

Bowlby, J. (1982). Attachment and loss: Retrospect and prospect. *American Journal of Orthopsychiatry, 52*(4), 663–678.

Bowman, B. T. (1990). Educating language minority children. *ERIC Digest: ERIC Clearinghouse on Elementary and Early Childhood Education* (EDO-PS-90-1).

Bradbard, M. R., & Endsley, R. C. (1982). How can teachers develop young children's curiosity? In J. F. Brown (Ed.), *Curriculum planning for young children.* Washington, DC: National Association for the Education of Young Children.

Braine, M. D. S. (1963). The ontogeny of English phrase structure: The first phrase. *Language, 39*, 1–13.

Brasch, W. N. (1981). *Black English and the mass media.* Amherst: University of Massachusetts Press.

Braun, S. J., & Edwards, E. P. (1972). *History and theory of early childhood education.* Worthington, OH: Charles A. Jones.

Bredekamp, S. (Ed.). (1987). *Developmentally appropriate practice in early childhood programs serving children from birth through age 8: Expanded edition.* Washington, DC: National Association for the Education of Young Children.

Bressan, E. S. (1990). Movement education and the development of children's decision-making abilities. In W. J. Stinson (Ed.), *Moving and learning for the young child.* Reston, VA: American Alliance for Health, Physical Education, Recreation, and Dance.

Brittain, W. L. (1979). *Creativity, art, and the young child.* New York: Macmillan.

Britton, G., & Lumpkin, M. (1983). Basal readers: Paltry progress pervades. *Interracial Books for Children: Bulletin, 14*(6), 4–7.

Broadhurst, D. D. (1986). *Educators, schools, and child abuse.* Chicago: National Committee for the Prevention of Child Abuse.

Bromwich, R. (1977). Stimulation in the first year of life? A perspective on infant development. *Young Children, 32*(2), 71–82.

Bronfenbrenner, U. (1969). Preface. In H. Chauncey (Ed.), *Soviet preschool education: Vol. II. Teacher's commentary.* New York: Holt, Rinehart & Winston.

Bronfenbrenner, U. (1979). *The ecology of human development.* Cambridge, MA: Harvard University Press.

Brooks, D. (1978). Impedance screening for school children: State of the art. In E. Harford, F. Bess, C. Bluestone, & J. Klein (Eds.), *Impedance screening for middle ear disease in children.* New York: Grune & Stratton.

Brown, C. C. (Ed.). (1984). *The many facets of touch. The foundation of experience: Its importance through life, with initial emphasis for infants and young children.* Skillman, NJ: Johnson & Johnson Baby Products.

Brown, R., & Bellugi, U. (1964). Three processes in the child's acquisition of syntax. *Harvard Educational Review, 34*, 133–151.

Bruner, J. S. (1964). The course of cognitive growth. *American Psychologist, 19*, 1–15.

Bruner, J. S. (1966). On the conservation of liquids. In J. S. Bruner, R. R. Olver, P. M. Greenfield, et al., *Studies in cognitive growth.* New York: John Wiley.

Bruner, J. S. (1970). *Poverty and childhood.* Detroit, MI: Merrill-Palmer Institute.

Bruner, J. S. (1974). Nature and uses of immaturity. In K. Connolly & J. S. Bruner (Eds.), *The growth of competence.* New York: Academic Press.

Bruner, J. S. (1975). The ontogenesis of speech acts. *Journal of Child Language, 2*, 1–19.

Bruner, J. S. (1978). Learning the mother tongue. *Human Nature, 1*(9), 42–49.

Bryan, J. H. (1975). Children's cooperation and helping behavior. In E. M. Hetherington (Ed.), *Review of child development research* (Vol. 5). Chicago: University of Chicago Press.

Burchinal, M., Lee, M., & Ramey, C. (1989). Type of day-care and preschool intellectual development in disadvantaged children. *Child Development, 60*(1), 128–137.

Burn, J. R. (1989). Express it with puppetry: An international language. In S. Hoffman & L. L. Lamme (Eds.), *Learning from the inside out: The expressive arts.* Wheaton, MD: Association for Childhood Education International.

Butler, A. L., Gotts, E. E., & Quisenberry, N. L. (1978). *Play as development.* Columbus, OH: Merrill.

Caldwell, B. (1973). The importance of beginning early. In J. B. Jorden & R. F. Dailey (Eds.), *Not all little red wagons are red.* Arlington, VA: Council for Exceptional Children.

Caldwell, B. N. (1977). Aggression and hostility in young children. *Young Children, 32*(2), 4–13.

Campbell, K. C., & Arnold, F. D. (1988). Stimulating thinking and communicating skills. *Dimensions, 16*(2), 11–13.

Cannella, G. S. (1986). Praise and concrete rewards: Concerns for childhood education. *Childhood Education, 62*(4), 297–301.

Carlsson-Paige, N., & Levin, D. E. (1985). *Helping young children understand peace, war, and nuclear threat.* Washington, DC: National Association for the Education of Young Children.

Carter, J. (1983). Vision or sight: Health concerns for Afro-American children. In G. J. Powell (Ed.), *The psychosocial development of minority children.* New York: Brunner/Mazel.

Cartwright, G. P., Cartwright, C. A., & Ward, M. E. (Eds.) (1981). *Educating special learners.* Belmont, CA: Wadsworth.

Cartwright, S. (1988). Play can be the building blocks of learning. *Young Children, 43*(5), 44–47.

Cartwright, S. (1990). Learning with large blocks. *Young Children, 45*(3), 38–41.

Cassidy, J., & Vukelich, C. (1980). Do the gifted read early? *The Reading Teacher, 33,* 578–582.

Cazden, C. (1970). Children's questions: Their forms, functions and roles in education. *Young Children, 25*(4), 202–220.

Cazden, C. B. (1972). *Child language and education.* New York: Holt, Rinehart & Winston.

CDF Reports. (1990). A child care victory: Child care bill finally becomes law: Special report. Washington, DC: Children's Defense Fund.

Chafel, J. A. (1990). Children in poverty: Policy perspectives on a national crisis. *Young Children, 45*(5), 31–37.

Chaillé, C., & Young, P. (1980). Some issues linking research on children's play and education: Are they "only playing"? *International Journal of Early Childhood, 12*(2), 53–55.

Chandler, L. A. (1982). *Children under stress: Understanding emotional adjustment reactions.* Springfield, IL: Charles C. Thomas.

Chattin-McNichols, J. P. (1981). The effects of Montessori school experience. *Young Children, 36*(5), 49–66.

Cherry, C. (1972). *Creative art for the developing child: A teacher's handbook for early childhood education.* Belmont, CA: Fearon.

Cherry, C. (1981). *Think of something quiet: A guide for achieving serenity in early childhood classrooms.* Belmont, CA: Pitman Learning.

Chhim, S. H. (1989). *Introduction to Cambodian culture.* San Diego: Multifunctional Resource Center, San Diego State University.

Child Care Employee Project. (1988). *Child Care Employee News, 7*(3) (entire issue).

Children Today. (September–October, 1982), 30.

Children's Defense Fund (1989). *A children's defense budget: FY 1989.* Washington, DC: The Fund.

Chomsky, N. (1987). Language: Chomsky's theory. In R. L. Gregory (Ed.), *The Oxford companion to the mind.* Oxford: Oxford University Press.

Ciaranello, R. D. (1988, Summer). Autism: The prison of self. *The Stanford Magazine,* pp. 18–21.

Cicerelli, V. G., Evans, J. W., & Schiller, J. S. (1969). *The impact of Head Start on children's cognitive and affective development: Preliminary report* (PB 184 328 & 329). Washington, DC: Office of Economic Opportunity.

Clark, K. B. (1963). *Prejudice and your child* (3rd ed.). Boston: Beacon Press.

Clewett, A. S. (1988). Guidance and discipline: Teaching young children appropriate behavior. *Young Children, 43*(4), 26–35.

Cohen, D. L. (1990). Early childhood educators bemoan the scarcity of males in teaching. *Education Week, X*(3), 1, 12, 13.

Collins, C. J., Ingoldsby, R. B., & Dellmann, M. M. (1984). Research: Sex-role stereotyping in children's literature. *Childhood Education, 60*(4), 278–285.

Conte, J. R., & Berlinger, L. (1981). Sexual abuse of children: Implications for practice. *Social Casework, 62*, 601–606.

Cook, R. E., Tessier, A., & Armbruster, V. B. (1987). *Adapting early childhood curricula for children with special needs* (2nd ed.). Columbus, OH: Merrill.

Coopersmith, S. (1967). *The antecedents of self-esteem*. San Francisco: W. H. Freeman.

Corrigan, R. A. (1984). Campus child care: Value to the college community. *Focus on Learning,* Spring(10), 5–7.

Corsaro, W. (1988). Children's conception and reaction to adult rules: The underlife of the nursery school. In G. Handel (Ed.), *Childhood socialization*. New York: Aldine De Gruyter.

Corsaro, W. A. (1981). Friendship in the nursery school: Social organization in a peer environment. In S. R. Asher & J. M. Gottman (Eds.), *The development of children's friendships*. New York: Cambridge University Press.

Cotton, K., & Conklin, R. R. (1989). *Research on early childhood education: Topical synthesis 3: School Improvement Research Series*. Portland, OR: Northwest Regional Educational Laboratory.

Cotton, N. (1983). The development of self-esteem and self-esteem regulation. In J. E. Mack & S. L. Ablon (Eds.), *The development and sustenance of self-esteem in childhood*. New York: International Universities Press.

Council for Early Childhood Professional Recognition. (1990). *The Child Development Associate credential*. Washington, DC: The Council.

Council on Interracial Books for Children. (1976). Racism and sexism in children's books. *Interracial Digest, 1*.

Cox, F. N., & Campbell, D. (1968). Young children in a new situation, with and without their mothers. *Child Development, 39*, 123–131.

Cratty, B. J., & Martin, M. M. (1969). *Perceptual-motor efficiency in children: The measurement and improvement of movement attributes*. Philadelphia: Lea & Febiger.

Cummings, J. (1984). *Bilingualism and special education*. San Diego: College Hill.

Curry, N., & Bergen, D. (1988). The relationship of play to emotional, social, and gender/sex role development. In D. Bergen (Ed.), *Play as a medium for learning and development: A handbook of theory and practice*. Portsmouth, NH: Heinemann.

Curry, N. E., & Johnson, C. N. (1990). *Beyond self-esteem: Developing a genuine sense of human value*. Washington, DC: National Association for the Education of Young Children.

Curtis, S. R. (1982). *The joy of movement*. New York: Teachers College Press.

Damon, W. (1977). *The social world of the child*. San Francisco: Jossey-Bass.

Damon, W. (1983). *Social and personality development: Infancy through adolescence*. New York: W. W. Norton.

Damon, W. (1988). *The moral child: Nurturing children's natural moral growth*. New York: Free Press.

Davis, C. M. (1939). Results of the self selection of diets of young children. *Canadian Medical Association Journal, 41*, 257–261.

Day, B. A. (1988). What's happening in early childhood programs across the United States. In C. Warger (Ed.), *A resource guide to public school early childhood programs*. Alexandria, VA: Association for Supervision and Curriculum Development.

Day Care Special Report. (1986). The future of military child care: Can there be a role for the private sector? *Day Care Information Service, 15*(13).

Day, N. (1984, January). Day care comes to the campus: Colleges have found the key to luring a new kind of student. *Working Mother,* pp. 36, 38, 40–41.

Deci, E. L., & Ryan, R. M. (1982). Curiosity and self-directed learning: The role of motivation in education. In L. G. Katz (Ed.), *Current topics in early childhood education* (Vol. IV). Norwood, NJ: Ablex.

Denk-Glass, R., Laber, S. S., & Brewer, K. (1982). Middle ear disease in young children. *Young Children, 37*(6), 51–53.

Dennis, W. (1960). Causes of retardation among institutional children: Iran. *Journal of Genetic Psychology, 96*, 47–59.

Derman-Sparks, L., & the ABC Task Force. (1989). *Anti-Bias curriculum: Tools for empower-*

ing young children. Washington, DC: National Association for the Education of Young Children.

Derman-Sparks, L., Higa, C. T., & Sparks, B. (1980). Children, race, and racism: How race awareness develops. *Interracial Books for Children: Bulletin, 11*(3 & 4), 3–9.

Deutsch, M. (1971). The role of social class in language development and cognition. In E. M. Bower (Ed.), *Orthopsychiatry and education.* Detroit, MI: Wayne State University Press.

DeVries, R., & Kohlberg, L. (1990). *Constructivist early education: Overview and comparison with other programs.* Washington, DC: National Association for the Education of Young Children.

DISTAR. (1969). Englemann, B., & Osborn, K. *DISTAR, Language 1.* Chicago: Science Research.

Dobbing, J. (Ed.). (1987). *Early nutrition and later achievement.* London: Academic Press.

D'Odorico, L., & Franco, F. (1985). The determinants of baby talk: Relationship to context. *Journal of Child Language, 12*(5), 567–586.

Doescher, S. M., & Sugawara, A. I. (1989). Encouraging prosocial behavior in young children. *Childhood Education, 65*(4), 213–216.

Dorwick, P. W. (1986). *Social survival for children: A trainer's resource book.* New York: Brunner/Mazel.

Duer, J. L., & Parke, R. D. (1970). The effects of inconsistent punishment on aggression in children. *Developmental Psychology, 2,* 403–411.

Dugan, T. F., & Coles, R. (Eds.). (1989). *The child in our times: Studies in the development of resiliency.* New York: Brunner/Mazel.

Dunn, J., & Kendrick, C. (1981). The arrival of a sibling: Changes in patterns of interaction between mother and first-born child. In S. Chess & A. Thomas (Eds.), *Annual progress in child psychiatry and child development, 1981.* New York: Brunner/Mazel.

Durkin, D. (1982). *A study of poor black children who are successful readers. Reading Education Report No. 33* (ED 216 334). Urbana, IL: Center for the Study of Reading.

Dyson, A. H. (1990). Research in review: Symbol makers, symbol weavers: How children

link play, pictures and paint. *Young Children, 45*(2), 50–57.

Dyson, A. H., & Genishi, C. (1984). Nonstandard dialects in day care. *Dimensions, 13*(1), 6–9.

Eastman, P. D. (1960). *Are you my mother?* New York: Random House.

Edgerton, R. B. (1979). *Mental retardation.* Cambridge, MA: Harvard University Press.

Edmonds, M. H. (1976). New directions in theories of language acquisition. *Harvard Educational Review, 46*(2), 175–195.

Edwards, C. P. (1980). The comparative study of the development of moral judgment and reasoning. In R. L. Munroe, R. Munroe, & B. B. Whiting (Eds.), *Handbook of cross-cultural human development.* New York: Garland.

Edwards, C. P., & Ramsey, P. G. *Promoting social and moral development in young children: Creative approaches for the classroom.* New York: Teachers College Press.

Education Week. (1991, March 13). Health Education Week, p. 11.

Eisenberg, N., McCreath, H., & Ahn, R. (1988). Vicarious emotional responsiveness and prosocial behavior: Their interrelations in young children. *Personality and Social Psychology Bulletin, 19,* 848–855.

Eisenberg, N., & Mussen, P. (1989). *The roots of prosocial behavior in children.* New York: Cambridge University Press.

Eisenberg, N., Shell, R., Pasternack, J., Lennon, R., Beller, R., & Mathy, R. M. (1987). Prosocial development in middle childhood: A longitudinal study. *Developmental Psychology, 23,* 712–718.

Elkind, D. (1987). *Miseducation: Preschoolers at risk.* New York: Alfred A. Knopf.

Elliot, O., & King, J. A. (1960). *Psychological Reports, 6,* 391.

Endres, J. B., & Rockwell, R. E. (1990). *Food, nutrition and the young child* (3rd ed.). Columbus, OH: Merrill.

Emery, R. E. (1989). Family violence. *American Psychologist, 44*(2), 321–328.

Eriksen, A. (1985). *Playground design: Outdoor environments for learning and development.* New York: Van Nostrand Reinhold.

Erikson, E. (1950). *Childhood and society.* New York: Norton.

Erikson, E. (1958). *Young man Luther.* New York: W. W. Norton.

Erikson, E. H. (1959). Identity and the life cycle. *Psychological Issues,* Vol. 1 (1), Monograph 1.

Erikson, E. (1963). *Childhood and society* (2nd ed.). New York: W. W. Norton.

Erikson, E. H. (1982). *The life cycle completed: A review.* New York: W. W. Norton.

Evers, W. L., & Schwarz, J. C. (1973). Modifying social withdrawal in pre-schoolers: The effects of filmed modeling and teacher praise. *Journal of Abnormal Child Psychology, 1,* 248–256.

Faber, A., & Mazlish, E. (1980). *How to talk so kids will listen, & listen so kids will talk.* New York: Avon Books.

Fagot, B. I. (1977). Consequences of moderate cross-gender behavior in preschool children. *Child Development, 48,* 902–907.

Fein, G., & Rivkin, M. (Eds.). (1986). *The young child at play: Reviews of research* (Vol. 4). Washington, DC: National Association for the Education of Young Children.

Ferrara, A. (1985). Pragmatics. In T. A. van Dijk (Ed.), *Handbook of discourse analysis: Vol. 2. Dimensions of discourse.* Orlando, FL: Academic Press.

Feshbach, N., & Feshbach, S. (1972). Children's aggression. In W. W. Hartup (Ed.), *The young child: Reviews of research* (Vol. 2). Washington, DC: National Association for the Education of Young Children.

Flavell, J. H., Botkin, P. T., Fry, C. L., Wright, J. W., & Jarvis, P. E. (1968). *The development of role-taking and communicative skills in children.* New York: John Wiley & Sons.

Folb, E. A. (1980). *Runnin' down some lines: The language and culture of black teenagers.* Cambridge, MA: Harvard University Press.

Forman, G. E., & Hill, F. (1980). *Constructive play: Applying Piaget in the preschool.* Monterey, CA: Brooks/Cole.

Fraiberg, S., with the collaboration of Louis Fraiberg. (1977). *Insights from the blind.* New York: Basic Books.

Freidrich, W. N., & Einbender, A. J. (1983). The abused child: A psychological review. *Journal of Clinical Child Psychology, 12,* 244–256.

Friedman, B. (1984). Preschoolers' awareness of the nuclear threat. *California Association for the Education of Young Children Newsletter, 12*(2).

Frost, J. L., & Sunderlin, S. (Eds.). (1985). *When children play: Proceedings of the International Conference on Play and Play Environments.* Wheaton, MD: Association for Childhood Education International.

Frost, J. L., & Wortham, S. (1988). The evolution of American playgrounds. *Young Children, 43*(5), 19–28.

Furman, E. (1974). *A child's parent dies: Studies in childhood bereavement.* New Haven, CT: Yale University Press.

Furman, E. (1982). Helping children cope with death. In J. M. Brown (Ed.), *Curriculum planning for young children.* Washington, DC: National Association for the Education of Young Children.

Furman, E. (1984). Children's patterns in mourning the death of a loved one. In H. Wass & C. A. Corr (Eds.), *Childhood and death.* Washington, DC: Hemisphere.

Furman, W., & Masters, J. C. (1980). Affective consequences of social reinforcement, punishment, and neutral behavior. *Developmental Psychology, 16,* 100–104.

Gagné, R. (1968). Contributions of learning to human development. *Psychological Review, 73* (3), 177–185.

Galdone, P. (1981). *Three billy goats gruff.* New York: Ticknor & Fields.

Galdone, P. (1985). *The three bears.* New York: Ticknor & Fields.

Galinsky, E. (1988). Parents and teacher-caregivers: Sources of tension, sources of support. *Young Children, 43*(3), 4–12.

Gallagher, J. J. (1990). A new policy initiative: Infants and toddlers with handicapping conditions. *American Psychologist, 44*(2), 387–391.

Garber, H. L., & Heber, R. (1981). The efficacy of early intervention with family rehabilitation. In M. J. Begab, H. C. Haywood, & H. L. Garger (Eds.), *Psycho-social influences in retarded performance: Vol. II. Strategies for improving competence.* Baltimore, MD: University Park Press.

Garber, J., & Seligmann, M. E. P. (Eds.). (1980). *Human helplessness: Theory and applications.* New York: Academic Press.

Garcia, E. E. (1990, Fall). Bilingualism, cognition, and academic performance: The educational debate. *Houghton Mifflin/Educator's Forum*, pp. 6–7.

Garcia, E., & August, D. (1988). *The education of language minority students*. Chicago: C. C. Thomas.

Gardner, H. (1986). Notes on cognitive development: Recent trends, new directions. In S. L. Friedman, K. A. Klivington, & R. W. Peterson (Eds.), *The brain, cognition, and education*. New York: Academic Press.

Garvey, C. (1977). *Play*. Cambridge, MA: Harvard University Press.

Garvey, C. (1979). Communicational controls in social play. In B. Sutton-Smith (Ed.), *Play and learning*. New York: Gardner Press.

Garvey, C. (1984). *Children's talk*. Cambridge, MA: Harvard University Press.

Genishi, C. (1987). Acquiring oral language and communicative competence. In C. Seefeldt (Ed.), *The early childhood curriculum: A review of current research*. New York: Teachers College Press.

Genishi, C., & Dyson, A. H. (1984). *Language assessment in the early years*. Norwood, NJ: Ablex.

George, B., & Tomasello, M. (1984/85). The effect of variation in sentence length on young children's attention and comprehension. *First Language, 5*, 115–128.

Geraty, R. (1983). Education and self-esteem. In J. E. Mack & S. L. Ablon (Eds.). *The development and sustenance of self-esteem in childhood*. New York: International Universities Press.

Gesell, A., Halverson, H. M., Thompson, H., & Ilg, F. (1940). *The first five years of life: A guide to the study of the preschool child*. New York: Harper & Row.

Getzels, J. W., & Jackson, P. W. (1962). *Creativity and intelligence*. New York: John Wiley & Sons.

Gibson, L. (1989). *Literacy learning in the early years: Through children's eyes*. New York: Teachers College Press.

Gittler, J., & McPherson, M. (1990). Prenatal substance abuse: An overview of the problem. *Children Today, 19*(4), 3–7.

Gleason, J. B. (1981). Code switching in children's language. In S. Kaplan-Sanoff & R. Yablans-Magid (Eds.), *Exploring early childhood: Readings in theory and practice*. New York: Macmillan.

Glick, P. C., & Lin, S. (1986). Recent changes in divorce and remarriage. *Journal of Marriage and the Family, 48*, 737–747.

Glueck, S., & Glueck, E. (1950). *Unraveling juvenile delinquency*. Cambridge, MA: Harvard University Press.

Goffin, S. G., & Lombardi, J. (1988). *Speaking out: Early childhood advocacy*. Washington DC: National Association for the Education of Young Children.

Golden, M., Bridger, W. H., & Montare, A. (1974). Social class differences in the ability of young children to use verbal information to facilitate learning. *American Journal of Orthopsychiatry, 44*(1), 86–91.

Goldenring, J. M., & Doctor, R. (1983). California adolescents' concerns about the threat of nuclear war. As cited in P. Skeen, C. Wallinga, & L. P. Paguio (1985), Nuclear war, children, and parents. *Dimensions, 13*(4), 27–28.

Gonzalez-Mena, J. (1976). English as a second language for preschool children. *Young Children, 32*(1), 14–19.

Goodson, B. D. (1982). The development of hierarchic organization: The reproduction, planning, and perception of multiarch block structures. In G. E. Forman (Ed.), *Action and thought: From sensorimotor schemes to symbolic operations*. New York: Academic Press.

Goodwin, M. T., & Pollen, G. (1980). *Creative food experiences for children* (rev. ed.). Washington, DC: Center for Science in the Public Interest.

Gottman, J. M. (1983). How children become friends. *Monographs of the Society for Research in Child Development, 48*(3), Serial No. 201.

Gottwald, S. R., Goldbach, P., & Isack, A. H. (1985). Stuttering: Prevention and detection. *Young Children, 41*(1) 9–14.

Gray, S. W., Ramsey, B. K., & Klaus, R. A. (1982). *From 3 to 20: The early training project*. Baltimore, MD: University Park Press.

Greenberg, P. (1970). *The devil has slippery shoes: A biased biography of the Child Development Group of Mississippi*. New York: Macmillan.

Greenberg, P. (1988). Ideas that work with

young children: The difficult child. *Young Children, 43*(5), 60–68.

Greenberg, P. (1989). Ideas that work with young children: Parents as partners in young children's development and education. A new American fad? Why does it matter? *Young Children, 44*(4), 61–75.

Greenberg, S. (1985). Educational equity in early education environments. In S. S. Klein (Ed.), *Handbook for achieving sex equity through education.* Baltimore, MD: Johns Hopkins University Press.

Greenfield, P. M., & Smith, J. H. (1976). *The structure of communication in early child development.* New York: Academic Press.

Greenman, J. (1988). *Caring spaces, learning places: Children's environments that work.* Redmond, WA: Exchange Press.

Griffin, E. F. (1982). *Island of childhood: Education in the special world of nursery school.* New York: Teachers College Press.

Gruber, K. (1978). Water play I. Water play II. In C. Kamii & R. DeVries, *Physical knowledge in preschool education: Implications of Piaget's theory.* Englewood Cliffs, NJ: Prentice-Hall.

Grusec, J. E., & Arnason, L. (1982). Consideration for others; Approaches to enhancing altruism. In S. G. Moore & C. R. Cooper (Eds.), *The young child: Reviews of research* (Vol. 3). Washington, DC: National Association for the Education of Young Children.

Grusec, J. E., & Redler, E. (1980). Attribution, reinforcement, and altruism: A developmental analysis. *Development Psychology, 16,* 525–534.

Guilford, J. P. A. (1958). A system of psychomotor abilities. *American Journal of Psychology, 71,* 146–147.

Guilford, J. P. (1981). Developmental characteristics: Factors that aid and hinder creativity. In J. C. Gowan, J. Khatena, & E. P. Torrance (Eds.), *Creativity: Its educational implications* (2nd ed.). Dubuque, IA: Kendall/Hunt.

Gundersen, B. H., Melas, P. S., & Skar, J. E. (1981). Sexual behavior of preschool children: Teacher's observations. In L. L. Constantine & F. M. Martinson, (Eds.), *Children and sex: New findings, new perspectives.* Boston: Little, Brown.

Guttentag, M., & Bray, H. (1976). *Undoing sex stereotypes: Research and resources for educators.* New York: McGraw-Hill.

Hakuta, K., & Garcia, E. E. (1989). Bilingualism and education. *American Psychologist, 44*(2), 374–379.

Hale, J. (1986). *Black children: Their roots, culture, and learning style* (2nd ed.). Baltimore, MD: Johns Hopkins University Press.

Hallahan, D. P., & Kauffman, J. M. (1986). *Exceptional children: Introduction to special education.* Englewood Cliffs, NJ: Prentice-Hall.

Haller, J. A. (1967). Preparing a child for his operation. In J. A. Haller (Ed.), *The hospitalized child and his family.* Baltimore, MD: Johns Hopkins Press.

Halpern, D. F. (1986). *Sex differences in cognitive abilities.* Hillsdale, NJ: Lawrence Erlbaum.

Hamilton, M. L., & Stewart, D. M. (1977). Peer models and language acquisition. *Merrill Palmer Quarterly, 23*(1), 45–55.

Harley, R. K. (1973). Children with visual disabilities. In L. M. Dunn (Ed.), *Exceptional children in the schools: Special education in transition* (2nd ed.) New York: Holt, Rinehart & Winston.

Hartup, W. W. (1977). Peer relationships: Developmental implications and interaction in same- and mixed-age situations. *Young Children, 32*(3), 4–13.

Hartup, W. W. (1989). Social relationships and their developmental significance. *American Psychologist, 44*(2), 120–126.

Hartup, W. W., Glazer, J. A., & Charlesworth, R. (1967). Peer reinforcement and sociometric status. *Child Development, 38,* 1017–1024.

Hawkridge, D., Chalupsky, A., & Roberts, A. (1968). *A study of selected exemplary programs for the education of disadvantaged children.* Palo Alto, CA: American Institutes for Research in the Behavioral Sciences.

Hayes, C. D., Palmer, J. L., & Zaslow, M. J. (Eds.). (1990). *Who cares for America's children? Child care policy for the 1990s.* Washington, DC: National Academy Press.

Heath, S. B. (1989). Oral and literate traditions among Black Americans living in poverty. *American Psychologist, 44*(2), 367–373.

Heber, R. (1961). Modification in the manual

on terminology and classification in mental retardation. *American Journal of Mental Deficiency, 46,* 499–501.

Heber, R., Garber, H., Harrington, S., Hoffman, C., & Fallender, C. (1972). *Rehabilitation of families at risk for mental retardation: Progress report.* Madison: Rehabilitation Research and Training Center in Mental Retardation, University of Wisconsin.

Helfer, R. E., & Kempe, C. H. (1987). *The battered child* (5th ed.). Chicago: University of Chicago Press.

Hendrick, J. B. (1973). *The cognitive development of the economically disadvantaged Mexican-American and Anglo-American four-year-old: Teaching the concepts of grouping, ordering, perceiving common connections, and matching by means of semantic and figural materials.* Unpublished doctoral dissertation, University of California at Santa Barbara, CA.

Hendrick, J. (1990). *Total learning: Developmental curriculum for the young child.* (3rd ed.). Columbus, OH: Merrill.

Hendrick, J. B. (1968). Aggression: What to do about it. *Young Children, 23*(5), 298–305.

Hendrick, J., & Stange, T. (1990). *Do actions speak louder than words? An effect of the functional use of language on dominant sex role behavior in boys and girls.* ED 323 039 PS 019 059.

Hendricks, G., & Wills, R. (1975). *The centering book: Awareness activities for children, parents and teachers.* Englewood Cliffs, NJ: Prentice-Hall.

Herzog, E., & Sudia, C. E. (1973). Children in fatherless homes. In B. E. Caldwell & H. N. Ricciuti (Eds.), *Review of Child Development Research* (Vol. 3). Chicago: University of Chicago Press.

Hess, E. H. (1960). In L. Uhr & J. G. Miller (Eds.), *Drugs and behavior.* New York: John Wiley.

Hetherington, E. M. (1989). Coping with family transitions: Winners, losers, and survivors. *Child Development, 60*(1), 1–14.

Hibbard, R. A. (1988). Evaluation of the alleged sexual abuse victim: Behavioral, medical and psychological considerations. In O. C. S. Tzeng & J. J. Jacobsen (Eds.), *Sourcebook for child abuse and neglect: Intervention, treatment,* *and prevention through crisis programs.* Springfield, IL: Charles C. Thomas.

Hilgard, E. R., & Bower, G. H. (1966). *Theories of learning* (3rd ed.). New York: Appleton-Century-Crofts.

Hill, D. M. (1977). *Mud, sand and water.* Washington, DC: National Association for the Education of Young Children.

Hitz, R., & Driscoll, A. (1988). Praise or encouragement? New insights into praise: Implications for early childhood teachers. *Young Children, 43*(5), 6–13.

Hodges, W. (1987). Teachers-children: Developing relationships. *Dimensions, 15*(4), 12–14.

Hofferth, S. L. (1989). What is the demand for and supply of child care in the United States? *Young Children, 44*(5), 28–33.

Hofferth, S. L., & Phillips, D. A. (1987). Child care in the United States, 1970–1995. *Journal of Marriage and the Family, 49,* 559–571.

Hoffman, M. L. (1970). Moral development. In P. H. Mussen (Ed.), *Carmichael's manual of child psychology* (Vol. 2). New York: John Wiley.

Hoffman, M. L. (1975). Moral internalization, parental power, and the nature of parent-child interaction. *Developmental Psychology, 11,* 228–239.

Hohmann, M., Banet, B., & Weikart, D. P. (1979). *Young children in action: A manual for preschool educators.* Ypsilanti, MI: High/Scope Educational Research Foundation.

Hollifield, J. (1989). Trends in early childhood and elementary education. In J. Hollifield et al., *Children learning in groups and other trends in elementary and early childhood education* (#204). Urbana, IL: ERIC Clearinghouse on Elementary and Early Childhood Education.

Hom, J. L., Jr., & Hom, S. L. (1980). Research and the child: The use of modeling, reinforcement/incentives, and punishment. In D. G. Range, J. R. Layton, & D. L. Roubinek (Eds.), *Aspects of early childhood education: Theory to research to practice.* New York: Academic Press.

Honig, A. S. (1982a). Language environments for young children. *Young Children, 38*(1), 56–67.

Honig, A. S. (1982b). Parent involvement in

early childhood education. In B. Spodek (Ed.), *Handbook of research in early childhood education*. New York: Free Press.

Honig, A. S. (1985a). Compliance, control, and discipline. *Young Children, 40*(2), 50–58.

Honig, A. S. (1985b). Compliance, control, and discipline. *Young Children, 40*(3), 49–51.

Honig, A. S. (1986a). Research in review: Stress and coping in children. In J. B. McCracken (Ed.), *Reducing stress in young children's lives.* Washington, DC: National Association for the Education of Young Children.

Honig, A. (1986b). Stress and coping in children: Part I. *Young Children, 41*(4), 50–63.

Honig, A. S. (1986c). Stress and coping in children: Part 2. Interpersonal relationships. *Young Children, 41*(5), 47–60.

Honig, A. S., & Wittmer, D. S. (1982). Teacher questions to male and female toddlers. *Early Child Development and Care, 9*(1), 19–32.

Howes, C. (1986). *Keeping current in child care research: An annotated bibliography.* Washington, DC: National Association for the Education of Young Children.

Howes, C. (1988). Peer interaction of young children. *Monographs of the Society for Research in Child Development, 53*(1), Serial No. 217.

Howlin, P. (1986). An overview of social behavior in autism. In E. Schopler & G. B. Mesibov (Eds.), *Social behavior in autism.* New York: Plenum Press.

Hunt, J. M. (1961). *Intelligence and experience.* New York: Ronald Press.

Hunter, I., & Judson, M. (1977). *Simple folk instruments to make and play.* New York: Simon & Schuster.

Huston-Stein, A., Freidrick-Cofer, L., & Susman, E. J. (1977). The relation of classroom structure to social behavior, imaginative play and self-regulation of economically disadvantaged children. *Child Development, 48,* 908–916.

Hutchings, J. J. (1988). Pediatric AIDS: An overview. *Children Today, 17*(3), 4–7.

Hyman, I. A. (1990). *Reading, writing, and the hickory stick: The appalling story of physical and psychological abuse in American schools.* Lexington, MA: Lexington Books.

Hyson, M. C., & Hirsh-Pasek, K. A. (1990). Some recent Spencer studies: Academic environments in early childhood: Challenge or pressure? *The Spencer Foundation Newsletter, 5*(1), 2–3.

Ianotti, R., Zahn-Waxler, C., Cummings, E. M., & Milano, M. (1987, April). *The development of empathy and prosocial behavior in early childhood.* Paper presented at AERA, Washington, DC.

Imhoff, G. (Ed.). (1990). *Learning two languages: From conflict to consensus in the reorganization of the schools.* New Brunswick, NJ: Transaction.

Infant Health and Development Program. (1990). Enhancing the outcomes of low birthweight, premature infants: A multisite, randomized trial. *Journal of the American Medical Association, 263*(22), 3035–3042.

Ingram, D. (1989). *First language acquisition: Method, description, and explanation.* Cambridge: Cambridge University Press.

Inhelder, B. (1968, Fall). *Recent trends in Genevan research.* Paper presented at Temple University, Philadelphia.

Institute of Medicine. (1989). *Research on children and adolescents with mental, behavioral, and developmental disorders: Mobilizing a national initiative.* Washington, DC: National Academy Press.

Irwin, D. M., & Moore, S. G. (1971). The young child's understanding of social justice. *Developmental Psychology, 5*(3), 406–410.

Jackson, P. W., & Wolfson, B. J. (1968). Varieties of constraint in a nursery school. *Young Children, 23*(6), 358–368.

Jacobson, E. (1976). *You must relax* (5th ed.). New York: McGraw Hill.

Jalongo, M. R. (1989). Career education: Reviews of research. *Childhood Education, 66*(2), 108–115.

Jalongo, M. R. (1985). When young children move. *Young Children, 40*(6), 51–57.

James, J. C., & Granovetter, R. F. (1987). *Water works: Waterplay activities for children aged 1–6.* Lewisville, NC: Kaplan.

Jenkins, J. K., & Macdonald, P. (1979). *Growing up equal: Activities and resources for parents and teachers of young children.* Englewood Cliffs, NJ: Prentice-Hall.

Jennings, L. (1990, April 11). Child-abuse reports in 1989 up over 10% over '88, state by state survey finds. *Education Week, 8.*

an early childh[...]
can Science &[...]
Lavatelli, C. S.[...]
lum. Boston: [...]
ing.
Lay-Dopyera, [...]
Strategies for[...]
The early child[...]
rent research. [...]
Press.
Layman, C. (19[...]
at Arkansas [...]
Six, Little Roc[...]
Lazar, I., & Da[...]
Lasting effects[...]
cation Commis[...]
ERIC/ECE.
Lazar, I., & Da[...]
fects of early [...]
Consortium f[...]
graphs of the S[...]
opment, 47(2–[...]
Lazar, I., Hubb[...]
M., & Royce,[...]
persistence of [...]
Washington,[...]
Education, ar[...]
Leacock, E. (19[...]
titudes on ch[...]
Case studies.[...]
cial life of chil[...]
dale, NJ: Law[...]
Leavitt, R. L., &[...]
day care. Lexi[...]
Leavitt, T. J. (1[...]
Bleck & D. A[...]
capped childrei[...]
(2nd ed.). Ne[...]
Lectenberg, R.[...]
Cambridge, [...]
Press.
Lee, L. C. (197[...]
infants: The be[...]
sented to the [...]
Study of Beh[...]
bor, MI.
Lee, P. R., Orn[...]
man, A., & T[...]
sciousness (pa[...]
ence). New Y[...]

Jensen, M. A. (1990). Multiple voices for advocacy: The story of WIC. In M. A. Jensen & Z. W. Chevalier (Eds.), *Issues and advocacy in early education*. Boston: Allyn & Bacon.

Jensen, M. A., & Chevalier, Z. W. (Eds.). (1990). *Issues and advocacy in early education*. Boston: Allyn & Bacon.

Johnsen, E. P., & Peckover, R. B. (1988). The effects of play period duration on children's play patterns. *Journal of Research in Childhood Education, 3*(2), 123–131.

Johnson, J. E., & Roopnarine, J. L. (1983). The preschool classroom and sex differences in children's play. In M. B. Liss (Ed.), *Social and cognitive skills: Sex roles and children's play*. New York: Academic Press.

Johnson, S. E. (1987). *After a child dies: Counseling bereaved families*. New York: Springer.

Johnson, V. M., & Werner, R. A. (1975). *A step-by-step learning guide for retarded infants and children*. Syracuse, NY: Syracuse University Press.

Joint Commission on Mental Health of Children. (1970). *Crisis in child mental health: Challenge for the 1970's*. New York: Harper & Row.

Jones, M. (1977). Physical facilities and environments. In J. B. Jordan, A. H. Hayden, M. B. Karnes, & M. M. Wood (Eds.), *Early childhood education for exceptional children*. Reston, VA: Council for Exceptional Children.

Jorde, P. (1982). *Avoiding burnout: Strategies for managing time, space, and people in early childhood education*. Washington, DC: Acropolis Books.

Jorde-Bloom, P. (1988). *A great place to work: Improving conditions for staff in young children's programs*. Washington, DC: National Association for the Education of Young Children.

Kadushin, A., & Martin, J. A. (1981). *Child abuse: An interactional event*. New York: Columbia University Press.

Kagan, J., & Lamb, S. (1987). *The emergence of morality in young children*. Chicago: University of Chicago Press.

Kagan, S. L., & Zigler, E. F. (1988). *Early schooling: The national debate*. New Haven, CT: Yale University Press.

Kamii, C. (1973). Pedagogical principles derived from Piaget's theory: Relevance for educa-

tional practice. In M. Schwebel & J. Raph (Eds.), *Piaget in the classroom*. New York: Basic Books.

Kamii, C. (1975). One intelligence indivisible. *Young Children, 30*(4), 228–238.

Kamii, C. (1982). *Number in preschool and kindergarten: Educational implications of Piaget's theory*. Washington, DC: National Association for the Education of Young Children.

Kamii, C. (1985). *Young children reinvent arithmetic: Implications of Piaget's theory*. New York: Teachers College Press.

Kanner, L. (1944). Early infantile autism. *Journal of Pediatrics, 25*, 211–217.

Kaplan-Sanoff, M., Brewster, A., Stillwell, J., & Bergen, D. (1988). The relationship of play to physical/motor development and to children with special needs. In D. Bergen (Ed.), *Play as a medium for learning and development: A handbook of theory and practice*. Portsmouth, NH: Heinemann.

Karnes, M. B., & Johnson, L. J. (1989). Training for staff, parents, and volunteers working with gifted young children, especially those with disabilities and from low-income homes. *Young Children, 44*(3), 49–56.

Kastenbaum, R. J. (1986). *Death, society, and human experience* (3rd ed.). Columbus, OH: Merrill.

Katz, L. (1969). Children and teachers in two types of Head Start classes. *Young Children, 24*(6), 342–349.

Katz, L. (1974). *Closing address*. San Diego: California Association for the Education of Young Children.

Katz, L., & Chard, S. C. (1989). *Engaging children's minds: The project approach*. Norwood, NJ: Ablex.

Katz, P. A. (1982). Development of children's racial awareness and intergroup attitudes. In L. Katz (Ed.), *Current topics in early childhood education* (Vol. IV). Norwood, NJ: Ablex.

Kempe, C. H. (1962). The battered child syndrome. *Journal of the American Medical Association, 181*(17), 17–24.

Kendrick, A. S., Kaufmann, R., & Messenger, K. P. (Eds.). (1988). *Healthy young children: A manual for programs*. Washington, DC: National Association for the Education of Young Children.

Kent, J. (198
NJ: Prenti
Kessler, J. V
Separation
children. P
vention of
Associatic
King, N. R.
perspectiv
87.
Kinsey, A.
C. E. (194
Philadelp
Kinsey, A.
& Gebha
human fen
Kinsman, C
the block
in play ai
35(1), 66–
Kirk, S. A.
(2nd ed.)
Kirk, S. A.,
exceptiona
ton Miffl:
Kliman, G.
childhood.
Kline, P. (1
children's
Arlingtor
Koblinsky,
Sex educ
Children,
Kohl, M. F
dough, ai
WA: Brig
Kohlberg,
dren's o
quence i
In P. B.
developm
Kohlberg,
and prac
Damon
ment: M
cisco: Jo
Kohlberg,
Vol. II: '
nature ai
cisco: H

tions for Head Start in the 1990s. *Young Children, 45*(6), 22–30.

Lord, C. (1982). Psychopathology in early development. In S. G. Moore & C. R. Cooper (Eds.), *The young child: Reviews of research* (Vol. 3). Washington, DC: National Association for the Education of Young Children.

Lorenz, K. (1966). *On aggression.* New York: Harcourt, Brace & World.

Lowenfeld, V., & Brittain, W. L. (1987). *Creative and mental growth.* New York: Macmillan.

Maccoby, E. E. (1980). *Social development: Psychological growth and the parent-child relationship.* New York: Harcourt Brace Jovanovich.

Maccoby, E. E., & Jacklin, C. N. (1974). *The psychology of sex differences.* Stanford, CA: Stanford University Press.

Maccoby, E., & Martin, J. A. (1983). Socialization in the context of the family: Parent-child interaction. In P. H. Mussen (Ed.), *Handbook of child psychology* (4th ed.), E. M. Hetherington (Ed.), *Vol. IV: Socialization, personality and social development.* New York: John Wiley & Sons.

Macfarlane, J. W. (1943). Study of personality development. In R. G. Barker, J. S. Kounin, & H. F. Wright (Eds.), *Child behavior and development.* New York: McGraw-Hill.

Macnamara, J. (1966). *Bilingualism in primary education: A study of Irish experience.* Edinburgh: Edinburgh University Press.

Manning, M., Manning, G., & Kamii, C. (1988). Early phonics instruction: Its effect on literacy development. *Young Children, 44*(1), 4–9.

Margolin, E. (1968). Conservation of self expression and aesthetic sensitivity in young children. *Young Children, 23,* 155–160.

Marland, S. P. (1972). *Education of the gifted and talented.* Washington, DC: U.S. Department of Education.

Marshall, H. H. (1989). The development of self-concept. *Young Children, 44*(5), 44–51.

Martin, H. P. (1976). *The abused child: A multidisciplinary approach to developmental issues and treatment.* Cambridge, MA: Ballinger.

Martinson, R. (1973). Children with superior cognitive abilities. In L. M. Dunn (Ed.), *Exceptional children in the schools: Special education in transition.* New York: Holt, Rinehart & Winston.

Maslow, A. (1965). *Eupsychian management.* Homewood, IL: Dorsey Press.

Mattick, I. (1981). The teacher's role in helping young children develop language competence. In C. B. Cazden (Ed.), *Language in early childhood education* (rev. ed.). Washington, DC: National Association for the Education of Young Children.

May, R. (1975). *The courage to create.* New York: W. W. Norton.

Mazur, S., & Pekor, C. (1985). Can teachers touch children anymore? *Young Children, 40*(4), 10–12.

McAfee, O. (1976). To make or buy. In M. D. Cohen & S. Hadley (Eds.), *Selecting educational equipment and materials for home and school.* Wheaton, MD: Association for Childhood Education International.

McAfee, O. D. (1985). Circle time: Getting past "Two Little Pumpkins." *Young Children, 40*(6), 24–29.

McCartney, K., & Phillips, D. (1988). Motherhood and child care. In B. Birns & D. F. Hay (Eds.), *The different faces of motherhood.* New York: Plenum Press.

McCord, W., McCord, J., & Howard, A. (1961). Familial correlates of aggression in nondelinquent male children. *Journal of Abnormal Social Psychology, 62,* 79–93.

McCurdy, H. G. (Ed.). (1966). *Barbara: The unconscious autobiography of a child genius.* Chapel Hill: University of North Carolina Press.

McFadden, E. J. (1990). Helping the abused child through play. In J. S. McKee & K. M. Paciorek (Eds.), *Early childhood education* (11th ed.). Guilford, CT: Dushkin.

McKey, R. H., Condelli, L., Ganson, H., Barrett, B. J., McConkey, C., & Plantz, M. C. (1985). *The impact of Head Start on children, families, and communities: Final report of the Head Start evaluation, synthesis, and utilization project.* Washington, DC: CSR Incorporated for the Head Start Bureau, ACYF, U.S. Department of Health and Human Services.

McLane, J. B., & McNamee, G. D. (1990). *Early literacy.* Cambridge, MA: Harvard University Press.

McLaughlin, B. (1987). *Theories of second language learning.* London: Arnold.

McLoyd, V. (1986). Scaffolds or shackles? The role of toys in preschool children's pretend play. In G. Fein & M. Rivkin (Eds.), *The young child at play: Reviews of research* (Vol. 4). Washington, DC: National Association for the Education of Young Children.

McMillan, M. (1929). *What the open-air nursery school is.* London: The Labour Party.

McTear, M. (1985). *Children's conversations.* New York: Basil Blackwell.

Mecca, A. M., Smelser, N. J., & Vasconcellos, J. (1989). *The social importance of self-esteem.* Berkeley: University of California Press.

Meeker, M. N., Sexton, K., & Richardson, M. O. *SOI abilities workbook.* Los Angeles: Loyola-Marymount University.

Meisels, S. J., & Anastasiow, N. J. (1982). The risks of prediction: Relationships between etiology, handicapping conditions, and developmental outcomes. In S. B. Moore & C. R. Cooper (Eds.), *The young child: Reviews of research* (Vol. 3). Washington, DC: National Association for the Education of Young Children.

Meisels, S. J., & Shonkoff, J. P. (1990). *Handbook of early childhood intervention.* Cambridge: Cambridge University Press.

Mejia, D. (1983). The development of Mexican-American children. In G. J. Powell (Ed.), *The psychosocial development of minority group children.* New York: Brunner/Mazel.

Menyuk, P. (1963). Syntactic structures in the language of children. *Child Development, 34,* 407–422.

Meyer Children's Rehabilitation Institute. (1974). *Meyer Children's Rehabilitation Institute teaching program for young children. Handicapped children in Head Start series.* Reston, VA: Council for Exceptional Children.

Midlarsky, E., & Bryan, J. H. (1967). *Journal of Personality and Social Psychology, 5,* 405–415.

Miel, A., & Kiester, E. (1967). *The shortchanged children of suburbia.* New York: Institute of Human Relations Press, The American Jewish Committee.

Miller, C. S. (1984). Building self-control: Discipline for young children. *Young Children, 40*(1), 15–19.

Miller, K. (1985). *Ages and stages: Developmental descriptions & activities, birth through eight years.* Marshfield, MA: Telshare.

Miller, L. B., & Dyer, J. L. (1975). Four preschool programs: Their dimensions and effects. *Monographs of the Society for Research in Child Development, 40* (5–6, Serial No. 162).

Milner, D. (1981). Are multicultural classroom materials effective? *Interracial Books for Children: Bulletin, 12*(1).

Mirandy, J. (1976). Preschool for abused children. In H. P. Martin (Ed.), *The abused child: A multidisciplinary approach to developmental issues and treatment.* Cambridge, MA: Ballinger.

Mitchell, A. (1985). *Children in the middle: Living through divorce.* London: Tavistock.

Moffit, M., & Omwake, E. (no date). *The intellectual content of play.* New York: New York State Association for the Education of Young Children.

Montagu, A. (Ed.). (1978). *Learning non-aggression.* New York: Oxford University Press.

Montagu, A. (1986). *Touching: The human significance of the skin* (3rd ed.). New York: Harper & Row.

Montessori, M. (1912). *The Montessori Method: Scientific pedagogy as applied to child education in "The Children's House" with additions and revisions by the author* (A. E. George, Trans.). New York: Frederick A. Stokes.

Moor, P. (1960). What teachers are saying—about the young blind child. *Journal of Nursery Education, 15*(2).

Moore, S. G. (1982). Prosocial behavior in the early years: Parent and peer influences. In B. Spodek, (Ed.), *Handbook of research in early childhood education.* New York: Free Press.

Moore, T. E., & Harris, A. E. (1978). Language and thought in Piagetian theory. In L. S. Siegel & C. J. Brainerd (Eds.), *Alternatives to Piaget: Critical essays on the theory.* New York: Academic Press.

Morada, C. (1986). Public policy report: Prekindergarten programs for 4-year-olds: State involvement in preschool education. Part 2. *Young Children, 41*(6), 69–71.

Morgan, J. (1984). Reward-induced decrements and increments in intrinsic motivation. *Review of Educational Research, 54*(1), 5–30.

Morland, J. K. (1972). Racial acceptance and preference of nursery school children in a southern city. In A. R. Brown (Ed.), *Prejudice in children.* Springfield, IL: Charles C. Thomas.

Morrow, R. D. (1989). What's in a name? In particular, a southeast Asian name? *Young Children, 44*(6), 20–23.

Moshman, D., Glover, J. A., & Bruning, R. H. (1987). *Developmental psychology: A topical approach.* Boston: Little, Brown.

Moukaddem, V. (1990). Preventing infectious diseases in your child care setting. *Young Children, 45*(2), 28–29.

Moyer, J. (Ed.). (1986). *Selecting educational equipment and materials for school and home.* Wheaton, MD: Association for Childhood Education International.

Murphy, L. B. (1976). *Vulnerability, coping and growth.* New Haven, CT: Yale University Press.

Murray, F. B. (1972). Acquisition of conservation through social interaction. *Developmental Psychology, 6,* 1–6.

Musick, J. S., & Householder, J. (1986). *Infant development: From theory to practice.* Belmont, CA: Wadsworth.

Mussen, P. H., Conger, J. J., & Kagan, J. (1969). *Child development and personality.* New York: Harper & Row.

NAEYC. (1985). *In whose hands? A demographic fact sheet on child care providers.* Washington, DC: The Association.

NAEYC. (1990). NAEYC position statement on guidelines for compensation of early childhood professionals. *Young Children, 46*(1), 30–32.

National Academy of Early Childhood Programs. (1991). Personal communication. Washington, DC: National Association for the Education of Young Children.

National Academy of Sciences (1986). *Confronting AIDS: Directions for public health care and research.* Washington, DC: National Academy Press.

National Association for the Education of Young Children. (1989). The National Association for the Education of Young Children code of ethics. *Young Children, 45*(1), 25–29.

National Association of Children's Hospitals and Related Institutions. (1989). *Profile of child health in the United States.* Alexandria, VA: The Association.

National Association of State Boards of Education. (1988). *Right from the start: The report of*

the NASBE Task Force on early childhood education.* Alexandria, VA: The Association.

National Center on Child Abuse. (1975). *Child abuse and neglect: The problem and its management: Vol. II. The roles and responsibilities of professionals* (OHD 75:30074) Washington, DC: U.S. Department of Health, Education, and Welfare.

National Committee for Prevention of Child Abuse. (1985). *"Think you know something about child abuse?" Questions and answers.* Chicago: The Committee.

National Governor's Association and the Center for Policy Research. (1987). *Focus on the first sixty months: A handbook of promising prevention programs for children zero to five years of age.* Washington, DC: The Association.

National Institute of Neurological Diseases and Stroke. (1969). *Learning to talk: Speech, hearing and language problems in the pre-school child.* Washington, DC: U.S. Department of Health, Education, and Welfare.

Nedler, S., & Sebera, P. (1971). Intervention strategies for Spanish-speaking children. *Child Development, 42,* 259–267.

Neisworth, J. T. (Ed.). (1986). Topics in early childhood education: Gifted preschoolers. Austin, TX: *Pro-Ed, 6*(1).

Nemerowicz, G. M. (1979). *Children's perceptions of gender and work.* New York: Praeger.

Neugebauer, R. (1991). How's business? Status report #7 on for-profit child care. *Child Care Information Exchange, 77,* 31–34.

Nieto, S. (1983). Children's literature on Puerto Rican themes—Part 1: The messages of fiction. *Interracial Books for Children: Bulletin, 14*(1/2) 6–9.

Northcutt, W. H. (1970). Candidate for integration: A hearing impaired child in a regular nursery school. *Young Children, 25*(6), 367–380.

Numeroff, L. J. (1987). *If you give a mouse a cookie.* New York: Harper & Row.

O'Connor, R. D. (1972). Relative efficacy of modeling, shaping, and the combined procedures for modification of social withdrawal. *Journal of Abnormal Psychology, 79,* 327–334.

Olson, S. L., Bayles, K., & Bates, J. E. (1986). Mother-child interaction and children's speech progress: A longitudinal study of the first two years. *Merrill-Palmer Quarterly, 32,* 1–20.

Olweus, D. (1980). Familial and temperamental determinants of aggression behavior in adolescents: A causal analysis. *Developmental Psychology, 16,* 644–660.

Orata, P. T. (1953). The Iloilo experiment in education through the vernacular. In *The use of vernacular language in education: Monographs on Fundamental Education* (VIII). Paris: UNESCO.

Orlick, T. (1982). *The second cooperative sports and games book.* New York: Pantheon.

Ornstein, R. (1977). *The psychology of consciousness* (2nd ed.). New York: Harcourt-Brace-Jovanovich.

Ornstein, R. (1978). The split and whole brain. *Human Nature, 1*(5), 76–83.

Osborn, D. K. (1980). *Early childhood education in historical perspective.* Athens, GA: Education Associates.

Otis, N. B., & McCandless, B. R. (1955). Responses to repeated frustrations of young children differentiated according to need area. *Journal of Abnormal Social Psychology, 50,* 349–353.

Pacific Oaks College (1989). *The anti-bias curriculum.* Papers presented at national conference of the National Association for the Education of Young Children, New Orleans.

Paley, V. G. (1979). *White teacher.* Cambridge, MA: Harvard University Press.

Parke, R. D., & Duer, J. L. (1972). Schedule of punishment and inhibition of aggression. *Developmental Psychology, 7,* 266–269.

Parke, R. D., & Slaby, R. G. (1983). The development of aggression. In P. H. Mussen (Ed.), *Handbook of child psychology* (4th ed.), E. M. Hetherington (Ed.), *Vol. IV: Socialization, personality, and social development.* New York: John Wiley & Sons.

Parrillo, V. N. (1985). *Strangers to these shores: Race and ethnic relations in the United States* (2nd ed.). New York: John Wiley & Sons.

Parten, M. B. (1932). Social participation among preschool children. *Journal of Abnormal and Social Psychology, 27,* 243–269.

Parten, M. B. (1933). Social play among preschool children. *Journal of Abnormal and Social Psychology, 28,* 136–147.

Patterson, C. (1977). Insights about persons: Psychological foundations of humanistic and affective education. In L. M. Berman & J. A. Roderick (Eds.), *Feeling, valuing, and the art of growing: Insights into the affective.* Washington, DC: Association for the Study of Curriculum Development.

Patterson, G. R. (1982). *Coercive family practices.* Eugene, OR: Castalia Press.

Patterson, G. R., DeBaryshe, B. D., & Ramsey, E. (1989). A developmental perspective on antisocial behavior. *American Psychologist, 44*(2), 329–335.

Patterson, G. R., Littman, R. A., & Bricker, W. (1967). Assertive behavior in children: A step toward a theory of aggression. *Monographs of the Society for Research in Child Development, 32*(5), 1–43.

Pediatric Mental Health. (1986). Parents overnight in the hospital. *Pediatric Mental Health, 5*(4), 1–4.

Pellegrini, A. D. (1986). Communicating in and about play: The effect of play centers on preschoolers' explicit language. In G. Fein & M. Rivkin (Eds.), *The young child at play: Reviews of research* (Vol. 4). Washington, DC: National Association for the Education of Young Children.

Pence, A. R. (Ed.). (1988). *Ecological research with children and families: From concepts to methodology.* New York: Teachers College Press.

Pepler, D. (1986). Play and creativity. In G. Fein & M. Rivkin (Eds.), *The young child at play: Reviews of research* (Vol. 4). Washington, DC: National Association for the Education of Young Children.

Perry, S. K. S. (1978). *Survey and analysis of employer-sponsored day care in the U.S.* Milwaukee: University of Wisconsin.

Peterson, R., & Felton-Collins, V. (1986). *The Piaget handbook for teachers and parents: Children in the age of discovery, preschool–third grade.* New York: Teachers College Press.

Petty, W. T., & Starkey, R. J. (1967). Oral language and personal and social development. In W. T. Petty (Ed.), *Research in oral language.* Champaign, IL: National Council of Teachers of English.

Pflaum, S. W. (1986). *The development of lan-*

guage and literacy in young children (3rd ed.). Columbus, OH: Merrill.

Phyfe-Perkins, E. (1981). *Effects of teacher behavior on preschool children: A review of research.* Champaign: ERIC/ECE, College of Education, University of Illinois.

Piaget, J. (1926). *The language and thought of the child.* New York: Harcourt, Brace & World.

Piaget, J. (1932). *The moral judgment of the child.* London: Routledge & Kegan Paul.

Piaget, J. (1948). *The moral judgment of the child.* Glencoe, IL: Free Press.

Piaget, J. (1950). *The psychology of intelligence.* London: Routledge & Kegan Paul.

Piaget, J. (1959). *The construction of reality in the child.* New York: Basic Books.

Piaget, J. (1962). *Play, dreams and imitation in childhood.* New York: W. W. Norton.

Piaget, J. (1963). *The origins of intelligence in children.* New York: W. W. Norton.

Piaget, J. (1965). *The child's conception of number.* New York: W. W. Norton.

Piaget, J. (1977). *The development of thought: Equilibration of cognitive structures.* New York: Viking Press.

Piaget, J. (1983). Piaget's theory. In P. H. Mussen (Ed.), *Handbook of child psychology* (4th ed.), W. Kessen (Ed.). *Vol. I: History, theory, and methods.* New York: John Wiley & Sons.

Piaget, J., & Inhelder, B. (1967). *The child's conception of space.* New York: W. W. Norton.

Piaget, J., & Inhelder, B. (1969). *The psychology of the child.* New York: Basic Books.

Piper, W. (1980). *The little engine that could.* New York: Putnam.

Pitcher, E. G. (1969). Explaining divorce to young children. In E. A. Grollman (Ed.), *Explaining divorce to young children.* Boston: Beacon Press.

Pitcher, E. G., Feinburg, S. G., & Alexander, D. A. (1989). *Helping young children learn* (5th ed.). Columbus, OH: Merrill.

Pitcher, E. G., & Prelinger, E. (1963). *Children tell stories: An analysis of fantasy.* New York: International Universities Press.

Poest, C. A., Williams, J. R., Witt, D. A., & Atwood, M. E. (1989). Physical activity patterns of preschool children. *Early Childhood Research Quarterly, 4,* 367–376.

Polito, J. T. (1989). Current trends in employer-supported child care. *Early Child Development and Care, 46,* 39–56.

Portage Project. (1976). *Portage guide to early education.* Portage, WI: The Project.

Powell, D. R. (1978). Interpersonal relationship behavior: Parents and caregivers in day care settings. *American Journal of Orthopsychiatry, 48*(4), 680–689.

Powell, D. R. (1989). *Families and early childhood programs.* Washington, DC: National Association for the Education of Young Children.

Powell, D. R. (1990). Home visiting in the early years: Policy and program design decisions. *Young Children, 45*(6), 65–69.

Power, C., & Reimer, J. (1978). Moral atmosphere: An educational bridge between moral judgment and action. In W. Damon (Ed.), *Moral development.* San Francisco: Jossey-Bass.

Prescott, E. (1981). Relations between physical setting and adult/child behavior in day care. In S. Kilmer (Ed.), *Advances in early education and day care: A research annual* (Vol. 2). Greenwich, CT: JAI Press.

Project Head Start. (1990). *Project Head Start: Statistical fact sheet.* Washington, DC: Administration for Children, Youth and Families, Office of Human Development, Department of Health and Human Services.

Provence, S., Naylor, A., & Patterson, J. (1977). *The challenge of day care.* New Haven, CT: Yale University Press.

Ramsey, P. G. (1979). Beyond "ten little Indians" and turkeys: Alternative approaches to Thanksgiving. *Young Children, 34*(6), 28–52.

Ramsey, P. G. (1982). Multicultural education in early childhood. *Young Children, 37*(2), 13–24.

Reese, H. W., & Lipsitt, L. P. (1970). *Experimental child psychology.* New York: Academic Press.

Reifel, S. (1982). The structure and content of early representational play: The case of building blocks. In S. Hill & B. J. Barnes (Eds.), *Young children and their families: Needs of the nineties.* Lexington, MA: D. C. Heath.

Reifel, S. (1984). Block construction: Children's developmental landmarks in representation of space. *Young Children, 40*(1), 61–67.

Reifel, S., & Greenfield, P. M. (1982). Structural development in a symbolic medium: The representational use of block constructions. In F. E. Forman (Ed.), *Action and thought: From sensorimotor schemes to symbolic operations.* New York: Academic Press.

Reis, S. M. (1989). Reflections on policy affecting the education of gifted and talented students. *American Psychologist, 44*(2), 399–408.

Resnick, L. B. (1989). Developing mathematical knowledge. *American Psychologist, 44*(2), 162–169.

Resnick, R., & Hergenroeder, E. (1975). Children and the emergency room. *Children Today, 4*(5), 5–9.

Rest, J. R. (1983). Morality. In P. H. Mussen (Ed.), *Handbook of child psychology* (4th ed.), J. H. Flavell & E. M. Markham (Eds.), *Vol. III: Cognitive development.* New York: John Wiley & Sons.

Reynolds, M. C., & Birch, J. W. (1988). *Adaptive mainstreaming: A primer for teachers and principals.* White Plains, NY: Longman.

Rheingold, H. L. (1982). Little children's participation in the work of adults: A nascent prosocial behavior. *Child Development, 53,* 114–125.

Rice, E. P., Ekdahl, M. C., & Miller, L. (1971). *Children of mentally ill parents: Problems in child care.* New York: Behavioral Publications.

Richman, N., Stevenson, J., & Graham, P. J. (1982). *Preschool to school: A behavioural study.* New York: Academic Press.

Riley, S. S. (1989). Pilgrimage to Elmwood Cemetery. *Young Children, 44*(2), 33–36.

Robertson, J., & Robertson, J. (1989). *Separation and the very young.* London: Free Association Books.

Robinson, B. E. (1988). Vanishing breed: Men in childcare programs. *Young Children, 43*(6).

Rogers, C. R., & Dymond, R. F. (1954). *Psychotherapy and personality change.* Chicago: University of Chicago Press.

Rogers, C. S., & Morris, S. S. (1986). Reducing sugar in children's diets. *Young Children, 41*(5), 1–16.

Rogers, D. L., Perrin, M. S., & Waller, C. B. (1987). Enhancing the development of language and thought through conversations with young children. *Journal of Research in Childhood Education, 2*(1), 17–29.

Rohe, W., & Patterson, A. H. (1974). The effects of varied levels of resources and density on behavior in a day care center. In D. H. Carson (Ed.), *Man-environment interaction.* Milwaukee, WI: EDRA.

Rohner, R. P. (1986). *The warmth dimension.* Beverly Hills, CA: Sage.

Roopnarine, J. L., & Honig, A. S. (1985). The unpopular child. *Young Children, 40*(6), 59–64.

Rosenhan, D. (1972). Prosocial behavior of children. In W. W. Hartup (Ed.), *The young child: Reviews of research* (Vol. 2). Washington, DC: National Association for the Education of Young Children.

Rosenthal, A. R. (1981). Visual disorders. In E. E. Bleck & D. A. Nagel (Eds.), *Physically handicapped children — A medical atlas for teachers* (2nd ed.). New York: Grune & Stratton.

Rosenthal, R., & Jacobson, L. (1968). *Pygmalion in the classroom: Teacher expectation and pupil's intellectual development.* New York: Holt, Rinehart & Winston.

Ross, J. B., & Pate, R. R. (1987). The National Children and Youth Study II: A summary of findings. *Journal of Physical Education, Recreation and Dance, 58*(9), 51–56.

Rothman, R. (1990). Survey reveals wide latitude in reporting abuse. *Education Week, IX*(23), 1, 28.

Routh, D. K. (1986). Attention deficit disorder. In R. T. Brown & C. R. Reynolds (Eds.), *Psychological perspectives on childhood exceptionality.* New York: John Wiley & Sons.

Rowe, M. B. (1974). Wait-time and reward. Part 1: Wait time. *Journal of Research on Science Teaching, 11,* 81–94.

Rubin, A. (1980). *Children's friendships.* Cambridge, MA: Harvard University Press.

Rubin, K. H. (1977). The play behaviors of young children. *Young Children, 32*(6), 16–24.

Rubin, K. H., & Howe, N. (1986). Social play and perspective taking. In G. Fein & M. Rivkin (Eds.), *The young child at play: Reviews of research* (Vol. 4). Washington, DC: National Association for the Education of Young Children.

Rubin, K. H., & Pepler, D. J. (1980). The relationship of child's play to social-cognitive growth and development. In H. C. Foot, A. J. Chapman, & J. R. Smith. *Friendship and social relations in children.* New York: John Wiley & Sons.

Rudigier, A. F., Crocker, A. C., & Cohen, H. J. (1990). The dilemmas of childhood HIV infection. *Children Today, 19*(4), 26–29.

Rutherford, E., & Mussen, P. (1968). Generosity in nursery school boys. *Child Development, 39,* 755–765.

Rutter, M., & Garmezy, N. (1983). Developmental psychopathology. In P. H. Mussen (Ed.), *Handbook of child psychology* (4th ed.), E. M. Hetherington (Ed.), *Vol. IV: Socialization, personality, and social development.* New York: John Wiley & Sons.

Sacks, J. J., Smith, J. D., Kaplan, K. M., Lambert, D. A., Sattin, R. W., & Sikes, R. K. (1989, Sept. 22/29). The epidemiology of injuries in Atlanta day-care centers. *Journal of the American Medical Association, 262*(12), 1641–1643.

Safford, P. (1978). *Teaching young children with special needs.* St. Louis, MO: C. V. Mosby.

Safford, P. (1989). *Integrated teaching in early childhood: Starting in the mainstream.* White Plains, NY: Longman.

Saifer, S. (1990). *Practical solutions to practically every problem: The early childhood teacher's manual.* St. Paul, MN: Toys 'n Things Press.

Saltz, E. D., & Johnson, J. (1977). Training disadvantaged preschoolers on various fantasy activities: Effects on cognitive functioning and impulse control. *Child Development, 48,* 367–380.

Samalin, N., & Jablow, M. M. (1987). *Loving your child is not enough.* New York: Viking Press.

Sameroff, A. J., & Seifer, R. (1983). Familial risk and child competence. *Child Development, 54,* 1254–1268.

Saunders, R., & Bingham-Newman, A. M. (1984). *Piagetian perspectives for preschools: A thinking book for teachers.* Englewood Cliffs, NJ: Prentice-Hall.

Schachter, F. F., Kirshner, K., Klips, B., Friedricks, N., & Sanders, K. (1974). Everyday preschool interpersonal speech usage: Methodological, developmental, and sociolinguistic studies. *Monographs for Research in Child Development, 39*(3), Serial No. 156.

Schachter, F. F., & Strage, A. A. (1982). Adults' talk and children's language development. In S. G. Moore & C. R. Cooper (Eds.), *The young child: Reviews of research* (Vol. 3). Washington, DC: National Association for the Education of Young Children.

Schaefer, C. E. (1979). *Childhood encopresis and enuresis: Causes and therapy.* New York: Van Nostrand Reinhold.

Schaefer, C. E. (1984). *How to talk to children about really important things.* New York: Harper & Row.

Schaefer, C. E., & O'Conner, K. J. (1983). *Handbook of play therapy.* New York: John Wiley & Sons.

Schickedanz, J. A. (1986). *More than the ABCs: The early stages of reading and writing.* Washington, DC: National Association for the Education of Young Children.

Schickedanz, J. A., Hansen, K., & Forsyth, P. D. (1990). *Understanding children.* Mountain View, CA: Mayfield.

Schirrmacher, R. (1986). Talking with young children about their art. *Young Children, 41*(5), 3–7.

Schirrmacher, R. (1988). *Art and creative development for young children.* Albany, NY: Delmar.

Schweinhart, L. J., Weikart, D. P., & Larner, M. B. (1986). Consequences of three preschool curriculum models through age 15. *Early Childhood Research Quarterly, 1*(1), 15–46.

Scott, D. K. (1985). Child safety seats—They work! *Young Children, 40*(4), 13–17.

Scott, K. P., & Schau, C. G. (1985). Sex equity and sex bias in instructional materials. In S. S. Klein (Ed.), *Handbook for achieving sex equity through education.* Baltimore, MD: Johns Hopkins University Press.

Schwartz, J. C., & Wynn, R. (1971). The effects of mother presence and previsits on children's emotional reaction to starting nursery school. *Child Development, 42,* 871–881.

Seaver, J. W., Cartwright, C. A., Ward, C. B., & Heasley, C. A. (1983). *Careers with young children.* Washington, DC: National Association for the Education of Young Children.

Secord, W. (1985). The traditional approach to articulation treatment. In P. Newman, N.

Creaghead, & W. Secord (Eds.), *Assessment and remediation of articulatory and phonological disorders*. Columbus, OH: Merrill.

Seefeldt, C. (Ed.). (1987). *The early childhood curriculum: A review of recent research*. New York: Teachers College Press.

Seibel, P. (1981). Physical handicaps and health problems. In B. P. Cartwright, C. A. Cartwright, & M. E. Wards (Eds.), *Educating special learners*. Belmont, CA: Wadsworth.

Seligman, M. E. P. (1975). *Helplessness: On depression, development and death*. San Francisco: W. H. Freeman.

Seltzer, M. M., & Seltzer, G. B. (1983). Classification and social status. In J. L. Matson & J. A. Mulick (Eds.), *Handbook of mental retardation*. New York: Pergamon Press.

Selye, H. (1981). The stress concept today. In I. L. Kutash, L. B. Schlesinger, & Associates (Eds.), *Handbook on stress and anxiety*. San Francisco: Jossey-Bass.

Serbin, L. A., Connor, J. M., & Citron, C. C. (1978). Environmental control of independent and dependent behaviors in preschool boys and girls: A model for early independence training. *Sex Roles, 4*, 867–875.

Shafer, M. (1982). *Life after stress*. New York: Plenum Press.

Shapiro, J., Kramer, S., & Hunerberg, C. (1981). *Equal their chances: Children's activities for non-sexist learning*. Englewood Cliffs, NJ: Prentice-Hall.

Shelton, H., Montgomery, P., & Hatcher, B. (1989) *Bibliography of books for children: 1989 edition*. Wheaton, MD: Association for Childhood Education International.

Shirah, S., & Brennan, L. (1990). *Sickle-cell anemia*. Paper presented at the conference of the National Association for the Education of Young Children, Washington, DC.

Sholtys, K. C. (1989). A new language, a new life. *Young Children, 44*(3), 76–77.

Shotwell, J. M., Wolf, D., & Gardner, H. (1979). Exploring early symbolization: Styles of achievement. In B. Sutton-Smith (Ed.), *Play and learning*. New York: Gardner Press.

Shweder, R. Q., Mahapatra, M., & Miller, J. G. (1987). Culture and moral development. In J. Kagan & S. Lamb (Eds.), *The emergence of morality in children*. Chicago: University of Chicago Press.

Sickle Cell Disease Association. (1987). *About sickle-cell trait and anemia*. South Deerfield, MA: Channing L. Bete.

Siegel, I. E., & Brainerd, C. J. (Eds.), (1978). *Alternatives to Piaget: Critical essays on the theory*. New York: Academic Press.

Siegel, L. S. (1972). Development of the concept of seriation. *Developmental Psychology, 6*, 135–137.

Sigel, I. (1987). Does hothousing rob children of their childhood? *Early Childhood Research Quarterly, 2*(3), 211–225.

Sigel, I. E., & McBane, B. (1967). Cognitive competence and level of symbolization among five-year-old children. In J. Hellmuth (Ed.), *The disadvantaged child*. Seattle, WA: Special Child Publications.

Sinclair, H. (1971). Sensorimotor action patterns as a condition for the acquisition of syntax. In R. Husley & E. Ingram (Eds.), *Language acquisition: Models and methods*. New York: Academic Press.

Singer, D. G., & Singer, J. L. (1990). *The house of make-believe: Children's play and the developing imagination*. Cambridge, MA: Harvard University Press.

Skeen, P., & McKenry, P. C. (1982). The teacher's role in facilitating a child's adjustment to divorce. In J. F. Brown, (Ed.), *Curriculum planning for young children*. Washington, DC: National Association for the Education of Young Children.

Skinner, B. F. (1974). *About behaviorism*. New York: Alfred A. Knopf.

Skolnick, A. S. (1986). *The psychology of human development*. New York: Harcourt Brace Jovanovich.

Slobin, D. (1975). On the nature of talk to children. In E. H. Lenneberg & E. Lenneberg (Eds.), *Foundations of language development*. New York: Academic Press.

Smart, M. S., & Smart, R. C. (1972). *Child development and relationships* (2nd ed.). New York: Macmillan.

Smedslund, J. (1966). Les origines sociales de la centration. In F. Bresson & M. De Montmalin

(Eds.), *Psychologie et epistemologie genetiques*. Paris: Dunod.

Smilansky, S. (1968). *The effects of sociodramatic play on disadvantaged children*. New York: John Wiley & Sons.

Smilansky, S., & Shefatya, L. (1990). *Facilitating play: A medium for promoting cognitive, socioemotional and academic development in young children*. Gaithersburg, MD: Psychosocial & Educational Publications.

Smith, A. B., Ballard, K. D., & Barham, L. J. (1989). Preschool children's perceptions of parent and teacher roles. *Early Childhood Research Quarterly, 4*(4), 523–532.

Smith, C. A. (1988). *I'm positive: Growing up with self-esteem*. Manhattan, KS: Cooperative Extension Service, Kansas State University.

Smith, J. A. (1966). *Setting conditions for creative teaching in the elementary school*. Boston: Allyn & Bacon.

Smith, J. (1990). *The frugal gourmet on our immigrant ancestors: Recipes you should have gotten from your grandmother*. New York: William Morrow.

Smith, N. R. (1983). *Experience and art: Teaching children to paint*. New York: Teachers College Press.

Smith, P. K., & Connolly, K. J. (1980). *The ecology of preschool behavior*. Cambridge: Cambridge University Press.

Smitherman, G. (1977). *Talkin' and testifyin': The language of Black America*. Boston: Houghton Mifflin.

Snider, W. (November 21, 1990). Parents as partners: Adding their voices to decisions on how schools are run. *Education Week*, pp. 11–20.

Snow, C. E. (1989). Understanding social interaction and language acquisition: Sentences are not enough. In M. H. Bornstein & J. S. Bruner (Eds.), *Interaction in human development*. Hillsdale, NJ: Lawrence Erlbaum.

Soderman, A. K. (1985). Dealing with difficult young children. *Young Children, 40*(5), 15–20.

Spodek, B., & Saracho, O. N. (1990). Preparing early childhood teachers for the twenty-first century: A look to the future. In B. Spodek & O. N. Saracho (Eds.), *Yearbook in early childhood education: Vol. 1. Early childhood teacher preparation*. New York: Teachers College Press.

Sprafkin, C., Serbin, L. A., Denir, C., & Connor, J. M. (1983). Sex-differentiated play: Cognitive consequences of early interventions. In M. B. Liss (Ed.), *Social and cognitive skills*. New York: Academic Press.

Sprung, B. (1975). *Non-sexist education for young children: A practical guide*. New York: Citation Press.

Sroufe, L. A. (1983). Individual patterns of adaptation from infancy to preschool. In M. Perlmutter (Ed.), *Proceedings of the Minnesota Symposium on Child Psychology*. Hillsdale, NJ: Lawrence Erlbaum.

Starr, R. H. (1988). Physical abuse of children. In V. B. Van Hasselt, R. L. Morrison, A. S. Bellack, & M. Hersen (Eds.), *Handbook of family violence*. New York: Plenum Press.

Starr, R. H., Jr. (Ed.). (1982). *Child abuse predictions: Policy implications*. Cambridge, MA: Ballinger.

Stebbins, L. B., St. Pierre, R. G., Proper, E. C., Anderson, R. B., & Cerva, T. R. (1977). *Education as experimentation: A planned variation model. Vol. IV-A: An evaluation follow through*. Cambridge, MA: Abt Associates.

Steele, B. F. (1987). Working with abusive parents. In R. E. Helfer & C. H. Kempe (Eds.), *The battered child* (5th ed.). Chicago: University of Chicago Press.

Stephens, K. (1988). The First National Study of Sexual Abuse in Child Care: Findings and recommendations. *Child Care Information Exchange, 60*, 9–12.

Sternberg, R. J. (Ed.). (1988). *The nature of creativity: Contemporary psychological perspectives*. Cambridge: Cambridge University Press.

Stevenson, J. H. (1990). The cooperative preschool model in Canada. In I. M. Doxey (Ed.), *Child care and education: Canadian dimensions*. Scarborough, Ontario: Nelson.

Stith, M., & Connor, R. (1962). Dependency and helpfulness in young children. *Child Development, 33*, 15–20.

Stott, L. H., & Ball, R. S. (1957). Consistency and change in ascendance-submission in the social interaction of children. *Child Development, 28*, 259–272.

Strayhorn, J. M. (1988). *The competent child: An approach to psychotherapy and preventive mental health*. New York: Guilford Press.

Strickland, J., & Reynolds, S. (1989). The new untouchables: Risk management for child abuse in child care. *Child Care Information Exchange, 65*, 37–39.

Strom, R. D. (1981). The merits of solitary play. In R. D. Strom (Ed.), *Growing through play: Readings for parents and teachers*. Monterey, CA: Brooks/Cole.

Strom, R., Johnson, A., & Strom, S. (1990). Talented children in minority families. *International Journal of Early Childhood, 22*(2), 39–48.

Sussman, S. W. (1984). Cooperative child care: An alternative to the high cost of campus child care. *Focus on Learning, 10* (Spring), 45–47.

Sutherland, A. (1986). *The best in children's books: The University of Chicago's guide to children's literature*. Chicago: University of Chicago Press.

Sutton-Smith, B. (1971). A syntax for play and games. In R. E. Herron & B. Sutton-Smith, *Child's play*. New York: John Wiley.

Sutton-Smith, B., & Roberts, J. M. (1981). Play, toys, games and sports. In H. C. Triandis & A. Heron (Eds.), *Handbook of developmental cross-cultural psychology* (Vol. 4). Boston: Allyn & Bacon.

Swedlow, R. (1986). Children play, children learn. In J. S. McKee (Ed.). *Play: Working partner of growth*. Wheaton, MD: Association for Childhood Education International.

Swick, K. J. (1987). *Perspectives on understanding and working with families*. Champaign, IL: Stipes.

Swick, K. (1989). Review of research: Parental efficacy and social competence in young children. *Dimensions, 17*(3), 25–26.

Talbot, J., & Frost, J. L. (1989). Magical playscapes. *Childhood Education, 66*(1), 11–19.

Tardiff, T. Z., & Sternberg, R. J. (1988). What do we know about creativity? In R. J. Sternberg (Ed.), *The nature of creativity: Contemporary psychological perspectives*. Cambridge: Cambridge University Press.

Task Force on Pediatric AIDS. (1989). Pediatric AIDS and human immunodeficiency virus infection. *American Psychologist, 44*(2), 258–264.

Tavris, C. (1982). *Anger: The misunderstood emotion*. New York: Simon & Schuster.

Taylor, K. W. (1981). *Parents and children learn together* (3rd ed.). New York: Teachers College Press.

Thomas, R. M. (1985). *Comparing theories of child development* (2nd ed.). Belmont, CA: Wadsworth.

Thompson, G. G. (1944). The social and emotional development of preschool children under 2 types of educational programs. *Psychological Monographs, 56*(5), 1–29.

Tillotson, J. (1970). A brief theory of movement education. In R. T. Sweeney (Ed.), *Selected readings in movement education*. Reading, MA: Addison-Wesley.

Tizard, B., Mortimore, J., & Burchell, B. (1983). *Involving parents in nursery and infant schools: A source book for teachers*. Ypsilanti, MI: High/Scope Press.

Torrance, E. P. (1962). *Guiding creative talent*. Englewood Cliffs, NJ: Prentice-Hall.

Torrance, E. P. (1970). Seven guides to creativity. In R. T. Sweeney (Ed.), *Selected readings in movement education*. Reading, MA: Addison-Wesley.

Torrance, E. P. (1977). *Discovery and nurturance of giftedness in the culturally different*. Reston, VA: Council for Exceptional Children.

Torrance, E. P. (1988). The nature of creativity as manifest in testing. In R. J. Sternberg (Ed.), *The nature of creativity: Contemporary psychological perspectives*. Cambridge: Cambridge University Press.

Trawick-Smith, J., & Thompson, R. H. (1986). Preparing young children for hospitalization. In J. B. McCracken (Ed.), *Reducing stress in young children's lives*. Washington, DC: National Association for the Education of Young Children.

Truax, C. B., & Tatum, C. D. (1966). An extension from the effective psychotherapeutic model to constructive personality change in preschool children. *Childhood Education, 42*, 456–462.

Trueba, H. T. (1990). The role of culture in the acquisition of English literacy by minority school children. In G. Imhoff (Ed.), *Learning two languages: From conflict to consensus in the reorganization of schools*. New Brunswick, NJ: Transaction.

Tureen, P., & Tureen, J. (1986). Childhood speech and language disorders. In R. T. Brown & C. R. Reynolds (Eds.), *Psychological perspectives on childhood exceptionality*. New York: John Wiley & Sons.

Turiel, E. (1973). Stage transition in moral development. In R. Travers (Ed.), *Second handbook on research in teaching*. Chicago: Rand McNally.

Tzeng, O. C. S., & Hanner, L. J. (1988). Abuse and neglect: Typologies, phenomena and impacts. In O. C. S. Tzeng & J. J. Jacobsen (Eds.), *Sourcebook for child abuse and neglect: Intervention, treatment, and prevention through crisis programs*. Springfield, IL: Charles C. Thomas.

U.S. Consumer Product Safety Commission. (1981). *A handbook for public playground safety: Vol. 1. General guidelines for new and existing playgrounds*. Washington, DC: U.S. Government Printing Office.

U.S. Department of Labor. (1984). *Occupational projections and training data, bulletin 2206*. Washington, DC: Bureau of Labor Statistics.

Valentine, C. W. (1956). *The normal child and his abnormalities* (3rd ed.). Baltimore, MD: Penguin Books.

Van Riper, C., & Emerick, L. (1984). *Speech correction: An introduction to speech pathology and audiology*. Englewood Cliffs, NJ: Prentice-Hall.

Vaughan, B. E., & Waters, E. (1980). Social organization among preschool peers: Dominance, attention and sociometric correlation. In D. R. Omark, F. F. Strayer, & D. G. Freedman (Eds.), *Dominance relations: An ethological view of human conflict and social interactions*. New York: Garland STPM Press.

Viadero, D. (1988). Corporal punishment foes gain victories, see "Best year ever." *Education Week, VII*(3), 1, 38, 39.

Vygotsky, L. S. (1978). *Mind in society: The development of higher psychological processes*. Cambridge, MA: Harvard University Press.

Wadsworth, B. J. (1989). *Piaget's theory of cogni-tive and affective development* (4th ed.). New York: Longman.

Wakefield, H., & Underwager, R. (1988). *Accusations of child sexual abuse*. Springfield, IL: Charles C. Thomas.

Walk, R. D. (1981). *Perceptual development*. Monterey, CA: Brooks/Cole.

Walker, J. E., & Shea, T. M. (1991). *Behavior management: A practical approach for educators* (5th ed.). Columbus, OH: Merrill/Macmillan.

Wallach, M. A., & Kogan, N. (1965). *Modes of thinking in young children: A study of the creativity-intelligence distinction*. New York: Holt, Rinehart & Winston.

Wallerstein, J. S. (1983). Children of divorce: Stress and developmental tasks. In N. Garmezy & M. Rutter (Eds.), *Stress, coping, and development in children*. New York: McGraw-Hill.

Wallerstein, J. S., & Blakeslee, S. (1989). *Second chances: Men, women and children a decade after divorce*. New York: Ticknor & Fields.

Ward, W. C. (1968). Creativity in young children. *Child Development, 39*, 737–754.

Warger, C. (1988). *A resource guide to public school early childhood programs*. Alexandria, VA: Association for Supervision and Curriculum Development.

Warren, R. M. (1977). *Caring: Supporting children's growth*. Washington, DC: National Association for the Education of Young Children.

Washington, V., & Oyemade, U. J. (1987). *Project Head Start: Past, present and future trends in the context of family needs*. New York: Garland.

Weber, E. (1984). *Ideas influencing early childhood education: A theoretical analysis*. New York: Teachers College Press.

Weikart, D. P. (1971). *Relationship of curriculum, teaching, and learning in preschool education*. Ypsilanti, MI: High/Scope Educational Research Foundation.

Weikart, D. P. (1990). *Quality preschool programs: A long-term social investment*. New York: Ford Foundation.

Weikart, D., & Lambie, D. (1970). Early enrichment in infants. In V. Denenberg (Ed.), *Education of the infant and young child*. New York: Academic Press.

Weisberg, R. W. (1988). Problem solving and creativity. In R. J. Sternberg (Ed.), *The nature of creativity: Contemporary psychological perspectives*. Cambridge: Cambridge University Press.

Weiser, M. (1982). *Group care and education of infants and toddlers*. St. Louis, MO: C. V. Mosby.

Weiss, B., & Weisz, J. R. (1986). General cognitive deficits: Mental retardation. In R. T. Brown & C. R. Reynolds (Eds.), *Psychological perspectives on childhood exceptionality*. New York: John Wiley & Sons.

Weiss, G., & Hechtman, L. T. (1986). *Hyperactive children grown up: Empirical findings and theoretical considerations*. New York: Guilford Press.

Wender, P. H. (1973). *The hyperactive child: A handbook for parents*. New York: Crown.

Wenning, J., & Wortis, S. (1984). *Made by human hands: A curriculum for teaching young children about work and working people*. Cambridge, MA: Multicultural Project for Communication and Education.

Wenning, J., & Wortis, S. (1988). Work in the child care center: A curriculum about working people. *Day Care and Early Education, 15*(4), 20–25.

Werner, E. E. (1984). Resilient children. *Young Children, 40*(1), 69–72.

Werner, E. E., & Smith, R. S. (1982). *Vulnerable but invincible: A longitudinal study of resilient children and youth*. New York: McGraw-Hill.

Werner, R. H., & Simmons, R. Q. (1990). *Homemade play equipment*. Reston, VA: American Alliance for Health, Physical Education, Recreation, and Dance.

Wessel, M. A. (1983). Children, when parents die. In J. E. Schowalter, P. R. Patterson, M. Tallmer, A. H. Kutcher, S. V. Gullo, & D. Peretz (Eds.), *The child and death*. New York: Columbia University Press.

Weston, J. (1980). The pathology of child abuse and neglect. In C. H. Kempe & R. E. Helfer (Eds.), *The battered child* (3rd ed.). Chicago: University of Chicago Press.

White, B. L. (1979). *The origins of human competence*. Lexington, MA: Lexington Books.

White, R. W. (1968). Motivation reconsidered: The concept of competence. In M. Almy (Ed.), *Early childhood play: Selected readings related to cognition and motivation*. New York: Simon & Schuster.

White, R. W. (1976). *The enterprise of living: A view of personal growth* (2nd ed.). New York: Holt, Rinehart & Winston.

White, S., & Buka, S. L. (1987). Early education: Programs, traditions, and policies. In E. Z. Rothkopt (Ed.), *Review of research in education* (Vol. 14). Washington, DC: American Educational Research Association.

Whitebook, M., & Granger, R. C. (1989). "Mommy, who's going to be my teacher today?" Assessing teacher turnover. *Young Children, 44*(4), 11–15.

Whitener, C. B., & Keeling, M. H. (1984). *Nutrition education for young children: Strategies and activities*. Englewood Cliffs, NJ: Prentice Hall.

Whitmore, J. R. (Ed.). (1986). *Intellectual giftedness in young children: Recognition and development*. New York: Haworth Press.

Wickstrom, R. L. (1983). *Fundamental motor patterns* (3rd ed.). Philadelphia: Lea & Febiger.

Wiggins, M. E. (1976). The cognitive deficit-difference controversy: A Black sociopolitical perspective. In D. S. Harrison & T. Trabasso (Eds.), *Black English: A seminar*. Hillsdale, NJ: Lawrence Erlbaum.

Willer, B. A. (1990). *Reaching the full cost of quality in early childhood programs*. Washington, DC: National Association for the Education of Young Children.

Williams, C. K., & Kamii, C. (1986). How do children learn by handling objects? *Young Children, 42*(1), 23–26.

Williams, V. B. (1982). *A chair for my mother*. New York: Greenwillow Books.

Wilson, G. L. (1980). Sticks and stones and racial slurs do hurt: The word *nigger* is what's not allowed. *Interracial Books for Children: Bulletin, 11*(3 & 4).

Wilson, L. V. C. (1990). *Infants and toddlers curriculum and teaching*. Albany, NY: Delmar.

Wiszinckas, E. (1981–82). Preparing children for situational crises. *Journal of Children in Contemporary Society, 14*(3), 21–25.

Witt, J. C., Elliott, S. N., & Gresham, F. M. (1988). *Handbook of behavior therapy in education*. New York: Plenum Press.

Wolfe, D. A., Wolfe, V. V., & Best, C. L. (1988). Child victims of sexual abuse. In V. B. Van Hasselt, R. L. Morrison, A. S. Bellack, & M. Hersen (Eds.), *Handbook of family violence*. New York: Plenum Press.

Wolfle, J. (1989). The gifted preschooler: Developmentally different, but still 3 or 4 years old. *Young Children, 44*(3), 41–48.

Woodard, C. Y. (1986). Guidelines for facilitating sociodramatic play. In J. L. Frost & S. Sunderlin (Eds.), *When children play: Proceedings of the International Conference on Play and Play Environments*. Wheaton, MD: Association for Childhood Education International.

Yarrow, L. J. (1948). The effect of antecedent frustration on projective play. *Psychological Monographs, 62*, 6.

Yarrow, L. J. (1980). Emotional development. In S. Chess & A. Thomas (Eds.), *Annual progress in child psychiatry and child development*. New York: Brunner/Mazel.

Yarrow, M. R., Scott, P. M., & Waxler, C. Z. (1973). *Developmental Psychology, 8*, 240–260.

Yawkey, T. D. (Ed.). (1980). *The self-concept of the young child*. Provo, UT: Brigham Young University Press.

Young Children. (1989). New guidelines on HIV infection (AIDS) announced for group programs. *Young Children, 44*(2), 51.

Young Children. (1990). [Entire issue.] *45*(6).

Young, L. L., & Cooper, D. H. (1944). Some factors associated with popularity. *Journal of Educational Psychology, 35*, 513–535.

Youniss, J. (1975). Another perspective on social cognition. In A. Pick (Ed.), *Minnesota Symposia on Child Psychology* (Vol. 9). Minneapolis: University of Minnesota Press.

Zahn-Waxler, C. Z., Radke-Yarrow, M. R., & King, R. A. (1979). Child rearing and children's prosocial initiations toward victims of distress. *Child Development, 50*, 87–88.

Zavitkovsky, D. (1990). Enjoy a Docia story. *Child Care Information Exchange, 74*, 62.

Zigler, E. (1984). Handicapped children and their families. In E. Shopler & B. G. Mesibov (Eds.), *The effects of autism on the family*. New York: Plenum Press.

Zigler, E., & Balla, D. (Eds.). (1982). *Mental retardation: The developmental-difference controversy*. Hillsdale, NJ: Lawrence Erlbaum.

Zimmerman, B. J., & Bergan, J. K. (1971). Intellectual operations in teacher question asking behavior. *Merrill-Palmer Quarterly, 17*(1), 19–26.

Acknowledgments for Chapter-Opening Quotations

1. From *Growing Minds: On Becoming a Teacher* (p. 16) by Herbert Kohl, 1984, New York: Harper & Row: "The National Association for the Education of Young Children Code of Ethics" (p. 25), 1989, *Young Children, 45*(1).

2. From *Young Man Luther* by Erik Erikson, 1958, New York: W. W. Norton.

3. From *Teaching Young Children* (p. 124) by Evelyn Beyer, © 1968 by Western Publishing Company, Inc., reprinted by permission of Bobbs-Merrill.

4. From *What the Open-Air Nursery School Is* (p. 3) by Margaret McMillan, 1929, London: the Labour Party; from "Magical Playscapes" (p. 17) by James Talbot and Joe L. Frost, 1989, *Childhood Education, 66*(1); from "Resource Sheet 11" by the Canadian Child Day Care Federation, no date, Ottawa, Ontario: The Federation.

5. From *Early Education and Psychological Development* (p. 5) by Barbara Biber, 1984, New Haven, CT: Yale University Press.

6. From *You and Your Child's Self-Esteem* (p. 33) by J. M. Harris, quoting John Dewey, 1989, New York: Carroll & Graf.

7. From *Last Poems*, XII, by A. E. Housman, 1922.

8. From the Preface (p. 5) by Urie Bronfenbrenner in *Soviet Preschool Education* (Vol. 2: Teacher's Commentary) by H. Chauncey (Ed.), 1969, New York: Holt, Rinehart & Winston; from *Starting School: From Separation to Independence* (p. 64) by Nancy Balaban, 1985, New York: Teachers College Press.

9. From *Constructivist Early Education: Overview and Comparison with Other Programs* (p. 379) by R. DeVries and L. Kohlberg, 1990, Washington, DC: National Association for the Education of Young Children.

10. From "Avoiding 'Me Against You' Discipline" (pp. 26–27) by P. Greenberg, 1988, *Young Children, 44*(1).

11. From *The Good Preschool Teacher: Six Teachers Reflect on Their Lives* (p. 70) by W. Ayers, 1989, New York: Teachers College Press.

12. Author unknown. A particularly well-sung version of this gospel tune is available on the record *Songs of My People* with Paul Robeson. An RCA Red Seal rerelease, LM-3292.

13. From "The Nature of Creativity as Manifest in Testing" (p. 68) by E. Paul Torrance, 1988, in *The Nature of Creativity: Contemporary Psychological Perspectives* by R. J. Sternberg (Ed.), Cambridge: Cambridge University Press; reprinted by permission of the publisher from Eleanor Fitch Griffin, *Islands of Childhood* (p. 140), Teachers College Press. © 1982 by Teachers College, Columbia University. All rights reserved.

14. From "Magical Playscapes" (p. 11) by James Talbot and Joe L. Frost, 1989, *Childhood Education, 66*(1).

15. From Kenneth Rexroth quoted on a calendar; from "The Motivation to Be Creative" by Teresa Amabile, 1987, in *Frontiers of Creativity Research: Beyond the Basics* by Scott G. Isaksen (Ed.), Buffalo, NY: Bearly.

16. From "Learning the Mother Tongue" by Jerome S. Bruner, 1978, *Human Nature, 1*(9), 42–49.

17. By permission from *Developmentally Appropriate Practice in Early Childhood Programs Serving Children from Birth Through Age 8* (p. 55) by S. Bredekamp, 1987, Washington, DC: National Association for the Education of Young Children.

18. From "Children Come First" (p. 70) by John Coe, 1987, *Childhood Education, 64*(2).

19. From "What Do Young Children Teach Themselves?" (p. 9) by Nancy Balaban, in *Early Childhood: Reconsidering the Essentials: A Collection of Papers,* 1984, New York: Bank Street College.

20. From *Education for Parenting* (p. 6) by Mary Lane. Reprinted by permission from *Education for Parenting.* © 1975, National Association for the Education of Young Children, 1834 Connecticut Ave., NW, Washington, DC 20009.

21. From "Handicapped Children and Their Families" (pp. 32–33) by Edward Zigler, in *The Effects of Autism on the Family,* by Eric Shopler and Gary B. Mesibov (Eds.), 1984, New York: Plenum Press.

22. Hubert H. Humphrey. Speech delivered at dedication of Hubert H. Humphrey Building for the U.S. Department of Health, Education, and Welfare, November 1, 1977.

INDEX